D1605899

The Idea of Hegel's *Science of Logic*

The Idea of Hegel's
Science of Logic

STANLEY ROSEN

The University of Chicago Press
Chicago and London

Stanley Rosen is the Borden Parker Bowne Professor and University Professor Emeritus at Boston University. He is the author of many books, most recently *Plato's Republic: A Study.*

The University of Chicago Press, Chicago 60637
The University of Chicago Press, Ltd., London
© 2014 by The University of Chicago
All rights reserved. Published 2014.
Printed in the United States of America

23 22 21 20 19 18 17 16 15 14   1 2 3 4 5

ISBN-13: 978-0-226-06588-5 (cloth)
ISBN-13: 978-0-226-06591-5 (e-book)
DOI: 10.7208/chicago/9780226065915.001.0001

Library of Congress Cataloging-in-Publication Data

Rosen, Stanley, 1929–
    The idea of Hegel's Science of logic / Stanley Rosen.
        pages cm
    Include bibliographical references and index.
    ISBN 978-0-226-06588-5 (cloth : alk. paper) — ISBN 978-0-226-06591-5
(e-book) 1. Hegel, Georg Wilhelm Friedrich, 1770–1831. 2. Hegel, Georg
Wilhelm Friedrich, 1770–1831. Wissenschaft der Logik. 3. Logic. I. Title.
    B2949.L8R668 2013
    160—dc23

                                                            2013014451

CONTENTS

ACKNOWLEDGMENTS

I gratefully acknowledge the invaluable contributions of my friend Dr. Paul C. Good in preparing this book for publication. Though he is not a philosopher by training, Paul's intelligence and common sense, and his assistance as a technologist, patient listener, advisor, and laborer helped make this book possible. Together we look toward future accomplishments.

Introduction

Shortly after Hegel's death, the school he established dissolved into at least three main segments, known as the left, center, and right Hegelians. The comprehensiveness of this articulation exhibits two closely related points. First: not even Hegel's personal students could furnish a widely acceptable and lucid account of the master's central doctrines. Second: the absence of any agreement about the content of Hegelianism encouraged a resurgence of positivist and empiricist doctrines of various kinds, loosely unified by the slogan "Back to Kant." There is a deep connection between this process and the debate between the so-called analytical and phenomenological schools of the twentieth century. It would be a mistake simply to identify Hegel himself as the grandfather of phenomenology and the neo-Kantians as the ancestors of analytical philosophy. But it is certainly true that the collapse of Hegelianism was instrumental in the subsequent repudiation of systematic and, of course, speculative philosophy. The apparent failure and, indeed, absurdity of Hegelian "science" (*Wissenschaft*) was a major factor in the subsequent rise to dominance of scientific rationalism in the sense of that expression that is illustrated by the mathematical and natural sciences and their associated technology.

I will not attempt here to describe in detail the doctrinal history of the past hundred years. It is enough to say that if the picture of a quarrel between analysts and phenomenologists was ever an accurate representation of philosophical discussion, it is today largely outmoded. Something similar to, if not identical with, what happened following the dissolution of the Hegelian school is now taking place in contemporary philosophical debates. To mention just one highly relevant illustration of this, Hegel himself has come back into fashion among academic philosophers, and one sees a steadily increasing effort to reformulate Hegel's "plastic" texts into

documents of sufficient lucidity and analytical precision to be useful to
the more adventuresome and imaginative members of what I have loosely
characterized as the neo-Kantians.

What makes the present moment philosophically exciting is at the same
time a cause of danger. Despite the continuing popularity of analytical philosophy in the academic community, the old enthusiasm and rather dogmatic conviction of intellectual rectitude has evaporated. More and more
self-styled analysts are turning to the study of Hegel, Nietzsche, Husserl,
and Heidegger, to mention only the most important examples. Even in
the latest manifestation of vigor among analytical philosophers, namely,
philosophy of mind both natural and artificial, one finds a broad spec-
trum of interest in phenomenological thinkers. As to the "hard-headed"
analysts in this line of development, they seem to be closer to neurophysi-
ology and computer science than to philosophy, and there is considerable
opposition to this hyperscientific approach among analytical philosophers
themselves.

In sum, there are many signs of a new willingness to explore ostensibly
outmoded and even ridiculed styles of thought. I am therefore encouraged
to enter into this ecumenical process with my own interpretation of Hegel's *Science of Logic* (hereafter *SL*). As is well-known, Hegel figures promi-
nently in the development of analytical philosophy in England. One of the
central issues in the early stage of that development is virtually the same
as the problem that underlies Hegel's critique of traditional rationalism.
It will thus be doubly useful to begin my exposition with an introductory
statement of the problem. The problem is where one stands with respect to
the question whether logical atoms exist. Are there, in other words, formal
elements of such simplicity that they cannot be further reduced by analysis, and each of which is directly intelligible as itself, without reference to
the others? Otherwise stated, if it is impossible to arrive at formal atoms
by the process of conceptual analysis, and necessary that the analysis of
any formal element make use of others, does this mean that the atoms
are intrinsically interrelated in a dialectical manner, or can we distinguish
between the irreducible complexity of analytical language and the ontological simplicity of such formal elements (or concepts) as being, nothing,
same, other, and so on? The question can also be phrased as follows: If the
analytical philosophers were correct to repudiate logical atoms, does this
not force them to fall back upon a kind of Hegelian dialectical ontology?
Is it possible that the apparently dominating influence of Kant among analytical thinkers is a simulacrum of the subterranean influence of Hegel? Or
can we say that the explicit repudiation or derision of dialectical ontology

is undercut by its implicit presence within the broader theoretical doctrines of post-Tractarian analytical philosophy? Could one not plausibly argue that modern science is itself dialectical, as for example in its recognition of the reciprocal influence of one aspect of reality upon the others? I am not, then, raising an obscure question from the history of traditional philosophy. The issue goes to the heart of the relation between language and reality. The question, rendered canonical by Kant, is whether the discursive intelligence produces the world-order by the very activity of the conceptual analysis of experience. Still more precisely, is experience itself a production of cognition? If it is not, then how does cognition grasp (and so refer to) experience? If it is, then how can we distinguish between better and worse productions other than by personal preference or the fashions of intellectual history?

Hegel, like many contemporary (or late-modern) analytical philosophers, contends that the logical structure of experience is independent of its variable content. Otherwise put, it is this structure that orders historical variability into a conceptually coherent, and so complete, understanding of human experience. This formulation already shows, of course, how Hegel differs from the analytical proponents of logic. I mean by this something much more important than the rejection of formalism by Hegel, or even the agreement by many philosophers of logic that logic is itself a historical creature. The sharpest statement of the difference is that for Hegel, logic is ontological. And this is closely connected with the thesis that ontology is dialectical, that is, that the elements or atoms of the structure of intelligibility are interrelated intrinsically and not "merely" in the process of cognition. Finally, it means for Hegel that history is not some random agency that lies outside our philosophical doctrines and exchanges them in an arbitrary and hence meaningless way. Instead, history is the human exhibition of the very conceptual structure that constitutes experience.

These are extraordinarily difficult issues, and I have stated them in a prefatory manner, but not, I hope, so obscurely as to make unintelligible to the prospective reader what this book is about. In order to set out upon this path, I have tried to assimilate as much as possible of the best secondary literature, and it goes without saying that one must render Hegel's own views as accurately as possible. But the reader should know from the outset that this is not in the first instance a historical or philological commentary. Commentaries of this sort are extremely useful, but for my purposes they have served as instruments rather than models. One cannot comment upon something that one has not understood, and this book is devoted to the effort of understanding Hegel by thinking through the problems that give

Logic
↓
ontological
↓
dialectical

Logic is ontological.
Ontology is dialectical.

life to the letter of the text and, indeed, that render his always obscure and sometimes—let us simply admit it—unintelligible language a legitimate object of philosophical *eros* rather than a curiosity for antiquarians. Without this kind of effort, the commentaries are in fact useless to the student who is not already an expert. For how can we know which commentator has understood Hegel correctly? What we want here is neither a paraphrase of the text in Hegelian jargon nor a radical oversimplification that trivializes the difficulties in an effort to make Hegel acceptable to an English-speaking audience. I repeat: our goal must be to rethink the problems that animate Hegel's dialectico-speculative logic. On this point, I follow Dieter Henrich, one of the most learned and thoughtful Hegel scholars of our time, when he says that "whoever wishes to understand Hegel is always alone with himself. He will find no commentary that helps us in reading him, unless one wishes merely to replace [*ersetzen*] him."[1]

It is therefore no part of my task to justify every phase of Hegel's doctrine. Thinking about Hegel is in the first instance thinking about philosophy with Hegel's assistance. Hegel is of help at the very outset in our understanding of what it means to think about philosophy. There was a time when this statement would have been characterized as an invocation to metaphilosophy. The expression derives, I believe, from formal or mathematical logic, that is, from the practice of formalizing one language within another. Since the language within which one carries out the formalization may itself presumably be formalized within yet another metalanguage, the entire process lies within the domain of what Hegel would have called the "bad infinity." For a Hegelian, whether in the literal sense or in the somewhat metaphorical use that I shall often make of that term, metaphilosophy is an absurdity; thinking about philosophy is just philosophizing. This is so for at least two reasons.

First: Hegel was entirely opposed to the formalization of philosophy, and this includes his own science of logic. Odd and even absurd as it may sound to uninitiated ears, Hegel was to a considerable extent a philosopher of natural and, up to a point, ordinary language. He had no respect for commonsense versions of ordinary language, but he knew that technical philosophical terms must originate within natural language if they are to be adequate to the experience of the human spirit. As one could also put this, Hegel's logic is not deductive but developmental. For reasons that we shall explore in due course, Hegel does not detach the forms of argument from the motions or processes of conceptual thinking. His primary concern is to describe these processes in language that itself exhibits the movements it describes. This may strike the contemporary reader as a lapse into psychologism, but I think it can be shown that Hegel is not open to such a criticism. Stated with introductory concision, his point is rather that formal conceptual structures are themselves internally "excited" in ways that exhibit the excitation of the process of conceptual thinking. One can, so to speak, "read off" the laws of the formal order from those of the cognitive process, and vice versa. This is not because the laws are equivalent but rather because they are the same. The attempt to formalize these processes would immediately suppress the dialectical movement that is the mark of the life of the spirit and transform it into the skeleton of a corpse.

NB
2

Second: the expression "metaphilosophy," if it means anything at all, must refer either to something higher than philosophy or else to the philosophical consideration of the nature of philosophy. The second alternative is obviously just philosophy. It is of course true that one may philosophize about restricted or specific aspects of experience without thinking directly about the fundamental nature of philosophy. But what makes our thinking about a specific aspect of experience philosophical is precisely its connection with or derivation from what we take to be the fundamental nature of philosophy. A good example of this is the history of philosophy. Hegel is one of the first of the great modern thinkers to concern himself with a serious study of his predecessors. But his reading of these predecessors is always an expression of his underlying doctrine of the historical development of conceptual thought, or what he often refers to simply as "the concept." Hegel's lectures on the history of philosophy, exactly like those on the philosophy of history, religion, or art, are popular versions of his philosophy, which he took to be the possession rather than the love of wisdom. For better or worse, Hegel is a systematic thinker. All of his texts have their place within his system, and the fundamental text, the text that contains the purest and most authoritative expression of the structure of the system itself, is the *SL*.

As a systematic thinker who addressed himself to "the whole" and who is notorious for the assertion that "the true is the whole" (or "totality": *das Ganze*),[2] Hegel had no place in his thought for metaphilosophy in the sense of an activity that is external to or more universal than philosophy. Metaphilosophy would be for Hegel, if anything, then prephilosophy. There is a curious resonance between Hegel's assertion that the true is the whole and the Quinean or Duhemian thesis that the empirical meaning of a sentence is determinable only within the context of a theory or even science as a whole.[3] But Hegel's meaning is, if not the reverse of, then certainly quite different from, that of his successors. For Hegel, it is the "scientific" in the sense of the theoretical whole that determines not the empirical but the ontological truth of a sentence. He knew very well the difference between physics and philosophy, for example, although he often opened himself to ridicule by attempting to express the philosophical significance of physics. But this was precisely his intention: to provide a philosophical explanation of philosophy as an expression of the totality of the human spirit. Hegel accepts the scientific nature of philosophy, but he distinguishes philosophical from natural science.

The immediate point is this. Nothing lies "beyond" philosophy for Hegel, because it is the task of philosophy to explain the structure of totality. It should go without saying that this explanation is accessible only to philosophers. But it is part of the task of philosophy, as conceived by Hegel, to demonstrate that a nonphilosophical understanding of physics, mathematics, history, or any other sphere of human experience is inadequate for the genuinely speculative person. One is tempted to call this circular and to take it to mean simply that nonphilosophical explanations are inadequate for philosophers but by definition adequate for nonphilosophers. But Hegel means something much more than this, however objectionable it may sound to contemporary ears. He means that philosophy is the highest expression of the human spirit and that its fulfillment in wisdom is equivalent to the manifestation of the divinity of that spirit.[4]

There is an important corollary to this extended remark. We frequently speak of the philosophy of history, the philosophy of science, the philosophy of art, and so on. In our professional training of philosophers, we provide a general account of the various branches of philosophy, an account that expresses the philosophical presuppositions of the school to which the dominant professors belong, and then set the student to the task of mastering a specific aspect, or more usually a subaspect, of the discipline. This procedure is modeled upon the division of labor intrinsic to the study of the natural sciences. I am aware that in the best cases, mathematicians and scientists transcend their "areas of specialization," and that they sometimes do so in the direction of philosophy. It is these cases that conform more directly to the Hegelian paradigm of philosophy. From a Hegelian standpoint, there is no such thing as a genuinely philosophical mastery of a special branch of knowledge that is not itself invigorated—literally, given its conceptual and spiritual life—by the system of philosophy as a totality. In the last analysis, this means that there is no genuinely philosophical mastery of a special branch of knowledge or practice that is not grounded in an understanding of Hegel's dialectico-speculative logic.

Thinking about Hegel, then, means thinking about everything, but not at all about each thing or branch of human experience in its own terms, where "own" refers to the first principles, methods, and technical terminology of a specific discipline. In other words, to think about Hegel is not at all to think about physics in the manner of the physicist or even history in the manner of the scientific or professional historian. It is rather to think about how all aspects of human experience constitute a whole, and how that whole is the necessary presupposition for the possibility of explaining anything whatsoever. Stated with respect to the primacy of the science of logic, then, philosophy is ontological in the sense that it exhibits the categorial structure of anything whatsoever.[5]

In an age that has been not merely dominated but saturated by the mathematical and experimental sciences, talk about knowledge of the whole must seem extraordinarily vague and even pretentious. To this objection, there are several responses. The first is to repeat the previous assertion that knowledge of the "whole" is not for Hegel a replacement for the individual sciences. In terms that illuminate Hegel's Kantian heritage, it is the account of the conditions for the existence and intelligibility of anything whatsoever.[6] As such, it is the theoretical counterpart to what Aristotle meant by *phronesis*, which, he says, is concerned with the whole of life, that is, with how each practical act contributes to the perfection of life as a whole and not just to the given context of activity. But, also like *phronesis*, a theoretical account of the whole is a "science" in its own right, by which I mean that it addresses itself to a particular subject matter, namely, the set of the most general properties of experience. This science has its own methods and its own technical terminology. And the problems it studies are direct consequences of the particular sciences or still more fundamentally, of the nature of discursive thinking.

Very far from being an unscientific thinker, Hegel suffers from the opposite affliction. The Hegelian system, and in particular the *SL*, is entirely dominated by the scientific goal of complete explanation. Hegel will argue in exhaustive detail that if anything whatsoever is intelligible, then everything is. This thesis itself depends upon a radical revision of the Kantian doctrine that nature conforms to the workings of the human intelligence, to which must be added the corollary that this work is itself intelligible or that it could not take place except as intelligible to the worker. The Kantian claims to know the general (transcendental) structure of rational work, which is the cognitive production of the world of experience and science. This in turn provides us with knowledge of the "phenomenal" world, that is to say, the world that appears to us as the direct result of our own productive activity. But it leaves in total darkness whatever lies beyond or outside the horizon of perceptual and conceptual cognition.

Hegel takes the next step by purporting to demonstrate that *nothing* lies beyond the horizon of conceptual thinking, and that "nothing" is itself the name of a concept, and so of a constituent of the process by which things come into existence and pass away. To put this difficult point in an entirely introductory way, Hegel's logical revolution rests upon the conceptual mastery of nothing, or his demonstration that it is the same as being, or a bit more fully, that being and nothing are the two aspects of becoming. If this sounds obscure, we have only to think of the way in which modern logic and set theory define "not" or negation as a syntactical operator or concept. Propositions within a given language are true or false depending upon whether they correctly express what is or is not the case. We use the expressions "true" and "false," or their symbolic representatives, such as "1" and "0," to designate propositions in which a predicate is correctly or incorrectly assigned to a subject, or an instance is correctly or incorrectly subsumed under a concept, or an element is said correctly or not to "belong" to a set. But "is" and "is not" are uneliminable and reciprocally intelligible expressions of the most general structure of the universe of discourse.

It is impossible, for example, to provide an intelligible analysis of the modern form of the proposition, in which the copula has ostensibly been replaced by a function, without the concept of truth-value. But "truth" is just another way of saying "is the case," and this in turn is intelligible only through an antecedent grasp of "is" and "is not," or in the Hegelian formulation, being and nothing. These are not "entities" but logical constituents or the moments of becoming, and hence of any element of genesis whatsoever. Parenthetically, this is why "existence" is not a satisfactory replacement for "being" in Hegel's view. Whereas everything is, only individuals of a certain sort exist. But I will discuss this at greater length in the appropriate place.

I do not wish to press this example, which I have introduced here for purely introductory purposes. A fuller account would bring out the fact that Hegel is interested not in "truth-functions" of logical calculi but in what we would perhaps call the "ontological" categories that are employed, consciously or otherwise, by all those, logicians and others, who engage in rational discourse. The main point for the moment is that Hegel's logic is not propositional or deductive, in the sense of providing criteria by which to determine whether one proposition follows from another by virtue of its form alone. He is centrally concerned with the categorial structure of rational discourse, of which propositional speech is a species. That is to say, he is interested in how one form or category follows from another by the very attempt to think the first form in itself. In this sense, Hegel aspires to the cognitive constitution of the world, but to a constitution that is itself both the world and its cognitive account. In another formulation, Hegel's is a logic of judgments, not propositions, and a judgment is already a synthesis of cognition and intelligible form.

This requires some expansion. Hegel is neither a monist nor a dualist. He does not reduce everything to cognition or to extension (to use the Cartesian terms that were familiar to him). But neither does he hold that cognition and extension, or spirit and nature, are separate. Hegel is neither an idealist nor a materialist. He holds that cognition and extension are two dimensions of a common actuality (in conventional language, "reality") or totality, a totality that can be described as an identity within difference.[7] This is not a purely "speculative" or (as we would say today) "metaphysical" statement for Hegel. It is a conclusion that is forced upon us by the facts of experience.

I will illustrate this point with an example from contemporary philosophy of language. Hegel could be understood to pose the following question: how can we refer to anything at all? There are two parts to any answer to this question. First: how can there be anything at all to which to refer? Second: what is the process by which the cognitive act of the referential agent "grasps" and identifies an item? We can give empirical rules for establishing the truth of referential statements, or what comes to the same thing, we can formalize these rules through the tacit acceptance of "common" or "intuitive" experience. In both cases, we assume the success of reference and proceed to describe it as rigorously as possible. And there is nothing wrong with this, so long as we admit that no explanation of reference has been offered. Hegel offers us an explanation. I mean by this that he explains how it is possible for the *ego cogitans* to escape from solipsism and to "grasp" (the literal sense of "conceive") anything at all, including itself. This last qualification is crucial, since Hegel holds that we cannot grasp ourselves except as other than another, or in less unfamiliar terms, except through the same concepts that explain the separateness or distinctness of the items in our ostensibly private experience. In terms more appropriate to an analysis of the *Phenomenology of Spirit* (hereafter *PS*), I am you because you are me, not as it were empirically but as manifestations of the process that underlies and constitutes all of human consciousness. This "identity," however, does not cancel out our difference. Indeed, the identity could not have been stated except because of the givenness of the difference.

So much for examples of the problems that will concern me in the following pages. We begin with Hegel in an effort to understand the fractures that developed in our conception of philosophy, fractures that have subsequently replaced the stable guidelines of the great rationalist tradition in Western thought. To sum up, there are three main problems, central to the history of Western philosophy, which Hegel claims to solve, and which he denies can be solved by traditional or nondialectical thinking. The first problem is that of analysis: how can we grasp the fundamental structure of discourse if we cannot grasp the atomic elements of cognition? Second is the problem of reference: how do we overcome the split between terms and their referents without collapsing the distinction between being and thinking, that is, without falling prey to subjective monism and thereby transforming the world into a product of convention? Third: is there a logic that is appropriate to the conceptualization of the unity of the process of life, as distinguished from the traditional rationalist logic of static and finite forms? These three problems can be restated as one general problem: how can we overcome the nihilism that is the consequence of Eleatic monism on the one hand, which leads to silence, and of Platonic-Aristotelian dualism on the other, which leads to the endless chatter of the history of philosophy? Hegel's logic is the fundamental step in his attempt to rescue us from estrangement and nihilism by the replacement of philosophy with wisdom.

ONE

The Historical Context

In this chapter, I shall be primarily concerned with the manner in which Hegel's understanding of the history of European philosophy contributes to the formation of his central problematic. My presentation of these problems is designed to cast light on Hegel's appropriation of the tradition and not to write a potted history of Western philosophy. Only those topics that are essential for an understanding of the *SL* will be included. I have postponed the consideration of excessively difficult material, such as Fichte's *Doctrine of Science*, for a more appropriate stage in our investigation. The interested reader will find additional historical material, in particular with respect to Plato and Aristotle, in my earlier book on Hegel.[1] It should also be admitted at the outset that Hegel's treatment of the history of philosophy is sometimes excessively general and that he often overinterprets points of interest to his own agenda.

I have not hesitated to introduce my own interpretations of familiar doctrines or problems when this seemed the best way to bring the serious student into the heart of the matter. The main intention of these pages is to think about or with Hegel, unrestricted by his own terms. Still more precisely, it is to arrive at a plausible representation of the spirit or inner dynamic of the Hegelian solution to the problem of traditional rationalism. I would almost go so far as to suggest that Hegel is appropriated in these pages, not merely interpreted. We shall attempt to learn from Hegel without becoming his disciples. This places upon us the burden of deciding which parts of the *SL* require extensive expansion and which may safely be put to one side.

Before I turn to the main order of business, I want to mention that Hegel's interpretation of his philosophical predecessors, and the use he makes of some of their doctrines, is not separate from the main doctrine of the

SL, in particular from the relation between temporality and eternity. To put this in an introductory formulation, human existence is for Hegel historical in the sense that it develops in a chronological order that somehow approximates to the dynamical development of the world at the dialectico-speculative level. In other words, the historical order in which the major stages of philosophy unfold toward its completion in Hegel's system is the same as the order of development in the logical derivation of the conceptual determinations of the idea of the whole. History mirrors logic. Or at least it mirrors a scientific presentation of logic.[2]

This peculiar doctrine deserves a restatement. History, and in particular the history of philosophy, is the story of the process by which human beings discover more and more about the structure of intelligibility, until at last the stage is set for Hegel, who arrives at the critical moment at which the whole has in principle been revealed and awaits only Hegel's explanatory description of it. In other words, the truth about the whole exhibits progressively more complex stages of its development within the thought of the most perspicuous thinker of each epoch, culminating with Hegel. This is surely one of the most obscure facets of Hegel's teaching; it is connected to his appropriation of Christian eschatology, in which the pivotal moment is the entrance of Jesus Christ into human history, but with this radical difference. Christ's *parousia*, or the entrance of eternity into temporality, sets the stage for a series of events that culminate in the "second coming" in the persona of Hegel, whose teaching is thus judgment day for all preceding doctrines and the establishment of heaven upon earth.[3] Strictly speaking, Hegel does not create a new doctrine but reports on the cumulative historical process by which the truth is realized. The chronological order of the history of philosophy thus mirrors, not just the human description of the revelation of truth, but the inner dynamic of that revelation itself.

It is not easy to explain the Hegelian doctrine of the coincidence of history and logic. Things become clearer when we recognize our own post-Hegelian age as the dissolution of the European Enlightenment, that is, the failure of Hegelianism. We can see Hegel as offering a choice between two versions of the future. The first version leads to scientific socialism and the second to Georg Lukács. But this by the way.

I note here only that this coincidence of history and logic is the foundation of Hegel's attempt to overcome modern nihilism. Another related question is what to make of expressions like the "life-pulse" of the concept or reiterated "spirit," human or absolute. Hegel applies the former to the dialectical process itself, and not just to the thinking of that process. "Spirit,"

on the other hand, does not refer to a psychological or self-conscious being, but, as Stephen Bungay puts it, "it is rather a concept in terms of which
anthropological and psychological phenomena can be understood."[4]

The "demystification" of Hegel's logic is sometimes convincing and
sometimes not. One finds with some frequency in the secondary literature
the view that Hegel accommodated his doctrines to Christianity in order
to avoid trouble with religious and political authorities. One problem with
this approach is that it attributes to Hegel a practice that he rejects. For
whatever it is worth, Hegel denies in his lectures on the history of Greek
philosophy that philosophers can conceal their ideas in their pockets.
He does hold that philosophy in its own nature is esoteric, but by this he
means that it is difficult, not that it can be concealed.[5] The aforementioned
difficulty does not arise explicitly in the *SL*; it belongs more properly to
the *PS* as well as to the *Encyclopedia* and Hegel's various university lecture
courses. Let us also remember that in the *SL*, the movement of thinking is
a response to the movement or "life-pulse" of the determinations of thinking. If that were not so, dialectic would itself disappear, and (in the Kantian
sense of these terms) reason would be reduced to understanding.

Plato and Aristotle

It is by now a platitude to all those trained in academic philosophy that
the Socratic school, and in the first instance Plato, initiates the tradition
of Western philosophy by a synthesis of the main teaching of Parmenides
and Heraclitus. To the extent that this is true, we may regard that tradition
as a debate between the partisans of the one and the many for dominance
in the attempt to discover, and later to construct, a comprehensive understanding of the world. Hegel as it were resolves the debate by transforming it into his new version of dialectic. Simply stated, the palm is awarded
neither to the one nor to the many, but to their agreement to disagree. This
can be illustrated by the problem of "nothing" or what Parmenides apparently calls "the altogether not." He warns us never to think or mention it
in any way but illustrates the inadequacy of this admonition by its very
formulation. Historians normally follow the Eleatic Stranger, the hero of
Plato's *Sophist*, from which we derive our knowledge of the Parmenidean
admonition, in speaking of a "parricide" by Plato, the actual student of
father Parmenides. By this is meant the ostensible fact that Plato rejects the
admonition and proceeds to offer us an analysis of the meaning of negation. But there is no parricide here; instead, Plato begins the long tradition
of rationalist adherence to Parmenides by avoiding the altogether not in

favor of one form or another of a rule or concept for syntactic negation. It is as if Parmenides were to have said that "the altogether not" has no semantic weight whatsoever, thereby persuading his successors to provide it with a syntactic function.

In fact, there is no radical distinction between semantics and syntactics, since rules of syntax themselves have meanings or express concepts. Plato interprets "not" to mean "other" or, more abstractly, "otherness." To say that the cow is not brown is then in fact to mean that the cow has some *other* color than brown. I cannot go into the details of this patently unsatisfactory analysis. I will mention only the case of negative existentials, such as "Socrates does not exist," which certainly cannot mean that Socrates is actually some other person. It is not necessary to give the history of the doctrine of predication, first systematically developed by Aristotle, for our present extremely restricted purpose. Suffice it to say that in a negative statement, we deny that a certain property "belongs to" a certain substance. I put "belongs to" in quotation marks because it is an unanalyzed or primitive concept in modern set theory as well as in Aristotle's doctrine of predication. A negative statement is thus not at all an attempt to say something about a self-contradictory entity called "nothing" (self-contradictory because it is a referent of a statement that denies that it possesses a referent). Instead, it records the absence or privation of something in particular within something else in particular. Stated somewhat awkwardly, to refer to the absence of something is not to refer to absence. In deference to Parmenides, we refer to the concept of absence, which has particular but never universal application. Something in particular can be absent from some other particular, but it makes no sense to try to utter true statements about total absence, because that would require a listing of its properties, of which it has none.

On the other hand, we can and do talk about the concept of total absence. In making use of this concept, we do not define the (nonexistent) properties of a (nonexistent) entity called "nothing." Instead, we explain how to use the expression "total absence" or "nothing" in rational discourse. In my opinion, which I have expressed elsewhere at considerable length, this is not a satisfactory solution to the paradox of Parmenides. But our concern here is with Hegel, and he resolves the paradox by applying the previously mentioned principle that we cannot think of anything that is outside our thought. "Nothing" is for Hegel the most universal form of the concept of the absence of all categorial determinations. But these determinations are absent in the unity of thinking and being that is the inescapable horizon or theater within which we think of anything whatsoever. There is, so to speak, nothing outside this horizon, because the moment we posit that there is, we have in fact situated it within our thinking. This is the background to the otherwise unintelligible statement that being and nothing are the same.

Pure being cannot possess any determinations whatsoever, for then it would no longer be pure. That is, it would be some other category, such as becoming or existence. As nothing in particular, being just is, or is inseparable (but not, as we shall see later, indistinguishable) from nothing. Being and nothing are thus the first stage in the process by which we identify the universal horizon of the world or, more precisely, what Hegel calls "the whole." Hegel calls the universal horizon "the concept," which we can gloss as follows. Thinking begins with the mind's act of grasping within itself whatever it thinks about. "Grasp" is the literal sense of the German word for "concept": *Begriff*. It should already be obvious that Hegel is going to have to explain the relation between the world of existing things (what the Greeks called *onta*) and the process of thought. To anticipate, he will not say that the world of things is identical with the thought processes of each existing thinker, since this would amount to filling up our thought with existing stones, trees, and so on. But he will say that the laws of thought are the same as the laws of existing things. There is thus a structural, or (in the dialectical sense of the term) logical, connection between thinking in general and being in general.

Despite all signs to the contrary, Hegel is thus firmly within the rationalist tradition in obeying Parmenides's command not to think of or mention the altogether not. Hegel is entirely concerned with the category "nothing," which is itself a primitive structural component, along with being, of the concept, that is, of the universal horizon for thinking altogether. Hegel's understanding of the structure of negativity is, however, more complicated than the usual rationalist view. For the time being, let me say that what is normally called "logical negation" is in Hegel's terminology "determinate negation." That is, the positing of a particular as not some property p (i.e., the negation of p) highlights the particular as some other particular q. We can see here quite plainly the concept of what Plato called "otherness." For Platonists, each "other" is logically or ontologically distinct from all the rest, and this is also true at the logical or ontological level of the universal forms (Plato's "greatest genera") or categories that underlie all discourse. For Hegel, the determinate negation is the first step in a dialectical process through which the formal properties or categories implicit in anything whatsoever are gradually made explicit and shown to be interconnected. Stated as simply as possible, negation introduces a connection between two terms as well as a separation. To think p is also to think non-p.

The transformation of the altogether not into the concept of negation can be understood dialectically as the resolution of the debate between the one and the many in such a way as to give a proper role to each in the construction of intelligible discursive thinking. The many are in fact many ones or units, and this makes it possible for the many to retain their independent natures when they combine into identifiable unit-multiples (or units with inner articulation). For example, "red" and "ball" combine into "red ball," a unity that does not destroy its component units. Conversely, each one may combine or not combine with any of the others, which makes it possible for us to speak about any given unit in terms of its "properties" or the other units with which it combines (and similarly for those properties with which it does not combine). Thus the world is neither simply one nor simply many but a unification of the two that gives equal weight to each. The world is a unity of unit-multiples. Hegel calls this an identity of identity and nonidentity (or difference). I shall frequently refer to this expression as "the identity of identity and difference" in order to preserve its positive resonance. That is, the identity of the world (= the whole) is not in addition to, but is essentially defined by, the nonidentity or difference between one unit and another.

This apparently peculiar expression can also be understood as the dialectical version of Aristotle's use of *qua* or "with respect to." The various respects in which we can speak of something are its collective differences, and the substance or entity of which we are speaking in each case is the identity that stands under or unifies the differences without dissolving them. For example, the substantial unity "ball" unites without dissolving the units "red" and "round" to form the unit multiple "red round ball." To be anything at all is to be both identity and difference (a red ball rather than a blue one), and these jointly constitute the complete nature of the entity, which is brought out by referring to the identity of identity and nonidentity. It is not enough to say that the entity is both identity and difference, because these two expressions are opposites. They need to be reconciled or united at a higher level to which each contributes by the retention of its own nature. A word of warning: the one that unites with no other units, and thereby exhibits no differences at all, is nothing, or rather the sameness of being and nothing. Conversely, the many, in which each element is entirely detached from the others, is neither being nor nothing but the concept of quantity.

Earlier in the chapter I mentioned that Plato attempts to overcome the problem of the one and the many by a noetic alphabet of pure formal letters or elements, each of which is a determinate form as well as a unity. In his simile, we can distinguish, say, change from rest just as we distinguish the letter alpha from the letter beta. In both cases, the element or letter presents a unified form that is distinct from every other form. This unity remains undisturbed and indeed untouched in its identity by attempts to analyze it, all of which attempts are predicated upon its antecedent existence as just what it is. The complex structures of formal discourse are built up of atomic elements, just as words (or, as we can say, the names of concepts) are built up out of letters. We cannot give an analytical account of the formal element by reducing it to some simpler constituents; these elements are themselves the simplest constituents of the intelligible. So too the letters of the alphabet are simples with respect to the "spelling" or structure of the word. This thesis is obviously the ancestor of the early-twentieth-century doctrine of logical atomism.

It is Hegel's contention that the impossibility of explaining a primitive formal element by itself, without making use of the others, or in other words of the initial interconnectedness of these elements with respect to human cognition, is due to an ontological interconnectedness such that the elements not only are not individually conceivable but do not exist independently of each other. The heart of the matter for Hegel is that what Plato claims to be independent and stable properties are in fact dialectically excited moments of a complex process that is continuously transforming one property into the other. If the elements were static and independent, the coherence and life of the world would be unintelligible. Otherwise stated, Plato's world is not one cosmos but two: the cosmos of pure formal structure and the cosmos of genesis. Hegel intends to overcome this dualism, not by reducing one cosmos to the other, or reinstituting monism, but by his doctrine of sublation (*Aufhebung*) or the identity of identity and non-identity. This expression, to repeat, refers to the preservation of opposing moments at a higher level, which moments both contribute to the richer meaning or structure of intelligibility. Hegel intends to show that genesis, which, if understood to be separate from intelligible form, has the status of an "illusory shining" (*Schein*) or image of being, is in fact the shining forth (*Erscheinung*) of essence. Genesis is not separate from but is rather the presentation of form, but form understood as formation process. The motion or change of genesis is thus not *essentially* different from the motion or change of the *koinonia* (communion) of formal elements.

The crucial contribution of Aristotle is to bring down the forms from heaven and to allow them to "actualize" within the activity of thinking it-self. Two Hegelian theses may be traced back to this step. First: there is no separation of being, in the sense of formal intelligibility, and thinking. Second: whereas Plato's forms are entirely static, Aristotle's form is defined as *energeia* or actuality, where "actuality" can be interpreted as a kind of ac-tivity or (in anachronistic terms) a transcendental motion. The Aristotelian *eidōs* is a "being at work," which from a Hegelian standpoint may be con-ceived as expressive of the life or spirit of the thinking by which the form moves from potentiality to actuality. Note that Hegel adapts in his own way the Aristotelian distinction between the divine or active and human or passive intellect. In the *SL*, we are studying divine intellect, hence thinking God's thoughts just prior to the creation of the universe. Just as in Aristotle the human intellect can "perceive" the actualization of the form effected by the divine or agent intellect, so in Hegel the finite human being can grasp the conceptual structure of absolute spirit as it manifests itself in the quasi-categorial dialectic that constitutes the structure of intelligibility. In sum: Aristotle furnishes the prototype of the Hegelian conception of being and thinking as excitation, interconnection, and development. Thinking is thus the work of the spirit, a work in which human spirit and absolute spirit are unified by the content of their thought. As we saw previously, this unity is an expression of the life of the concept. It should be added here that Hegel's view of Aristotle is distinctly influenced by Christian Neopla-tonism and in fact exhibits one of his most fundamental intentions: to rec-oncile the biblical and in particular the Christian religious tradition with the Aristotelian version of classical philosophy.

The *Ego Cogitans*

Hegel begins his presentation of logic with a reference to Kant. In order to make the reference intelligible, we have to start with a preliminary reflec-tion on the Cartesian founding of modern philosophy. For Hegel, the cru-cial feature of the Cartesian revolution is the doctrine of subjectivity. Other-wise stated, Descartes begins with the dualism of mind and body. Whereas metaphysics (as we can call it) deals with the mind, modern science pro-vides knowledge of the body. The question naturally arises: how can we bring together these two types of knowledge into a unified account of the whole? If we apply the techniques of science to the study of the mind, the latter is soon reduced to an epiphenomenon of the body. The contrary ef-fort to apply the techniques of metaphysics to the study of the body leads to subjective idealism or what Hegel would call estrangement from the actual world. Leibniz attempts to overcome this reductivism, or its alternative, dualism, by introducing the doctrine of a preestablished harmony between the two domains of nature (body) and grace (the soul). This is the preparation for Kant's two domains of the phenomena and the noumena.

It should be noted that Descartes speaks of mind rather than soul in formulating the central theoretical question of dualism. He treats the soul separately in a treatise on the passions, which in effect interprets the soul as an epiphenomenon of the body. Leibniz attempts to reconcile the Greeks with the Bible; in this important respect he sets the stage for Kant and Hegel. But there is an intermediate stage in which Rousseau is without doubt the most important figure. This stage prepares a kind of alternative to the soul in the form of "spirit" (*esprit*), sentiment, and inner reflection, or what Kierkegaard will later call "inwardness." As is well-known, Kant was initially influenced by Hume but later found a deeper source of inspiration in Rousseau. Hume taught him that we cannot establish necessity (a priori principles, causal connections, mathematics) so long as the intellect is subordinated to nature. Rousseau taught him of the moral conscience and the sentiment of interiority as independent of and higher than the conceptual knowledge of nature. Instead of attempting to reduce one dimension to the other, or to relate the two by recourse to a theological metaphysics of predetermination, which among its other disadvantages threatens the fact of freedom, Kant preserves dualism by fixing the limits of each domain. In his famous words, "I had to deny knowledge [of the domain of pure reason] in order to make room for *faith*."[6] He attempts to overcome the disadvantages of dualism by means of his critical philosophy, that is to say, by the very definition of the conditions that establish the limits of each domain. From a Hegelian standpoint, this is a modification of Spinozism: We are free because we know the limits of determinism, but this freedom is purchased at the price of the most important knowledge about ourselves. We cannot know but only hope that we are free, that we possess immortal souls, and that there is a God.

Hegel in effect resolves the impasse of Kantianism by adapting the Kantian doctrine of asymptotic development toward an infinitely distant historical resolution of human suffering, together with Kant's presentation of the dialectic of the antinomies of pure reason. To state this in a concise and introductory manner, Kant argues that the attempt to think the whole issues in a series of contradictions, namely, that the world is spatiotemporally finite and infinite; that with respect to the spatiotemporal finitude or infinitude of the universe, composite substances do and do not consist of simple parts; that human beings are and are not free; and that there is and is not a necessary being that belongs to the world.[7] Hegel attempts to show that the dialectic of reason is itself progressive in a positive sense; the contradictions of the antinomies unfold as it were into an all-encompassing conceptual structure of the whole. In so doing, they also overcome the split between eternity and history, or in another vocabulary, between categories and concepts on the one hand and historico-political existence on the other. The subjective interior of mankind and the corporeal or natural exterior are shown to be both preserved and yet overcome within the total development of what Hegel calls the absolute. It is at this point that the various left-Hegelians deviate from Hegel by demoting the absolute to the level of endlessly continuing history, or else, as in the case of the Marxists, into endless post-history.

The notion of historical development that is central to Hegel is a characteristic of modern philosophy, which may be understood in its entirety as an ongoing revolution against the ancient and medieval worlds of the pagans on the one hand and the biblical tradition on the other. This revolution is carried out in two parallel ways. With respect to nature or the body, science proceeds analytically or genetically, by what we can call the genealogical method of discovering the original principles and elements. With respect to human affairs, and so the soul or mind, the elements and first principles seem to be inaccessible. Philosophers therefore attempt to infer them from the historical process itself, by constructing theoretical models of human nature, as in seventeenth- and eighteenth-century doctrines of the state of nature. It is at this crucial point that Hegel deviates from the standard progressive character of modern philosophy in a way that reminds us of Leibniz. Hegel combines the historical conception of human nature with the Christian doctrine of eschatology. The "end of history" takes place here and now, in Hegel's own exhibition of the truth about human existence. History of course continues; but it is the eternal return of the same logical structure, and so the contingent events of historical existence provide us with no new knowledge of the structure of intelligibility, that is to say, of the thesis that human nature reveals itself in its actions, or that it emerges historically.

The various accounts prior to Hegel of the historical character of our moral and political nature are not sustained by an ontological or epistemological account of the ego or subject. Sensation is the theoretical counterpart to the practical concept of history. In the empiricist tradition, best represented by Locke and Hume, we begin with a study of the mind by reflection on its experience, which is initially sensation or *representation*, and we end with Hume's conclusion that the mind in itself is inaccessible.

The only thing we can know is the discontinuous flow of experience, that is to say, of the representation in our sensations of an inaccessible self. The *ego cogitans* knows its cogitations but not the ego. In the idealist tradition (within which we can situate Kant, who is assimilated to Fichte by Hegel), the same result obtains. For neither Kant nor Fichte can we say that the ego is knowable in itself. What we can know is the conceptual activity of the ego or, in Fichtean language, its positings (the projection of objects of cognition).

To clarify this last point: the subject projects or produces the object as a limitation of its own nature; as a result, the subject is concealed by its own cognitive activity. Despite the ostensible accessibility of transcendental structure, or rather because of it, we have cognitive access only to our own representation of ourselves, in other words, to the idealist version of sensation. We should not forget that for Fichte as well as for Kant, the overcoming of dualism is by way of practice, not theory. And for both, this overcoming is linked to history in such a way as to play an essential role in the subsequent development of the philosophy of history (a development in which figures like Montesquieu, Rousseau, Herder, and Schiller also play an important part).

Hegel's view of the deficiencies of the Kantian-Fichtean doctrine can be illustrated by the concept of the synthetic unity of apperception. This is the unity of thinking that underlies the structure of necessary connections by which our experience is constituted. It is, however, as Hegel objects, a logical or empty thesis that tells us nothing about the ego that enacts the synthesis. Knowledge of the inner nature of subjectivity is missing here; instead we get the condition for the possibility of subjective experience. Instead of knowledge of subjectivity, Kant gives us a version of Rousseau's doctrine that we are certain of ourselves in moral experience, through the phenomenon of the moral conscience. This leads us to hope for freedom and immortality; in so hoping, we place our credence in a hypothesis that must be the case if freedom is to obtain. Kant is unable to overcome the division between belief and knowledge or the dualism of pagan philosophy and biblical religion.

On this basic point, Kant has not advanced beyond Hume; with respect to subjectivity, Kant is for Hegel, odd though it sounds, an empiricist. Spirit is not self-conscious in the Kantian doctrine of the transcendental ego. How can this be rectified? Kant himself has unknowingly stumbled onto the right road. His antinomies show the dialectical character of experience. The antinomies of pure reason arise from the attempt to think the totality of the world in space and time; they culminate in the attempt to reconcile the necessity of nature and the freedom of the soul. Kant assigns the task of thinking elements or series of elements within totality to the understanding, and it is here alone that genuine scientific knowledge is accessible. This is the domain of necessity, that is to say, of the phenomenal world.

The thinking of totality, and so too of freedom, is assigned to the reason. Whereas the knowledge acquired by the understanding is constitutive of the structure of the world of experience, the thinking of totality and freedom is regulative. We can call this a thinking of ideals that are required to render coherent our knowledge of natural necessity and our moral sense of the dignity of a rational person. This is of course the briefest sketch of a complicated aspect of Kant's teaching, but it is enough to indicate that from a Hegelian standpoint, there is a dualism between understanding as the instrument of knowledge and reason as the instrument of faith. It is Hegel's goal to bring together understanding and reason in such a way as to show that the ideals of the latter are achieved or fully manifested in the structure of the former. This in turn depends upon the transformation of the synthetic unity of apperception from a logical condition of consciousness to a principle of subjectivity, namely, the principle that underlies the unity of subject and object.

Kant thus provides Hegel with the elements of dialectical reasoning, without himself having achieved a genuine resolution of the dualism of knowledge and belief. He shows that thinking is self-contradictory, or in other words that there is a contradiction between understanding and reason. But he is unable to resolve this contradiction because he cannot bring reason within the domain of cognitive knowing. For Hegel, on the other hand, the antinomies exhibit not the limitations of thinking but rather the dialectical structure of actuality. Differently stated, the antinomies are a feature of abstract understanding, which deals with static forms and is obedient to the principle of noncontradiction in its traditional form. The correct shift from the Kantian understanding and reason to the Hegelian sense of a comprehensive conceptual thinking depends upon recognition of the dynamical structure of contradiction, and so too of forms or predicates. Every determination is a negation or limitation (the principle stems from Spinoza) in two senses. First, each thing is this particular entity and nothing else. But second, it can be distinguished from everything else only through the incorporation of what it excludes within the conceptual analysis of its formal structure or definition.

It should be mentioned here that Hegel's thinking on this point was criticized by Bertrand Russell as rooted in a failure to distinguish between identity and predication,[8] but this is not correct. I will come back to this later in much more detail, but we ought to make an introductory response to Russell's criticism in order to remove an initial obstacle to the appreciation of Hegel's technical doctrine. I note that Hegel's doctrine is entirely compatible with the modern scientific notion of the interdependence of all elements of a system and, in the extreme case, of the cosmos. Hegel's logic is one not of identity and predication but rather of the interpenetration of formal determinations, of the development or evolution of complexity from initial simplicity. Hegel is attempting to explain the seamlessness of genesis in terms of the process by which one constituent element involves, or more precisely is transformed into, another.

Hegel does not deny that each moment in a structure of formal properties (or predicates) has its individual identity. His point is rather that the attempt to think and so to define with precision the identity of a given property entails a reference first to the logical complement of that property and second to the total underlying structure of analytical or identifying discourse. Thus Hegel would explain the identity of a predicate as itself rooted in its logical interconnectedness with all other predicates. But this interconnectedness has nothing to do with predicational logic, which belongs to the level of understanding, not of dialectico-speculative reason. In dialectical logic, the identity of a thing is itself a consequence of the participation of complementary or contradictory properties. In other words, the dialectical logician is concerned with the analysis of formal or categorial structure, not with the form of logical inference.

Russell contends that for Hegel, since Socrates is mortal, "Socrates" and "mortal" are identical; since they are different, they must constitute an identity in difference. In fact, Hegel is not concerned with propositions like "Socrates is mortal" in the *SL*. Propositions of this sort belong to the domain of understanding. One could, however, assert that the identity of Socrates depends upon, or includes necessarily, the predicate of mortality. The proposition in question would become dialectical if and only if Socrates were simultaneously immortal as well as mortal, but not if he were mortal in this life and immortal in the next. On the other hand, Socrates is, as identical with himself, different from everyone else. The identifiability of Socrates depends upon his separateness. Identity and difference are thus ingredient in each other. In traditional rationalism, we pay no attention to this reciprocal interpenetration of formal determinations; or if we do, we call them abstractions. For Hegel, on the contrary, reciprocal interpenetration is the pulse beat of life. The abstractions of analytical understanding are brought to life by dialectical logic.

In the *SL* we are given the conceptual structure of experience in the order in which its elements must be thought if the result is to be a presup-positionless and systematic science, or in other words, a unified wisdom rather than a dualism of knowledge buttressed by belief. The next step, not taken in the *SL* itself, is for the content of the universe to emerge from within its logical structure by further stages of development. This emergence corresponds to the creation of the world by the God who has just completed the process of conceptualizing its structure. The rhythm of this development, or its logical life-pulse, is exactly the same as that described in the *SL*. Otherwise stated, there is no actual separation of structure and content, but in the *SL* we study the structure independent of the content. The form, so to speak, *is* the content of logic.

In the actual world, however, there is no split between God and creation, although their underlying unity (as an identity within difference) is not manifested until the entrance of God into human history in the form of Jesus. The historical process by which God becomes man is as it were conceptualized in Hegel's retrospective assimilation of the twin processes of eternal and historical development. Our task in this study is in principle restricted to grasping the conceptual structure of the world, not its actualization as a spatiotemporal cosmos. We are not required to assimilate the cosmos in its full manifestation; our task is the more modest one of becoming God. By thinking God's thoughts, Hegel becomes God; by thinking Hegel's thoughts as presented in the *SL*, we do the same.

In the preceding remarks, I have described the central theme of Hegel's *SL* in a way that concentrates upon his appropriation of ancient and modern philosophy. Plato and Aristotle define the ontological problem; Descartes introduces subjectivity, the tool that prepares the solution to the problem. Hegel claims to describe the self-articulation of the abstract *ego cogitans* into the self-consciousness of absolute spirit. The subsequent history of Kant's transcendental ego shows not only that the ego is the absolute (Fichte), and so too the thing-in-itself, but also that the absolute reveals or manifests itself in the activity of thinking (Hegel). Kant is thus the transition-point between what we can call the empirical history of Locke and Hegel's absolute history.

From a Hegelian standpoint, Locke was correct in holding that the mind observes itself after it has developed. But Locke was unable to supply the structure of this development. What he observed, so to speak, was an unstructured account of the phenomenal experience of mind. His *Essay concerning Human Understanding* is thus the prototype for Hegel's *PS*. Hume, the crucial precursor of Kant's theoretical philosophy, is the prototype for the *SL*. Kant supplies the essential elements of the transcendental machinery as well as the emphasis on contradiction. Fichte explicitly identifies the ego as the absolute and introduces the notion of transcendental history. This is further developed by Schelling, for whom the Kantian ego (*Ich*) or synthetic unity of apperception is not an original or immediate synthesis but the result of a thesis (*Ich*) and antithesis (*nicht-Ich*). Stated succinctly, Hegel provides us with the transcendental history of contradiction. He shows how contradiction at the level of categorial thinking is the first moment in a resolution of the two apparently irreconcilable terms at a higher level of complexity.

Hegel's appropriation of Kant can also be understood in terms of his interest in Greek skepticism, which he very much admired, regarding it as entirely superior to the modern variety.[9] Ancient skepticism doubts the results of sense perception, not of reason (*Vernunft*). It serves the valuable function of dissolving the commonsense understanding of the world. Hegel expresses this by saying that ancient skepticism shows the negative moment of the understanding (*Verstand*: common sense rooted in sense perception) that has not reached or infected reason. Modern skepticism, on the contrary, doubts reason while accepting the testimony of sense perception. It thus leads to a dogmatism of the sciences of experience, together with those of mathematics or analytical formalism.

This doubt of reason (except in its mathematical or purely formal use) and acceptance of sense perception amounts to a division between thinking and being. The world is taken for granted as the referent of sense perception; i.e., it is essentially extension. The source of thinking, however, is not accessible. Mathematics alone can and must serve as a bridge from the inaccessible *ego cogitans* to the accessibility of sensation. Since mathematics is nondialectical formalism, it has no internal principle of development through contradiction and serves not merely to structure experience but to mark the boundary between the rational and the nonrational. It is the enforcer of dualism. And the world of science is a dogmatic construction that is lacking in human significance because it is devoid of spirit. The false synthesis of mathematics and sensation is unstable and deteriorates into a bad because endless infinity, disguised by scientific rhetoric as infinite progress. From this standpoint, Kant is still a modern skeptic in the style of Hume.

In the preceding sketch of Hegel's appropriation of the tradition, I have said next to nothing about a crucial strand in his early development: the influence of Rousseau, Schiller, Hölderlin, and others in the attempt to overcome Kantian dualism with a doctrine of moral sentiment as the anticipation of the categorical imperative or love as the unification of opposites, a unification that preserves both the integrity of the individual person and

finite experience. Important though this influence may be in understanding the sources of Hegel's thinking, it appears in the *SL* only in the abstract
form of the identity of identity and difference. I have therefore restricted
myself to touching upon the logical and metaphysical themes of Hegel's
predecessors that play a direct role in the *SL*. In this context, let me mention that I shall have to discuss Fichte at some length, but it will be better
to do so as a preface to the logic of reflection in book 2[10].

A Note on Religion

In the doctrines of Descartes and his followers, there is a dualism of mind
and body within an unknowable substance (the ghost of the Eleatic one).
In Kant, there is a Leibnizian "preestablished harmony" of mind and body
within an unknowable substance that is, however, accessible to practice
or the conscience. In Hegel, mind and body are initial manifestations of
spirit (*Geist*), which develop neither separately nor identically but differently within identity. Hegel thus prepares decisively the ground of late-
modern "process" philosophies by shifting attention from mind and body
to the process by which they develop and through which they are united.
The theological consequence of this Hegelian version of the modern shift
from substance to function (in Cassirer's phrase) is the overcoming of the
separation between God and the world, an overcoming that is mediated
by the figure of Jesus Christ. There cannot be a transcendent God for Hegel, namely, a God that is separate from creation and hidden from human
intelligence. On this point one can say that orthodox Christian interpretations of Hegel, whether from the right like that of Ivan Iljin or from the left
like that of Michael Theunissen, despite their great interest, are certainly
mistaken. The creation of the world is an externalization of God's thought;
in other words, the apparent separation is actually overcome in the very
act of creation, because to understand the structure of creation is to understand God.

In the *Lectures on the Philosophy of Religion*, the crucial step in this process of understanding is provided by the entrance of God into human history in the person of Jesus, who translates the ontological process into a
historical or teleological one. Jesus is as it were the concrete manifestation
of the biblical statement that God created mankind in his image. But this
formulation of the issue belongs to what Hegel himself calls in the *PS*
"representation" or the popular language of religion. Despite rhetorical or
metaphorical passages like the one in which we are invoked to think the
thoughts of God prior to the creation of the universe, religion plays no

explicit role in the logical articulation of the concept. In fact, as is pointed out by a leading expert on Hegel's religious thought, Walter Jaeschke, the "philosophico-theological dimension," i.e., the ostensible identity of the traditional God and the absolute idea, "is, however, only indirectly derivable from the chapter on the absolute idea at the end of the *Logic*. It is only the philosophy of religion that makes it fully clear that the absolute idea is the proper object of philosophical theology. For it is only here that the content of the idea of the identity of concept and reality has become sufficiently concrete for the idea of God not to remain abstract."[11] Jaeschke does not seem to notice that this makes Hegel's views ambiguous, indeed, entirely obscure, since the lectures on the philosophy of religion are exoteric works, not part of the system. In other words, the whole question of Hegel's religious views remains open. I will say only that it strikes me as impossible to identify the traditional conception of God with the absolute idea. Whatever the exact content of Hegel's religious views (he always insisted that he was a Lutheran), there cannot be any doubt about the role that the Christian interpretation of divine and human history plays in his own account of human experience. We can say with considerable support from the texts that Hegel was neither a pantheist (= monist) nor a dualist. The divine spirit, as expressed in the Christian trinity, is for Hegel at the very least a representation of the identity within difference of eternity and temporality, that is, of the indispensable condition for the knowledge of totality. In the *SL*, however, this condition is defended in conceptual rather than representational terms. Metaphors to one side, we shall follow Hegel in our exposition.

TWO

The Prefaces

We are now ready to turn to the text of the *SL*. Hegel has given us two prefaces and an introduction to the *SL*. One preface is to the original edition of 1812 (as is the introduction); the second preface is for a new edition and is dated November 1831; it is thus one of the last writings from Hegel's pen, and we will study it very carefully. I will begin with a brief consideration of the first of Hegel's two prefaces.

The Preface of 22 March 1812

Hegel's major works, the *PS* and the *SL*, were composed during the height of Napoleon's consolidation of his empire. Shortly after seeing Napoleon at the battle of Jena in 1806, Hegel referred to him as "reason on horseback." In other words, both the *PS* and the *SL* are postrevolutionary works. We can characterize Hegel's general understanding of the French Revolution by borrowing an expression from the *PS*; the Revolution corresponds to "the Terror" or mutual destruction of the leading factions that is the practical analogue to the "night in which all cows are black."[1] Hegel refers with this phrase to Schelling's absolute idealism; the sense of the metaphor is to criticize conceptions of the absolute that fail to preserve individual determinations and that thereby dissolve the actual world. More generally, Hegel understands human history as a dialectical process of continuous development through the posing of contradictory positions and their reconciliation in a more comprehensive stage. Within each stage, the negation of the initial position results in a temporary nihilism that is overcome by the formulation of the succeeding stage. The French Revolution, and in particular the Terror, is the nihilism that precedes the "final" stage, which Hegel seems to understand as a kind of synthesis between the Protestant

Prussian monarchy and the Napoleonic code.² Schelling is the philosophical expression of this penultimate nihilism.

I say "penultimate" because Hegel intends to transform the exhausted
relics of the philosophical tradition into an exposition of the truth, the
whole truth, and nothing but the truth. The true, as Hegel says, is the whole.
Hegel is thus like the surprise witness in a complex trial whose testimony
makes intelligible the previously obscure and mutually inconsistent assertions of his predecessors. He begins the preface with a remark about philosophical revolution. In the past twenty-five years, he says, there has been a
"complete transformation" in philosophy; more precisely, the period has
exhibited the extirpation of what was previously called "metaphysics" (by
the Leibniz-Wolff-Baumgarten school). But this transformation has not yet
had much influence on logic (3).³ Hegel means that even Kant accepts the
Aristotelian logic as final, whereas interest in earlier ontology, rational psychology, cosmology, and natural theology is no longer manifest.

It is what Hegel refers to as Kant's "exoteric teaching" that is responsible
for the renunciation of speculative thinking. The term "exoteric" means not
that Kant is concealing his genuine views but rather that his distinction
between understanding (*Verstand*) and reason (*Vernunft*) leads to the vulgar
or superficial thesis that the former cannot go beyond experience without
transforming the powers of knowledge into a pseudotheoretical *Vernunft*,
which can give birth to nothing but ghosts. In an especially striking passage,
Hegel says: "To the extent that science and the commonsense understanding of human life [*der gemeine Menschenverstand*] work together in order
to achieve the destruction of metaphysics, so the peculiar spectacle seems
to have been brought about of *a cultivated people without metaphysics*" (4).⁴
This passage is interesting because it could easily have been written to describe our own time, or let us say the situation of philosophy in 1968, just
prior to the advent of the various movements conveniently joined together
under the title "postmodernism." But there is a crucial difference from a
Hegelian standpoint between the French Revolution of 1789, which is a
world-historical event that proves its seriousness by the bloodshed it initiates, and the revolution of 1968, which is a bourgeois uprising that proves
its triviality by the amount of verbiage it engenders.

However this may be, Hegel is not advocating a return to the metaphysics of the disciples of Leibniz, any more than postmodernists advocate a
return to what they call the metaphysics of Platonism. Hegel recognizes
the spiritual poverty of the alliance between positive science and common sense, which resembles "an otherwise completely ornamented temple
without what is most holy" (4). These dark periods in the spiritual history

of mankind are, however, incomplete negations in the sense that the inner restlessness of spirit will negate the negated content and thus give rise to a new period of fecundity.[5] Hence the emergence of Hegel as the historical agent of double negation, that is, the dialectical transformation of nihilism into the final epoch of world history. Marx will later modify this transformation by replacing Schelling with the universal proletariat, whose lack of all property, including their own children and even their bodies, makes them the negative basis for world revolution.

It would therefore be a great mistake to attribute to Hegel a doctrine of uniform progress. A related error is to take his statement in the *Philosophy of Right* (hereafter *PR*) that the actual is the rational to mean that whatever occurs is rational and so a genuine manifestation of the absolute. On the contrary, most of what occurs is not rational; only the whole is true or *wirklich* in Hegel's special sense of the term.[6] One could say that the dark spots in the book of history are necessary, but only as a preparation for the next stage of development, not in themselves. In colloquial language, great mistakes are fruitful because the despair they engender serves to stimulate a new outburst of creativity. The separation of *Verstand* from *Vernunft* is a mistake because it leads to the triumph of common sense in everyday life and to the replacement in theology of rational speculation by feelings or sentiments (*Gefühle*), the practico-popular and historical doctrines of thinkers like Schleiermacher, F. H. Jacobi, and (at a much lower level) J. F. Fries. History has thus presented us with the penultimate stage in this discipline. Not so with logic, however, which remains at the level of its Aristotelian beginnings. Innovation in logic must therefore at the same time amount to the "negation" or dialectical dissolution of the rigid structure of a method that is independent of and imposed onto its content. As one could put it, Hegel must show that logic is the life of thinking, not its taskmaster. Hegel employs a more brutal metaphor. Logic is today a method external to the sciences, by which we are supposed to learn how to think, "as if one should first learn how to digest and move one's bowels by studying anatomy and physiology" (4).

Once again, we must never forget that Hegel does not wish to abolish traditional or (as we often call it) formal logic. He wishes to exhibit the pattern intrinsic to the development of the thinking of the whole. The whole is an organic unity; it cannot be captured by analysis into rigid and lifeless structures. Even if there were a "complete" logical calculus, whether of the Aristotelian or Fregean-Russellian variety, it would provide us with the structure of understanding in the Kantian sense, but not with the process by which that structure and its content could be expressed as a unified totality. The forms of Hegel's logic grow into each other in a cumulative development toward completeness or circularity. The task of the expositor seems therefore odd, not to say implausible, to the traditional rationalist. We can as it were name or identify the individual components in the unified structure of the whole, but as soon as we list the predicates or attributes of each component, it turns into its opposite. In order to understand at the outset what Hegel is arguing, we must remember that he intends to describe the process of world formation through the interaction of formal determinations or categories. Hegel's categories are alive, dynamic, and interactive. They can no more be, or be thought to be, independent and rigid than can the greatest genera of Plato's *Sophist*.

To continue with the preface, despite the retention of the old logic, Hegel is confident that the philosophical revolution will extend itself to this science as well: "Once the substantial form of spirit has transformed itself, it is vain to want to preserve the forms of earlier cultivation [*Bildung*]" (5). Hegel exhibits here the conviction of the revolutionary theorist that history is on his side. And this raises an extremely important point. It is one thing for an age to be ready for a new logic; it is something else again for that logic to be successful. Hegel is confident that the new epoch has completed its period of fermentation, as is evident even in those who oppose it but are unable to resist its transformation. It is now time for the reworking and cultivation (*Ausbildung*) of the new content of the age, but this is to say that it is a time for the formation (*Bildung*) of an age, as well as of the individual resident therein, through the acquisition and assertion of the new principle. In other words, the revolution of philosophy is itself a free act of the human spirit. It must be carried out by human activity. History provides us with the materials for transformation or fulfillment, but success depends upon human work.[7] When we lose the intensity of conceptual thinking, that work deteriorates, and the Hegelian system, which cannot be superseded by something more comprehensive, collapses into fragments, each of which presents itself as an original philosophical "position."

The inverse situation obtains at the moment in which Hegel presents his *SL* to the world. The work of developing the philosophical systems that will constitute the building blocks of Hegel's system has now been completed. But there is an important lacuna: the new logic, or the exposition of the true significance of all this work, has not yet appeared. As Hegel puts it, the logical science that constitutes "genuine metaphysics or pure speculative philosophy" (6) has hitherto been neglected; in other words, the conceptual structure of the new principle of subjectivity has not yet been understood. Hegel is thus starting from scratch as a dialectico-speculative logician in the *SL*. He has no predecessors in this field, nor could he, since his work is the decisive step in the unfolding of the last because fully rational stage. In keeping with the radical novelty of his attempt, Hegel has been unable to give his treatment a greater completeness (6). He means by this not that there are more categories or moments of the concept to be discovered but that his exposition of logic leaves room for greater detail and more refinement.

His essential point is the need for a new concept of scientific procedure (6). Philosophy, which ought to be a science in its own right, cannot borrow its method from a subordinate science like mathematics, nor can it rest content with the categories secured by previous methods, in particular by inner intuition (*Anschauung*) or by external reflection. Hegel means by this last expression the linear or nondialectical and finite logic of traditional rationalism, in which the determinations of conceptual thinking are imposed onto philosophical content by a separate, independently devised method. This makes philosophy dependent upon an external science. In genuine reflection, the content "poses and produces" its own logical determination (6).

The new logic thus produces its own content by transforming the old logical determinations. Hegel gives what is even for him an extremely condensed introductory statement of the heart of his new logic (6–7). Let us examine this statement with some care. "*Verstand* fixes and preserves determinations." This is a reference to the predicative activity that lies at the heart of traditional logic. In the language of the logic of Hegel's day, S is p, and p is predicated of the subject S. But as Hegel learned from Spinoza, every determination is a negation. Precisely as p, S is not non-p. Reason shows us that negativity (the dialectical version of negation; one could call it the negative work of *Das Nichts* or nothing) plays a role in determining the structure of S. "*Vernunft* is negative and dialectical because it dissolves the determinations of *Verstand* into nothing." That is, the attempt to think through the structure of the cosmos of traditional rationalism founders in contradiction, of which the most important example for Hegel is that of the Kantian antinomies "[But] reason is [also] positive because it produces the universal and grasps the particular therein." It rescues the negated fragments of traditional rationalism and generates the universal process that is the condition for the possibility of thinking these fragments as moments in a coherent whole.

Hegel next makes a distinction between two different types of reason. "Just as understanding (*Verstand*) tends to be taken as something separate from reason (*Vernunft*) in general, so too the dialectical reason tends to be taken as something separate from the positive reason." Dialectical reason can also be called negative reason because its function is to dissolve finite determinations. Positive reason reconstitutes these fragments. "But in its truth, reason is spirit [Geist], which, as higher than both, is *verständige Vernunft* or *vernünftiger Verstand*. Spirit is [on the one hand] the negative, that which constitutes the quality of both dialectical reason and understanding. It negates the simple; thus it posits the determinate difference of the understanding [by means of a predication]; but it just as much dissolves that determinate difference [by showing that non-p, as the boundary of p, is an essential part of its intelligibility], and it is thus dialectical."[8] In other words, spirit defines the object by a predication or negation, but it also dissolves that object into the steps of dialectical logic. In Hegel's own words: "But it does not restrict itself to the nothing of this result but is therein equally positive and has also produced therewith the first simple [*das erste Einfache*], but as [a] universal that is concrete in itself."

The universal to which Hegel refers is a category. Each of these categorial determinations is constituted by the unity of position and negation or, more precisely, an identity within difference. Each category thus constituted is richer in formal content and more inclusive than its predecessor. Thus the whole or absolute is built up in a step-by-step process of logical formation. I call the reader's attention to the unmistakable animism of Hegel's concept and its logical development. Hegel is talking not about the metaphorical motion of human thinking but of the ontological excitation and life of the absolute or whole.[9] It may also prove helpful to call attention to Hegel's treatment of negativity in the passage we have just analyzed. There will be an extensive treatment of the concept of nothing at a later juncture. It will be sufficient for the moment to say that we are here concerned with the work of negation as an active transformation of logical determinations into components of a more inclusive degree of complexity.

Hegel spells out the sense of the negative in four steps (7):

1. It negates "the simple" (e.g., "A") and so poses the "determinate difference" (e.g., "non-A"); in other words, "non-A" does not annihilate "A" but distinguishes its logical complement. "A" is therefore preserved as the determination that is different from the complement represented by the negation. This is determinate negation.

2. It dissolves that difference, and so is dialectical. In other words, "A" and "non-A" are reciprocally entailed in the definition of each. At the level of understanding, this would be a contradiction.

3. Reason, however, does not remain within the "nothing" or negativity of this result; from the fact that "non-A" involves "A" in its meaning, we

see that the negative is also positive in that it produces "the first simple" or a universal that is concrete in itself. Hegel refers here to the result of the reciprocal entailment of "*A*" and "non-*A*," which between them form a concrete universal, say "*B*." "*A*" is delimited and thus defined by "non-*A*," which in turn, as the negation of "*A*," presupposes it. This universal is the source for the generation of particulars by the posing and dissolving of the various determinations (= negations) of "*A*" that it contains within itself. These determinations are produced by the activity of negativity within the concrete universal.

4. It is thus "the absolute method of knowing," a spiritual excitation that is the immanent development of the concept. When the concept is fully revealed, the recipient of that revelation (i.e., Hegel) has overcome the split between subject and object. The history of philosophy is complete and the absolute is present within human time. Being and thinking are the same. Hegel must begin from this assertion or it will be impossible for him to overcome the various dualisms of traditional philosophy. At the same time, he claims that his assertion is not an unsupported axiom but a tautology. For an intuitive justification of the tautology, the reader may recall my discussion in the introduction. To think something is to possess it within thinking. The rules that govern thinking are the same as the rules that govern the world process. To the objection that we cannot know what we cannot know, Hegel would claim that his system is circular in the precise sense that it exhibits the impossibility of conceiving any further determinations. We shall have to decide eventually whether this contention is valid, or even plausible. Meanwhile, it is clear that without the identity within difference of the orders of thinking and being, philosophy cannot be replaced by wisdom, or in Hegel's own term, *Wissenschaft*. "Only out of this self-constructing way, I assert, is philosophy capable of being objective, demonstrated science" (as I shall translate *Wissenschaft*: 7).

Hegel then makes a comment about the relationship between the *PS* and the *SL*. In the former, consciousness was exhibited as a process of self-construction. By consciousness, Hegel means concrete spirit that is "knowledge trapped in externality," or the stages of world-historical existence. In other words, the *PS* shows us the development of the human spirit toward self-completion as absolute spirit. It is the exhibition of "appearing" in the sense of self-manifesting spirit, not in the straightforward chronology of empirical history but as a deeper process that animates history. Still more deeply embedded within the spiritual formation process of the spirit, however, is the dialectico-speculative structure of logic. The development of spiritual formation "depends only . . . upon the nature of *pure essentialities* [*reinen Wesenheiten*] that constitute the content of logic" (7). These pure essentialities are not directly visible in the *PS*. At the outset, they are clothed in immediacy and external concreteness, from which they must be freed by negative work, i.e., by the existential or spiritual contradictions arising from the collision of one spiritual moment or fundamental human type with another. The sum of these collisions is the dialectical process by which the spirit is transformed from the simple givenness of sensuous certitude into a pure knowing "that gives to itself those pure essentialities themselves, as they are in and for themselves, as the object" for future study by logic.

Stated as simply as possible, the human spirit grows toward completion through the process of contradiction between its successive stages of experience. This takes place at the historical level, but only as a reflection of the inner process of development of the spirit. And this inner process of development culminates in the raising up of the spirit to the level of the absolute, that is, of the science of logic. Spirit is now ready to think its conceptual determinations. The structure of its own development is also the structure of the concept.

I will take up the question of the relation between the *PS* and the *SL* at greater length in subsequent chapters.

The Preface of 1831

The text we are about to study is dated November 1831. Hegel was in the process of revising the *SL;* he completed the first book before dying unexpectedly a week after dating the new preface. In my analysis, I will omit discussion of points already treated, except for references that are indispensable to sustain the flow of Hegel's argument. The first thing to notice is that Hegel refers to the imperfect exposition in the first edition of the *SL* and the intrinsic novelty and difficulty of logic itself, but not to any incompleteness in his system. We should not therefore assume that Hegel's precipitate death prevented him from recording new discoveries in the list of logical categories or in the order of their development.

As we have already seen, Hegel's logic is a radically new enterprise in the history of philosophy. The obvious difference between Hegelian and traditional logic, whether of the Aristotelian or Fregean-Russellian varieties, has not prevented a number of efforts to formalize Hegel's logic. That this effort is misconceived from the outset has been argued in detail by David Lachterman.[10] Lachterman makes the following major points. Hegel deals with concepts, not with propositions; he treats the evolution of one conceptual determination from another, not the deduction of conclusions from premises; each conceptual determination is dynamic, or more radically, each violates the so-called laws of deductive thinking (the principles of identity, noncontradiction, and excluded middle); this violation at the lower level of understanding is in fact intrinsic to the establishment of those principles at the higher level of reason; there are no singular terms in Hegel's logic; negation is intrinsic to the concepts and is not an external operator; the activity of negation is essential to the overcoming of the separation between subjects and predicates; and, finally, the Hegelian equivalents to logical operators are all characterized by self-applicability or so to speak "self-predication."

To this I would make the following crucial modification. The laws of deductive thinking are "violated" in the sense that they cannot themselves be grasped conceptually except as developing dialectically. But the conceptual description of the dialectical nature of the laws of logic must itself be composed in a discursive prose that obeys those laws. In other words, to show that p includes non-p in the full structure of its intelligibility is not the same as the simultaneous assertion and denial of p. The statement that the positive and negative moments combine in a richer structure is not itself simultaneously asserted and denied. The key to understanding Hegel's logic is to see it as the effort to set into motion, and thereby overcome the separation between the two "hands" of Aristotelian conceptual analysis, "on the one hand this" and "on the other hand that," the distinction between which is itself expressed by the particle *qua*. The two hands of Aristotelian conceptual analysis are unified as it were into a living being, of which the life-spirit is an identity of identity and nonidentity.

Hegel presents a vivid exhibition of the transformation of distinct formal elements into each other, thanks to the activity by which we think them. It is important to remember that for Hegel, we do not create logical forms by thinking them, but rather the laws of formation are the same as those of dialectical thinking. Not surprisingly, Hegel is less successful in providing us with a conceptual account of the unity of life as lived. Just as materialists must assume that the body accounts for the mind, so Hegel must assume that our direct experience of consciousness refutes the reductivism of the materialist. But he is unwilling to rest content with a dualism of mind and body; dialectic is the method by which Hegel attempts to overcome dualism in a third or total structure of the two distinct moments. The fundamental disputes surrounding the interpretation of Hegel are all about the nature of the "third" or what Hegel calls "the absolute." No interpretation will be satisfactory that reduces one factor (e.g., the mind) to the other (e.g., the body). But this does not prove that a satisfactory interpretation, in the sense of a coherent discursive account, is itself possible. For the time being, I leave it at this: Hegel must justify dialectic in the prose of what he calls reflective understanding. If he cannot do this, then each utterance will immediately be canceled by its conceptual complement. If the structure of sheer process is itself in process, then a stable *logos* is impossible.

To continue, as Lachterman also demonstrates, it would be more accurate to say that foundational investigations in mathematical logic show the need for dialectical thinking, rather than that mathematical formalization is useful in exhibiting the structure of dialectic. We can establish the main point in an informal or nontechnical manner by noting that Hegel's intention is to exhibit the conceptual articulations of the whole, which is in turn to be understood as both subjective and objective. That is to say, the whole is spirit; it is alive, and the articulations of life are themselves living. Formal analysis is a version of what Socrates calls "cutting at the joints" in the manner of the butcher's art.[11] But butchers work on corpses, and much the same is true of mathematical logicians; let us say that the latter study the structure of skeletons, whereas Hegel's logic is addressed to the living person.

Hegel thus has no predecessors in the field of logic as he conceives the discipline; previous work in metaphysics and logic has furnished him with external materials only (9).

On the other hand, the history of philosophy is for Hegel the gradual discovery of the essential ingredients in a comprehensive system that includes dialectical logic. As Hegel states on numerous occasions, the decisive step is the Kantian doctrine of the antinomies. In this part of the First Critique, Kant ostensibly demonstrates opposite arguments on the beginning and finitude of the world, its composition out of simple parts, causal determinism versus freedom, and the existence of a necessary being that is the cause of the world. What is demonstrably unthinkable from the standpoint of the phenomenal world of the understanding, and so of natural science, becomes possible from the standpoint of the noumenal world and reason. Kant believes himself to have shown the contradiction in the heart of thinking, as represented by the separation between understanding and reason, whereas according to Hegel, he has actually discovered the dialectical nature of pure thinking.

It is as Kant's successor, then, that Hegel proudly claims that "the philosophical exposition of the domain of thought, that is, in its intrinsic inner activity, or what is the same thing, in its necessary development, must therefore be a new undertaking and so be begun from the beginning" (9). The beginning is the reconceptualization of the inner dynamic of intelligible form, or the reconciliation of understanding and reason from the higher standpoint of Hegel's logic. As to the formal elements of this reconciliation, they have been transmitted to us by the philosophical tradition. *Sprache* (speech or language) is the medium of transmission of traditional logical categories. More fundamentally, we differ from the brutes in our ability to interiorize external experience and make it into *Vorstellung*, thereby appropriating it as our own. The term *Vorstellung* has a variety of meanings, but we should be sensitive to the special importance of the literal meaning, "to place before," or in other words to make into an object. The term is often translated as "representation," that is, to re-present something that has presented itself antecedently, where "antecedently" may refer to logical or chronological order. A *representation* of exteriority is thus an artifact of consciousness. This notion underlies British empiricism as well as German idealism and no doubt goes back at least to the ambiguity in Descartes between the direct apprehension of the *lumen naturale* and the symbolical or constructive nature of mathematical thinking.

In British empiricism, thinking is representation understood as sensation. I cite an early example from Hobbes's *Leviathan*. The thoughts of men, says Hobbes, "are every one a *Representation* or *Apparence*, of some quality, or other Accident of a body without us; which is commonly called an *Object*."[12] It is important to see that the same foundation underlies Hegel's conception of thinking. Hegel's praise for the identification by the ancient Greeks of thinking and being is incomplete in itself. Greek philosophy leads to dualism or the separation of formal being from the world of genesis. On the other hand, the British empiricists, by limiting themselves to representation, lose all contact with formal being, despite their inconsistent and ungrounded acceptance of the certitude of mathematics. Kant attempts to unite representation and formal thinking but does so in such a way as to restrict the latter to the former; in other words, there is no original presentation of the external world of things in themselves but only a representation of what we cannot know in its own terms. Hegel will try to show that the process of representation exhibits the intrinsic process of presentation and that this exhibition takes place at the level of logic or categorial thinking. But the process of presentation is not immediately visible in the act of representation; it has to be elicited, first by phenomenology and then by logic.

Hegel does not quite state that speech is identical with thought, but he says that speech penetrates into everything interior, and what man brings to speech and externalizes in it contains a category (10). Speech thus plays a crucial role in two processes: internalization of what must be "silent" while external, and then externalization in language, as structured by categories. In other words, nature as physical extension is silent, that is, inaccessible to discursive thinking, until it is transformed by "the logical," i.e., categorial or conceptual thinking. Such thinking constitutes the genuine nature of man, but it must be called supernatural in the sense that it governs or makes genuinely its own the processes of external nature (10).

This is what I meant when I said that representation in itself does not make presentation immediately accessible. It is thus a mistake to refer to representational thinking as connected to a doctrine of being as presence, as Heidegger does. At the very least, we must modify the thesis by adding that being does not present itself without mediation but has to be reconstituted by the discursive transformation of representational consciousness. This means also that physical nature has no significance in itself. Science is an activity by which thought orders nature or gives it conceptual and so spiritual meaning. Otherwise stated, nature as *res extensa*, taken as the mere exteriorization of spirit, is not in itself dialectical.

There are then two distinct senses of "externalization" in Hegel, corresponding to two different stages in his reference to "nature." The human animal is initially separated from the silence of nature by the discursive articulation of desire. At this stage, nature is an obstacle to, but also the potential satisfaction of, desire. The potentiality is actualized by human work, or the incorporation and "digestion" of the external object. This digestion process evolves into the conceptualization of the external world and so eventually into the reunification of subject and object. In short: nature is the external environment or the horizon within which human history unfolds, but it is also the external exhibition of the internal activity of spirit. The shift is not between two empirical states of nature but rather between two stages in human experience. The two senses of "externalization" correspond to these two stages.

In his analysis of speech, Hegel adapts to his own terminology the Aristotelian definition of the human being as the *zoon logon echon*. The human animal possesses *logos* in the dual sense of speech and proportion or order. Initially, to be sure, this possession is only potential. Speech and order are actualized by the work of the spirit; from a Hegelian standpoint it is appropriate to translate *energeia* as "being at work." Furthermore, the speech or sense-attributing process must be carried through to completion, or else human beings will be alienated from their discourse by its very partiality. By the completion of speech or *logos*, Hegel is referring to the completion of philosophy in wisdom or a discursive account of the structure of intelligibility. Logic is the basis of this account, but not its entirety;

the wise man is also able to explain the unification of theory and practice, or the identity within difference of the interiority and exteriority of spirit. Partial philosophical speeches come into conflict with one another and are reduced thereby to mutual cancellation, or meaningless chatter; in other words, to silence.

Hegel goes on to praise the German language because of its richness in logical particles as well as in substantive and verbal realizations of the determinations of thought. He also singles out the number of German words that have opposed meanings and so prefigure the speculative integration of these meanings into a dialectical unity. German (like Greek, as Hegel says elsewhere) is thus a uniquely philosophical language and stands alone among modern languages in this respect. Hegel goes on to say that "philosophy requires therefore no particular terminology" apart from a few foreign words that have been given rights of citizenship (10–11).

The intrinsic philosophical spirit of German is sufficient to supply us with the vocabulary of logic. It goes without saying that this vocabulary will not be the same as that of ordinary language, just as the syntax of logic is supplied by reason (*Vernunft*) rather than understanding (*Verstand*). The vocabulary of ordinary German, inflected by its logical advantages, will be dialectically transformed into the extraordinary speech of Hegel's logic. But it remains true that the language of this logic is German. German is Greek suffused with the spirit of Luther.

Ordinary language develops into the technical terminology of science by the process of abstraction and renders the educated person familiar with logical categories like part and whole, subject and predicates, and so on. But familiarity or "acquaintance" (*bekannt*) is not knowledge (*erkannt*) (11). And in the usual philosophical education, the logical terms are precisely these familiar products of the process by which we apply abstraction to everyday language. It is in other words necessary to discuss the relation of "natural" (ordinary) to scientific thinking (12). By this Hegel means that we must show how science in the usual sense is not the same as philosophical science. The static logical categories of pre-Hegelian science have themselves suppressed the inner dialectic of ordinary language. Paradoxical as it may seem, Hegel must take a step back toward everyday language by setting the logical forms of thought into motion. At the same time, this step back is by way of the very categories that were obtained by abstractive purification from the ordinary language of need and desire as expressed in the unreflective (*selbstbewussten*) intuitions of everyday life.

I mean by this that Hegel does not reject the progress of European rationalism in favor of a prescientific, natural speech but instead coordinates at a higher level the living spirit of the former and the conceptual discoveries of the latter. The passage on which I am commenting is also rendered ambiguous because Hegel refers to "scientific" in two different senses, that of traditional rationalism on the one hand and, on the other, that of his own dialectico-speculative thinking. The suggestion is that the latter arises thanks to a revivification of the former by the spiritedness and protological structure of natural language, which was jettisoned in the process of preparing the traditional categories that serve as the external content of Hegel's logic.

Also to be praised is the traditional philosophical detachment, epitomized by Aristotle, from the concerns of everyday life, a detachment upon which philosophical progress depends. "In the still places of thinking that has arrived at itself and exists only in itself, those interests are silenced by which the life of the folk and the individuals are stirred up" (12–13). For Hegel, philosophy as a way of life is still essentially the Aristotelian *theoria*; what differs is the content, which is as it were transformed by the assimilation of the Christian spiritual *logos* and is accordingly united with production. This is the paradigm for the overcoming of the separation of theory from practice through the completion of human history as captured in *logos* by Hegel.

At first glance, logic would seem to correspond to pure theory. As Hegel goes on to say, as philosophy deals with "concrete objects" like God, nature, and spirit, logic treats them in their complete abstraction (13). I call the reader's attention, however, to the fact that by producing its own objects, logic is not an abstract method or subject independent of the intellect that studies it; it is the productive working of spirit. In that sense, there is from the outset no complete split between theory and practice. We have to distinguish between theoretical practice, which is a logical production, and historico-political practice, which is the everyday enactment of the inner life-pulse (*Lebenspuls*: 16) of logical production. In this context it should also be noted that Hegel follows Plato rather than Aristotle by not distinguishing between practice and production. More fundamentally, both theory and practice are productive; the intelligible world is an *enactment* of intelligence. This is how Hegel attempts to overcome all forms of dualism and their attendant skepticism and nihilism.

It is helpful to bear in mind the phenomenon of love when considering Hegel's account of theoretical productivity. As a young man, Hegel was very much interested in the unifying function of love as a preservation of the separate identities of the united lovers. At a more abstract level, the same identity-preserving unity is visible in the Christian *agape*. In the logic, this unity is discernible as a self-differentiating one; in other words, the ortho-dox doctrine of the divine creation of humanity is now represented as an emanation of absolute spirit. The human spirit is indeed the "breath" of God; what one could call the logical transformation of love into the living concept is also the process by which we discover the identity within differ-ence of the human and the divine.

Hegel's doctrine of unification as the preservation of difference is a re-vised version of the Fichtean doctrine of *Streben* or striving, by which term Fichte refers to the activity of the absolute ego, in which the subjective side projects a determinate object in the very act of consciousness. The ego as it were seeks to discover itself within its products, which (in a way that an-ticipates Heidegger's doctrine of the veiling over of Being by beings) them-selves conceal the original source. The activity of cognition is thus a striving for completeness through the production of the intelligible world; but that very act of production preserves the separation between the subjective and objective dimensions of the ego. Fichte's "striving" is thus something like a Platonic Eros that produces the very entities it desires. Love is an expression of a one differentiating itself, but in such a way as to make reunification impossible, except as an ideal limit. One sees here the Kantian notion of asymptotic progress toward wisdom and the coincidence of happiness and goodness.

Hegel is much closer to Kant and Fichte than he is to Plato, but he can-not be identified with either teaching. On the one hand, spirit does not in Hegel's doctrine obscure its own nature by the "projection" of the objective world but progressively reveals it. On the other hand, the Platonic separa-tion between thinking and being is overcome in the Hegelian conception of a common structure of intelligibility that is also the living spirit of both dimensions of actuality. Plato comes closer to Hegel in his metaphorical representation of Eros as continuously dying and being reborn, or in other words, as a kind of anticipation of the inner contradiction of the living intelligence that seeks resolution at the higher level of pure noetic vision. From a Hegelian standpoint, this seeking is very much like Fichtean *Streben* (the striving of the ego to find itself through the production and cognition of the objects in the world). Kant and Fichte, to exaggerate slightly, are still Platonists, despite the fact that they replace the eternal and detached Pla-tonic forms with transcendentally constituted categories, concepts, rules, and ideals. Nevertheless, it is this replacement that serves as the basis for the Hegelian completion of the Platonic doctrine of blessedness as con-templation of pure forms. In Hegel, contemplation is also conceptual uni-fication; it is consciousness of the unity of theory and practice.

To return to the preface, Hegel is distinguishing between the desires and intentions of everyday life, which are regulated by what he calls the "natural logic" (14), i.e., the use of categories in concrete life, and two kinds of theoretical logic, his own and Aristotle's. In everyday life we attempt to possess the categories through the mediation of the objects we desire. They are instruments of passion, will, and, in general, of the interests of concrete consciousness. Aristotelian logic strips the categories from concrete objects and renders them static; they stand to the life of spirit as does the skeleton to the living body. Hegel combines Aristotelian detachment from the objects of everyday life, and the subsequent mastery of the passions and desires, with a revitalization of the determinations of thought. He therefore subscribes to Aristotle's dictum that philosophy, or in the minimal case, ontological logic, has no end beyond itself, that we must not attempt to approach the determinations of thought from within the restriction of a subjective interest in the objects they define or whose nature they constitute. Freedom of thought is the domain of pure abstraction, hence of freedom from things as opposed to their concepts. At the same time, however, freedom, exactly as for Spinoza, is knowledge of the necessary order of conceptual structure.

This leads Hegel to a criticism of Kant's doctrine of things in themselves, a criticism with which we are already familiar and which can be passed over (15–16). I do want to emphasize Hegel's expression "life-pulse," which is applied to the subject or thinker as well as to the object or cognized category. The passage just cited also makes clear that Hegel's logical determinations are alive, contrary to those of Aristotle. Abstraction in Hegel is thus only superficially like its Aristotelian counterpart, despite Hegel's implication to the contrary. Once more, the similarity lies in the fact that both Aristotle and Hegel recommend a rising beyond everyday passion, desire, will, or in general "interests," and a residence within the domain of pure thought. But Hegel's pure thought is the life of the spirit, and his logical determinations are the activity of that spirit; they have the same life-pulse as does spirit. One would have to spiritualize Aristotle's reference to "work" in the term *energeia*, and thereby to overcome the separation between form and thought, in order to make him into a Hegelian. Hegel's "logical nature that ensouls spirit, that works and acts in it in order to bring it to consciousness" (16), is separated from Aristotelian logic and ontology by its assimilation of the Neoplatonist interpretation of Christianity.

There is thus a historical line of development by which Hegel gives a Neoplatonist interpretation of Spinoza's pantheistic revision of Cartesianism. Fichte and Schelling play an important role in this development because they, unlike Kant, identify the Cartesian *ego cogitans* with God (the subjectivized or spiritualized interpretation of the transcendental ego), and the world is for them the result of the divine infinite activity of thinking. As to the absolute ego itself, it is *causa sui* (a Spinozist expression) and in that sense spontaneous (a Kantian expression): Necessity actualizes out of itself in accord with its own rules. The spontaneity of conceptual thought is the same as the actualization of the transcendental ego within the cognitive activity of the human intellect, but there is still in Kant a separation between the two. The transcendental ego is not alive; it is neither God nor man but the structure of intelligibility. Nevertheless, it does actualize within human intellectual activity; this is the point of contact with Neoplatonism for the assimilation of Kant by Fichte, Schelling, and Hegel.

In Schelling's formulation, the being of the last or highest principle, namely, the *Ich*, which is *causa sui*, cannot be known through some other principle. We think it as it is in itself directly or immediately, not through the mediation of a quasi-Cartesian argument ("I think, therefore I am") but from our own thinking. More precisely, I intuit intellectually myself as thinking, rather than inferring the I from an analysis of its activity or productions. Any such external deduction would determine or limit the I and so divide it into a being on the one hand and its intelligibility on the other (compare here Kant's argument that if thinking conforms to the nature of the things thought, then we can never be sure that we have grasped the things in their essence). The identity of being and intelligibility, and so the overcoming of Greek dualism, depends upon the immediate intuition of the absolute as the unconditioned I.[13]

I do not need to emphasize the unsatisfactory nature of Schelling's appeal to intellectual intuition, which has no content other than the immediate affirmation of the I and so can be neither derived from some conceptual structure nor discursively described. The first derivation would limit it externally; the second would divide it or mediate it internally. This is why Hegel refers to Schelling's absolute in the *PS* as the night in which all cows are black. But he does not simply repudiate the Schellingian absolute; on the contrary, he accepts it, while claiming that it manifests itself in its activity. This is the aforementioned "one differentiating itself" or the synthesis of Parmenides and Heraclitus.[14] The activity of manifestation is precisely the life-pulse of the soul or spirit as described by Hegel's logic.

Hegel's logic is thus alive; the connection with Schelling's absolute can be restated as follows. The immediate identity of being and thought is an identity that contains a difference; it is therefore unstable and spills out into production or self-differentiation. "Instinctual activity distinguishes itself from intelligent activity in general through the fact that the latter takes place with consciousness. Insofar as the content of the work [or 'impulse': *des Treibenden*] is brought out of immediate unity with the subject to become its object, there begins the freedom of spirit, which is [before this] trapped in the instinctual work of thinking, in the bonds of its categories, and is fractured into an infinitely manifold material" (16). The transition from Schelling to Hegel must therefore initially resemble a sundering of the unity of subject and object, a sundering that will finally be revealed as self-differentiation or the complete manifestation of the absolute within its appearances.

One could therefore say that logic is the soul of spirit, and not vice versa. "The most important point for the nature of spirit is the relation of what it is *in itself* [*an sich*], not only to that which it is actually, but to that which it knows *of itself*" (17). The first part of this statement is a repudiation of Schelling, for whom the indeterminate absolute (Hegel's *an sich*) is still distinguished from the determinate or empirical world. The task of Hegel's logic is to bring spirit to freedom and truth, which, one may add, are the same within the identification of self-consciousness with what it knows. In knowing itself, spirit knows the world. This is Hegel's Spinozistic version of the Cartesian invocation to mankind to become as masters and possessors of nature.

Hegel concludes the second preface with an extensive discussion of the difference between his living logic and the static logic of the tradition. The issue is posed in terms of the erroneous distinction between form and content that is for Hegel fundamental to Greek metaphysics, and this means for him primarily Aristotle. Aristotle perfects the Socratic insight that to be is to be something, this particular thing, and so a thing of such and such a kind. To the shape or *morphe* of the particular thing there corresponds an *eidōs*, which Hegel calls a *Denkbestimmung* (17). This is potentially misleading, since for Aristotle the form enables the thing to be and to be thought, whereas for Hegel it is the emergence of the essence within thought. Otherwise put, Aristotle's form is defective from a Hegelian standpoint precisely because it is detached from matter on the one hand and distinguished from the intellect on the other.

Hegel assumes that the Aristotelian *eidōs* is characterized by the same separation (*chorismus*) from the world of genesis that Aristotle attributes to the Platonic form. On this view, the form is "stamped" onto matter from the outside and in such a way as to produce a finite determination from matter. The form is separated from the world of genesis; as "this such" it is detached from all other determinations and thereby conceals rather than reveals the infinite truth with a finite seal or look. And finally, as detached from intellect, it is external to spiritual excitation, to the power of the negative by which the finitude of formal determinations is overcome. As finite, form is a negation, and hence not actual or genuinely true. To anticipate, the negation of the particular determination, which excludes itself from all other determinations, must itself be negated. The form must show itself to be related to the other, that is, to the different forms, precisely by virtue of its identity.

According to Hegel, the *Grundbestimmung* or fundamental formal determination common to all finite forms is the law of identity, $A = A$, which regulates traditional logic as the principle of noncontradiction (18). In the traditional version, this principle tells us that we cannot say both p and $\sim p$ of S. In Hegel's terminology, the principle holds that the attribution of opposite predicates to the same entity would deprive it of its identity. The law of identity is thus also equivalent to $A \sim= \sim A$ (A is not identical with not-A). Traditional logic is unable to explain the movement from the first to the second A in the law of identity, which for Hegel is explained by the work of negation intrinsic to, if not explicitly stated within, that law, and which becomes visible only by the statement of its equivalent. Otherwise expressed, the positive and the negative forms of the law of identity are the essential content of the principle of noncontradiction. From a Hegelian standpoint, this principle is accordingly both positive and negative; it contains an inner excitation. The traditional logician would reply that the second A in the (positive) law of identity has only notational existence; the law does not identify two distinct entities but asserts the identity with itself of any entity whatsoever. To this, Hegel would object that the traditional explanation amounts to the assertion "A," which is meaningless, a mere sound, and which, if it expresses anything, represents the unthinkableness of monism or Eleaticism. In order to think identity, the intellect must perform a movement or doubling. That is to say, the intellect grasps identity by distinguishing it from nonidentity (A is identical with A *and not with non-A*).

The law of identity in its unanalyzed form is the fundamental determination of what Hegel calls the logic of common sense. As soon as we see the inner structure of this law, as we do when we grasp properly its articulated version, the law of noncontradiction, we are prepared for the shift from lifeless to living logic; that is to say, we see negation not as a static syntactical operation but as the product of the *activity* of negativity. Negative activity differentiates; this assertion is also central to the importance assigned to difference (or *différance*) in late-twentieth-century continental philosophy, which mistakenly believes itself to be "post-Hegelian." For Hegel, however, position and negation are equal partners within identity-as-difference, the beginning of Hegel's logic. This has an important consequence for the first moment in the logic proper. To anticipate, being and nothing are pure abstractions when considered separately and lead nowhere; it is their identity within difference as becoming that generates the subsequent determinations of the concept.

It is crucial to see here that Hegel is not denying the intelligibility, at the level of understanding, of finite or separate entities such as tables and chairs. In order to assert truly the proposition "this table is brown," I do not have to add that the table is not a chair. There is no internal relation between the table and the chair, but rather the relation is between the manifestations or comings to be of the table and the chair. If I wish to understand the manifestation process or formation process, then I do have to take the table and the chair together as elements manifested by the process of becoming. At this level, however, it is not the table and the chair that interest me but the structure of becoming. This is Hegel's version of the distinction between the transcendental and the immanent, or between the ontological and the ontic. In one more formulation, what the British idealists call "internal relations" hold between the concepts or pure logical determinations that form the conceptual substratum of the thinking of tables and chairs, but not between tables and chairs as elements of our experience.

Considered simply as an object of experience (and so as a suitable candidate for scientific investigation), a stone is what it is; in order to understand what it is, we do not have to study something else, except incidentally. To be more precise, in order to study a stone, we do not have to study at the same time, as part of our attempt to identify the nature of the stone, the soil upon which it sits. The stone *qua* stone is not also the soil. We may, however, have to investigate the underlying soil as part of our attempt to understand the stone, for example, in order to see whether there is any chemical process within the soil that leads to the existence of the stone. In conducting this investigation, we will turn our attention from the stone to the soil, each of which can be studied independently precisely as must be the case if we are to establish a causal connection between the two. And the discovery of such a connection, should there be one, does not erase the separation of the stone *qua* stone from the soil *qua* soil. If we could not study things separately, we would never be able to discover any connections between them. The entire investigation begins in the desire to determine whether the soil has any relation to the stone other than proximity; it begins with the soil and the stone as separate and investigates them separately, even when some link is established. The establishment of that link does not result in the production or discovery of some new, third object that is at once both the stone and the soil and neither of them.

The situation is quite different when we ascend from the level of the empirical investigation of stones to the level of the formation process that gives rise to any object of experience whatsoever. Position and negation are functioning jointly within the "ontological" process by which one thing is manifested as different from another and identical to itself. The entire logical process that is presented in a step-by-step development by Hegel's exposition is not a process in which individual objects are produced seriatim. The three stages of Hegel's logic correspond to three different ontological levels in the coming to be of the totality (*das Ganze*) that can also be expressed as the identity within difference of the subject and the object. Hegel is describing the paradigm for the creation of the universe, not the creation of stones, tables, or human beings. He is describing the process that gives rise to anything whatsoever; within this process, all things are related, not as things but as instances of creation. This is what Hegel means when he says, in opposition to the study of finite or entirely separated formal determinations by logicians of the understanding: "With this introduction of content into logical reflection, it is not the things that become [the] object [*Gegenstand*], but *die Sache*, the concept of things" (18). *Sache* corresponds approximately to the Greek *pragmata*, which can refer to either things or events, and so to the state of affairs; it means here the process of formation itself. The content of logic is logical form, understood as active and developing. Logic has as its content the concept, which is the process by which things are manifested through a continuous development of form.

Hegel's logic is one not of syntactic form but of conceptual determination. His is a logic not of deductive inference but of the structure of the constitutive process by which human experience is conceived as a totality. His "concept" (*Begriff*) is the grasping of the totality of time and eternity, of the human and the divine, of history and nature. It is not so much "logic" in the Aristotelian sense, a sense that still underlies the modern use of the term, as *logos* in a sense that expands the Greek notion of "giving a rational account" (*logon didonai*) to include the word of God. Hegel's logic is intended to fulfill the promise of Kant's doctrine of the transcendental ego, not to replace the Aristotelian doctrine of syllogistic. In this sense we can call it a logic of objectification, provided we bear in mind that it is subjectivity that objectifies or grasps by rendering determinate.

Hegel makes this point implicitly when he observes that no exhibition of an object (*Gegenstand*) is able to bring out the development of its thinking in its necessity "with strict and total immanent plasticity" (19). If it could do this, its scientific nature would surpass that of mathematics. "For no object has in itself this freedom and independence" (20). In other words, mathematics can proceed entirely from within its inner necessity, or as we say, purely formally, in a purely deductive order, because it has no object or is not "about" any object other than deductive structure. In order to do mathematics, we must proceed in the precise order in which each successive determination of thought emerges from its antecedent.

This kind of mathematical rigor and purity will be impossible in logic, which has the categories as its content. In other words, human exposition is unable to achieve the level of necessity exemplified in the inner development of the concept. Hegel must supply external observations that are designed to prevent us from infecting the exposition of logical development with the by-products of "representation" (the concepts of understanding) or unregulated thinking. We can learn to do pure mathematics more easily than pure logic (in his sense of that term). Hence remarks and clarifications will be required that are contingent in comparison with the inner necessity of the development of the concept. "The peculiar restlessness and dispersion of our modern consciousness allows nothing other than also [i.e., in addition to logical exposition in the strict sense] to have recourse to obvious reflections and thoughts that occur at the moment [*Einfälle*]" (20). It remains to be seen whether this "external necessity" compromises the inner necessity of logic or in other words prevents us from achieving a systematic science.

Why is Hegelian logic more difficult than mathematics? Because in mathematics the order of necessary inference, or the discerning of pure formal structure, taken in abstraction from all content of any sort whatsoever, already detaches us from the confusions of ordinary experience, the distractions of opinion, dogma, or philosophical doctrine, and in particular from the reflexive task of apprehending the very process by which we understand mathematical reality. It goes without saying that one must have the requisite technical ability, but Hegel is referring to the subject or science of mathematics itself, as compared with the science of logic. The purity or abstractness of mathematics makes it in a sense self-evident; if we can perceive mathematical structure at all, it stands forth with what Husserl called "evidence" of a kind that does not require any further justification or paraphrase. But this is at the same time a sign of the philosophical inferiority of mathematics to logic. *Philosophical* inferiority, I hasten to underline. Mathematics, while as it were perfect in itself, does not provide us with an account of the concrete totality of our experience. It thus does not account for itself or its own role in the economy of the sciences.

This to one side, Hegel also clearly asserts that the "restlessness" and "dispersion" of the modern consciousness prevents a purely immanent exposition of logic. The selfless and restful attention to the *Sache* that one finds in a Platonic dialogue is no longer accessible in modern times. This is an extremely interesting comment, especially since Hegel is very far from advocating a return to classical thought, nor is he finally endorsing the "calm" of the ancients in preference to the "restlessness" of the moderns, since the latter attribute is a necessary feature of the development of self-consciousness or modern subjective inwardness. I understand Hegel to be making two points here. The first is that the ancient theoretical tranquility is an essential ingredient in the *Aufhebung* or surpassing of the difference between the ancients and the moderns. The second point is that in Hegel's immediate generation, we have not yet achieved the practical implementation of the unification of theory and practice that is symbolized by Napoleon and ostensibly manifested in the Prussian Lutheran monarchy. In sum, we must not confuse the excitation of Hegelian logic with the restlessness and dispersion of the modern spirit.

It is quite striking that Hegel carries through this comparison between his audience and work and those of Plato, not Aristotle. The initial reason for this is that Hegel is thinking of the character of his addressees and the kinds of objections raised against a "plastic" presentation of logical categories. Hegel uses the term *plastisch* regularly here to denote the purity of development of his exposition. He takes the plasticity or spontaneity of the Platonic dialogues as an accurate portrait of the classical openness to pure thinking, not simply on the part of the philosopher-lecturer but also on the part of his interlocutors. Plato, in other words, presents us with philosophical pedagogy in a direct and dramatic form, as Aristotle does not. Plato shows us why it is possible for Aristotle to speak as he does, a level of discourse that Hegel cannot adopt because the modern situation is more complex than its ancient counterpart. Odd though it sounds to the contemporary student of Hegel's logic, he is stating that his presentation is so to speak exoteric rather than esoteric.

One might suppose that the proper beginning is to establish with complete security the origin or ground upon which everything is built (21). But far from securing a foundation for a "plastic," that is, purely immanent development of the logical categories, this procedure in fact leaves room for arbitrary reflection and thoughts of the moment. The attempt to establish with perfect security the initial simple categories, such as being and nothing, is impossible without the introduction of other, later categories or concepts, which must in turn be clarified and grounded. What I am calling an esoteric presentation depends upon the formation and cultivation or breeding (*Zucht*) of one's audience, and this is accomplished only "through progress: through the study and production of the entire development."

Plato, Hegel reminds us, is said to have rewritten his *Republic* seven times. Hegel indicates the greater magnitude of his own task by wishing that he could have rewritten his logic seventy-seven times. But the very circumstances that make the task of the modern philosopher more difficult, namely, the greater depth of the modern principles and the more comprehensive material to which they apply, as well as "the unavoidable dissipation due to the magnitude and many-sidedness of the interests of the time," also force Hegel to present us with an imperfect result of his labors. He also doubts whether "the noisy confusion of the day and the deafening chatter of the imagination" leave room for the participation in "the disinterested stillness of purely thoughtful knowing" (22). It goes without saying that we who are unable to study Hegel's logic seventy-seven times must face the text with the same doubts. Let us at least attempt, in a post-Hegelian and ostensibly postmodern age, to disregard the noisy clamor of the day and the chatter of imagination, in order to hear Hegel's thought as it emanates from an age that has already become classical in comparison with our own.

One last comment. For Hegel, there is no simple superiority of moderns to ancients or vice versa. The Greeks were more open to pure philosophical reflection than the busy and distracted moderns; but the dispersion of the modern soul is already a sign of its greater and more comprehensive enterprise. What we require is a unification of the virtues of the epochs, in particular, of Greek plasticity and German industriousness.

THREE

The Introduction

As Hegel explains at the end of the second preface, the *SL* is an exoteric book in the sense that neither the subject matter nor the nature of the contemporary philosophical *Bildung* (formation) permits a purely immanent, plastic, and rigorously developmental exposition of the categories of the concept. Let me cite a famous passage from the preface to the *PS*: "The mode of study of ancient times has this difference from that of modernity, that the former mode was the authentic education [*Durchbildung*] of the natural consciousness. Investigating itself in particular in each part of its existence and philosophizing about everything that came before it, it generated itself as a thoroughly active universality. In modern times, on the other hand, the individual finds the abstract form already prepared; the straining to grasp it and to make it one's own is more the unmediated impelling to external work of the inner and fragmented production of the universal than an emerging of the universal from the concrete and the multiplicity of existence. Today the work in front of us is not so much to purify the individual out of its immediate sensuous modalities and to transform it into a thought and thinking substance, but rather the opposite, namely, to actualize and instill with spirit the universal through the sublation of fixed determinate thinking."[1]

In other words, the ancients were in direct contact with natural experience because there was no philosophical tradition to separate or mediate the two. They were accordingly able to carry out the conceptualization of natural experience, which is our heritage. Now we must actualize or set into motion this conceptualization within dialectico-speculative logic. Note that we cannot go back to the natural experience of the initial philosophical situation. There is no question here of a new beginning or a fresh conceptualization of everyday existence, which is rather thoroughly historical and

contains the whole development of previous ages. The ancients were superior to us because of their direct contact with natural experience, because
of the freshness and spontaneity of their philosophizing. But the moderns
are superior to the ancients in that they inherit the first stage of the work
of the spirit, namely, the conceptualizing of natural existence. This inheri-
tance is to be not repudiated but completed. But the task of completion
is not direct or spontaneous, as was the thinking of the ancients. We have
to overcome the alienating effects of the history of partial truths, each of
which is presented as the whole story. Not only is our historical experience
the necessary presupposition for the last stage of philosophy; it is also an
obstacle to the carrying out of that last stage. We have so much experience
and we know so much that we are restless and dissipated. Reason has been
dissipated by the imagination and must recover its concentration.

An example of what Hegel has in mind is illustrated by the Platonic dialogue *Parmenides*, in which the young Socrates proceeds directly from his
first encounter with Zeno to the philosophical gymnastics of Parmenides.
The question of the one and the many is accessible to the ancients in ordinary experience, as it were on the surface of things; there is no need to pass
through a conceptual tradition in order to acquire it. We on the other hand
require the prefaces, introduction, and notes to the *SL*, because of both the
greater complexity of our task and the distracted, harried, and dispersed
nature of our consciousness.

Modern philosophy in general begins in the repudiation of the classical orientation by ordinary experience or the domain of opinion.[2] The
attempt to master nature, or to replace the inconclusive and inconsistent
domain of opinion and traditional philosophy, leads to the construction
of models or hypothetical artifacts by which we express a precise interpretation of the structure of intelligibility. Transcendental philosophy and
Hegelian dialectic are expressions of the same spirit. Philosophy, or more
generally, theoretical construction, turns away from the everyday or given,
although this rejection is not always explained in the same way. Hegel's
explanation is that the given has already been transformed into concepts;
theoretical speculation must now go to work on the historical product of
this transformation.

What Hegel calls the exoteric presentation of logic is determined in its
content by the need to effect the transition from the penultimate stage of
European *Bildung* to its completion in his own system. Hegel refers to this
situation in the opening pages of the introduction. There is a difference
between the subject of logic and the preparation of the students for that
study. The first step in our preparation is to see the difference between logic

and all other sciences. "In every other science, the object that it treats and the scientific method are separated from one another; in addition, the content does not make an absolute beginning but depends upon other concepts and in each case is connected with other content" (25). Even mathematics depends upon definitions, postulates, and axioms that are not an absolute beginning because they are not produced by the unfolding of the science itself but regulate this development. In logic, on the contrary, the rules and laws of thinking cannot be presupposed; they are not external to and in that sense the foundation of logic but a part of its content and must be grounded within logic. This is also true of scientific method and of the very concept of science, both of which belong to the content of logic and constitute its final result. We cannot therefore "introduce" logic by an external definition, nor can we begin with a method that is drawn from the other sciences.[3] The introduction is not part of logic and does not contain the ground of what follows but is intended merely to bring the student's conception (*Vorstellung*) to the proper viewpoint for thinking the present science by means of clarifications and observations of a discursive and historical sort (26). I note that there is no reference here to the *PS* as the required immediate antecedent to the study of logic.

The task of philosophy is thus to grasp the first principles, and on this point it resembles Aristotle's first philosophy (*prote philosophia*) or, as it has traditionally been called, metaphysics. Aristotle, however, derives the concepts of the first principles from a pure intellectual perception. This has two implications. The first is that the given, or everyday life, is theoretically transparent or presents no obstacle to the direct apprehension of pure forms. The second is that the concepts are themselves rooted in silence. But how can we give a discursive justification of our first principles? Certainly not by a logical deduction in the usual sense from other, still higher principles, since the ones we seek to ground are by definition the highest. Other than by simply seeing that the first principles hold, there is no way in which to ground them at the beginning; and simple "seeing" is for Hegel unsatisfactory because it leaves the starting point arbitrary. We might have seen some other ostensible first principles. Hegel silently excludes Aristotle's actual starting point, namely, the direct accessibility of everyday or natural experience because, as we have just seen, he holds that natural experience has already been conceptualized by the tradition.

It is not the world that is given to modern man, but the concept of the world. But this "givenness" is already mediated by its own history. The first principles are grounded not at the beginning, since there is no ground prior to and apart from their development, but rather at the end, that is to say, by their consequences. And this is what Hegel claims. That is why he said previously that the justification of the laws and rules of the science of logic, including its method and the very conception of science it endorses, is securely acquired only by carrying out the study of the subject. Hegel holds to the view that we cannot understand something by analyzing its origin; instead, we must grasp its entire development. The last stage is the decisive one. This is as it were one side of the complex structure of modern philosophies of history. The other side is the apparently opposite thesis, visible in such disparate texts as Rousseau's *Second Discourse* and Heidegger's *Being and Time*, that one must return to the origin by a kind of deconstruction of subsequent developments that obscure the first principles.

The presuppositionlessness of the science of logic is possible if and only if the first step is wholly given, and this in turn is tantamount to saying that the whole or totality must be given in the first step. But how can this be, if the task of science is to show the development of the whole? Hegel's answer is that the whole is given initially in its simplest or most abstract sense, without any determinate content whatsoever. It must then be possible to initiate the development of subsequent stages, i.e., the stages of the progressively more concrete content of the whole, from an inspection of the initial abstract presentation of the whole. So the presuppositionlessness of the first step of the logic is not at all the same as the justification of the laws and rules of the science of logic. This latter justification is immanent to logic as a process. There is thus to be found in Hegel's procedure *both* steps of what I have called the philosophy of history; we must go back to the original or simple situation *and* trace out the entire development.

Hegel turns next to the task of distinguishing between his logic and that of the tradition (26). He does so by repudiating the traditional distinction between the content of knowledge and its form, that is, the distinction between truth and validity. A form detached from content is for Hegel an empty abstraction; knowledge consists in the conceptual grasp of the totality of form and content. In the case of logic, the content is precisely form in the process of development, and this in turn is the comprehensive structure of the process by which content assumes a determinate form.

The next two paragraphs are confusing because Hegel seems to shift from the opposition between content and form to that between the matter or object of knowledge on the one hand and thinking on the other. According to Hegel it is presupposed by the tradition that the matter (*Stoff*) of knowledge is like a completed world external to thinking, "present in and for itself" (*an und für sich vorhanden*). Thinking is then like an empty form that approaches the matter, fills itself up with it, and thereby acquires content and real knowledge (26–27). This terminology makes us think of Heidegger's account of the traditional metaphysical view of Being as "presence" (although Heidegger uses *Vorhandenheit* to refer to the mode of being of tools). The picture here is of an intellect separate from and conforming to the content of an independently existing world; the conformity is described as a filling up of the empty intellect with the content of the independent world.

In what sense can empty thinking be called a form? Hegel is not referring here to logical or even metaphysical forms that are supplied by the intellect. In Aristotelian language, the intellect becomes the form of what it thinks. But this assumption of form depends upon the passive apprehension of the entity by an intrinsically empty intellect. On this view, the only sense in which the intellect is a form is that it has no content of its own yet nevertheless is the *topos eidon*, the "place" in which forms occur.[4] For Hegel, Kant's doctrine of the synthetic unity of apperception is very much like a formless form of concepts. For Aristotle, the form that actualizes in the formless intellect or place of all forms is the genuine essence or *ousia* of the thing itself. For Kant, the form that actualizes in the activity of the formless form of the synthetic unity of apperception is the structure of the phenomenon and not of the thing in itself. On the traditional view as Hegel presents it, the object (*Objekt*) is complete and finished in itself and does not require thinking in order to be what it is, whereas thinking is defective and must complete itself through some content or matter (*Stoff*), with respect to which it is like "a weak, indeterminate form" that must make itself conform to or measure its matter. This is not the view of Aristotle; it seems to be some general characterization of the precritical doctrine according to which truth is the correspondence of thought to an external object. On this view, the "subject" or intellect is independent of the "object" it apprehends, and this leads directly to the Kantian position, as Hegel indicates in the next paragraph.

The clarification of the correspondence theory reveals that, on the terms of that theory, the intellect or act of thinking (= form) is separate from the object (= matter). "Thought therefore does not arrive at a position external to itself in its reception and shaping [*Formieren*] of the matter" (27). That is, modern philosophy prior to Kant arrives at a representation of the object rather than the object itself. Instead of working on, and thereby assimilating, the object, the *ego cogitans* takes a mental photograph of it. What began as the independence of the subject from the object is thus revealed as dependence of the subject on its own representation. This is "subjectivism" in the pejorative sense of the term. It is also the direct ancestor of the

Kantian phenomenon, which is a representation of the thing in itself, and one that cuts us off from the external world. Hegel refers to such an alienated world as a "beyond" (*Jenseits*), and he calls the thing in itself a *Gedankending* or product of thinking, that is, an illusory phantom or residue of representational thinking.

The unity of being and thinking underlies Hegel's claim that the conceptual constitution of the object, and in the limit case, the whole, does not terminate in subjective idealism but instead allows for the externalization of thinking as actuality. This is why Hegel praises the ancients as superior to the moderns in their recognition not merely that the true properties of things are established by thinking but also that the determinations of thought belong to the things themselves, so that thinking and being coincide (28). This can be understood as a consequence of the aforementioned direct access of thinking to the things of natural existence, as is especially evident in Aristotle. Note that this is neither subjectivism nor the modern correspondence theory of truth; correspondence rests upon separation, which leads to subjectivism in the pejorative sense of the term, whereas in ancient philosophy there is unification and so a kind of synthesis of subject and object. As Hegel sees the history of philosophy, everything from the Neoplatonists to Kant is a working out of the dialectical oppositions generated by the two key standpoints of Plato and Aristotle. Kant combines all of these oppositions in a way that makes Hegel possible. In this sense one could say that there is a decline in overall quality after Aristotle that extends to Kant; nevertheless, each position generated by the Platonic-Aristotelian dialectic constitutes a necessary moment in the advance from the ancients to the Kantian doctrine and its Fichtean development.

The ancient unification of subject and object, although intrinsically correct, is too simple or abstract; it lacks the dialectical development of its inner determinations. First we note the defect of modern "reflective understanding," by which Hegel means "the abstracting and thereby separating *Verstand* that persists within those separations" (28). Hegel is referring to traditional rationalism that is based upon identity, predication, and the law of the excluded middle. In other words, reflection is grounded in common sense and the stability and separateness of logical forms. The objects of common sense are derived from sense perception by the external application of the stable forms of *Verstand*. Reason, on the other hand, is isolated from empirical objects and, left to itself, produces only ghosts (such as the Kantian thing in itself). The truth of reason is replaced by *Meinen*, which carries the sense of "mine," "opinion." and "meaning" or, in other words, of subjective opinion

In sum, reflection combines the representationalism of perceptually oriented empiricism and the separation of the object into finite and rigid determinations, namely, predicates, which are both separate from and essential to the nature of the object. In reflection, there is no dialectical development from a subject to its predicates, no expression of the inner connection between a predicate and its negation. Nevertheless, the deviation from knowledge into opinion (that is, from the Greek unity of being and thinking to the subjective epistemologies of the modern period), which appears as a deficiency and a step backward, contains a deeper stratum that leads to "the higher spirit of the newer philosophy." This higher spirit manifests itself as the Kantian antinomies of pure reason. In other words, it is not so much the positive doctrines of Descartes, Leibniz, Locke, Hume, and Kant that prepare us for the great advance made by Hegel beyond the Greeks as it is Kant's formulation of the limitations of modern rationalism. This conforms with my previous remark about Hegel's view of the history of philosophy. Kant purports to show that we can have no conceptual knowledge of the whole and that the very attempt to acquire such knowledge leads to contradictions. Hegel will show that this manifestation of contradiction is the very pathway from the finite understanding to a genuinely cognitive reason. It is a bit melodramatic and perhaps even misleading to say merely that for Hegel, the whole *is* contradiction. But this melodramatic assertion can be refined and developed into a sound description of the motor of Hegel's logic.

Here is a provisional account of the dialectical situation. Understanding seems to arrive at an impasse in which both members of a fundamental opposition can apparently be demonstrated, for example, that the world is both eternal and has a beginning in time. It looks as though reason has negated itself, or sunk into the night in which all cows are black. In historical terms, the moment immediately preceding the exhibition of wisdom by Hegel is nihilism, as represented by Schelling's identity philosophy. But this is the necessary presupposition for "the great negative step to the true concept of reason" (29). In the present context, Hegel does not give an adequate explanation of why this is so.[5]

The main point is that the antinomies demonstrate "the negativity of the categories of finitude with respect to content" (*SL*, I. 198). In other words, they show the dialectical nature of reason, but from the negative side only. Understanding is incapable of overcoming the perpetual opposition of contradictory propositions. When the opposition is sufficiently comprehensive, there is a dialectical inversion of the two opposing assertions, within which neither is annulled but both are preserved at a higher level. That is to say, it is for Hegel not the case that the world is finite from one standpoint and infinite from another. He means instead that it is both finite and infinite, and this from the standpoint of the absolute.

This is what Hegel means when he says that contradiction lies at the heart of things. He means not that chaos is the essence of being, as Nietzsche will later proclaim, but instead that contradiction is the engine by which structural complexity unfolds. I must emphasize, however, that a genuine difference between Hegel and Nietzsche is sustained only by a demonstration of the completeness or circularity of the formation process. Without such a demonstration, Hegel's circular, eternally rotating absolute deteriorates into the Nietzschean myth of the eternal return of the same. In sum: the finite understanding works itself out by posing one thesis or determination after another but, in the absence of completeness, is unable to discriminate between any two fundamental and contradictory claims. This process is terminated not by the assertion of some new doctrine but rather through a conceptual grasp of the underlying rhythm of assertion and counterassertion. It is this grasp that shows us the structure in its totality. And that is why history must complete itself. There cannot be any philosophical advances after Hegel, but only retreats disguised as advances. The post-Hegelian epoch is in fact the pre-Hegelian epoch.

Modern philosophy, i.e., Kant, provides us with the contradictions of finitude, and so of understanding, as if these were an intrinsic defect of reason. It does not see that the contradiction is the movement of reason beyond the limitations of the understanding and the dissolution of these limitations (29). This shortcoming leads to a fall back into sensuous existence, as if it contained a basis for a stable unified life. The result is to identify the object of knowledge as appearance, which, says Hegel, is as unreasonable as the claim that one is able to understand untruth but not truth. The forms of understanding have no application to the things in themselves.

This should be compared to the previous distinction between intellect as empty form and the independent object as content of knowledge. The independent object has now disappeared, to be replaced by the unknowable thing in itself, and the empty form of intellect or cognition has now been filled up with forms of appearance, or as one could also say, with *apparent forms*. Their insubstantial nature has already been demonstrated by the antinomies, which, since they are held to apply to reason (but in fact are as limitations characteristic of understanding), also apply to the forms that are now the self-generated content of reason. The forms are therefore untrue, since they purport to belong to the object. But the subject is also "untrue" because it is constituted by its untrue forms. In dramatic terms, the construction of the intelligible world by the mutually inconsistent or self-contradictory acts of the transcendental ego is a farce or shadow play.

To summarize: the defects of Kant's critical philosophy can be overcome neither by transcendental idealism, which errs on the side of subjectivism, nor by the abstract forms of traditional logic that are sundered from one another and thus deprived of spirit and organic unity (31), a deficiency that I will call excessive objectivism. The content of logic is then the living concretion and unification of logical determinations, whereas logical reason is not the previously cited empty intellect but rather "the substantial or real [intellect] that holds together within itself all abstract determinations and is their pure, absolute-concrete unity" (31). Hegel repudiates both the conformity of the intellect to the independent object and the constitution of the object by forms that are intrinsic to the cognitive process. Nevertheless, he is much closer to the latter than to the former. With all his criticism of Kant and his praise for the ancients, Hegel never advocates a return to the pre-Copernican standpoint. The doctrine of the coincidence of thinking and being prevents our return to the natural situation. We should also note that Hegel tends to interpret the ancients as idealists.

Hegel turns next to a brief discussion of the relation of the *SL* to the preceding *PS*. As he makes at least three different statements on this relation, the issue has naturally caused a good bit of discussion in the secondary literature. I have analyzed the problem at some length in my book on Hegel.[6] Reduced to its simplest terms, the situation is as follows. In the *PS* (1807), Hegel says that the phenomenology is the first part of his system. In the current text, the introduction of 1812, phenomenology is called a presupposition of the system. In the *Encyclopedia* of 1817, Hegel changes his terms once more and says that phenomenology is the introduction to the system. I believe that the last statement should be taken as indicating Hegel's mature view. But it is not entirely incompatible with the 1812 statement that phenomenology is a presupposition. At first inspection, an introduction to the system does seem to be a presupposition. If we were indeed gods or could be shot from a pistol into the absolute, then no introduction to logic would be necessary. For ordinary mortals, the situation is different. This or that particular introduction may be a matter of contingency and relative to the circumstances of the time, but at any time a ladder to the absolute is required, as Hegel himself notes.

In his well-known study of this problem, H. F. Fulda grants that Hegel's later attitude toward the status of the *PS* is very unclear.[7] He does, however, arrive at a general conclusion, namely, "that an introduction which justi-

fies the ascent into pure thinking is still necessary even for the encyclope-
dic form of the Hegelian systematic; further, that this introduction is to be
treated in a particular discipline which must be the science of consciousness, but which *cannot be the first part* of the system nor be restricted to the
form of consciousness, and which has its foundations in the conclusion of
the system."[8] As Fulda very reasonably observes, we require an introduction separate from the system "in which science brings the unscientific consciousness to an understanding about the former."[9] Since it is science that
is effecting this understanding, the introduction must itself be a science;
since the introduction must come to terms with the unscientific consciousness, it must take place outside of, and so not be a part within, the system.
Unfortunately, this results in two sciences, one antecedent to the system
and the other identical with it. In this case the system is not really *the* system; it is not the science of the whole. In other words, the science recorded
in the *PS* is the necessary presupposition of the system of which the logic is
the first part, but there is no part of the system that explains its own necessity. I see no recognition on Fulda's part of this paradoxical consequence of
his analysis. That Fulda is himself unable to overcome the confusion inherent in Hegel's presentation is evident from later passages in his book. For
example, Fulda says that the *PS* is the first step in the process of the unfolding of spirit toward science. He adds that this is not simply the beginning
of a historical process but without restriction "the first part of the system
of science, while this cannot begin with the complete transparency of its
elements, and so also not with that part of itself which makes the beginning of its absolute content."[10] Five pages later, Fulda returns to the earlier
formulation that the *PS* is an introduction to the system but not a part of it;
it is a formation (*Gestaltung*) of the foundation of the scientific treatment
of consciousness but not the same as that scientific treatment; it produces
the concept of science, and so on.[11]

Fulda's book is filled with many interesting remarks about Hegel's procedure, but I cannot find a satisfactorily precise resolution in it to the problem it addresses. The science of logic requires an introduction that is not
itself the first part of that science. This introduction must make clear to
the pre-Hegelian or unscientific neophyte what is meant by science and
system, and so in what sense the logic must be presuppositionless. This is
in fact the intention of my introductory discussion of Hegel's preliminary
material, which discussion is based on a wide range of texts, including a
number of Hegel's other writings, crucial works in the history of philosophy, examples of the secondary literature, and my own reflections. I could
not have written precisely these chapters if I had not studied the *PS*, but

this is not the same thing as to say that the *PS* is itself the necessary presupposition of the system. If that were true, then we would first have to master the *PS* before studying the *SL*. Yet Hegel could hardly assume that all those who followed his lectures on logic had already mastered the *PS*. Furthermore, the science of logic is the first part of Hegel's *Encyclopedia*, which he intended as a textbook of the system. Phenomenology now appears as a short subsection of the philosophy of spirit and falls between anthropology and psychology. I cannot see any compelling reason to accept Hegel's early statement about the indispensability of the *PS* to the *SL*.

This does not alter the fact that in writing the *SL*, Hegel speaks of the *PS* as the necessary presupposition of the science of logic. The problem we are investigating can perhaps be best resolved by saying that the *PS* is part of Hegel's system but not a part of the science of logic. A possible justification of this view is that the system contains a variety of sciences, as the *Encyclopedia* shows. This is not the same as to say that the *PS* is a science falling *outside* the system, as follows from Fulda's analysis. On this simple solution, the *PS* should be studied *after* the science of logic, not before it. However this may be, I doubt that Hegel himself had successfully resolved the problem of the relation of the two books. His thought was clearly in flux on this point, and we are at liberty to follow what seems like the best solution. This is, I believe, to take the exoteric material in the *SL* as Hegel's own way of preparing the student of logic for the absolute standpoint. And that is what I am doing. In my analysis of the exoteric material, I feel free to introduce any thoughts at all, whether from Hegel's works, the history of philosophy, or my own reflections, that will serve to introduce us to the science of logic. We cannot as it were excise those passages in the *SL* in which Hegel insists upon the scientific priority of the *PS* to the *SL*. But we are required to show that even if Hegel was right to retract or modify this claim in later years, the integrity and plausibility of the logic itself are not affected.

I regard it as quite plausible to admit that no one can plunge directly into the categorial development of the concept without any introductory preparation. It is also plausible to say that part of this preparation is a discussion of the relation between phenomenology and logic. What I deny is that we must assimilate the content of the *PS* in order to understand the *SL*. It may perhaps be true that we cannot become Hegelians without proceeding via the *PS*; but that is not my intention. What Hegel seems to mean is that, at best, by our having worked through and assimilated the *PS*, we acquire the "material" of the totality of human experience, the logical structure of which we are about to study. But since it is not evident how knowledge of the totality of phenomenal experience would play a role in clarifying or explaining the categories of logic, we can simply assume that in studying the logic, it is precisely the structure of totality that we are learning. In sum: for our purposes, there is no necessary dependence of the *SL* on the *PS*.

We must nevertheless understand the point that Hegel wishes to make in the introduction of the *SL* about the relation of phenomenology to logic. Hegel says that in the *PS* he has exhibited "consciousness in its progressive movement from the first immediate opposition of itself with its object [*Gegenstandes*] to absolute knowledge . . . This way proceeds through all forms of the relation of consciousness to the object [*Objekt*] and has as its result the concept of science" (32). The distinction between *Gegenstand* and *Objekt* seems to be that the latter term refers to the correlate of *Subjekt* whereas the former has no fixed technical sense but represents an opposition that is turned into the subject-object distinction by the development of experience. In neither sense of the term is an "object" the presence of an independent being, not even to the so-called natural consciousness. From the outset, consciousness is an opposition of itself to an object, to that which "stands opposite to" immediate awareness, which is not yet conscious of itself as a subject that projects the object. Thinking is from the outset representation. The object of consciousness is necessarily within the penumbra of consciousness for Hegel, just as it is for Kant and Fichte. Again I emphasize that if Hegel is to make good on his promise to avoid subjectivism, it can only be as a *result* of the logic, not because of anything in the *PS*, which itself amounts to the self-differentiation of the appearing spirit into a totality of subjective conceptual experience.

This is evident from Hegel's explanation of the concept of absolute knowing that is provided us by the *PS*. "Absolute knowledge is the truth of all modes of the consciousness because, just as the process of consciousness produced it, the separation of the object from self-certitude [*die Gewissheit seiner selbst*] has been completely dissolved only in absolute knowledge" (33). In other words, absolute wisdom is the complete assimilation of the object into "self-certitude," which we can call "spirit" rather than "the subject" because it contains both the subject and the object. The *PS* shows us how spirit produces and reassimilates in completely developed form all fundamental ways of cognizing the object. The *SL* shows us the complete development of the logical moments of the process through which this antecedent assimilation occurs. What was previously an indissoluble separation of the "I" from the "not-I" within consciousness is now an identity within difference of subject and object. But this identity within difference is the very structure of "the concept."

Hegel goes on to restate what has been contributed to the study of logic by the *PS*. "Pure science presupposes the liberation of consciousness from opposition. It contains thought insofar as the latter is the *Sache in itself*, or [it contains] the *Sache in itself* insofar as *it is just as much pure thought*" (33). There is no externalization in the sense of alienation, i.e., no separation of subject and object or, rather, no separation of intellect and thing. However we finally articulate the science of wisdom, it cannot be a return to the independence of being from thinking. If we have correctly understood the *PS*, then we have reached the absolute standpoint in the sense that all apparent externalizations have been internalized, all oppositions of consciousness have been overcome. This provides us with the key premise of the *SL*: the concept is equivalent to totality. In the terms of the tradition, we cannot think about "being" or ontology except by thinking about thinking. Our experience has completely appeared, not as "mere appearance" or what Hegel calls *Schein*, but as fully understood. "Appearance" here is full disclosure: In the subsequent language of the *SL*, the inner or ostensibly hidden essence is now seen to be identical with the complete set of its appearances. But this is not conceptually grasped until we actually complete our study of the logic. Full disclosure is one thing; wisdom or the discursive account of what has been disclosed is something else.

There follows a striking passage in which Hegel insists that the content of pure science (i.e., of logic) is "objective thinking" and not something purely formal in the traditional sense of that term. Nevertheless, this content is pure thinking or absolute form itself. The logic is therefore "the system of pure reason," "the domain of pure thought," or "the truth as it is without any husk, in and for itself." In an expression that we have already had occasion to notice, Hegel says that this content is *the exhibition of God, as he is in his eternal essence before the creation of nature and finite Spirit*" (33). This makes it quite clear that the *SL* does not contain an external nature or a realm of objects that are independent of consciousness. In addition, we are told that the world of man and nature is implicit within God. Nevertheless, Hegel will later deny that he is a pantheist. The justification of this denial will depend upon whether or not Hegel's doctrine of the relation between the interior and exterior of spirit as one of identity within difference can be sustained.

Hegel's denial that he is a pantheist comes down to the following point. The pantheist says that God is everything. Hegel, whether he speaks of

God, spirit, or the absolute, distinguishes between God and the world. God creates, and thereby separates himself from, the world. But, as is symbolized in religious terms by the figure of Jesus Christ, the world is not simply detached from and other than God; Hegel is not a dualist. In the language of logic, God is in the world in the form of the logical process by which anything whatsoever acquires objectivity. But he is separate from the world since the life-pulse of objectification is not simply identical with the totality of objects making up creation.

In short, the logical structure of the world, and so too of humankind, is contained within God, that is to say, absolute spirit, prior to the creation. God is identical to his creation before it has occurred. But the act of creation or the externalization of the world from the inwardness of God the spirit does not render the world contingent; on the contrary, as created by God, it exhibits its creator. That is what it means to say that the world is the externalization of spirit. God is accordingly also different from his creation, not as sundered from or radically independent of it, but as an original is different from its image. However, we must not forget that in this case, the image is not a kind of Platonic simulacrum of the *eidōs* or original; the relation between image and original is here not so much reflection as isomorphism of structure. God shows himself in his creation; the "show" is indeed of God, but of God as manifested in the world. Hence God and the world exhibit an identity within difference. The holy trinity exhibits the same structure in Hegel's analysis.

Hegel's conception of logic is thus closer to Anaxagoras's doctrine of *nous* than to the Platonic ideas; the former contains implicitly the thought "that the essence of the world is to be defined as thought" whereas the latter reifies the truth (34). In the next several pages, Hegel repeats points that we have already encountered in the two prefaces. I therefore pass directly to his statement on method (38ff.). According to Hegel, the central insight into the method is quite simple: It is "the knowledge of the logical rule [*Satz*] that the negative is equally positive, or that what contradicts itself is dissolved not into nullity, into the abstract nothing, but essentially only into the negation of its particular content."

Hegel now says that the negation "non-p" is "determinate" because it depends upon and is restricted to p, which stands for a property that is preserved within the negation as its defining content. "Non-p" thus designates something else, say q, that is itself defined with respect to the negated content p. Hegel also says that non-p is a "result" of p or in other words depends upon it as an antecedent determination. He adds that the determinate negation is richer than the original concept or content p; this added richness comes from the negation, which thus opposes that content to itself. That is, non-p is opposed to p, but non-p is not the erasure of p; on the contrary, it raises p to a higher and richer level. "It is the unity of itself and its opposite" (39).

Hegel goes on to say that whereas the exposition of the details of his system could undoubtedly be improved, he knows that this method "is the only true one." This is exhibited already by the fact that there is no separation between logic and its object and content, "for it is the content in itself, the dialectic, that it contains within itself and that moves it forward" (39). This last phrase requires comment. Dialectic is not synonymous with logic but refers to the work of negativity by which logical content is produced and accumulated (see also 40). It is thus closely connected with contradiction. As we shall see later, logic taken as a totality is not dialectical because there is no higher stage to which it could attain. Whereas the work of negativity continues forever within the circle of totality, or, alternatively expressed, whereas the circle of totality is continuously being reconstituted, since totality is itself this continuous activity, there is no higher conceptual activity in opposition to which it could itself be negated and into which it would accordingly be raised. There is no infinite progress in logic. The negation of the negation of the determinate concept thus passes over into the world of nature, or in theological language, God creates the world. Logic is raised beyond or outside itself into genesis.

It also follows from the nature of negative activity that logic is in itself seamless or continuous. The division of the *SL* into chapters and sections, and the clarifications and historical remarks, are all external to logic, products of "external reflection," that is, of Hegel in his pedagogical or expository identity, which he can assume because he has already carried out the thinking of the totality of logic and can therefore anticipate for the convenience of the novice each stage before it is produced by the inner dynamic of the concept.

None of this is intended to imply that the order of exposition, that is, of the unfolding of the moments of the concept, is anything but necessary. The order of exposition follows the immanent development of God's thinking through the "recipe" (my phrase) of creation. At this point, we can already discern what will be a central difficulty. Can Hegel actually show that the order in which he treats the development of the concept is necessary, i.e., the only one possible? In the language of his own metaphor, why must God, in creating the world, or in preparing to create the world, think through its structure step by step, beginning with the emptiest of all determinations (being) and proceeding thence in a predetermined order to the whole? Hegel can reply, of course, that the order of the logic is necessary to the articulation of a system or science for human beings. But how can he prove that the process of conceptual development that he describes is in fact the procedure followed by God? Certainly the actual creation did not occur stage by stage, i.e., as a series of determinate negations that are then preserved at a higher level.

We may pass by the following passage, which repeats the difference between Hegelian dialectic and that of Plato and Kant. I proceed directly to the conclusion of the introduction. Hegel observes that the science of logic looks different to us depending upon whether we are studying it for the first time or returning to it after the mastery of the other sciences. This is because, looked at initially or in itself, "the system of logic is the domain of shadows, the world of simple essentialities, freed of all sensuous concretion" (44). At the same time, this abstractness allows us to develop our logical powers independent of all worldly concerns, and then to fill up the forms of logic with the content of all truth, "thereby bestowing upon it the worth of a universality that is no longer a particular next to other particulars, but that goes beyond all these and whose essence is the absolutely true" (44). In other words, like God, we must first prepare the structure of intelligibility and then create the world.

FOUR

The Beginning of Logical Science

In this chapter, we shall be concerned primarily with two technical points: (1) the difference between subjective and objective logic, and (2) the sense in which the science of logic is presuppositionless. This brings us more directly into the details of Hegel's logic than was necessary in the previous chapters. It is my hope that the extensive introductory analysis will have equipped us to deal with Hegel's idiosyncratic terminology, and to render perspicuous his general intentions.

The General Division of Logic

In the last part of the introduction, Hegel presents us with the general divisions of logic (45). The fundamental point to grasp is that despite the division of the *SL* into the objective and subjective logic, we are never literally external to subjectivity. In this context, "internal" and "external" refer primarily to a shift in attention or focus within self-consciousness. Stated in simple terms, we may focus upon the objective properties of experience, but "objects" are already products of, and in that sense fall within, the domain of subjectivity. To speak of beings that are cognized as they exist independently of cognition is for Hegel to contradict oneself. As we have seen, this contradiction of the natural consciousness, which latter underlies Greek metaphysics, sets into motion the development of dialectical logic. The development is from the outset one of the concept (*Begriff*), a term used with great frequency in the *SL*, the most general sense of which is that of a reflexive or self-conscious grasping by subjectivity of itself as the unity within difference of subject and object. Being and essence, the first two parts of the central division of Hegelian logic, constitute objective logic; these parts are united within part 3, the concept, from which the final and all-inclusive manifestation of the whole exhibits itself as the absolute idea. At every stage, including all of objective logic, we are within the domain of thinking.

We can therefore restate the development leading up to the science of logic as follows. Kant defines the subject-object structure of experience, but his account suffers from two major defects. The first is that finite subjectivity is detached from and subordinate to essentially static logical conditions of intelligibility. In other words, Kant's conceptual structures of intelligibility are for Hegel as separate from the subjective process of thinking as are Plato's ideas from their sensed particulars. Kant does not answer the question how formal universals are ingredient in particulars. The second defect is that objectivity is equated with the domain of phenomena; this leaves a *Jenseits* or domain beyond and inaccessible to subjectivity, so that knowledge is reduced to the status of knowledge of appearances. Fichte and Schelling begin the process of rectifying the first defect; Hegel perfects this correction and also removes the second defect. In short, Hegel claims to fulfill the promise of the discovery of the *ego cogitans* by Descartes, a promise that has thus far been unfulfilled thanks to the retention of traditional formalist rationalism. The abstract ego becomes the concrete productive subject; human beings thereby overcome estrangement or alienation from the products of their conceptual labor. The productive process of thinking is thus the unity between universal form and particular instances. This unity is present from the outset in the abstract identity of being and thinking. The process of logic is one in which this abstract identity differentiates itself, that is, becomes richer in content and ever more concrete. In the *SL*, the content is that of logical determinations. But the interplay of these determinations constitutes the matrix within which particulars appear; it is not a separate and static formal structure of a transcendental or Platonist variety.

At least as originally conceived, the *PS* is intended to carry out those perfections of the modern revolution that culminate in the *SL*. Hegel is referring to the *PS* when he says that "the concept of logic is itself given in the introduction as the result of an external [*jenseits liegende*], i.e., antecedent science and so here at the same time as a presupposition" (45–46). This passage seems to contradict the subsequent characterization of the presuppositionless nature of the science of logic. As I have already shown, there was some confusion in Hegel's mind about the relation between the *PS* and the *SL*, which he stated differently in different contexts. In the present passage, Hegel is referring to the fact that we do not ascend to the level of logic as if shot from a pistol. An elaborate preparation is necessary before we can take this step. This preparation is itself given the form of a science in the *PS*. In this work, Hegel describes the unification within consciousness of the empirical opposition between subject and object, of which the result, as he now claims, is the concept of logic as the science of pure thinking (45–46). To repeat Hegel's earlier remark, the way of phenomenology "goes through all *forms of the relation of consciousness to the object* and has the *concept of science* as its result" (32). In a more colloquial formulation, the *PS* provides us with the conceptual appropriation of the process by which human experience is produced. Still more simply, I first produce something by separating it from myself, and then overcome this separation by understanding that I have produced it, that it is an expression of my own creativity. The relation of consciousness to its object obviously falls within consciousness; otherwise put, the objective and subjective aspects of consciousness are in a more fundamental sense both modes of subjectivity.

As the science of pure thinking, which has pure knowing as its principle, logic "is not abstract but rather concrete living unity; and in it the opposition within consciousness of [on the one hand] a subjective existent for itself [*einem subjektiv für sich Seienden*] and [on the other hand] a second such existent, namely, an objective one, is contained as overcome; being as pure concept in itself and the true concept as the true being are known" (46). In other words, the content of the science of logic is the pure thinking, not of static logical form as distinct from subjectivity, but of the conceptual development of the process of spirit, that is, of the life-pulse or unity of being and thinking. The conceptual moments of this process are accordingly alive; they are self-moving and interactive. We can think them independently or one at a time only up to a point, beyond which they turn into their opposites and thereby rise to a higher and more complex level of inner structure. The last stage of this journey is the appearance or self-presentation of the actual world of particulars, not as brute matter somehow shaped by an external and static or transcendental form, but as the "appearances" or self-exhibitions of the reciprocal motions of the logical determinations.

In order to make sense out of this bizarre-seeming conception, we must remember the cardinal point of Hegel's underlying argument. The point is that there is no way in which to account for our experience if we restrict ourselves to the finite analytical terms of traditional rationalism. Experience is a unity as well as an exhibition of diversity. One might grant this even while denying the possibility of capturing the unitary nature of experience within a conceptual articulation. But this is precisely Hegel's goal. He is not sorting out finite and mutually independent categories but rather describing the growth of the pure concept into a fully articulated totality. It is easy to be incredulous at the extravagance of this enterprise. Hegel insists, and in my view not entirely without reason, that if we repudiate his enterprise, we are doomed to the nihilism of multiple and mutually exclusive partial views, perspectives, interpretations, or opinions about human life. But he does not leave it at an edifying rejection of nihilism. He insists that a rigorous analysis of human experience itself provides us with the starting point for the overcoming of the night in which all cows are black. This starting point is the fact of intelligibility, which is already a unity of diverse elements, or in Hegel's own language, the identity of identity and nonidentity (in my paraphrase, "an identity within difference").

With these remarks in mind, the difference between the *PS* and the *SL* now becomes somewhat easier to see. In the *PS*, we begin and end with spirit (*Geist*) and pass through the various stages of subjective experience; it is precisely subjective experience that we are studying. In the *SL*, on the other hand, despite the presupposition of the underlying unity of subject and object, we begin the actual description of the development or self-differentiation of that underlying unity with the excitation of the object, and therefore we must derive the subject from our thinking of the object. This is necessary if we are to exhibit the objectivity of the subject, that is, as sharing the universal logical structure of the objective world. As always in Hegel, unity, however abstract, must precede and indeed be the condition for subsequent development. In that development, unity is not dissolved but unfolded in a determinate order. It cannot be "glued" together from independent static elements like form and matter or the subject and object of traditional rationalism. In short, the *SL* begins with the concept as "existing" or "in itself" and afterward as "for itself" (47). That is, it begins with being and ends with thinking. And this twofold process is the development of the primitive unity of being and thinking.

I would then describe the starting point of the science of logic as follows. The introductory or pedagogic material explains that and why we require a presuppositionless science of the structure of the whole. A science is necessarily conceptual and discursive; a presuppositionless science is grounded in a first step that is both indisputable and rests upon no antecedent assumptions. Spinoza is the primary example of a philosopher who attempts to give a logical account of the whole but who begins with unjustified definitions and axioms. Hegel intends to rectify this oversight. I emphasize this point: Although the presuppositionless step takes place within, i.e., as the opening of, the science, its necessity and its general nature are described in the pedagogical or propaedeutic material. What then is indisputable about conceptualization? Hegel's answer is: the being of the concept. The concept is indispensable; without it, there is no thinking, let alone science. But it cannot be derived from anything else, since whatever we conceive, we conceive by way of concepts. That is, all content is relative to or dependent upon conceptualization. The opening of the logic is thus with the pure concept, the concept as empty of all content or determinations and so of anything that could itself be said to depend upon some prior cognitive act. We begin with nothing but the pure form of the concept, about which nothing can be said except that it exists (and "exists" is here a more euphonious surrogate for "is").

Now comes the peculiarly Hegelian maneuver. Having emptied the concept of all content, we have nothing to think but its being. But Hegel shifts our attention from the being of the concept to being itself; he assumes that the process of abstraction or emptying of the concept directs our attention, not to the concept as thought, but rather to its mere being. The fact that we are thinking or conceiving of each category in turn is obvious enough, but it can be disregarded because our initial task as practitioners of logic is to think the categories, not to think the concept that as it were owns these categories. We will think the concept itself only at that stage of the logic at which it emerges dialectically from the development of the categories themselves. That stage is the transition from the objective to the subjective logic. The history of metaphysics is thus marked for Hegel by what one could call the forgetting of thinking, rather than of being. By penetrating deeper and deeper into the excitation that underlies the false surface calm of being, we gradually liberate the imprisoned or concealed subjectivity. This penetration is *Erinnerung*, literally, "going within," but in its normal sense, "recollection."

If we possess the conceptual power to resist the easy blandishments of nihilism, or the endless multiplication of mutually incompatible because finite interpretations of this or that aspect of human experience, we are prepared to undertake the task of mastering Hegel's logic. The first step in that task is to understand the presuppositionlessness of the first step. And it is here that Hegel is at his most problematical. As we have already seen, it seems to be impossible on Hegelian grounds to begin in a presuppositionless manner. To begin with, a great deal of experience and conceptual labor is required in order to render evident the necessity of a presuppositionless science. But this is not in itself a difficulty from Hegel's standpoint. The prescientific preparation required to make us understand the need for science is not itself a part of science. The difficulty of the prescientific presuppositions lies in Hegel's ambiguous account of the role of the *PS*.

We have already discussed this problem in the previous chapter. To re-iterate the main point, if the science of phenomenology is the necessary mediation of our historical experience on the one hand and the science of logic on the other, then it must be the first part of the Hegelian system. There cannot be a science that is outside the system of science itself. In this case the *SL* is not intelligible without a prior understanding of the *PS*. But what does it mean to understand the *PS*, or in other words to accept its exhibition of the experience of the overcoming of the separation of subject and object? Does this not in turn depend upon our grasp of dialectico-speculative logic? Without such a grasp, Hegel's exhibition of human expe-rience remains at the level of a rhapsody or myth.

The first step in the logic must then be presuppositionless in the follow-ing precise sense. Regardless of the experience that was needed to arrive at this science, or as Hegel put it previously, to rise to the level of the abso-lute, the logic itself must begin with the assertion of what is most universal and therefore lacks any determination except itself. I note that, *sub specie aeternitatis*, there is no such self-subsisting category, since each category en-tails the others. The actually true is the whole. But the scientific account of the system must lead us step by step to this comprehensive insight into the perpetual circularity of the concept. In other words, the linear or step-by-step presentation of the science of logic is itself an accommodation to pedagogic necessity.

But we are not quite ready to analyze this opening moment within the science of logic. I allude to it here in order to clarify the difference between the presuppositionless beginning of logic and the external approach to logic. Logical presuppositionlessness has nothing to do with the kind of historical experience or antecedent knowledge required to begin the sci-ence of logic. Hegel is now engaged in the process of preparing us to take the first step. The preparation consists in persuading us that we can con-ceive of the process of thinking itself in two ways. First, we can represent it as an activity or process of such and such a kind, with the following set of properties. Second, we can think of it simply with respect to its being. In this case, we disregard what Kant calls its real predicates and concentrate upon being as a logical predicate. More precisely, we concentrate upon be-ing as antecedent to the distinction between subject and predicate.

Inside the science, we are thinking of pure being, and thus not even of thinking. Outside the science, we know that the pure being of which we think is just the being of thinking. The reason for this is that we have come to understand, as the preparation for the science of logic, that there is no being for us that is outside of or entirely separate from thinking. We cannot think of something of which we are not thinking. Therefore when we discard or disregard every positive determination of experience other than that it exists, what remains is the being of thinking. And there is nothing left over outside this being. There is no residue of unthought being. To suggest otherwise is at once to think that residue and so to incorporate it into thinking.

Throughout what follows, we must keep in mind the two points that have just been established. The distinction between presuppositions and the absence of presuppositions has a different meaning when it is applied outside the system from its meaning inside the system. Second, the distinction between objective and subjective logic is one of attention or focus, not of two distinct ontological domains. Subject and object can be reintegrated because they were never radically separate. The initial difference between them is the bridge through which they implicate one another at a higher level of development. It is this bridge that allows Hegel to overcome the dualism intrinsic to traditional metaphysics. This is expressed with extreme concision by Hegel when he says that the key to the logic is the exhibition of substance as subject. In book 1, we are at the level of substance.

With this explanation at hand, we can return to the text and consider the following passage, which summarizes succinctly the most important of the points I have just made: "Thus it is the total concept that is to be thought, once as existing [*seiender*] concept and then as concept" (47). In other words, the first part of the logic deals with being, and so with the being of the concept. The third and last part deals with the concept as such. And the being of parts 1 and 2 taken together is the being of thinking, although we do not focus on thinking as is done in part 3. Continuing: "In the first case it is only the concept in itself, of reality or of being. In the second case it is the concept as such, the concept that is for itself" (in other words, as aware of itself and not simply as existing).

In one more formulation of this crucial point, the objective logic has two main parts, treating respectively being and essence. Essence mediates between being and the concept. Subjective logic deals with the concept, or the emergence and development of the subjectivity of substance. Objective logic shows us the inner breakdown of the traditional doctrine of substance as independent of subjectivity. In the part on essence, we study the determinations of the concept of being as in relation (*Beziehung*) to one another and not, in other words, as discontinuous interpretations of that concept. Traditional ontology posits one determination after another as if each were the essence of being, such as quantity, quality, existence, and so on. Because none of these determinations can bear the weight of independence, each deteriorates into the next in the very process by which we try to think it as independent. The result is as it were a heap of candidates for the title "essence." This heap is accordingly the collapse of traditional ontology (31). The next step is to show how the internal excitation of the collapse leads to the reconstitution of the heap as essence. This amounts to a reinterpretation of disorder as the gradual appearance of order. As Hegel will put it, essence *is* appearance; conversely, appearance is precisely the appearance of essence. But this by way of anticipation.

With What Must the Origin of Science Be Made?

According to Hegel's opening statement in the section "With What Must the Origin of Science Be Made?," the problem of a beginning in philosophy first rose to the level of consciousness in modern times (55). I need to comment on this point at some length. In the main classical school of Socrates, philosophy begins from opinion (*doksa*) or the views (*endoksa*) of the most thoughtful persons. One could therefore describe philosophy as an ascent from everyday life to the forms or categories that constitute the structure of the whole. There is, however, a disjunction between the discursive account of everyday life and the intellectual apprehension of the forms, whether these be Platonic ideas or Aristotelian species forms; and the same could be said of Aristotle's categories, which are neither deduced from a first principle nor justified systematically. Both Plato and Aristotle speak as if the forms and categories are directly accessible to theoretical intelligence.

On the other hand, the separateness of the ideas from one another is never overcome by an actual science of dialectic. The identity within difference, as Hegel might call it, between the Good and its participant ideas is purely formal; there is no inner excitation, no dialectic between the two elements. We cannot derive the ideas from the Good, nor can we express conceptually the Good as the ground of the ideas. One of Hegel's most pervasive assumptions is that formal elements cannot be unified except through the mediation of subjectivity, that is, the work of thinking their difference. In a Hegelian metaphor, thinking is digesting; life grows by assimilation and in that process brings to life what it assimilates, only at a higher level of completeness. No such life is present in Platonic *noēsis* of the ideas, and a similar observation holds good for the Aristotelian categories. Note that when Aristotle speaks of god as thought thinking itself, he adds that god does not think the very forms that pure thinking actualizes.[1] According to Aristotle, our own ability to think the forms depends upon our possessing two intellects or at least two different but related intellectual powers. Stated as simply as possible, we must both "activate" the form within thinking and then think it. And Aristotle never gives the slightest explanation of how these two types of noetic activity are related.

Wherever we look in ancient philosophy, then, it is evident that opinion and myth serve to bind the fragments of a rational or discursive doctrine into a total account. From this standpoint, the ancients, even Aristotle among them, provide us with a myth of the whole, not a *logos*. The fundamental change in modern times may be expressed as consisting of two points. First: the blending of the Judeo-Christian tradition with Greek philosophy gives rise to a doctrine of subjectivity that prepares the way for the modern account of thinking as assimilating and reforming, or in other words, as constituting or creating rather than simply apprehending independent external forms.

Second: the paradigm of mathematics may be detected as underlying the Socratic conception of theoretical intelligence with respect to the criteria of universality and certitude. But this paradigm does not hold for human life or knowledge of the spatiotemporal cosmos; this leaves a dualism of eternity and temporality, of the divine and the human. Modern philosophy, on the contrary, has at its disposal the experimental and theoretical science that is rooted in modern mathematics, which does in fact apply to the spatiotemporal world. It is an easy step to the hypothesis that the same methods by which we have acquired exact knowledge of physical nature can be applied with similar results to human experience. Certitude is now accessible, at least in principle, to philosophy, which can at last become scientific or genuinely epistemic.

From a Hegelian standpoint, the great significance of Descartes is not only that he introduces the prospect of a *mathesis universalis* by which to transform opinion into knowledge, but that he also founds the science of subjectivity in his discovery of the *ego cogitans*, the *punctum inconcussum* (the unmovable point or foundation) of metaphysics. Certitude is not merely mathematical in the usual sense of that term; it applies first and foremost to self-consciousness. The course of modern philosophy from Descartes to Hegel is that of the steady overcoming of the separation of the two modes of certitude, mathematical and subjective. What one could call Descartes's formal Platonism, most obvious in his doctrine of the intellectual intuition of pure mathematical forms by the *lumen naturale* or natural light of the intellect, must be overcome by an assimilation of mathematical or ontological forms into the cognitive activity of the *ego cogitans*. Intellectual intuition must be replaced by dialectic, and this in turn requires completion by speculation. Kant is the mediating term between Descartes and Hegel with respect to this process.

It is true that Hegel replaces the rigid and separate nature of mathematical elements with the formation process in which individual forms are dialectically interrelated, but he preserves the criterion of certitude that underlies modern philosophy from Descartes forward. His goal is to present a complete and consistent system of knowledge, although not quite in the sense that these terms are employed in post-Hegelian formalisms. Hegel claims that his system is complete because all essential stages of the concept have been exhibited; this is evolutionary, not deductive, completeness. His system is consistent in the sense that it explains contradiction rather than eliminating it; that is, Hegel shows how *A* and not-*A* are consistent with one another at a higher level of development. This is not at all the same as the demonstration that if *A* is deducible from a set of axioms, then one cannot deduce not-*A* from the same set. It is rather the demonstration of the interdefinability of axioms.

In sum: it is Hegel's intention to carry out in fact the elimination of opinion and myth from philosophy by transforming it into scientific knowledge and, in that sense, wisdom. By so doing, Hegel also intends to carry out with respect to the whole tradition what Aristotle attempted to accomplish with respect to his teacher Plato. At the same time, however, Hegel wishes to preserve freedom, something that at least initially does not seem to be compatible with mathematical systematicity, an incompatibility that is already visible in Spinoza, who attributes geometrical necessity to the order that unites thought and extension and thereby defines freedom as knowledge of determinism. Spinoza lacks a doctrine of subjectivity; to this extent he is a step backward from Descartes. The latter, on the other hand, fails to provide a mediating principle between the principle of subjectivity and the geometrical necessity that is visible to the *lumen naturale*. There is in Descartes a subjectivist dualism, represented by the distinction between mathematics and metaphysics, that remains to be overcome. At the same time, this dualism must be overcome in such a way as not to reduce the subject to the bondage of determinism.

The correct beginning is therefore one that leads to both certitude and freedom. We are now in a position to see that one characteristic of this beginning is that it will not be mathematical. Hegel in one sense rejects the Cartesian *mathesis universalis* by replacing it with dialectic; in another sense, he accepts the need for a single and infallible method, but not a method that is external to the content of philosophy in the way that mathematical formalism is external to the formalized content. Experience is not "subjected" to the method of dialectic; it is rather dialectical in its very nature. Dialectic is already present in the preliminary opposition between subject and object; opposition is relation, not exclusion or cancellation. As we recall, according to Hegel's original claim, the *PS* is the complete exhibition of the modes of opposition or relation between the subject and its object, an exhibition that necessarily occurs within subjectivity itself. In terms of the preceding discussion, this exhibition is the dissolution of the rigidity and separateness, typical of mathematics, that are attributed to ontological forms. It is precisely by thinking them conjointly that we overcome the rigidity and separateness of forms.

This point can be restated independently of taking a position on the function of the *PS* in the acquisition of Hegelian wisdom. Our own experience confirms the lesson of history that there is a finite number of comprehensive philosophical positions, each of which is internally inconsistent. When we think through this inconsistency in a given case, we thereby generate one of the other comprehensive positions, and this process continues until we see that we are repeating ourselves and so that there are no more comprehensive positions. What now passes for novelty or progress in philosophy is instead a retreat or a narrowing of vision that leads us to take one aspect or another of a previously considered position as a new approach. But the incompleteness of this ostensible advance leads sooner rather than later to a dialectic of fragments, each supposedly original, and thereby to a reconstitution of the already traversed comprehensive positions from the collision of the aforementioned fragments. We arrive at a recognition of the reciprocally canceling relations that govern any and all of our examined positions. The penultimate stage of wisdom is thus nihilism, or what is today called "postmodernism" and sometimes "post-Hegelianism." *Logos* is replaced by the chatter of transient intellectual fashions.

The ultimate stage, or the escape from nihilism, can be called the "negation of negation," that is, the understanding that the apparently destructive excitation of colliding positions is actually the expression of a dialectical logic of totality. What looks from the immanent or finite or historical viewpoint like permanent dissolution is actually, that is, from the standpoint of logic, permanent reconstitution or preservation. Even granting that Hegel succeeds in his effort to think the whole as an eternal or circular consequence of the formation process, what has this to do with freedom? I believe that there can be no doubt about Hegel's fundamental Spinozism on this point. To be free is to be reasonable and thus to know the necessary structure of the circular activity of formation. But knowledge is in fact possible, as, strictly speaking, it is not for Spinoza, because the formation process is a process of life, that is, of subjectivity as the inwardness of absolute spirit. Hegel does not reject the essence of Spinoza's conception of freedom on behalf of post-Hegelian romanticism about the individual person; he rather brings it to life by showing the rational core of individual human existence. What is understood in the post-Hegelian period as the contingent freedom of the purely historical individual is thus raised by Hegel himself from irrational because arbitrary and evanescent chance to the level of rationality and universality, thanks to the exhibition of the identity within difference of the individual person with God.[2] This exhibition is provided for the sage by the Hegelian teaching and for the non-sage by participation in rational political institutions.

It should now be evident that the expression "identity of identity and not-identity" is not a rhetorical flourish but captures the nerve of Hegel's teaching and thereby points out the correct beginning in Hegelian *Wissenschaft*. This correct beginning cannot be an abstract principle like the law of identity or an ontological *prius* like the idea of the Good. It cannot be substance, because substance lacks subjectivity; but neither can it be subjectivity alone, as in the teaching of the German Idealists, for what lacks objectivity cannot be known. And finally, it cannot be a "harmony" of subject and object, because this merely brings together two dimensions that remain external to one another, with no explanation of their inner relation. The beginning can only be the simplest instance of the totality of logical determinations, an instance that is not itself the result of an antecedent determination but that originates the process of the development of all determinations. Note carefully: this is a completely general assertion and does not refer to some particular set of opposed terms that are identical and different. So far as particular sets of logical oppositions are concerned, it makes no difference where one begins. It is through identity that we think difference and through difference that we think identity. Stated succinctly, not-*A* does not cancel out or obliterate *A* but is an ingredient in its form at a level more encompassing than that of each by itself.

All this is necessary, but it is not yet sufficient to explain to us what Hegel regards as the correct beginning of *Wissenschaft*. We must now add to the preceding analysis that two entities are in opposition, not in themselves, but in and for thought. The distinction "subject-object" is not the expression of an arbitrary doctrine of subjectivity but the only possible way of representing how one may think anything at all. When the ancients and their imitators speak of the noetic apprehension of beings or forms, what are they saying if not that apprehension takes place within thought? Do they wish to suggest that thought and being are glued together in such a way that they remain separate even as attached? Why should the attachment constitute thinking rather than mere contiguity? This is no more intelligible than the solipsism of subjective idealism, according to which beings are appearances within thought. In the first case, there is no explanation of how things are thinkable; in the second, there are no things but only thoughts. In order to preserve both the thinkability of beings and their independent reality (so that they are genuine *res* and not phantoms or illusions), we must begin by accepting their identity within difference.

And now the term "within" becomes crucial. Thoughts and beings are different, but this difference occurs within a common medium. That is, thoughts and beings are the interior and the exterior of a process that exists by manifesting itself, a process that Hegel calls absolute spirit. The manifestation is in the first instance that of the absolute to itself. This corresponds to the thinking by God of the universe just prior to its creation. In other words, the absolute is not in itself an empty universal or abstraction but the universe as created in addition to its creator. The universe is the exhibition of God to himself, but to himself as both creator and created. God would not be God if he did not create and thereby render actual the glorious possibilities of his thinking. This is not simply an expression of piety that I am attributing to Hegel as an ostensibly devout Lutheran; if it were an expression of piety, it would have nothing to do with philosophy. Hegel arrives at the thesis that God must create the universe because of a healthy respect for *Wirklichkeit*; in other words, he rejects all forms of idealism or doctrines that attribute a higher excellence to ideas than to the actualization of these ideas in spatiotemporal, and so historical, existence. Stated provisionally, Hegel claims that essential possibility must actualize fully, thanks to the inner excitation or drive toward self-exhibition that is the heart and soul of the absolute. The meaning of this claim will be made more precise when we study the dialectic of being and nothing.

Hegel's doctrine of absolute spirit must be understood as an attempt to validate the splendor, not of the universe as external to self-consciousness, but of our self-conscious appropriation of the visible universe. As he frequently says, the most insignificant thought of the least intelligent human being is intrinsically more valuable than the entire world of nature. To those who insist upon the glory of nature, Hegel replies that this glory is entirely dependent upon its presence to thought. And as I have already emphasized, the presence to thought occurs only within thought. In sum: the sense of "within" is supplied by the absoluteness or comprehensiveness of spirit. Conversely, absolute spirit is not a hypothesis or an arbitrary assumption motivated by religious faith rather than philosophical analysis.

It is the necessary and immediate consequence of the identity within difference of subject and object. In plain English, it is the condition for the possibility of the thinking of anything whatsoever.

I can now come back to my earlier assertion that subject and object are both subjective in the sense that the relation of the two takes place within thinking, which is obviously an activity of the subject. This assertion does not need to be withdrawn, but it does require deepening. The relation in which the subject thinks the object does indeed occur within the subject. But this is not to say that the object occurs within the subject. The object is the exterior of spirit, just as the subject is the interior. In other words, subject and object are the two dimensions of spirit, which is neither the one nor the other but their identity within difference. As thought, the two are the same; as existing, they are different. What Hegel does contend is that the whole (*das Ganze*) is alive; and it is the life-pulse of the formation process that is the sign of this life. This raises the problem of the relation between God and his creation. Some have accused Hegel of pantheism, some of atheism. I doubt whether he would accept either designation. The same formula of the identity of identity and not-identity applies to God and the creation. The world is the externalization of God, or the object that corresponds to the divine subject. Neither could exist without the other (since to be a God is to create), and the two together are the two sides of absolute spirit.

We can now continue with Hegel's own exposition of the problem of a beginning. The beginning must be either immediate or mediated, and yet it is easy to show that neither of these is possible (55). Hegel means that each is self-contradictory. A mediated beginning is one that arises out of antecedent terms; it is therefore not a beginning. But an immediate beginning is impossible, because everything in heaven or on earth or in spirit contains *both* immediacy and mediation (56). What we call "immediate" is always the result of a previous mediation. Hegel does not explain this point in the present context, but it follows directly from the dependence of what is immediately present upon the subject to which it is presented. Consider those who believe themselves to begin with a divine revelation, an intellectual intuition, and so on, as if they were shot from a pistol without any prior deliberation on objective or subjective criteria for the origin of philosophizing (55). The initial absence of deliberation does not alter the fact that the content of the revelation stands as the object to the subject-recipient.

Let us note the connection between the relation of immediacy and mediation to the problem of presuppositionlessness. Assuming that we can indeed begin our science with an undeniable assertion that rests upon no presuppositions, we must still be brought to the level of science by our historical experience (or as Hegel puts it, the PS is the presupposition of the *SL*). Inside the science of logic, being is immediate. But we arrive at this immediacy by emptying our experience of all other determinations. That is, being is initially experienced as mediated. The turn to the immediacy of being is thus accomplished with the assistance of a series of negations, which collectively mediate our progress from mediation to immediacy. We do not start immediately with immediacy. But we can *arrive* at immediacy because it was already present within the total situation. In the present case, we do not invent the pure category of being but rather identify it through a narrowing of conceptual focus. On the other hand, if we had not narrowed our focus, we would never have perceived pure being.

The upshot is that life itself is never simply immediate or mediated, but it is both at once. These two aspects of the unity and process of life cannot be existentially sundered. But neither can they be completely separated in pure thought. Each attempt to isolate one is dependent upon the other. In contemporary language, logical atomism is impossible because logical atoms are self-canceling. In Hegelian language, subjective activity must combine from the outset with objective truth. Hegel is here alluding to the claim that the *PS* is the necessary presupposition for the *SL*. In the present context he says: "The beginning is logical insofar as it shall be made in the element of a thinking that is free for itself, in pure *knowing*. The beginning is here mediated because pure knowing is the last absolute truth of consciousness" (57).

In other words, the beginning of the *SL* is the conclusion of the *PS*. Hegel goes on to say that pure knowing, as the beginning of logic, must now be considered just as it presents itself, as "ready to hand" (*vorhanden*), apart from all previous reflections or opinions about it (58). I note that the idea of pure knowing has the same role in logic that is assigned by phenomenology to sensuous certitude. It is, however, much more difficult to understand what Hegel means by "pure knowing." To begin with, he says that it is *das Unterschiedslose*, "that which contains no inner distinction or determination." In sensuous certitude, this corresponds to the absence of a conscious distinction between the subjectivity of sensuous awareness and the content of sensation. It must therefore be the case that the corresponding "simple *immediacy*" attributed by Hegel to pure knowing is the absence of a separation between the subject or knower and the object, which has been entirely assimilated by the completed development of spirit.

"Simple immediacy is itself an expression of reflection and refers itself to the distinction from the mediated. In its true expression, therefore, this simple immediacy is pure being" (58). This looks as though Hegel has forgotten his preceding assertion that everything whatsoever contains both immediacy and mediation; but that is not so. He is rather taking the first step in his attempt to explain that the beginning is both immediate and mediate. It must be immediate in order to serve as a beginning; but it must be mediate if it is to have any consequences. The immediate is, precisely as immediate, and so as lacking in determinate distinctions, distinguished from mediation, and therefore immediacy is mediated *by* mediation. The first step in the analysis of the beginning is to consider its immediacy. That Hegel has not forgotten mediation is indicated by the words "refers itself to the distinction from the mediated." Stated in a preliminary and general manner, immediacy is intelligible only as contrasted with mediation; our thinking of the one is therefore mediated by our thinking of the other.

Much of the obscurity in the present section comes from the fact that Hegel wishes to make two claims at once that seem to be incompatible with each other. On the one hand, he denies that logic begins as if shot from a pistol, that is to say, in a purely arbitrary and unjustified manner. As we have seen, in at least the initial conception of the *SL*, the *PS* supplies us with the presupposition of logic. On the other hand, Hegel needs to insist upon the difference between phenomenology and logic. The content of the idea of pure knowing, that is, the details of the development of spirit as recorded in the *PS*, is not as such a part of the beginning of logic. What we utilize here is the state of pure knowing without reference to the details of what is known. One may think here of Spinoza's remark that to know is to know that one knows. Hegel is as it were isolating knowing that one knows from the more concrete and detailed knowing itself. This state of pure knowing contains no separation between subject and object (any more than does the state of sensuous certitude); it is therefore complete, and so immediate in the sense that it refers to nothing outside itself. In this sense, it is pure being. As soon as this is established, however, Hegel will turn to the reference of immediacy to mediation; that is to say, pure being is immediate in lacking inner determinations and in being complete, but it is mediate by virtue of its self-reference to nothing.

This is how Hegel proposes to justify the assertion that the beginning of logic is the result of phenomenology but that logic differs from phenomenology in such a way as to be independent of it. Phenomenology makes logic independent by providing it with the idea of pure knowing. Let us, however, remember that the transition from the *PS* to the *SL* is anything but immediate or straightforward. Apart from the prefaces and introduction, the present section is necessary in order to show how pure knowing is pure being. This identification is made for us by Hegel, who has already negotiated the transition, but who therefore stands outside and above those of us who are attempting it for the first time. And a similar distinction between Hegel and us is equally necessary with respect to the *PS*. It is not the case that we are automatically transformed from philosophers into sages by the necessary course of history. We require to be instructed by Hegel, who has himself alone understood and exhibited the truth of that course in his writings and speeches. One could no doubt say that if Hegel had not existed, history would have produced a suitable substitute. But what one cannot plausibly maintain is that no teacher is required, or that what the Marxists call the dialectical process of historical materialism will itself produce wisdom, any more than it will produce the classless society or the posthistorical Utopia. In sum, a preface to logic is necessary, whether or not this preface includes the science of phenomenology. My own view is that even the science of phenomenology would require a prescientific or pedagogical preface, and that such a preface could well dispense with the *PS* itself, as Hegel in effect does in the *Encyclopedia*, and as I am doing in this book.

Being, then, is the beginning (*das Anfangende*), and it is exhibited as such solely through mediation with nothing (58). That is, being, as empty of determinations, is not itself the result of a mediation. It is not the result of a previous simpler determination. But as the same as nothing (which is also not the result of a previous determination), being is mediated by nothing. We should, however, bear in mind that we must be able to distinguish between being and nothing in order to show their sameness, namely, that the attempt to analyze either logical determination leads us directly to the other, and so to becoming. Becoming contains the two determinations of being and nothing, and their interaction engenders a dialectical step forward, or what Hegel calls an *Aufhebung*, a rising up to a more inclusive level of development. Neither being nor nothing is by itself capable of this step forward. Allow me to underline this point. Becoming is the first logical moment to emerge from two simpler and complementary terms. It therefore seems to be the case that dialectic begins with becoming.

Hegel turns back to the previous point of how logic can be both dependent upon the *PS* and yet be independent or constitute an immediate, and so presuppositionless, beginning. It is true that pure knowing as the result of finite knowing or consciousness is presupposed here. "But if no presupposition is to be made and the beginning is to be taken as itself immediate, it then determines itself only in this way, that it shall be the beginning of logic, of thinking for itself. Only the resolve [*Entschluss*], which one can also take as arbitrariness, that one wills to contemplate thinking as such is at hand" (58).

The sentence just quoted is highly ambiguous and turns upon two occurrences of *sollen* ("shall" or "ought") as well as upon references to arbitrariness (*Willkür*) and the will (*wollen*). But the intention is straightforward. As I said a moment ago, the idea of pure knowing and its identity as pure being are actual for Hegel but only possible for us. Just as for the most sophisticated Marxist thinkers of the past there would be no revolution without an act of will on the part of the participants, so too there will be no ascent to wisdom for us unless we will ourselves as it were to the level of the absolute.

The invocation of *sollen* leads us to *necessity*; stated with a certain direct awkwardness, it ought to be (or shall be) that the beginning must be immediate ("So muss der Anfang absoluter oder . . . abstrakter Anfang sein"). To restate this slightly, necessity is a consequence of the will. Hegel does not say so, but I take the implication of what he does say to be something like this. In Kant, freedom is hypothetical or possible only, because it is compatible with the noumenal domain only, which is inaccessible to conceptual understanding. We cannot know that we are free. Knowledge is of necessity; it is equivalent to the assertion of a rule or law. In Hegel, the necessary knowledge of the conceptual structure of the absolute is dependent upon the act of the will by which we accomplish the transition from phenomenology to logic. One *might* call this free act of the will "arbitrary," but Hegel clearly does not, since then it would be irrational. The act is rational in the precise sense that our rationality depends upon our performing it and so passing over to the science of logic. This performance is free but not arbitrary; we are free to be persuaded to rise to the absolute, whether by the *PS* or in some other way. We are persuaded to be both free and rational by our human understanding. And as both free and rational, we unify freedom and necessity as an identity within difference, something that Kant could not accomplish.

Summary and Transition

We are studying the preliminary essay entitled "With What Must the Origin of Science Be Made?" The general problem as posed by Hegel is this: In order to arrive at wisdom rather than mere philosophy, we must possess a systematic exposition or, as the Greeks called it, a *logos* of totality. In traditional terms, we must explain the essence of the whole. But a genuine explanation of the essence also accounts for its relation to its appearances. The same point can be made in theological terms. Wisdom is knowledge of God or the divine. But complete knowledge of God includes knowledge of the creation. We need to know not every empirical detail of the creation but rather how it is a manifestation of God. In the other terminology, we need to know not every empirical appearance of essence but how appearances are themselves presentations of essence (and note that even as differing from essence, they present it as different from themselves, as that with respect to which they are defined as appearances).

Hegel's fundamental premise is that the Greek, and in the best sense Aristotelian, conception of philosophy as *logon didonai* (giving a rational account) is correct. Furthermore, Hegel accepts without question the Socratic thesis that whoever seeks wisdom must give an account of form in the sense of the Platonic ideas or Aristotelian *eidōs*. To understand is to understand formal structure. However, Hegel also accepts the modern doctrine, associated with and in the most important sense derived from Christianity, that wisdom includes knowledge of soul or spirit understood as inwardness or subjectivity. He also accepts the Kantian thesis that the relation between knower and known is one of subject and object, or that the subject "projects" its object. Hegel modifies this thesis in two important ways. First, he conceives of the subject and the object as the two dimensions of a more comprehensive totality, namely, spirit. Second, he denies the Kantian distinction between phenomena and noumena or things in themselves. According to Hegel, the phenomena are actually the appearances of the noumena; that is to say, the noumena appear as the phenomena. There is no dualism of subject and object because there is no separation, in the last stage of the development or manifestation of spirit, between what we know and what we cannot know. It is the nature of spirit to manifest itself, and the two sides to this manifestation are subjectivity and objectivity.

In sum, Hegel both carries out the Greek intention to explain intelligible form and reinterprets what the Greeks called *psuchē* and *nous* as *Geist* and *Selbstbewusstsein*. Hegel purports to give a comprehensive account of the formal structure of the whole (*das Ganze*), God and creation or (in the secular terminology) essence and appearance. Stated more abstractly, Hegel will explain the essential structure that unfolds from the reciprocal excitation of being and nothing. This excitation, expressed generally, is becoming. We have seen that the first moment of Hegel's dialectic contains the whole, if in a peculiarly abstract manner. And this is necessary if we are to arrive at a complete development of the whole. As we have also seen previously, Hegel overcomes the split between form and thought (and so between object and subject), but redefines form as *formation process*. In the last analysis, there are no separate pure forms but instead a process of interrelated conceptual moments of the concept, that is, the *logos* of absolute spirit.

As to presuppositionlessness, Hegel's solution to this problem is that the first step of science is both immediate and mediate. In his initial version of this solution, the science of logic is mediated by phenomenology, which transmits to the putative logician its own result, the idea of pure knowing. This idea is the necessary starting point of the science of logic. But the idea of pure knowing contains no determinations, i.e., no determinate knowledge, and so no opposition of subject and object within the unity of negated difference. It is like sensuous certitude in this respect; the knower knows that he knows but does not actively know this or that as an object of his cognition. In this sense, it is a totality without determinations, and so it is immediate relative to the logician.

There is, however, a disjunction between the final result of the presentation of phenomenology in the *PS* and the immediate beginning of the *SL*, a disjunction that can be filled only by the will of the putative logician. We must will to contemplate thinking as such. This act of resolve is therefore equivalent to a fresh start. Hegel insists that we are put into the position of being able to make this fresh start by the successful completion of the *PS*, but he offers no persuasive arguments to sustain this assertion. At best there seems to be a rhetorical force inherent in the assimilation of the *PS* that allows us to will to begin logic with an immediate in the sense of entirely undeveloped concept of totality. But I see no reason why one could not make the same beginning without having traversed the *PS*.

There follows a very obscure discussion of the question whether philosophy must return "into the ground" of natural experience or rather into that of the absolute. In the former case, the result is empiricism; in the latter, empirical growth is transformed from the outset into logical development. I will paraphrase this passage as follows. In the empiricist conception of philosophy, the model is that of progress from a simple beginning (sensations) to a continuously more complex account of experience. One may ask whether this complex account is acquired from nature by observation and analysis or whether we ourselves produce it by cognitive labor. The answer is initially that the account is a mixture of observation and production. Eventually, however, what we mean by "nature" itself comes to be regarded as a product of cognitive labor, as for example in the Kantian doctrine of the transcendental ego, and eventually as an outright creation of historical human beings. In Hegel, on the other hand, the acquired complex account is a product of, and in a deeper sense is identical with, the manifestation-process of the absolute. To be sure, human work is an essential ingredient in this process; but it is intrinsically the work of the absolute. Progress is therefore for human beings a return back into the ground in the following sense: in our "phenomenological" motion forward, we are making history; but in the "noumenal" core of this motion, we are repossessing or recollecting the absolute. From this standpoint, history is *Realphilosophie* or the rendering actual of God's thoughts just before the creation.

The return to the ground is the return to the origin. This may seem to contradict my earlier assertion that for Hegel there is no return to the origin. But I was there speaking of origin as a source or ground that is independent of what emerges from it, and so of opinion as the origin of knowledge. In the present context, the origin is neither opinion nor for that matter an archaic gift or manifestation of being. The origin is instead the grounded world or structure of intelligibility. In other words, each step forward by which we observe the unfolding of another stage of conceptual development is also a step backward into the first principle, the idea of pure knowing, by which we find the step of the historical future already present in the structure of eternity. What is enacted in history is "the whole story" of eternity, which is not static but always enacting or "telling" itself to itself. The absolute is thus a perpetually rotating circle. "The essential requirement for science is not so much that the beginning be a pure immediacy, but rather that the totality of science describes a circle into itself, within which the first is also the last and the last is also the first" (60).

Human history is the temporal enactment of the paradigm of eternity. From this standpoint, history stands to eternity as does the subject to the object. But we recall that absolute spirit is both subject and object, both history and eternity. The development forward into history is as it were the recollective manifestation of what is contained "backward" or "already" in the ground of the eternal paradigm. The transcendental or absolute excitation of eternity, by which the moments of the concept are positing themselves and being transformed into their opposites, is the paradigm of historical excitation, by which the dialectic of the concept is translated into the course of human history. History exhibits or "mirrors" the life-pulse of the eternal circular excitation of logic; this life-pulse is the absolute.

This line of reflection must now be related back to the problem of immediacy and mediation in the beginning of science. Once again, a science must be immediate or presuppositionless, and yet this is evidently impossible. Either one begins arbitrarily and so contingently, or one assumes a hypothetical first principle, which once more renders our science contingent. Hegel has now explained the sense in which logic is a circle, such that each step forward (the exhibition to the knowing subject of a determination of the concept) is also a step backward (into the concept, in order to "recollect" the particular determination). Hegel can thus maintain that we are always making an immediate beginning no matter what we do. To begin is necessarily to begin on the circle, and the circle is immediate because it is totality; we do not arrive at the circle from some point external to it.

Nevertheless, as the simultaneity of forward and backward motion (explained by the fact that history mirrors eternity), the circle, and every step that we take on it, is mediated. This brings us once more to the ostensible relation between phenomenology and logic. Presumably phenomenology is not "on" the circle of logic but projects us onto it. But logic is not the only circle; there is also the circle of history or temporality, and the identity within difference of these two circles constitutes a third, all-encompassing circle, the absolute. Within the absolute, we move from the phenomenological organization of history onto the logical articulation of the concept, i.e., eternity. This "move" is accomplished by the comprehensive negation of all stages of phenomenological experience into "the night in which all cows are black" and by the negation of this negation, or the recognition that total truth is precisely the sum of self-contradictions of all attempts to explain human experience that fall short of totality. If we know that we have exhausted all comprehensive approaches to the whole, then we have a negative understanding of the whole itself. Totality is the sum of the self-cancellations of partial philosophies. Or so Hegel seems initially to have thought.

We see here the same lacuna that was noticed previously in Hegel's account of the transition from phenomenology to logic. Let us assume that we have explored every philosophical account of human experience that identifies an essential perspective yet falls short of the whole. Why should our perception of shipwreck transform itself (via negation of the negation) into the idea of pure knowing, or (as the last chapter of the PS is entitled) into "absolute knowing"? Hegel does not claim that we arrive at the whole by a steady addition of parts; on the contrary, the process is dialectical in the sense just described. One "part" (= philosophical position) negates itself or turns into its opposite. These opposing terms are then sublated into a higher stage, in which each is present as negated; i.e., each is no longer independent but functions merely as one aspect of a larger totality. In order for us to arrive at the ultimate stage by a negation of the negation, the penultimate stage must itself be a negation. The historical representation of this stage is for Hegel the philosophy of Schelling, which is equivalent to nihilism, or the negating of all previous sublations. How then do we emerge from nihilism into absolute knowledge?

If there is an answer to this question, it depends upon a later stage of the exposition, namely, the claim that essence manifests itself fully as its appearances. But this transfers the problem to a higher level. How do we know that we have witnessed all interpretations of the appearances? To reply that we are complete when we begin to repeat ourselves leaves open the possibility that we have overlooked some philosophical account of the whole. In the present passage, Hegel goes on to say that the first is last and the last is first: The beginning is the ground and the ground is its derivative. Since progress is also return, the immediacy of the beginning is mediated by this reciprocal motion or excitation, that is to say, by the establishment of the circularity of excitation (61). There is then nothing provisory or hypothetical about the progress of logic, which not only depends upon but is the same as the reappropriation of what has already been established. I must say that this is not very persuasive. Hegel here as elsewhere confuses what is said to hold in the absolute with what we human beings discover as we pursue our thoughts sequentially. The only way in which our study of logic can be freed of its provisory quality is by our completing it. What Hegel must mean to say is that the manifestation of the absolute in history has already completed itself and been both grasped and described by Hegel himself. In the *SL*, Hegel records the circle of logic. But we who are beginning to study it cannot know that each step forward is a step back into the ground. We have to take Hegel on faith, at least to the extent that we are prepared to follow his account and see whether it is persuasive. In other words, we cannot know that Hegel has presented us with the system of science until we complete it and thereby know ourselves to be wise. If this should happen, we will then be in a position to affirm Hegel's account of the identity within difference of forward and backward progress. Meanwhile, we can only go forward.

As Hegel himself puts this point: "that which constitutes the beginning, insofar as it is as such the still undeveloped and is lacking in content, is not yet truly known at the beginning," nor is the science of logic available at the outset in its complete development as truly grounded knowledge (61). The intrinsic identity of the beginning with the ground, which we have just studied, is thus not available to the student at the outset, and presumably not until the completion of his studies, at which time the circle of the concept is completed. Logic can then be understood to have been a return into the ground, and so to have been grounded from the outset. The beginning is pure and without content; it is pure being and as such could offer no information on the process of progress and return that we have just studied. This raises a new difficulty. The idea of pure knowing, which we have presumably inherited from the *PS*, is absolute knowing taken apart from its internal determinations. This presumably requires the suppression even of the distinction between subject and object, that is to say, between the act of knowing and what one knows. As a consequence, this idea contains no subjectivity for the same reason that it contains no objectivity; it is pure being.

It might appear initially that in the transition from the *PS* to the *SL*, we have lost self-consciousness along with the determinations of absolute knowing. Hegel's point is that what we require for the beginning of logic is the pure form of being that is common to the subjective and the objective dimensions of the experience of totality achieved by spirit at the end of the *PS*.

Hegel is going to show how all formal determinations of the concept arise from the initial excitation of pure being. This excitation arises, as we are about to see, from the fact that pure being, as pure, is no thing whatsoever, and so nothing. Hegel will claim that this dual identity of our beginning constitutes an opposition that sets both poles into motion; the result is becoming. I will return to the details of this excitation. Here we need to see that the process of the development of pure being will lead to the production of the objective and the subjective structure of absolute spirit. We need to begin with pure being precisely to demonstrate the order of development of totality by steps, each of which emerges from its antecedent (with the exception of the initial step); this process goes on until the entire structure of the concept is visible.

To say this in another way, suppose that we begin our dialectical reflections with some intermediate opposition, say, quality and quantity. Our analysis of this opposition will lead us to discover not only their conceptual connectedness but also the substructure of forms that is part of their nature. In the case of quality, this will include existence, becoming, nothing, and being. One cannot understand an intermediate form without also understanding its substructure. And the task of understanding the substructure entails the understanding of how it is composed of syntheses that are themselves generated by the work of negativity from the opposition of simpler elements. This process takes us back inevitably to the first step, namely, the pure being that is identical with the idea of pure knowing. Pure being and pure nothing are reached by the search for transparent simplicity. In sum: not only do the moments or categories that constitute the concept grow out of one another, but they do so in a necessary order.

In this sense, one could speak of the study of logic as "deductive," namely, in the sense that we must understand how one level of formal structure follows from its predecessor.

To come back now to the idea of pure knowing and its identification with pure being, Hegel says: "This pure being is the unity into which pure knowing returns; or if this [pure being] is itself still to be distinguished as form from its unity, so too is it the content of that same [unity]" (61). This confirms my previous explanation of the loss of self-consciousness that occurs in the shift from the *PS* to the *SL*. Pure being is so to speak the residue remaining when one squeezes an elaborated self-consciousness, and with it objective determinations, out of the idea of pure knowing. Needless to say, this "squeezing-out" process does not take place within the consciousness of the beginning student of logic. *But neither does it take place in the ontological actuality of totality*. Where then does it occur? In the concept of a pure beginning, in other words, in that absolute limit to which the student reduces his resources when commencing to do logic. Paradoxical as it sounds, the correct beginning of logic is one in which the novice places himself at the outset in the position of God, in order to duplicate, under the guidance of Hegel, who has already completed the process, the thinking of the creator immediately prior to the act of creation.

In the continuation to the previously quoted statement on page 61, Hegel says that pure being, as the content of unity (i.e., the pure unity of subject and object), is absolute mediation, and this is in addition to its identity as absolute immediacy (which arises from its lack of finite determinations). This is a particularly obscure move in the dialectic, and one that is quite typical in Hegel. Pure being is empty; hence it is unity, like the Eleatic one. But pure being is also the content of unity; it is so to speak the predicate by which we identify pure unity. This is in effect the Platonic criticism of Eleatic ontology. When we say that being is one, we are mentioning two items, being and unity or the one.

Having established the mediated nature of pure being, Hegel warns us to put it to one side. Pure being must be taken "essentially only in the one-sidedness of pure immediacy, precisely because it is here the beginning" (61). This is quite irritating, but it is not entirely unintelligible. We remember that everything, including immediacy, contains the immediate and the mediate. But pure being is mediated by nothing other than itself, in other words, by nothing as the empty content of its own unity.

This dualism will set off an internal excitation within pure being and cause it to dissolve or to multiply; but this will occur only in a later stage of our analysis. The first stage is the immediacy of this particular mediation of immediacy and mediation. Thus Hegel says: "Pure knowing offers only this negative determination, that it is to be [*soll*] the abstract beginning. Insofar as pure being is taken as the content of pure knowing, the latter must retreat from its content, leave it secure for itself, and give it no further determination" (62). The continuous circular excitation of the spirit that flows within the concept as its life-pulse, and that relates formal elements to their opposites within higher levels of structure, does not dissolve these elements but exhibits their complex or totalizing natures. If the elements were simply dissolved into one another, then we could not isolate them in thought; more radically, there would be no experience, no self-consciousness, nothing but a blur. Hegel is not a postmodern partisan of *différance*.

With the retreat of pure knowing from being in its role as content, we are left with what I called above the residue of the abstract beginning of philosophy, namely, the unity of being and knowing: "Insofar as pure being is to be thought as unity, in which knowing coincides with its object at its highest peak of unification, so [the element of] knowing in this unity has vanished and has no difference from it and so retains no determination [by which it can be known]" (62). But we can also discard the determination of being and require nothing except that a pure beginning be made. In short, we can move from being as content to being as unity to the absence of being. Bear in mind that being as unity is one aspect of a *Vorstellung* or "concept" in the usual sense of an idea or representation, even the product of imagination; in the given concept, being as content and being as unity are connected representations of the presuppositionless beginning in the science of logic. The fact that we can consider being as pure unity does not mean that it cannot also, and from another standpoint, be considered as the content of unity. This is extremely important because it illustrates a general truth. We do not "create" the objects or contents of our thoughts. Being is what it is; however, part of its nature is to be accessible to thinking. If being could be said to be produced by anything at all, it would be by absolute spirit, not by the temporal thinking of the individual philosopher who is taking the first step in Hegelian logic.

We now shift our attention from beginning with being to beginning with nothing. There is an essential difference between these two beginnings. Whichever we employ, it is obvious that there must be a consequence: the development of the determinations of the concept must be contained implicitly in our beginning, so that progress is also a return into the beginning as ground. Pure being contains a mediation, namely, the opposition between itself as pure and itself as content of unity. As we may anticipate, pure being already contains the moment of nothing. But pure nothing is vacuous. "The beginning is not the pure nothing but a nothing from which something is to [*soll*] emerge; being is thus already contained in the beginning. The beginning therefore contains both being and nothing; it is the unity of being and nothing—or it is not-being [*Nichtsein*] that is at once being, and being that is at once not-being" (63).

This passage is of extreme importance. As I have prepared for its analysis at some length, I can here be brief. Hegel is in effect repeating the step taken by the Eleatic Stranger in Plato's *Sophist* (258d1ff.), namely, the rejection of "the altogether not" (*to mēdamōs on*) in favor of what Hegel has just called *Nichtsein*. The Stranger defines nothing as not-being, and not-being is in turn defined as otherness. Hence when we say "not," we are actually referring indirectly to something, to some content or determination. To say that "Socrates is not an ape" is to refer indirectly to the fact that he is a human being, and so on. "Not," in other words, is intelligible or used legitimately only as attached, or with reference, to a predicate. Hegel does not simply adopt the definition of "not" as "other." Instead, he incorporates otherness into the *Vorstellung* of nothing that is qualified to serve as a beginning for logic. Note that for Hegel, *Nichtsein* is the generalized form of determinate negation, i.e., of a negation of some definite object or predicate. Since *Nichts* understood as *Nichtsein* contains being, it also contains implicitly all of the determinations of being. But the role of the negation is to hold these determinations in suspension, not to erase them. In short, *Nichts* as defined by Hegel contains being, but in suspension.

We could not begin with a pure *Nichts* because it has no consequences, and this is because it has no opposing determination. The Aristotelian assertion that being has no contrary applies for Hegel to the pure *Nichts*. In the logic proper, Hegel actually begins with being, which, as we have just seen, contains an opposition between itself as content and itself as unity. It therefore contains nothing in the sense of not-being. Contrary to Parmenides, there is already a difference within pure being, as was brought out in Plato's *Parmenides*, since to say that being is one is to mention two things, being and unity. For this reason, but without calling it explicitly to our attention, Hegel shifts in his very discussion of a beginning with *Nichtsein* to a beginning with *Sein* and *Nichts* (63). He simply rules out a beginning with pure nothing, and in discussing its ostensible alternative, the beginning with a generative *Nichts*, identifies its generative capacity with the fact that it contains being. The actual import of this passage is that we cannot begin with either being or nothing, but rather must begin with both as opposed to one another: "Further, being and nothing are present at the beginning as distinct" (63). In other words, if we want to begin at all, we have to begin with something. This rules out the pure nothing. But the "something" with which we begin must be presuppositionless in the sense that it is in no way arbitrary. As this can also be expressed, the "something" must be universally present no matter how we begin. The opposition of being and nothing is just the "something" we need. We therefore take it apart from the particular determinations in which it is manifested and make it the beginning of the science of logic.

The analysis of the beginning has thus provided us with the concept (i.e., our own understanding) of the unity of being and not-being, or in terms of reflection, i.e., of the relation of determinations, of the unity of being distinguished and of not being distinguished. This in turn is the same as the identity of identity and nonidentity. As I pointed out previously, this last concept "could be viewed as the first, purest, i.e., most abstract definition of the absolute" (63). Hegel next adds a lengthy remark on the by now familiar point that the beginning of a science cannot be contingent or depend upon oppositions imported tacitly into the ostensible first step by the accidental circumstances of the investigator. The initial opposition must be immediate or, in the sense just explained, universal, and it must emerge from the chosen unity (i.e., being and nothing) by the inner excitation of the opposed elements (64).

But this is not yet precisely stated. The opposed elements cannot be concrete, since in this case their reference to one another would be the result of a sublation of an antecedent opposition. For example, "something" cannot be the beginning, because it contains a concrete determination, namely, being and nothing understood conjointly as becoming; and the elements of this determination are simpler components out of which our ostensible beginning has been constituted. So however we regard the matter, there is no other way in which to begin but with the unity of being and not-being. This depends upon nothing antecedent, and yet it contains a distinction or mediation from which content can be generated.

Nevertheless, says Hegel, one other thesis about the beginning, dating from recent times, must be briefly considered. This is the doctrine of Fichte, according to which the beginning is with the "I" (*Ich*). At first glance, the I seems to be both immediate and universal or free of contingency. But the I in question is not the immediately known ego of everyday consciousness; it is instead the pure knowing that Hegel himself has previously identified as the beginning of science. However, Fichte simply postulates the pure I as the beginning without showing how we must arrive at it through the progressive and necessary inner excitation of the ordinary ego. The Fichtean beginning is thus a subjective postulate, and Fichte (as Hegel says elsewhere) is a subjective idealist (65–66). Hegel, on the contrary, arrives at his beginning by demonstrating its necessary priority as the ultimate presupposition of any concrete beginning whatsoever. In this sense it is presuppositionless, and so a genuine beginning.

Hegel next makes the objection to Fichte that, on his grounds, we can reach the I of pure knowing only by an absolute act of self-ascent from within immediate or ordinary consciousness, and this creates the impression that the beginning of philosophy is accessible to that consciousness, an impression that is exposed as a deception by the discovery that the absolute I is unfamiliar to the everyday ego (66). It is true that Hegel's own beginning is accessible only by an act of abstraction, but it differs from Fichte's on two points. First, there is no illusion of familiarity or accessibility to ordinary consciousness; second, the beginning is not a subjective postulate but the unity of subject and object; more precisely, it is that unity apart from any inner determinations.

It is also a disadvantage of Fichte's doctrine that objects are always posed in contrast to the I; we never overcome the split between subject and object, as does Hegel by denying the separation of the two elements, which he instead characterizes as an opposition within unity. Hegel sees Fichte in essentially Kantian terms, that is, as retaining the split between phenomena and noumena. On the one hand, objects are subjectivized by being defined as objects in and for subjects; on the other hand, objects are themselves detached from their noumenal identity as things in themselves. The opposition of subject and object is thus trapped within appearance (67).

In a later chapter, I will discuss the technical details of Fichte's doctrine at length. This brief treatment was required by Hegel's reference to the central deficiency of that doctrine. Hegel concludes that he has himself arrived at the only possible and indeed the one necessary beginning of a presuppositionless science.

Universal Division of Being

Book 1 of the *SL* has three main sections: determinateness or quality, quantity, and measure. Being is the first moment of determinateness; to be is to be something. But to be something is to possess a formal identity, and this is not true of quantity. Quantity, like Aristotelian *hulē*, is individuated by form, and form is qualitative, "suchness" (69). Hegel calls quantity *aufgehobene Bestimmtheit* (sublated determinateness) because it is lacking in formal identity; here one can think of Aristotle's "prime matter" as that which receives form. Prime matter is in one sense without form, but in another, its *dunamis* to receive *eidē* is itself a quasi-form. So too Hegel's quantity is the capacity to receive qualitative determination; as such, it is not the complete lack of determination but the potentiality to be qualitatively determined. This is itself a determination, corresponding to the potentiality of Aristotelian matter. This is what Hegel means when he says that quantity is "quality become negative" (70). Or again: quality represents the alterability of being but not alteration itself. Hegel takes this to show that quality is not yet distinguished from being, as it becomes through sublation within quantity or magnitude (70). Measure stands to quality and quantity as does becoming to being and not-being.

We note next that being appears in three places in the structure of the *SL*. Book 1 of the *SL* is entitled "The Doctrine of Being." This designation is distinguished from "The Doctrine of Essence," which mediates between it and "The Doctrine of the Concept." These titles express the general development of the science from objective to subjective logic; they do not in themselves make clear that the subjective logic is not an external supplement to, but a sublation of, the objective logic. Objective logic corresponds to traditional ontology; in Hegel's revision, we first study the categorial structure of the thing (*on* or *res*) and thereby exhibit its development into essence (*ousia, essentia*). The crucial point here is that the traditional distinction between essence and attributes is circular. We cannot identify the attributes of a thing unless we know its essence; yet we are supposed to know the essence via knowledge of the essential attributes. Furthermore, we cannot distinguish between essential and accidental attributes unless we already know the essence. This circularity leads to the dissolution of the essence into its attributes or "appearances" (as in nominalism and British empiricism). Hegel must show that the circle is dialectical or a sublation rather than a contradiction in the pejorative sense of traditional rationalism. That is, he must show that the appearances are the essence and that the essence is nothing other than its appearances.

I postpone discussion of the difficult question of the transition from objective to subjective logic to the appropriate place. To stay with the organization of book 1, I note that the two additional chapters of the first section ("Quality") are called in German "Das Dasein" and "Das Fürsichsein." So "being" (*Sein*) is present within these chapters, but in a more developed way. It must of course also be present in the second and third sections of book 1, but evidently not as visibly as it is in the first section. In Hegel's version of ontology, then, one could almost say that being becomes *less* visible, not more so. This is because it is virtually invisible from the start, as we have already seen. The attempt to think being in itself forces us to introduce other logical determinations, or in other words to enrich our concept by the addition of logical structure. This addition is not arbitrary but forced upon us by the effort of thinking itself and, initially, by the effort of thinking being. There is one further problem here. Strictly speaking, the additional determinations, which are Hegel's version of what Aristotle and Kant call "categories," are not properties of being. "Nothing" is not "predicated of" being. Yet Hegel often speaks as though it is the structure of being that we are elucidating. We should guard against falling into this way of speaking. The additional determinations grow out of the concept of being, but thereby surpass it. Being is not the owner of these determinations in the sense that the traditional essence is the owner of its attributes or properties. I will have more to say on this point in a later chapter.

The term *Sein* no longer appears in the names of the logical determinations after the first section. The German term *Dasein* means literally "being there" and is often translated as "existence." The problem here is that Hegel also uses *Existenz* as a technical term. The traditional procedure is to translate the technical uses of *Dasein* as "determinate being," a procedure not without its difficulties, as we shall see later. Since "there-being" and "being-there" are unusually cumbersome to the English-speaking ear, I will follow tradition while signaling the German term when it seems necessary to do so. In ordinary passages, where the term does not designate a logical moment of the concept, I will translate *Dasein* as "existence." *Fürsichsein* will be translated literally as "being for itself," and its sense will be explained in the appropriate place.

It would not be useful to present a more detailed analysis of Hegel's preliminary sketch of the universal division of the treatment of being. In the next chapter, we will turn directly to the first section of book 1.

FIVE

From Being to Existence

Book 1, Section 1: Determinateness (Quality)

We are about to study section 1, "Determinateness (Quality)," the first moment of the development of the structure of the concept. Like any science, this is an activity of self-consciousness, but unlike other sciences, the activity is what Hegel calls "pure thinking." This expression refers in the first instance to the fact that the content of our thought is thinking itself and nothing else. It would be cumbersome but not inaccurate to refer to logic in Hegel's sense as the science of science, since "science" means literally "knowing." The structure of the concept is a fortiori the structure of knowing anything whatsoever, for example, physics or history. It is not the structure of physics or of world history as a determinate body of knowledge but rather the structure of the *topos* of every determinate body of knowledge. One could perhaps refer to this *topos* as "transcendental" inasmuch as it is the condition for the possibility of knowledge of anything whatsoever.

It would be tempting to continue the previous point by adding that the *topos* is also the condition for the possibility of the being of anything whatsoever. But this Kantian turn of expression, if it is to be used at all, is subject to the following restriction. For Kant, "to be" is to have phenomenal location within the network of categories, concepts, rules, schemata, forms of intuition, and sensations that constitute the phenomenal experience of rational thinking, and thus to be a possible subject of scientific knowledge. But this notion of being cannot be attributed to Hegel. Kant's sense of being or existence (terms that he uses synonymously) applies to a thing or "object" (*Gegenstand*). There is no use of "being" in Kant that stands for the totality of the actual world and certainly not for the transcendental conditions by which the world is constituted as a theater of possible experience. As Heidegger correctly puts it, being is for Kant positionality within the phenomenal world.[1] For Hegel on the contrary, being is not positionality;

that term would correspond, if to anything, then to *Dasein* or determinate being. *Sein* in the *SL* is not a determinate being but the narrowest or simplest thinkable determination of the concept understood as the *topos* of anything whatsoever. One could, however, refer to being in the Hegelian sense by the Kantian expression "logical predicate," since being is a determination or quality of the concept in the most comprehensive sense of that term; that is, being is a quality of the structure of the continuum of becoming, rather than the essence of this or that particular item within that continuum. All of the determinations in Hegel's logic are "logical predicates" in this sense.

In this context I might also mention Heidegger's well-known criticism of what he calls the traditional definition of being as the most universal and so the emptiest concept. Being is for Heidegger not a concept and not a determination, however universal, of the concept of totality; it is instead the process whereby beings are manifested. It would not be entirely wrong to see here a resemblance to Hegel's doctrine of totality as a process of becoming, although Heidegger would no doubt reject the analogy. There is also a certain kinship between Hegel's conceptual articulation of the structure of the whole and the early Heidegger's account of the "existentials" or categories of the hermeneutical ontology of human being, which is in turn intended as the basis for the never-achieved doctrine of the sense of Being. In his later philosophy, Heidegger gives up the attempt to derive the categories of historicity and turns away from predicational discourse toward "the other way" of speaking about, or more precisely bespeaking (= evoking), Being.

Heidegger's criticism of the universal concept of being (as opposed to "Being" in his sense of the term) seems to be based upon the assumption that the richness of Being must somehow correspond to the richness of beings, or in other words that Being is the source of everything whatsoever and cannot be less fertile than its consequences. At the same time, Heidegger disapproves of all "ontic" descriptions of Being, namely, those that employ real predicates or qualitative determinations and thus conceal Being by the language appropriate to beings. The consequence of these joint theses is the turn away from predicative discourse in an attempt to discover an alternative manner of speaking and thinking about Being.

For the Hegelian, Heidegger's "other way" is myth or poetry as opposed to conceptual discourse. Hegel might also say that the turn back to poetical speech is based upon the mistaken notion that being is too rich to be captured by predicative discourse. On the contrary, being is too empty to be grasped in that way. What corresponds in Hegel's philosophy to the Heideggerian "Being" is not being but, if anything, then the absolute, which is for Hegel not empty but the most concrete or all-inclusive. Otherwise put, the absolute is not a predicate or property but rather the ultimate owner of all properties, including being. Finally and perhaps most important, it makes no sense to speak of the "emptiness" of being except in a provisional or nondialectical sense. Being is the simplest property of the conceptualization of the absolute, but the attempt to think it transforms it into its opposite and thus initiates the process whereby being grows or expands into the totality of determinations constituting the concept.

This point requires emphasis. The *SL* is especially obscure because it attempts to capture the inner excitation and evolving nature of the structure of unity, even while doing justice to the independent identity of each unit in that structure. Hegel's language is thus on the one hand static and finite; that is, it obeys the principles of the syntax of traditional rationalism. But on the other hand, the content of this language is alive, coming to be and passing away, and so it violates the ontological principles of classical rationalism. No single sentence in Hegel's exposition disobeys the principle of noncontradiction, but the content as it were flows beyond the syntactic boundaries of the individual sentences in the effort to convey the plasticity and organic unity of the diverse properties of living thought. According to the traditional version of the hermeneutical circle, one must understand the whole to understand the parts; yet, in order to understand the parts, one must understand the whole. We can adapt this circle to Hegel as follows. In order to understand the unity of diversity, one must in fact master seriatim the diverse components of that unity. But in mastering the diverse components, we detach them from unity and thereby deprive them of both life and their place within the whole.

For Hegel, then, being is the first (or last) condition of discourse, and the discourse that interests Hegel is here conceptual. No doctrine of being is possible because being has no inner complexity, nothing with which to sustain a doctrine. All doctrines that purport to be ontological in the sense of describing the nature of being are thus from a Hegelian standpoint actually describing something else, namely, something that *has* being, or that *is* or *exists*. Note that this is true in particular and par excellence of doctrines of categoricity. Hegel's own "table" of logical determinations or categories is not intended as a definitive analysis of the structure of being; on the contrary, being is the simplest or emptiest of the categories of the concept, namely, the concept of actuality (*Wirklichkeit*).

So much by way of introduction. Let us now turn more directly to the text. The first section of book 1 is called "Determinateness" (*Bestimmtheit*), which Hegel himself glosses as "Quality" (71). The priority of quality to quantity (the gloss on "Magnitude," the title of the second section) exhibits the previously noted adherence by Hegel to the traditional doctrine of the priority of form to matter. Just as form, in traditional ontology, shapes matter, so for Hegel it is qualitative determination that gives identity to extension or difference. However, as we shall see, for Hegel, quality itself evolves into quantity; more precisely, the effort to think through the nature of quality leads us to quantity as its dialectical consequence. These two elements of a conceptual opposition are then resolved into an identity within difference that Hegel calls "measure" (*Mass*), the title of the third section.

It follows directly that, for Hegel, being and nothing are both qualities; that is to say, they are logical determinations, or what I called previously "logical" rather than "real" predicates. I note in passing that in giving priority to quality, Hegel seems to differ sharply from the mathematical logic of Gottlob Frege and Bertrand Russell, in which existence is expressed as a quantifier. If we look more closely, however, we see that the statement "x exists" means for the mathematical logician "there is at least one thing that has a certain property (or set of properties)." In other words, x is said to "instantiate" a concept or set of concepts. The identity of x is accordingly fixed by a real predicate, that is to say, by a formal structure. But this by the way.

To say that something "is" (or "exists") is to make the minimal intelligible statement about it. Those who complain about the emptiness or incompleteness of the attribution of being are in a sense right to do so. But its very emptiness or indeterminateness is already a determination. This determination carries the name "nothing." The determination "nothing" does not erase or destroy pure being; it expresses the movement or excitation within being, an excitation that is exhibited in our thinking as the process back and forth between being and nothing. Our attempt to think pure being thus drives us to equate it with nothing, in the sense of nothing definite or enduring, yet this indefiniteness or transience does not suppress or destroy being. This continuous movement back and forth from being to nothing and vice versa is the simplest logical characterization of becoming. In sum: we cannot "think" pure being, if to think means to describe its structure or nature, because pure being, as pure, has no structure or power. The only way in which to describe pure being is by negation; the ostensibly positive terms "pure" and "simple" mean "indeterminate," "nothing in particular." As soon as we think through what it means to speak of, and hence to conceive as opposed to merely intuiting, pure being, we engender the dialectic of being and nothing. This dialectic is the process of becoming; that is, it is the structure of the continuum of the whole.[2]

In considering Hegel's logical transitions, it would be a complete mistake to ask whether something, for example being, "actually" turns into something else, for example becoming, through the emergence from itself of nothing and their subsequent opposition. The correct question is whether we are compelled to think nothing by the thinking of being, and so whether this jointly necessary result of thinking leads necessarily in turn to the thinking of becoming. We are engaging in logic or conceptual thinking, not in the physical construction of the universe from the bricks and mortar of divine masonry. Plato's mythical divine artificer is replaced by the Hegelian logician.

Book 1, Section 1, Chapter 1: Being

I have now concluded a rather lengthy preliminary discussion of the logical moves to be accomplished in the first book of the *SL*. This provides us with the general context within which to study the moves themselves. We begin with paragraphs A, B, and C in chapter 1, entitled "Being" (*Sein*). In the broader sense of the term, the teaching about being includes quality, quantity, and measure. In the narrower sense, being is quality. We are not yet in a position to understand the broader teaching, but the location of the first category of being under quality is already partly intelligible to us in view of my discussion of the Kantian definition of being.

In order to see why this is so, let us take up once more the Kantian thesis that being is not a real predicate. This means that it is not a property of a *res*, thing, or *Gegenstand*, understood as a phenomenon accessible to perception and hence to conceptual knowledge. Being is not part of the inner structure of an object of experience. "It is merely the positing of a thing, or of certain determinations, as existing in themselves. Logically, it is merely the copula of a judgment"; i.e., it serves only "to *posit* the predicate in its relation to the subject."[3] Real predicates can be added to the concept of a thing in such a way as to enlarge that concept. This is Kant's way of saying that a real predicate picks out a defining property within the structure of the thing. If I say that human beings are rational, then I have enlarged the concept of human being by identifying a constituent property. If, however, I say that human beings exist, or that this human being exists, I have posited an object as ingredient within the structure of phenomenal experience without saying anything about the inner constitution of that object. In this sense, we can say that being is for Kant the possibility of being an object; but in another, we would have to add that the object itself is not possible but actual, since otherwise it would not exist, i.e., not be contained within the structure of experience as a possible object of science.

In other words, the total structure of phenomenal experience makes *possible* the *actual* being of this, that, or the other object. Being as possibility is not at all empty but instead consists of the structure of experience. Strange as it may seem, however, the being of an actually existing object is empty in the sense that it is nothing other than the taking up or filling of a position. We could contest this by insisting that the being of any individual existing object is precisely the structure of intelligibility. Kant would reply that as such, the structure is the being of every object and hence determines none of them as the precise object it is. Otherwise stated, the being of the object is not at all the structure of intelligibility or of the totality of experience but the assuming of a position within that structure. So far as I am aware, Kant does not, nor could he, speak of the "being" of the structure of the totality of experience. For that structure, which we can abbreviate as the functioning or working of the transcendental ego, to "exist" or possess being, not merely would it have to exhibit the properties that define or constitute it, but it would in addition require to be added synthetically to our concept of that structure, as Kant says that the 100 existing thalers are added synthetically to my concept of them.[4]. But to speak of the synthetic addition of an object to our concept of it is just to speak of that object's indeed becoming an object for us, i.e., an object of experience. This is impossible for the working of the transcendental ego, which cannot be added synthetically to my concept of it, since it is precisely the ground of all syntheses. In more straightforward language, the transcendental ego cannot become an object within experience, because it is not empirical but the condition for the possibility of experience.

The upshot is that for Kant, the word "being" cannot refer to "the whole" either as a sum or totality of parts, or as a unity of the ground; to repeat, every unity is for Kant a synthesis. The transcendental ego is outside being, just as it is "outside" (if that is the right word) the world that its work actualizes. The situation in Hegel would seem at first glance to be quite different from this, inasmuch as for Hegel, the transcendental ego is replaced by absolute spirit or, to give it its colloquial name, God. Nevertheless, Hegel never speaks of God as "being" or even as the "source" or "cause" of being. Instead, he speaks of the concept as the pure thinking of God, and of being as the minimal manifestation of the concept. Being is for Hegel, just as for Kant, never a real predicate. It does not pick out or identify a constitutive property of anything whatsoever because it belongs to anything whatsoever.

In addition, as we have seen on more than one occasion, there is no separation between thinking and the concept. Let me make a distinction between two senses of the expression "pure thinking." In the first sense, pure thinking refers to the science of logic in its entirety. But in the second sense, pure thinking is the same as the pure concept; that is to say, it is just thinking in the sense of awareness or attentiveness—what Hegel will call empty *Anschauen*, i.e., an attending with nothing to which one attends (71). We arrive at pure thinking in this second or narrow sense by a process of abstraction, a process that Hegel summarizes metaphorically as an ascent to the absolute, whether through an arbitrary act of the will or by some other manner. In this sense, our thinking is pure when it is empty. Note that this does not nullify our thinking. Instead, we come here as close to the exemplification of the Aristotelian *noēsis tēs noēseōs* (thought thinking itself) as possible. This will be important at the conclusion of our studies when we see how the end is also the beginning.

I note further the fact that the arrival at pure thinking or *noēsis tēs noēseōs*, which is also the arrival at the thinking of pure, empty being, is accompanied by the process of abstractive activity through which we as students of logic arrive at pure being. That there are two processes here and not one is evident from the fact that if we merely arrived at pure being, we would come to a complete standstill. To be attentive to empty being (i.e., thinking) is not the same as to see that the thinking of being is the same as the thinking of nothing. What I will call the accompanying or pedagogical thinking is represented by Hegel's text, which describes how we arrive at the first, presuppositionless stage and how we proceed from one step to the next.

Let me underline this. It is Hegel who calls to our attention that the thinking of pure being is also the thinking of nothing. Without this signal, there would be no movement from the first to the second moment. After all, as Hegel himself insists, despite their sameness, nothing is a separate determination from being; as he says in subsection C, the truth about being and nothing "is not their indistinguishability [*Ununterschiedenheit*], but that they are *not the same*, that they are absolutely distinguished," and so on (72). In thinking pure being, I am thinking nothing; but this has to be brought to my attention by the act of attempting to understand *what is involved* in the task of thinking, and so understanding, pure being.

This helps us to resolve an apparent aporia. Taken as logical categories, being and nothing are the same; i.e., they do not "go over" into one another but each has *already* "gone over" into the other. In thinking or attending to one, I am attending to the other. But that is not the same as the "reflexive" act by which I know that I am attending to both through my attention to either one. This reflexive activity is supplied by Hegel, who as it were whispers into our ear: "notice that empty being is the same as nothing." And in so whispering, he distinguishes what is from the standpoint of pure thinking indistinguishable. The whisper is no longer pure thinking in the second or narrow sense; it is pure thinking in the first or broader sense.

It make no difference if we rephrase this distinction as transpiring within the thought processes of the logician rather than between Hegel and the student. The distinction is analogous to that between the "we" and the "I" in the *PS* and goes back to Fichte's distinction between the positing and the reflecting ego, the ego that activates the world of determinations and the ego that observes and describes this activity. There are differences among these several versions of the distinction, but each is the attempt to come to terms with absolute beginning and the process by which we apprehend the absolute beginning as well as its systematic consequences.

In the introductory paragraph just prior to chapter 1, Hegel says: "Being is the undetermined immediate" (71). Strictly speaking, this assertion is false. We arrive at being by a process of abstraction that, even though Hegel barely alludes to it, is not itself immediate. And this is in addition to the whole question of how we arrive at the absolute standpoint of pure thinking in the broader sense of the expression. Nevertheless, within the logic understood as system, the statement is true. Being is immediate because it does not arise from still simpler elements by a sublation or synthesis. It is mediated by its relation to nothing (which in itself is also immediate).

As immediate and hence lacking in determinations, being is without quality. But now Hegel makes his characteristic and highly controversial move: the character of indeterminateness pertains to being *an sich* (in itself) "only in opposition to the determinate or qualitative" (71). Just as the immediate is conceived by opposition to mediation and is thereby mediated by it, so the indeterminate is conceived by opposition to the determinate and is thus determined by it. This is the necessary consequence of the unified process of actuality. We can attend to some moment of totality in itself, as for example the category of "something." But we cannot think in the sense of explain any such moment without delimiting it from its opposite. The two opposing moments can once again be regarded at the level of analytical thinking or reflection as conceptually juxtaposed and static, just as we write down "*A*" and "not-*A*" on the blackboard. The symbol "*A*" does not turn into the symbol "not-*A*," but the conceptual significance of "*A*" is dependent upon that of "not-*A*" and vice versa.

In this preliminary paragraph, Hegel is describing the overall movement of the first section of book 1 from being through existence (*Dasein*) to being for itself. The reciprocal implication of immediate and mediated or determined being leads to the shift from being as mere positionality (to use the Kantian expression) to being as a positioned entity. We are not ready to study this shift (or its sequel) into being for itself. I pass directly to subsection A.

Book 1, Section 1, Chapter 1, Subsection A: Being

Pure being in its undetermined immediateness is the same as itself and "not unlike in opposition to another" (71). In other words, taken as the presuppositionless because altogether simple beginning, being is not defined by limitation through another, complementary determination, as we shall see to be the case, for example, with "something" and "another." In particular, it is not the case that being is defined in opposition to nothing; there is no dialectical movement from one to the other because, to anticipate, the two are the same. Each is already, as itself, the other; whichever we examine, it has already "gone over" into the other. To look ahead to subsection C on becoming: *Pure being and pure nothing are therefore the same. The truth is neither being nor nothing but that neither does being go over into nothing nor nothing into being; each has rather gone over* [already] *into the other*" (72).

Hegel is thus confirming, in his own cryptic way, my previous observation that it makes no difference whether we begin with being or nothing, because nothing is the same as being, namely, the sheer givenness of the concept, and not the Parmenidean "altogether not." More precisely, it is a mere illusion to suppose that we can begin with nothing whatsoever. Such a start would be self-canceling; it would not be a start at all. To start is always to start with something, in the hypothetical case with the "something" that is nothing in the sense of an empty thought or concept, hence nothing in particular but still the being of the thought of nothing. This is undoubtedly very awkward, but that should not surprise us, since we are attempting to understand what is involved in the attempt to conceive nothing. Hegel claims in effect that we can do this only in the sense that our conceptual activity is functioning as openness or receptivity, and so as the same as sheer positionality. Nothing and being are the same empty continuum. It is like a radio that is turned on but not yet tuned to any station.

It should by now be obvious that being is the beginning of the science of logic only with respect to the expository goal of classifying the categories or logical determinations in the order of ascending complexity. For exactly the same reason, nothing is not a genuine beginning of scientific analysis in the usual sense of studying formal structure, because it has no structure to study. Otherwise put, there is no genuine dialectical movement between being and nothing; they are not logical complements that define each other reciprocally by limitation. For this reason, it cannot be the case that the shift from being-nothing to becoming is an instance of *Aufhebung* or dialectical sublation. What happens instead is that to think being and nothing as independent formal elements is virtually impossible; that is, it is unstable and turns directly into the thinking of becoming, which Hegel defines as the immediate disappearance of the one into the other (i.e., being into nothing or vice versa).

In my opinion, the upshot of this odd initial situation is that we try to begin with being and/or nothing but find that we are instead beginning with becoming. Becoming just is the identity within difference of being and nothing; it is not the dialectical resolution of their complementarity. This is a crucial result because it exhibits one of Hegel's fundamental doctrines. It is impossible to conceive of a nullity or altogether not "outside" being, because being is the minimal qualitative determination of conceiving. Furthermore, becoming is the first independent structure or prototype of the whole; structure is in other words from the outset "excited" (*bewegt*) rather than static. Being and nothing are thus abstractions from becoming, and abstractions that collapse into each other; each is, as itself, that which has already gone over into the other.

One last point in this connection: dialectic in the proper sense of the term is the development of becoming into the structure of intelligibility. Dialectic proper thus begins with an excitation that is intrinsic to the attempt to begin with the predialectical stability of a completely simple determination. The same point could be made by mounting a Hegelian criticism of the effort by Plato's Eleatic Stranger to begin with static formal atoms such as being. No such beginning is possible because the ostensible atoms are themselves internally excited. The inner motion of being and nothing is the basis of dialectic (but not dialectic itself) as exhibited within apparently complete simplicity.

I have moved to subsections B and C in the attempt to explicate subsection A because being is not thinkable in isolation; in a limited sense, Hegel thus echoes the Platonist criticism of Parmenides. In addition, Hegel is a Platonist in the sense that he obeys the Stranger's admonition to avoid entirely the altogether not. But Hegel is a Heraclitean in the sense that for him the truth of being and nothing is becoming. What the Eleatic Stranger calls "otherness" (the formal element corresponding to negation) has two different forms in Hegel's logic. Otherness is in Plato a static and independent formal property that does its work by "communion" with the other formal elements. In Hegel, otherness appears as the dialectical counterpart to somethingness in the pair of determinations called "something" and "another." But this refers to the dialectical opposition of two positive elements or moments in a manifold. The inner excitation by which one logical determination is transformed into another is "negative activity" or "negative work." In other words, the first type of otherness is ontic whereas the second type refers to the absolute activity of the formation of the concept.

Now we must look at some of the details within this general picture. In subsection A, Hegel says that if it is permissible to speak of apprehension (*Anschauen*) with respect to immediate being, "there is nothing in it to apprehend . . . or it is only this pure, empty apprehension itself" (71–72). Why is there a question about the permissibility of speaking of *Anschauen* here? In its usual sense, the word refers to the apprehending or viewing of some determinate content. In the present case, however, there is no content. But we must not forget that the absence of content is not the same as a total void. Thinking is present; the emptiness or absence of determinations is that of the concept. And by "concept," Hegel is referring not to a finite and separate artifact of thinking but rather to the living activity of the thinking of spirit. The pure *Anschauen* of being is attentiveness to attentiveness, or the initial manifestation of *noēsis tēs noēseōs*. Being is the being of the concept.

That is to say, it is not the thinking of anything, but "empty thinking" (72). Empty thinking, however, is still thinking. Since there is nothing else available, it must be the thinking of thinking, not in the sense of grasping its own nature or structure but in the sense of being "at the ready" or attentive. One might object to this that I have built self-consciousness or complexity into Hegel's formulation, but that is not what I have in mind. Pure being is pure thinking; if there were no attentiveness, there would be no thinking. "Thinking of thinking" has nothing as such to do with self-consciousness; this is a later stage of development.

Nevertheless, there remains a difficulty for my analysis in the shift from being to nothing. Immediately after identifying empty being as empty thinking, Hegel says: "Being, the indeterminate immediate, is in fact *nothing* and nothing more nor less than nothing" (72). It is one thing to say that empty thinking is not the thinking of anything definite. But it is something else to say that empty thinking *is* nothing. Hegel has just identified empty thinking as being, and being is surely the being of the concept in its initial conceptual status as lacking all subsequent determinations. "Nothing" must therefore refer to the absence of all subsequent determinations. But being, more precisely the being of the concept, is not nothing. Let's take this up by turning to subsection B.

Book 1, Section 1, Chapter 1, Subsection B: Nothing

"Nothing, pure nothing; it is simple sameness [*Gleichheit*] with itself, complete emptiness, lack of determination and content, undifferentiatedness in itself" (72). This seems to be very close to the opening account of pure being, but the resemblance conceals an important difference. The emptiness of pure being is not the same as the emptiness of pure nothing. Pure nothing would also be the absence of being. In other words, pure nothing is the "altogether not" against which Parmenides warns us, whereas the Hegelian nothing is the absence of determinations *within* pure being. Hegel's "pure" nothing is not pure, despite his assertion that it is so. As Hegel himself makes explicit, the concept, or thinking, and so pure being, has not disappeared in the transition from subsection A to subsection B. Hegel proceeds to develop the same point about *Anschauen* with respect to nothing that he developed with respect to being. "Insofar as *Anschauen* or thinking can be mentioned here, so it counts as a difference if something or nothing is apprehended or thought. The attending to or thinking nothing has therefore a meaning [*Bedeutung*] . . ."

I break off the quotation to comment. It is as meaningful to speak of apprehending nothing as it is to speak of apprehending something, but the meaning is different. There is a difference between saying "I see the table" and "I see nothing." But there is also a difference between saying "I see nothing" as a result of attempting to see something in particular, and saying "I see nothing" when one is referring to the absence of any particular visual object or to one's blindness. To continue with the quotation: "The attending to or thinking nothing has therefore a meaning; the two are distinguished; thus nothing is (exists) in our attentiveness or thinking; or rather it is empty attentiveness or thinking itself, and the same empty attentiveness or thinking is pure being." Hegel distinguishes between thinking something and thinking nothing. There is a meaning associated with thinking nothing. But note carefully: Hegel does not say that the meaning (*Bedeutung*) is the same in both cases. On the contrary, the flow of the clauses of his statement entails that the meanings are *distinguished* (*unterschieden*). What is the same in both cases is attentiveness or thinking.

The thinking of being is the same as the thinking of nothing. In both cases, we have mere attentiveness. The nothing in question is the absence of any determinations other than being, and being is the same as the thinking concept. In thinking being, we do not think any determinations. In thinking nothing, we do not think any determinations. The thinking that is the same in both cases is not the void or altogether not but the emptiness of being. It follows that in thinking nothing, we are also thinking being. Or so Hegel contends. I would say instead that we are thinking thinking (or the concept) as both being and nothing. But furthermore, we are thinking thinking as being in general, whereas we are not thinking nothing as nothing in general. Instead, we are thinking nothing as neither this nor that determination of thinking or being.

In short, Hegel has silently, perhaps even inadvertently, followed the injunction of father Parmenides not to mention or think the altogether not. He assimilates nothing into being by defining it as the absence of any determinations. But he never suggests that it is the absence of being. Instead, he asserts very cryptically that it is the same as being. Being and nothing are the same in that neither is anything in particular. *But both "are."* "Nothing is thereby the same determination or rather lack of determination and so in general is the same as *pure being*" (72).

Book 1, Section 1, Chapter 1, Subsection C: Becoming

Hegel infers from the previous conclusion, as we saw above, that "the truth is neither being nor nothing but that neither does being go over into nothing nor nothing into being; each has rather gone over [already] into the other" (72). In other words, the truth is that neither subsists without the other. We have distinguished them analytically and therefore in a fundamental sense we have falsified actuality. This was necessary in order to take the first step of a presuppositionless science. But we can see that this science is itself very much like a second ladder to yet a higher level of the absolute. Once we have completed this science, or arrived at a systematic exposition of the structure of the absolute, we can become divine only by contemplating the absolute absolutely, that is, as actuality, not as a sequence of dialectical steps that culminates in the absolute. Presumably this is possible if and only if intellectual intuition or simultaneous apprehension of the whole is possible.

Hegel now seems to contradict flatly his previous conclusion that pure being and pure nothing are the same. "But neither is the truth their indistinguishability but that they are not the same, that they are absolutely distinct, but also unseparated and inseparable, and each immediately disappears in its opposite." Hegel means that the sameness of being and nothing arises from their each already having gone over into the other. They are distinguishable as having done so, but as having done so, they are inseparable. We can think, in the sense of attending to, each apart from the other, but as soon as we think each in the sense of understanding its nature, or better, its activity, we necessarily think the other.

"Their truth is thus this excitation of immediate disappearance of one into the other: becoming, an excitation in which both are distinguished, but through a difference that has even as such dissolved." The excitation in question comes from our attempt to think each in isolation. It is present within the logical moments themselves, but not directly or with respect to their role as the intention of a concept, i.e., what we think about. This presence rather derives from the fact that the logical moments are moments of thinking, i.e., of the concept.

At this point, a general remark is in order. I noted a while ago the difference between the Heideggerian "Being" and the Hegelian "being." It is nevertheless interesting that Hegel conceives of being as both present and absent, as is made evident by the sameness of being and nothing. This sameness recurs at every level of the development from our beginning. Heidegger is undoubtedly correct from a Hegelian (and not just from a Hegelian) standpoint to insist upon concealment or absence as a component of the meaning of Being; he is wrong to assert that he is the first to have understood this. For Hegel, in any event, thinking is the presence and absence of being; that is to say, it is speculative contemplation of the process of position and negation of elements as well as of their opposition and their preservation within that opposition at a higher level. What Hegel calls "self-consciousness" is the presence and absence of thinking to itself.

SUBSECTION C, PARAGRAPH 1: UNITY OF BEING AND NOTHING. In what sense are pure being and pure nothing the same? Consider the following objection to Hegel. Pure being and pure nothing cannot be the same insofar as pure being is pure position whereas pure nothing is pure negation, because position and negation are conceptually distinguishable. It is all very well to say that the boundary of position is defined in opposition to, and so via, the boundary of negation. But to be defined with respect to something else is not to be that something else. The sublation of position and negation is an internally articulated structure, not an erasure of the distinctness of its elements, an erasure that would also cancel the structure. Suppose we were to start with negation or pure nothing. We can define it by opposition to pure being if and only if we already perceive or cognize pure being. And if we already grasp it, then we are not starting with pure nothing. This shows that it is impossible to start with pure nothing, and therefore pure nothing cannot be literally or entirely the same as pure being. The pure nothing that Hegel starts with is determinate negation, namely, the negation of a definite quality, in this case, being. Hegel's nothing, namely, determinate negation, always assumes an antecedent, namely, the determination or property of which it is the negation.

Hegel would reply that pure being and nothing are the same in the sense that neither has an inner determination. There is no inner structure, antecedently available, out of which pure being and pure nothing are constituted. But this does not make them the same. Hegel is entitled to say only that they *have become* the same by the attempt to conceive them in their separateness. And what "has become" the same was initially distinct. In other words, the force of Hegel's unification of being and nothing rests in our ability to distinguish them as discursively indistinguishable. Similarly, being is position, and this is not the same as negation. It is not even true that in order to conceive of position, one must conceive of negation. If I teach you how to walk by saying, "Move your left foot forward one step and then swing the right foot ahead of and parallel to it," I have not said anything about negating the previous position of the feet.

This does not settle the matter in Hegel's favor, because he claims that everything contains both immediacy and mediation. What he has to say is that the mediation of being and nothing has already occurred in thinking either as the same as the other. He must therefore both assert and deny that being and nothing determine each other. They do not determine each other in the sense that no determining predicate exists with which to state the determination: both are immediate. But they do determine each other in the sense that we cannot think one without seeing that it has already gone over into the other. I find this rather forced, but that is the nature of dialectical logic.

To continue, being is a quality, and precisely the quality that it is. When it is taken purely or abstractly as itself, namely, as pure being, there is no reason to expect it to possess any other, additional property. But that does not alter its own simple identity of being, which is not nothing. The sameness of being and nothing arises when we take two different conceptual determinations and attempt to analyze them. Neither can be analyzed because both are entirely simple. In that sense they are the same. But they are the same in the sense that two distinct simples are the same—namely, as simple. If they were the same in a stronger sense, i.e., as *the* same simple, then being would really be nothing, and there would be no becoming.

And this brings us again to Hegel's statement that the truth is neither being nor nothing, but that each has gone over into the other. Once again, this does not assert that they are literally or ontologically or even conceptually the same. If A has already gone over into B and B into A, it does not follow from this that A is B and vice versa. What follows is that every attempt to distinguish the two conceptually must fail. I can say "being is position" and "nothing is negation," and this is a perfectly intelligible distinction of the two logical determinations. But the point is that within the totality of the concept, and disregarding all subsequent determinations of that concept, being and nothing can be distinguished only as inseparable, because nothing whatsoever can be said of either, other than to give the name: position, negation. In failing to say anything more about being, I am succeeding in indicating the further unspeakableness of nothing.

In sum: being has already gone over into nothing by virtue of the very effort to define it, and not because it has ceased to be itself. On the contrary, in order to observe the identification or sameness of the two terms, we must have both independently in mind. For this reason, it is impossible to begin with nothing; to begin is to think, and this immediately grants being to thought. By the same token, it is wrong to think of becoming as a construction from two independent elements, being and nothing. The inseparable distinguishability of being and nothing is precisely the primitive or founding structure of becoming that gives rise to dialectic. Our attempt to think pure empty being is itself imbedded within our apprehension of sheer succession. By succession I refer to the continuity of the *reine, leere Anschauen selbst* (pure empty apprehension itself), which Hegel identifies with pure being and nothing. This continuity is as it were the substratum of the concept, a substratum that is nothing but openness or receptivity. We have to remember that Hegel is not talking about the physical universe here; "becoming" is a logical category, not spatiotemporal genesis. The inner excitation of the logical category of becoming is that of pure thinking, i.e., the pure thinking of genesis, the apprehension in pure thought of the conceptual structure of genesis.

It is therefore not possible for Hegel to explicate becoming in terms of space and time; on the contrary, space and time are the external manifestation of becoming. The being of continuity is openness to positionality; the nothing of continuity is the emptiness of sheer openness. Each has "already" gone into the other with respect to our attempt to think their relation. The inner excitation is not that of a spatiotemporal coming into being and passing away but rather that of the pure thinking of being and nothing as categorial determinations of pure thinking. The difference between being and nothing is the dimensionality of the continuum; the sameness of being and nothing is its seamlessness.

Subsection C, paragraph 1, note 1. In the first of four notes appended to the paragraph on the sameness of being and nothing, Hegel is obviously keenly aware of the obscurity of this crucial initial stage of the logic. He begins the first note by distinguishing between determinate and pure nothing. The first is the nothing that is opposed to something (*Etwas*). The second, with which we are now concerned, is the pure nothing of indeterminate simplicity. This nothing can be expressed equally in German as *Nichts, Nicht-Sein,* or *Nicht* (73). In all cases, we designate abstract, immediate negation. It is therefore not conceived as determinate, that is to say, as the negation of a term or property that is distinguished in contrast to the affirmation of that same term or property. I remind the reader that although pure nothing lacks an opposing term of which it is the negation, it is nevertheless mediated as well as immediate. The mediation is precisely the aforementioned difference between, on the one hand, being, or more precisely in this case, the absence of being, i.e., the absence of anything about which to think, and, on the other, sheer empty viewing and thinking.

Pure nothing is thus, as empty thinking, the same as pure or empty being, more precisely, as the pure being of thinking, which latter is itself the presence of being to conscious cognitive activity. Despite its purity or lack of a reference to an external determination that is reflected within its own interiority, pure nothing is not "the altogether not" (which is by definition not the same as thinking in any sense whatsoever).

After reviewing the ancient references, both positive and negative, to nothing, Hegel states the following conclusion: "the philosophical insight that holds as a principle 'being is only being, nothing is only nothing,' deserves the name 'Identity system'; this abstract identity is the essence of pantheism" (74). He means by this that in pantheism being is separated from nothing, which is rejected and so plays no role in the interior of being, which is accordingly static, as in Eleaticism (under which rubric Hegel includes Spinoza). As one, it encompasses everything, including God; as static, God and the world cannot be differentiated from one another in an identity within difference. There is no difference but only identity. This criticism is meant to apply to Schelling as well.

After criticizing the tendency to wonder at the introduction of expressions into philosophy that deviate from the ordinary understanding, Hegel goes on to emphasize the fundamental nature of the unity of being and nothing (74–75). He adapts a previous remark about immediacy and mediation to this unity: "*There is nothing in heaven and on earth that does not contain within itself both being and nothing*" (75). This unity is the first truth of logic and the ground for every subsequent logical determination. We should note that all subsequent determinations of the initial unity are "reflected" being and nothing that contain the pure versions as their abstract foundation. The sameness of being and nothing as abstract ground is thus independent of whether any particular thing exists or not. A particular is an instance of determinate being that defines itself by reference to another particular thing; "one thing leads to another," as we might paraphrase Hegel's point. The totality of necessary interconnections of content arises from the reciprocal relations of the underlying logical determinations that define the structure of the whole, and these in turn are grounded in the unity of abstract being and nothing (76).

Hegel proceeds to illustrate his point with a brief inspection of the Kantian example of 100 thalers. The main point is that Kant does not distinguish between being (*Sein*) and existence (*Dasein*). He therefore does not see the Hegelian distinction between being as an abstract ground of logical determinations and *Dasein* as the determinate particular: "It is *Dasein* that first contains the real distinction between being and nothing, namely, a something [*Etwas*] and another [*Anderes*]" (78). For Kant, "to be" is to be posited by a subject as a *res* (real thing) within the structure of rules that constitute phenomenal experience.[5] Being is thus the possibility to receive real predicates. Hegel shifts this possibility to the next level of logical determination. The primitive or grounding level of being-nothing-becoming is not present in Kant. By collapsing the two levels, Kant covers over the unity of being and nothing, or as one can also put this, he does not see that nothing is a primitive ontological dimension. For Kant, "nothing" is the same as "not" or determinate, i.e., reflected negation, hence, not a *res*. In addition, Kant confuses contingent properties (designated by real predicates) with genuine being, or as Hegel puts it, he confuses an alterable and transient subjective content with a genuine or logical *sich auf sich Beziehendes*, i.e., with the logical structure of self-referentiality that underlies the reflected determinations of this or that content (79).

Hegel turns next to a contrast between doctrines of a Kantian sort and his own. He then makes the following extremely important assertion: "What is first in science had necessarily to show itself historically as the first. And we must regard the Eleatic one or being as the first [result] of knowing by [philosophical] thinking" (79). I note in passing that Hegel again emphasizes the inseparability of thinking and being. But the new and crucial point here is the assertion of a connection between logical and historical priority. We recall that logical priority refers not to the chronological constitution of the universe but to the order in which we must think logical development so as to exhibit the necessity and systematicity of totality. The present assertion implies that this logical order is reflected in the chronological order of the history of philosophy. If this is the correct reading, then Hegel is committed to an isomorphism between the thinking of eternity and history that entails the *scientific* but not of course the empirical or temporal end of history. For otherwise it could not be the case that the circle of logical science had completed itself; future essential determinations of the concept would be possible.

At a deeper level, it is not simply the human temporal thinking of eternity that is isomorphic to the history of philosophy but also the very structure of eternity itself, which is not detached or concealed, whether altogether or partially, from conceptual thought. And this is indeed the assumption that underlies Hegel's various writings, published or unpublished by him personally, on the conceptual mastery of the main spheres of human experience. It is of course extremely difficult, and in my view impossible, for Hegel to carry through this isomorphism of all spheres of experience with the inner excitation of absolute spirit. But it seems to be necessary that he do so, inasmuch as the identity of identity and difference is the life-pulse of the whole as well as of whatever determinations exhibit themselves within it.

Subsection C, paragraph 1, note 2. Hegel calls our attention to the fact that the assertion "Being and nothing are one and the same" is an incomplete rendition of the results of our contemplation of the two abstractions. The assertion or sentence (*Satz*) seems to exclude the distinction between the two terms of the judgment (*Urteil*), in which the predicate *P* expresses a property of the subject *S* (81). Note that *Satz* is not here "proposition" or sense independent of the thought of the logician, but rather, exactly as in Kant, a cognitive act by which one "judges" *S* to be *P*. The main point here is that *S* and *P* are indeed different, even though the judgment seems to unite them. Hegel has in mind here a judgment of identity; he is ignoring predicative judgments in which *P* is said to be a property of *S* but not to be identical with it. In fact, predicative judgments are irrelevant to the point under discussion, which is that the unity of being and nothing is an identity of identity and difference. As such a unity, the judgment is marked by an internal contradiction, which Hegel calls a *Bewegung* or excitation through which the initial judgment vanishes. Hegel's exposition is here faulty, since, as is immediately made explicit, he means not that judgment vanishes but that it sets into motion its own deeper content, namely, becoming. In other words, the two terms, being and nothing, are simultaneously being identified and sundered. Hence the unity is continuously coming into being and passing away; and this is exactly what we mean by becoming, considered as the continuum within which this or that existing entity appears and disappears.

We should also notice that the result or content of the judgment is not expressed by the literal wording of the judgment; "it is an external reflection that discerns the result in the judgment" (82). And this shows us that the form of the judgment is not suitable for the expression of speculative truth, namely, the fuller exposition of the sense of the unity of logical determinations that we have just illustrated in the fundamental case of being and nothing. In passing, Hegel licenses us to disregard what is in effect the difference between identity and predication, i.e., the fact that subjects possess more than one predicate and that predicates are broader than their subjects. The main point, that in speculative content the two terms are both identical and not identical, holds in the case of logical opposites, which would normally be expressed by two mutually contradictory judgments. For example, we would say both that "the positive is the negative," which is a dialectical truth, and also that "the positive is not the negative," which is a logical or ontological truth in the traditional sense. What Hegel refers to as "speculative content" thus requires two judgments for its complete expression, judgments that are mutually contradictory. A speculative judgment would be one that expresses the full content in one assertion that exhibits the inner contradiction as well as its *Aufhebung* or preservation of both terms at a higher, more inclusive level of structure. Judgments of the normal predicative sort, e.g., "Socrates is mortal" or "the rose is red," are not dialectical in their normal usage; they express empirical facts, not the internally excited structures of logical relations.

Hegel next warns us about a deficiency in the sense of "unity," which normally refers to a bringing together of two separate items and is thus an external or subjective reflection, whereas what we want to express is that the unity is ingredient to the two terms of the judgment (83). We could call the unity "unseparatedness" or "inseparability," but this fails to capture fully the affirmative content of the relation.

In the balance of the note, Hegel repeats various points, of which I emphasize the distinction between being and existence. "We shall preserve the expression *Existenz* for being that is mediated" (84). Later Hegel will say that *Dasein* is determinate being. But there is no conflict here, since to be mediated is precisely to possess a determination. This seems to confirm that for Hegel, *Dasein* and *Existenz* can be used interchangeably. We should also note Hegel's observation that one sees as little in the absolute clearness of pure light as in the absolute darkness (85); in other words, Hegel defines being not as *parousia* or *Anwesenheit* but rather as both presence and absence, and in that sense as indistinguishable from nothing; this indistinguishability establishes the priority of becoming over either of the two previous terms taken separately. Each is determined through the other; this is the mediated nature of pure being and nothing. Nevertheless, pure being is immediate because it is mediated (literally) by nothing, and vice versa.

Subsection C, paragraph 1, note 3. Hegel begins note 3 with an obscure statement that is typical of his logical reasoning. "The unity whose moments, being and nothing, are as inseparable, is itself at once distinct from them, and so is a third in opposition to them, [a third] that in its most personal form is becoming" (85). As we recall, being and nothing are each pure, immediate, lacking in inner determinations; this allows them to serve as the presuppositionless beginning, which would be impossible if they possessed a content that is itself the result of an antecedent logical beginning. At the same time, everything whatsoever contains both mediation and immediacy, including being and nothing. The immediacy of each is its pure abstractness. But what is mediation in each case? Hegel's reply is that the very indeterminate immediacy of each is a quality that stands in opposition to, and so is mediated by, mediation (71–72).

Hegel's view is thus more radical than the assertion that everything contains both immediacy and mediation. He holds that immediacy is *itself* a determination (*Bestimmung*), and is therefore mediated. So the immediacy of pure being is as such the mediation of indeterminateness in opposition or with respect to determination. The absence of a determination in some "determinate" sense, as a distinct formal property, does not affect the issue, because we cannot conceive of immediacy or indeterminateness except in opposition to, and so as in conjunction with, determinateness or mediation. I repeat: it is not simply that pure being *contains* immediacy and mediation; on the contrary, immediacy is inseparable from mediation. Conversely, mediation is inconceivable except as opposed to, and so via, immediacy.

A very similar kind of reasoning obtains in the derivation of becoming from the unity of being and nothing. As lacking in determinations *other than themselves*, being and nothing are each immediate and so indistinguishable from one another. But since both are determinations (being is quality, and nothing is the same as being), the two terms mediate one another. Strictly speaking, the unity of immediacy is different from the unity of mediation. Although both are the same, they are nevertheless distinguishable. There is a "difference" or determination within unity here, which enables us to distinguish it from the two terms that constitute it *as* a unity. Unity is here also multiplicity. But conversely, multiplicity is also unity (namely, the immediate inseparability of being and nothing). So unity falls apart into multiplicity, which reconstitutes itself as unity. More concretely, by continuously collapsing into and separating from one another, being and nothing generate becoming.

The upshot of all this is that for Hegel no single logical property, including the most primitive, pure, or abstract properties of being and nothing, is stable, independent, of a single enduring nature that excludes all others, and in particular its own opposites. None can be thought in pure isolation from all others; consequently, no logical term is univocal. This is why Hegel regularly seems to contradict himself in what looks like a nondialectical way. We soon become familiar with the standard form of the dialectical contradiction, according to which A and non-A are united by their opposition in the more comprehensive B. But we find it harder to grasp that A and non-A do not represent two distinct and independent properties. *They are the same property, looked at from two different sides.* In popular language, not merely does every thesis have an antithesis; every thesis *is* its own antithesis.

In the balance of this note, Hegel discusses some of the errors that arise in the history of philosophy from *Räsonnement*, i.e., false, finite, nondialectical reasoning about the transition between being and nothing that constitutes becoming. The source of the errors lies in the positing of what Hegel calls *Reflexionsformen* or *Reflexionsbestimmungen*. These amount to the assertion of individual logical forms as immediate, separate, self-identical, stable, and independent. There is a consequent failure to observe the transition (*Übergehen*) of one form into its ostensibly independent opposite; forms are taken as static rather than as marked by excitation (*Bewegtheit*). The thinking intellect is thus external to the inner development of the observed structure and "reflects" upon that structure as opposed to it, i.e., as not sharing in the inner movement of thinking itself. *Räsonnement* does not grasp the identity within difference of the elements to one another, or of the structure being studied to the thought of the student. I have already discussed the essential point of these examples (Parmenides, Fichte, Kant, and Jacobi); we can therefore pass over the balance of the note, as well as note 4, in which Hegel says that Kant makes becoming unintelligible by the conceptual separation of being and nothing (97–99).

SIX

Transitional Remarks

Transitional Remarks

We have now completed our examination of the identity within difference of being and nothing. Hegel's argument on this fundamental point can be summarized as follows. Being is the presence of the concept as mere presence. Since mere presence is nothing in particular, being is also nothing in particular. But "nothing in particular" names a determination. Taking these two results together, being is also nothing and nothing is also being. This is an odd claim, but it is, I think, possible to see what Hegel is getting at. Let us restate the point in simpler language. Whatever exists has a certain nature. This nature can be divided into two sets of properties. One set gives the properties that are intrinsic to the identity of the existing thing itself. For example, a cow is brown, has four legs, chews the cud, yields milk, and so on. "Brown, four-legged," and so on make up the set of properties intrinsic to some particular cow. It is not necessary for my present purposes to distinguish between essential and accidental properties, and to do so would only complicate the exposition.

There is, however, another set of properties that define the conditions for the existence of the cow. These include being made of matter (however this term is subsequently interpreted), possessing a certain perceptual shape, occupying space, persisting through time, and so on. We normally do not include "being" as a separate property in either of these two sets. In everyday language, we would say instead that "cows exist" means that there are things having the aforementioned properties. If asked "What does 'are' mean in the expression 'There are things'?," we would probably reply that it means "Things of that sort exist," and so on. In short, we would rotate in a circle, not because we have no understanding of words like *is* or *exists*, but because their sense is so fundamental that it cannot be expressed in simpler terms.

In so-called mathematical logic, that is, the logic of Frege and Russell, no distinction is (normally) drawn between "being" and "existence." In accord with the analysis of this kind of logic, to say that something exists is to say that it is the instance of a concept. For a Hegelian, and not only for a Hegelian, this simply bypasses the question of the being of the instance as well as of the concept. The question "What does it mean to be an instance?" is not answered by giving a list of the concepts in which the instance participates. The list in question presupposes the existence of the instance to which it is said to belong, or which is said to exemplify it. And the general reply, "An instance is a structure of concepts," is hard if not impossible to distinguish from the traditional Platonist assertion that a spatiotemporal particular is an instance of a community of pure forms or ideas. In other words, an instance *qua* instance is not the same as a structure of concepts. Nor do instances spring into existence simply by the conjunction of a set of predicates or concepts. Furthermore, the question of the being or existence of the concepts or predicate terms has yet to be answered. If we quantify over predicates, as logicians put it, do we not then reduce these predicates to the status of second-order instances, and thereby point to a second-level domain of concepts of which the first-level concepts are instances?

Without in any way questioning the depth, power, or utility of modern "mathematical" logic, I conclude that it casts no light on our problem. It is designed not to answer the question "What is being?" but, if anything, to render that question superfluous. And no doubt it is superfluous for many purposes. But philosophy is not one of the cases in which we can dispense with being. This becomes evident as soon as we begin to think philosophically about logic; or at least it should become evident. To come back to the individual cow, whom we shall baptize "Elsie," we can certainly analyze her concept (but not Elsie herself) into a set of conceptual determinations, or into a plurality of such sets, of which we can select two that were noticed previously. In so doing, however, we are in all cases talking about properties or determinations, each of which may in turn be analyzed into subproperties, and perhaps these again into subsubproperties. But eventually we come to the end of the line, and this end is "being." The being of the various properties is just what allows us to grasp them conceptually. If they had no being, we could not isolate or discuss them, or even try to discuss them. Note also that whereas the existence of Elsie the cow, or some other perceptual entity, may be an illusion, or imaginary, the same cannot be said of the properties that constitute the illusion. The brownness of an imaginary cow is just as real as the brownness of a perceived cow, although it may not be as vivid in its manifestation.

Hegel's implicit contention, then, is that whereas being, precisely because it is the simplest, emptiest, or most universal property, cannot be paraphrased or expressed in still simpler terms, it is nevertheless intelligible. Being is what is left when one disregards every other determination. If, in discarding all the other determinations, we also discarded being, then we would be left with the altogether not. We would literally disappear, along with everything else.

On the other hand, there is in Hegel no "ontology" or conceptual doctrine of being. How could there be, if being is itself empty of content? But if it is empty of content, we are tempted to respond, is it not nothing at all? Hegel's reply is surprising. He agrees that being is nothing, but he means by this that it is nothing other than itself, namely, sheer openness to further determination. At this point, Hegel is very close to the Kantian doctrine of being as positionality. For Kant, to be is to be a possible item within the spatiotemporal world of entities that are subject to investigation by science. Hegel generalizes upon the possibility. That is, being, taken by itself, is not for Hegel "presence" but rather the possibility of presence. Being is the field or horizon within which everything presents itself. But by the same token, it is also the field or horizon within which everything absents or conceals itself.

I remind the reader that for Hegel, being is the most universal determination of thinking, or what he calls the concept. In the opening moment of the logic, we disregard, or attempt to disregard, the concept, and to think pure being in isolation. But our effort to think this determination cannot be disregarded; it is precisely the effort of thinking that renders anything accessible. The effort to think pure being leads us to identify its content as nothing. But this amounts to the replacement of the determination "being" by the determination "nothing." It does not, as I noted above, result in our dissolution into nullity. Again, those who say that there is no such thing as being are correct, because being is not a thing. But neither is nothing, and yet we must understand what it means when we say "being is nothing," since otherwise the assertion could not be subjected to critical analysis. In other words, when someone says that being is not a thing and only things exist, this entails that there is nothing but things. The expressions "not a thing," "no thing," and so on, are themselves intelligible only if we understand "not," and this cannot be understood as "not a thing" or "no thing." To say that it can is to spin one's wheels. It is to claim that we do not in fact understand "nothing" and so that we do not understand the expression "not a thing," but that we understand only thing-expressions. In this case, negations are finally all affirmations.

Being and nothing cannot be thought in themselves without our seeing that in the effort to think one of the pair, we arrive immediately at the other. Being is indeed the emptiest determination, but it is so empty that it resists our capacity to describe it in ways that do not assume the accessibility of other determinations. This emptiness of being is what Hegel means by "nothing." And nothing can no more be described analytically than can being. In short, the two are inseparable. But they are just barely distinguishable. And they are distinguishable as two inseparable and fundamental constituents of everything whatsoever. As such, they are determinations of the concept, that is, the articulated formal structure of the continuum of the whole.

I underline the fact that the absence of all content of a concept is not the same as the absence of the concept itself. We would not therefore say that the Hegelian concept "is and is not" if we mean by this that it comes into and passes out of being. The concept "exists" always and everywhere. What changes is our attention, which is directed initially to being and then to nothing. In attending to each of these, we find that we cannot think it except as its having already gone over into, and thereby showing itself to be the same as, the other. The net result of this "already having gone over" is that the attempt to think pure being or pure nothing results directly in the thinking of becoming. I want to repeat that the concept is not becoming in the sense that it enters into and exits from being. Hegelian actuality is circular and continuous; it is not disjunctive at each moment like the continuous creation of Malebranche or the discontinuous temporal sequence of Sartre. Hegel means that the distinguishable yet same moments of being and nothing are the categorial and so conceptual foundation to the continuum of spatiotemporal genesis. It will be helpful if we reserve the term "becoming" (*Werden*) to refer to the logical category and employ "genesis" to name the production of the world.

We can now take together the very brief second and third parts of Hegel's tripartition of the analysis of becoming. Having already established the unity of being and nothing, Hegel next considers the two moments of becoming, emergence and departure, and the logical transition to the sublation of becoming in *Dasein* or determinate being. Becoming is everywhere the unity of emergence and departure (*Entstehen und Vergehen*, 99). This implies that being is presence and nothing is absence, but we cannot take either of these as stable and independent of the other. The movement of thinking back and forth from being to nothing is the process by which becoming evolves as emergence and departure. Note that these two are not the same as presence and absence. What is present has already emerged; if it were now emerging, it would be partially absent. Conversely, what is absent has already departed. If it were now departing, it would be partially present.

The reciprocal transformation of emergence and departure into each other is the process that preserves the continuum of becoming. Without that transformation, we would have only the nondialectical simultaneity of presence and absence. Becoming is not dissolution; it is the continuum within which dissolution and regeneration recur forever. "Becoming is an unceasing unrest that sinks down into a tranquil result" (100). This expression might be given a Christian interpretation as follows. The unceasing unrest is the categorial excitation of absolute spirit or God, whereas the tranquil rest is the eternal circle of genesis. But this leaves unanswered the question why unceasing unrest would produce only one universe; it leaves unanswered the question of the relation between eternity and temporality.

A much more likely interpretation of the sentence just quoted is that the process of becoming, precisely through its continuous preservation of the structure of genesis, allows for the tranquil existence of something or another, which retains its identity within the internal excitation of becoming. Becoming "vanishes" as a process without position by emerging as *Dasein* or determinate being, as "being there" and so as something that can be further identified and therefore assigned a position within the process of becoming. The distinguishable sameness of being and nothing gives definiteness to the anonymous moments in the perpetual flow of becoming. In this sense, being and nothing are the limits of becoming.

To summarize: let us reserve the expression "identity within difference" (identity of identity and nonidentity) for sublations of dialectically opposed determinations and refer to the primitive relation of being and nothing as distinguishability within sameness. This relation is the basis for the next conceptual step in the development of the structure of intelligibility, namely, the grasping of emergence and departure, which together constitute becoming, the logical or ontological foundation of genesis. Being and nothing are empty abstractions from becoming; Hegel's vision of totality is dynamic, not static. This is revealed at the outset in our attempt to grasp being independently, an attempt that sets into motion each of the succeeding stages studied thus far. As the conceptual version of genesis, becoming is a continuum of the emergence and departure of identifiable elements. Hegel's word for these elements is *Dasein*, "being there," i.e., having a location within the continuum.

Book 1, Section 1, Chapter 2: Dasein

"Dasein ist bestimmtes Sein," Hegel says on page 102. A *Bestimmung* is a determination or even a definition. We can call it a predicate in the sense of a name of a qualitative modification of the pure continuum of becoming, a modification by which the continuum is stamped with location by virtue of its occupant. Let us be as precise as possible here. *Dasein* does not refer to any existing *res* or object. It is a general category, the first determination of becoming. As such, it belongs to every subsequent specification of the conceptual structure of the absolute. Whatever emerges or departs does so by occupying and relinquishing position within the continuum of becoming that is itself seamlessly woven out of being and nothing. Position is occupied and relinquished by something that endures long enough to make available to thought its presence and absence. This endurance depends upon identifiability.

There are two moments to the identifiability of *Dasein*, one finite and the other infinite. The finite moment is quality; this predicate is invoked when we state that the *Dasein* is a such-and-such. To be, or to come into being, and so to be identified as having passed away, is to be a so-and-so of such and such a kind. This is an Aristotelian formula that holds good for Hegel as well. Note an important consequence. Hegel begins with quality, not quantity. According to the traditional view, quantity is the principle of individuation because it makes possible the instantiation of form. But the reverse is equally if not more pressingly true. Form is the paradigm that organizes anonymous or potential matter into individuals of identifiable kinds. The entire first section of book 1 of the *SL* is entitled "Quality." "Quantity" comes afterward. Suppose that being were quantity rather than quality. There would be no way in which to distinguish between the homogeneous moments of becoming and the distinct positions of identifiable and reidentifiable entities that emerge and disappear. Without quality, there would be continuous quantity. Disjunctions between one heap of quantity and another would lack qualitative significance; there would be chaos at the heart of being, as Nietzsche asserts on behalf of his own materialism.

The infinite moment in *Dasein* is the negation of its finite moment. The reason for this should now be familiar to us. *Dasein* is defined by a finite quality; an infinite quality would be useless in distinguishing this determinate existent from that one. In fact, anything possessing an infinite quality is by definition not determinate, not a this thing here of such and such a kind. But the very finitude of the defining quality is itself shaped through limitation from or opposition toward infinity, i.e., an infinitude of qualities or, what comes to the same thing, an infinite quality. Hegel says that *Dasein*, thanks to the negation of its finite by its infinite moment, shifts from the "abstract opposition" of its positive and negative sides and dissolves into "oppositionless infinity" or "being for itself" (103). This is too cryptic to interpret as it stands; Hegel is here preparing us for the more elaborate subsequent analysis. We can, however, guess at part of what he means. As this rather than that, *Dasein* is finite. But as opposed to every other finite identity, it is infinite (that is, its identity depends upon an infinite series of negations: not this, not that, and so on). The abstract opposition of the finite and the infinite sides of qualitative determination defines the *Dasein* as whatever it happens to be. *Dasein* draws sustenance from this abstract opposition. It endures, and in that sense, it is oppositionless. Nothing deprives it of its identity as long as its existence has positionality or location within becoming. As oppositionless, it is infinite in the sense that nothing annuls it. This is being for itself.

So much for our preliminary inspection of *Dasein*. The chapter consists of three subsections, (A) *Dasein* as such, (B) something and another, or finitude, and (C) qualitative infinity. These correspond to locatability, identifiability, and subsistence.

Book 1, Section 1, Chapter 2, Subsection A: *Dasein* as such

Subsection A again falls into three parts: *Dasein* generally, quality, and something existing (103). *Dasein* is locatable thanks to its qualitative determination; it is a *res* as so determined, but every determination is a negation. To be this locatable *Dasein* is not to be any other. As delimited from every other, it is "reflected" into itself and stands forth as an existing something. In other words, Hegel thinks of "nothing" as exerting a kind of substantive force upon the finite qualitative determination, thanks to which the latter is held together in its locus within the excitation of becoming. In this sense, nothing does not dissolve but rather preserves.

SUBSECTION A, PART A: *DASEIN* IN GENERAL. Note that "Quality" and "Something" are the titles for parts b and c of subsection A. "*Dasein* in general" is obviously synonymous with "*Dasein* as such." This is not the first time that Hegel uses a general title as the name of both a section and one of its subsections. The most obvious case is that of "being."

Subsection A begins as follows: "*Dasein* emerges from becoming. It is the simple *Einssein* of being and nothing" (103). *Einssein* or " being one" means something like "that which is one through the superordination of being over nothing." It would make no sense to say that *Dasein* is the simple "nothing-one" of being and nothing. And yet, strictly speaking, if being and nothing are the same, such a statement ought to be legitimate. But they are not the same here, as they are at the initial level of the logic. The negativity of nothing at the level of *Dasein* is that of determinate negation, that is, the negation of something in particular (a qualitative particular thing).

I interpolate an observation about Hegel's terminology. The logical determinations, and in particular the simplest ones that we have studied thus far, are not intelligible except through the use of terms like "identity," "difference," "one," "unity," "sameness," "generality," "immediate," "mediate," and so on. We might do worse than to refer to these as *syncategorematic* terms. That is, the categories depend upon other terms that are not themselves categories, and so are not derived dialectically within the science of logic proper. Hegel does not address the important question of the status of these terms. Are they given by the exoteric thinking of the logician? Similarly, Hegel will sometimes have to make use of later categories, whether implicitly or explicitly, in order to explain earlier ones; examples of this are multiplicity and infinitude. This last procedure is not a contradiction of the order of development; it is required by the discursive nature of human intelligence.

Hegel continues: *Dasein* as the unity of being and nothing "has, thanks to this simplicity, the form of an immediate. Its mediation, becoming, lies behind it. *Dasein* has sublated it and appears therefore as a first out of which there will be emergence" (103). Becoming is the mediation of being and nothing. *Dasein* has unified being and nothing in the superordination of being over nothing. Hence it stands in the initiating position that was previously occupied by being. *Dasein* is negatively enriched being, out of which more concrete determinations are about to emerge. To say this in a slightly different way, becoming is itself accessible only as the mutual positing and negating of existing things that represent for us the otherwise invisible becoming by way of their own sustenance and position, and as we are about to see, thanks to their relations with one another.

I have now explained most of page 103, but let us note the following assertion. *Dasein* is, with respect to its becoming, "überhaupt Sein mit einem Nichtsein," and so on. The *Nichtsein* is so contained or subordinated within the concrete totality that *Dasein* takes the form of being and immediacy. In other words, despite its shaping, differentiating, and supporting work, nothing cannot stand forth on its own but only as pertaining to being. Being predominates as that upon which the negative activity of nothing works. This point is also to be found in the commentary by Alexander of Aphrodisias on Aristotle's *Metaphysics*.

At the top of the next page (104), Hegel supplies one of his reminders that there is a difference between how the categories are posited within themselves (*an sich*) and how they appear in our reflection upon them (*für uns in unserer Reflexion*). For us, *Dasein* exhibits itself as a being that has only a moment to endure (before it is taken away by the flow of becoming, in other words); as such, it exists as already removed or sublated, as negatively defined (i.e., as transient). In itself, it is posited as part of the content of the concept we are thinking. Hegel then draws the following distinction: "That the totality, the unity of being and nothing, lies in the one-sided determination of being is an external reflection. In negation however, in something and another and so on, that unity [of being and nothing] will arrive at the being of positedness." He means that nothing can be conceptualized via being only (without recourse to negativity) so long as we engage in the nondialectical thinking of traditional rationalism. It is from this standpoint that we are first introduced to *Dasein*. Since each *Dasein* is at the level of logic structurally the same as every other, we see each as a being, i.e., a being *there*, but without seeing the negation implicit in the difference of one "there" from another. This difference emerges into view only when we further refine our analysis of *Dasein* into *Etwas und Anderes*, "something and another." Not only is there a multiplicity of locatable existents, but multiplicity itself consists of identifiably many elements. If we cannot distinguish between something and another, then the distinct locations will themselves collapse into a homogeneous continuum of indistinguishable possible positions. One location or possible position does not genuinely negate another; instead, each is, that is, continues to exist in an unbroken sequence. Identifiability requires that the sequence be articulated by difference, and it is nothing or negativity that differentiates. In other words, "location, location" is replaced by "something in this location, something other in the next location."

In the final paragraph on page 104, Hegel repeats that *Dasein* is in the place of *Sein*; it is determinate being, a concrete being, although we are hardly in a position to identify it or to distinguish one from another as yet.

SUBSECTION A, PART B: QUALITY. *Dasein* is determinate being. The determination is not particular (105); i.e., it is the general openness of being to take a particular determination that will identify it as something or another. "The determinateness, as isolated for itself, as existing determinateness, is quality, something altogether simple, immediate" (105). It is not yet specified as this or that quality. We may think of this whole section of the *SL* as the gradual assemblage of the structural shell of an existing object. The actuality of the shell increases at each step, but the object remains possible until such time as all of its determinations are added.

In the first part of (b), Hegel has considered the immediacy of *Dasein* as a being. In paragraph 3, he shifts his attention to its negative dimension. This negativity is the measure for the "one-sidedness" of the determination; that is to say, it fixes the identity of the determination by excluding all other identities. That identity is posited as "differentiated, reflected" (105). The qualitative determination is the "denial" of all other identities; hence it must be contrasted to them or grasped with respect to them; Hegel refers to this as "reflected," a term always associated by him with the thinking of a determination in contrast to or in conjunction with one that is external to it. "Reflection" is contrasted to "dialectic," by which we think one determination as growing out of another from the inner excitation of the former. When reflection takes place, we know that we have not yet moved from how things look to the student of logic to how they are to be grasped from within the concept. Thus Hegel says that the qualitatively determined *Dasein* is grasped negatively; its quality serves as a border or limit between it and all the other qualities that it lacks. In more straightforward language, the *Dasein* is grasped as a *Realität*, as a merely positive, nondialectical *res*.

One might object to Hegel's critique of reflection in the following terms. Since the human intellect is discursive and temporal, it must state separately the moments of whatever structure it wishes to grasp conceptually. One sees this in the science of logic itself, in which we always formulate logical determinations independently of their dialectical relations; in other words, one cannot state the dialectical relation obtaining between A and non-A except by stating the two as external to one another. Only then can we go on to state that the externality is dissolved by the inner dynamic of the relation of opposition, or in other words that a new, more inclusive concept emerges from the dynamic opposition between the two simpler terms. The assertion of the dialectical relation itself is carried out in the language of external reflection. We are incapable of speaking a truly dialectico-speculative language that exhibits accurately the dynamic transformations of the absolute concept. This objection is reinforced by my previous remark about (what I called) syncategorematic terms, namely, terms that are not categories emerging from being, nothing, and so forth, but upon which logic depends fundamentally.

Hegel's invention of logical terminology is very much in the spirit of the invention by the late Heidegger of an ostensibly new way of speaking about being, a way that avoids the discourse appropriate to beings or things. But the new way contains thing-words and relies upon poetic incantation to carry us beyond the immediate references of its constitutive vocabulary to the higher dimension of thinking.[1] So too in the case of Hegel, external reflection remains the heart of dialectico-speculative discourse. We cannot arrive at dialectical thinking except through the use of the thinking of external reflection. The most Hegel can claim is that external reflection is employed to point out its own sublation; but this does not change the fact that the higher or sublated stage is itself intelligible only through the juxtaposition of separate and finite terms, which serve as the basis for the attempt to transform juxtaposition into dialectical development.

To return to the text, the appended note repeats and expands on previously mentioned points. Quality identifies by limiting; it serves as a border and thereby negates what is outside that delimitation. *Omnis determinatio negatio est.* This negation results in the loss of *Dasein*'s immediacy. As immediate, it is one of an infinite series of *topoi* or ontological possibilities of becoming. The particular and hence negative determination (whatever it may be) renders *Dasein* distinct from the flow of immediacy and so to speak "qualifies" it as *something* (106–9).

SUBSECTION A, PART C: *ETWAS*. *Dasein* is a moment of becoming that is separated from other moments by a determinate property. The property in question transforms the existent moment into something real; it does so by a negation (by the attribution of an identifiable quality). The aforementioned separation (the quality in question) is also sublated, i.e., raised to a higher level of development in which the existing moment and its identifying quality are united. In other words, the shift from *Dasein* to *Etwas* consists first in an opposition of *Dasein* and its quality, which opposition is a separation of the two, but second, the opposition is overcome and thus we are raised to something or another. The point at issue is the logical (not temporal) process by which a moment of becoming, in its development into *Dasein* (109), acquires a qualitative determination that allows us to locate that moment in logical space and so to be something in particular. If I understand this correctly, *Dasein* or "being there" presents the moment of becoming and its qualifying property as separate from one another, as in traditional logic, whereas *Etwas* arises when we grasp the interrelatedness of existence and its identifying quality.

This seems to be what Hegel means when he says that "the *Etwas* is the first *negation of negation* as simple existing reference to itself" (110). In other words, the *Etwas* cancels the separation between a *Dasein* and its quality and raises them up to an identity within difference. *Dasein* corresponds to the Aristotelian *tode ti* or "this thing here," whereas *Etwas* corresponds to a *tode ti* that is also a *toionde*, "of such and such a kind." *Etwas* is the developed stage of *Dasein*.

Note also that negation of negation first appears with respect to *Etwas* because it is here that we first introduce properties as external or opposed to the category they determine. It is by negation of negation that we move from reflection to dialectic. The first negation is the opposition of category and determining property; the second negation raises up this opposition into a more complex and hence dialectical process. This does not occur in the case of being, nothing, and becoming, because there the categories emerge from the inner excitation of pure thinking, rather than by the opposition of one logical determination to another. Otherwise stated, being is not *opposed* to nothing but has already gone over into it. Hegel also emphasizes that we must characterize existing somethings with participial rather than infinitival terms. We have moved beyond the universal structure of the shell of an existing entity and have arrived at thinking *ein Reelles* (a *res* or real thing, 110).

Book 1, Section 1, Chapter 2, Subsection B: Finitude

In the last moment of *Dasein*, *Etwas*, as a subsisting structure of becoming, is a transition to another such structure. Something, in other words, is defined in opposition to another; this is the unending self-differentiation of becoming (111). We now consider this process from the two sides of the finitude of the individual moments and the infinitude of the process as a whole.

The process of something and another is introduced with the aid of a new technical distinction. Previously Hegel anticipated his later discussion of being in itself and being for itself. Now he distinguishes between being *an sich* and being *für Anderes*. It has become customary to translate *an sich* as "in itself," but this is not precise and leads to confusion between *an sich* and *in sich*. The preposition *an* is better rendered here as *qua*, "as far as" or "with respect to." Something, considered as such, is defined in opposition to another such, and, indeed, we say "something or another" in ordinary speech to bring out the inner sense of the term. In another locution, to be something is to be limited by a boundary that is at the same time its mediation or transition to something outside itself. In studying this transition or externalization process, we shift from the affirmative determinations of

Dasein (quality, something) to the negative determination of otherness. More precisely, we shift from first negation (determination as such) to second negation or negation of negation (the unity within difference of the something with another, 111–12).

It would be excessively tedious to go through each step in the dialectic of something and another. Suffice it to say that the identity of any "something" whatsoever is maintained by its sharing in a process of self-externalization of the following sort. Consider two elements that exist in a relation of reciprocal definition. For convenience we shall call them A and non-A. A is something and non-A is another, that is, other than A and so part of its boundary or definition. But if we shift our perspective, non-A is itself a something, say, B, and as such is something other than A, which is thus non-B. Stated abstractly or generally, this is the process of self-externalization, in which each something is also the other of another, and so is both the same as and other than itself.

I note Hegel's criticism of Kant on page 116, when he says that it is a mistake to regard "the *Ansich*" as something lofty, like inwardness (he is referring to the Kantian *Ding an sich*). In fact, what is merely *qua* itself has no dialectical relationship to other things and so no structure of its own; it neither is nor is not. Metaphysicians, Hegel contends, are interested exclusively in being *qua* being or the existent *qua* existent (*Ansichseiendes*). In other words, they are oblivious to the dialectical distinction between being *qua* itself and being for another (118). They fail to realize that the nature of a logical determination depends upon a relation to its complementary determination. In Hegel's own jargon, "being for another and being for itself are identical in the unity of the *Etwas*" (116).

Hegel illustrates these complicated dialectical relations with the example of the human being. "The determination of the human being is thinking reason. Thinking in general is his simple determinateness. Through it, he is distinguished from the brutes; he is thinking *an sich* insofar as he is distinguished from his being-for-another . . . But thinking is also *an ihm* [intrinsic to his nature] . . . it is his *Existenz* and his actuality [what traditional metaphysics calls man's essence]." But this *Bestimmung* "is again only *an sich*, as a *Sollen*," which Hegel explains as the opposition of the corporeal thinking human to immediate nonhuman sensuousness (119). The separation between the human being and immediate nature remains to be overcome; this depends upon the development of human nature.

Something is what it is by virtue of a determination that defines it and so distinguishes it from anything else. But the same determination (*Bestimmung*) conceived with respect to external relations and influences is called a

Beschaffenheit, a condition, quality, or nature. Each "something-or-another" is defined by its quality as what it is both *qua* itself and with respect to another; the quality determines it, makes it what it is in its independence from another but also what it is in terms of the other. The unity of these aspects is the unity of *an ihm* and *an sich* (119). In short, *Ansichsein* is a structural moment in tandem with *Sein für Anderes*, whereas existing *an ihm* is the actuality of the something (in the example, man) in its own right.[2] To complete the example, thinking is *an ihm* what each human being is in his own right; and so it is concrete, full of content, and what Hegel calls a *Bestimmung* or concrete quality. But it is also *an sich* "as a *Sollen*," i.e., as a potentiality that stands in contrastive opposition to sensuous, nonreasoning nature. We can therefore distinguish two aspects of quality. As ingredient in actual existence, it is a *Bestimmung*; as involving externality or otherness, it is a *Beschaffenheit*, and the two together constitute determinateness (*Bestimmtheit*, 119).

The main point of these peculiarly arid distinctions is not, so far as I can see, stated clearly by Hegel. The point is as follows: the analysis of becoming as the continuous reciprocal overcoming of being and nothing arises from the attempt to begin with no presuppositions whatsoever. This beginning is one of thinking; we think away or abstract from every logical determination until we arrive at one that cannot be removed without canceling the entire process. In Hegel's presentation, pure being is the simplest determination. Even further, it is the first presuppositionless determination, since it is the first to present itself from the sheer act of thinking, and not as a consequence of the overcoming of an external opposition.

Two objections arise almost immediately. First: Hegel assumes that being is not the separate "object" of thinking; it is rather the being that one thinks. As I put it in an earlier chapter, we cannot think of anything that is outside our thought. Unfortunately, this axiom does not guarantee us that there are no beings, and indeed, no logical determinations, that are inaccessible to our thinking. The foundation for the refutation of dualism thus dissolves. The second objection is not decisive. There seems to be an abrupt, predialectical shift from the determination of becoming to that of *Dasein*. Hegel would justify it by noting that one cannot proceed in the analysis of becoming to more complex determinations, except by introducing properties. We are studying the steps by which to build up in a dialectical manner the structure of the intelligible world. *Dasein* is the next step; we require it in order to say something about the content of becoming. But the quality "being there" does not emerge from the structure of becoming as the integration of being and nothing. Just as Hegel is forced to admit that our starting point is not with being and nothing but with becoming, so, the objection goes, he must admit that the introduction of location (*Dasein*) and the various modalities of quality must be introduced by the logician in order to keep the process of development going. They are not furnished by becoming alone. In other words, according to this objection, Hegel has not explained why the structure of the world exists within the continuum of becoming. What he can claim to have shown is that, given the existence of the world, it must have emerged as he describes it.

After a minute consideration of the modalities of the independence of a something and its relation to another (119–22), Hegel turns to the determination (= quality) understood as a limit or border (*Grenze*). The limit both holds the something together and connects it to the other (which from its standpoint shares the same limit). The momentum of the dialectical excitation of each component in this relation (that is, the shift from one delineated form to the other) is transferred to the limit that binds and distinguishes them. As Hegel puts it, a something undergoes restlessness within its limit, the restlessness to transcend itself. Let us say that finite things, or more generally, finitude itself is self-contradictory; each moment negates its own existence and so that of the other with which it is dialectically connected. The limit, as definition or border of something, is negation. As always for Hegel, a border both donates positive form to an existing thing and also negates it (the form is what it is by not being its others). The other, however, is negation of negation. This means that there occurs a mediation of what the border is with what it is not (122–23). France is distinguished from Switzerland by their common border, which both gives form to the territory of France (position) and exhibits the dependence of the form of France upon the adjacent nations that it is not (negation). The simultaneous occurrence of position and negation is referred to by Hegel as the negation of negation. We return to a positive moment, but one in which the content of the negation is preserved. Negation is thus not simple cancellation but a formally productive force.

The excitation of the border or limit is exhibited by the aforementioned restlessness of each finite something that drives it to go out over its border, to externalize and become other. This is the very nature of finitude (125). As we noted previously, the *Ansichsein* of something, or its being as both distinguished from and related to the being of another, is stamped by a *Sollen*. This can now be expressed as the restlessness of finitude, the inner motion toward externalization, and so toward completion. The *Sollen* looks suspiciously like a *deus ex machina* that is designed to remove the objections I raised a moment ago.

This *Sollen* is an anticipatory revelation of the inner presence of spirit in being. One sees this in Kant and Fichte, for whom, however, the limits of understanding preserve *Sollen* (or in Fichte's term, *Streben*) within reason in conjunction with morality and a teleology of endless striving. The result of making *Sollen* the permanent limit or boundary of philosophy, or its final principle, is to preserve us within finitude or genesis, understood (in Hegel's terms) as a bad infinity, an infinity that continuously negates itself but with no dialectical self-preservation. Instead we must see that *Sollen* overcomes every obstacle. To posit (*setzen*) a limit is in itself metaphysics, or external reflection; it is not dialectical (125–35).

All of Hegel's fundamental logical distinctions have now been exhibited within the first stage of the development of structure, commencing with the interplay of pure being and nothing and proceeding through the differentiation of becoming into *Dasein*. This does not mean that all of the categories are available; we still have to traverse the *SL*. But the inner engine of logical excitation is now visible. I will simply list the main motions for the sake of convenience:

1. Every form is internally excited; even unity spills out into multiplicity. This means that no formal atom can be understood in itself because it has no independence or inner stability.

2. The fundamental process of inner excitation leads to the self-affirmation of a finite moment of becoming as both integral in itself and as defined by its opposition to another finite moment. This is true at the purely abstract level of the dialectic of something and another but also at every successively more complex stage of development.

3. We can therefore say that to come into existence is both to posit and to negate oneself. To be is to become, and to become is to exhibit self-contradiction. One may object that only assertions are self-contradictory, but this is idle pedantry, especially with respect to Hegel, for whom thinking and being are the same. It is this sameness, masked by the inner excitation that transforms it into an identity within difference, that allows us to think anything at all, and so the process of development from being to actuality. This sameness can also be expressed as the identity within difference of soul and body, God and the world, or the interior and exterior of absolute spirit. In sum: by thinking form, we are also thinking life.

4. To be anything at all is to be stamped by a quality. Taken apart from anything else, a quality is a simple negation, namely, this but nothing else. Taken in conjunction with the "nothing else," as represented initially or generally (and so abstractly) as anything other, the otherness of what is ex-

terior to simple quality negates that simplicity, and so functions as the negation of negation. This is dialectical affirmation; it is also the inner mechanism of sublation (*Aufhebung*), the principle by which elementary levels of logical form differentiate and accumulate into ever greater complexes.

5. In order to understand any logical moment whatsoever, we must consider it first in itself, then in opposition to its complement, and finally as preserved with the complement in a relation of identity within difference. This can be carried out by Hegel in tedious detail, but the general procedure is always the same.

6. The externalization of something or another, i.e., of finite moments of becoming, has no end in itself. It can be brought to an "end" only in the sense that we exhibit the circularity of its logical structure. Infinitude is the perpetually self-excited, self-differentiating structure of becoming. God is thus the *logos* or concept, the form of the world. But Hegel denies that this is pantheism. Pantheism is the nondialectical identity or unity of God and world; Hegel's doctrine is that of the identity within difference of God and the world, that is, the manifestation of God's inwardness in the exteriority of his creation.

Whoever has fully grasped these six points has understood Hegel's logic in principle. What remains is to master the details. As our next step in the attempt to acquire that mastery, we move on to infinitude.

Book 1, Section 1, Chapter 2, Subsection C: Infinitude

We have now reached subsection C of chapter 2 (*Dasein*). This brings us to the dialectic of infinity or infinitude (*Unendlichkeit*). The essential point in this subsection (135–58) is the distinction between the bad infinity of understanding and the (good) infinity of reason. The key to the subsection is as follows. Reason is dialectico-speculative or marked by the full panoply of inner excitations that we have now studied completely, albeit in their most general forms. Reason thus encompasses and indeed *comprehends* not merely contradiction within the whole but the self-contradictory form of the whole or totality. Remember that the life-pulse of the absolute is the identity of identity and difference or, as we can now also express it, the structure that arises from the preservation of two negated, i.e., logically complementary moments, within a relation that shows them to be mutually responsible for each other's existence and intelligibility. Understanding, or nondialectical logic, is on the other hand linear or finite; it founders on the thesis of the static and independent nature of formal elements or logical atoms. Accordingly, understanding tries to exclude, and so falls into, self-contradiction. This exclusion is rather an act of self-dissolution, the guarantee of the unending position and negation of the bad infinity of finite elements.

We should not make the egregious error of assuming from this that Hegel repudiates the understanding. The understanding becomes "bad" only when it attempts to replace or to dispense with reason. This is Hegel's Kantian heritage. As previously noted, our main task is to distinguish between what Hegel calls "the finitized infinite" or bad infinity of the (nondialectical) understanding and the infinitude of reason. The infinite is initially the absolute defined as "determinationless self-reference posed as being and becoming" (135). In other words, it is the most general logical structure of what we traditionally call the spatiotemporal continuum (but not that continuum itself), within which all individual existing things emerge and pass away in their identities as something or another. In this unfolding continuum, each antecedent finite moment is negated by its successor, even as the continuum remains forever (since the dialectic of becoming has no cessation).

This negation is thus affirmation; more precisely, it is the affirmation of the continuum through the positing of a finite moment. One moment follows another and is a different moment, yet the continuum of moments remains the same. The collapse or departure of one finite moment is the origin of another. As an item within Becoming, each moment has a definite structure of its own, which structure will thus differ from moment to moment, whereas the continuum of moments has its own inner structure. A tree is a *Dasein*, not Becoming, but the existence of the tree requires the matrix of the continuum. This affirmation is also a reciprocal modification of the finite and the infinite, since the positing of finite moments is endless. The total process of the endless affirmation and negation of finitude constantly repeats itself, but the complete manifestation of the logical categories of the continuum of finite appearances and disappearances completes presence or actuality of the continuum as a whole. This is the absolute in its first or logical manifestation: a circle that rotates perpetually upon its axis, a structure that consists in the reciprocal shaping or defining of finitude (*Dasein*) and infinitude (one *Dasein* after another). We arrive at the genuine infinity of reason. It should be clear on the basis of our preceding analysis that this corresponds to the internal structure of absolute spirit, as represented by the two dimensions of God and the creation, or eternity and temporality (135–36).

Each finite moment is a negation in the familiar sense that it stands forth or "exists" (= "is there") in opposition to infinite passing away. But as the process that cancels each finite moment by the positing of its successor, infinity is the negation of the negation. In the first negation, this *Dasein* is posited as other than every other; in the second negation, each and every *Dasein* is dissolved by and is other than the endlessness of becoming.

Bear in mind that Hegel is discussing here not concrete events like the existence of human beings or the objects of everyday life but rather the conceptual structure of the process by which these concrete things come into being and pass away. From the standpoint of logic, the "cancellation" of a finite moment of becoming through the positing of its successor is not pure annihilation; if it were, becoming would be discontinuous, in which case the conceptual and physical connections that bind the concrete objects and events of becoming would also dissolve; there would be no becoming at all, but rather chaos.

To those who argue against Hegel that it does not violate the law of noncontradiction to posit continuous creation *ex nihilo*, or a discontinuous infinite series of momentary manifestations of stages of the universe that are well ordered or produce the illusion of a continuum, Hegel has already replied in the dialectic of being and nothing. The ability to conceive a discontinuous continuum is itself self-contradictory or self-sublating because it rests upon the reciprocal transformation of being and nothing into one another. In short, the hypothesis of discontinuity is just the assertion of dialectical community. We enact the sameness of being and thinking by posing a discontinuity; when asked to explain or analyze the conception of discontinuity, we say that it is an infinite series of positions and negations, which is exactly what Hegel means by becoming.[3]

"It is the nature of the finite itself to go out beyond itself, to negate its negation and to become infinite. The infinite does not thus stand apart from the finite as something finished for itself, so that the finite has its station outside or beneath the former" (136). This is now clear. There are not two entities, the finite and the infinite, standing separately and in opposition to one another. This has been excluded by the previous stage of the dialectic. We can restate the point as follows. There cannot be two opposing infinities, since there would be nothing to distinguish them. But one infinity is made up of an endless sequence of finite moments, not of two separate sequences, one finite and the other infinite. Someone could say that there are two finitudes here, the past and the future, separated from one another by the point or instant of the present. But this is to confuse the experience of everyday time by the understanding with the inner dialectic of reason, according to which the present is assimilated upward (sublated) into, that is, it is shown to possess, the circular reciprocal transformation of being and nothing.

It is perhaps desirable to add here that my reference to the spatiotemporal continuum should not be misinterpreted to refer to the physical space-time that is studied by natural science. I would never deny that in his *Realphilosophie* or philosophy of nature, Hegel is limited by the scientific knowledge of his epoch and in addition makes egregious blunders due to exaggerated trust in his speculative machinery. But in the *SL* we are not studying the empirical world or even mathematical models of that world. We are in *conceptual* space-time. Hegel must contend, in other words, that all conceivable scientific theories about spatiotemporality, magnitude, dimensionality, causality, and so on exhibit at their most general level exactly the structure that he is in the process of articulating. That structure is not a "scientific" theory in the usual sense of a theory of mathematical or experimental science; it is instead the conceptual shape of any theory whatsoever, or more precisely, of being and thinking, the "ground" out of which all theories about the world emerge.

In sum, "infinitude does not arise through the sublation of finitude in general, but the finite is just this, itself to become the infinite through its own nature. Infinitude is its affirmative determination, that which it truly is in itself" (136). And this affirmative determination is a negation of negation, i.e., a removal in the sense of a passing across the boundary of the finite *qua* finite. Otherwise stated, the finite and the infinite determine each other reciprocally; neither moment could be what it is apart from the other (137–38).

I turn now directly to the distinction between the bad and (as we may call it) the good infinity. And first a general remark. As opposed to the finite moment, the infinite is an empty "beyond" (*Jenseits*) that lacks all concrete content. This is the bad infinity or highest truth of the understanding. But precisely as opposed to the finite, the bad infinity is bounded or limited by it. It is thus itself a finite infinity. One might think here of the hierarchy of types or levels of complexity in set theory and logic, each of which is infinite within, yet finite externally because bounded by another well-defined level of infinity. For Hegel, there are only two "levels," the finite and the infinite, but his dialectic of these two levels is a generalization of the alternation of finitude and infinitude that one finds in mathematical analyses of the transfinite. From a mathematical standpoint, as long as each level can be indexed, there is no end to the process (that of taking the power-set of a given level). But each level is both finite and infinite, each is defined by the other.

To continue, a finitized infinity is in fact finite; i.e., we have finitized it by transforming the linearity of the bad infinite into a circle, the circle of the conceptual grasp of its endlessly repeating and mutually defining affirmations and negations. The finite and the infinite are thus "internally" or conceptually the same, but externally they manifest themselves as two distinct "worlds," heaven and earth, or the dualism of eternal form and temporal genesis, of essence and existence, that is the heart of traditional metaphysics. Hegel is in the process of attempting to overcome dualism by arguing that form or essence is the self-manifesting interior of genesis (138).

We have now stated the process by which the bad infinite, or "the perennial ought-to-be" (*das perennierende Sollen*, 141), that is, the continuous exchange between finite and infinite, or the so-called infinite progress, is generated. "This infinite has the firm determination of a *Jenseits* [beyond] that cannot be reached because it ought not to be reached [*nicht werden soll*]" (142). To this is opposed as its other the *Diesseits* of finitude. As we can now anticipate, the dialectic of "here" and "there" or of something and another will lead to a sublation of the perpetual opposition of finite and infinite into an identity within difference, as was already visible in the fact that each dimension is the other's boundary and so participates in its shape and intelligibility (142–44).

Looked at more closely, the unity of finitude and infinitude is achieved by the summation of the dialectical excitations marking each element. Each element, as opposed to and so delimited by the other, is finite. On the other hand, as passing over into the other, their identities are reversed: the finite recurs infinitely, and the infinite is posed at each moment as finitude (144–45). We have to grasp this process, not as an external bringing-together of two separate elements, but as an inner reciprocal process: "each is *an ihm selbst* this unity" (145). The German expression, we recall, is the expression of an integral identity that is more fundamental than a determination of something by its opposing other. Both elements are finite *and* infinite. Their sublation is thus not alteration but the inner development of what each is *an ihm* (145–46). We can also express this by saying that each exhibits the two forms of negation. Each is a simple determination or first negation. But as that very determination, each is also the other, not through opposition but via its own inner development. Hence the first negation is itself negated; the result is an affirmation that contains two instances of first negation in an identity within difference (146–47).

Hegel emphasizes that this process, in which each element affirms the whole, is a result or totality (*Ganze*), not a beginning (147). It makes no difference whether we begin with the finite or the infinite; the result is in each case the same. Furthermore, insofar as each is a moment in the total process, each is finite; insofar as each element is negated by the process, each is infinite (148). Thus we arrive at the genuine, true, or (in my term) good infinite, or the totality of becoming, that is to say, the entire dialectic as studied thus far, and not simply at the abstract formula "unity of finite and infinite" (149). Whereas the bad infinity is represented as a straight line, the genuine infinity is "bent back into itself" and its true image is the circle, the line that has reached itself, that is closed and entirely present [gegenwärtig], without a beginning point and end (149–50). In other words, eternal or transcendental or absolute excitation must be both distinguished from and yet the same as temporal excitation. The two are distinguished because temporality is the form, so to speak, of the created world in which human history, including the history of the philosophical reappropriation of eternity, transpires. But the two are the same because the eternal excitation is itself the pulse beat of temporality or creation.

Hegel next introduces a double distinction, first between *Realität* and *Idealität* and then between *das Ideell* and *das Ideal*. Reality is the domain of *res*, hence of the *onta* of classical or pre-Kantian ontology. But the genuine reality is the idea; that is to say, the truth of things is accessible only in and through thinking. So genuine *Realität* is *Idealität*, but not in the sense of the subjective idealists. *Das Ideelle* refers to the dependent existence of finitude as a determination that is a moment within a larger whole. In other words, it captures the popular sense of "ideal" as "what is not is not fully present or actual." If one follows the normal procedure of taking reality to correspond to *Dasein* and ideality, in the sense of *das Ideelle*, to correspond to the concept, then one will fall back into the abstract determinations of the bad infinity (150–51).

There follows a "Transition" to chapter 3 (*Fürsichsein*) consisting largely of two notes. In the first and longer note, Hegel reconsiders the relation of the finite and the infinite; his main point here is that the infinite does not "become" finite but is *für sich selbst* both finite and infinite (154–55). In the second note, Hegel criticizes idealism, which he defines as "the assertion that the finite is *ideell*," in other words, that it does not possess genuine being (*wahrhaft Seiendes*) (156–57). In a sense Hegel agrees with this, but it has to be explained correctly. A philosophy that takes finite existence to be true being has forfeited the name of philosophy (157). But finite being is not "ideal" in the sense that it is a mere opinion of my own (*Meinen*), a "thought" or "representation" in my imagination. The reality of finite being is its manifestation or externalization of infinite being, i.e., spirit.

Summary and Transition

Before we enter into chapter 3 (*das Fürsichsein*), let's take stock of our position. Hegel's method of dividing the *SL* into sections and subsections is unusually cumbersome. We are currently in the first of three books, each of which is divided into three sections (*Abschnitte*). Book 1 is called "the doctrine of being" and is divided into chapters called "Being," "Dasein," and "Fürsichsein." We can look at this basic structure in two different ways. On the one hand, book 1 moves from being and nothing to becoming, which in turn transforms itself (or is transformed by dialectical thinking) into *Dasein*, "being there," that is, holding a location within the flow of becoming. In other words, in order for becoming to transpire, it must be *somewhere* at each moment. I believe what is implied here is that *Dasein* is present. For example, an existing tree is present to an observer. Hegel generalizes this or renders it fully abstract: the existence of an object depends upon its being somewhere or another, and to be this, it must be *something* or another. And this entails that the thing be for or in itself, independent of its being observed. Perhaps we can say that it is observable. To sum up, for Hegel to be is to be present. But being is itself coming to be and passing away. And in my view, this too entails the primacy of presence.[4] For Hegel, temporal presence depends upon transcendental presence (= absolute spirit).

In chapter 2, *Dasein* develops in two senses. First, its attribute of being, namely, location, is in itself too anonymous to be identified and re-identified. Position becomes intelligible only if it belongs to something or another. I have raised an objection at this point. One can arrive at the constituents of form by analysis, but this would require us to reverse the motion of Hegel's logic or move from the complex to the simple. If we go from the simple to the complex, we must have already acquired the elements of form by a previous intuition, sensory or cognitive, or by a prior analysis, which leads to an infinite regress. Briefly stated, Hegel does not explain how the empty continuum of becoming acquires formal articulation. I argue that form must be acquired from outside the continuum, and so that dualism is not overcome.

The second sense in which *Dasein* develops is as finite and infinite. This takes place in parts B and C of chapter 2. Before we return to chapter 2, I want to make a summary remark about chapter 1. In chapter 1, we studied the predialectic of being-nothing-becoming. This is the basic structure of the entire development of the concept; it repeats itself in the form of ever increasing determinations until the last stage, at which it becomes fully concrete and so externalizes as God's creation even while remaining itself.[5] In other words, at every subsequent stage, we will find a more complex or richer version of each of the three moments, being-nothing-becoming. Everything is in process (becoming), but process has the inner structure of determination and negation, something and another, unity and multiplicity, and so on. These pairs all correspond to being and nothing. Stated concisely, nothing works on being at every stage of Hegel's logic to produce further structure; more precisely, this holds true until all structure has been revealed. After this, no new structure is produced, but the process of production is repeated forever.

In chapter 2, *Dasein*, "existence," "being there," or "determinate being" is the immediate manifestation of becoming. In other words, becoming cannot be grasped as pure process or flow; the analysis of the process of becoming into being and nothing was so abstract as to take place prior to dialectic. We cannot as it were gain a conceptual grip on becoming except as a sequence of existents, literally, entities that possess location in the flow of becoming. This is why Hegel attributes immediacy to becoming taken as "being there" or existence. It is this immediacy to which I referred when formulating my objection concerning the appearance of form (*Etwas und Anderes*) a moment ago. The whole process can also be understood as the dialectic of finitude and infinitude. Previously, i.e., with being-nothing-becoming, we had no grip on things, and so could conceive neither of the finite nor the infinite.

In chapter 2, parts B and C, Hegel develops the dialectic of the finite and the infinite. The transformation of the *Dasein* as a something or another is accomplished by the attribution of a predicate or quality. As a finite, determinate entity, each thing (= *Etwas*) is defined by opposition to some other thing (including some other stage of the same thing). There is a limit or border that both separates one thing from another and defines each thanks to the other. Hegel refers to the restlessness of the finite to exceed its border, by which he means that the isolation of finite entities is overcome by their dependence upon that which defines them by exclusion. France may or may not desire to assimilate Switzerland, but no one can fully understand France without having understood its difference from Switzerland (my example). In more Hegelian terms, the *Etwas* is defined by its border, which is also the border of that which it is not. The attempt to understand one thing leads us inexorably to something else that it is not; the broader, more inclusive concept includes both within its domain. In short, each thing is and is not itself; each thing is also its opposite or negation.

It should be easy to see that the transition from finitude to infinitude arises from the restlessness of the finite. Stated concisely, this means that each finite thing is defined by its complement and thereby becomes infinite. But the attempt to conceive of this infinite is itself possible only by contrast to the finite that it transcends. Since this process is linear and has no end, each stage erases what has been established by its antecedent. Hegel calls this the bad infinity. We are now at the point we reached last time, and I return to a more leisurely exposition of the text.

Book 1, Section 1, Chapter 3: Das Fürsichsein

Our main business is now with chapter 3: *Das Fürsichsein* or being for itself. The continuum of becoming diversifies itself into moments, each of which is the concentrated thereness of the full process. Each moment is a unity and, as such, finite; but it is a unity precisely as a manifestation of the infinity of the process of becoming. Becoming can manifest itself only as this and this and this, as something or another, as a multiplicity of existing units. Each unit is a subsisting moment of becoming (a being *there*), but it is also the emblematic representation of the infinite process of which it is a moment, a process that shows or manifests itself moment by moment. These moments fall apart into the finite and the infinite; that is to say, as present, each is finite. But as coming into being and passing away, as the emblem of the totality of becoming, each is infinite. But the same process that separates or dissolves the finite moments reunites them as the point-by-point unfolding. So each is infinite in two senses, one, as exhibiting the flow of infinity, and two, as exhibiting the finitude of the exhibition of infinity. Hegel calls this reunion "being for itself." He wishes to indicate by this expression that being is not canceled within becoming by nothing. Becoming persists or maintains itself.

Perhaps it will be helpful to precede the technical analysis of *Fürsichsein* with a statement of its human manifestation. Thinking initially detaches us from the wholeness or continuity of becoming by the projection of the subject-object structure. We remain in this dualism only through a failure to carry out our thinking completely. If we do persevere, however, or in other words come to a full understanding of the absolute as the identity of identity and difference, thinking repairs the schism or diremption that it itself caused. To understand the whole is to be reintegrated into it without losing one's personal identity or self-consciousness, or in Hegel's expression, one's *Fürsichsein*. We preserve our finitude precisely through a conceptual grasp of the infinite. But it is only a finite being, a being marked by the property of "for itselfness," i.e., a being that is not only a subsisting

unity but also self-conscious, that is capable of conceptually grasping totality, or the absolute. This is very important. Intelligence comes in finite
units.[6] Hegel's "absolute" is not an infinite deity that exists separately from
the finite or immanent domain. That is the *deus absconditus* of Judaism.
Neither is God identical with the world. That is the God of pantheism. It is
the interrelatedness of all the finite elements or "monads." And this is the
identity within difference or according to Hegel the God of Christianity, as
interpreted by himself.

In a previous text, I illustrated the Hegelian thesis that knowledge of the
whole or wisdom heals the wound of consciousness by making it fully self-
conscious. In consciousness, we are separated from ourselves, and in that
sense lacerated, by the subject-object distinction. The object represents our
completeness through work, but the work has the effect of "alienating" us
from our labor. Self-consciousness is the recognition that the object is contained within the subject *as* my work, whereas this is not evident to mere
consciousness. There is a fine illustration of this point in Hegel's treatment
of the biblical account of the Garden of Eden. Knowledge separates mankind from nature, and by showing us what we are not, it separates us from
God; it is thus the cause of evil. But this is necessary in order to show the
human being what he is in himself, i.e., what he ought to be as a result of
the labor of understanding. In Hegelian language, the work of cognition
is also the activity of recognition, that is, of recognizing the object as my
work, and so as assimilated into my own spirit. "Erkennen heilt die Wunde,
die es selber ist" (Knowing heals the wound that it is itself).[7]

Book 1 of the *SL* contains the teaching of being. By a slight simplifica-
tion, we can say that this teaching has three parts. Part 1 sets out as though
it were treating pure being, but it soon becomes evident that being and
nothing are conceptually accessible only as becoming. Becoming in turn is
first accessible as "being there" or *Dasein*. This can be glossed as "pure location." Becoming is articulated into a flow of locations. But one location can
be distinguished from another only by content: "something and another."
To be something is to have a predicate or determination: a *quality*. This is
why Hegel subtitles the first section of book 1 "Quality." Being/nothing is
the most primitive form of quality, which, as we shall see, develops into
quantity. Note: the reason why terms like being and quality appear in more
than one division of the *SL* is to show that one logical category flows or
develops into the next; this is a seamless process, not an abstract list of distinct categories as in Aristotle or Kant.

A quality distinguishes one thing from another; no such distinction occurs in the initial subsections on being/nothing/becoming. Hegel tries to escape from this problem by claiming that a lack of a predicate or determination is itself a determination. But he also claims that location or *Dasein* mediates between being/nothing/becoming and something and another. Location is already implicit in being/nothing/becoming. It is therefore implicit in becoming, which is so to speak the truth of being/nothing. Location as it were makes room for *Dasein*. But where does being for itself come from? This category expresses the first manifestation of the content of each location. In sum: what is there? Something or another. What is that? It is a determinate quality, the content of the moments of becoming. We can consider this content as it is "for itself," i.e., prior to its conceptual development as existing relative to a different determination. It is the something taken as itself, before we consider it in opposition to another. Hegel will develop this in his analysis of one and many. Note that this is a prefiguration of quantity, which emerges from quality. For Hegel, quantity is already a quality; if this were not so, we could never make a seamless ascent from quality to quantity. Footnote: to think is to think something in particular, i.e., a quality. We cannot think formless or entirely indeterminate quantity. The quality of thinking has been presupposed from the outset: being is the first quality that we think. And there is no qualitative distinction between being and thinking at the initial step. They will never be completely separated but will develop into a unity within difference or the absolute.

Now let's look at some of the details in the dialectic of "being for itself." As usual, the dialectic of *Fürsichsein* has three parts. The general sense of the term is self-subsistence; the entity has not yet moved out beyond its border thanks to the inner excitation of its qualitative determination (159). Hegel refers to being for itself as "infinite return into itself" (160). At this stage, the existing entity is considered apart from antecedent dialectical steps. Bear in mind that being for itself is a property of *Dasein* or existence and is immediate in the sense that this is the first stage of the development of the concept that we can actually grasp. As an example, Hegel contrasts consciousness with self-consciousness. Consciousness contains the intuition or thought of its object *within itself* (*in ihm*) as *Ideelles*, i.e., as subjectively represented and so as external to itself. It does not recognize that the object, not just the subjective representation, is contained within itself; consciousness is thus "for itself" as separated from the external object. Hegel calls it "dualism." Self-consciousness, in contrast, is the completion of being for itself; there is no reference to an object outside of and other than itself (160). (Self-consciousness is accordingly the presence of abstract infinity, i.e., of the continuum of pure self-awareness.) This example is an anticipation; we are still within the objective logic and have not yet arrived at self-consciousness, which is a part of the subjective logic.

I note in passing Hegel's discussion of *Sein-für-Eines*, "being for one." This peculiar expression introduces one of the most obscure passages in the entire *SL*. It designates the general condition of self-subsistence in which there is no opposite determination, even though one is required at this point in dialectical thinking. Hegel is criticizing standard idealism here, in which God and spirit are for themselves, i.e., static, because lacking another determination through which to be set into excitation and thus to proceed on the dialectical path to self-consciousness (161–62). Hegel expands upon this point in the note, which turns into a general discussion of idealism. In traditional idealism, self-consciousness is taken as the something for which or with respect to which it is itself a something or another, and the same holds for God. Again, there is no genuine engagement between God or spirit and anything else. In effect, this dooms both God and spirit to isolation from the world, and so from humankind. This renders them merely *Ideell* while it bestows genuine existence on finite things. In other words, there can be no unifying identity within difference here, because the separation is not one of an internally excited negativity that draws the two opposing moments into its orbit (162–63). Note also that Hegel uses the term *Kategorie* on page 163 to refer to the stage of dialectic under discussion.

Hegel observes that there is no being for itself in Eleatic or Spinozist monism because there are no determinations leading to distinct beings. Nothing can define itself or stand forth as what it is, because this requires a standing apart with respect to something else. In particular, there can be no subject or spirit. In general, one can say that even those who, like Malebranche and Leibniz, attempt to introduce subjectivity into Spinozistic monism succeed only in rendering *ideell* the entities or thoughts that exist properly only within the thinking of God (163–66).

I will be as brief as possible with respect to the two remaining determinations of being for itself: one and many and repulsion and attraction, which I will take together for the sake of simplicity and then consider the notes interspersed through the main sequence of the text. Being for itself is initially self-subsistence or the simple unity of itself and its properties, including the property of being for something: in the first instance, it is itself that something. That is, it is a more concrete way of characterizing the existent, the concentration of becoming into a location or *there*. In other words, it is one (*Eins*), immediate, and an existent. At this point, however, it has to be remembered that despite its simple unity, the one nevertheless contains as it were in suspension all of the determinations studied thus far. More precisely, the unity of the one is a development of being, whereas the indeterminateness or lack of content of unity is a development of nothing.

I remind you that the existent is the developed form of the being-nothing relation that we described as the finite manifestation of the infinite process of becoming. It is as though these determinations are concentrated into a point, a point that holds in dialectical suspension the moments of independent existence out of which the continuum of becoming is constituted: "Being for itself is in [the] one the posited unity of being and existence as the absolute unification of reference to another and reference to itself" (167). To clarify this statement: in the determination of unity, or the "oneness" of any unit, there is no being for another; unicity is the same in every case. So being for another is here absolutely the same as being for itself.

Remember that the initial stage of being for itself is that of the static independence of a qualitatively determined *Dasein*. As independent of every other object or determination, it cannot define itself. Whatever seems to be other than itself is therefore taken as subjective (*ideell*).

On the other hand, it is obvious that in order to be anything at all, something must be a one or (more felicitously in English) a unit. Being for itself cannot be defined by its qualitative determinations, which, as static and independent of dialectical transitions, are unknowable. Remember that these static determinations are available to us only as subjective and illusory appearances. They reduce to unity. But it is impossible to think unity as independent for two reasons. First, unity possesses no qualities that make a concrete definition possible. Second, unity can be thought only in opposition to, and hence in conjunction with, multiplicity. But each unit of existence is stamped by unity, which we take here as what permits the unit to be identified and so contrasted with other existing moments, even though the *unity* of one unit cannot be distinguished from the unity of another unit. Hegel is nevertheless attempting to think unity or oneness in itself.

Let me restate how we got to unity. We have moved from becoming to location, and from location to content. This content is both independent of other content or formal determinations and dialectically related to its antecedent and subsequent determinations. Hegel wants to show that we cannot think independent content as such because it collapses into unity, i.e., a point; and this in turn leads us to multiplicity. The point develops dialectically. This is the immediate ancestor of quantity.

We might imagine that the description of unity, i.e., the one, is possible only with reference to the many as itself a distinct category. For example, a single point, which exemplifies abstract unity, can be grasped only with respect to many points. But in order to employ the notion of manyness, we must have some way of expressing unity, and thus of how unity is dialectically excited into the generation of its opposite, namely, manyness. Hegel himself refers to the extreme difficulty of this enterprise (166–67).

Hegel is attempting to think unity as a distinct category of anything whatsoever, which first becomes conceptually accessible to us at the level of existence (of which "being for itself" is a further determination, namely, the one that exhibits the property of unity). Taken as itself and in general, it is the being of unity not to be existence, to have no determination as a reference to another and so no constituted nature; "it is just this, to have negated this circle of categories" (168). Under this supposition, we would return to being and nothing. Hegel means that if unity possessed logical determinations, it would become multiplicity. So it must negate all determinations other than sheer unicity (to coin a term). He goes on to say that as just described, unity possesses the determination of indeterminateness, not, however, as does pure being, but as reference to itself, as "posited being in itself" (*gesetztes Insichsein*, 168). Unity is therefore quite empty; Hegel refers to it as "the abstract reference of negation to itself" (169). But how does this differ from the initial stage of being, of which much the same thing is said?

I think that Hegel must be understood here as follows. Unity consists of position and negation: to posit unity is to locate it; but we locate it as lacking in inner structure. Unity is thus a development of being and nothing. Stated informally, unity manifests itself as the simplest property of anything whatsoever. As Aristotle says, there are as many senses of "one" as there are of "being." Whatever is, is a unit. If this is so, and if to be is to be knowable, can we define the property of unicity itself? Hegel's answer is "no." The attempt to define unity forces us to introduce multiplicity. This is the abstract version of the claim that "being for self" cannot be understood in itself but requires a reference to what I will call "being for another." This is a product of the *Etwas und Anderes*. Something is intelligible in terms of something else. Unity is intelligible in terms of multiplicity. The finite is intelligible only in terms of the infinite, and so on and so forth.

These instances of dependence were not available to us at the initial level of being/nothing/becoming. They show themselves only in the transition to *Dasein*. And note: it is a characteristic of Hegel's dialectic that at each stage of transition from a lower to a higher level of conceptual development, there is a collapse or disintegration of inner structure. At the initial level of being/nothing, there is no inner structure to collapse; these determinations are immediate. Hence they cannot be separated from each other; as soon as we think one, we are thinking the other. And this initial step is the forerunner of many subsequent steps.

Being, in its reciprocity with nothing, does not subsist as a unity or existing moment. It is radically simpler and radically more undifferentiated than unity. So unity, as a property of an existing being for itself, is a development of being. In other words, being does not mark off an existing thing as does unity, which is a property of *Dasein* or being there, a determination subsequent to that of being. As such, unity possesses a *dialectical* relation to the negative aspect of the same existing thing. Both aspects are then preserved at a higher level of complexity. This level is that of the one and the many, which will itself turn subsequently into quantity (169).

I will make a general remark in this connection. Unity has a stability and logical independence that being does not. Nevertheless, it is discursively inaccessible in itself; the attempt to grasp or describe it conceptually leads directly to multiplicity, for example, as the limit between two sets of points (think of a midpoint on a line). To say this in another way, unity *qua* unity has no defining properties, no properties that distinguish it from something else. This vacuousness negates its stability and independence because we can distinguish one point only by contrasting it with others, all of which are in turn vacuous or lacking in content. This initiates the dialectic of the one and the many.

Now let us consider the relation between two types of negation introduced by Hegel in his discussion of the one and the many, namely, unity as positive, on the one hand, and its emptiness or lack of qualitative determinations on the other. "The one is negation in the determination of being; the empty is negation in the determination of nonbeing" (*Nichtseins*, 171). This is the point that I made earlier; unity is a developed form of being, which is as such also something positive (unity) and something negative (vacuousness of defining or distinguishing characteristics). In other words, the attempt to think unity *per se* leads to a continuous negation or extinction of the given instance, but at the same time to the positing of some other unity as the external referent by which we were able to grasp the first instance. Otherwise stated, the process by which unity is transformed into multiplicity is that of the separation of the positive element (being) from the negative element (lack of content). Each unit is actually a dyad, that is, a multiplicity.

It is appropriate to refer here to the remark on page 170 from the note beginning on page 169 about classical atomism, or the doctrine of atoms and the void (as one may also translate *das Leere*). "The insight that the empty constitutes the ground of excitation" does not mean, according to Hegel, merely that atoms require a void in which to move about, something that would be impossible if space were filled up, but also "contains the deeper thought that the ground of becoming, of the restlessness of self-excitation, lies in the negative, in which sense, however, the negative is to be taken as the true negativity of infinitude."

Hegel means by this that the motion of the atoms is a generalized case of the inner excitation of unity or one atom, which, by virtue of the fact that it is its own other, "is thereby the coming to be of many ones" (171). We have here another form of the previous Hegelian thesis, already to be found in Plato's *Parmenides*, that to say, and so to think, that "being is one" is to multiply it into the dyad of being and one—but with this crucial Hegelian addition. The "not" or negation employed in the assertion "being, taken as one, is not one," itself taken as one, is a third term in the dialectic, not a simple syntactic operator external to the ontological substance of the discourse. Negativity is internal to, and itself brings about, the separation of being and unity. And this in turn has as its result that being is one, and one or unity is being; we now have two atoms or units, each of which will undergo the same process of inner separation and multiplication, thanks to the labor of the negative.

This crucial process allows us to restate an equally crucial general feature of Hegel's logic. Each time we make a syntactic distinction, we have identified a category of the concept, that is to say, of the formation process that both unifies and differentiates being and thinking. I see only one difference between this thesis and the assumption of contemporary philosophies of language, for which to be is to be speakable, that is to say, for which being is equivalent to one's definition of language, to linguistic categories, to logic. The difference is that Hegel takes negation seriously: He understands it to be negativity, and so work or activity.

These remarks were necessary in order to clarify Hegel's excessively cryptic account of how the one or unity multiplies itself. In Hegel's own language, the one is both negative and existent; "thus the one pushes itself away from itself. The negative reference of one to itself is repulsion," that is to say, the posing of many ones through oneness or unity itself (171–72). The many ones then go through the usual process of (i) repulsion as external opposition to one another or mutual indifference thanks to their emptiness or negation of all determinations and (ii) attraction through the very nullity of what distinguishes each one from the others (172–73).

The dialectic of repulsion and attraction (174–84) may be restated as follows. The reciprocal excitation of being and nothing results in the immediacy of existence as "being there," i.e., as concentrated at a point. Hegel tries to study the unicity of this point, not as "this" or "that" point but as a general category. Unicity is being for itself, namely, as self-subsisting rather than as defined through a reference to something external. On the other hand, to be for itself is always to be for or with respect to something else; even the pure one is determined by negativity or opposition to nothing. Every determination whatsoever, however simple, is constituted by its relation to other determinations. Logic is the demonstration of the fact that our very effort to understand a simple determination in itself, beginning with the most simple (pure being), leads us necessarily to its defining relata. So too unicity, the "oneness" of "existence at a point" (my terms), is necessarily manifested at *many* points, not because of the pre-givenness of multiplicity as the external relation of atoms, monads, or any other ontological entities, but thanks to the inner diremption, the "tornness" or separative function of unicity itself. The engine of diremption is negativity.

It follows from the preceding discussion that what I have called here the self-diremption or self-multiplication of unicity is not some arbitrary or mysterious self-multiplication of one into many. "Self-multiplication" is unintelligible only when considered externally, that is, from the standpoint of the usual static conceptions of being and nothing. A static one could hardly become anything other than itself, including a replica of itself. When Plato points out that to say "being is one" is to identify two elements, he has not yet shown how the external relation of being and one is capable of producing a continuum of points of existence. Dualism, in other words, is as inadequate as monism. We require a third, dynamic element, namely, the active negativity that is concealed within the assertion that "being is one," to which we must add explicitly that "being is not one." Note that these are not predication statements but statements of identity. Taken jointly, they constitute a contradiction. But the contradiction is an identity within difference that exhibits a vacillation within the unity, a vacillation deeper than the surface opposition of being and one. The deeper vacillation is that between being and nothing, of which the result is becoming.

Prior to becoming, which manifests itself at a point, and furthermore as a sequence of points, unicity does not emerge as a determination possessing being for itself. The statement that being is one is already an inference from the analysis of the continuum of becoming; it is the denial of the attribution of stability to multiplicity on the grounds that each element of the many presents itself and subsists as a one. The monist claims that unicity is the being of the many, which is not a genuine entity in its own right but a sequence of units. The true being of each transient unit cannot be its transience; it must be its permanent determination of unicity, which is always and everywhere the same, and which may thus be captured in the assertion that being is one. But this line of argument is clearly unsatisfactory, since it forces us to jettison manyness, which is an undeniable ontological dimension of our experience and upon which ontology or rational speech, or more generally, human existence altogether, obviously depends. Since the elevation of manyness to the level of exclusive ontological principle is as unsatisfactory as monism, the only alternative is to preserve the one and the many in their integrity by adding a third term that accounts for the dynamic, reciprocally modifying nature of their relation. This third term is negativity.

Let me underline this point. Unicity alone cannot account for multiplicity; but conversely, multiplicity is already characterized by and does not explain unicity. So long as we continue to insist that unicity is *not* multiplicity and that multiplicity is *not* unicity, while refusing to acknowledge the active or transforming role of the "not," we shall never be able to account for the logical construction of the world. Furthermore, as has already been indicated by Hegel, it is precisely through the aperture of the "not" that spirit or consciousness makes itself visible. The "not" is the mark of conceptual thinking that both unites and separates.

The ensuing detail of Hegel's analysis of the one and the many consists of the attempt to describe each moment in the process of the self-multiplication of unicity in three ways, as itself, as opposed to its opposite, and as "negation of the negation" of that opposition, which is now a richer level of structure. The upshot of this tripartite process is the establishment of a manifold of ones or points of existence (*Dasein*), of being *there* as "this" or "that," i.e., as something or another. These points are themselves defined by quality, the exhibition of thisness or thatness. Quality is here considered as a logical category, not as this or that concrete property. But as so considered, it is indistinguishable from quantity. The existing "something" is united to its "other" by the very qualitative determination that serves as its limit, and so as the border between the two, and so too with the "other" considered as a "something" (183). The result is a manifold of unified ones, or quantity.

In the note on pages 169–71, Hegel indicates the application of the dialectic of one and many to human political existence. There is no abstract freedom of the independent individual antecedent to political life. Such an individual would be equivalent to an undifferentiated monad, and so to all other individuals. This is tantamount to the assertion that man is by nature the political animal, but with the somewhat sharper corollary that human beings have no "rights" in the state of nature. In the note on pages 173–74, Hegel complains that Leibniz begins with a multiplicity of monads, each of which is independent of the others; the whole is thus constituted as abstract externality. There is no dialectical development of the sort we have just studied; Leibnizian idealism thus turns out to suffer from the flaws of traditional atomism. Finally, in the long note on pages 184–91, Hegel criticizes Kant's doctrine of matter. The basic defect is that Kant assumes matter as given and then proceeds to analyze it; again, there is no dialectical construction. More precisely, Kant defines matter as impenetrability in the sense of repulsion and says that attraction belongs to, but is not contained within, this concept. In effect, Kant showed that attraction and repulsion belong to matter, but he left them external to one another.

We have now completed the first section of book 1 of Hegel's *SL*. Stated very broadly, it is obvious from the continuum of becoming that quality is inseparable from quantity. Nevertheless, what is inseparable is a unification of distinct elements, and as always in Hegel's logic, we study the elements in the order of increasing concreteness. We cannot start out with a fully concrete speech about totality or actuality; a random beginning with some arbitrarily selected part or aspect of totality would be entirely contingent and fail to reveal the conceptual structure that is the goal of philosophy. We would thus remain within the domain of *doksa*, of fragmentary opinions or in the best case of myths about the whole. In order to give a *logos* or rational account of the whole, we have to exhibit the individual identities but also the concrete interrelationships of its fundamental constituents. In other words, we cannot give a list of each concrete individual, which would be a bad infinity and in any event totally lacking in significance. What we want is the categorial structure of concreteness. But once again, this categorial structure cannot be given as a totality, as though we approached something complete and static from the outside and proceeded to describe it in external detail.

Otherwise stated, the structure of the whole or totality (*das Ganze*) is alive, not a dead collection of bones. As both alive and total, it includes intelligence; it includes the process by which we attempt to grasp it conceptually. The correspondence between subject and object is possible only because both elements emerge from within a more general unity. In order to understand the subject-object relation as an opposition *and* an identity, we have to understand the process by which these two apparently separate elements emerge from the more general, and so more abstract, unity. The study of the whole is the study of the development or emergence of its fundamental parts. One might ask why we cannot begin with the whole and proceed analytically to the parts. But this is impossible, because the whole is too complicated to serve as a starting point for the human intellect. We arrive at a proper conceptualization of the whole only through having grasped each stage of its development into circularity or totality. Thinking the whole *is* thinking the sequence of its parts as they are in themselves and hence as they are related to the other parts. Hence we must begin with the simplest or most abstract part and proceed to derive each subsequent part in the order of increasing concreteness, until we have derived all parts, i.e., categories. Only then can we think the whole.

Being is the most general, most abstract, and in that sense simplest category of the whole. It is the first determination of anything whatsoever. It is true that nothing is also a primitive and completely abstract determination of anything whatsoever, but it is nevertheless subordinate in the order of exposition to being. One might wish to claim that nothing is primary, but this would be to grant that nothing "is," and even further that at the beginning it is what we mean by "being." In other words, the nothing with which we try to begin is not sheer vacuity, the *mēdamōs on*, but indeed, as a beginning, it is something, namely, the origin of anything whatsoever. As I expressed the underlying point previously, Hegel accepts the Greek adage that out of nothing, nothing comes to be. The truth is that neither being nor nothing "comes to be"; on the contrary, both are eternal within becoming or coming-to-be itself.

Becoming is thus not quite the beginning but rather totality itself. Being and nothing are the beginning of logical demonstration; they are the inner excitation or categorial structure of becoming. But they are never completely separate from one another; this ostensible external reflection is in fact impossible. It is inconceivable that being and nothing should be radically separable within eternity, let alone within temporality. Furthermore, becoming is not just a perpetual movement or blur; it takes its shape from the externalizations of the dialectical relations of its inner structure. The first of these externalizations is *Dasein*, literally "being there" but often translated as "determinate being." As I have expressed this, becoming as a process manifests itself at a point; it is a sequence of points, each of which has location and each of which concentrates at a point the process as a whole. The "determinateness" of *Dasein* is initially being for itself or sheer subsistence as a point, and so as independent of any other points, and this independence is a limit induced by a property or quality.

I will not summarize all the determinations that arise in the course of this development. Suffice it to say that to be anything at all is to be something or another, and so to manifest a quality, but any quality whatsoever. Since we do not identify concrete qualities at the categorial level of logic, the structure underlying the capacity to be qualified is just the attraction and repulsion of mutually defining points or moments of existence. More precisely, this abstract structure *is* quality at this level of development. In short, quality "goes over" from within itself into quantity. One might wish to call this structure "quantity" from the outset, but Hegel would object that quantity is a multiplicity of distinguishable units, and it is quality that allows us to distinguish one unit from another.

In the next chapter, we turn to the second section, entitled "Magnitude (Quantity)." It will come as no surprise by now to learn that the third section, "Measure," is in effect the identity within difference or "second negation" of the categories of quality and quantity (each of which is a "first negation" or determination).

SEVEN

Quantity

Book 1, Section 2: Quantity

We are about to shift from the study of quality to that of quantity. This section of the *SL* will strike the contemporary reader, especially one with a training in modern mathematics, as especially odd. The specialist in the history of mathematics will find more familiar Hegel's long discussion of the infinitesimal in early nineteenth-century versions of the calculus. I will give the main point of this well-known section at the appropriate place, but it cannot detain us for long, because the details are tangential to our central concerns, and the whole issue, which was also anticipated by Bishop Berkeley, has been rendered obsolete by the transformation of calculus in the period following Hegel by figures like Augustin-Louis Cauchy. In order to bring out the philosophical significance of Hegel's analysis of quantity in something like the terms of traditional metaphysics, and of course Hegel's revision of this tradition, I have been led to deviate frequently from a close paraphrase of the text. My reconstruction of the argument will be illustrated with enough quotations and sample summaries to give an authentic flavor of the original without weighing the reader down with the apparent eccentricities of Hegel's own formulations. My intention is not to replace Hegel with some presumably superior doctrine of quantity but to let Hegel's doctrine speak as plausibly as possible to contemporary ears.

I begin with a brief summary of our progress to this point. And first, a word about the general structure of book 1 of the *SL*. It is entitled "The Doctrine of Being" and has three sections, "Determinateness" (*Bestimmtheit*), "Magnitude," and "Measure." "Determinateness" has the parenthetical extension "Quality," and "Magnitude" has the parenthetical extension "Quantity." So our first impression is that there are three levels of the structure of being: determinateness or quality, magnitude or quantity, and measure. A closer look reveals that the first chapter of section 1 on determinateness or quality is also called "Being." So too the first chapter of section 2 is called "Quantity." If we had looked initially at section 2, we might have expected chapter 1 of section 1 to be called "Quality." How are we to understand this apparent disorder in the titles, and also the recurrence of "Being" in the general and subtitles? In order to approach this question, we have to move back from the titles and consider Hegel's overall conception. The key point is that Hegel wants to begin as simply or as abstractly as possible, or as he also puts it, with what is first because it has no presuppositions. This in turn is necessary in order to develop a genuinely scientific account of the structure of totality.

Let us recall that the account or *logos* is not the same as the various procedures by which we arrive at the level of the absolute from which the *logos* is to be produced or demonstrated. The ascent to the absolute is an arbitrary act of the will; i.e., it can come from anywhere. We might therefore arrive at any point on the circle of the absolute. Then we can go forward or backward, but in either case, if we reason correctly, we will return to our starting point. This is not the process that Hegel records in the *SL*. He presents the circle of the concept of logic in terms of a comparison to the thought of God prior to the creation of the universe. In other words, Hegel presents the circle, not as eternal, but as though we were generating it from a point, but not any point; the point corresponds to the self-evident beginning of an evolutionary account of the absolute.

I have to emphasize this obscure but crucial conclusion. The *SL* is entirely artificial in the precise sense that the absolute is an eternally rotating circle. It is always entirely what it is and so both present and absent everywhere as exactly the same total process of position and negation, identity of identity and difference, and so on. But human beings have a discursive intelligence. We have to proceed one step at a time in thinking out the dynamic structure of the circle of the absolute. Wisdom is the metaphorical representation in the finite human spirit of the eternal excitation of the whole or actuality (*Wirklichkeit*). In order to arrive at wisdom, we must have a "deduction" of the structure of the whole. But deductions in the traditional sense all rest upon presuppositions. As long as the presuppositions are themselves not part of the deduction, wisdom is impossible. Hegel must therefore find a presuppositionless beginning, namely, he must begin with the whole or absolute in its simplest, indispensable sense, a sense that rests upon nothing because it is entirely evident as that which presupposes nothing, yet is presupposed by everything. And I repeat, he must do this in order to demonstrate to the human intellect that his *logos* of the absolute is indeed complete, that he has begged no questions, presupposed nothing, left nothing outside the deduction.

In sum, we have to distinguish between human time and what I shall call the transcendental activity of the absolute. The absolute process by which the continuum of totality preserves its total structure as an identity within difference is not the same as the finite order in which the structure of totality is presented discursively to the finite human intellect. But the purpose of the discursive presentation is to reveal to the finite intellect its transcendental status within the absolute. It is the peculiar function of the finite intellect to understand the conditions of its activity as an identity within difference of the finite and the infinite. This stage of Hegel's teaching is perhaps the one that is most alien to the late-modern spirit of neo-Kantianism, and it has been dropped by the various forms of left-Hegelian interpretation. To do so, however, is to abandon Hegel's own teaching, and in particular to jettison what is for him the key to the solution of the outstanding philosophical problem of our tradition: how to explain the unity of thought and being. As a result, left-Hegelianism has from the beginning taken on the limited form of philosophical anthropology and the philosophy of history, including political and sociological theory. In other words, Hegel is mutilated in such a way as to reduce him to empiricism, if an empiricism with a Kantian flavor. But nothing more than a flavor, since Kant's transcendental ego is itself replaced by the historical ego, and this in turn by the *Zeitgeist*.

Let me also remind the reader that by "deduction" is not meant the usual logical deduction of a conclusion from premises that themselves rest upon axioms or principles serving as the presuppositions of the demonstration. In Hegel, to "deduce" is *deducere* in the sense of "to lead out one logical determination from the other," to show how they evolve from one another by the very process of our thinking them. And this in turn is rooted in the identity within difference of being and thinking. In the case of God or the absolute, this identity refers to spirit and extension, the two principal predicates or substances of modern philosophy (*res cogitans* and *res extensa*). In the case of the finite human being who is beginning the study of Hegel's logic, it certainly does not mean that our thoughts are the same as the whole, except in the potential sense that we can think the whole by wholly completing the process of thinking. And this in turn is possible because the whole is wholly accessible to us; there is nothing thinkable external to thought.

At first this looks like Kantianism, and in a sense it is. Putting to one side Hegel's idiosyncratic interpretation of Aristotle, we see that he accepts the Kantian version of the modern Cartesian enterprise to replace "being" or "substance" or "essence" with a world that is entirely the product of human thinking. But he goes beyond the modern version of which Kant gives us the most developed form. To put the main point as concisely as possible, Descartes says that it makes no difference what lies outside human thought because we can replace it with our own version of nature. Kant says that we can replace nature conceptually; but this leaves us with the need for morality or more generally for the domain of freedom and purpose. Hence we need to make use of what lies outside the cognitive or conceptual powers of the human mind in order to postulate freedom and purpose. No attention whatsoever is paid to this problem in Descartes, so far as I can see. We are free to do whatever we wish, depending upon the degree of our power to shape ourselves and our environment. Hegel orients himself by Kant, but with the intention of assimilating what lies outside the conceptual dimension. In other words, Hegel, taking a clue from Kantian dialectic or the antinomies and paralogisms of pure reason, revises conceptuality as dialectical speculation and attempts to think conceptually the dimension of freedom and purpose. Hegel understands, as Descartes either did not or thought irrelevant, that traditional science is spiritually empty and even that it is hostile to spiritual life. But he regards the Kantian approach as unsatisfactory because it retains a dualistic separation between scientific necessity and spiritual freedom.

So much by way of a brief reminder of the general intentions of Hegel. To come back to the text, the first book of the *SL* is about the progressive evolution of the concept of being into the concept of essence by virtue of our thinking of the three substages of quality, quantity, and measure or the ratio of these first two determinations. Again, we are *not* studying the ontological development of being into essence because being always is essence; the actual is always actual and does not itself "grow" chronologically into maturity. We are studying or enacting science, and this can be done only by thinking actuality or the absolute as though it were constructed from progressively more complicated layers of structure. At each step of our study, we are studying actuality, not something else, e.g., a "theory" in the sense of an arbitrary interpretation of experience. But we are studying it as it needs to be considered in order for us to arrive at a complete and circular *logos* of totality.

At this point, I raise a difficulty for Hegel that I shall develop later. It could be contended that the *SL* is in fact written in the language of what Hegel calls "external reflection," which (the objection goes) he falsely claims is transcended by dialectico-speculative thinking. Every sentence of the *SL* is an example of external reflection, in which we are forced by the finite nature of our cognitive faculties to conceive of a determination as opposed and hence as external to its complement. The very assertion that not-*p* is the limit or boundary of, and hence ingredient within, the concept of *p* is intelligible to us only through the separation of *p* and not-*p*. We cannot think either except as separate from or external to the other. External reflection is overcome within the absolute by absolute spirit (assuming that there is such a spirit), which can think totality, but the closest we can come to this is by giving the definition of the life-pulse of totality as the identity of identity and difference, and this itself depends upon the externality of one term from the other.[1]

So much for why we begin with being. There is no other conceivable beginning of equal simplicity or emptiness. We might try to begin with nothing, but such a beginning is in fact with the concept of nothing, and so with the being of the concept. "Nothing" refers to the emptiness of the empty concept of being. But why is being a quality rather than a quantity? Again I come back to the difference between the title of book 1 and the subtitle. "The Doctrine of Being" is in fact quite misleading because it sounds as though we are going to be presented with an analytical explanation or definition of being. But as I have just shown, this is impossible. The expression "doctrine of being" instead refers to the process by which the attempt to think being leads first to the distinction between essence and appearance and then to the understanding that it is essence that appears, or in other words that there is an identity within difference between essence and appearance.

A crucial question here is whether Hegel is correct. He seems to assume the traditional account of metaphysics according to which being is composed of essence and appearance. However, we are not yet in a position to try to answer this question; I simply raise it here. The question is whether the thinking of being follows the three stages of quality, quantity, and ratio in such a way as to arrive at the concept of essence, and so inevitably of appearances. This assumption is based upon the prior assumption that predication exhibits the structure of being, i.e., that the way we talk, namely, by saying that something belongs to, or does not belong to, something else, is a direct grasping of how things are themselves. In ordinary life we sometimes succeed in identifying things through their properties and sometimes we fail. This success is in fact circular, because we would have to know who owns what in order to identify something as belonging to the correct owner. How then do we identify the correct owner? It is circular to say that we do so by identifying his belongings.

If this set of commonsense assumptions is wrong, then being does not consist of essences and appearances. More precisely, essences cannot consist of essential properties because it is the essence that allows us to distinguish between essential and accidental properties. By "appearance" is meant the confusion of accidental for essential properties. Something appears to be such and so, but it is actually something else, namely, thus and such. And it seems that this is just what Hegel is heading toward when he claims that essence appears, i.e., that there is no dualism between essential and nonessential or accidental properties.

Furthermore, Hegel denies that being consists of anything whatsoever; it is non-Hegelian to refer to being as composed of essences and attributes or properties. For this reason, his distinction between essence and appearance cannot refer to the inner structure of being, but instead we recall that essence "is" and appearance "is." That is, "is" names a more simple determination, in fact, *the* most simple determination. So by "appearance," Hegel cannot mean "accidental properties of being." Neither can "essence" mean "essential properties of being." It is better to say that "essence" and "appearance" both *appear* in the sense that we think them to be separate whereas they are not.

Being is the emptiest, most abstract, hence minimal and indispensable beginning. It has no presuppositions in the table of logical determinations. But this is within the *logos*. The presupposition of being is the didactic process by which Hegel is leading us into the heart of systematic knowledge of the absolute. We come back to why being is introduced as quality. The short answer is that for Hegel, any logical determination is a quality. Quantity is "indifferent" to quality; in its primitive form it contains no traits by which we could distinguish one thing from another. As I noted in the previous chapter, we cannot even distinguish one monad or point from another except by way of a multiplicity of monads or points, a multiplicity in the sense not simply of a heap but rather of a number or answer to the question "how much?" And this in turn leads to the reinstitution of quality, that is, to the treatment of quantity as quality or rather as defined in opposition and so in relation to quality. Stated colloquially, you can't identify anything by a number unless you can state what it is about which you are answering the question "how many?" We don't say "how much apples?" but "how many apples?" "Much" is purely quantitative, whereas "many" is qualitative; it refers to a kind of which there are many instances.

Quantity, says Hegel, is "determinateness become indifferent to being"

(192). This in itself is not fully intelligible. The point is that every determination is a quality or *quale*, a such and such or so and so that defines a difference or distinguishes a type of being. Being is itself neither a "how much?" nor a "how many?" but the precondition for answering the question "of what sort?" In that generalized sense, it is a *what*. In one sense, it is therefore like the Greek *eidōs* or form that serves as the basis for "how much" and "how many" questions. On the other hand, it is not like the Greek form because it is the sheer positedness of any form whatsoever. One could almost compare it to Aristotelian prime matter. As such it is also negation or absence of any form whatsoever. Restated: being is the capacity to occupy a position in the continuum of becoming. As such it is a "what" that is not yet "this" or "that." In this sense it is like being as positionality in Kant.

So we cannot begin with quantity as our minimal presuppositionless exhibition of the determinations of the concept. The categories or determinations tell us "what's what." Being is a continuum but not a heap. If one tried to begin with quantity by calling being the continuum of points, each of which defines a position for the concatenation of qualia, one would have explained the "what" of the continuum. In other words, by focusing upon its multiplicity of points, one would not have explained its nature as a continuum of logical determinations, but instead one would have made those points in principle visible or thinkable by virtue of their function as positions for positings. What illuminates is not their multiplicity or quantitative nature but their role as placeholders; and it is this role that allows us to speak of a *manifold* or multiplicity of points at all. The manifold is derived by abstraction from the multiplicity of differences or "whats" in terms of which we are able to speak of presence and absence, i.e., position and negation.

None of this is to say that being is quality but not quantity. Being is *a* quality, namely, quality in general and so neither this quality nor that. If we go one step farther and abstract from quality in general while thinking only "neither this quality nor that," then we come to quantity as determinateness that has become indifferent to being. In thinking quantity, we look away from the quality that allows us to say "neither this quality nor that" and think only the multiplicity of "neither this nor that."

Once again, what does it mean to say that "being is quality" or "being is both quality and quantity"? Or that "being is the ratio of quality and quantity"? Being is these things as it develops from its initial empty manifestation as positionality toward the complex logical structure that underlies the identity within difference of essence and its appearances. I want now to revisit briefly the determination "being" and the difference between logical and real predicates. In Kant, being is not a real predicate; i.e., it is not the name of a property of a *Gegenstand* that designates a formal difference in that object. Real predicates are for Kant elements in the concept of that thing, whereas its being is simply its occupation of a position within the conceptually defined stream of appearances constituting our experience. Since everything that we encounter in experience "is," that word does not distinguish one thing from another and so does not belong to the defining concept of any thing at all. For Hegel, being is also one of the various logical categories that constitute the conceptual structure of anything whatsoever. "Being" is a qualitative determination or the name of a form, namely, of the minimal and so not further analyzable property of thinking. It is the concept as the precondition of all conceptual determinations. But these conceptual determinations collectively define the intelligible structure of totality or actuality, not of *res* or *onta*. One could say that being is a predicate of totality, but this does not make it a real predicate.

It follows from these considerations that the word *being* is used in a somewhat different sense in the title of book 1 of the *SL* from its use in the first chapter of the first section. We can say of being as it is the theme of book 1 that it is quality, quantity, and measure or ratio. But we cannot say this of being as the first logical determination. As presuppositionless beginning, being is nothing; i.e., it has no predicates or complex inner structure. As it develops in the course of our attempt to think it in its initial form, it takes on further determinations. These determinations are not elements in the inner structure of being; on the contrary, being is the simplest element in the inner structure of every subsequent determination. This is easy to see in the case of *Dasein*, where being (*Sein*) is the basis of "thereness" or location (*Da*).

It is not so easy to see in the case of quality, quantity, and ratio. Being is an instance of these determinations, not the basic element in their inner structure. We do not think "quality" as such in our initial thinking of being and nothing; and in fact, there is no separate chapter devoted to quality, as there is to quantity in the second section. This is because every determination, including that of quantity, is a quality. Quality is not a separate logical category or determination, but it is determinateness as such; this is the subterranean link between Hegel and the classical philosophers of form. Every logical question is an instance of the paradigmatic "what is *x*?," the classical Socratic question. This is true of quantity as well. Quantity is "determinateness become indifferent to being." But it does not cease to be a determination; to be indifferent to being is to be something, a determination of indifference as opposed to being concerned with, or however we define the opposite of indifference.

Hegel does not say so, but I believe that it is a defensible hypothesis to regard "quality" as a syncategorematic term in his logic. Quality is not an element within the structure of being, which has no structure. But neither is it a later or more complex category that contains being as an element, because being is already a quality. The same is not true of quantity, because being as quality is not yet a quantity. This is an extremely obscure situation. We have to distinguish between two senses of category. The first sense is that of the determinations of Hegel's logic: being, nothing, becoming, and so on.[2] The second sense includes the terms by which we speak about categories in the first sense. This includes quality; one might think that it must also include terms like same, other, one, and so on. But Hegel seems to make no such distinction; same and other are obviously categories in the first sense for him, and I am not aware of any passage in which he distinguishes between two senses of "category" or, to use his favorite term, "determination."

Thus far I have been approaching Hegel's treatment of quantity by a consideration of its difference from quality, and in particular by consideration of the fact that being is as such a quality but not yet a quantity. As an introductory formulation, we can say that the question "how much?" is inappropriate with respect to being, and the question "how many?" refers to instances of a particular kind of being, and not to the being of that kind. Being is not found, so to speak, as an independent element in nature. Strictly speaking, it is a *Gedankending* or product of thought. It is the simplest determination we can think. On the one hand, it has no structure, no properties, and so is not derived from anything else or reducible into simpler constituents. On the other hand, we cannot do without it, which is equivalent to the assertion that it belongs to the conceptual structure of anything whatsoever.

In other words, suppose that we ask what it means from a Hegelian standpoint to say, for example, that "trees exist." Existence (i.e., being) is a property not of individual trees but of the absolute formation process, of which trees are a contingent consequence. Now it is true that any of Hegel's logical determinations can be applied metaphorically to things or *res*. A tree is identical with itself, other than a stone, shares in finitude and infinity, and so on. I call this a metaphorical application because, as we learn in the *SL*, these determinations are all articulations of the initial continuum of being. In Kantian language, they are collectively the conditions for the possibility of trees or anything else: any *res* or thing So the logical categories, taken in themselves, do not constitute actuality or *Wirklichkeit*. This term refers to the identity within difference of the interiority and exteriority of the absolute, i.e., to the logical structure for the possibility of a world and to the world itself as the exemplification or consequence of that structure. The *SL* describes not actuality but rather possibility, if by "possibility" one means "a possible world" and so by extension "possible things."[3]

To continue, being (*Sein*), existence (*Dasein*), and being for itself (*Fürsichsein*) designate the irreducible minimum of intelligibility. *Dasein* and *Fürsichsein* are the properties by which being takes a stand or shows itself as a point that persists as the locus of any existing thing whatsoever. As we learn more concretely from the discussion of quantity, a point is accessible only in distinction from another point; the *Dasein* and *Fürsichsein* of two points in a dyad also apply to that dyad itself, which thus reduces to a monad, namely, this unique dyad; and as such, it is intelligible only in opposition to another dyad, and so on forever. This constitutes the simplest level of the structure of becoming, which is a logical process. I mean by "logical" that it is not actuality but the intelligibility of actuality that we are here studying; we are doing logic, not physics. The process *qua* process would be invisible if we could not see or think the *nunc stans* of the point as *Da* and so as "for itself" or enduring simply as what it is, whereas a pure standing or (to coin a term) unicity would not exhibit process. To speak of these determinations as qualities is thus to retain the traditional thesis of form as the principle of intelligibility.

However, as we now know, Hegel introduces a drastic modification into the classical doctrine of form. He attributes formal or qualitative status to nothing (*Nichts*) or nonbeing (*Nichtsein*). Nothing, understood actively as negativity, takes two forms of its own. As simple or first negation, it is equivalent to a determination or positive quality that "takes shape" or acquires its defining boundary from opposition to its logical complement. Hegel does not bring this out satisfactorily, but we should note that there are always two related instances of first negation, since every quality is defined by its complement, which stands as a positive determination and so a first negation with respect to its opposing determination. Second negation (= negation of the negation) is a canceling of the separateness of these two simple negations; their negativity is transformed into the positive affirmation of an identity within difference.

We are now prepared to grasp the transition from quality to quantity. There is no chronological transition but only a logical or transcendental one. This can be most simply described as follows. We have just thought the tripartite structure of being as (1) the identity of presence and absence or position and negation, as well as the process or shift back and forth from the one to the other; (2) the locatability or thereness of each moment in the process; and (3) its persistence simply as what it is, that is to say, as containing but not yet as having unfolded the various determinations by which it will be dialectically implicated with the other moments in the process. This dialectic is of the one and the many and thus of attraction and repulsion.

As one or unity, being for itself is the unity of *Sein* and *Dasein* (167). But the one, like everything else in Hegel's logic, is what it is only by relation to something else, as I noted above. We cannot think the one except as in relation to another (171). If there were a single one, it would have to be thought via the relation of opposition to itself, and so it would immediately double. That is to say, there are many "ones." Each one, as intelligible only through another, is thus negatively related to itself; it repels itself. But each one can be intelligible in opposition to another if and only if it is attracted to that other. Stated somewhat more simply: unity both asserts itself and dissolves itself into a multiplicity. Previously we studied these determinations as belonging to quality, that is, as producing the structure of becoming. Now we are going to look at the multiplicity of that structure, not at its structuredness. Differently stated, as an articulated whole, the structure is a unity. But as consisting of homogeneous elements, it is a multiplicity. The articulation of unity is quality; the multiplicity of the manifold of articulated unity is quantity.

This is what Hegel means by saying that the points of multiplicity are, as sheer manyness, indifferent to their qualitative determination, i.e., to being as quality. What is already implicit within the logically separate moment of subsistence, namely, within the unicity of the point or moment of existence, emerges through the instigation of negativity. The suspended structure of "something" and "another" emerges; the point collapses from momentary subsistence as a unity into a "double," i.e., itself and the other with respect to which alone it can be designated a subsisting point. The point, precisely as unique or one, is its own other. To conceive a point or one at all is necessarily to conceive it in terms of some other point or one.

Furthermore, since we are now disregarding structure *qua* structure and regarding instead only the unity or unicity, i.e., the abstract property of each unit as a unity, the result is the same everywhere. As expressions of unity, the points or moments of becoming are indifferent to their qualitative structure. They are "indifferent to being," not in the sense that they cease to exist or are separated from being, but in the sense that their being (and so their qualitative determination) is sheer manyness. This is how Hegel moves from the one-many and attraction-repulsion dialectic to quantity.

The three main divisions of the section on magnitude (quantity) are (1) quantity, (2) quantum, and (3) the quantitative relation. I have already given the main argument of the first division, but we will look at it again. We can represent the defining characteristic of quantity as manyness or multiplicity; a quantity is an *Anzahl* or "heap" of monads. A quantum is most succinctly defined as number or *Zahl*, a determinate amount of monads, of which in each case we can ask "how many monads?" or more generally still, "how much?" The ratio of the two gives us a heap measured by a number; i.e., it gives us both multiplicity and unity.

The following simple example may be of help here. What is the difference between questions of the form "how many thousands of dollars do you earn in a month?" and "how much money do you make?" In the first question, "dollar" names a unit of money; it is a type or form of money that serves as the standard by which to count individuals exhibiting that form. The term "money" is distinct from "length" or "weight," but it is too general to serve as a standard for "how many?" This is easily seen as follows. I can reply to the question "how many money?" by saying "five hundred," but the questioner will not know *how much* I make because the five hundred pieces of money could have varying monetary values. Similarly we can ask "how much do you weigh?" but not "how many do you weigh?" Here we have to be more precise: "how many pounds do you weigh?" and so on.

Similarly we can ask "how many monads?" and expect an intelligible answer only in those cases in which the quantity can be brought into one-to-one correspondence with an initial segment of the natural numbers. If this can't be done, we might ask "how much of a quantity is that?" where "quantity" is too general, just as "money" was in the previous example, to sustain a reply of "how many." So we reply to "how much?" with expressions like "a lot" or "not too many" or something of that sort. Even these responses are intelligible only by tacit reference to some accessible standard of measurement by which we decide the difference between "a lot," "a medium-sized amount," and "a little." If we generalize on these cases of quantity, and disregard all standards of measurement, then we have manyness in the sense of sheer quantity. Why don't we have "muchness"? I think it is because manyness implies that we can in principle count the constituent units or monads. In other words, we get to quantity by the dialectic of one and many; a quantity consists of many ones, whether we can in practice count them or not. I hope that this interpolation will cast some light on Hegel's obscure formulations.

Note that these considerations apply to number itself. We can have "many" numbers but also "too many to count" or so many that we have to invent ways of counting them, as with transfinite numbers. In other words, "quantum" as number is the limit of a quantity. But as such, it can apply to endless quantities; as number in general, it is indifferent to any limit in the sense that the number series increases endlessly. Each quantum is thus indifferent to itself as determination, goes out beyond itself, negates itself (192). And here is the next dialectical "jump." As endless progress, quantum sublates or cancels each "going beyond" from one limit to another; it cancels the indifference of one number to another's limit and thus reestablishes quality. Hegel means by this that the very ability of quanta to "go beyond" each limit itself depends upon the limit structure by which one number is said to be more than another. A countable "infinity" is articulated or rendered accessible to calculation by its formal structure, by the quality or qualities of which it is a "many." An uncountable infinity is itself rendered accessible to conceptual determination by its formal properties such as "point," "attraction," "repulsion," and so on, that is, by the properties through which we grasp it as infinite rather than finite. In contemporary language, uncountable infinities are defined by a rule, that is, by a qualitative specification of the nature of the infinity.

Hegel, of course, knew nothing of the transfinite. What he knew is that no quantity can be defined, or for that matter, counted, except through qualitative determinations. First we studied "muchness"; then we studied "manyness." Third, we study their ratio, i.e., the ratio of muchness and manyness or of quantity and quantum. Each quantized quantity is what it is in relation to its *Jenseits* (350); in plain English, there is a dialectical relation of "something" (the quantized quantity) and "other" (the as yet unquantized quantity). This is the structure of qualitative determination. So quantity has been reunited with quality in measure or ratio (193); we can no longer disregard the structure of multiplicity and concentrate upon sheer multiplicity.

In note 1, Hegel makes the important point that the qualitative identity of a thing remains the same through quantitative change; when the quality changes, the very being changes (193). We have now studied at considerable length Hegel's very brief introduction to quantity by reconsidering the transition from quality to quantity. The main argument of the chapter on quantity should now be accessible if not entirely lucid. It remains to buttress this statement of the main argument with the most important details.

Book 1, Section 2, Chapter 1: Quantity

The first chapter of the section on quantity covers eighteen pages of text (194–212), of which fifteen are given over to notes, the longest of which concerns the Kantian antinomies. This is enough to show that Hegel regarded the main discussion as unusually concise and difficult to follow. I have already expanded and paraphrased the main thread of the argument in my preliminary remarks. With respect to pure quantity, I will therefore add only that attraction is the moment of continuity in quantity (194); obviously enough, repulsion corresponds to the moment of distinction from the other through which each quantum of quantity is defined, and so to what Hegel calls in note 1 the being-outside-itself of space and the coming-outside-itself (*Aussersichkommen*) of time (196–98).

It should be carefully noted that quantity is a concept or logical determination and is not to be confused as such with spatiotemporal extension or matter. The dialectic of attraction and repulsion thus unfolds the conceptual continuum or categorial structure of extension: "quantity is the pure thought-determination; matter is its external existence" (*Existenz*, 197). One does not find the traditional dualism or separation of thought from extension in Hegel: "The determination of pure quantity belongs even to the I as it is an absolute coming-to-be-other, an endless distancing or all-sided repulsion [that moves] toward the negative freedom of being for itself" (197). In other words, the "stream of consciousness," as one might call it, is coextensive with but distinguishable from the spatiotemporal continuum; everything is thinkable or intelligible because there is an identity within difference of being and thinking. The difference is one between pure inwardness and exteriority (the union of consciousness with the concept of a spatiotemporal content).

The pure unity of each quantum of quantity is indistinguishable from any other; this "simple unity of discreteness and continuity" leads to the antinomy, treated by Kant, of the infinite divisibility of the extended world (198), which Hegel discusses in a long note. If we consider discreteness alone, we are led to the indivisible as the standard of endless divisibility (i.e., the discrete is a sequence of indivisible units); conversely, a one-sided reflection on continuity leads to infinite divisibility (since discreteness must itself, as continuous, be divisible into parts).

Hegel will resolve this antinomy and all others like it by emphasizing the inner relation between discreteness or unicity and continuity, which arises from the inner repulsion in the one of itself as its own other; i.e., the attempt to think a one is inevitably rooted in distinguishing it from something else. But the "something else" is just another unit or one. In this sense, we are thinking the same unicity in all cases. But we are also thinking the continuous production of units.

Hegel praises the four cosmological antinomies of Kant as the outstanding impetus that has led from previous metaphysics to his own dialectical logic, and in particular because they bring about the conviction of the nullity of the nondialectical categories of finitude with respect to [extended] content. He criticizes Kant for attempting to understand the antinomies solely with the use of finite categories (199). In other words, Kant has not attained to dialectical logic. From this standpoint, the dialectical treatment of motion by the Eleatics is superior, because it shows the inner identity of the being of Parmenides and the becoming of Heraclitus (207–8).

In general, Kant establishes the antinomies by separating continuity from composition. Our study of the structure of becoming has shown us that these two are the same (i.e., an identity within difference); continuity arises, not by the composition of discrete or stable and independent points, but through the pure transition from one point to another. This is the same as to say that Kant studies the relation between continuity and composition in the form of the actual extended world of space, time, matter, and so on, rather than "in the concept itself" (199). On the other hand, his resolution of the antinomies by way of the "so-called transcendental ideality of the world of perception" (200) renders the entire conflict subjective, that is to say, leads to the thesis that we conceive of bodies as appearances only. There is a sense in which Hegel would use the same words, but *Erscheinung* means for him the exteriorization of the concept itself within the bodies of space-time. Thus in conceiving of bodies as appearances, we also grasp the concept that appears in them; in other words, Hegel abolishes, or let us say makes accessible, the thing in itself.

I cite the following important passage that bears on the entire logic, not merely on the resolution of the antinomies: "Two determinations, insofar as they are opposed and inhere necessarily in one and the same concept, cannot be valid in their one-sidedness, each for itself, but . . . they have their truth only in their having been sublated [*in ihrem Aufgehobensein*], in the unity of their concept" (200). Note that the dialectical relation holds only between complementary determinations that inhere in a concept, i.e., in another determination. "Something" is dialectically related to "another" but not to "infinity" or "ground." Kant makes the mistake of isolating each determination from the other. Since they can never be united once they have been sundered and opposed in a relation of mutual exclusion, Kant has no recourse but to appeal to a shift in cognitive stance; cf. *First Critique*, B519ff and in particular B534: "Thus the antinomy of pure reason in its cosmological ideas vanishes when it is shown that it is merely dialectical, and that it is a conflict due to an illusion that arises from our applying to appearances that exist only in our representations, and therefore, so far as they form a series, not otherwise than in a successive regress, that idea of absolute totality which holds only as a condition of things in themselves." For Kant, dialectic is illusion; for Hegel, it is the statement of the self-contradictory nature of understanding, a contradiction that is not an impasse so long as we restate it as a totality. But this in turn depends entirely upon Hegel's new interpretation of negation as negativity.

We now have the fundamental idea of the two remaining subsections of chapter 1. Continuity is the moment of quantity that is first completed by discreteness; i.e., it is the self-composition of the continuum of pure quantity. On the other hand, as considered in itself, it is continuous magnitude (209–10). Correlatively, discrete magnitude, as distinguished from the continuity of quantity, is an existent something (*Dasein und Etwas*, 212).

In sum: to be is to be something or another, hence marked by quality but also, as an existing point or unit, to possess quantity. Quantity is the externalization of a point (cf. Nicholas of Cusa: space is the unfolding of a point), induced by the attempt to grasp it in its unicity; what externalizes constitutes a quantum or number even as it retains its qualitative identity. This brings us directly to chapter 2.

Book 1, Section 2, Chapter 2: Quantum

In chapter 1, we studied quantity as a moment of the continuum, and so as itself continuous. In chapter 2, we turn to quantum, "how much," as a moment of quantity. The complete form of quantum is number (*Zahl*, 212).

Whereas pure quantity is indifferent to its numerical limits or is the same throughout all of them, these limits are not indifferent to quantity but give it unicity by articulating it as a series of sets of units. In other words, number defines a unit that is itself an assemblage of units, an assemblage to which the question "how many?" can be correctly addressed. It follows that the unity and multiplicity of a set of units (a natural number) are both formal or qualitative properties, as distinct from the heap or endless reiteration of uncounted points. Unity is formally prior to multiplicity because we can grasp multiplicity only as a particular unity (a definite number of units).

Furthermore, as a unit, every number is the same as every other number. As a multiplicity of units, every number is again a unit, but this time a unit that differs in each case. So each number possesses both discreteness (it is distinct from every other number) and continuity (it has its unique and unalterable position within the number series) and is the fullest determination of quantity (213). Or in slightly different terms, "*Anzahl* and *Einheit* constitute the moments of *Zahl*" (214). This is very close to the Greek definition of *arithmos*. The unity of number is a unity of multiples, whereas the (uncounted) heap of multiples is a heap of units. Hegel calls this a contradiction and says that it is the quality of the quantum; in other words, to be a quantum (in the fullest case, a number) is to be a unity of multiples and a multiple of unities (215).

Why is this a contradiction? Let us first recall that Hegel is not here trying to give a mathematical definition of number. He does not seem to be concerned with properties like well ordering or transitivity; this is understandable because he is arriving at number from a logical genesis of the concept of becoming, not from modern set theory. A number has two properties, unity and multiplicity. As this particular number, say, 7, it is a unity; but as constituted by a heap of seven units, it is a multiplicity. It is thus the same number, e.g., 7, that is at once a unity and a multiplicity. There is not some distinct essence of 7 that owns two distinct properties corresponding to the predicates "unity" and "multiplicity." Otherwise stated, the properties in question are equally essential; one could not know them except by knowing the essence, yet in order to know the essence, one must know them. This is why Aristotle says that there is no predication with respect to essences. Hegel concludes that the "essence" of 7 (or number in general) is a contradiction, because the predicates "unity" and "multiplicity" exclude one another. Yet both belong necessarily to the essence of the number.

There follow two long notes, of which the main point is the nondialectical nature of number (215–30). Number is an externally defined heap of units that is intrinsically inert and that can be activated only by the modes of calculation that are applied to it (216). The various formal excitations of the determinations of the concept of number are logical, not mathematical. Thus. for example, in speaking of the Kantian treatment of arithmetic as synthetic a priori, Hegel holds to the contrary that the synthesis is a mere external combination or analytical synthesis that involves no concepts; in adding 7 and 5, we begin with 7 and proceed unit by unit to 12 in the same way as we extend a line. This is an analytical procedure in the sense that nothing emerges from the numbers that is not introduced from the outside (218–19). There is no conceptual growth, which is what Hegel means by a genuinely synthetic process. What Kant calls a synthetic a priori judgment, and what is according to Hegel one of Kant's greatest and imperishable accomplishments, is the concept of distinct elements that are inseparable, in other words, an identity within difference (221). For example, to say that A is the cause of B is to unite two separate things or processes by the inner dynamic of conceptual understanding. Exactly as Hume points out, the causal connection is not perceived or given; but neither does it arise by a mere juxtaposition or combination from outside by an act of intuition. Instead, A and B are (in Hegelian language) *aufgehoben* into a more comprehensive conceptual structure of cause and effect as defined by a rule.

The same point is reiterated in the second note. "Arithmetic is an analytical science because all connections and distinctions that arise in its object do not lie in that object itself but are applied to it entirely externally." Furthermore, the "object of arithmetic does not contain the concept and thus the task for conceptualizing thought, but is the opposite of that concept" (225). Number "is the pure thinking of the authentic externalization of thinking" (226). It does not and cannot represent concrete, living thoughts (227). It is therefore altogether erroneous to regard mathematical categories as capable of expressing philosophical concepts. The opposite is the case; the conceptual significance of mathematical categories must be expressed in philosophy. "Such consciousness of them is logic itself" (229–30). I note in passing Hegel's observation that an excessive emphasis on calculation in education vulgarizes the spirit of the young. Machines can calculate; this shows how unsatisfactory calculation is for the development of spirit (230).

Emile Meyerson has criticized Hegel for not seeing the dialectical nature of mathematics itself; from a different perspective, some philosophers of mathematics have discussed the dialectical consequences of the circularity of the foundations of set theory, and I have noted the dialectical relation between the finite and the infinite in the hierarchy of sets. For Hegel, all such considerations have nothing to do with the nature of number as the first mathematical category to emerge from the quantitative determination of being. Reflections on the foundations of mathematics would belong for him to philosophy, and more precisely to logic in his sense of the term. We gain a better light on Hegel's intentions when we understand him to be rejecting the identification between conceptual thinking or reason on the one hand and *ratio* on the other. This identification marks the Cartesian tradition and has its roots in Greek thought, for which *logos* or reasoning and *logismos* or calculating are branches of the same root. In Plato, every *logos* (and so too all *logismos*) is embedded in a myth: the dialogue form. Aristotle begins the attempt to repudiate the mythical context and to liberate *logos*. Thanks to the influence of thinkers like Galileo and Descartes, this "liberation" is transformed into the mathematicizing of *logos*; myth remains, however, in the form of rhetoric or ideology.

Summary and Transition

A quick reminder of the overall structure of the immediate argument will be useful. We are studying magnitude or quantity, the second of the three sections of book 1 of the *SL*, which is devoted to being. We began with quality, which is the defining mark of anything whatsoever. Otherwise put, the study of quality corresponds to the study of the unity of identity. This turns into the study of quantity, or the multiplicity of identity. The section on quantity has three chapters, quantity in its pure form, the quantum or number, and quantitative relation. The chapter on quantum is again divided into three parts: number, extensive and intensive quantum, and quantitative infinity. Magnitude is the external or analytical combination of units; it is itself divisible into quanta. There are two main kinds of quantum; the first is the number or heap of units. We are now ready to turn to the second type, namely, extensive and intensive magnitude.

In the first subsection on the quantum, we studied the categories of the continuous magnitude, namely, continuity and discreteness, which are determinations of quantity as such; that is to say, they express the extendedness of magnitude without attention to the boundaries or numbers taken as limits apart from the extended magnitude they articulate. It is essential to bear in mind that the continuum to which Hegel refers here is not primarily that of space-time but rather that of intelligibility. Stated a bit more fully, he is referring to the continuum of pure thinking, within which one determination after another of the thinkable entity is exhibited. Spatiotemporality is itself a condition for the possibility of an object of thought (note the Kantian resonance); the concept of spatiotemporality consists in the determinations that we are currently studying. The main property of space-time, considered as a condition for the appearance of entities, is that it is a continuum of moments of becoming. The continuum is one of the unfolding of positions that may be "filled" with a spatiotemporal slice of anything whatsoever. The various modalities of quantity arise from the acts by which we conceive of this continuum. For example, number is of interest to Hegel as a property by which we distinguish segments of the continuum and, thereby, objects from one another.

One could almost say that Hegel's treatment of quantity is a primitive species of point-set topology, but it is in no sense anything like set theory (despite the historical relation between the two branches of mathematics). He is trying to describe the properties of the points on the continuum of cognition and how these properties cooperate to allow objects to take shape. For example, extensive and intensive magnitudes are properties of numbers as boundaries (*Grenze*, 230–31). This distinction can be illustrated by considering the German words *Anzahl* and *Zahl*, which are normally translated into English as "number," although *Anzahl* can also mean "magnitude." The distinction is as follows: *Anzahl* refers explicitly to plurality or sheer quantity, that is, to a multitude of numerical units that are indifferent and external to one another, whereas *Zahl* expresses the numerical unity. The sheer externality of *Anzahl* disappears in the unity of number considered in itself as boundary, in Hegelian jargon as "reference of number to itself" (232). In other words, the seven monads that are unified into an identifiable number by the *Zahl* 7 are themselves indistinguishable from one another and also from the monads making up the other numbers, considering them too apart from their respective sums (*Zahlen*).

Hegel is here much closer to ancient Greek conceptions of number than to modern mathematics. Note, however, that he does not adopt the Platonist conception of pure number forms in order to explain how seven indeterminate monads are unified and determined as the number 7. So far as I can see, in discussing the various motions of attraction, repulsion, and so on, Hegel says nothing at all on this crucial issue. In short, number (e.g., 7) simply appears in Hegel's exposition as the unification of sheer multiplicity; it is not dialectically derived from anything else. On the contrary, Hegel says explicitly that numbers lack dialectical properties. In contemporary language, Hegel seems to hold that the natural numbers are intuitively obvious. But this is unsatisfactory for an evolutionary ontology of the intelligible structure of totality. If numbers are constituents in this intelligible structure, then they must be derived dialectically from some previous, simpler stage.

Extensive magnitude is the number or boundary considered as an *Anzahl* or heap of units; it looks backward, so to speak, toward continuity and discreteness, but from the standpoint of the number as boundary. Intensive magnitude is measured by degree rather than as a multitude of units; here the notion of ordering enters into the picture: "When one speaks of ten or twenty degrees, the quantum that has so many degrees is the tenth or twentieth degree, not the *Anzahl* and sum of those degrees, for then it would be extensive. It is rather only one, the tenth or twentieth degree" (232–33). Hegel says that the distinguishing mark of intensive magnitude is *Mehrheit*, "plurality" or, perhaps better, "moreness." One is reminded in this passage of Socrates's discussion of the more and the less in *Philebus*. "More" and "less" are difficult to define because they are not sums of monads or units; it would seem that intensity is a qualitative rather than a quantitative concept, but Hegel does not say this.

The same basic point is confirmed in the next section. "Extensive and intensive magnitude are thus one and the same determination of the quantum; they are distinguished only in that the former contains the *Anzahl* within itself and the latter contains it as external to itself" (235). This presumably means that the intensive magnitude is external to the quantum because it is not a heap of monads. In this case it is not plain why Hegel refers to them as an identity. In any event, this identity introduces the "qualitative something" (*qualitative Etwas*) or unity of number as both *Zahl* (unifying border) and *Anzahl* (multiple of units). The difference within number that arises via quantity is thus negated; since this initial difference is itself the relation between two determinations or simple negations (each is itself but not the other), the result is a double negation or the reinstitution of quality out of quantity. This last statement needs to be translated into more straightforward English, and this will lead to a serious criticism of dialectical logic.

A "qualitative something" is a thing possessing an identity of which we can ask: "what is it?" So far as we have studied it in this chapter, the identity is quantitative; that is, it occupies a stretch of the continuum of intelligibility or thinkability. And it is an identity by virtue of its unified (*Zahl*) extension (*Anzahl*). In other words, each identifiable thing, considered as a complex structure of unity and multiplicity, is both these mutually canceling determinations at once. But since these mutually exclusive properties are essential to the nature of number, the latter cancels or negates that mutual exclusion. Hegel refers to this as the negation of negation. He then claims that this restores quality out of quantity. It is at this claim that my criticism is directed. What precisely is the nature of the quality that ostensibly reappears at this stage? It can only be the aforementioned qualitative something. But this was just shown to be a quantitative structure, or in other words what Aristotle calls the "noetic *hulē*" or intelligible matter that is a metaphorical reference to the sense in which any formal structure consists of elements that are external to one another. This is the intellectual equivalent to the spatial extension of any object of sense perception. We cannot conceive unities in the sense of points; the conception of points as positions or elements of location is not that of a qualitative something, but instead that of the conceptual extension of that something.

In short, the reciprocal negation of unity and multiplicity does not produce a higher, more comprehensive formal structure. Instead, it provides us with an analysis of the conceptual extension of anything whatsoever. What keeps the contradictory properties (unity and multiplicity) from dissolving is the look or form of something or another, that is, a "this thing here of such and such a kind," in the familiar Aristotelian expression. As I noted previously, Hegel cannot explain the emergence of qualitative form out of the dialectic of quantity. To do so is as impossible as it would be to attempt to derive being from nothing. Otherwise stated, he cannot produce number out of unity and multiplicity; on the contrary, we arrive at unity and multiplicity only through the analysis of number. If this is right, then it is impossible to exhibit the quantitative substratum of a qualitative form with no reference to already present qualities. In order to escape this difficulty, Hegel must grant that expressions like unity and multiplicity are already qualitative, not quantitative. In this case, we can speak of a unity of some manifold as the substratum of intelligible form that corresponds to spatiotemporal extension in the case of sense perception.

Two brief notes are appended, which we do not need to consider. There follows an extremely obscure passage that I will paraphrase as follows. We can conceive the unity of a qualitative something, apart from thinking or perceiving the particular thing that it is. The concept of unity, however, itself consists of identity (what the unity is) and difference (the multiple parts or elements that are unified and upon which the intelligibility of the unity rests). Since Hegel is here disregarding the qualitative or actual identity of any object and restricting himself to the quantitative structure common to all, he represents the real object (which is not at issue here) by the concept of quantum or number. As we have just seen, Hegel claims that the reciprocal negation of unity and multiplicity transforms quantity into quality. I have challenged this assertion and claimed in effect that Hegel presupposes the presence of a particular qualitatively defined object, from which he arrives by abstraction at its noetic *hulē*, that is, the part of the continuum of intelligibility over which it extends. But what he needs to do is to produce quality from quantity, that is, show how the inner dialectic of quantity reinstitutes quality. Only thus will he be able to claim that the full possible object consisting of both quality and quantity has emerged from the earlier stages of the dialectic.

So much for my criticism of this portion of the argument. What Hegel asserts is that each quantum is an identity of identity and difference; it is both the sameness of quantity and quality and their distinctness from one another. Let me refer to this structure as a second-level identity (an appropriate terminology since it alludes to the structure as the product of double negation). The second-level identity is in fact primary with respect to the procedure of identification, since it exhibits the comprehensive structure of the quantum. It is therefore the case that the primary identity, through which we identify quanta, is indifference (namely, to either species of the genus quantum). Hegel calls this indifference "self-negation." To negate oneself is to become something other, of such a kind, however, as not to obliterate the self-negated item but rather to preserve it as referring to its opposite within a higher level of categorial structure. A quantum is the answer to the question "how much?" We can also call it a finite amount. But the opposite of "finite amount" is "infinite amount." Each finite or definite quantum is defined by reference to an infinite amount. However, the converse also holds true; the infinite amount is itself limited or defined by the opposed finite amount and so itself becomes finite or a quantum. This fluctuation of the infinite and the finite, with its attendant lack of stability, results in what Hegel calls the bad infinity.

I want to emphasize that the last paragraph contains my analysis of, not Hegel's explicit argument in, the part of subsection B entitled "The Alteration of the Quantum" (239–40). What Hegel actually says is that the qualitative side of a quantum is in absolute continuity with its externality or "being otherwise" and can therefore exceed each determination of magnitude. In other words, the form of the flower remains in "place" despite the growth of the flower. Not only is this possible; it is in fact necessary. Why? Recourse to examples like that of a growing plant will not help us here. Hegel is talking about continuous alteration of magnitude as a fundamental characteristic of the continuum of becoming. This continuum is generated by the impossibility of the literally understood assertion that being is one. There cannot be, in other words, just one "one"; in order to be itself, it must be opposed to and so defined by something else, as is actually exhibited by the very assertion "being is one," in which being is distinguished from (the) one.

One thing leads to another, as we can somewhat facetiously put it. Quantity "quantizes," as a Heideggerian might say, and not without justification. The quantizing process is rendered intelligible by qualitative determination, the first manifestation of which is quantity itself, in the form of a quantum, i.e., a "number" in the dual sense of *Zahl* and *Anzahl*. In the study of a still relatively pure or abstract becoming, there are no qualitative determinations like that of my example, the flower, or for that matter of anything other than being and its categories (determinateness, existence, being for itself, and the various modifications of quantity that we have studied thus far). The process of self-multiplication of a hypothetically initial singularity is just the generation of extensive magnitude, which has no intrinsic capacity to terminate or to bend back upon itself into a circle. The intensive magnitude is number or quantity, whose "form" or qualitative determinateness is just the dialectical moments of quantity itself. We have numbers, whether cardinals or ordinals, but we have no actual forms like flower or dog, no qualitative determinations like color or any of the so-called real predicates. Being, nothing, and so on are themselves determinations and so qualities, but qualities that are indistinguishable from quantity.

We can now supplement Hegel's statement with my previous paraphrase or interpretation. The self-multiplication of one (*Eins*) is the reiteration of *Zahl* as *Anzahl*, i.e., of unity as multiplicity. And that is what it means to say that "a quantum is with respect to its quality in absolute continuity with its externality, with its being otherwise" (240) and that "the one is infinite or negation that refers itself to itself, and therefore the repulsion of itself from itself" (240). In other words, no number can be conceived except through its position in the number continuum. Hence each number not only points outside itself but is in fact defined by that which is at once inside and outside its concept. There is a continuous transformation of the quantum as a limit into the negation of limit, and hence from internality into externality, or in short, the generation of infinite extension.

Book 1, Section 2, Chapter 2, Subsection C: Quantitative infinity

In his discussion of quantity thus far, Hegel has established the following main points:

1. Continuity and discreteness are interdependent in quantity.
2. Finite quanta are continuous within a range of grades or degrees of magnitude, all of which collectively are equivalent to being as quantity.
3. That which lies beyond (*Jenseits*) every quantum falls within quantity.
4. The nature of quanta as nondeterminate externality is its quality, *Fürsichsein*; that is to say, quanta have no external determinations other than them-

selves; these arise from the inner dialectic of the quantum, which is equivalent to externalization.

To this we may now add:

5. "Das Quantum ist ein Sollen" (241); i.e., it is determined to be for itself as another; to exceed its own boundary or extend itself in this way is its intrinsic nature.

This leads to the following difference between quantitative and qualitative determination. Quantitative determination is such that each quantum contains its own other (each is defined by way of its predecessor and successor and, in fact, by the whole number-series); to be a quantum *qua Anzahl* is to negate oneself and thus to come to be other than oneself, simply stated, to depend upon an endless series of numbers for one's own definite nature, which for that reason is indefinite. This is the previously studied dialectic of finitude and infinitude. But qualitative determination refers to its other as that which is essentially another being than itself. "It is not posited so as to contain within itself its negation, its other" (242). Magnitude on the other hand exists precisely by negating or sublating itself; it defines itself through another that is just the same as itself, namely, extension. But a quality defines itself through another that is qualitatively (and not quantitatively) different from it.

The dialectic of quantity, taken in itself, produces the bad infinity of endless progress. In fact, there is no genuine progress or development here but only a repetition of positing, sublating (i.e., of the finite into the infinite magnitude), and repositing (since sublation simply leads to an extended magnitude), and so on forever (244). In the first note to part c of subsection C, Hegel points out that Kant and Fichte both fall victim to the bad infinite. Kant places the overcoming of the infinite extension of the *Jenseits* of the natural world in a return to the pure I. It is, however, impossible to master nature through the pure will, so long as they are opposed to one another. Morality is thus permanently inaccessible. Similarly in Fichte there is an unending "progress" toward the inaccessible overcoming of the split between the I and the not-I (245–51). Fichte reduces the opposition between the I and the not-I to one of quantitative determinations of absolute substance; their endless sequence of positings can therefore never be terminated, as we have already shown. In general, we require a complete opposition of qualitative determination in order to produce a genuine unification at a higher level of formal structure. Quantitative opposition produces only a continuum of quanta.

In note 2, Hegel returns to the Kantian antinomies concerning the temporality of the world. His main point here is that Kant begs the question in the manner in which he formulates the antinomies. I will skip this discussion, since it simply repeats the previous dialectic of quantity.

In the next section, Hegel calls our attention to the fact that since each quantum exceeds itself by turning into another quantum, there is no genuine "beyond" to quantity, no formal opposite; but instead, quantity is defined as *Sollen*, i.e., as endless striving to complete itself (as is obvious in Fichte, for example). The actual "beyond" or unachieved termination to the endless self-externalizing of quantity is quality (256–59).

There follow three very long notes on mathematical infinity, with special attention to the infinitesimal in calculus. We cannot study them in detail since they are based upon the state of the calculus as it was conceived in Hegel's time; the problem that engages him was presumably eliminated by the new notation of Cauchy and Richard Dedekind, among others. I will simply state the main point of Hegel's argument. Hegel wishes to distinguish between the right and the wrong way in which to understand infinity within mathematics. The infinity to which he refers is that of the real numbers. He proceeds by attempting to establish that infinite magnitudes are not quantities but qualities, namely, relations or proportions.

Here is an example of Hegel's argumentation. We can distinguish between a qualitative and a quantitative proportion, e.g., $2/7$ (qualitative) and $0.28574\ldots$ (quantitative). In the latter expression, the qualitative infinity is replaced by a quantitative row that could be continued forever. In $2/7$, the 2 and the 7 could be replaced by an infinity of other numbers without altering the proportion, which is a quality, not a quantity. In the decimal, however, there is no defining quality external to the quantity, which would serve to define it. There is always something missing from the decimal expression that is essential to its meaning and is represented by dots (. . .) that are themselves a sign of the need to continue the expression, which thus continues itself, as it were, forever and is never bounded by a quality a/b. Hegel concludes that the decimal is infinite in what it lacks; the proportion is the genuinely mathematical or qualitative infinity (264–71).

Before turning to a second example, that of the infinitesimal, let us recall that for Hegel, a quality is defined via its difference from something other than and external to itself. Quantity, on the other hand, has itself as its own other; simply stated, there is no qualitative difference between one quantum and another, except for their *Zahl* or number. But number is itself a quantum, i.e., the answer to the question "how much?," and so is essentially quantitative. In a ratio or proportion, it is not the particular numbers being compared that define the nature but the formal structure of comparison itself; thus the numbers can be replaced by letters (a/b). Stated somewhat pleonastically, one proportion is qualitatively other than all others. This is the basis for Hegel's analysis of the infinitesimal. The infinitely decreasing magnitude Δ is not a real number (how could it be written?) but a quality, or that which is what it is in opposition to or as different from something other than itself, some other quality that can be sublated together with its opposed relatum in a higher, more complex formal structure. In Hegel's analysis, Δ exists only in a proportional comparison of magnitudes Δ. This proportion expresses limits of proportions. In calculus, dx, dy have the definite meaning of a qualitative determination of the quantitative, of a proportional moment as such. That is to say, there are not just negative magnitudes or infinitely diminishing quantities (275–301).

We can restate the main point of Hegel's discussion of mathematical infinity as follows. Quantity is unintelligible in itself, except with respect to its own formal structure, which is dialectical. The moments constituting the development of the continuum of quanta may be understood as the first qualitative determination of pure being (or nothing). Other than this, however, quantity is empty of formal content. Mathematics is itself form or quality, not content; on this point, Hegel is a "formalist," although obviously not in the same sense as that term is used today.

APPENDIX

In the following remarks, I shall present the nub of the issue that vexes Hegel with respect to the use of infinitesimals in calculus. Consider a diagram of a continuous curve (I) located in the x-y axis, and let y = distance and x = time. The curve then represents the velocity of a body. We calculate the average velocity of a body between times x_1 and x_2 by noting the distance covered between the co-ordinate points y_1 and y_2. So

$$\frac{y_2 - y_1}{x_2 - x_1}$$

gives us the answer.

Now the question arises: can we calculate the velocity of a body at a given point in time, i.e., the instantaneous velocity? This is an intrinsically ambiguous question, because it would seem that at a given instant, the body has no velocity at all, whereas on the other hand, continuous velocity runs through the curve without a break, so that the body is moving through all the points on the curve (each of which, incidentally, presumably corresponds to a real number). Here is how Leibniz attempted to solve the paradox of instantaneous velocity. The particular interpretation I am about to give should be called the "Bos-Tragesser interpretation"; it is a modification of Henk J. M. Bos's account by Robert Tragesser of Connecticut College.

I remind you first that the constant velocity of a body is a straight line represented by the equation $y = cx + b$, where c is a constant. Let the instantaneous velocity be the velocity at a point at which all external forces on the moving body are removed. Now consider the two lines A and B as arbitrary representations of the situation at every point on the curve. Line A is the tangent to the curve at some point p. Line B is the straight line of constant velocity that the body assumes if all external forces stop acting on it at that point. We want to show that the two lines are the same. In order to convince ourselves of this, we take two points on the curve that are arbitrarily close to each other, considered with respect to the change in y (distance) relative to the change in x (time). Now we want to show that the two lines have the same slope, namely, the constant c in the equation $y = cx + b$. The slope is the rise over the run, or $\Delta y / \Delta x$.

Now consider a small piece of curve I, labeled II. Let $x - 1$ and $x - 2$ be the two points taken to be arbitrarily close to one another on the curve. Then Δx is the difference between the two times and Δy is the difference between the two covered distances. It is obvious that the smaller Δx is (the shorter the difference between the two points in time), the more the curve II will look like a straight line. In other words, it will look more and more like the tangent at $x - 1$. Furthermore, the smaller the ratio $\Delta y/\Delta x$ becomes, the more it becomes, not an average velocity, but an actual velocity at the moment designated by the point, i.e., an instantaneous velocity. So we have reduced the problem of computing instantaneous velocity to the task of computing the tangent at any point on the curve.

The problem here can be represented geometrically by looking at the following situation. Let $s(t)$ be the distance covered at time t, whereas $s(t + h)$ is the total distance covered at time $t + h$. What we want to do is to make h as small as possible. In other words, we want to reduce the difference between times $x - 2$ and $x - 1$, as noted in the previous version of curve II. As h tends toward 0, the chord or secant between $x - 2$ and $x - 1$ $(= t + h$ and $t)$ will move closer and closer to the tangent line at $x - 1$ $(= t)$. So the triangle of which the base is $(t + h) - t$ and the altitude is $s(t + h) - s(t)$ will come closer and closer to area zero. The problem is that it never actually disappears in our calculation. In other words, the problem concerns the nature of h.

This problem does not arise when $y = cx + b$, i.e., in the case of a straight line representing constant velocity. This is shown by the following calculation:

$y = cx + b$

So $f(x) = cx + b$ and this equals y or the distance-point at which we take the tangent $y' = c(x + h)$ or the distance-point that tends toward y as h tends toward zero.

The times are represented by x and x'. Recall that we are calculating $\Delta y / \Delta x$, the ratio of the changes in y and x.

$$\Delta y / \Delta x = \frac{f(x+h) - f(x)}{\Delta x},$$

which equals $\dfrac{(c(x+h) + b - (cx+b)}{(x+h) - x}$

$$= \frac{cx + ch + b - cx - b}{h}$$

$$= \frac{ch}{h} \text{ or } c.$$

So h drops out algebraically. Note also that it makes no difference which two points we take on the straight line. By the law of similar triangles, $\Delta y / \Delta x$ will always be the same.

Quantitative Relation

Like the previous treatment of quantity, Hegel's treatment of quantitative relation is unusually difficult to render into more accessible language. It will be helpful to understand at the outset that for Hegel, quantity is itself a logical determination of being and in that sense counts as a quality. If this were not so, we could not grasp quantity at all; to grasp is to understand discursively, or in other words to be able to answer the question "who am I?" In order to understand Hegel's treatment of substance, it is necessary first to examine the earlier work of Locke and Fichte, to which I now turn.

Locke and Fichte

The main points in this section are based upon an earlier discussion in my book on Hegel.[1] In order to make the present work self-contained, it seemed best to take up the topic again. Locke exhibits the modern empiricist consequences of the Platonic-Aristotelian tradition with respect to the problem of essence or substance, as well as the root of the problem that Kant and his idealist successors attempt to resolve.

First, a terminological point. Locke speaks of "substance" rather than "essence," but the latter term brings out more accurately his inner sense. "Substance" means literally "that which stands beneath" and so supports or sustains. It is derived via Latin from the Greek *hupokeimenon*, which itself has two senses or is employed in two different contexts. In the first sense, *hupokeimenon* refers to the material substrate, as that which "stands beneath" and so supports the form. But in the second sense, it refers to the form as the essential nature of a thing, or in other words as the underlying foundation of the essential properties. So in English a "substance" is either the material out of which something is made or else the ground of predication. In this latter sense, we speak of a substance and its attributes. Unless the term "attributes" is already taken to designate essential properties as distinct from "accidents," we have to make a further distinction within the attributes between those that are essential and those that are not. If "attributes" is taken to refer to all properties, essential or otherwise, then the reference of the term "substance" is, to say the least, obscure. The temptation is then very great to identify substance with matter. Whether or not one succumbs to this temptation, the problem of identifying the essentiality of essential attributes is the same in principle as that of identifying the formal bond through which the substance may be said to "own" its attributes.

This is, briefly stated, exactly the problem in Locke. It arises from the failure of Socrates and his students to explain the meaning of the question with which they initiate traditional rationalism: "what is X?" Let me emphasize that the problem is not to answer the question but rather to analyze it. Of course it is frequently the case that we cannot identify elements in our experience. But more frequently we can, and these cases constitute collectively the paradigm for proceeding in the cases in which we are unsuccessful. In all cases, however, successful or unsuccessful, it is one thing to say what X is, for example, a cow or a horse, and something else again to explain why X is a cow or a horse rather than something else, or for that matter nothing.

One finds an alternative within the Socratic school to the general analysis of being and intelligibility as form, and of form as essence and attributes, in the conception of being as *dunamis* or power. This definition is introduced by the Eleatic Stranger in the Platonic dialogue *Sophist* (247d8–e4), and it is somehow implicit in Aristotle's conception of form as *energeia*, a word that is difficult to translate into English but that carries the notion of activity or work. In Aristotle's doctrine of form, however, *dunamis* refers not to power but to potentiality, of which the *energeia* is the actuality or "work" by which the thing is exhibited in its integrity, identity, and independence. Interestingly enough, the Eleatic Stranger's definition, which is never developed by him, is at least in part closer to the modern notion, according to which we know the essence of a thing by its external effects rather than by its inner nature. The Stranger says only that to be is to act or to suffer (i.e., to undergo action); he does not analyze how we know this, but his words are at least compatible with the interpretation that we know this by modifications in our experience. It is a decisive step forward (or backward) to say in addition that the modifications are all that we know, or in other words that the underlying agents or patients are invisible and that we know them only by what they do. Thus for example Locke: we have no idea of what substance is but "only a confused, obscure one of what it does" (I. 230).[2] The deeds are then emancipated: essence is transformed initially into attributes, but then the attributes are reduced to the status of accidents. Locke is the crucial figure in this process of emancipation.

Hence the close connection in modern philosophy between the notion of substance as "something, I know not what" and the related notions of power and will (I. 230. According to Locke, "man's power, and its ways of operation" are "much the same in the material and the i0ntellectual world" (I. 390ff., 397, 400). Man makes complex from simple ideas; hence he makes species and genera. The real essences of simple ideas cannot be defined (I. 214; cf. I. 44, 145). Instead, the constitution of the intelligible world by thought arises from an uneasiness or a desire for absent pleasure, which in turn leads us to exercise our will, and hence our powers, in the consideration of some idea or chain of ideas that will satisfy, or contribute to the satisfaction of, our desire for pleasure (II. 6, 16ff., 23ff., 32).

In short, the intelligible world is not an independent formal structure that we discover by perception and conceptual analysis; it is an artifact of desire, will, and the exercise of power. It would be an overstatement to say that substance is for Locke the will to power, but the ingredients for the emergence of that much later Nietzschean doctrine are already visible. The world is a representation of the human will's work to satisfy desire. And this satisfaction depends for its motivation upon the unintelligibility of substance, but for its validation upon the irrelevance of substance to the satisfaction of desire. From the irrelevance of substances, it is a short step to the denial of their existence. Unfortunately, this leaves us in a world of accidents, with the consequent trivialization of the significance of the satisfaction of desire.

This is of course not how Locke sees the picture. For Locke, the invisibility of substance means that human beings are free to the extent that they possess the power to modify their sensations in such a way as to act in accord with their preferences or volitions. Closely connected to this is Locke's assertion that the ideas of relations can be more perfect and distinct than those of substances (the relata, I. 430). Relations are consequences of human desire; that is, they are man-made and subject to the will or to technical power as directed by the will. This view plays its part in the prehistory of the development of modern logic, and it anticipates the later doctrine of logical conventionalism. More immediately, what Locke interprets positively as the condition of human power is from a Hegelian standpoint *Schein* or the illusion of freedom, which in fact reduces the properties of things to contingency. Locke anticipates the idealist doctrine (explicitly stated by Fichte) that freedom is prior to in the sense of higher than being.[3]

Kant retains the Lockean notion of freedom in his doctrine of the spontaneity of reason but attempts to distinguish freedom from chance by making the products of spontaneity the rules of cognitive thinking. In Fichte, these rules, categories, concepts, and ideals are redefined as products of the self-limitation of the free activity of the absolute ego. This amounts to the separation of freedom from rational structure and the subordination of the latter to the former. In Fichte's version of idealism, there is no being in itself but only activity (*Handlung*). Being is the negation of the freedom of the ego or a derivative concept to be understood in opposition to freedom. Even though it is a necessary consequence of the activity of the absolute ego, being, or the intelligible world of reflection, must be negated or transcended in order for man to return to the original freedom of absolute spontaneity. Reflection is the attempt to understand oneself in the objective products of subjective work, that is to say, in the objects as separated from but reflected or represented within human thought, which is itself a limitation on and concealment of the absolute ego. It follows that reflection is alienation.

We should note that the situation in Fichte is a more complicated version of the Lockean analysis; the crucial difference is that Fichte fills up the empty space left by Locke's unknowable substance with the absolute ego. For all practical purposes, there are no substances in Locke but only accidents and the human cluster of cognitive powers, rooted in will or desire. Freedom is therefore not a problem in Locke, that is, not one that he explicitly notices. It is instead a given of the initial situation. Alienation, to the extent that it is visible in Locke, appears disguised as the insatiable nature of human desire, which makes life into continuous labor, or a "joyless quest for joy."[4] Hence the emphasis in modern philosophy on "satisfaction" as opposed to personal happiness, an emphasis that is common, for example, to Hegel and Nietzsche. In Fichte, satisfaction depends not upon avoidance of alienation or work, which is coeval with finite existence, but instead upon our capacity to reconcile work with the principle of human activity. In other words, work, or the projection of objects, and the consequent reinforcement of the subject-object distinction, is simultaneously the satisfaction of human striving and the concealment of the goal of that striving. The dilemma of Fichte's idealism, never resolved by him through all the versions of the *Doctrine of Science*, is how to arrive at the absolute through procedures that separate us from it.

To return to Locke, he refers to sensation and reflection as the two sources of ideas. This is the modern empiricist revision of the classical distinction between sense perception on the one hand and the two intellectual powers of formal perception and discursive thinking on the other. Locke in other words eliminates intellectual perception; the complex truths of mathematics are made by the reflective intellect together with the rules of morality from a straightforward inspection of ideas whose ultimate source is sensation (I. 47–48, 144–45, 213–14). There are no innate ideas but only innate appetites (I. 69). Reflection, or the turning inward away from sensation to our own thoughts, is thus rooted in appetite. This is the basis for the separation of the subject from the object as the foundation for the production of objects (I. 122–23). It is also the anticipation of Fichte's doctrine of *Streben*.

According to Locke, in the absence of intellectual perception, the intellect must produce its own formal structure or scientific truth. It does so by reflection, "that notice which the mind takes of its own operations, and the manner of them, by reason whereof there come to be ideas of these operations in the understanding" (I. 124). Subjectivity, or consciousness of the self, arises from reflection; it is impossible to perceive or to think without perceiving that we do so (I. 316, 327, 331, 345; the echo of Descartes is obvious). The turn inward toward the self is rooted not so much in a primordial separation of the subject from the object as in the contention that the complex subject and object are both *products* of the power of the self. This follows from the absence of an original absolute, or from what I would call primordial solipsistic dualism, that is to say, a self that is entirely immersed within its sensations but that possesses the power to modify them in accord with its appetites. Locke knows that the subject-object distinction is produced by the self through reflection, but he lacks the concept of absolute reflection or the dialectical understanding of the power of the self.

For Locke, the complex subject and object are both constructed from simple ideas. The self knows itself by its operations or work, but neither as substance nor as subject. The self is visible only in the vague sense of the power of an invisible substance. For this reason its works are not known directly through the self (as must be the case if the split between the subject and the object is to be overcome); there is no dialectic of identity within difference and so no possibility of ever arriving at absolute spirit. In fact, by turning inward, and thereby constructing the subject, the self turns away from its essential self. No wonder that human life is for Locke perpetual uneasiness or dissatisfaction (I. 332–33, 344, 448ff.). It is the eternal striving for pleasure, or alienation from oneself, caused by the very appetites that drive the human being to work, and so to construct the intelligible world (note the similarities between this strand of Locke's doctrine and Hegel's *Phenomenology of Spirit*). Mankind is thus doomed to dissatisfaction or infinite striving thanks to the fall into reflection, and so into being rather than freedom.

Idealism transforms the labors of reflection into obedience to the categorical imperative, or the command that one ought to strive for the infinite. In Fichte, Locke's dissatisfaction is overcome through the comprehension of human life as an expression of the absolute spontaneity of the activity that actualizes in the opposition of subject and object. The activity of the human ego exemplifies the spontaneous activity of the absolute or divine ego. Just as in Locke, however, this exemplification is not accessible to conceptual intelligence. On the other hand, Fichte's revision of Locke is the immediate precondition for Hegel's own analysis of reflection. I turn now to Fichte's *Wissenschaftslehre* (*Doctrine of Science* of 1794, hereafter cited as WL) for the details.

Fichte on Reflection

In the first three sections of the WL of 1794, Fichte presents his interpretation of the three laws of thought: identity, difference, and the ground, which is his version of the law of noncontradiction. These are the principles of reflection. Like Hegel, Fichte is obsessed with the need to arrive at a presuppositionless beginning, in order to transform philosophy into a deductive or systematic science. He begins his search for the "first, strictly unconditioned principle" with a distinction between thinking as activity and the principle as an expression of that activity (I. 11).[5] This is a Kantian distinction that is based upon the premise that thinking synthesizes its objects or is present within every principle of thought as the synthesis of the antithetical subject and predicate. In his analysis of the synthetic unity of apperception, Kant insisted that the activity of thinking is accessible only as what we may call the antithetical articulation of a synthesis. Whereas Fichte accepts this restriction with respect to analytical thinking, his purpose is to lead us beyond the antithetical structure to an intuition of synthetic or productive activity itself.

Each of the principles of reflective thinking is already an instance of the subject-object distinction, which, we recall, is the primordial structure of the activity by which the absolute ego thinks or poses itself by limitation from a non-ego that is nevertheless within the ego (since there is no "place" outside the absolute in which it might reside). The various determinations of the world as object of the subject of consciousness are all modifications of the non-ego, produced by the successive efforts of the ego to overcome the limitations that are the necessary result of its own thinking. In other words, the absolute ego cannot simply think itself from the outset, thereby bypassing the various self-limitations that, speaking colloquially, constitute the creation of the world. This would be like God thinking himself not as a creator but as pure potency. God is not God unless he creates the world; so too the absolute ego is not absolute except by activity; it is, so to speak, *energeia*, not *dunamis*. But *energeia* is the formation process, and this is what it is by the production of forms, i.e., of limitations on the absolute. This is the general background to the difficult analyses that we are about to study.

We begin with the principle of identity, $A = A$. Fichte says that the certitude of this principle is formal or hypothetical rather than existential, by which he means that it does not depend upon the value or identity, that is, upon the actual being, of A. What it actually asserts is that "if A, then A." This distinction is reminiscent of the distinction drawn by the Eleatic Stranger in the *Sophist* between sameness and being. I call attention to the fact that in stating the principle of identity, it is necessary to double the variable A and so to elicit an act of reflection on our part, or a bending-back from A onto itself. We can conceal this moment of reflection by saying "A is the same as itself," but "itself" is just a synonym for the second A. If we were merely to say "A," our expostulation would be a meaningless noise, to be granted whatever meaning one wishes. It would be an interesting question to ask whether "$A = A$" is a result of analysis or synthesis. Do we divide A or double it? Suffice it to say here that the principle of identity mirrors the subject-object structure of the absolute ego, which is the inaccessible unity (the "A" within the two symbols A) that underlies and manifests itself as a duality. According to Fichte, every attempt to grasp the underlying unity of this principle must proceed by concealing it in the division or multiplication of what we are seeking. As we have seen, Hegel will analyze this principle as already pregnant with the principle of difference, and so as containing negativity, or more precisely the labor of negativity, through whose work the identity within difference of all three principles of reflection will emerge.

It is also crucial to notice that in Plato's *Sophist*, the Eleatic Stranger is unable to speak about being without mentioning sameness, or about sameness without mentioning being. This is the famous problem, still perplexing to Wittgenstein and Russell, of the intelligibility of formal atoms. The question is whether those things of which we cannot speak except by weaving them together in discourse can exist independently from one another apart from discourse. The fundamental point of Hegel's dialectical logic is to demonstrate that they cannot. Certainly the prima facie evidence is on Hegel's side, since experience constitutes a seamless web. Otherwise stated, no one has ever observed an atom of sameness independent of atoms of being, nor could they, since an atom of sameness, in order to *be* that atom, must also be an atom of being, and so on with the other primitive forms. Hegel does not deny that we can distinguish one property from another in a complex formal structure; the very names "being" and "sameness" would have no sense if this were not possible. His point is that we cannot explain what we mean by these names except through the instrumentality of dialectical logic, which is not simply a type of discourse but the discourse that exhibits the internal relations of formal elements themselves. Our ability to name separately "being" and "sameness," very far from resting upon some obscure metaphysical doctrine, is very much a part of commonsense rationalism as grounded in the Socratic axiom that to be is to be this thing here of such and such a kind, and not something else. This commonsense rationalism gives rise to the metaphysics or ontology of Western rationalism, which is from a Hegelian standpoint simply a hardening of vulgar commonsense understanding.

To come back now to Fichte, it is impossible to communicate the principle of identity (or sameness) by saying merely "A" or even "A is." The first expression says nothing at all, whereas the second is an assertion of being, not of identity. On the Fichtean analysis, whereas we are saying "A = A," we mean "if A then A." One could object to Fichte that the "if . . . then" schema has nothing to do with the identity of the two terms but instead links them in an inference pattern. The schema, of which the present instance is a tautology, does not comment on the tautology as such, namely, the sameness of the two *As*, but rather asserts that if the first *A* holds, then the second *A* follows. It is only when we notice that the two letters are the same that we shift from the "if . . . then" syntax to the identity equation. The equation, as the assertion of a principle, is rooted in an intuition of the sameness of the two *As*.

This is not to deny that the principle of identity is indeed one of the three fundamental laws of discursive thought. But as such a law it holds for everything, including nonexistent or imaginary beings. To be is to be identical, or in the Platonic idiom, the same as itself, and this holds also for "to be imaginable" or "to be mentionable," where what we mention does not in fact exist. This is a law of possible being, not a statement of identity as distinct from being. In other words, we arrive at the same result as we found in the consideration of Plato. Identity and being cannot be separated. There are no nonidentical beings (and in the case of beings that are changing their identities, the statement holds with respect to each thinkable or mentionable moment in the change).

However this may be, Fichte himself takes the "if . . . then" schema as a third item in addition to the two *A*s, an item designated by the letter *X* that serves as the identifying ground of, or the necessary connection between, the first two. Granting that we have already noticed the identity of the two terms, I think we can grant to Fichte that the assertion of identity in a formula is a kind of inference. What else are we to call the attribution of the identity predicate to two terms, or alternatively, applying to them jointly the logical operation of identity? This is something more than intuiting sameness; it is the transformation of our intuition into a logical principle. What is for the contemporary logician syntax, however, is for Fichte ontology. His *X* is the license to say "*A* is *A*," a license that is issued by none other than the reflecting ego, i.e., the absolute ego as both concealed through and accessible in the guise of the finite ego of the individual thinker. "For the ego is that which judges in the above proposition, and, indeed, it judges in accord with *X* as a law" (I. 13). In this context I remind the reader that the law is an exhibition of its own activity as the ground of all thinking. The doubling of the *A* corresponds to the distinction between the ego and the non-ego; the identity sign or its licensing *X* corresponds to the sameness of the ego and the non-ego (in place of which Hegel would say, "to the identity within difference of the ego and the non-ego").

The establishment of the ego/non-ego (or subject-object) structure as the basis of discursive thinking reflects the fact that thinking is intrinsically dual. The activity of thinking is distinguishable from the content of thought. Even where the two are the same and thinking is thinking itself, it must appear to itself as the object of its own subject. In order to penetrate the doubling structure of thinking and to seize the underlying unity of the ego, we should have to transcend discursive thought altogether or achieve an intellectual intuition (different from the previously mentioned type that apprehends the sameness of two forms) in which the dividing structure of conceptual understanding is surpassed. To employ a metaphor from one of Fichte's later versions of the *WL*, intuition is a seeing that sees itself, but directly or immediately and not reflexively. The principles or laws of thought are obviously laws of discursive thought, and so exhibit the doubling structure of thinking, but not of intellectual intuition, which has no laws and is free spontaneity. Otherwise stated, in the act of issuing a license *X* to itself to think *A* = *A* in the sense of "if *A* then *A*," the ego is articulating the implications of the primordial act by which it poses the objective world as a mirror image of the very act of positing.

The objective world is thus thinkable because its structure is that of discursive thought. In this sense, the problem is not too little intelligibility but too much, since each act of discursive thinking perpetuates the subject-object structure that conceals the primordial ground of the unity of thinking and being. The grasping of one determination is the producing of another. Since Hegel essentially agrees with this, his task is to overcome the endlessness of production without attempting the impossible task of rising above it to pure intellectual intuition. His solution is to bend reflection into a circle, not by limiting the number of determinations, but by shifting his attention from the determinations as novelties to the dialectical structure through which they are produced. The sum total of the categories is then the circular structure of the identity within difference of the subject and the object, or in Fichtean terms of the ego and the non-ego. It is entirely insufficient to keep chanting "identity within difference," which serves merely as an abbreviation of the content of the SL, or the actual description of the working of the formation process of the absolute.

To come back to Fichte, the ego is initially accessible not through intellectual intuition but by way of the aforementioned doubling, which we can represent as $I = I$. Let us refer to this as the licensing agent that issues all permissions for the establishment of subsequent cognitive structure, such as the aforementioned X ("if . . . then"). Intrinsic to the authority to license is the property of intellectual agency; in other words, the "ego" is not itself a form but a self-conscious agent of formation. Fichte is obviously within the Cartesian tradition, for which self-consciousness or ego-accompanied thinking is more immediate than the beings or objects of which we think. And the same is true of Kant, whose teaching Fichte believes himself to be perfecting, not surpassing or replacing. In this tradition it is self-evident that thinking exhibits the structure of a thinker and the content of thought, but also that the thinker is an I, not some anonymous cogitator. For the idealists, this is true even of the absolute. In the case of Hegel, the issue is ambiguous and the cause of much dispute; witness the split between left- and right-Hegelians. For the time being we can postpone our own response, noting only that left-Hegelianism requires the demonstration that Hegel was an atheist.

Since "$A = A$" is a license issued by the ego, it is not a proposition but a *judgment*; its structure exhibits the "primordial division" (the literal meaning of *urteilen*) of the field of cognition. In general, the logic of Kant and his immediate successors is one of judgments, not propositions, as is still visible in what Frege calls "the assertion sign" and is brought out even more explicitly in L. E. J. Brouwer's intuitionistic logic (although the ego symbol is suppressed by his students and followers). To repeat, judgment originates in the spontaneous activity of the self-identification of the ego as *I* = *I*. The ego identifies itself as a being that thinks; Fichte revises the Cartesian *cogito ergo sum* into *sum qua cogitans*. No doubt in the correct Cartesian spirit, despite the reversal of order of the key terms, Fichte wishes to avoid even the appearance of a deduction from thinking to being. Since "being" is posed by thinking, and the original position is self-position, I am in the act of posing myself (I. 16). "What is not for itself is not an ego." Perhaps more self-evident than the associated assumption concerning the egological nature of all thinking is Fichte's claim that the ego exists (= is) only to the extent that it is self-conscious (I. 17). The ego does not acquire self-consciousness, nor can one ever abstract from self-consciousness (I. 17).

Fichte turns next to the law of difference: "not-*A* is not equal to *A*." Let me underline the fact that this is a second law independent of, not deduced from, the law of identity. Both, however, are reached by a process that begins with a "fact of the empirical consciousness" and proceeds by what we may call an analysis of analysis to the original or "genetic" situation (and I note parenthetically that in the *WL* of 1804, "genetic" occurs regularly to refer to the constituting activity of the absolute ego). Fichte accepts the traditional (and still dominant) view that one cannot "deduce" difference from identity because "not" (or "negation") is the name of a primitive operation that is absent from the entirely positive "*A* = *A*." As Fichte puts it, not-*A* stands to *A* as opposition to position. All one can say is that, just as "position" appears in "op-position," so the empty form "*A*" appears in *A* and not-*A*. But the "op-" prefix no more appears in "position" than does the "not" in *A*. This is the unpassable border between the two; for otherwise opposition would be indistinguishable from position (II. 21–22); we would retreat from "*A* = *A*" to "*A*" and so to silence.

I emphasize this simple point because the step from Fichte to Hegel turns upon its denial. For Hegel, Fichte's ego, and so his logic, is discontinuous. The accusation leveled by Fichte against Kant, that there is no deduction of the categories, is applied by Hegel to Fichte's laws of thought. If position and negation are genuinely separate, then how can we construct a unified conceptual account of the world? In somewhat different terms, Fichte's understanding of "not" is, for all the peculiarity of his terminology, no different from that of the orthodox logician. It is a static syntactic operation that applies only to finite, independent forms but is incapable of capturing the excitation of negativity as a living force, as the formation process of life or spirit. It can therefore not overcome the dualism of being and thinking.

The two principles of identity and difference are thus separate possibilities of the activity of the ego; neither is grounded through the other (II. 22). On the other hand, as I have already shown, the content ("A") of the principle of difference is dependent upon identity, and so upon the underlying $I = I$ of the thinking ego, which is itself not a principle but what Fichte will later call the "image" (*Bild*) of the unity of the absolute ego. To repeat, $I = I$ is already a product of reflection: "I am originally neither the reflecting nor the reflected, and neither is defined by the other, but *I am both in their unification*, which unification I cannot indeed think, precisely because in thinking, I separate the reflected and the reflecting."[6]

It follows from all this that the unity of identity and difference is not formal but inheres in the activity of the ego. Unfortunately this mode of inherence is invisible to discursive thought, for which identity and difference are separated from one another exactly as the subject is separated from, or is "not," the object. This allows us to say that difference is dependent upon identity in the sense that one cannot distinguish elements that lack an identifying coherence of their own. Again, the "A" in the two laws is the same. But the *difference*, as symbolized by the "not," is not the same. Negation is a distinct power of thought. I repeat: identity and difference are given simultaneously in the self-positing of the ego through limitation, or as in opposition to the non-ego. But we cannot understand or analyze further the "given simultaneously," because to analyze it is to divide it in accord with the subject-object distinction. The ego presents us with identity and difference in one act, but *as already divided*.

The problem of the self-generating obstacle of reflection is visible in Fichte's contention that just as "$A = A$" is grounded in "$I = I$," so too is "not-A is not equal to A" grounded in "not-I does not equal I." This last formula, in other words, cannot be deduced from "$I = I$." It is thus separate from the initial form of reflection by a further act of reflection. But where then are we to find the origin of "not-I does not equal I"? Everything that is posited must be posited within the ego, *including the non-ego*. In other words, as absolute, the ego must be distinguished from the nonabsolute; otherwise it will have no identity or be simple indeterminateness or nothing. But the act of distinguishing the absolute from the nonabsolute can take place only within the absolute; there is no other place in which it can occur. The ego therefore posits itself by way of delimitation from the non-ego that is paradoxically both within and outside it. The "outside" is already contained within the "inside." Once more we see that the initial self-positing of the absolute ego can be grasped conceptually or expressed discursively only in the language of reflection. The ego is accordingly both itself and not itself, or more precisely, itself and its not-self. The step from Fichte to Hegel consists in grasping the dialectical implications of this ostensible contradiction.

In the teaching of Fichte, however, a proper dialectic is missing; we see a discontinuous continuity of the laws of identity and difference. Fichte offers us an explanation of why reflection or analytical thinking is grounded in the identity structure of self-consciousness, but the ground gives rise to dualism or discontinuity, because these are the only terms in which it is itself accessible to cognition. Furthermore, Fichte is from a Hegelian standpoint a *subjective* idealist because there is no genuine positing of the world as external to the ego. He is a dualist because the second principle or law cannot be deduced from the first. One could reply on Fichte's behalf that his intention is quite different from Hegel's. Fichte is attempting not to explain actuality (*Wirklichkeit*) but rather to deconstruct it in the attempt to achieve the absolute. He studies the sequence of positings or self-limitations of the ego in order to surpass them, not in order to preserve them as the coordinate to the subject pole within the absolute. For Hegel, in other words, the created or posited world is itself part of the absolute. Not so for Fichte: the absolute is the absolute ego, and it is concealed by the world, not exhibited within it, except as in an image.

In any case, Fichte claims that once we possess the first two principles, we are able to deduce a third: the principle of the ground (III. 26). One would expect here the principle of noncontradiction. But Fichte wishes to give an interpretation of that law that enables him to unite identity and difference. This cannot be done so long as we interpret the law of noncontradiction in the usual way. As we shall see, Fichte is required to shift from more or less traditional logical notation in the case of the first two laws to a metaphysical or ontological formulation of the third law; more precisely, he shifts from logical laws to a statement about the nature of the absolute ego.

In traditional notation, the law of noncontradiction reads "S is not both p and not-p." Suppose we were to represent the third principle as "A is not both A and not-A." This is equivalent to saying that A is either A or not-A (but not both). If A is A, then of course we assert the first principle. But the second alternative, "A is not-A," is not the second principle. Nor is it the law of noncontradiction; on the contrary, it is a contradiction. The actual path to noncontradiction proceeds something like this. A is A because it consists of a set P of essential properties $(p_1, p_2, \ldots, p_n)$ that are the same in every instance of A. We cannot negate any p in P without changing the identity of A to not-A. In other words, the move from identity and difference on the one hand to contradiction on the other is by way of an analysis of the inner structure of *A* and not-*A*. This analysis was not necessary in order to formulate the first two principles. But it would have become necessary if anyone had asked for further clarification of what we mean by identity and difference.

It is, I think, a simple logical mistake for Hegel to say that the negative form of identity is the equivalent of the law of noncontradiction. We will see later, when we return to Hegel's text, whether this carries any fatal consequences for his own dialectical logic. For the moment, the more important point is how to reformulate the law of noncontradiction so that it can be the ground of identity and difference. I note first a feature of Fichte's terminology. Normally we would say that the ground serves as a kind of axiom from which to deduce the laws or principles of which it is the ground. But Fichte does not start with his third law or *Satz vom Grunde*, as it would be called in the German tradition, and deduce from it identity and difference. Instead, he starts with the latter and derives the ground from them. His reason is undoubtedly that identity and difference are much simpler than the law of the ground. Unfortunately, by starting as he does, Fichte gives independent status to position and negation. These two cannot be synthesized in some third law expressing a logical operation that does not presuppose them as separate. So we are not going to get a logical law of thought at all, but something quite different.

In fact, the ensuing argument, which is extremely complicated and which I can only summarize here, is not so much a deduction as a statement of the infinite task facing intellectual activity in its effort to close the gap between subject and object (III. 26). Here is my summary. The ego initially poses itself as ego by opposing itself to the non-ego, which is, however, posed as within itself (since the ego is, so to speak, "everywhere"). In other words, the original determination "non-ego" originates not through the need to indicate an object external to the subject but as an indispensable part of establishing the identity of the ego. All subsequent objects are determinations or delimitations of the original non-ego. In the original moment, the ego is itself, thanks to a process in which it is also not itself. Note that this seems to violate the traditional law of noncontradiction. In all subsequent moments, the posited objects are, I repeat, refinements of the non-ego. The original or absolute ego thus expresses its own nature by posing itself in the divided form of ego and non-ego. Furthermore, each act of position subsequent to the original results in an alteration of both the ego and the non-ego (III. 30).

In other words, the pure spontaneous activity of the self-conscious synthetic unity of apperception (Fichte's revision of Kant) takes the original self-concealing form of an image, in which the original and concealed unity appears as a reciprocally determining or modifying ego and non-ego, the borders between which vary from one act of position to another. Thinking is visible as *judging* (= dividing). The absolute ego presents itself in an infinite series of images, each of which divides the appearance into the two finite poles of ego and non-ego. Fichte calls this the principle or law of the ground: *opposites are unified within the absolute ego.* This is a reinterpretation of the traditional law of noncontradiction. Fichte's tacit premise is as follows: In thinking the law of noncontradiction, we violate it. And we must think it in order to understand it. But the violation is not a cancellation of the opposed terms; it is instead their preservation. Here *in nuce* is Hegel's doctrine of *Aufhebung* or the identity of identity and nonidentity, i.e., identity within difference.

From a Hegelian standpoint, there are two defects in the Fichtean formulation. First: affirmation and negation remain distinct as ontological categories. Second: the unintelligibility or inaccessibility of the absolute ego as the unity underlying the original position of ego and non-ego leaves hanging in the void the ostensibly dialectical assertion of the law of noncontradiction as a contradiction, and so as an *Aufhebung* of identity and difference. It possesses significance only as a hypothesis, exactly like Kant's transcendental ego; it is a *Sollen* or infinite project for analytic thinking. So long as we remain within analytic thinking, each step in our ostensible demonstration of original unity will be accomplished only by the posing of a new subject-object opposition.

We have to take one more step in our analysis of Fichte's treatment of reflection. According to the principles of identity and difference, the non-ego is both posed within and opposed to the ego. The conjoint assertion of these two principles is thus equivalent to their cancellation. Yet the ego remains; we must now find a principle that expresses the preservation of the identity of self-consciousness despite its internal contradiction. This principle will be something like the assertion prohibiting contradiction, which, precisely as such a prohibition, must itself assert and so preserve that contradiction. In other words, the intelligibility of the law of noncontradiction is rooted in our ability to think, i.e., to understand conceptually, the contradiction against which we legislate. The situation here is thus similar to the one signaled by the Eleatic Stranger in Plato's *Sophist.* Parmenides's prohibition against thinking or mentioning the altogether not requires us to think or mention the altogether not.

Fichte's principle, however, as I indicated previously, is not analogous to those of identity and difference; it cannot be stated as a logical law. Instead, it describes the activity, represented by Fichte as X, that unifies the oppositions in question. Previously, X stood for a license, issued by the ego to itself, to say "$A = A$" in the sense of "if A, then A." The license, in other words, was the law of identity. But in the present context, X is not a law; it is the original activity of the absolute ego that produces the relation of the finite ego and non-ego (III. 26–27). More precisely, the absolute ego spontaneously poses itself by an original activity of limitation, designated as Y, that results in the ego/non-ego distinction. This distinction or limit within Y, that is, the boundary between the reciprocally determined ego and non-ego, is X (III. 28). The reason for the distinction between Y and X is to establish the production of the structure of reflective analysis (X) by an activity (Y) that is itself inaccessible to reflection. X is thus an analytic image of Y.

Since X is the act by which I, an empirical agent, pose myself as a finite, reflecting ego, and since X is itself actualized by the Y activity, which acts as it were covertly, having assumed the persona of X, it turns out that the act by which I pose myself is the same as the activity by which the absolute ego poses me. I am myself an image of the absolute, which, in posing me, serves as primordial ground for the ontologically derivative laws of identity and difference (III. 29–30). This is the penultimate stage of a line of development from Aristotle via neo-Platonism to Spinoza, Kant, and Fichte. The law of noncontradiction combines with the doctrine of thought thinking itself to provide the structure of self-consciousness. In this structure, I think myself as both opposed to and the same as my object. The law of noncontradiction is the assertion of my identity with myself as opposed to what I am not. But the law of noncontradiction can be formulated only through its violation by the act in which I think it. What remains is the unification of identity and difference from within, in a way that exhibits the conceptual structure of that unity rather than masking it by the finite structure of reflection that is a consequence of primordial activity. That step is taken by Hegel, to whom we will return in the next chapter.

NINE

Transition to Book Two

Monism and Dualism

I suggested that book 1 of the *SL* can be understood as the analysis of Greek ontology prior to Plato. Parmenides is the first to develop a doctrine of being as one or unity. As we can put it, each being, despite its different configuration of properties, is the same as every other being with respect to its unity. Since being is the same everywhere, we cannot distinguish between any two (or more) beings. But this formulation cannot be satisfactory. If we disregard every property of an entity other than its unity, then all talk, and so all ontology, is talk, not about being but about the things that are. So talk about unity reduces to silence.

Heraclitus introduces multiplicity into the discussion, as well as continuous change, which latter opens a space for the dialectical transformation of one ontological property into another. But this flow is ungrounded. From a Hegelian standpoint, it constitutes a bad infinity or endless chatter. And endless chatter is self-canceling; hence it turns into silence.

Plato presents this problem in a slightly different way. To say "being is one" is to say two things, namely, "being" and "one." I add that the distinction between the two itself rests in a third term, "is," whether in the sense of identity or the copula. Furthermore, being must be the same as itself, whereas it is other than identity. This line of thinking, which we need not pursue, leads Plato to the doctrine of the "greatest genera," of which being is just one. Plato anticipates Hegel by showing that being, taken entirely apart from same, other, and so on, is nothing. But he does not take the step that is crucial to Hegelian dialectic. He makes his genera static. They do not evolve from one another but are all at the same level of ontological givenness. Therefore one cannot say anything about being in itself but must always invoke the other genera in order to define it. So the characterization of being is once more silence. Nothing as the opposite to being is the total cancellation or absence of anything whatsoever. It has no properties, and so can be referred to only by attaching the other genera to it as properties or predicates. But then to speak of being—or to try to speak of being—is actually to speak of something else. So there is not only no ontology, but when we do succeed in saying something about the greatest genera, the result is chatter.

In sum, the basic philosophical problem is that of the one and the many. To be is to be both one and many. But without an adequate analysis of the relation between the two, our attempt to understand them turns into silence on the one hand and chatter on the other. Plato's solution is to hypostatize the one-over-many, i.e., to turn it into a form—the Platonic idea. But this is merely to pose the problem as the solution. What unites the one and the many? In such a unification, does not manyness erase unity? Or else, if each unit of a manifold is *qua* unit the same as all the others, then all such units are one and the same, and we are left with a nonunified many, i.e., the heritage of Heraclitus. Finally, Plato offers no solution to the problem of thinking or (as he calls it) subjectivity. Since the intellect does not participate in the ontological elements or greatest genera, the domain of formal structure is lifeless and inert. Thinking is disconnected from the content of thought, and so there can be no dialectic movement that overcomes the various aporiai that I have just summarized. Aristotle takes the next step by saying that the forms or essences "actualize" in the intellect, but he retains the Platonist notion of the static nature of form. One could almost say that the balance of the history of philosophy is the attempt to bring Aristotle's forms to life, and in so doing to show that the logical determinations by which we think are the same as those by which the structure of the absolute constitutes itself. Subjectivity is the truth of objectivity.

I want next to express this general Hegelian interpretation of the history of philosophy with respect to the traditional doctrine of essence and attributes. The essence, we can say, is the owner of its properties. To attribute a property to an essence is to say that the essence "owns" that property (and the word for essence, *ousia*, meant originally "property" of material "substance"). Now in the case of human beings, we can say that a man owns his house if he has a document of ownership, a mortgage that has no encumbrances. No one would confuse the man for the house or the house for the man. But we need proof that the man owns the house. Stated with maximum simplicity, the proof is the mortgage or title of ownership. And this in turn is a social document that, if we analyze its own properties, brings into play all aspects of the society or civilization within which the owner and house in question reside,

Think of an Aristotelian instance of essence and property in this way. The essence owns the property if the fact of ownership has been defined with sufficient rigor that we can use it to prove the fact of ownership. Aristotle defines this fact as follows. The owner (substance, subject) is identified by the structure of essential properties that constitute it. But the essential properties are determined by our grasp of the essence. In our example, the essential property of the owner-property connection is the mortgage. Now a mortgage is obviously something artificial or conventional, whereas we are looking for the natural foundation of the essence-attribute relation. That is, we make up the rules of property ownership in a way that is convenient for us, and so for our society. In nominalist philosophies, this is exactly what we do with rules of set membership or the relation of "belongs to." We define this relation to suit our convenience.

Why do we need essences in the first place? There are none in standard predicative logic, although they appear at least as pure forms in modal logic, which works with necessity and contingency. If there are no essences, then everything is contingent. This leads us back to Heracliteanism. If we can define essences to suit our convenience, then philosophy is transformed into poetry. If we claim to intuit essences, then speech, and so conceptual thinking, is reduced to silence. Put as simply as possible, Hegel solves this problem by making essence the appearance of appearances. But we cannot leave it at this. Hegel says in effect that at the level of dialectical logic there is just one essence, namely, all of appearance. Essence is not hidden and it is not simply defined. Essence appears. And this is not Heracliteanism, because essence appears completely as the circular structure of the concept or absolute.

This point is indicated by the titles of books 1 and 2. Book 1 is called *Being* and book 2 is called *Essence*. Bearing in mind that Hegel's presentation is evolutionary, we note that there is no essence in book 1, whereas being is present in book 2. Book 1 contains the articulation of being into quality and quantity; measure is a ratio of quality and quantity. Quality corresponds historically to the being of Parmenides, which is itself indistinguishable from nothing. Quantity corresponds to the becoming of Heraclitus. Quality taken apart from quantity is abstract empty unity; quantity taken apart from quality is equally abstract and empty or formless, but now multiplicity, not unity. This sheer multiplicity corresponds to the *Anzahl* or "heap" of the continuum understood as comprehensive change. Such

change has no forms, not even the form of number. Analogously, quality as abstract unity is formless. A thing can first be perceived, identified,
and so conceived only if it is a relation or ratio of quality and quantity.
The relation of abstract quality and abstract quantity yields the numbers of
Pythagoras or the atoms of Democritus. But these are unstable; the units
or monads in each of these cases, which may be called the ancestors of
idealism and materialism respectively, cannot be distinguished from one
another.

There are two cases to be distinguished here. We are dealing either with
ideal units or with pure points on the logical continuum. The units constituting the Pythagorean ideal number "7" (to take an example) are either
homogeneous or heterogeneous. If they are homogeneous, there is no difference between the units constituting "7" and those constituting "8." The
relation between the pure form "7" or "8" and the homogeneous units is
then arbitrary or external. If the units are heterogeneous or (as I shall call
them) number-specific; that is, if the units in the ideal "7" belong to it and
it alone, and could not be constituents in any other ideal number, then
there are two forms at play here. The form "7" has to be distinguished from
the form of the units constituting "7" since a unit is not seven units; in
other words, the number "7" cannot be the form of the individual units
composing it. But what could this form be? The idea of an ideal number
composed of ideal units that belong to the individual number and it alone
is circular. Seven-units are identified by inherence in "7" and "7" is identified by the seven-units of which it is constituted. This is an abstract version
of the puzzle of essence and accidents or substance and attributes.

Now we turn to the case of points on the logical continuum. Each of
these points is a unit, indistinguishable from every other unit. But in order
to count these units, i.e., to transform a heap into a number of units, we
must first discern them. Yet this is impossible, since one logical point, like
a mathematical point, is indistinguishable from all the rest. We do not in
fact distinguish units, or unities, by counting them, but we know what to
count because we have first apprehended the entity in question as a unit, or
in other words as a unity of some multiplicity.

Bear in mind here that Hegel is discussing the way in which we attempt
to conceive of pure quantity, or rather, he is trying to show us that it is
impossible to conceive of pure quantity. And the attribution of numbers
to sets of points results in artifacts, that is to say, in definitions of members
of a more complex conceptual structure. For example, what does it mean
to say that the cardinality of the natural numbers is Aleph-Null, or in other
words that there are Aleph-Null elements in the set of natural numbers? It

certainly does not mean that we can count out the natural numbers one by one until we arrive at the final number and say, "this is the Aleph-Nullth member of the set." We define the members of the set by an axiomatic definition of what it is to be a natural number. The axiomatization of arithmetic is a complex formal structure, and it is to this that we appeal when we identify any member of the set of natural numbers. Each member of this set is said to possess certain properties, to be related to the other members in various ways, and so on. But no member is discernible in itself; we identify it via its set-theoretical equivalent, e.g., for the number "0" we employ the null set, or the set containing no members.

Even the counting numbers of ordinary experience are members of a complex formal structure that is not the same as the continuum of logical or mathematical points. In order to conceptualize quantity, it has to be formalized, that is to say, be replaced by a formal artifact that possesses qualitative properties. But this is already true in the Pythagorean ideal mathematics of antiquity. The eidetic units in the ideal number "7" are indistinguishable from those in the ideal number "5," which is to say that the collocation of seven units in one case and five in the other is purely arbitrary. It is not the nature of the units (the ancestors of modern points) that we conceive but the numbers we use to count them; and these are conceivable via the concept of counting numbers, i.e., of arithmetic or *logismos*. Why numbers should apply to units or points cannot be inferred from an apprehension of the units or points, which are in themselves invisible or inconceivable as unities. Since the unity of every unit is the same, how could we distinguish one unit from another, or see the boundary between one unit and another? This is part of the problem arising from the fact that between any two points, we can always insert, or imagine ourselves to be inserting, another point.

In sum, nothing binds the form (the determinate number or answer to the question "how many?") to the matter or content; the units thus as it were overcome the boundaries of their numbers and dissolve into heaps. As to atomism, the constant flux of the atoms makes all collocations arbitrary; in other words, no answer to the question "how much?" is permanent, and what is an atomic structure at one time is a dissolving heap at another. The atoms are thus points on a continuum that is dissolving into the abstract negativity of the void.

In both cases, quality is primordial, first as being and then as number. But quality is constantly dissolving into quantity, as we saw above; between any two points, there is always another point. This is to say that being is dissolving into becoming through the inner negative activity of nothing (namely, the "nothing" that stands between any two points). From one standpoint, the multiplicity of points is collapsing into the Eleatic One; from another standpoint, it is continuously dividing itself into the ceaseless flow of becoming. The attempt to articulate the continuum into intelligible units is impossible on the basis of ratios of numbers alone. The next step is to develop a sense of form as the paradigm by which the relation of quality and quantity is preserved. In traditional language, we require a doctrine of essence that binds together the unity of quality and the multiplicity of quantity. As to numerical structure, it cannot be Pythagorean, despite Plato's attempt to incorporate the latter doctrine in his hypothesis of the pure ideas. Numbers are not conceptual or discursively meaningful; every formula has to be explained in conceptual language. But the same flaw holds good of the "pictorial" forms that serve as essences in Plato and Aristotle, to mention no other defects of this hypothesis.

In sum: we do not abolish the continuum of becoming as defined through unity and multiplicity, or in other words becoming as an uninterrupted sequence of points, each of which serves as an ontological place for the emergence of an existing thing (*Dasein*) that has spatiotemporal coordinates and thus can be distinguished from other existing things to that extent. What we must do is to render stable the natures of the existing things by attributing to them a thinkable structure. The unity of the thing must consist in a ratio of attributes; it must be a unity of multiplicity. But these dimensions cannot be simply numerical; the qualitative determination of things cannot be simply quantitative. There must be superimposed onto the quantitative structure a new structure of attributes that correspond to the predicates of discursive speech. The attributes are the defining features of the unities that own them, but that reciprocally provide an identity to these attributes, and accordingly a conceptually accessible nature.

The unity is identified through its multiplicity of properties (not through the number of its quanta). Unities that possess identities are the owners of those properties; they "stand beneath" the multiplicity as its unity in each case. But as we are about to see, there is an insoluble problem here. Which properties, which elements in the multiplicity of a given unity, serve to constitute its identity and so to render its unity intelligible? Must we not first grasp the identity of the unity before we can say which properties constitute it? But how are we to grasp the identity of the unity except via the properties that constitute it? This is the fundamental aporia of the Socratic thinkers, i.e., Plato and Aristotle, so far as we are concerned. But it also underlies the history of modern philosophy, that is, the history of the attempt to find the inner unity of substance in the *ego cogitans* or the activity of thinking. Plato and Aristotle attempt to grasp the inner substance (called "essence" traditionally; the Greek word is *ousia*) as if it were intrinsic to the existing thing independent of the activity of thinking. The modern philosophers prior to Kant attempt to construct the essence through thought, but through a thought that is still external to the object constructed. Kant revolutionizes philosophy by making thought the structure of the existing thing, but in so doing, he does not escape subjectivism or the detachment of thinking from the independent substance of classical philosophy, now called "the thing in itself." Schelling and Fichte attempt to overcome Kantian dualism through a dialectic of thinking as ontological constitution, but they remain within a Kantian framework. Only Hegel (or so he claims) solves the problem by making the subject as well as the object of thinking the two dimensions of the triple structure of spirit, i.e., the identity of identity and difference (and note that the first or comprehensive identity is not the same as the second identity that it incorporates).

I remind the reader that the discussion of Greek ontology in book 1 (which is continued in book 2) is in no sense a return to the pre-Kantian standpoint of the Greeks themselves. The objective logic, as Hegel calls the first two books of the *SL*, is a presentation of the incoherent conceptual structure of classical and modern (i.e., pre-Hegelian) ontology. But one can present this conceptual incoherence only *conceptually*. One could go so far as to say that the central inadequacy of Greek ontology is for Hegel its failure to understand the role of the subject or alternatively to define thinking in terms of being, rather than the reverse. Note that this is true even of Parmenides, who says, or who is taken by Hegel to say, that being and thinking are the same. The sameness here is equivalent to the abstract emptiness of being, i.e., of nothing. This abstract emptiness is retained in the Platonic-Aristotelian doctrine of pure *noēsis*, i.e., the pure contemplation of separate forms by a structureless and inactive or nonproductive intelligence (Plato) or the apprehension in empty intelligence of forms that are actualized therein by a mysterious, entirely separate deity, the connection of which to the human intelligence is never explained (Aristotle).

Allow me now to restate the central theoretical flaw of pre-Socratic philosophy as follows. Quality and quantity can be neither distinguished nor unified. Quantity is itself a kind of quality, but what kind? It is the quality of qualitatively indifferent exteriorization. Accordingly, it can itself be identified, i.e., thought conceptually, only if it is unified by a determinate form. The obvious candidate is number. But which number? I mean by this: how do we determine how many units there are in a given quantity? The only way in which this is possible is through a standard other than that of sheer multiplicity, a standard that delimits the points on the continuum that we are to count and provides us with a number to assign to the quantity we have just selected, thanks to that standard. So the counting of points on the continuum is a purely arbitrary process; more precisely, it is impossible, since points are mathematical entities, not existing things. Number thus dissolves into the continuum; i.e., unity dissolves into multiplicity, which itself dissolves into chaos.

One last observation is in order. The shift from book 1 to book 2 is a shift from being to essence. The dialectic of abstract unity and multiplicity is continuously collapsing into unity and expanding into multiplicity. In that dialectic, nothing endures to preserve the two dimensions of unity and multiplicity in their reciprocal integrity. It is not wrong, but it is not sufficient, to say that "essence" (*Wesen*) is Hegel's name for the third dimension that holds together unity and multiplicity. The problem remains that essence has an inner tendency to dissolve itself into unity on the one hand and multiplicity on the other. As distinct from its accidents or attributes, essence is unity; as the structure or manner of coherence of its accidents or attributes, essence is multiplicity. If one cannot describe conceptually or discursively the nature of essence, one has simply doubled the already existing and unstable structure of unity and multiplicity studied in book 1.

To look at the same problem from another angle, quality is determinateness and one such quality is quantity, or the determination of indeterminateness. Let us say simply that the primary level of intelligible structure is that of quality and quantity or unity and multiplicity. Since that structure is unstable or self-contradictory, we seem to require a new level of structure, or some third category in addition to quality and quantity or being and becoming, to act as the agent of stability. The third element must be richer or more concrete than pure being and becoming. It must contain being and becoming, but in addition to these, it must contain something more. This something more must be capable of furnishing us with an answer to the question "what is it?" in the case of each individual existent (*Dasein*). If the third element is something additional to being and becoming, then it must contain within itself the explanation of how it holds these two dimensions together as an existing entity. If this holding together is not to be external or arbitrary, it must grow out of the inner excitation of being and becoming themselves. Essence in other words must be the process of the dialectic or inner self-contradiction of being and becoming, but now understood as inverting or preserving itself at a higher level of inner complexity, a complexity that also stabilizes instead of collapsing or dissolving its elements.

Hegel hints at this on page 3,[1] when he says that *Wesen*, which means literally "what was," is "past—but timelessly past—being." In the first instance, this means that essence is the accumulation—i.e., the preservation at a higher level of complexity—of the entire development of being described in book 1. The "past" in question is timeless because it refers to the logical order in which we think what is in actuality always fully or completely present.

But what precisely is the preservation at a higher level of complexity of the evolution of being? Since that evolution terminates in collapse, i.e., in implosion or dissolution, we can say that the result of book 1 is chaos or nihilism. The attempt to grasp conceptually the structure of the cosmos on the basis of pre-Socratic ontology leads directly to the conclusion that life is illusion, i.e., that the appearance of cosmic order is an "appearance" in the pejorative sense of the term, namely, the pure "shining" (*Schein*) that lacks stability or substance. It is precisely this collapse or descent into nihilism that forces us to begin our search for essence, to find the ground of conceptual structure we must first "go to ground." Hegel obviously takes it for granted that the genuine philosopher is not immobilized by going to ground or being plunged into illusion. In addition, he tacitly assumes that the philosopher is sober enough not to attempt to transcend illusion in some imaginary and so equally illusory heaven or fanciful metaphysical construction. We start from illusion because it is to illusion that we have been brought by metaphysics or philosophy in its initial manifestation. Restated: it is realistic to begin with the reality of illusion; reality is precisely illusion and nothing else. We have to find order within chaos; that is, we must derive order from the chaotic motions of illusion itself.

We are thus continuing to study negative activity in book 2, and so we retrace all of the dialectical stages in book 1, but at a deeper level. Negativity is for us both a problem and the solution to the problem. The problem is that negativity dissolves what it produces, or transforms it into its opposite. As we shall see, in book 2, negativity produces essence as the inner excitation of chaos or illusion, but it also dissolves essence into its opposite, namely, accidents or attributes. The solution to the problem, which I can only state here, is that essence is recaptured through the recognition that the process by which it dissolves is also the comprehensive manifestation of the categories or logical determinations that constitute it.

The Problem of Essence and Attributes

At the end of the previous chapter, I gave a preliminary characterization of the turn from being to essence. This turn has nothing to do with what the textbooks call the "traditional" account of essence and attributes. Hegel is perfectly aware of the fundamental deficiency of this doctrine, which I will restate as follows. From the standpoint of ordinary experience, there is no question about the existence of individual things of an identifiable nature. The commonsense observer does not attempt to prove the existence of tables and chairs, rocks and trees, persons and individual artifacts, because existence is more certain than proof. We attempt to prove the existence only of things whose existence we doubt, and here too there must be some reason to assume existence, or there would be nothing to prove. Thus for example we try to prove that something is not a dream or an illusion but "actually" exists. But this means that the thing in question is already known to exist at the least as a dream or an illusion. So here the investigation is not about existence, in the minimal or most general sense of the term, but about "actuality" or *Wirklichkeit*.

Those things whose existence we do not doubt possess a stable identity that we refer to as their natures. By this I do not mean in the first instance a nuclear identity or set of properties that must be present in order for us to agree upon the thing's identity. At this level of cognitive perception, the words "look" or "appearance" are satisfactory ways of designating what we identify. If something "appears" to be a human being, this is because it exhibits the "look" of a human being as a whole, i.e., as what Hegel would call a "unity of unity and multiplicity," an expression that is of course not employed in ordinary discourse. Now obviously, things that normally look like human beings can vary in such a way as to raise a doubt concerning their identity. To take a simple case, an infant might be born with no legs. Note that this would lead us to doubt not the existence of the infant but only its identity. However, exactly the same is true of a shadowy figure in the distance that we perceive only vaguely, but the identity of which we cannot discern.

Debates about the existence of the gods, or about God, like those about the status of the individual human soul, take place at what one could call the margins of ordinary experience. They seem to arise wherever there are human beings, yet they point beyond ordinary experience. Nevertheless, they do not violate the previous assertion that we do not debate the existence of entirely unknown entities. The soul is known as one's own existence or life or consciousness; this fact requires no proof, nor would there be any way in which to go about proving it. What requires proof is the thesis of the immortality or incorporeality of the soul, in other words, its "actual" identity. As to the gods, we infer them from natural forces or visions of supernatural spirits. Again, if one experiences a visitation from a spirit, the question is not whether the spirit exists but whether it is illusory or actual. To say that spirits do not exist is to say that their existence is illusory. In short: we cannot properly discuss our experience without a distinction between existence and actuality. Whatever can be mentioned exists, but not everything that exists is actual. Note that this distinction is normally suppressed in the paradigm of formal logic, but it could be represented by appropriate rules and symbols.

To come back now to the larger issue, the distinction between existence and actuality arises from ambiguous experiences that raise the question of correct identification. Very often we answer this question by modifying the perceptual experiences that gave rise to the initial ambiguity. For example, we can move closer to a figure that is too distant to identify, or increase the level of illumination in a dark room, and so on. In these cases, what we perceive when the modifications have been successfully made is an identifiable entity, that is, one with a normal look or appearance. But sooner or later we come upon cases in which elementary procedures do not resolve the ambiguity, and this in turn leads eventually, by a series of events that we do not need to analyze here, to the question of the actual nature of an existing thing. Note that "actual nature" is a kind of expansion of the everyday use of the term "actual." In the normal course of events, someone may perceive what he or she takes to be a ghost, only to find upon closer inspection that it is a trick of the light, or a mirror image, or some familiar object that has been only partially apprehended and thereby subjected to imaginary distortions. The person in question then says, "oh yes, it was actually a mirror image" or something of that sort.

In order to explain the occurrence of the illusion in the language of everyday experience, we have to distinguish between the actual and the perceived or imagined nature of the entity or event. More generally, wherever there is a dispute about identity, some criterion has to be established. To repeat, we can often settle the dispute simply by taking another look, by rectifying the initial perceptual circumstances, so that the "look" or "appearance" of a familiar entity comes indisputably into view. "Oh yes, it is a man." Here no further discussion of essential attributes need emerge; everyone knows what a man looks like. But often the dispute cannot be settled by bringing a familiar identity into view. Or what comes into view is only partially familiar. In the case of partially familiar looks, we have to decide what features are to count as necessary and sufficient identifying properties. And so the distinction between essential and accidental attributes is born.

The preceding remarks were intended only as an introductory sketch, not an exhaustive analysis of the origin of the distinction between essence and attributes. I wanted in particular to show that the question of essence is different from that of existence. To ask what is the essence of man is not to ask whether men exist. In fact, the questions are addressed in two different but related directions. We ask not whether man exists but whether men exist. But we do not ask whether men have essences, except as an indirect way of expressing the underlying question of whether the existing individuals that bear the look or appearance of men share through that common look an essence, namely, the essence of man. To ask whether essences exist is not to ask whether men or any other individuals bearing familiar looks exist. It is to ask what has been traditionally called the "metaphysical" question concerning the existence of abstract entities. If essences exist, then this means that the individual essences corresponding to classes or families of individuals bearing a common look themselves exist as individuals of a higher order or different type, or in some way that distinguishes them from the existing things whose essences they are.

To say this in another way, we know that human beings exist whether or not there is an existing essence that bears the name "human being." Or at least this is what the dispute is about. Some say that there are no essences, or that even if there were, we could never discern them. But those who hold this view do not also assert that nothing exists. Nor would all of them say that nothing is actual, or that to exist is to be an illusion. But whether they would say this or not, we have to understand the implications of the denial of essences. The first point to be made is that it is one thing to say that essences do not exist, and something else again to say that there are no essences. There is a difference between being and existence, as is brought out in book 1 of Hegel's *SL*. Existence (*Dasein*) is "determinate being." To exist is to be something or other, or what Aristotle calls a *tode ti*. But to be something or another is to be of such and such a kind, or a *toionde ti*. At this point, however, there is a parting of the ways between Aristotle and Hegel, a parting that is not made explicit anywhere in the text, any more than is the level of agreement.

The disagreement is as follows. Aristotle has no doctrine of being as entirely general and all-comprehensive. What Aristotle means by "being *qua* being" is what we would call a concept or abstract definition of what it is to be any being whatsoever, i.e., any individual. To be in this sense is to instantiate the categories. The first category is *ousia*, which I shall translate for the time being as "essence." But *ousia* is not being *qua* being. Being *qua* being is the exhibition of each of the subsequent categories through the representation of properties that inhere in an *ousia*. But it is no being or thing in particular. And neither is any of the categories, the number of which, incidentally, varies from one Aristotelian text to another. Aristotle does not discuss the mode of being of the table of categories; in fact, he never applies the verb *is* to the categories. Nor does he say that *ousia* "is" or "exists." What exists is a particular individual or instance of a property-bearing essence, an instance that Aristotle sometimes calls a "primary *ousia*" or what we would have to designate by a different English translation of *ousia* here as "an existing thing."

In other words, existing things all exemplify being *qua* being because to exist is to be constituted of an essence together with attributes. But Aristotle does not apply the general term "being" to all aspects of his conceptual analysis of "the whole." He frequently speaks of *to on* or "being" as the general property of *ta onta* or existing instances of being *qua* being, but that has nothing to do with a being that encompasses essences and attributes, and more specifically essential and accidental attributes, together with primary *ousiai* or existing things. This is not the place to enter further into the details of Aristotle's doctrines, as for example the question of whether he distinguishes between being and existence in any systematic way. The only point I wished to establish is that Aristotle no more than Plato has a doctrine of being, whereas Hegel has no ontology, nor could he have one, given the absence of any internal structure to the pure concept of being; being is for him the whole at a primordial level and not at all equivalent to *Wirklichkeit*. One could say that *das Ganze* (the whole) is for Hegel the complete development or actualization of being. As we have seen in sufficient detail, simply to say that being is the whole or the all is to make an uninformative statement, one that must develop by its internal dialectical movement through the excitation of the work of negativity.

Now we are ready to see Hegel's deviation from the "tradition" with respect to essences and attributes. The Aristotelian doctrine on this point is itself closely related to the ordinary experience of commonsense reasoning that I summarized in the initial paragraphs of this section. I restrict myself to the crucial point. How do we identify an essence according to Aristotle? The answer is, and can only be, by intellectual apprehension, perception, or intuition (*noēsis*). *Noēsis* corresponds to the act of cognitive perception in ordinary experience by which we identify something by its look or appearance "as a whole," by how its features are arranged into a distinct unity. It is simple nonsense to try to turn Aristotle into a nominalist or in other words to claim that for him, essences are defined. First of all, Aristotle is explicit on the point of *noēsis*. Second, he states explicitly that there is no predication, no "before" and "after," in *ousia*. Third, the attempt to define an essence is always circular. In order to define an essence, we would have to state its essential properties. But we could not know its essential properties unless we had grasped the essence. To say that we must come to some agreement on the question of which attributes are to count as essential in each case is the same as to say that essences are conventional entities, artifacts, and so *accidental*. In other words, it is to deny that there are essences, not to define them.

I will certainly come back to this topic later; in particular, we shall have to look more closely at the notion of "belonging" that underlies the Aristotelian table of categories and so the traditional doctrine according to which the essence is the "owner" of its properties, which therefore "belong to" it. It should be obvious that "belonging" is a notion that cannot be analyzed in a noncircular manner. We can define abstractly what it means for something to belong to something else, but it is another matter to determine ownership by the articulation of formal structure in any particular case. "Belongs to" is like "is the cause of." As Hume showed, we cannot perceive necessary connections. But neither can we simply define them, since then they are relative to the perceptual and cognitive schemes by which we constructed the definition. In my view, Aristotle is right to say that we perceive essences, even though we cannot always identify essential attributes. But this is a side issue. The main point here is that the intrinsic circularity of the Aristotelian definition, or the patent impossibility of explaining discursively or analytically what belongs "essentially" to the looks or appearances of things, leads to nominalism and conventionalism, and so to the view that the identities of things are arbitrary or perspectival, or to the doctrine that we can call "nihilism."

We have now rejoined the point made at the end of the previous chapter. Western European philosophy, which receives for Hegel its decisive formulation in the attempts by Plato and Aristotle to reconcile the opposing and apparently mutually contradictory theses of Parmenides and Heraclitus, leads to the night in which all cows are black, that is to say, to the conviction that the world, or more precisely human existence, is an illusion. Hegel's tacit reply to this conviction is in principle the same as that of Leibniz to the assertion that life is a dream. Leibniz says somewhere that life may indeed be a dream, but what is of importance is its structure. In the explicit terms of the end of book 1 of the *SL*, measure, the identity within difference of quantity and quality, dissolves because of the indifference of each to the other, and so of both to their unity in the continuum of becoming. Hegel means by this that quality and quantity are continuously turning into each other, but not in such a way as to allow this process to preserve the integrity of each, together with the integral dependence of each upon the other. There is a kind of identification of quality and quantity, and so of being with itself, but as a totality of indifferences, or what Hegel also calls negative totality.

And now we see once again the power of the negative. On the one hand, the various articulations are effaced; a process of mere reciprocal transformation has no significance or inner essentiality. This returns us to Parmenides and Spinoza: the unity is empty of enduring determinations. Nevertheless, this unity is indeed filled with determinations, namely, those that come and go with no stability or inner connectedness. The coming and going, or reciprocal negation, is the movement that will lead to the reemergence of the as yet mutually indifferent qualitative and quantitative determinations. In other words, they will "reappear" as "appearance," at first in the sense of *Schein*, "show" or "illusion" (because not yet connected with essentiality), but then as the show or appearance of the inner itself, namely, essence. Hegel will thus have demonstrated that even if we begin with the assumption that the world is an illusion, the analysis of that illusion returns us to actuality. We can also understand this demonstration to be Hegel's attempt to rescue European philosophy from nihilism.

Foundationalism

The main theme of book 2 can be stated as the solution to the problem of the grounding of philosophy. This problem is today much discussed as a dispute between foundationalism and antifoundationalism. It is easy to see that the contemporary discussion has made no essential progress beyond the Hegelian analysis; in fact, it falls short of that analysis. Stated as simply as possible, the dispute amounts to this. The foundationalists claim that philosophy is grounded in or built upon an indubitable, entirely secure, i.e., *absolute* starting point, whether this be a first principle, a universal method, an intellectual intuition of pure forms, or something else. The antifoundationalists deny this; for them, philosophy is the ungrounded multiplication of differences through language of one kind or another. In other words, not even language is the ground, because there is no privileged manner of discourse.

The defect of foundationalism is obvious enough. There is no noncircular way in which to validate one's starting point. A first principle cannot be deduced from or justified by something else that is antecedent to and higher than it, precisely because it is *first*. But everything that we deduce from the first principle is already determined through our acceptance of it.

Foundationalism thus leads to a multiplication of philosophical systems or positions, and the task of choosing among them becomes arbitrary. In other words, the attempt to enforce foundationalism leads to antifoundationalism, or the conviction that there are a multiplicity of systems, i.e., perspectives or points of view. But antifoundationalism in turn leads to foundationalism, namely, the arbitrary assertion of the ungroundedness of philosophical discourse, which amounts to the thesis that chaos is the ground or first principle of all points of view. One cannot, in other words, stop at the assertion that there are multiple interpretations of experience, all of them of equal merit, because this is merely a cheerful way of expressing the conviction that no interpretation is correct, and so that, as interpretations, all are worthless.

It may be the case that some interpretation or another is necessary in order for life to be endurable. But if this is so, it simply proves Nietzsche's contention that art is worth more than the truth for life. In this case, we must determine *which* artwork, i.e., which viewpoint or interpretation, is best suited to preserve life. Antifoundationalism thus proceeds to foundationalism by two stages. It first negates all foundations, thereby establishing chaos or nothing as the foundation. But second, it thereby endorses the priority of art to truth, or defines truth as a work of art. Nietzsche's doctrine is a specification of antifoundationalism, in which life, or more precisely "life enhancement," is the foundation.

I emphasize that nothing is accomplished by calling antifoundationalism "postphilosophy" or something of that sort. Antifoundationalism, whether or not in the Nietzschean version, makes a statement about the fundamental nature of truth, namely, that it is a work of art and, further, that as such it is a "groundless" or arbitrary shaping of chaos. Everything is derived from and reduced back into chaos, which is thus the ground of artistic discourse. In the SL, Hegel attempts to provide us with the inner structure of chaos. In other words, he starts with the antifoundationalist thesis and demonstrates how it turns into foundationalism. But this process is reciprocal or unending in itself; it amounts to a bad infinity

The resolution to the dispute can come only from the demonstration that the totality of the excitations of chaos constitutes an identity within difference of foundationalism and antifoundationalism. "The true is the whole [*das Ganze*]." There is no foundation external to experience, whether in a Platonist, Kantian, or Nietzschean sense. But it is preposterous to infer from this that we are incapable of discriminating among modes of discourse; in particular, the mere assertion that chaos is at the heart of everything is cognitively worthless and nothing but an ideological slogan.

One has to *demonstrate* that chaos is the ground. And this is equivalent to demonstrating the categorial structure of the *concept* of chaos, or to give it its Hegelian name, of becoming as the identity within difference of being and nothing.

If we take the term in its traditional sense, and in particular as it is used today, then one cannot call Hegel a "foundationalist." In particular, Hegel does not beg the crucial question from the outset by assuming the principle of the absolute spirit. Hegel denies that we can begin to philosophize by abandoning everything that we know, including the knowledge that we are philosophizing. Chaos is our origin only in an ontological sense; existentially, it can only be our destination. The Cartesian *cogito* is indubitable, but it is not a ground or foundation in itself, since it is quite compatible with the thesis that life is an illusion. Whatever one may think of Descartes's proofs for the existence of God, it is obvious that, as proofs, they cannot express a foundation or absolute starting point; and without their validity, the *cogito* cannot protect us from solipsism and its twin, hermeneutics. The correct way in which to philosophize is not to assume the starting point or first principle from which everything follows, but rather to assume nothing. Hegel is as it were a more rigorous Cartesian than Descartes, because he abstracts from the divine guarantor of the truth of clear and distinct ideas and begins with the sheer emptiness of thinking, namely, with the thinking of pure being.

Whatever the empirical stages that led to Hegel's conceptualization of his logic, the logic itself purports to start *ex nihilo* and thereby to derive the world (totality) from nothing. As we have already seen, nothing is for Hegel not sheer vacuousness but rather itself something. It is the concept of nothing, as is obvious from the fact that we are thinking it. Accordingly, it is the emptiest or purest form of being. To start with nothing is thus to start with being, and to start at all is to think. Being and nothing are the logically first because simplest forms of thinking. They are in other words categories of the concept. But it is pointless to try to distinguish between the concept and some sense of being as external to or beyond thinking, since the effort to make this distinction takes place within thinking itself. Hegel's *SL* can therefore also be described as the demonstration that all appearances of a being external to thought are instead appearances of thinking.

I repeat: Hegel rejects the thesis that the ground is separate from the grounded. This is a more general version of the denial that being is separate from thinking. We cannot think of what lies outside of thought. If the ground lies outside of thought, then it cannot serve as the ground of thinking, and so of human existence, which thus dissolves into illusion, and so into chaos. But Hegel also rejects the thesis that there is no ground; this is a self-contradictory assertion because it amounts to the thesis that nothing is the ground, or in other words that the truth of being is its essential illusoriness. In much simpler terms, if the ground is separate, then things fall apart; but if there is no ground, the result is the same. So far as we humans are concerned, there is no difference between these two doctrines. The serious question is therefore whether things fall apart. In other words, can the thesis of essential chaos be sustained? Or is Leibniz correct to say that it makes no difference whether life is a dream but that what counts is whether the dream possesses a structure?

The thesis of essential chaos grants that chaos is the essence of appearance. It is therefore already on the way toward overcoming the split between essence and appearance. What has to be shown is that the inner excitation of chaos is precisely the formation process by which appearances appear. And this can be done as soon as we begin to speak: to speak is already to contradict the claim that life is sheer chaos. This is why Alexandre Kojève says in his commentary on the *PS* that the only way in which to remain impervious to Hegel is by remaining silent. Even the assertion of nihilism is grounded in a structure of meaning that is the object or content of comprehensive negation. And negation is itself unintelligible except in conjunction with affirmation. That is, negative discourse is a modality of affirmative discourse; the two taken together exhibit the dialectical interrelationship between position and negation, or, in the abstract categorial language of book 1 of the *SL*, of being and nothing.

I can render more specific the previous point by means of three simple examples of a Hegelian account of negativity. In general, it is unsatisfactory to speak of "not" as a syntactic operator, because the rule that defines the operation must derive its sense from a category of conceptual thinking. The examples are as follows:

1. Conceptual thought is the same as the Aristotelian *nous* that has the capacity to become "somehow" the forms or beings it thinks. As the receptacle of forms, *nous* cannot itself possess a form that would give it a rigid structure and thereby prevent it from receiving or "becoming" all other forms.

2. What separates one intelligible form from another? Not a third form, since that would lead to an infinite regress. We are inclined to say that the forms are separated from one another by their boundaries, but if these are immediately contiguous, why do they not constitute one comprehensive form? In fact, Hegel holds that all formal elements are modes or categories of one circular, internally articulated form or concept. Nevertheless,

individual determinations can be distinguished from one another, and the question again arises as to what makes this possible. In order to grasp any form, we must discern it as identical to itself, and thus as not the forms that bound it. Since there is no third boundary between any two others, it must be nothing that distinguishes them from each other. This "nothing" is negative activity; it is the differentiating power that engenders formal distinctions.

3. According to Christian theology, God created the world out of nothing. As we have already seen, Hegel's logic is a conceptual analysis of the act of creation. Either the world comes directly from God, in which case pantheism is correct, or else it is distinguished from God by nothing. But pantheism leaves unintelligible contingency or the dualism of essence and appearance. This failure to explain contingency amounts to a collapse of pantheism into the traditional separation between God and creation, or in effect licenses the assertion of the second alternative, namely, that nothing separates God and the world. If "nothing" is a name for sheer vacuity, then God is not actually separated from the world and the result is pantheism. In order to avoid this vicious circle, we have to conceive of nothing as negative activity, or the principle of divine creative labor. God then creates the world out of himself or exhibits himself within it through the instrumentality of human being. In other words, the intelligibility of the world to human beings is the mark of God or absolute spirit; it is the same work or life-pulse by which God creates the world.

As these examples indicate, negativity plays a structural role in the differentiation of formal moments, but also in the process of thinking. There are not two separate "nothings," one at work within the domain of form and the other the mark of the receptivity of intellect. The "nothing" that produces formal difference is the same "nothing" that assimilates these differences into thought. And note carefully that this assimilation, i.e., the act of thinking, is a preservation rather than an annihilation of what is thought. Hegel is not averse to comparing conceptual thinking to the process of digestion. We can apply this metaphor in the present context as follows. The intellect ingests external form and transforms it into the concept; there is accordingly an identity within difference between the being of the form and that of the intellect. This identity within difference is the activity of thinking, which, precisely as an activity, is *negativity*. Forms are transformed by the formation process, the engine of which is negativity, into the conceptual structure of spirit.

In short, the key to Hegel's reinterpretation of the Eleatic thesis that being and thinking are the same is his new understanding of nothing as negativity. What separates being from thinking, according to the traditional, pre-Hegelian doctrines? But there is nothing other than being on the one hand and thinking on the other. The answer to the question is therefore "*nothing.*" This is why the dualism of common sense soon collapses into the monisms of materialism on the one hand and idealism on the other. But these monisms are in direct contradiction to common sense, that is, to the phenomenon of life as it is lived. They do not save the phenomena but destroy or at the very least obscure them. In Hegel's teaching, it is the dialectical activity of negativity that both separates and identifies being from thinking. Hegel is thus neither a monist nor a dualist but a trinitarian. On his view, being and thinking were never separated but instead have always constituted an identity within difference.

To those who find the preceding line of analysis excessively obscure, I can at least mitigate the obscurity, although I cannot remove it, by the following consideration. Hegel is the only philosopher who offers an explanation to the central question of how we can know anything about the external world. If the intellect is separate from the things it knows, then it cannot know those things directly, but only through internal modifications or thoughts. In this case, the so-called external world is reduced to the status of a *Gedankending*. If the intellect is the same as the things it knows, the same result follows. It is hardly a solution to the problem to deny the existence of the intellect or to claim that the intellect is merely an epiphenomenon of the body. The former assertion leads immediately to comprehensive silence or sheer noise; the second leaves all questions in place.

How for example are we to interpret AI, the contemporary philosophy of artificial intelligence that takes the world of human experience to be a product of neurophysiological processes? Is it idealism or materialism? Materialism leads directly to nihilism, but thereby to the thesis that chaos or nothing is the first principle or ground of all things. As we saw above, if this is to be something more than a mere ideological slogan, its analysis leads us directly to Hegelian logic. Idealism on the other hand, rather than reducing the mind to the brain, interprets the brain as an epiphenomenon of the mind. We are then faced with the task of accounting for neurophysiological processes on the basis of thoughts, which is absurd. Such an explanation would be like running the film of Darwinian evolution backward. Or more accurately put, the scientific idealist has to account for the persistence of empirical order on the basis of something like the absolute ego of Fichte and Schelling, while at the same time explaining the functions of the absolute ego on the basis of empirical psychology and physiology.

It should be carefully noted that Hegel does not advocate the view that to be is to be a thought. His claim is rather that to be is to be thinkable, which, without further modification, is identical with the fundamental assumption of the Socratic school represented most powerfully by Plato and Aristotle. However, the Socratics cannot explain *how* being is thinkable. I note that Plato apparently follows Socrates by leaving the pure forms external to the intellect, whereas Aristotle attempts to resolve the subsequent aporia by relocating the forms within the intellect. But since Aristotle is unable to account for the preservation of difference between form and intellect, he must be regarded as the great-grandfather of modern subjectivism or, as it was called by Hegel's contemporaries, idealism. For Hegel, beings are thinkable because they are united to thinking by negativity. In the traditional terminology, there is literally nothing that stands between being and thinking. But this leaves their relation unintelligible. Hegel attempts to explain that relation by so to speak bringing the traditional nothing to life.

I want next to illustrate how Hegel constitutes an advance upon idealism by taking up the topic of intellectual intuition. This topic arises in conjunction with the question as to how (or whether) thought thinks itself. In the Socratic tradition, to think is to think a form, i.e., not the form of the intellect, since there is no such form, but some other form. Even if the intellect becomes the form of which it thinks, to think is to think that form, not the intellect or thinking itself. The apparent exception proves the rule; Aristotle speaks of god as thought thinking itself, but he says nothing whatsoever about the "content" of that thought.

At the same time, it is obvious that the dualism of being and thinking cannot be overcome unless we are able to think thought itself. More precisely, if there is no being outside of thinking, then all thinking of being is at once a thinking of thinking. And yet, if thinking is accessible to us only as the being that it thinks, then it is inaccessible to us as itself; and this inaccessibility casts a shadow of ignorance over the being that is the content of thought. Thought *appears* as being; being is the appearance or *Schein*, i.e., the illusion of thought. Note the relation between this formulation of the problem and Heidegger's criticism of the history of metaphysics, according to which the thinking of beings covers over being.

Fichte and Schelling attempt to resolve the problem of thought thinking itself by recourse to intellectual intuition. This is not the Greek *noēsis* or grasping of pure forms. We may describe it instead as a direct vision (with the eye of the intellect) of the pure process of posing and negating forms. As a vision of the process, however, it is not an apprehension of the forms as forms, and so, from Hegel's standpoint, it is empty or a vision of nothing in the static sense of that term. In other words, the idealists approach the doctrine of dialectic by attempting to grasp the process of position and restriction through which the absolute ego constructs the world of determinate form. But they lack a doctrine of negative activity and so fall back into a dualism of thinking and being.

No doubt the most powerful statement of the doctrine of intellectual intuition is to be found in the late versions of Fichte's *WL*. But Hegel was not familiar with these versions; he bases his criticism of Fichte on the versions of 1794/97. All of these versions proceed by attempting to explain the production of the world of finite or determinate forms as the result of a process of self-limitations by the absolute ego. But the purpose of Fichte's account is not to analyze the categorial structure of the formation process. It is instead to proceed backward and to remove the determinations in order to return to the pure self-reflection of the absolute ego, or in other words to see the absolute ego as it is prior to the production of the world. I shall call this Fichte's inverse version of Hegel's divine standpoint (i.e., the standpoint of God immediately prior to the production of the world). Fichte's dialectic is thus a kind of *via negationis* or return to one's own divinity by the removal of the determinations through which this divinity conceals itself by the creation of the world. In Hegel, God is exhibited in the world; this is impossible in Fichte, not only because the determinations conceal rather than manifest the absolute, but also because the determination process can never come to an end. Every apprehension of a relation between the I or subject and the object results in a further production of the subject-object opposition, and it is just this opposition that makes inaccessible the complete unity of subject and object in the absolute. Again note the similarity between Fichte and Heidegger, despite the difference in terminology. For Fichte, the world is produced by an absolute spiritual process that conceals its intrinsic nature by the very activity of revealing itself as the ground of the world.

Fichte's logic is "dialectical" because it leads us "up" from one inadequate formulation of the logical world, by a series of contradictions or *reductiones ad absurdum*, by which we are to see that the world cannot be thought in its own terms (i.e., as a series of objects of the subject). It is in other words a spiritual exercise designed to show us that the world cannot be its own ground and is therefore unthinkable in its essential nature. Unthinkable, not just unknowable; as ungrounded, the world is sustained only as an infinite series of (1) positing, (2) contradiction between positing subject and posited object, and (3) cancellation that is in effect a new positioning. The net result of the various versions of Fichte's logic is nihilism or the disappearance of the world. Even if intellectual intuition were to succeed, it would arrive at itself, or in other words at Aristotle's *noēsis tēs noēseōs* but in complete isolation from the series of finite determinations that produce the world. But intellectual intuition cannot succeed; hence the series of finite determinations is infinite, which is to say that the world is ungrounded, and so the attempt to know it collapses into nihilism. (By the version of 1804, Fichte makes it explicit that in the achievement of intellectual intuition, we leave altogether behind our own worldly or finite selves.)

Hegel, needless to say, entirely rejects this version of intellectual intuition. Its most obvious deficiency is that it preserves the separation of the ground from the grounded. Many of Fichte's admirers insist that Hegel's criticisms are no longer valid for the editions of the *Wissenschaftslehre* of 1804, which is widely regarded as the most mature of the various versions, and which was not published during Fichte's lifetime. It is, however, obvious even from Fichte's earlier writings that an intellectual intuition of the absolute can have no finite content and so makes self-consciousness impossible (since self-consciousness is reflexive and thus rests upon a determination of the self from itself, or upon formal content). Any attempt to intuit oneself is necessarily circular. I cannot intuit myself unless I already know myself; otherwise I would not know that the act of intuition was indeed of myself. This is the problem of "reflection," one that Fichte made various efforts to resolve; he ended up, however, in repudiating the self.

Fichte attempts to overcome the theoretical gap between the finite ego and the absolute in another way. This time he turns from theory to praxis, in a sense of the term that includes the notion of production. I will give a brief sketch of this process later, but first I want to finish the present series of remarks about the question of the sameness of being and thinking. Let me say here only that Fichte's practical solution, which is based upon Kant, leads to another version of the bad infinity, or what Hegel calls *Sollen*. The overcoming of the split is posited as a categorical imperative to be reached. Unfortunately, it is not and cannot be reached in any discursively accessible way.

It should be evident from the preceding remarks that Fichte anticipates Hegel in attempting to solve the problem of foundationalism, namely, that of the ground, or of dualism (the separation of being from thinking or of the subject from the object), by establishing an identity within difference between the ground and the grounded. The absolute is the infinite series of finite determinations or self-limitations that constitute the world. But in the absence of a dialectical understanding of negative work, no genuine identity within difference can be established. The Fichtean identity within difference is a *Sollen* or what ought to be accessible once we have removed all finite determinations (or on the opposite end, completed the infinite series of those determinations). Lacking the dialectical conception of negativity, Fichte cannot bring together identity and difference into a discursive structure. His doctrine amounts to this: the world is a *Bild* (picture or image) of the absolute. But it is a *Bild* that conceals rather than reflects or exhibits the absolute.

For Hegel, the correct understanding of the ground emerges from the realization that the doctrine of reflection (or external examination of the structure of the subject-object distinction) is incapable of explaining the relation between substances and attributes, or in other words the Aristotelian doctrine of predication. Aristotle's *ousia* or subject of predication is intrinsically unknowable; as such, it is the ancestor of Locke's unknowable substance, which disappears altogether in Hume's sensationalism, and which remains invisible in Kant's critical philosophy as the thing in itself as well as in the idealist doctrine of the inaccessible absolute ego, which is the invisible ground of the substance-attribute structure that it produces by a process of self-limitation.

So much for a general introduction to the problems treated in book 2. In the next chapter, I shall discuss in greater detail the Fichtean basis for what Hegel calls "external reflection."

TEN

The Fichtean Background

In this chapter, my procedure will be as follows. First I shall conclude the introductory discussion of Fichte as Hegel's immediate predecessor. Then I will analyze in detail pages 3–6 of the second volume of the *SL*, in which Hegel introduces book 2 on *Wesen*. These pages contain in extremely condensed form Hegel's general doctrine of the shift from being to essence on the one hand and from essence to the concept on the other. With this general background in place, I will turn in chapter 11 to a technical account of Fichte's treatment of reflection in the *WL* of 1794, restricting myself to the indispensable minimum for understanding Hegel's own treatment of reflection at the beginning of book 2. I move back and forth between Fichte and Hegel in this way, because it allows me to follow a path of developing conceptual difficulty. Hegel presupposes a knowledge of Fichte, but Fichte can himself be best explained at some points by a knowledge of Hegel.

The Fichtean Background

As I have emphasized throughout, it is a major defect of Aristotelian logic that essences are identified by essential predicates, which cannot be known unless we first know the essence. Fichte attempts to overcome this defect from within a Kantian framework. The paradigm case of the subject-predicate relation is for him the self-knowledge of the ego. In other words, the paradigmatic predicates are those of the paradigmatic subject: the ego. If we can explain the relation of "belonging" (my expression) in this case, then we know how substance in general "owns" its attributes.

In the Kantian perspective, however, the predicates of the ego are connected to the subject ego by a transcendental synthesis of apperception, which as primordial for discursive thinking is itself obviously not know-

able via such thinking. We have no analytical access to its originating structure, because for Kant every analysis is rooted in a prior synthesis, and there
could not be a synthesis of structure prior to the primordial synthesis. We
can therefore say that there is an initial "identity within difference" of the
transcendental and the empirical ego. But this structure (if that is the right
word) cannot be captured conceptually, since Kant has no dialectical logic
(except in a pejorative or sophistical sense). Hence there can be no deduction of the empirical from the transcendental ego. Nor can there be
a deduction of the categories from the synthetic apperception that is the
precondition of cognitive thought, for the reason just given. The entire apparatus of cognitive conditions is separate from and the same as its empirical instantiations, but the sameness and separateness are invisible. In other
words, the bonds of necessity that tie together the world are inaccessible to
conceptual understanding. We have in effect returned to the condition of
British empiricism.

Fichte attempts to rectify this situation, that is, to correct the defect of
Kant's version of Kantianism, by means of an intellectual intuition of the
working transcendental ego, an intuition that is not simply "of" an external object but the point of unity between the empirical and the transcendental ego. This leads to the transformation of what is for Kant a set of
logical conditions into the absolute or living ego of idealism. But the absolute ego, although it produces formal structure through an infinite series
of self-limitations, has none of its own, nor could it have, since structure is
limitation and characterizes the domain of the finite ego as established by
the absolute ego and by which the latter is concealed.

At least for the Fichte of 1794, the ground is the absolute, but an absolute that is unknowable either conceptually or discursively. From a Hegelian standpoint, Fichte thus makes clear the deficiencies of Kantianism:
knowledge is grounded in belief, a belief expressed theoretically as the hypothesis of the transcendental and practically as *Sollen*. Hegel's analysis of
the determinations of reflection in the *SL* is an interpretation of the logical
deficiencies of Fichte's doctrine. Fichte, we should remember, states explicitly that there is no theoretical knowledge of the whole. Just as in Kant,
practical knowledge is higher than theory. We therefore ask whether the
subject-object opposition can be overcome in the domain of practice. The
answer is "yes and no." No, because there is an unending process of striving for completeness by producing finite objects and assimilating them. At
each stage of assimilation, there results yet another product to be assimilated. In theoretical terms, conceptual knowledge of a finite object leads to
yet another structural determination that stands between us and the abso-

lute ego. Yes, in the sense that we pose the categorical imperative that the separation of subject and object *must be overcome*. As Fichte puts it: "Du sollst schlechthin." That is, thou must without restriction externalize, produce objective determinations, fill up eternity.

In sum: for Fichte, the human being is free spontaneous activity. The process of cognitive activity, which is also a production of objects, makes us conscious of ourselves in two ways: first, through the defining role played by the products of cognition themselves, and second, through our intuition of the process of production. As we have already seen, the highest version of that intuition is intellectual intuition. Fichte himself describes this intuition as given by the act of self-positing. I have only to think "I" in order to see that I and I alone am both subject and object . This thinking is an activity, not a logical concept of a separate structure. The intuition can be derived only through my own productive act. Philosophy is the exhaustive answer to the question, what is one really thinking when one thinks the identity of subject and object in the "I"? This intuitive act is a unity; it becomes a series of constructions in response to our analysis. The analysis is twofold. If we think of the I as object, we have the ground of things or beings; if we think of the I as subject, we have the ground of the concept. The unity of the concept and the things or objects within the self-production of the I as identity of subject and object is an obvious prototype of the Hegelian unity of subject and object in the fully developed concept. In Fichte, however, the unity is primary and is actually dissolved by the activity of analysis. In Hegel, the unity is primary only in the sense of an empty immediacy that does not dissolve but develops toward completion under the stimulus of analysis. Unfortunately, however, Fichte's two paths to self-consciousness lead in opposite directions. The more we produce, the farther we are from the absolute ego. The more we approximate to intellectual intuition of the absolute ego, the farther we are from the objective products of the empirical ego.

I want to emphasize three points of a historical nature with respect to Fichte's doctrine.

1. Fichte's analysis of human being as practico-productive is a reinterpretation of the Platonic doctrine of Eros. We strive to complete ourselves by the acquisition of perfection or eternity. In Plato, the striving and producing of beautiful speeches and deeds is intended to raise us to an intuition of the pure ideas. To the extent that it is accomplished, we leave behind the world of human existence, that is, the very world of deeds and speeches that we have produced for the sake of the vision. This is virtually the same situation that Fichte envisions, with one crucial difference. The

Platonic ideas are not produced and they are entirely lacking in subjectivity. From this standpoint, one could say that Fichte is a Neoplatonist because he brings the ideas to life as the conceptual determinations of divine spiritual activity, i.e., of the absolute.

2. In his role as Neoplatonist, Fichte spiritualizes Kant's transcendental ego, but he "platonizes" the categorical imperative by changing it from a moral to a practico-productive principle, the goal of which is not virtuous behavior but completeness or union with eternity.

3. Fichte's doctrine of *Streben* (striving) amounts to the definition of practico-production as will. This helps us to see that the modern emphasis upon the will, culminating in Nietzsche's doctrine of the will to power, is a descendant of the Platonic doctrine of Eros. In the modern version, however, the intermediate step of Neoplatonism, or the transformation of the Platonic ideas into the thoughts of God, leads to the subjectivizing of the ideas, and so to their subordination to the will. When the will is itself brought down from the transcendental to the historical level, the result is perspectivism, or in short the conquest of the intellect by the imagination.

We should be able to see that Fichte's doctrine is close to Hegel's, yet decisively different. For Fichte, the whole is an identity within difference of an absolute spiritual process and the articulated subject-object structure that it produces. But the produced world "conceals" the absolute process, and so the ground is inaccessible to conceptual thinking, which Fichte attempts to supplement, or rather to ground, with intellectual intuition. Hegel takes the next step of reassimilating intellectual intuition into the dialectical process of the development of the concept. We also see in Fichte the radicalization of the Kantian emphasis upon the productive dimension of conceptual thinking. It would be going entirely too far to say that there is no such dimension in Greek thought; see my book on Plato's *Statesman*, *The Web of Politics*.[1] Nevertheless, there is a continuous increase in the role played by constitution or projection within the history of modern philosophy; the upshot of this increase is the transformation of theory into interpretation (here see my *Hermeneutics as Politics*).

Now I turn to Hegel's opening statement on essence.

Book 2: The Teaching of *Wesen*

Hegel begins book 2 with a general remark about *Wesen* that we will study very closely. The first sentence reads: "The truth of *being* is essence" (3). I begin with a general remark about truth. We speak primarily of truth in two senses. The first sense is applied to propositions and is sometimes called "the truth predicate," especially if one is dealing with a formal language. Propositions consist minimally of a subject and a predicate; the predicate is "said of" the subject, or the subject is subsumed under the concept named by the predicate. It is not clear whether there is any difference between asserting a proposition and asserting that the proposition is true. Take the proposition "snow is white." Is there any difference between saying "snow is white" and "the proposition 'snow is white' is true"?

Let us restrict ourselves to what is most obvious here. We do not have to assert the more cumbersome expression with which we apply the truth predicate to the proposition, because we understand that this is what we are tacitly doing when we assert a proposition. Normally we determine from the discursive context whether or not a proposition is being asserted. We can ignore here the case of purely formal languages, since they have nothing to do with the attribution of truth in discursive or conceptual contexts. This is obvious from the fact that the application of rules in a calculus is itself intelligible only as a result of a discursive explanation of the calculus and its intended application.

The question immediately arises: what do we intend when we say in ordinary discourse that a proposition is true, whether we do this in the longer or the shorter way? It seems obvious that we are not simply engaging in a linguistic performance, as philosophers of language often state or imply. When I say that "snow is white," I mean to assert not simply that the subject term is subsumed under the predicate term but that snow is actually white. The truth that I attribute, explicitly or implicitly, to such a proposition is directed in the first instance only to the proposition as a linguistic entity. At bottom or fundamentally, I am making a claim about a state of affairs, that is to say, about what Hegel calls "actuality." More colloquially, I am talking about the color of snow, not about a linguistic convention for treating propositional utterances. In special circumstances, I can, of course, talk directly or exclusively about linguistic expressions and either apply or deny the truth predicate to those expressions. But this is a technical activity that itself treats linguistic expressions as the elements of actuality to which or about which further linguistic decisions are being made. These decisions are second-order linguistic decisions about first-order elements of actuality that happen themselves to be linguistic expressions. As such, the first-order elements are treated in the same way that the color white and the snow on the ground are treated in the previous example.

I believe that this suffices to make the needed point. It is entirely false to say that truth is a linguistic predicate only or even fundamentally. We understand what it means to employ the truth predicate only because we understand the ontological sense of truth. I could go on to discuss the various senses of truth as an ontological predicate, but I will leave it at the following remark. We can say that it is true that snow is white because snow is white, but we can also say that snow is truly white, or that this is a genuine diamond, or that someone is a true gentleman, and so on. When Hegel says that "the truth of *being* is *essence*," he is referring to ontological truth in two closely related senses. First: he means that truth is a property of states of affairs or processes of actuality. Second: not only is the "property" in question not a linguistic predicate or the name of a determinate structural feature of things, but it is the underlying process by which formal structure is produced. Hegel is not reiterating the traditional Aristotelian thesis according to which the true structure of an *on* is *ousia*, that is, the view that essences are distinct from their attributes and stand to these as owners to their properties. To say that the truth of being is essence is not to imply that there is a false part or dimension of being named *accident*. Aristotle would not say that accidents are false beings, but they certainly constitute an inferior dimension of being in contrast to the dimension of essence or *ousia*. As we should now be aware, Hegel has a quite different understanding. Being is in process of development into actuality, and the pivotal stage in this development is the emergence or "appearance," the *Erscheinung* or *Schein* of essence. Essence is not some part of being, not the "essential" part, but all of being at a higher level of development.

Once this is understood, it has to be added that there is no separation of being and conceptual discourse for Hegel. The restriction of "true" to its role as a truth predicate in the sense of a property of propositions leads inevitably to a thoroughly linguistic conception of being. If we cannot speak of things as true, then it makes no sense to speak of assertions that refer to things as true. One must always remember that for Hegel, it is impossible to "refer" to things through separate linguistic entities. In other words, it is impossible to "solve" the problem of reference merely by an analysis of language. We can make such an analysis only because we already understand the connection between linguistic artifacts and things, states of affairs, experience, and so on. And we already understand this because our conceptual discourse is already connected to things, states of affairs, experience, and so on. I am referring to the identity within difference of being and thinking, an identity that is itself absolute spirit, but that we are studying in logic as "the concept." The assertion "the truth of being is essence" is thus not exclusively an ontological statement; at a deeper level it is neither an ontological nor a linguistic statement. Being is the same as the concept; hence the assertion in question is not about a being that is separate from discourse any more than it is about discourse that is separate from being. We can therefore also say that essence is the truth of the concept, because the concept is the cognitive structure of the whole.

Such a statement is, however, anticipatory. At this moment, we are not describing the structure of the whole as the concept, i.e., as the cognitive dimension of absolute spirit. We are rather studying the process by which the collapse of being, as recorded in book 1 of the *SL*, is about to reconstitute itself as the process of the appearance of essence. It will be helpful in what follows to keep before us the following pedagogical statement of this process of reconstitution. The collapse of being is not the reinstitution of the *nihil* out of which, so to speak, God creates the universe. It is the reinstitution of chaos, that is, of the chaos of dissolved structure, namely, structure of quality and quantity as the most general dimensions of becoming (itself a process of being and nothing). This chaos can be considered in two ways. First: it is a return to the immediacy of being, which has lost its mediating structure. Second: the loss of structure means not that the continuum has disappeared but rather that it now appears to be discontinuous. This is the *appearance* of Heraclitean flux. In book 2, Hegel claims to show how the chaotic appearance of discontinuity, or in other words of sheer contingency, and so of pure accident, is itself the appearance of essence, the truth of being or the whole.

We have returned to the immediate, but we have the impression that there is something beneath it, "that this background constitutes the truth of being." What we logicians who are thinking the process of being wish to understand is the truth of being "in and for itself." It is as though we can still see the shadows left by the erasure of quality and quantity as independent categorial stages and wish to penetrate into the immediacy of being in order to grasp the still invisible logical entities that are the actuality corresponding to those shadows.

To continue with this metaphor, we begin with being and attempt to penetrate into its depths in order to arrive at the essence. "Knowing first finds essence through the mediation by which it recollects itself out of immediate being" (3). In other words, the activity of knowing (*Wissen*) has as it were been here previously, in the already completed first major stage of the dialectic of being, a stage that began with the immediacy of the abstract category. In fact, knowing was used here previously in two senses. I have just mentioned the first sense, namely, in the process of thinking by the logician. But underneath this presence is the antecedent identity within difference of being and thinking. We recall that the being of the first moment of logic is the *concept* of being. To say that we as logicians are thinking being is to say something more than that we are thinking it as separate from or outside of our thoughts. There is nothing outside our thoughts, since every assertion of existence is already a thought of what we assert.

One will object that there is a difference between thinking of things and positing them as existing within our thought, but this distinction is irrelevant to the Hegelian formulation. Hegel does not mean to assert that things or beings are just thoughts; he means that everything is thinkable and therefore knowable. And the reason why everything is thinkable is that there is no boundary between things and thoughts. The "nothing" that separates them also unites them. To think the structure of a being is to assimilate it conceptually without actually ingesting it in the sense that living beings ingest external items of food. So the abstract category of being, with which logic begins, is not a thing external to thought but is the being of anything at all, the being of thought itself. In other words, the abstract category of being cannot be distinguished from the abstract thought by which we think it. Otherwise put, a category *is* a thought; the most abstract category must be grasped by the most abstract thought. Since both are entirely abstract or empty of any determinations whatsoever, the two are one and indistinguishable. But therefore the dialectical development of the concept or thought of the abstract category of being is exactly the same as the dialectical development of being itself.

What then does *Wissen* or (as we may express it) thinking recollect? It recollects itself as originally posited, namely, as the abstract category of being. It recollects itself as having already come to pass, as "what was" or *Wesen*. "Language has preserved in the temporal word *Sein* the essence as 'having been' [*gewesen*] in the past time, for essence is the transpired [*vergangenen*] but atemporally transpired being" (3). I have translated *vergangenen* as "transpired." It would be perhaps more literal to translate it as "having gone away." In other words: essence is a development of being that is not present initially in the positing of the abstract category; it is like an accumulation of temporal process, and in particular of the process within which becoming is articulated and then collapses in on itself. This collapse is the return to the immediacy of being, immediate in the sense that it is not defined by relation to something external to itself. But this immediacy is in another sense mediated by what has gone before. Being must come back to itself in order to arrive at essence. This must be qualified, however, by underlining Hegel's assertion that the *Vergangenheit* is atemporal. The process in question is ontological and occurs at the level of the absolute, not within time but as the constitution of temporality.

It is hard not to think of the late Heidegger when reading this passage of Hegel's *SL*. Heidegger speaks of the "bewaying" of the *Wesen* in order to bring out the sense of process or occurrence that, strikingly enough, is implicit in the participial form of the English word "being." Hegel, for his part, relies on the forms of German in distinguishing between the abstract infinitive *Sein* and the participial sense of *Wesen*. In so doing, he has set into motion the Platonic doctrine of the *anamnesis* of the ideas. Knowing the essence is a turning inward (*das Wissen sich . . . erinnert*) that recollects what has already (i.e., in absolute time) been accomplished.

One could mistake this process for an activity of knowing that is externally applied to being, just as the Platonic *noēsis* is externally applied to the ideas. "But this process is the movement of being itself."[2] This is explained by the previously mentioned identity of the abstract concept of being and the logical determination itself. The grounding of our conceptual knowledge of the categorial structure of the whole is not something different from and external to the ontological growth or progressively increasing complexity of that structure. We are thinking the thought of God prior to the creation of the universe (i.e., prior to the actualization of the logical structure whose development we are studying); our thought is not in that sense chronological, although of course as students of the logic, we traverse its pages in human time. Is this a paradox or logical absurdity in its own right? Not for Hegel. Even the mathematician thinks eternity without quitting human temporality. Human existence is itself a dialectical isomorphism of eternity and temporality; we are ontologically constituted by the same web of categories that we are now in the process of studying.

The phrase *sich erinnert* (3) must therefore be understood in two senses, which I am distinguishing for the sake of convenience by the terms "ontological" and "conceptual," although it has to be remembered that the distinction is not complete; the terms are not external to one another but as usual constitute an identity within difference. Being "durch seine Natur sich erinnert," it turns inward through its own nature and arrives at *Wesen*, in Aristotle's Greek, *to ti ēn einai* or "what it was to be." But this result gives rise to an initial misunderstanding. "The reflection immediately forces itself upon knowing" that the pure being of the first stage of the logic, which is a negation of everything finite, "presupposes an *Erinnerung* and motion that has purified immediate *Dasein* to pure being."

Thus far in the logic, we have observed the following process. The abstract concept of being is inseparable from that of nothing; these together constitute becoming, which, as the pure continuum of (what I call) ontological "places" for all possible somethings or another, has two fundamental determinations: quality and quantity. The dialectic of quality and quantity leads to their identity (since quantity is the primary qualitative determination); but this is to say that they are indifferent to their distinct identities, and so to each other as distinct. Their difference collapses, and we return to being. So being is essence; it has no determinations within itself that could be distinguished as attributes belonging to a separate essence.

There are two different ways in which to conceive of being as essence. The first is through a kind of external abstraction in which we negate all finite determinations and are left with an opposition between them and pure being. But then "essence is neither *in itself* nor *for itself*" but derives its nature solely with respect to the determinations to which it is opposed. In this sense, essence is a product or artifact of external reflection (= juxtaposition of essence and attributes). The negations at play are applied by us to being and are accordingly external to it. The second way is to grasp the entire process as an inner development of being: "Essence, as it has here come to be, is that which it is, not through a negativity that is alien to it, but through its own, the infinite excitation of being" (4). These two ways correspond to traditional metaphysics on the one hand and dialectical logic on the other.

The aforementioned mistake is exemplified by Aristotle's doctrine of categories, which embody an external abstraction of properties from *ousia* and a consequent attempt to understand each pole in the opposition "externally," i.e., each from the perspective of its relation to its opposite. Stated crudely but correctly, the attributes are first detached from the being of immediate existence and then attached in accord with the prescriptions of analytical understanding. We have taken a quite different route. Although there is no talk as yet of particular properties (what Kant calls "real predicates"), we have shown how the basic categorial level of becoming emerges, indeed, grows, out of pure being and is negated *as a separate structure* by that same inner movement. Being is essence, not by abstraction, but in and for itself: in itself, because it is not dependent upon an external development; for itself, because it is itself the negation of those developments as something external to or other than being.

It should be clear that the shift from being to essence is a shift from one immediacy to another. We began with indeterminate being; we have arrived at indeterminate essence. The determinations of being have not been annihilated but are as it were in suspension at this level of immediacy. They have been sublated within essence, which contains them *an sich* but not as posited *an ihm* (4, bottom). In other words, they do not fix the identity of essence as they did of being. Essence initially has no *Dasein* or determination as a something or another, since this would be to divide it into essence and attributes. I suggest the following historical example. The Eleatic one has developed into Heraclitean multiplicity, which as yet cannot sustain itself; none of its moments is distinguishable from the others. These moments then do not disappear, but from the conceptual standpoint their status as determinations is entirely subordinate to the unity of the one.

In book 2 we will study the process by which this second-level one (= being as immediate or undetermined essence) regenerates its inner distinctions (i.e., the previous stages of dialectical development) in such a way as to establish the essence-attributes structure. The oppositions and negations that were delineated in book 1 will be integrated into that comprehensive structure. To anticipate, essence will show itself as its attributes. To cite Hegel: "Essence is absolute unity of being in and for itself; its determining remains therefore within this unity and is no becoming or going over [übergehen]" (5). Let us say that essence does not dissolve into the moments of becoming but achieves stability (i.e., not motionlessness but coherence of dialectical excitation).

Essence is simple negativity; as we have just seen, it has dissolved the antecedent determinations of being. But this is to say that it contains each of them within itself and is thus now in a position to give itself *Dasein*, i.e., to exist in the determinate form of its appearances, and hence too to acquire being for itself, thanks to the emergence of the defining structure of identity within difference of essence and appearances. Initially, however, essence as a totality corresponds at this level of dialectic to quantity in the previous level. Appearances correspond to qualities, and actuality is the identity within difference of essence and appearance.

Essence is like quantity in that both are indifferent to boundaries. But there is an important difference. In the case of quantity, the boundary is necessarily external to each stage of quantitative development, and it is that beyond which quantity goes in asserting itself. In the case of essence there is no external determination, i.e., no external boundary. All determinations are posed by essence and in relation to its unity. Hegel calls this negativity or self-containedness of essence *Reflexion*. This term, which we have encountered previously, is extremely difficult to define in a univocal manner. As we shall see, it refers here to the process by which essence poses its appearances initially in such a way that they lack independent status and return into essence itself. This is a merely negative reunification, not one that acquires actuality through the process of inner development. Simply stated: the appearances are not initially grounded by essence and so "show" themselves like images of it.

Looked at from the standpoint of the logic as a whole, essence is inter-mediate between being and the concept. Being must pass through the exci-tations of essence in order to arrive at the concept. In this light, essence is the first negation of being (that is, it negates all the determinations of first-level or abstract being). Its excitations are the process of achieving *Dasein* or determinate being, i.e., existence, in its appearances, and then reuniting with them. Hegel closes this introductory section with the assertion that the complete development of essence as being in and for itself is the con-cept, "for the concept is the absolute as it is absolutely in its *Dasein* or in and for itself" (5–6). This assertion is not intelligible at the present stage of our study. Hegel is referring here, not to the process of conceptualization by which we study the *SL*, but to the full development or rendering con-crete and hence actual of the abstractness of the concept of abstract being with which the *SL* begins. The problem will be to explain how subjectivity arises within objectivity, thanks to the development of categorial structure. Only then will the gap be closed between our finite intellects as students of Hegel and the absolute intellect or spirit of totality.

Reflection

Fichte's *WL* of 1794 is for Hegel the crucial text in his interpretation of traditional logic, understood not as a calculus of validity but as ontology. We should be clear at the outset, just as I pointed out when discussing Hegel's treatment of mathematics, that he is not attempting to replace tra-ditional with dialectical logic. Hegel is concerned not with the mechanism of deducibility but with the presuppositions concerning the structure of intelligibility. I have said that Hegel's logic is not a competitor but instead a philosophical interpretation of the traditional doctrine of inference and validity. This is correct as far as it goes, but it requires to be made more precise. The central Hegelian point is that traditional logic is not concerned with ontology and is not equipped to illuminate the inner development of the structure of intelligibility.

In slightly different terms, logic, including the so-called formal or math-ematical logic of the post-Hegelian epoch, is rooted in fundamental as-sumptions about the nature of intelligible form. The phrase "intelligible form" points us in the two directions of what Hegel and his contempo-raries called the subject-object relation. What counts as a form is clearly a function of the nature of intelligibility. It is not only pointless but also meaningless to say that there are forms of a determinate nature that, how-ever, we cannot know. Or rather it is impossible to say this, since as soon as we state the determinations, we know them. Nor do we begin with a clear-cut distinction between subject and object or knower and known. The so-called laws of thought, paramount among them the "law" of noncontradiction, are not discovered as independent of our experience and then applied to it. On the contrary, we arrive at the law, whether by induction or through a genial intuition, on the basis of our experience of the stability of beings and their relations. Nevertheless, it makes no sense to speak of "experience" as though it were something initially detached from thinking, and to which we subsequently apply our antecedent or separately discovered laws of thought. Experience *is* thinking. It is not, to be sure, philosophical analysis; but as soon as we begin to analyze experience, we find that it was already a kind of identity within difference of beings and thoughts.

We can thus formulate Hegel's central concern as the attempt to understand completely the subject-object relation that is the basic and indeed the comprehensive horizon of human experience. It has often been objected to Hegel and his predecessors that the conception of the subject-object relation is already a metaphysical assumption, characteristic of the modern epoch and absent in pagan philosophy, an assumption that conceives in advance of the being of a thing as the "object" or project of a "subject" or consciousness that is not simply open to but itself produces what it knows. One can reply to this objection on Hegel's behalf as follows. In Greek philosophy, the relativity of the known entity to the empirical knower is present exactly as it is to be found in the modern epoch. Plato and Aristotle attempt to overcome what we may call subjectivism and its attendant relativism by their doctrine of pure form and its cognitive counterpart, *noēsis* or intellectual intuition. Unfortunately, they are unable to provide us with a coherent account of the nature of pure form, and they cannot provide us with any account whatsoever of *noēsis*, since it is by definition without structure of its own. From a Hegelian standpoint, one can describe the classical doctrine of pure form as a doctrine of phantoms; it is the ancestor of the Kantian doctrine of "as if," in which the attempt to overcome subjectivism and relativism is rooted in a hypothesis of a transcendental ego that, very much like the Platonic forms as criticized by Aristotle, is both the "essence" of the appearances of cognitive experience and at the same time altogether separate from these appearances.

It is Hegel's tacit contention that one does not achieve stability and formal intelligibility by concealing the interdependence of being and thinking on the one hand or on the other hand by dividing our experience into two worlds, one of which is a phantom or *Gedankending*. If beings or forms are what they are independent of our thinking of them, and if, further, the thinking of forms is itself "formless," i.e., entirely empty and so unknow-able (since to know is precisely to apprehend forms), then how do we know that this thinking is not actually producing the forms it thinks? How in short do we know that the entire process of noetic apprehension is not simply the process of imagination? In practice, the only way we can know this is by demonstrating that order and stability are indisputable, incorrigi-ble features of experience. This experience might itself be imaginary (as in Nietzsche's doctrine), but as I have already pointed out, that is irrelevant. A more serious difficulty is that we are unable to achieve universal agreement about the nature of intelligibility, which itself seems to be a product of ex-perience or, in the now fashionable term, history. Still, even if we disregard this point, or reply to it that we are in the process of discovering more and more layers of structure, the layers we discover are hardly separate from the cognitive processes by which we discover them.

In sum: the attempt to verify the invalidity of the claim that the subject-object relation is the horizon of experience results in its validation. We can-not separate being from thinking except through an analysis of the thinking of being. Since this analysis takes place within thought itself, the separation can never be accomplished. Nothing is gained by calling the subject a locus of pure *noēsis*, any more than the problem is solved by shifting from *noēsis* to the transcendental ego. We still have to explain the disjunction between the *noēsis* or the transcendental ego on the one hand and the empirical thinker on the other, because this is the presupposition for the thesis that there are intelligible forms independent of our thinking of them. We know that such and such is the case only because we know that we possess *noēsis* or instantiate the transcendental ego. But this so-called knowledge is noth-ing but a hypothesis based upon our experience, i.e., upon the perturba-tions within the subject-object distinction.

Greek philosophy is from a Hegelian standpoint thus based upon a phantom of the imagination, namely, the phantom of the total transcen-dence of pure reason in response to the total transcendence of pure form. Aristotle prepares for the next decisive step, namely, Kant, by bringing the forms down from their Platonic heaven and locating them within *noēsis* or the potential intellect. But he offers no solution to the question of how the intellect thinks, or what it means to say, as he does, that the soul becomes *pōs* (somehow) the beings it thinks; even worse, his doctrine of the actu-alization of form by thinking does not rid us of subjectivism but simply transforms it into transcendental subjectivity, i.e., into a phantom being of a subjectivity without a subject. Kant and Fichte offer us two different in-terpretations of Aristotle's egoless transcendental subjectivity, and Fichte's version is preferable because it attributes the nature of ego or life to that subjectivity, thereby ridding us of the incoherent doctrine of a power of thinking that is not only disembodied but also despiritualized, without a soul, or in other words that does not know what it is doing, since its activity is simply to think itself, and itself as nothing other than the act of thinking.

No doubt more could be said on this topic, but the essential point has been made. From a Hegelian standpoint, traditional rationalism is a phantom. I do not mean by this that life is a dream or an illusion in the sense that it is governed by no laws or possesses no stable and intelligible structure. I mean that the structure attributed to experience by traditional rationalism is an inference or hypothesis based upon a failure to think through the implications of the subject-object relation. The inference is sound as far as it goes, and it is the basis of science and mathematics as well as ordinary experience. But it does not provide us with an ontological explanation of the structure of the whole, nor could it, since it does not address itself to the whole. Once more from a Hegelian standpoint, self-styled empiricism is below the level of philosophy, or rather of genuine *Wissenschaft*. A correct explanation of experience requires a correct understanding of the comprehensive structure of experience. It requires a correction of Kant and Fichte, not a new physics that, like Einstein's or Bohr's, corrects the old Newtonian physics, or a new logic like that of Frege, Georg Cantor, and Russell that corrects the old logic of Aristotle and Port Royal. "Logic" here means something like *logos*. In other terms, "dialectic" is not the study of how to argue validly on the basis of the classical laws of thought, namely, identity, difference or excluded middle, and contradiction; it is instead the study of the inner relations among these three laws, and so of the root process of formation by which they are constituted. Hegel will follow Fichte in interpreting the law of noncontradiction, correctly understood, as the ground of identity and difference. Let us now turn to these laws for a preliminary inspection.

The fundamental thesis of Western rationalist ontology as it originates in Plato and Aristotle is the assertion that to be is to be something in particular, and so an instance of a determinate kind. Let me first state the classical laws of thought as Fichte and Hegel state them. In this context, I shall use "is" and "exists" as synonyms. To say that A exists is to say that it is identical to itself: $A = A$. Needless to say, A may cease to exist or be transformed into some other entity, say, B, but in this case, the same situation applies. In order for B to exist, it must be true that $B = B$. In actual experience, our ability to apply the law of identity seems to be inseparable from our ability to apply the law of difference. To say that *A* is the same as itself is to distinguish it from whatever is not *A*; in other words, *A* does not equal non-*A*. So identity and difference are correlative terms, and it is impossible to understand one without understanding the other.

Someone might object to this that it is possible simply to perceive and so to silently recognize one thing as an identity without explicitly distinguishing it from anything else. But even if this objection were sound, it would not bear on Hegel's point, since he is concerned with the laws of discursive or conceptual thought, not with the prediscursive act of perception. Hegel might, however, defend the correlativity of identity and difference even on the prediscursive level by holding that to pick out some perceptual entity as an identity is already to separate it from its neighbors in the perceptual field. "Every determination is a negation." The cognitive correlation of identity and difference is rooted in their ontological correlation. Hegel could go on to claim that when the Socratic philosophers talk of the intellectual perception or intuition of a formal unity, they are describing a process of identification by separation or division from all other formal unities. Incidentally, it can already be discerned in the representation of the law of identity that we understand it thanks to our ability to distinguish "A" from "B," where "B" does not equal "not-A." In other words, negation is already at work in the very act of affirmation. But this in itself does not mean that negation is the same as affirmation, or that it is contained "within" affirmation as negative activity. All that can safely be said to this point is that the intellectual act of identification is correlative to the intellectual act of differentiation.

Let me underline this last point. From a classical rationalist standpoint, affirmation and negation are surds. One cannot be reduced to or derived from the other. We have to distinguish on the one hand the capacity of the active intellect to perform both operations together and, on the other, their ontological or logical distinctness. To anticipate, it is quite possible for thinking to violate the law of noncontradiction, and in fact it is necessary to do so in order to think the law of noncontradiction. In order to formulate this law, we must be able to understand that p and non-p cannot hold of S simultaneously and in the same sense. That is to say, we must predicate both p and non-p of S and see why this leads to an untenable result. We see that the result is a *contra*-diction in the sense that it cannot be affirmed in discourse that obeys the separation of identity from difference. Again, from the classical standpoint, correlation is not sameness. Everything therefore depends upon what Hegel means by the identity of identity and difference. If all that he means is that identity and difference are correlated from a higher standpoint in a structure that cannot be analyzed without employing both operations, then there is no difference between dialectical and traditional logic. Now Hegel certainly does not mean that there is no difference between identity and difference. He means that they can be distinguished as cooperating within the activity of thinking. Since it is impossible to separate being from thinking, this cooperation must also occur at the ontological level. This reflection suggests that the fundamental difference between Hegelian and classical logic lies in the unification (not "identification") of being and thinking, or in other words, in the transfer of the activity of thinking to being itself.

There is an additional consequence of the preceding reflection: the law of noncontradiction presupposes the laws of identity and difference. Why is it true that we cannot predicate p and non-p of S? The answer must be something like this: thinking rests upon the fact that S is identical to itself, i.e., that it can be identified, and hence that it is distinguishable from everything that differs from it, i.e., that cannot be identified with S. And how do we identify S as S? By its properties ($p_1, \ldots, p_n$). But note carefully: If the set of defining properties contained both p and non-p, this in itself would not prevent us from identifying S. All we would have to do is to list its properties correctly, thereby including p and non-p. We *assume* that contradiction is a fault because we assume that the properties represented by p and non-p cannot belong *ontologically* to the same entity. Once again, the difference between classical and Hegelian logic rests upon the question whether being is united to thinking.

This point is sufficiently important that it bears repeating. Take any simple proposition, such as the canonical "snow is white." Why do we reject "snow is white and not white" as defective and an example of the destruction of rational discourse? There is no discursive problem in saying "snow is white and not white." Presumably there is some problem in explaining what that means. But what it means is plain enough; it means that the substance "snow" has two properties, one of which is to be white and the other is not to be white. We take it for granted, of course, that snow is not multicolored, i.e., part white and part blue, or something of that sort. We also assume that the contradiction does not mean that snow is white with respect to color but not white with respect to shape, consistency, temperature, chemical composition, and so on. By a series of refinements of this sort, we gradually arrive at the following insight. It is possible to assert that snow is white and not white, but in so doing, we will "say the thing that is not," to borrow an expression from *Gulliver's Travels*. In other words, our speech in this case is measured or regulated by what is actually true; i.e., thinking is regulated by being.

It now looks as though Hegelianism stands or falls on the thesis that being is regulated by thinking, i.e., that thinking and being are the same. They constitute an identity of identity and difference in this sense. Whereas there is an ontological difference between thinking and being, there is no conceptual difference. We cannot conceive of the ontological status of being except by thinking it. Can we think of being as altogether other than thinking? Hegel agrees with Kant in rejecting this hypothesis. In fact, he rejects it more completely than does Kant, since for Hegel there is no possibility of an unthinkable, i.e., discursively or conceptually ungraspable, thing or being in itself. There is no point in pursuing the investigation of this pivotal thesis, since it cannot be resolved by a simple reflection on ordinary experience. In fact, the thesis is a contradiction of ordinary experience; it is a highly sophisticated "philosophical" thesis that can be confirmed or refuted, if at all, only by a comprehensive analysis of its consequences, and so, I would add, by a determination of whether the thesis or its denial enables us to arrive at a better understanding of ordinary as well as extraordinary experience. Hegel's philosophy is worth considering because it is a response to a very difficult, apparently insoluble problem that is inseparable from classical rationalism. The problem is how we can think of beings, i.e., in contemporary jargon, how we can refer to anything.

I come back now to identity, difference, and contradiction. Identity and difference are coordinate or correlative but not a homogeneous unity. Hegel is in the process of attempting to show us that their correlation is the sign of a deeper unity of a *process* of excitation, sometimes called by him "negative activity," but which we can for the time being call more simply "the formation process," i.e., the constitution of intelligible structure. And to speak of intelligible structure is obviously to speak of thinking as correlative to being, again, not in the sense of reducing to a homogeneous monad but in the sense that they are the two sides to the process of negative activity.

To continue where we left off, identity and difference work together, as becomes evident when we analyze the activity of cognitive thinking. Whether or not this correlation is obvious to infants, children, or nonphilosophers is for Hegel irrelevant. Hegel is not a child psychologist or a genetic linguist. Now the question we face is whether difference "follows from" identity or whether it is coordinate with it. The classical rationalist takes the latter view; Hegel holds the former position. There is no question of "deducing" the law of difference logically from the law of identity, by using standard or classical logic. We cannot infer a negative proposition from an affirmative one without making use of the negation operator, but this requires a law of negation or difference. What we can do is to point out that identity is inaccessible except through cooperation with difference. One could say that Hegel "deduces" difference from identity insofar as he derives both from an inner process of a "self-differentiating one," but even this is hardly a logical deduction. And in fact the concept of a self-differentiating one already includes identity and difference as coordinate or co-functioning. So the question is not whether one is logically prior to the other but whether their conceptual or logical coordination is intelligible only as a process or activity.

I emphasize that Hegel does not "deduce" negation from affirmation. He would have regarded my little exercise with simple logical formulae as a complete misunderstanding of his point. It is precisely the impossibility of deducing negation from affirmation in this way that constitutes for Hegel decisive evidence of the philosophical or conceptual inadequacy of classical logic. To continue with our present exposition, difference follows from our attempt to "think," or as one could legitimately say, to "analyze" what it means to identify. But now that we have both identity and difference, can we arrive directly at the law of noncontradiction? The law of identity requires us to say that "$A = A$." The law of difference requires us to exclude the possibility that "A = non-A." We are precluded from saying that "A and not-A," since "not-A" could not be "B" and so entirely distinct from "A," given the application of the law of identity to "A." All this being so, it follows that "not (A and not-A)." But this is not a deduction; it is a conceptual analysis of the interrelation of the three laws. Either equality ("$=$") is introduced into logical calculi as a primitive operator or a two-place predicate, or it is defined set-theoretically by saying that $x = y$ if and only if every element of x is an element of y. In other words, "equals" is defined in terms of "identity," which is in turn defined in terms of "same" (as in "same members, same set"). All this adds up to the tacit assumption that "equality" is the same as "identity" and that "identity" is immediately or intuitively obvious. In other words, no noncircular analysis of identity is offered.

To sum up, Hegel does not deduce logically contradiction from identity and difference. He claims that in thinking the first two, i.e., in trying to explain to ourselves what they mean, we must arrive at the third. Let me turn directly to pages 30ff. Hegel is here discussing identity as a thesis of Fichte's *WL*, not as the basis for a logical deduction. He says that the assertion of an identity is an empty truth that, because it contains no content, contradicts our request for a true proposition. If I ask, "what is God?" and you reply, "God is God," nothing has been said. Hegel clearly means here that the question demands a predicative statement; something must be said *of* God; a property of God must be enunciated. Identical statements like "God is God" contradict themselves. Instead of expressing absolute truth as "unexcited" or "unmoving" simplicity, an identity statement dissolves, shows itself to be the opposite of what we took it to be (namely, an informative or true utterance), and thus we move from abstract identity "to the pure excitation of reflection" (31), or analysis of what has happened, by replying to the question "what is A?" with the statement "A is A." We wanted something in addition to A, by which Hegel means a predicate; in my language, we wanted a deeper analysis of A. In this deeper analysis, A is not A but something else, i.e., B.

Note that what Hegel is actually saying is that identity is intelligible only on the basis of predication; he is not saying that identity *is* predication. Bertrand Russell accuses Hegel of confusing the two, but at least in the present context, the accusation is false. This is what Hegel means when he says that "in the expression of identity, difference immediately is found" (31). Again, no logical deducing is taking place. We ask "what is A?" and receive an identity statement. But we recognize that this statement tells us nothing about A and that in fact A is something other than just A. So it is empty, and in that sense false, to be told that A is A. The difference that arises is a difference of predication, but this is hardly surprising, since there is no difference of identity. We can say that every determination is a negation, but a determination is a predication, not a statement of identity.

So that is the sense in which an identity statement contains negativity within it. All statements of identity require further analysis or differentiation in order to become intelligible. Hegel holds, for reasons already given, that this differentiation is an internal excitation of the act of thinking identity. For the traditional rationalist, it is an additional step required by the attempt to think identity. Let me here add a clarification. There is no independent statement of a law of difference by Hegel in this text. Difference appears within identity from our attempt to think the latter, and it does so in such a way as to shift our attention from identity to predication. Hegel claims that there is a negative form of the law of identity, which is the law of noncontradiction. "A cannot be both A and not-A at the same time." I believe that we are more accustomed to state this law as "S cannot be both p and not-p at the same time," thereby bringing out the inner structure of predication, upon which the contradiction depends.

But Hegel as it were pushes the question of predication to one side and attempts to show how the law of contradiction, despite its negative form, follows directly from the positive form. He says that no further justification is required of how the form of negation arises within identity; putting this in contemporary terminology, he says that we already know why the law of identity is dialectically equivalent to the law of noncontradiction. Negation lies within identity "as the pure excitation of reflection," in other words, as the aforementioned critical analysis of the truth content of identity statements. Again I emphasize that the excitation in question, and so the emergence of negativity from identity, is due to the activity of thinking. Hegel insists that this activity is not separate from or imposed onto but the same as the excited or processual nature of being, understood as the structure of intelligibility.

Note that by moving from "$A = A$" to "not (A and not-A)," Hegel assumes, or seems to assume, that we can replace "=" by the combined operation of "not" and "and." But again, this is an illusion, because he is concerned not with logical calculi but with dialectical development. As is so often the case, his analysis of the development is not very clear. Speaking of the law of noncontradiction, he says: "An A and a not-A are expressed, [of which the latter is] the pure other of A. But [this latter] points itself out only to disappear. The identity is thus expressed in this proposition—as negation of negation. A and not-A are distinguished; these distinguished elements refer to one and the same A." I interrupt to make clear that Hegel is here taking A twice: "A is not at the same time both A and not-A." It is my impression that he does not mean by this to refer to A once as the subject of predication and once as one of the predicates. He is apparently thinking of the fact that the law of identity cannot be stated without a doubling of the A. I think he takes the first A to be the entity that is being identified initially (in "$A = A$") in relation to the second A, and in the law of noncontradiction with reference to the positive and negative forms. But this would mean that A is accessible to us as an intelligible monad prior to the assertion or thinking of the law of identity. And this seems to lead to an infinite regress, since it certainly looks as if the accessibility of A is itself intelligible only thanks to the use of the law of identity.

Continuing with the translation: "Identity is thus here exhibited as this distinction [Unterschiedenheit] in a single relation or as simple distinction [Unterschied] in itself" (31–32).What does this mean? Evidently that the mere assertion of identity as the claim that $A = A$ yields two distinct terms; that is to say, it yields the law of noncontradiction. And this is due to inner excitation or the work of the negative. Otherwise stated, negativity is already visible within identity in the duplicate structure by which A is divided in order to be identified. As Hegel says in a slightly earlier passage, his opponents do not see that "identity is already differentiated" (28). In other words, it is not enough to say that one cannot affirm and deny the same statement in the same way. We need to say that in order to analyze identity and difference, we have to explain how we identify and differentiate, and we do this by distinguishing between properties and their owners, i.e., by predication. The expression "not both A and not-A" means conceptually that it is not allowed to affirm and deny the same assertion in the same context of argumentation.

Now let us sum up the discussion to this point. Hegel does not wish to "infer" in the sense of "logically deduce" the law of noncontradiction from the laws of identity and difference. Instead, he claims that the first law grows out of or evolves from the laws of identity and difference by the very process of thinking them. Hegel expresses that law as follows (II. 31): A cannot be both A and not-A at the same time; he calls this the negative form of the law of identity. Identity presupposes difference (namely, the identity of A presupposes the difference of A from not-A), and difference presupposes identity (since one cannot distinguish A from not-A except by identifying A). Once A has been identified (with the assistance of difference), it is immediately evident that A cannot be both itself and its logical complement, or not-A. The nub of Hegel's reasoning might be expressed as follows. In formal inference, we cannot deduce difference from identity, because difference contains a negation whereas identity does not. We must therefore state both identity and difference as distinct laws in our logic and proceed to derive the law of noncontradiction from them. For Hegel, however, the entire process is implicit in our understanding of identity. That is, identity already contains negation.

As we shall see, both Fichte and Hegel are searching for a version of the law of noncontradiction that grounds both identity and difference. If by "ground" is meant "serves as the principle from which both can be deduced," then I have just shown this to be the case. However, the ground in question itself presupposes the intelligibility of affirmation and negation as distinct operations. The dualism of classical rationalism is in this sense retained. One cannot exhibit the dialectical interrelationships of affirmation and negation (or being and nothing) unless one can first distinguish them as conceptual moments. For Hegel, everything turns upon the impossibility of analyzing or conceptualizing any of these moments in isolation from the others. Once again we see that everything rests upon the identity within difference of being and thinking.

Once more to state the general point: according to the tradition that

Hegel is about to criticize, formal elements and the structures that are constituted of these elements are all independent of one another with respect to their being. We cannot perceive, intuit, or know discursively whatever is not identical to itself or stable and separate in its intrinsic nature from every other form. This means that even if it is possible to perceive or intuit a formal structure as a unified totality, there is a discontinuity between being and discursive thinking, and so between being and knowledge. Discursive thinking is analytical and synthetic; it takes complex unities apart by separating out their elements and combines elements in order to arrive at complex unities. But this means that there is no discursive knowledge of a formal unit, whether this unity be atomic or a complex structure of formal atoms. Whether they arise by analysis or synthesis, all discursive statements about unities are in fact about their structure and arise through specification of the order of their elements. It is obvious that there can be no discursive statement about the unity of a formal atom; as to complex unities, it is not their unity of which we can speak but their total pattern.

The kinds of difficulties to which this gives rise are well represented by Hume, who insisted upon the fact that we cannot perceive necessary connections. But neither can we describe them, since necessity inheres not in the order of formal elements but in their inner connection, which is itself unfortunately not a formal element. Another example is the previously mentioned impossibility of picking out essential properties without an antecedent knowledge of essence. A discursive knowledge of essence would depend upon knowledge of essential properties. Otherwise stated, an analytical description of the formal structure of a complex unity cannot establish the relation of owner and owned in the configuration that exhibits a formal unity. In sum: each formal element, as obedient to the laws of identity, difference, and noncontradiction, is separate from and *external to* every other element. "Necessary" connections, whether of predication or causality, are external relations. Since the relation is not grounded in the inner nature of the relata, one could say, and Hegel does say, that it is grounded in nothing. What we call "attributes" of "essences" or "predicates" of "subjects" are, as ungrounded in their ostensible owners, appearances in the sense of illusory properties of these owners. This is what Hegel means by *Reflexion*.

The relation of reflection holds between an essence and its appearances so long as the latter are not grounded within the former; as so ungrounded, or in Hegel's sense as grounded in nothing, they are a mere shine of appearance, i.e., *Schein* or illusion, like reflections in mirror surfaces. It therefore turns out that the laws of thought, together with their own grounding thesis about the integrity, stability, and independence of formal atoms and structures, which were taken to express both the inner nature of being and hence of intelligibility, lead instead to the dissolution of necessity, the loss of essentiality, and so to the rise of nominalism, sensationalism, and the desperate attempt to resolve these disastrous consequences by the transcendental turn, which itself leads to dualism and the grounding of knowledge in belief. Reflection is analytical discourse, which dissolves form and thereby reduces it to illusion, an image of nothing on the surface of nothingness.

ELEVEN

The Nature of Essence

Introductory Remarks

I began a previous chapter with a discussion of John Locke as a kind of anticipation of, or transitional state to, Hegel's treatment of essence. We recall that in the tradition started by the Greeks, the internal structure of a being or *on*, in its Latin derivative, entity (*ens, entitas*), is derived from a fundamental principle that is most fully articulated by Aristotle. To be is to be something, of such and such a kind. This basic axiom has two corollaries. First: to be is to be self-identical, i.e., to possess a differentiated unity that permits identification because it endures as the being of the thing itself. Second: we identify a thing in two steps; first by apprehending or grasping it as a unified structure by way of its particular look or form, but second, by expressing discursively what we have seen, i.e., by answering the question "what is it?" The answer to the question "what is it?" has two stages. We can answer by giving a name, if we happen already to know how the thing in question is referred to in our language, or if we have just decided upon the name we wish to use for such references. But the act of naming is not a real answer to the question "what is it?" because, if I am told that the thing in question is, say, an orange, the question legitimately arises, "what is an orange?" A genuine answer to our question is grounded in the internal structure of the differentiated unity. We cannot simply identify anything by calling it an identity, i.e., by applying to it the law of identity, "A = A," because this law applies to everything. Identification, or the accurate or at least satisfactory answer to the question "what is it?," requires us to restate the two features of the axiom noted initially in the particular terms of the internal structure about which we are speaking. The axiom, to repeat, says that to be is to be this particular thing of such and such a kind. The answer must state which kind. But this is not enough, as we can easily see in the case of the orange. An orange is a kind of fruit. But so is an apple and a grape. So we require a further characteristic of the orange that will tell us which kind of fruit it is. That is, we require some property of the kind "orange" that belongs to the more general kind "fruit" that differentiates the species (as we can conveniently refer to it) of the genus of fruit.

The structure that underlies definition by genus and difference is rooted in the assumption that we can distinguish the features of the differentiated unity of a thing into two kinds, essential and accidental. Let us pretend that the genus of the orange is "fruit" and the difference is "citrus." But fruit is marked by various properties like seeds, flesh, shape, color, and so on. For example, let us further assume that the shape of an orange is "oblate" and its color is "orange." The possession of seeds is clearly an essential property of fruit, whereas shape and color are ambiguous properties of any body whatsoever, but of fruit in general. Oranges are normally oblate and orange, but it is not certain that their shape and color might not vary. They could be yellow or green but presumably not chartreuse or taupe.

At this point I will leave the specific example of the orange and make the general point. It is possible to define something because to be a thing is to possess properties of two kinds. The first kind of property is like "citrus" and "fruit" relative to "orange." This kind of property must be present in order for the thing to be this thing here of such and such a kind. The second kind of property is like "red" and "hair" with respect to human hair. Human beings have hair as a rule, but they would not cease to be human beings if they were born without hair. Hair must have a color, but it need not be red. In defining human beings, we therefore do not make use of properties like "hair" and "red" but instead use "rational" and "animal," which are the analogues here to the properties "citrus" and "fruit" in the case of the orange.

In general, properties are called "essential" if they must be present in order for the thing to be the thing that it is. This is not a metaphysical or mystical or arbitrarily a priori thesis; it follows from the simple but careful analysis of how it is possible for anything to be anything at all. We call "predication" the linguistic activity by which we designate the properties of something. In this activity, we "say something of something" or "attribute" a property to an owner. At this point, uncertainty enters into the picture. It is not so difficult to defend the preliminary analysis I have given of the differentiated or internally structured unity, that is, of the general conditions of thinghood. There is a lot of talk today about how difficult it is to discern the things to which persons are referring, but these difficulties all arise at the level of discourse, that is to say, predication.

It makes no sense to suggest that people *cannot* refer, since we do so regularly and with no difficulty at all. In other words, I know what I am referring to, and there are various simple ways for me to indicate to you what it is. I don't believe that there is any real problem about identifying things of such and such a kind, whether we call these kinds "natural" or not. Identification is something else at which human beings are unusually good; the ambiguities that arise are all ambiguities about the identities in the sense of the internal structure of the things we are identifying. The question is not can we identify an orange but how do we do this. In general, the difficulties arise at the level of predication, and the root of the problem of predication lies in knowing which properties are essential and which are not. As I have pointed out on several occasions, in order to be able to distinguish the essential from the accidental properties, we must first know the essence. If the essence is an arrangement of certain properties but not of others, then it is the arrangement that allows us to identify the essential properties. But this duplicates the essence; we now have (1) the essence *qua* arrangement and (2) the essence *qua* elements in the arrangement. We have to know in advance which elements constitute the arrangement.

This can be easily shown. Assume that the essence is an arrangement of certain properties. How can we identify the essence? It is not enough to list the properties that are elements in the arrangement, since such a list must be correctly arranged. But it is not possible to give the arrangement without listing the properties, in their correct arrangement, of course. Now what does it mean to speak of the correct arrangement? Certainly it does not mean to give the list of the properties, because we have this already. It can only mean to give a list of some other set of properties constituting the arrangement. But we now have two sets of essential properties *and no statement of the reason why this arrangement of properties must always occur when a thing of such and such a kind occurs*. We can certainly say that nothing will count as a human being if it is not both an animal and rational. But what connects rationality to the genus "animal" in such a way as to distinguish humans from apes or aardvarks?

This little exercise shows us that rational discourse depends upon the arrangement of properties into patterns constituting internally structured unities. But it also shows us that we are unable to capture in discourse the "ground" of the relation between owner and properties in such a way as to reveal the underlying essence. Please note that this failure does not in itself dissolve the differentiated unity into a stream of randomly collocated properties. My inability to state the essence of an orange does not dissolve the orange or turn it into a tomato. The problem is rooted in discursive language, not in the orange. It is rooted in discourse, not in being. And here is the critical moment: without intellectual intuition or the direct perception of essences, discursive thinking cannot explain the intrinsic identities of things. But the very concept of intellectual intuition is unsatisfactory to discursive intelligence precisely because the latter is discursive.

If I may dramatize the situation, the discursive intelligence is always able to outtalk the intuitive intelligence because the latter cannot talk. Hence the charge that the intuitive intelligence "does not know what it is talking about" cannot be answered. This is the fundamental cause of nominalism. It is possible for the discursive intelligence to come to the defense of intuition and to construct arguments, for example *reductio* arguments, showing why it is necessary to assume the doctrine of essences that are intuited but that cannot be discursively described. But this requires a kind of bifurcation of the discursive intelligence into prosecutor and counsel for the defense. Intuition has to sit silently in the witness box. It cannot even send written notes to its attorney.

In less poetical terms, human beings by their natures like to give explanations; they like to clear up puzzles, find out how things work, how they are constructed, and so to give the laws of nature, language, and art. None of this can be done except because to be is to be something of such and such a kind. Yet all the usual ways of attempting to parse this axiom have failed. In order to understand the Hegelian strategy, we have to see *why* it was inevitable that they fail. And this is rather obvious, once one notices it, although it is so obvious that it is often not noticed. Discursive thinking is predominantly analytical. We cannot even synthesize unless we first take apart or equivalently discern particulars or elements as potential elements within our synthesis. This is the defect in the Kantian maxim that every analysis requires a prior synthesis. For Kant, synthesis is just the mirror image of analysis. Kant rejects, like all discursively dominated philosophers, intellectual intuition or the direct apprehension of a differentiated unity that is neither a synthesis nor an analysis. Now this is perfectly defensible; I have already noted the incapacity of intellectual intuition to defend itself against the charges that it is mute. Intellectual intuition, if it could speak, would say that it is apprehending something that cannot be captured in discourse because the latter proceeds analytically (or what comes to the same thing, synthetically), whereas the unity grasped by intellectual intuition is prior to analysis and synthesis and the ground of both. And this is of course unsatisfactory to the discursive intellect, for which silence is a mark of ignorance, not knowledge. "Say what you mean!" the discursive intellect protests, and after all, the demand is not entirely unreasonable.

Now for Hegel. He sees the inadequacy of the appeal to intellectual intuition, but he also sees the fundamental and necessary failure of traditional discursive reason to resolve the problem of the essence, i.e., of the ground of the structure of owner and properties, and so of the answer to the question "what is X?" Traditional discursive rationalism has accepted from the outset the claim of intellectual intuition that, since to be is to be something of such and such a kind, a being must possess a finite, determinate, stable structure of designatable elements arranged in a specific, i.e., itself fixed pattern or arrangement. Traditional discursive reason takes its bearings by the *construction* of the finite structure. Whether it is synthesizing or analyzing (and it is doing both), it proceeds as though dealing with a finite and stable entity that has been "glued together" from its properties, essential and accidental, into the particular thing that it is.

In Hegel's language, this is the assumption characteristic of external reflection. In external reflection, we proceed to take apart, or to try to take apart, what has presumably been put together by the divine artificer or some other agent in order to constitute this particular thing. And we assume that the elements are themselves independent, stable, finite things that, as the particular elements that they are, are *independent of*, although subservient to, the logical and ontological operations by which the entity is built up out of those elements. But this set of assumptions cannot do the job, and for two reasons. First: the arrangement of elements is not itself a further element in the structure of a differentiated unity or thing (just as a set is not a member of itself). Even if we picked out elements from our ontological warehouse in order to build an entity, we would not find the arrangement lying in the storehouse next to or as one of the elements. We might open our file of blueprints in order to find a suitable arrangement, but once we distinguish between the physical object of this drawing on this piece of paper, it is very quickly obvious that the physical entity of the blueprint in question is distinct from the form or structure of which the printed blueprint is itself a model or copy. Call the original the form or idea of the arrangement in question. And now the problem of construction is simply transferred to the form or idea, i.e., to the ideal blueprint. We have an arrangement of elements but no picture of which elements are essential to the being of the entity constructed in accord with the blueprint. To state this more sharply, we have no picture of what unites the properties of the blueprint into the pattern that constitutes the type of entity that we are proposing to construct.

And here the whole image breaks down, because the blueprint is something that we have ourselves designed. We have specified, or can do so if asked, which properties are essential to the existence of the object. An artifact is what it is because we say so. The essence of a chair, a table, a nuclear accelerator, and so on is the human soul or, if that word is too old-fashioned, the human intelligence. And what is the human soul or intelligence if not an activity that puts together elements? In other words, even at the level of human artifice, it is easy to see that the human intelligence is not an element among others and is in fact nothing like the elements that it fits together into this or that arrangement. Furthermore, the elements are no longer rigid or permanently in possession of natures that contribute a stable factor of identity to the structure into which they are combined. The elements themselves may be modified by the intelligent artificer. We can change their natures, for example by changing their atomic structure, chemical nature, genetic code, and so on.

To come back to synthesis and analysis or traditional discursive intelligence, it proceeds like the builder who has not reflected on the question of the blueprint but who assumes that the latter will be discovered in the rubble of the analyzed entity. The builder conceives of himself, if at all, as another entity external to the entity whose structure he is analyzing. He may of course come to recognize that by the activity of building, he is interacting with, and changing the natures of, the elements he uses in his syntheses and analyses. But the builder does not thereby assume that he is part of what is being built. I mean that a carpenter does not believe that he is modifying himself when he planes wood. A physicist does not assume that he personally is the photon or atomic particle that he is attempting to measure but says instead that he is interfering with the particle by virtue of his attempt to measure it. This interference could be construed as the modification of both parties, namely, the physicist and the particle, but the difference between them remains. A physicist is not the particle he is attempting to measure, and this attempt is by way of traditional discursive intelligence, namely, by the isolation of finite and stable formal factors of the measurement situation.

In order for this situation to be transformed into a model or example of the Hegelian doctrine, we have to conceive of the process by which the physicist and the particle are mutually modified, rather than of the physicist and the particle themselves. The same is true of my previous example of the builder. We will never get anywhere in our search for the essences of things, or the grounds of the essence-attribute relation, simply by taking things apart and putting them back together. This method is no doubt pragmatically fruitful, but with respect to our particular question, it leads to what Aristotle calls *empeiria* or a knack, not to *episteme* or science. What we have to study is, in the model of the builder, the activity of intelligence of the builder, and so too in the example of the physicist.

In other words, we have to shift from the level of stable and finite structure, of which the highest or most general principle is the law of identity, to the level of the interaction of finite elements, not in the construction of a table or a chair, or even in the measurement of the location or acceleration of an atomic particle, but in the process by which identity and difference themselves cooperate to produce identities or internally differentiated unities. This is the level of the formation process of the structure of intelligibility. And this level, according to Hegel, is not available to the faculty of intuition or to the discursive intelligence in the traditional sense, because both these types of intelligence take their bearings by identity, i.e., by finite, stable, enduring elements that constitute another finite, stable, and enduring identity. Hegel is not denying that such entities are encountered in experience; but he is not making a study of experience except in the sense that he is attempting to explain how there can be experience at all.

This is the general statement of the problem of the shift from Aristotle to Hegel. John Locke, with whom I began these remarks, is a way station who makes very clear to us the consequences of the failure of intellectual intuition to provide the needed structures to the discursive intelligence, needed, in other words, to make sense of the fact that things are this thing here, of such and such a kind, and that we rely on this in order to manipulate things, to describe them, to understand them, and so to understand or to know what we are talking about. This must suffice as a general statement of the problem intrinsic to classical rationalism that leads Hegel to his own attempt to overcome the dualism between essence and attribute.

Book 2, Section 1, Chapter 1: Schein

The key to understanding section 1 of book 2, titled "Essence as Reflection into Itself," is very simple. In traditional rationalist philosophy, essence is both separate from and defined via its attributes. The separation of essence arises paradoxically from the effort to account for the coherence of the properties of individual things. These properties are both multiple and changing, and yet the unity and identifiability of the individual thing seems to endure. The properties apparently belong to some principle of unity that preserves the identity of the individual, and this principle is called the *essence*. As we have already seen, however, there are only two ways in which to identify the essence itself. Either we do so by way of selected members of the set of the thing's properties, or we have recourse merely to the unity of the perceived form. The first alternative fails because we must already know the essence in order to determine which properties constitute it. The second alternative leads to the same result in all cases, namely, that essence is a way of unifying properties; but this amounts either to the vacuous identification of essence with unity, or to the tautology that the essence of a thing is its look, i.e., the thing itself. The identification of essence with unity is vacuous because unity is the same in every case. But if we say that the unity is individualized or given its peculiar identity by an arrangement of properties constituting that unity, then we arrive at the tautology that the essence is the precise look that everything of a given kind exhibits. And what look is that? The answer is: the essential look. So once again we have said nothing.

The net result of the attempt to grasp the essence as separate from, albeit the principle of coherence of, its properties is thus the same as the equation of the essence with its properties: the disappearance of essence. Either the essence is separate from its properties and so is inaccessible in them, in which case it cannot be the essence of these precise properties. Or else the essence is just the arrangement of the properties themselves, in which case we have to explain the arrangement as distinct from the properties, which is clearly impossible. Or finally we are led to identify the essence with the properties. On all three explanations, the essence disappears or turns out to be the reverse of itself, namely, its attributes. This reversal prepares us for the next shift in the history of essences, the shift from the admission that essences are invisible and inaccessible to the thesis that there are no essences but only appearances. In other words, if there are no essences, then there cannot be any attributes, in the sense of the properties of essences; there are only illusory appearances of essences and attributes.

Hegel points out that the denial of essences has the effect of rendering appearances essential. This consequence may be concealed by the skeptical interpretation of the situation, namely, nominalism and radical contingency. Life is then reduced to a dream or illusion. But the claim that chaos lies at the heart of all things is a slogan or rhetorical manifesto, not a philosophical proof. The ostensible dream status of experience does not reduce it to chaos but leaves it as it is: appearance. Leibniz's remark is here decisive; what counts is not whether life is a dream but whether the dream has structure. And it does have structure, namely, the structure of appearance. Hegel attempts to demonstrate that the structure of appearance is the structure of intelligibility, and so that appearance is nothing other than the full visibility of essence.

The underlying point of the treatment of essence is thus straightforward; unfortunately, the details of that treatment are complex and obscure. I shall try to make the main line of Hegel's account as clear as possible, but without betraying his thought by translating it into an idiom that is not his own. In the title of the section, "Essence as Reflection into Itself," "itself" refers to "essence," as is shown by the use of the personal pronoun *ihm* rather than the reflexive *sich* (7). In other words, the laws of identity, difference, and ground will be exhibited respectively as essence, appearances, and the identity within difference of the two stages of development. But the first step in this process is the separate manifestation of essence and its appearances, a manifestation that serves to negate both elements, thereby reducing the whole to illusion (*Schein*). This is equivalent to a comprehensive negation that is the precondition for affirmation at a higher level. The German expression *zu Grunde gehen*, "going to ground," is employed by Hegel in this dialectical sense.

We note that for Hegel, the laws of reflection are not expressed in terms of the activity of the ego, but are derived from the continuous inner development of becoming. Hegel wishes to avoid the subjective idealism of Fichte, for whom everything is posited within the ego. But this does not mean that he takes the opposite tack of trying to derive the ego (or subjectivity) from the object. It is true that the subjective logic comes after the objective logic, but we must not forget that the logic as a totality is the articulation of the pure *concept*, namely, the concept of empty, abstract being. And there are no concepts without thinkers or subjects. That is to say, there is no logic except as thought by logicians. According to Hegel, the *SL* is based upon the *PS*, which overcomes "phenomenologically" or empirically the split between the subject and the object. The *SL analyzes* this overcoming in categorial terms.

Essence can be regarded in two different senses. First, as having emerged from being thanks to the result of the internal excitations studied in book 1, essence is not immediately in and for itself; it is rather a determinate existent that derives its nature from standing opposite to the inessential. Hegel means by this that the inner determinations of quality and quantity have not yet been stabilized into an enduring structure. They are present within being, but as indifferent to one another and to being as well. This is the structure of external reflection; it remains for the determinations to be related inwardly by a process of growth. Until that occurs, essence is defined by the illusory presence of the inessential as external to it; these illusory accidents are in fact reflections of essence itself. Therefore "illusion is the authentic positing of essence" (7). In other words, essence is itself illusory or an illusion of essentiality.

It may be helpful to recall here that Hegel is talking not about any particular essences or concrete instances of essence; he is talking not about items of experience but about categories. Furthermore, we must remember throughout that he is not referring to the traditional essences of the rationalist or metaphysical tradition. We have already seen that the traditional doctrine is vitiated by an untenable distinction between an ontologically privileged owner and its subordinate properties. The distinction is untenable because we cannot establish through it the very properties that identify the owner. Hegel wishes to arrive at the interdefinability of owner and properties. The owner is not revealed within the properties as separate from them; this reduplicates the old metaphysical puzzles. Instead, ownership and propertyhood are redefined as a comprehensive *process*.

In the sense that we are concerned with the term, there are for Hegel no essences of individual things. "Essence" is a logical category, or an ontological rather than an ontic term. Essence is a stage or dimension of the formation process that gives rise to the structure of intelligibility. Hegel's "solution" to the classical problem of essence is thus to shift the issue to the level of the absolute. The true is the whole; essence is a determination of the whole, not of this or that *res*. Otherwise stated, it is the essentiality of the process of totality that gives stability to individual things. This is the Kantian foundation of Hegel's doctrine. Instead, however, of deriving essence from the purely formal activity of the transcendental ego, Hegel attributes it to spirit or the life-pulse of the whole. Thus far we have studied the dialectical process by which becoming acquires the inner articulation into determinate existing moments marked by an inner structure of quality and quantity. To be as a particular is to stand out in the flux of becoming as a ratio of quality and quantity. This result is the first appearance of essence. But the ratio keeps dissolving; quality and quantity are not preserved but are instead only turning into each other. Hegel expresses this as an indifference on the part of each moment in the process to the other two.

With this in mind, let us try to restate what Hegel means by illusion. In its initial appearance as what I will call for brevity's sake a ratio, each individual essence (which is, remember, a moment of becoming) is defined with respect to every other as external to itself. The stability of each thing derives not from itself as independent but from relatedness to another. To be is to be preserved from within and without by otherness, and so the being of the individual is the same in all cases; as one could put this, sameness is here preserved only as uniform difference. In this sense, all are formally the same; this is what Hegel means by saying that essence is being, i.e., not the abstraction with which we began, but a being articulated as the becoming of existents (*Dasein*). But each moment of becoming (= each existent ratio) is collapsing internally, thereby reestablishing the immediacy of the totality of the process. "Immediacy" means here that it is not defined relative to some other category or structure. Therefore the appearance of something "outside" a stable essence, in opposition to which essence is being defined, is an illusion. "Outsideness" is a reflection within essence itself. It is an extension of the instability of essence.

If this terminology seems peculiar, one should remember that Hegel is attempting to describe something quite peculiar, namely, the logical structure of an experience that is stable enough to be understood as lacking in stability. Instead of presenting us with a poetical description of impending chaos, he is attempting to conceptualize it. This conceptualization will serve as the basis for the steady transformation of impending chaos into an enduring circular order of coming into being and passing away. Hegel is in the process of saving the appearances by showing us that it is essence that appears.

Now consider Hegel's assertion that "essence as emergent from being seems to stand opposite to it; this immediate being is at first the inessential" (7). Essence is a series of ratios; taking this series as a totality, it can be opposed to the simpler process from which it emerged. The problem in understanding this opposition is that there seems to be nothing left over, once we arrive at essence. But this is from Hegel's standpoint a pseudo-problem rooted in our tendency to translate his discourse into the linear temporality of the understanding. The contrast between essence and being is not between two ontic entities existing side by side in the spatiotemporal world of experience. It is between two fluid moments of a living concept. We must, as finite, temporal beings, describe this living process in a step-by-step analysis. The peculiarity of Hegel's language arises from the need to invent an idiom of temporal language (as I will call it) that is faithful to the continuous excitations and transformations of the absolute.

From the absolute standpoint, being is neither outside nor something in addition to essence. It *is* essence; or rather, essence is being considered from a certain viewpoint, at a certain stage in its transcendental development. Both are aspects of the same concept. When we shift our attention to essence, being does not disappear but remains as it were patiently waiting for us to reconsider it. We should think of ourselves as God, contemplating now one feature, now another of the conceptual recipe for the creation of the whole (*das Ganze*). This is how we have to understand the appearance of opposition between essence and being. As we begin to think essence, it has been defined for us in juxtaposition with being, which is accordingly initially considered as the *inessential*. But the converse is also true. As inessential to essence, being is indifferent to it. But there is a difference between the two kinds of indifference. Once essence appears, it is coextensive with the entire process of becoming. There is "nothing" left over; and this "nothing" serves as the boundary or background against which the process of becoming *qua* essence takes shape. Therefore, essence, as defined by an external negativity, is itself a determinate negation (that is to say, a negation in the sense of an assimilation and development of being, 7–8). Hegel means by this that essence is a negation with respect to its determinate form (since every determination is a negation). As becoming, essence is not abstract being. Abstract being thus plays its part in fixing the determination of essence. It plays the part of the boundary. But abstract being is the same as abstract nothing. We arrive at the odd result that becoming is bounded by nothing; it is therefore itself everything, i.e., the totality at its present stage of development. And this is the same as to say that becoming is the essence of its own process of coming to be and passing away. Essence is the total process of appearances and disappearances.

What is the upshot of this entire process? Essence is as it were "accidentalized" or "deessentialized" by its having been defined through the inessential, and even worse, by the negative inessential. To paraphrase the general sense, as assimilated upward into the more complex level of essence, being has been negated; it no longer retains its initial abstract or empty and homogeneous identity. In order to conceive of this new manifestation of being as essence, however, we must contrast it with the old or initiating manifestation of being. Put colloquially, being is no longer this; it is now something more elaborate. The more elaborate stage has entirely sublated or transformed the initiating stage. It thus stands alone, or is defined in contrast to nothing, that is, nothing other than the no longer manifest abstract being. As defined with respect to the negation of the initial condition, essence is as it were infected with that negativity: essence "is not" abstract being. The very process by which it assimilated and developed being has also deprived it of being. That is to say, essence contains being, but in the form of becoming. Essence is thus shot through with negation. Its stability is instability.

One could also describe this situation as the temporary triumph of nothing over being within the genetic structure of the initial appearance of essence. Stated in Hegelian terms, being as inessential initiates a degradation in the nature of essence, which falls to the status of what Hegel rather confusingly calls *das Wesentliche*, "the essential" (8). This is a degradation or fall back to the level of *Dasein*, namely, the flow of one thing and another. The instability at work here can be described as an external positing in which it is not clear what belongs to the essential and what to the inessential. Here I believe we have to understand Hegel as follows. Since the emergent structure of essence is still unstable, nothing is predominant over being. Essence receives its defining determination, which is as such a first negation, as a something opposed to another, and is thereby rendered "essentially" contingent. At the same time, the shift from being to essence amounts to the absolute negation of being, not just to its appearance as another. Essence as it were projects its attributes onto mere otherness, hence onto the dominance of being by nothing, and so the projection is a mere illusion (8–9).

Summary and Transition

Let us restate the entire preceding argument in a synoptic manner. In the traditional understanding, things have essences and attributes. This is a fundamental structure of what it is to be something. Hegel takes the two moments of this structure, namely, quality and quantity, to be reciprocally posited; the structure is for him a process, not an abstract or static logical relation. The interaction between being and nothing, you will recall, produces becoming, followed by the development of existing things, each of which is a ratio of quality and quantity. This is the basic substratum of thinghood, a substratum, once more, that is a process, not an abstract structure. It is a process because each moment, i.e., each individual ratio, is defined by another, namely, its successor, just as each constituent category is defined by its opposite. Hegel describes this process as the transformation of being into essence, but it will be easier for us to envision the situation if we say rather that becoming, powered by the dialectic of being and nothing, has arrived at the complex category of essence. Remember that Hegel is talking not about any particular structure of essence and attribute but of the logical foundation for anything at all. Incidentally, although his analysis of essence is quite different from Aristotle's, to speak of essence at all is to grant that a thing has a structure that holds it together as this thing here of such and such a kind. Essences dissolve, but it is the Aristotelian essence that is dissolving. In an imperfect but not misleading metaphor,

Hegel wishes to put Aristotle's world of essences and attributes back together again. But he can do this only by grounding these essences in the excitations of dialectical logic. In a word, Hegel will show that the destructive motion of the collapse of traditional essences is in fact the emergence of dialectical logic.

To continue with our summary, the process of becoming as a whole has moved from being as a whole to essence as a whole. Whereas it makes no sense to speak of things with properties at the level of being or becoming, the emergence of existents, *Dasein* or determinate being, understood as a flow of "somethings," again, ratios of quality and quantity, clearly refers to particular items of existence. We are in other words at the structural level of "this" and "that." Now comes the peculiarity of Hegel's analysis. Each "this" or "that," each "something" or "another," is in one sense sufficiently stable to be conceived but in another not stable enough to provide a genuine identification of the thing via its essential properties. Each something is defined by something else, by another. But to be something or another is to be defined by essential properties. Therefore an illusory process occurs in which each something takes its other as its own defining properties. Each something seems to find its defining properties in the other; hence neither of any pair is actually defined. This is perhaps easier to see at the universal level. Each "something" is defined by everything else, namely, by the total structure of becoming, which is in flux. The traditional being of essential properties is an illusion; otherwise put, it is unstable. Hence the appearance of individual essences is also an illusion. But this means that the entire process of becoming, ostensibly the exhibition of essence, is in fact entirely illusion or *Schein*.

I have called this stage the dominance of nothing over being. Hegel says that illusion is "the negative posed as negative" (9), which we can paraphrase as the nonbeing of the nonessential. First we look at Hegel's expression of this point. "The inessential, in so far as it no longer possesses being, retains of otherness only the pure moment of *Nichtdasein* [not existing as determinate being]; illusion is the immediate *Nichtdasein* ingredient in the determinateness of being in such a way that it possesses *Dasein* only in relation to another, in its *Nichtdasein*, [and so it is] the dependent that subsists only in its negation" (9). We are now in a position to understand this formulation. Simply as an exercise, let us parse it in some detail.

The dissolution of the essence and its appearances, as these were traditionally conceived, has the initial effect of leaving us with nothing but appearances. But what seems initially like the disappearance of essence is in fact the reconfiguration of essence precisely *as* appearance. Now the traditional essences were individual, self-identical, and stable entities. Essence as appearance is something rather different. Whereas it is in a sense true to say that the persisting and independent or self-identical essences have been replaced by independent appearances, this independence is only relative to the moment of perception or identification. Since there is nothing to hold them together into enduring configurations, each is simply appearing and disappearing, that is to say, each is passing into, or is being replaced by, the other. What is essential here is not any enduring, self-identical unit but rather the process of the flow of appearances. "Appearance" is here the name of the process by which the stream of appearances is constituted.

To recapitulate, essence falls apart into its appearances, and these in turn fall apart into each other; that is, whereas previously the appearances were held together within a certain configuration by their respective essences, there are now no essences but only appearances. Since "essence" means nothing other than the underlying ground of the being or nature of what shows itself as what it is, essence is the flux of appearances. But we must also note that appearances owe their nature as appearances precisely to the essences that own them, the essences *of which* they are appearances. If there are no essences of this kind, then there cannot be any appearances. What we have just identified as the appearances of the essential process of appearance are in fact neither essences nor appearances. In colloquial language, ordinary experience is the illusion of regularity and intelligible structure, but the principles of regularity and intelligibility do not exist. Since these principles do not exist, neither do existing things. *Dasein* is *Nichtdasein*.

Nichtdasein is not sheer nullity; it is the categorial or quasi-categorial equivalent of indeterminate standing forth. And in fact, "standing forth" is too strong to capture the mode of "being there" of negative existence. Indeterminate being is like a phantom that flickers across a stream of flowing water. It is thus itself indeterminate in two different but coordinate senses. The intrinsic instability of the phantom itself is exaggerated by the flow of the water on the surface of which the phantom is fleetingly visible. In this image the stream of water corresponds to sheer becoming, and the phantom is the eviscerated appearance, i.e., the appearance that is deprived of its inner identity by the loss of essence.

Let us take one more step in our exercise. There are no essences and no attributes but only the illusion of both. In other words, what has dissolved is not everyday experience but our conceptualization of it. We have lost the ability to explain experience; the ground is gone, or, as one could also put it, experience has "gone to ground," i.e., collapsed into illusion. Our concept of experience is that of an illusion. This is the condition to which the Irish poet Yeats refers in his famous line "Things fall apart; the center cannot hold." We can also designate our illusion as a condition in which inessentiality is the essence of things. This is sometimes referred to as "the accidental universe." The essence is inessentiality, and this arises, not from the juxtaposing or distinguishing of two separate ontological elements, i.e., essence and appearance, but rather from reflection upon appearance as totality. Odd though it sounds, the inessential is both the essential and the inessential. In this odd situation, we are clinging to the illusion that has nonexistence as its form of being.

Now let us shift our attention from the fragile and threatening aspect of this situation to the security that is associated with clinging to illusion. I say "security" because if we are clinging to illusion, then we have not yet disappeared into the flowing stream of chaos. Hegel's expression for my "clinging" is "reflected immediacy" (9). Hegel does not say so, but I am reminded here of something like what he calls in the *PS* "the inverted world." Immediacy, that is to say, *Nichtdasein* or illusory existence, now becomes the essence of things in opposition to the traditional essence, which in turn becomes appearance in the sense of illusion. We can also understand this step in historical terms as corresponding to modern skepticism, i.e., the skepticism generated by British empiricism. "Thus *Schein* [illusion] is the phenomenon of skepticism; so also the *Erscheinung* [appearance, phenomenon] of idealism is such an immediacy that it is no *Etwas* or no *Ding*" (9). The Kantian phenomenon is for Hegel the same as the appearance of the empiricist, namely, not a subsisting or positively existing because grounded thing, but an illusion, a simulacrum that neither for the empiricist nor for the Kantian has any conceptual connection with an essence or the thing in itself.

From a Hegelian standpoint, the transcendental machinery that produces the Kantian phenomenon serves precisely to isolate the phenomenon from anything that could serve as its essence. As to the machinery itself, this is just a specious formalization of the immanent subjectivity of empiricism. The empiricist is in exactly the same position as the Kantian to say that it is his own psychological process of association that holds together sensations in the identity of a thing or object. Looked at from the opposite perspective, Kant's insistence that the immanent subjectivity of the empiricist can itself be explained in all of its powers only as an expression of transcendental laws does nothing to reconnect phenomena to their essences. Instead, it makes thinking the essence of appearances, i.e., of appearing objects. The separation from the thing in itself is equivalent to the connection of the intellect to phenomena, i.e., to what seem to us to be things but, apart from our own cognitive activity, are nothing but sensations. We can therefore understand Kant to be saying that humanity manufactures its illusion out of sensation by a reflected immediacy, that is to say, by reflection upon the immediacy of sensations. A Kantian is then an empiricist who insists upon the solidity and validity of his comprehensive illusion (which, bear in mind, from the standpoint of experience behaves in every way exactly like the experience of the empiricist)—who insists upon this stability and validity simply because he thinks it.

This discussion of Kant and empiricism is an expansion of Hegel's remarks on pages 9–10. He summarizes the inner identity of these two doctrines as follows: "Illusion is thus itself an immediately determined" (10). In other words, sensation in both cases simply "appears" or "shows itself." It does not rise up either from things in themselves (which are inaccessible) or from sense perception, which, vis-à-vis sensation, is receptive; the activity of perception comes only through the subsequent conjoint activity of cognition on raw sensations. And this is as true of Leibniz and Kant as it is of British empiricism. All of these "allow the content of their illusion to be given. It is for each immediate what content their illusion will possess" (10).

This will suffice as an account of the initial stage of the emergence of essence from the dissolution of the ratio in book 1 of the *SL*. Here is Hegel's transitional remark: "The sublation of this determinateness of essence rests thereby in nothing more than in the exhibition that the inessential is only illusion, and that essence rather contains illusion in itself as infinite excitation in itself, which defines its immediacy as negativity and its negativity as immediacy, and so it is *das Scheinen seiner in sich selbst*," that is, the shining of illusion within essence itself (13). I have now provided the elements of an explanation of this transitional statement. The determinateness of essence is "sublated" or negated at the level of traditional ontology; it is not erased but identified as illusion, which Hegel first calls "the inessential" because he is considering the negative dimension of the aforementioned sublation. Essence is revealed to be the inessential by the dissolution of traditional thought. Hegel says that essence contains illusion within itself as an infinite self-excitation from within; that is to say, essence *qua* the inessential, which we may gloss in turn as the flux that constitutes illusion, serves to negate the immediacy of illusion; i.e., each moment of illusion is disappearing into every other moment. The immediacy of illusion as illusion is negative, or as we could more fully describe it, negative activity. So essence shows itself to be illusion; illusion shines forth or shows itself within the essentiality of inessential, illusion-producing flux.

One last comment. Hegel speaks here of the distinction between essence and appearance as illusion. I have been discussing the question of essence throughout in terms of the traditional doctrine of essence and attributes and so with respect to the distinction between essential and accidental attributes or properties. But there is no real difference between the two presentations, since essences "appear" by virtue of their defining properties. If we cannot distinguish between the defining and the accidental properties, then the essence does not genuinely appear; its appearance is an illusion. I provided a fuller analysis in terms of the doctrine of predication because this analysis is all implied by Hegel's own discussion. By making it explicit, I have tried to render perspicuous the historical importance of Hegel's logic as a criticism of rationalism in the traditional sense of the term.

Schein is the illusory articulation of becoming into essence and appearance; each appearance "reflects" or lets shine forth its essence *as* the flux of appearances. All appearances of essence, i.e., all of its properties or attributes, are therefore illusory and so accidental; and so therefore is essence. Hegel makes an untranslatable pun concerning his choice of the word *Reflexion*, which is a "word from a foreign [*fremden*] language," i.e., Latin, for the process by which illusion is "alienated from its immediacy" (*seiner Unmittelbarkeit entfremdeten Schein*, 13). That is, it is a process "from nothing to nothing"; as I put it earlier, nothing predominates over being at this stage in the dialectic, and the result is nihilism. The process can be described in terms of three kinds of reflection.

1. *Positing Reflection*: Both essence and its appearance are negative (i.e., ungrounded or insubstantial, illusory); they constitute together an immediate identity of negatives or what Hegel calls a self-referring negation (i.e., it is ungrounded, and so the two poles are not preserved at a higher level). Illusion consists "in being itself and not being itself and, indeed, in their unity" (15). Becoming is reduced to a flow that is structured, not by a grounded identity within difference of essence and appearance, but by the illusory distinctions of reflection, namely, the "bending back" (*Rückkehr*) of the negative into itself. Bear in mind that throughout this section, Hegel is describing the flux of nihilism, or the illusion of a subject-object distinction that is a perturbation on the surface of nothing. Things "appear," but this appearance is a perspective of the subject, which is itself "defined" or literally dissolved by the nugatory products of its activity. The various obscure descriptive terms employed by Hegel in this passage all refer to the flow of illusory moments of becoming, which are posited by an insubstantial subject, and hence by nothing essential, and which are canceled thanks to their inherited insubstantiality by the next equally insubstantial

positing. Throughout this section, it will be helpful to think of Nietzsche, although Hegel has in mind the German tradition from Leibniz through Kant to Fichte and Schelling. The illusory structure of becoming is thus: posit, negate, posit, negate . . . (16). Indeed, each posit is already a nothing (i.e., it has no grounding) and is sublated as posited; that is to say, in what looks like position, it is in fact not being opposed to but rather being reflected back into the (insubstantial) subject. So what seemed to be *positing* reflection is rather *external* reflection.

2. *External Reflection*: The fundamental meaning of the state of external reflection is that illusion is a version of immediacy as related to nothing. The projection of an appearance is thus an immediate cancellation of the projecting or positing; in my terms, *nothing happens* (17). And yet it seems as if something is happening (even for the solipsist, who would not be a solipsist without an illusion of external reality). According to Hegel, whatever happens in the sense of being posed, even if the posing is illusory, must take place on the basis of something prior, which is its presupposition (in German, the word for presupposition is *Voraussetzung*, "that which precedes the *Setzung* or positing"). The only presuppositionless beginning, we recall, is the abstract concept of being, and even here, it is presuppositionless only with respect to all subsequent logical determinations. It depends as a presuppositionless beginning of logic upon the prior development described in the *PS*. And *that* development has no beginning; it starts anywhere.

What then is the presupposition for the illusion of position? Hegel's reply: it is external reflection itself, which is negated in advance by its own insubstantiality or illusoriness. The very movement toward positing is as it were an advance admission of its negativity; and yet since the illusion is effected, the pseudo-structure is exhibited of a negative opposed by the negative it posits. In slightly more accessible language, the presupposition is being, which has been reduced or transformed into illusion.

Hegel illustrates what he means by external reflection in a note on Kant's distinction between reflective and determining judgment in the *Third Critique*. Kant says that the former operates when a particular is given for which a universal is to be found. Hegel restates this as a movement from the immediate to the universal (18). His exposition is anything but pellucid; however, he seems to regard the beginning from the immediate or particular as demanding a movement outside itself to a universal that is consequently separated from it. The universal does not grow out of the particular or vice versa; instead, the two are externally connected.

3. *Determining Reflection*: Determining reflection is the unity of positing

and external reflection. In other words, a "something" is defined as a relation of essence and appearance by a process that is an externalization of nothing. Becoming is thus exhibited as essentially nonessential (20). More precisely, it is a process of positing in which the posits are illusory because insubstantial. The essence is reduced to illusion by the very process of showing itself in insubstantial or accidental properties. Essence and appearances are both reduced to nothing. So all moments of becoming are (thus far) at bottom negative. We presuppose that nothingness or (in Nietzsche's term) chaos is at the heart of all things, and on that basis we pose our nugatory determinations by an activity that is as empty as its consequences (21). Hegel repeats this basic point in a variety of ways on pages 21–22 that I will not analyze, since nothing new would result. This is the nihilism of becoming, in all of whose aspects negativity predominates.

Now let me try to state one last time what is at play in this chapter of Hegel's logic. Oddly enough, the underlying point is quite simple. Becoming is a continuous emergence out of nothing back into nothing; therefore each moment of becoming is ungrounded or negated by the very process that produces it. Becoming is *essentially* nothing. This is not to say that being has been annihilated or that it never appears. After all, illusion must exist if we are to understand its essentially illusory nature. It means rather that being is dominated or negated by nothing. So all forms of empiricism, process philosophy, or any other attempt to attach significance simply to the flow of appearances are whistling in the dark. At the same time, Hegel is not going to try to rescue us from nihilism by the hypothesis of a transcendental essence or *Jenseits*, which can only be the object of faith, but never of knowledge. Instead, he is going to show how the categorial structure that we must invoke in order to substantiate the rationality of our assertion of nihilism is itself the ground through which being is rescued from the dominance of nothing and restored to equal footing. Equal, but not superior. Becoming does not turn into abstract being simply by our conceptualization of it. Instead, the conceptualization of becoming preserves being and nothing in an identity within difference that cannot itself be negated or trivialized, since each attempted negation falls *within* it. The concept is circular or eternal, the eternal return of the same.

Book 2, Section 1, Chapter 2: The Essentialities or the Determinations of Reflection

Thus far in book 2 we have arrived at the insubstantial or ungrounded distinction between essence and appearance. This distinction is an illusion in the sense that we cannot distinguish the essential from the inessential. Essence "appears" as the inessential; its appearances are reflections of an inessential essence. The three moments of this process, namely, essence, the act of appearing, and what appears, are all negative. In making this point, Hegel distinguishes between two types of negation. "Negation as quality is negation as existing [*seiend*]; being constitutes its ground and element" (21). This is the familiar sense of determinate negation. Reflection, on the other hand, is "positedness as negation," i.e., the self-canceling flow of becoming, "negation that has being negated as its ground." As negative in all its moments, reflection possesses self-sameness that constitutes a peculiar kind of subsistence (*Bestehen*). Qualitative negation thus "goes over into another via its relation" to its logical complement, whereas reflection bends back into itself (23).

Thus Hegel says that "reflection is the shining [*Scheinen*] of essence into itself" (23). The next step is to show how illusion transforms itself into a self-grounding essence; in my previous terminology, it has to be shown how the structure of illusion is in fact the structure of the ground of the appearance of actuality. I will first express how he plans to do this in Hegelese and then restate it in my own language. Hegel will proceed by analyzing the identity of illusory essence (namely, as reflexive or comprehensive negativity) and its difference as the dialectic of the three negative moments noted above (essence, act of appearing, what appears). These two (the identity of illusory essence and the dialectic of the three elements just noted), taken together, constitute a contradiction that, seen as a totality, is self-grounding. In colloquial language, negativity is going to transform itself into positivity by the inner movement of its own negations. Still more simply: to those who say that things are continuously dissolving, Hegel replies that the essence of dissolution is precisely the force that produces the world. This is nothing other than an interpretation of the dual nature of becoming as emergence and disappearance, coming into being and passing away.

In the course of this analysis, Hegel explains contradiction as equivalent to Leibniz's law of the ground. I remind the reader that Hegel rejects the traditional interpretation according to which contradiction is a property of discourse only, not of things, being, or nature. As usual, we should keep in mind that logic is from the outset conceptual thinking; there is no separation between discourse and being. From this standpoint, one may regard Hegel as the fundamental ontologist of all philosophies of language. In Hegel's criticism of Fichte, identity and difference cannot be brought together by Fichte within a discursive explanation of contradiction or the ground because of the radical separation of affirmation and negation. This is because of the static nature of negation in Fichte. Hegel employs a dynamic conception of negativity. In his analysis, the illusory appearance of essence is positive to the extent that it appears, but negative as separate from essence (since essence is hidden or incapable of grounding its appearances except as illusions). This negativity is the impetus for the aforementioned return into the negativity of the hidden essence (or *deus absconditus*). The opposition of position and negation, again, of the illusory appearance of essence as a contingent semblance or phantasm, exhibits itself *as* a relation precisely by canceling itself as it "returns into its ground" (23).

In the next part of the *SL*, Hegel discusses the laws or determinations of reflection: identity, difference, and contradiction. The most important of these, which embraces the other two at a higher level of development, is contradiction. I will proceed directly to contradiction.

Hegel intersperses his discussion of the determinations of reflection with notes that are more interesting because more concrete than the main discussion itself. In the first note, Hegel asks why identity, difference, and contradiction alone serve as laws (*Sätze*) of thought. Why do we not express laws corresponding to all of the traditional categories, such as "Everything has existence" or "Everything has quality"? His answer is that categories are all determinations of being; as such, they are negations or "go over" into their opposites, which have equal right to be called laws. For example, "everything is a this-being-here" (*Dasein*) entails that this-being-here is some other being-here. Furthermore, each requires to be proved through the other; hence, neither of a pair of opposite quasi-laws can serve as a genuine, immediate, uncontradictable law of thinking (24).

Determinations of reflection, however, are not of a qualitative nature; they do not pose a property of being by way of its delimitation from its opposite but refer to themselves. We can paraphrase Hegel's meaning here by saying that in "$A = A$" and "not-A does not equal A," there is no predication and so no identification of a subject. The laws of identity and difference are entirely general and refer to subjecthood as such. I have pointed out in a previous chapter that identity and difference imply the doctrine of predication, but this has to do with an analysis of the structure of the entities to which the law applies and how we enforce that law. I think that Hegel is justified in saying that the form of the law is not qualitative, i.e., not predicative.

Predicative statements are called *Urteilen* or "judgments," not *Sätze*, here translated as "laws." In the *Satz*, the self-reference expressed is itself the content, i.e., the content of identity is $A=A$ itself, whereas in the *Urteil* the content is placed in the predicate as separate from the form or referential nature of the judgment itself, which is expressed by the copula. However, in order to express the determinations of reflections as universal laws, a subject is required for the reference in question, namely, "everything" or A, which signifies all and each being (25). Note that there is no distinction between subject and predicate here; A is both subject and predicate, which is just to say that the content of the *Satz* is a self-reference. Nevertheless, as Hegel observes, it is a fault of these laws that they require a subject in order to be expressed, since that "awakens" being once more, i.e., the structure of judgmental predication. We have to keep firmly in mind that the determinations of reflection have the form of total self-reference and in no way depend upon *Entgegensetzung*, a positing external to themselves. By this, Hegel means that each expresses a universal truth about anything whatsoever, not a specific attribute of something or another. They refer to themselves but also to one another, and are not at all immune to the dialectical processes of "going over" into their opposites, reciprocal contradiction, and sublation.

Book 2, Section 1, Chapter 2, Subsection A: Identity

If we consider everything simply as identical to itself, there is from that standpoint no difference; being is thus nothing and we return to the Eleatic one. "The negativity [of essence] is its being. It is the same as itself in its absolute negativity, through which otherness and reference to another has disappeared completely into itself in pure selfsameness" (26). Hegel means the following. Simply to say "$A = A$" is to say nothing, unless one is referring to individual "values" of A, and so to the distinctness of one value from another, a distinctness upon which the intelligibility of identity depends, and which is nothing other than *difference*. Despite the fact that the variable A has exactly the same values in both of its appearances in the law, that does not alter the presence of difference within the concept or intelligibility of the law. In terms of the previous discussion, essence as identity is essence without attributes, each of which would constitute a determination and so a difference. We can discern here the problem of the difference between essential and nonessential attributes. An essence cannot be the same as any set of attributes, since then there is no distinction between owner and owned, i.e., no ontological priority, no ground, no necessary order to the attributes. Nor can one say that the essence just is the necessary order of the essential attributes, since that necessary order is invisible. How would it be identified, if not through some other attributes? The upshot is that essence is prior to, i.e., devoid in itself of, attributes. Hence it is empty, invisible, or nothing.

In the first of two notes to this subsection, Hegel observes that the thinking of external reflection is incapable of knowing identity or essence as just defined. Such thinking treats identity as if it were the warp of reason, which binds difference together with it as the external woof (26). The identity of dialectical logic, on the other hand, is the sheer emptiness and hence unity of essence as independent of any other (i.e., any external difference). It is therefore its own other; that is, essence is comprehensive negation of its own content, and so of itself. Accordingly, it serves as its own other, and so is pure absolute difference as well (27–28). In other words, essence negates itself, thereby filling for itself the role played elsewhere by an opposing determination. Underlying this observation is the tacit thesis that identity depends upon difference in order to be what it is. Where there is no difference, identity or the identical must play both roles. The identity of essence is absolute nonidentity with anything else. Odd though this sounds, it is at bottom a restatement of the previous articulation of essence into three negative moments of what poses its appearances, the activity of posing, and the appearances that ensue. Becoming is essentially nothing projecting nothing out of nothing. The nothing that is identical with itself is nonidentical with or different from everything else (28).

In the second note, Hegel reiterates the previous conclusion: practitioners of external reflection who distinguish identity from difference "do not see that they are already saying thereby that identity is something differentiated; for they say that identity is different from difference" (28). Again, "the truth is completed only in the unity of identity and difference" (29). Those who fail to see this are deficient in the consciousness of the "negative excitation" by which identity exhibits itself. Let me underline the fact that Hegel is discussing the laws of thought, of which the third is contradiction. These laws must be expressed discursively, and the determinations they designate belong to discursive thinking. From this standpoint, it is wrong to say that Hegel detaches contradiction from discourse. But it is correct to say that Hegel extends discourse to being, because the being in question *is* the being of discursive thinking; the full sense of discursivity, however, is dialectical, not traditional. To note only the most important point, in traditional rationalism, predicates are attached externally to subjects; as we have seen, the result is an absence of groundedness or essence. In dialectical logic, predicates grow out of their opposites, and taken collectively, predicates are determinations or determinate negations. But the separate "laws" of discursive thinking also grow out of one another, as we have just seen in the case of identity and difference. The master law, as it were, is just this process of continuous reciprocal growth; this is the basic meaning of dialectic.

The main content of the balance of the note can be briefly expressed as follows. When we begin to assert the law of identity by saying "A is . . . ," we imply that we are about to make a specific determination, in other words, to make a predication, e.g., "A is B." But when we finish instead by saying "A is A," the expected B is present as vanished. Hegel means that the B is the negative presence of the fact that identity is identical with nothing other than itself. And so it goes out beyond itself into its opposite; that is, it goes out beyond identity and becomes difference (30–31). Hegel then says, in a previously discussed passage, that the negative form of the law of identity, "A cannot be simultaneously A and not-A," is the law of contradiction. I remind the reader that whereas in the standard or nondialectical forms of these laws, difference cannot be derived from identity, both can be derived from contradiction. In dialectical logic, however, since identity turns into, or is also, difference, the law of noncontradiction is nothing other than the simultaneous assertion of identity and difference.

Book 2, Section 1, Chapter 2, Subsection B: Difference

The key to Hegel's discussion of difference is the illusory nature of the distinction between essence and its ostensible appearances, which are inner reflections of essence rather than determinate existing moments external to essence yet joined to it by the relation of opposition. We should not be confused by the fact that Hegel calls "inner reflection" by the name "external reflection." The adjective "external" refers to the fact that the distinction between essence and appearances is not one of emergence or development; it does not present itself to us but we rather impose it onto becoming. In so imposing this distinction, which is external to genuinely essential growth, we nevertheless pose it *inside* essence, because there is nothing outside essence, no genuine subsisting appearances but only illusions. In other words, "inner" refers here to the subjectivity of the distinction; "external" refers to its static nature.

Hegel resumes this point in the assertion that the "absolute difference" of essence is contained within itself, and not via another (32). "This is the difference of reflection, not the other as of an other." Or again: "The *other of essence* . . . is the other in and for itself, not the other as other of another existent outside itself" (33). In short, essence as totality is both identity and difference; even further, each is totality, and as such, each contains or is the same as the other. "This is to be thought as the essential nature of reflection and as determinate *Urgrund* [originative ground] of all activity and self-movement." This crucial passage tells us that reflection is not an error in the sense of something to be avoided but an essential stage in the development of categorial structure. Identity and difference are posed as distinctions within the predominantly negative stage of becoming called "essence." But as we have seen, the identity of essence must serve as its own difference, since there are no genuinely existing appearances of essence at this stage of the dialectic.

Hegel moves next from absolute difference to diversity (*Verschiedenheit*, 34). Identity, as both itself and difference, is diverse. This diversity constitutes otherness (*Anderssein*) as such for reflection; in other words, diversity is the consequence of the inwardness or reflection of difference within identity. We note further that thanks to the identity of identity and difference at this stage, it is a matter of indifference whether we refer to one or the other in each moment of diversity. The distinction between identity and difference is in that sense "external," which we can understand as "arbitrary." Otherwise stated, in external reflection, the distinction between identity and difference is unstable (34). More precisely, identity and difference as united within difference each possess two logical properties. The first is "reflection in itself" (*an sich*) and the second is "external reflection."

Hegel explains the first property as follows: it is identity as identical with but indifferent to difference. By "indifferent" is meant here that the identity with difference is not dynamic or mutually sustaining thanks to the emergence of each from the other; hence this identity is merely *an sich* but not *für sich*. "External reflection" refers to the joint reflection of identity and difference into each other as indifferent to one another; it refers to the process as a whole rather than to the individual moments. There follows a long discussion of "likeness" and "unlikeness," which I summarize as follows. The external reflection that produces diversity out of identity and difference is the not yet dialectical logic of Kant and Fichte, which Hegel regularly treats as subjective idealism. In other words, the moments of identity and difference, as merely diverse, have no intrinsic stability except that which is given to them from "outside" by the subject. Again, the terminology is extremely confusing; actually, the moments of diversity and the properties of likeness and unlikeness are all *within* the subject. But the subject is "external" to the determinations, i.e., imposes them arbitrarily, in accord with how things look to it. In themselves, things have no distinct or stable identity; they are merely "diverse" (34–38). As Hegel summarizes this stage of his analysis in a note, the law of difference is external to the illusory appearance of identity and difference; as so external, it defines difference from a point of view or subjective perspective (40).

Hegel then proceeds to consider the moments of diversity as opposed to one another. The moments are likeness and unlikeness, which, as subjectively identified, can each be taken to be the other (41). Each is thus the other, or the totality of the opposition. If we take the totality as likeness, it is positive; if we take it as unlikeness, it is negative (41–42). Hegel then shows how the same dialectical transformations apply to the positive and the negative as to identity and difference (42–43). Each can assume the opposite identity. In an appended note, he illustrates this by means of positive and negative numbers. I call attention to the obscure discussion on pages. 43–44. The positive and the negative can each assume the other's identity in particular cases, but the relation between positive and negative is what gives that identity to each; it is in that relation that each is "in and for itself" either positive or negative. As we would perhaps say, the relation of opposition is objective whereas the particular determination of the positive and negative elements is subjective or depends upon circumstances.

I reserve for a separate chapter my discussion of contradiction.

TWELVE

Contradiction

Introductory Remarks

We turn now to the nature of contradiction. In order to understand the Hegelian doctrine of contradiction, it will be helpful to reconsider briefly the previously discussed operations of identity and difference. The first thing to be said is that we are not concerned with the laws or principles of formal reasoning as these are formulated within traditional rationalism. We have to understand that Hegel accepts the validity of these laws or principles within ordinary discourse. In other words, we must distinguish between the laws of the understanding and the laws of reason; the latter can also be called the laws of dialectic. For the sake of avoiding confusion, I will speak of the Hegelian situation as dialectical, and of traditional rationalism as ordinary.

In ordinary rationalism, the law of contradiction is said to apply to propositional discourse. What is meant by this latter expression? A proposition is a predicative statement that is said to be either true or false. We say something of something; in other words, the traditional grammatical and logical analysis that goes back to Aristotle is here assumed, either explicitly or in a disguised form. Modern functional logic is an example of what I mean by a disguised form of the Aristotelian analysis. In the explicit Aristotelian analysis, the proposition consists of a subject and a predicate. The subject term stands for the owner of the property for which the predicate term stands. "S is p" thus represents the attribution of a property to a subject. In other words, the subject term stands for the owner of the property; the subject term corresponds to the essence or substance of the "metaphysical" or (as we now say) the "ontological" analysis, which in turn underlies and is the ground or foundation of the grammatical or syntactical analysis.

We can say that p belongs to S or that it does not belong to S. "Is" and "is not" are thus verbally or grammatically distinct from S and p, but it is not at all clear that they are metaphysically or ontologically distinct. Let us take a simple example: "Socrates is mortal." On the one hand, "is" must be independent of "Socrates" as well as "mortal," because each of these might not be. Otherwise put, we can replace "Socrates" by "Plato" and "mortal" by "immortal" without changing the semantic role of "is." The relation between "is" and "not" is more complicated, and I will come to it in a moment. But first let me finish my remark about the two terms of the proposition. From another standpoint, neither "Socrates" nor "mortal" is independent of "is" (or alternatively of "is not"), because of the ordinary assumption that terms must have a reference of some sort. By "reference" we can mean either a "sense" or a "concept" as in the case of "mortal," or we can mean a spatiotemporal thing, or more generally a substance or primary *ousia*, such as Socrates. The Fregean distinction between *Sinn* and *Bedeutung*, usually translated "sense" and "reference," is ambiguous because the reference can itself be a sense. However, it would take us too far afield to pursue this line of inquiry.

Socrates is the person to whom we attribute the property "mortal" in our example of a proposition. We wish to indicate that if Socrates is indeed mortal, i.e., if he in fact owns the property of mortality, then the statement or proposition is true. But the truth of the proposition depends upon something, namely, upon the inherence of mortality in Socrates. Socrates must actually own the property in order for the statement to be a true proposition. So it is not satisfactory to restrict "true" and "false" to propositions or discursive thinking. In ordinary reasoning, we do not assume that there is any connection between whether or not Socrates is mortal and what we say about Socrates's mortality. On the other hand, we do assume that there is a connection between Socrates's mortality and whether what we say about it is true or false. So discourse does not regulate being, but the reverse is the case. This point is closely connected to the fact that there are at least two senses of "true" in ordinary discourse, one of which refers to propositions but the other of which refers to things or beings, in other words to substances and their properties, and thus to essences. For example, we often say "genuine" or "actual" or "really" when we are employing the ontological sense of truth.

All attempts to separate discursive from ontological truth rest upon metaphysical doctrines about the accessibility or ontological status of the referents of the words we employ in constructing propositions. I will say only that it is preposterous and incoherent to claim that words refer to other words only. If this were true, we could say anything we like. The claim that words refer to appearances rather than to things in themselves, i.e., to essences, is another matter, and it is this claim that we inspected in our study of the transition from book 1 to book 2. By way of transition from that discussion to this one, let me say that the claim that propositions refer to appearances but that there are no essences is from Hegel's standpoint also nonsensical. It leads to complete chaos. For if there are no essences, then there are also no appearances, but only *appearances* of appearances. Otherwise put, if there are no essences, then there are no owners of properties but only properties. In this case, however, there is no order or structure by which we can say that this belongs to that, but rather anything can—and does—belong to anything.

Considerations of this sort lead to the conclusion that the laws of thought in ordinary discourse themselves depend upon metaphysical or ontological order. In other words, when we say something like "Socrates is mortal," it is crucial as to what we mean by "is," and in parallel cases, by "is not."

Now barring eccentric cases, when we say that something is something, we mean to say that the two terms represented by "something" have actual references, and that they are in fact related by the relation of predication, so that the first something can truly be said to own the second something. If we break down this general situation into its components, we are saying that the subject and the predicate term both have referents that are different from one another, and that these two referents are connected to one another in such a way that they are both identical and different. To say "Socrates is mortal" is to say that Socrates is a man and mortality is a property and that Socrates possesses the property of being mortal. Socrates "is" and mortality "is." But the is-ness or existence or being or actuality, or even the illusory existence of each as independent, is itself independent of the connection between the two, and this connecting is represented by the copula "is," i.e., by the "is" in the proposition "Socrates is mortal." So it looks as if we have three different kinds of is-ness or being here; the conceptual or property existence of mortality, the essential or substantial is-ness of Socrates, and the ontological or connecting is-ness designed by the copula.

In functional logic, the copula is ostensibly eliminated and the predicate term is transformed into a function, e.g., "—— (is) mortal." Please note that in fact the copula is not eliminated at all, although no doubt one could write the predicate function in such a way as to make it appear as though we have eliminated it . What has actually happened, however, is that the copula is buried or concealed within the predicate expression.

Socrates now becomes an instance or value of a variable that stands for the universe of possible values of the function. For some strange reason it is assumed by philosophers of logic that this new analysis eliminates the old-fashioned substance-property analysis. But nothing metaphysical of any importance is accomplished by calling "Socrates" a value of the function "is mortal." We still need to know what it is to be Socrates, and we still need to know the status of the "is" that is buried within the predicate function.

This is as far as we can go in discussing the case of functional logic. I bring it up only to indicate that I reject entirely the today-dominant view that the new logic removes all the old traditional metaphysical problems. This is an absurd thesis and a kind of superstition of the enlightened, if I may so call it. It amounts to the assumption that we can change the world by altering the syntactical structure of our language.[1]

To return now to Hegel, "is" and "is not" in the ordinary rationalism are distinguishable from, and yet somehow the same as, the subject and the predicate terms. Socrates is, i.e., exists, and mortal is, i.e., exists, although Socrates exists in one way and mortality in another. But the way in which they exist is that mortality inheres in or is owned by Socrates. This is true, but unfortunately not true enough. I mean by this that Plato is also mortal, and Socrates is also rational. There are many independent substances and many independent properties, and these must all be said to exist or "be" in order for them to enter into true connections. But the connections are themselves not the same as the independently existing entities. There is some problem here of how to understand "is" (or "is not," a more complicated case), a problem that we avoid by speaking of the copula or linking verb. Incidentally, the difference between identity and predication does not remove any of these puzzles but is itself an expression of the puzzle, as we shall see later.

One might want to say that "Socrates" is just a name, albeit the name of a substance, and that "mortal" is a name for a property that has no independent existence but "is" only as an element within the being of a substance. This would leave us with the problem of the being of the concept "mortal," which does not inhere in Socrates as essentially owned by him; a concept is not a property. Similar considerations hold good in the case of so-called accidental properties, which I will not analyze for the sake of brevity.

This aside, the attempt to reduce the being of the referent of "mortal" to the status of element within the being of the referent of "Socrates" solves nothing because it is based upon the assumption of an internally articulated structure constituting the individual substance "Socrates." We would then have to repeat our analysis of this structure and explain the difference as well as the connection between the essence of Socrates and its attributes. In order to discuss this internal structure at all, we would have to use propositions of the form "something is something"; in other words, we would be back where we started.

Now what about "is" and "is not"? On the one hand, Socrates is mortal. Mortality is a property or predicate of Socrates. So he is not identical with mortality. But so what? Mortality is an essential property of Socrates, and hence it is an essential element in his *identity*. Socrates cannot exist apart from his mortality. We cannot reduce Socrates to mortality; Socrates is not a property of himself or of the living things on earth; he is not a property at all but a substance with an essence and attributes. But to be an essence is to have a definite nature that makes him what he is, and mortality is an essential ingredient in this nature. We thus have to distinguish between what I will call "reductive" and "essential" identity. X is reductively identical to Y if there is no difference at all between them, i.e., no ontological difference between the referents of the words or names represented by X and Y. In this sense, mortality is identical to itself, or in other words, reductive identity is represented as "$A = A$." But this is not the form of the assertion "Socrates is mortal." Socrates is essentially mortal; no mortality, no Socrates. The difference between Socrates and mortality is partially erased by their essential connection.

Let me draw this line of thought to a close: predication is itself a case of partial identity. We have been looking at a subcase, namely, essential identity; to this we would have to add "accidental identity." But essential identity is more interesting and keeps us closer to the heart of the Hegelian problematic. Socrates's identity not only depends upon but consists of differences. The statement that Socrates's identity consists of properties, and so that it is represented discursively by predications, is not a clarification of the more obscure statement that Socrates's identity consists of differences. Properties *are* differences; they are determinations of one kind and another, each of which makes something different from what it was before the predication or exhibition of the corresponding property.

Hegel does not deny that everything is identical to itself, nor does he confuse this with predication. It is impossible not to see that "$A = A$" is not the same as "A is B." Hegel's point is rather that "$A = A$" is already, precisely as the general form of the law of identity, the exhibition of the inner connection between identity and difference, and so by extension, of identity and predication. In order even to state the law of identity, one must distinguish the identical term from itself, i.e., double it. This doubling is self-differentiation. That differentiation is not disguised by the "=" sign. What does "equal" mean, if not "is identical with" or "is the same as"? But one thing cannot equal nothing; it must equal something, and the something is itself. In this analysis, we take one and the same thing and try to regard it from two different standpoints, in order to show that the two standpoints look out onto one and the same thing, and that this would be so regardless of how many standpoints we assumed. But none of this can be accomplished without the doubling or self-differentiation.

If this is persuasive, and I am simply trying to make out a plausible case for Hegel, then "—— is identical to itself" is a predicate by means of which we express the law of identity. Let us take identity as the limit case of difference, and hence of predication. As soon as we move beyond this limit case and add a difference to one of the terms in our equation, we arrive at difference. How is this to be symbolized? Not by "A not equal to A" since that is a contradiction, not at all what we want to say. "$A = B$" does not work in this case if $B = A$. We can say "A is not equal to non-A." But this depends upon the law of identity, namely, that $A = A$. So the law of identity is implicit within, i.e., is a part of the inner articulation of, the law of difference.

To come back to predication, in order to predicate B of A, we have to invoke both identity and difference. Both are essential ingredients of predication. In other words, they are not themselves reductively but essentially identical. But predication is thus seen to be a joint application of identity and difference in the discursive analysis of an ontological instance of truth, namely, in a case in which one thing is truly predicated of another. This entire process is represented by the law or principle of noncontradiction. So much for our preface to Hegel's discussion of contradiction.

Book 2, Section 1, Chapter 2, Subsection C: Contradiction

In the previous chapter we studied difference from three standpoints: (1) as containing moments of both identity and difference; (2) as diversity, and so as indifferent to either moment; and (3) as the relation of opposition, in which each (i.e., identity and difference) is defined through the other but as independent and reciprocally excluding the other. Hegel calls this "the independent determination of reflection" (48–49). He means to say that the moments of identity and difference, or positivity and negativity, are independent for reflection (the thinking by which the subject posits within itself a distinction between identity and difference, e.g., between essence and appearance), but that in fact they contradict one another. Why is this so?

Let us analyze the case of the opposition of positive and negative. In that opposition, each element is primitive. In other words, one cannot be reduced to or derived from the other, as is obvious, for example, in the primitive status of negation within traditional logic. Hegel refers to this primitive or independent status as "indifference." The reader will remember that what I am calling the primitive independence of the positive and the negative is itself negated by the ungrounded status of essence at this stage in our analysis. The distinction between essence and appearance is illusory; both terms are negativities and so too is their separation. But this illusion is imposed by reflection, which as it were enacts a subjective or perspectival distinction between the subject and its object. This distinction itself possesses the structure of identity, difference, and ground. But in the absence of a ground, identity and difference lack stability and undergo the transformations we have been studying. They both identify with and exclude one another. And this is to say that they are mutually contradictory. From the standpoint of reflection, this is a defect. Hegel intends to show that contradiction is instead a virtue; more precisely, it is the very ground for which we are searching.

As independent of each other, the positive and the negative are nevertheless opposed. But from this standpoint, each contains within itself its opposition to the other. More simply stated, in traditional rationalism, it is impossible to derive the negative from the positive. Nevertheless, we define each in terms of the other. This reciprocal process of definition is not, however, one of reciprocal evolution, as it is for Hegel. The positive, for example, does not lose its independence by being distinguished from the negative. It does not turn into or incorporate within its essence the moment of the negative. So far, so good. But Hegel's next step is considerably more obscure. Each moment, positive as well as negative, "possesses indifferent independence for itself through the fact that it possesses the relation to its other moment in itself; thus it is the total, self-contained opposition" (49). Hegel claims not only that one cannot derive the moments from one another but that therefore each is the entire opposition of positive and negative. The positive is independent of the negative in an evolutionary or developmental sense, but one cannot understand what it is to be positive except with respect to the negative, and vice versa.

I think that it is just possible to see Hegel's point in this passage. The assertion of positivity entails negativity, and vice versa. To assert either is to assert the relation of opposition. But it is not to identify or blend together the two moments of the relation. Each moment is the totality of the opposition, and in this sense each is mediated within itself with its other; but each moment is independent of the other and in this sense is mediated with itself through not being its other. In this second sense, each is a self-subsisting unity that excludes the other. It is easy to be frustrated by what looks like Hegel's unceasing nit-picking or hairsplitting, and to object that the various distinctions he extracts from the relation of a pair of complementary terms are all purely verbal. But what does this objection itself mean? Are not all logical relations "verbal"? More profoundly, Hegel insists that all of the relations of any two complementary terms are equally "real" in the sense of playing a role in the intelligible structure of the relation, and so of the terms themselves. This insistence is at the heart of the shift from reflection or the logic of understanding to dialectic or the logic of reason.

We may reply that it makes no sense to claim that the negative "grows" out of the positive or vice versa; the two are what they are, and as what they are, they stand in a relation of opposition. That, we may be inclined to say, is the end of the story. Hegel would reply as follows. I agree that the positive and the negative are what they are and as such stand in a relation of opposition. But each is independent of the other precisely because each includes the other in its independent concept. Therefore each includes the entire relation. These inclusions do not erase the initial independence; they articulate it. You may choose to disregard the articulations, but you will thereby forfeit any understanding of the structure of intelligibility.

The determinations of reflection are unstable because ungrounded, and they are ungrounded because they do not include a satisfactory analysis of contradiction. Each such determination contains and excludes its complement; each therefore excludes its own independence or contradicts itself. Indeed, "difference in general is already contradiction in itself, because it is the unity of elements that exist only in so far as they are not unified, and [it is also] the separation of those elements that exist only as separated in the same relation" (49). There is no point in arguing against Hegel that each atomic element is intelligible in itself when the opposite is obviously the case. No one has ever explained identity except via difference or difference except via identity. To insist that such explanations are concatenations of independent elements is to shift the problem to the concatenation. At what point are identity and difference concatenated in order to render each intelligible?

One cannot repeat too often that the problem is exactly that of the Eleatic Stranger in Plato's *Sophist*. The element of being is the same as itself and other than the other elements. How can it be separate from its sameness to itself? One could reply that we "conceive" of sameness as distinct from being but always combined with it in every complex instance. Hegel would not deny this claim; he would simply demand to know what it means. He too "conceives" of identity as other than difference; but this otherness is itself negated within the very activity of conceiving of the individual elements. Hegel does not so to speak deny the independence of each atomic element of intelligibility; instead, he points out the obvious fact that at the level of intelligibility, as opposed to mere enunciation of the name of an independent element, the elements are combined. But this is exactly what the Platonists claim. The problem is that they do not understand the implications of this claim. If to be is to be intelligible, and to be intelligible is to be compounded, then there is no independent being. The fact that I can verbally distinguish "being" from "sameness" is not a sign that they are actually or ontologically separate. As soon as I begin to analyze my words with the intention of understanding what they mean, it becomes clear that being is intelligible only through its sameness with itself, and that there is no sameness independent of being.

We should not commit the error of assuming that on the Hegelian analysis, everything is blurred together or that no individual things can be understood. On the contrary, in the *SL* Hegel is providing us with a micro-analysis of what it is to be intelligible, and so what it is to be, i.e., to be conceived as, an individual thing. Nor is he talking about stones, trees, stars, horses, or persons. He is explicating the logical, i.e., categorial structure of the concept of individuality. From this standpoint, the criticism of Hegel initiated by Schelling and Kierkegaard, to the effect that he tries to derive individuality from universality, is nonsense. Hegel does not hold that one can understand what it is to be Søren Kierkegaard by deducing him from the concept of the totality of categorial determinations. That is not the purpose of logic. Even Hegel's treatment of politics, religion, art, history, and so on is dominated by his intention of exhibiting the logical substructure of historical contingency. Even the *PS* is not an existentialist treatise on personal experience but a prolegomenon to logic. It is hardly by chance that there are no individuals in the *PS* with the exception of Rameau's nephew, an exception that proves the rule since that personage exemplifies the connection between individualism and nihilism. If we begin from the individual person, we can never rise above subjectivism, perspectivism, and nihilism, except by a leap of faith, a leap into the absurd. Hegel is the greatest enemy of such leaps who ever lived.

To come back to the text, the independence of identity and difference is such that each both includes and excludes the other. To be independent is to exclude one's opposite. But to exclude it is to become the entire relation, since neither element can be understood except via the other. As the entire relation, however, each element, in excluding its opposite, excludes itself from itself. This is contradiction. You cannot posit the positive without excluding the negative from it. But this "exclusion" is inclusion within the concept of positivity. And this is what Hegel calls "the absolute contradiction" of the positive and the negative: "The positing of both is a single reflection" (50). Note that the negative is more fundamental than the positive at this stage for the following reason. The positive is the same as itself and thus independent of the negative, which it becomes only by being related to it as its opposing element. But the negative is, precisely as negative, the same as itself and so positive, i.e., as one could put this, it is "positively negativity." I repeat: the positive as positive is not negative, but the negative as negative is positive, namely, positively what it is. It possesses the identity of negativity. Hegel makes this distinction by saying that the positive is only contradiction in itself, whereas the negative is "the posited contradiction, for in its reflection into self, by which it is negative in and for itself or, as negative, identical with itself, it has the determination that it is not identical, exclusion of identity. It is this: to be identical with itself as opposed to identity, and thereby to exclude itself from itself through its excluding reflection" (50).

In sum: the positive, as independent, is merely positive; the negative, as independent, is both positive and negative, or both identity and difference. Since it is both, in excluding its opposite, it excludes or contradicts itself. The next stage is to see how the contradiction dissolves itself. Not surprisingly, it does so by the process of "going over" that is engendered by, or is the same as, the negative activity that we have been studying in the various moments of the *Reflexionsbestimmungen*. In other words, what changes is our point of view, how we regard negativity. Whereas previously we viewed it as disruptive, this was because we had adopted the standpoint of reflection or finite, i.e., traditional analysis. If the various logical determinations were truly independent logical atoms, then the impossibility of thinking them without invoking their opposites or complements would lead to contradiction in the pejorative sense of the term. As soon as we see that contradiction is precisely the activity of thinking the conceptual connections that weave together the logical atoms, the pejorative assessment is dissolved. The initial nullity of contradiction that is produced by the reciprocal negations of each element is now seen as the extinguishing, not of the elements themselves, but of their independence (51). Each element is self-subsisting as or via its negative relation to its opposite.

Allow me to repeat that previously, becoming was envisioned as a fundamentally negative process, in which a transient and illusorily stable structure emerged from nothing, only to return to it. The analysis of reflection is an articulation of this negative process of becoming as seen from the standpoint of the understanding. Reflection is nihilism because it is unable to stabilize or sustain the self-differentiation of becoming, which continuously collapses into nothing. And this is exactly what has happened to traditional rationalism in its historical development throughout the nineteenth and twentieth centuries. The distinguishing feature of Hegel's thought is that he attempts to rescue us from nihilism not by begging the question with a leap into the absurd, or even into the absolute (as though we were shot from a pistol), but by a proper account of nihilation. Hegel's starting point is that even if being is nothing, that, so to speak, is already something. Illusion is something, not nothing in the sense of the void or complete vacuity. We think being; hence we think nothing. The structure of our thinking of nothing is the concept. The absolute is thus exhibited (not deduced) by its evolution out of the sameness of being and nothing into totality.

In my opinion, Hegel made a tactical error in insisting that the *SL* depends upon the *PS*. This error is compounded by his assertion at the beginning of the *SL* that we must rise to the level of the absolute by an act of the will. One could much more efficiently begin the defense of Hegelianism by starting with the radical aporiai of traditional rationalism and showing how these aporiai lead us directly into dialectical logic. An act of the will is required here, not to leap into the absurd, but to have the honesty to see what is staring us in the face, namely, the nature of conceptual determinations or intelligibility. As to the *PS*, the idea of absolute knowledge is no doubt a useful means of encouraging us to engage in the structural analysis of what we already know experientially or phenomenologically, but it is not logically necessary. All that Hegel needs in order to begin the shift to dialectic is the undeniable assertion that every statement about being is a statement about the thinking of being. We can distinguish between being and thinking, but the distinction is one of thinking. We can say: "it is one thing to be, and something else again to be thought of as so being." But the positing of a being independent of thought is a positing of thought. This is why to be is to be thinkable. We do not thereby erase the distinction between being and thinking but rather explain its structure as an identity within difference.

The purpose of this remark is to remind the reader of the larger context within which Hegel is shifting from reflection as contradiction to contradiction as the ground of identity and difference, and so of reflection itself. The attempt to understand traditional rationalism leads directly to dialectical logic. As independent, identity and difference depend upon one another; they are independent precisely through the negative relation that each bears to the other; or as Hegel puts it, their independence is *posited* (i.e., by the opposition in question, 51). At the same time, since each independent element negates the other, there is a negation of the initial negation (the determinative or excluding negation of moments as opposite) or an *Aufhebung* that raises us to the level of a totality in which each of the two fundamental elements is identical with as well as different from the other. In Hegelian jargon, to oppose is also to suppress the opposition or to unify (52). Now we have to apply this entire process to the case of essence. Essence shows itself as appearance, but this showing turns out to be illusory because it is ungrounded. We cannot know which appearances are essential without knowing essence, and we cannot know essence without knowing which appearances are essential. So the defining appearances are *merely apparent*. Since essence appears as mere appearance, it is itself mere appearance; both essence and its appearances are essentially negative, i.e., insubstantial, purely subjective. The positing opposition between essence and appearance is a self-negating as well as a self-defining relation. As self-negating, it reunifies essence and appearance; in the fuller statement, this reunification is established by the overcoming of the independence of identity and difference. Essence is the harmony of the positive and the negative moments; it is not a static or lifeless substance standing apart from its attributes but the process of excitation through which all categorial moments are produced, negated, and sublated by a proper grasp of contradiction; that is, they are raised to an identity within difference. Essence is thus the ground; I repeat that this ground is excitation, negative activity, process (52–53).

"The dissolved contradiction is thus the ground, the essence as unity of positive and negative" (53). As Hegel puts it, the determinations of identity and difference, positive and negative, "go to ground" (*zugrunde gehen*), This dialectical expression means both that the reflexive roles of the logical elements are destroyed through a sublation, and that they are preserved within the process of positing and negating as the ground. In radically oversimplified but intrinsically correct language: Previously we saw becoming as a negative process of negativizing. Now we see this same process in its positive identity as bringing into being; negativity is the essential condition for positivity or genesis.

The chapter closes with three notes, of which the last is the most important. In note 1 Hegel gives simple examples of the interconnectedness of the positive and the negative, e.g., light and darkness (54–56). He observes that one cannot take the first step in philosophy if one has not understood the interconnectedness of the *Reflexionsbestimmungen*. Note 2 contains a brief discussion of the opposition of identity and difference in the form of the law of excluded middle. I note that for Hegel, to say that everything is either +*A* or −*A* is to indicate a third term, namely, *A*, which, as neither the positive nor the negative variable, is itself what the law excludes.

In the third note, Hegel makes the general point that all things are "in themselves contradictory" (58). Remember that the "things" to which Hegel is referring are themselves modifications of discursive thinking or moments of the concept. They are not separate from discursive thinking. Since we cannot talk about them without generating contradictions, these latter are ingredient in the intelligibility of the things *as* things. It is therefore a much deeper truth to attribute contradiction to things than to attribute identity, which by itself is an attribute of dead being. As the "root of all excitation and life," contradiction is the exhibition of the negative (59). By this, Hegel refers to "negative unity," not annihilation, but the process itself, which we have now studied sufficiently. Finite things go to ground in two senses; they are "broken apart" by the contradiction of reflection, but at the same time they are grounded by the relations that they acquire through the breakup process itself (62). Thus the finite, precisely through its own not-being, is the absolute, namely, the negative activity of contradiction as the grounding of finitude.

Book 2, Section 1, Chapter 3: The Ground

The treatment of reflection culminates in the identification of contradiction as the ground of identity and difference. In somewhat more accessible terms, genesis is the exhibition of two opposing motions, coming to be and passing away. These motions are the constitutive structure of each moment of genesis, as is evident from the simplest reflection on the nature of time. We experience time not as a sequence of discontinuous moments or points but rather as a continuous process. What we call "the present" is emerging from the future and disappearing into the past. We can identify moments of time by naming them in accord with our systems of measurement, but this process of identification is an abstraction that is disregarded by time itself, which continues to flow regardless of which of its identified moments we choose to consider.

Notice that the concept of the past is not itself a moment of the past; it holds good for the present and the future as well. In other words, whereas we cannot exist outside of time, it seems that we can detach ourselves from its flow through conceptual thought. Numbers, geometrical shapes, ratios, values, and ends are some of the items that seem to be excluded from temporality, and hence to serve as gateways into, or at least windows onto, eternity. The least that can be said is that temporality itself exhibits a structure, or rather a series of structures, the most obvious of which we call "past, present, and future," and which include numbers, shapes, ratios, and so on. Furthermore, when I think about past events or imagine some future state of affairs, I do not cease to exist in the present, but I have extended myself via concepts and images into another segment of temporal flow than the one I occupy physically.

I want to generalize on these examples by saying that thinking enables us to move about in time. There are obvious limits to this capacity, but the limits themselves illustrate the point that time possesses a determinate structure or nature. We certainly do not understand time very well, but we know this structure from our experience. Differently stated, time is recalcitrant to our manipulations and even to our thoughts; it permits some procedures and forbids others. It is this regularity that enables us to think about time, and so about our temporality. In other words, life as temporality is not the same as our thinking about temporality. Furthermore, we have to think about time in at least two different ways. The first way corresponds to traditional rationalism, of which the first principle is the law of noncontradiction. This way is required in order to cope with our everyday experience of the independence and stability of things and events. I call this "everyday" for the following reason. Even if life is a continuous process, we cannot grasp it as a whole except by noticing its particular features. We take our bearings by identifiable and hence reidentifiable things, by what Aristotle calls "a this thing here of such and such a kind." This is in principle what Plato means by the ideas.

The second way of thinking about time corresponds to Hegel's dialectico-speculative logic, or at least leads directly to such a logic. In this way, we attempt to think about time as a totality. Once again, we cannot start by thinking the totality as a totality; we have to begin with particular features. These features are the logical determinations of the concept of time. The thinking of the concept of time, to repeat this crucial point, is not the same as living or the existential temporalization process. As living temporal creatures we are required *not* to think about time as a totality, but to respond to this or that particular temporal manifestation. As soon as we begin to think about time, even in the simplest way, as by noting that it is continuous, or that "time waits for no man," or that human beings cannot elude it as long as they live, or that we cannot physically move backward in time, and so on, our attention shifts from temporal things or events as such to the process as a totality, to how a thing or event occurs, and so to the general nature of occurrence. We discern that time is not itself coming into being and passing away but *is* the process of coming into being and passing away.

As that process, time is not a discontinuous sequence of two subprocesses. It is not the case that first there is a coming into being and then a passing away. Of course, this is precisely what happens at the intratemporal level of things and events, at the level, in other words, at which the law of noncontradiction holds good. But things and processes are not time; they are occurrences. Life is not a discontinuous series of time events, each of which is surrounded by eternity. It is rather the case that, wherever we look, including at ourselves as observers, occurrences are continuous. There are no holes in time; as we turn our attention from one event to another, we ourselves continue to exist temporally. We may not be measuring our own passing of time, but someone else can do so. And this holds true even when we are thinking about eternity or about eternal entities.

No doubt these remarks would have to be refined and elaborated, but they are not intended as an adequate philosophical treatment of time. I regard them as sufficient to illustrate the distinction between what I have called the two ways of thinking about time. The second way corresponds to time as a continuum or totality, and so as that which is continuously present in each of its moments, past, present, or future. As a totality, time is a contradiction in Hegel's sense of that term. Time manifests itself as a continuous series of moments, each of which is coming into being and passing away; otherwise stated, time is present as both past and future. It is thus both positive and negative at each moment, each of which is identical with and different from itself. We can and must regard each of these characteristics independently from one another; we must say "on the one hand this, on the other hand that," or apply our everyday version of rationalism to the task of studying temporal manifestation. But when we try to grasp this manifestation as a totality, then traditional rationalism breaks down.

I have used time as an example of what is in Hegel a completely general analysis of logical categories. It would be more Hegelian to say that time, considered as a totality, is eternity; in other words, eternity itself is not a nullity or a vacuity but a process. This is required if eternity is to possess any properties or content whatsoever. But even if we take the extreme case and equate eternity with nothing, Hegel presses his point. The equation of eternity with nothing is tantamount to the identification of nothing as being in the sense of essence. Such a statement is self-contradictory in the pejorative sense that to make it is to testify to the existence of something, namely, ourselves as speaking and so as thinking. And here our earlier conclusion enters into the picture. Life may be an illusion, but illusions exist. But putting to one side for the moment ourselves as thinking about nothing, Hegel holds further that nothing is not static but dynamic.

Suppose then a comprehensive nothingness. As such, it is neither temporal nor spatial, neither a totality nor a part, neither existing nor nonexistent, i.e., it is neither being nor nothing. But this is an absurdity; nothing is indeed nothing. It is identical with itself, since otherwise it would be non-nothing or something. But it is also different from everything else, for the same reason. Furthermore, if there is no time when anything occurs, and indeed, no time, then nothing is eternal. But the eternal is always what it is. We cannot say that the eternal is sometimes eternal but sometimes temporal. What then does it mean to attribute "always" to nothing? It could not mean anything other than that nothing is time, if a time in which nothing is happening. We have postulated that space and time do not exist; but this postulate prevents us from making the assertion that nothing is always. I do not need to continue with this line of reflection. It is clear that there is nothing to be said about nothing, about the "nothing" of total vacuity or what the Eleatic Stranger calls "the altogether not." As soon as we begin to speak, we are committed to a nothing that is indistinguishable from being, namely, to a continuum of ontological "places" in which things can come into being and pass away, but which itself is neither a thing nor an event, not a distinguishable or finite coming into being or passing away, but the ground of all such things and events.

Being is nothing; that is to say, the totality is becoming or genesis, and as such, it is a contradiction, not an annihilating contradiction but the ground of coming to be and passing away. Totality (*das Ganze*) is an identity of identity and difference, of position and negation; this is the inner dynamic of the identity within difference of being and nothing. "Just as *nothing* is at first in simple immediate unity with *being*, so here there is a simple identity of essence in immediate unity with its absolute negativity" (63). We can now see why time is for Hegel eternity; eternity exhibits itself as the continuous process of identity, difference, and identity of identity and difference, which is the grounding level of structure for anything whatsoever, that is, for the coming into being and the passing away of anything whatsoever, including conceptual discourse about anything whatsoever. The structure of excitation that constitutes totality is not something separate from conceptual discourse but the very same structure that constitutes it. It is the concept. This is why there can be no radical separation of being and thinking. The laws of thought are the laws of being. But being is process, not the dead being of traditional rationalism or identity philosophy.

We therefore require laws of thought that actually enable us to think a continuous process, as opposed to laws that govern static, finite, and independent forms. The key to laws of the required sort is the concept of negative activity. Without this activity, the moments of the process would dissociate; the process would dissolve and fall apart into the dead forms of traditional rationalism. If this form is radically separate from that form, there is a static "nothing" that stands between the two and prevents them from being connected. We as it were attempt to fill up that blank space with our thought; but thought is now itself separate from the forms it thinks and so is unable to reconstitute the continuum.

Note next that we have reached another level of immediacy with the attainment of the ground. Absolute negativity is the process of reflection; the identity of essence and absolute negativity is the *Aufhebung* of reflection (the first way of thinking) into the self-grounding process of contradiction (the second way of thinking). This process is immediate because it is not defined through opposition with some other process. The next stage in the development of the categorial structure of the concept must come from the inner articulation of the ground. To say this in another way, essence is grounded in itself; there is no ground apart from the reflective process of separation of essence and appearance, a separation that leads to the negation of both as the illusory appearances of illusion, and so to the conception that total negativity is the engine that drives the entire process of categorial development. "Essence, in so far as it is determined as ground, determines itself as the not-determined, and its determinateness is nothing more than the sublation of its being determined. In this being-determined as self-sublating, it has not come to be out of something else; in its negativity, it is essence as identical with itself" (63). The determinations of identity and difference have been sublated by contradiction. But contradiction sublates or cancels itself as a preservation of a positive and a negative term.

In one more formulation, reflection attempts to provide the ground for the distinction between essence and appearance by distinguishing between identity and difference, the underlying structure of all determinations of rational thought. However, identity and difference collapse into each other

as we try to distinguish them or keep them separate. This collapse is reflected at the level of essence, which is both the same as and other than
its appearances, or in other words, it is, precisely as essence, mere appearance, and precisely as appearance, essence. We escape this canceling effect
of negativity by rising to the level of dialectic or by seeing the process as a
totality. But for the time being we are still within reflection. Again I want to
emphasize that this is not a mistake on our part. We have to think through
the determinations of reflection in order to see their insubstantiality in isolation from one another.

The ground is initially determined as "the first" in the sense of the immediate, as just explained. This determination has two aspects. On the one
hand, as the sublation of identity, difference, and contradiction, it removes
all differences from within essence and so falls back to pure identity, the
first of the determinations of reflection, or reflection *an sich*, as Hegel puts
it. On the other hand, the determination proceeds from the ground itself, not as the result of a sublation of some previous opposition. In other
words, as lacking in attributes, essence is identity. But the identity is not
that of subcategories within the structure of the category of ground, not a
constituent of ground, because ground has no positive constituents. The
determination of ground is nothing other than essence. That is, ground is
now shown to be essence because it is the totality of the determinations of
reflection by which essential structure is constituted (64).

Hegel says next that reflection is pure mediation, whereas the ground
is the real mediation of essence with itself. "Pure" is not a complimentary
term here; Hegel means that the mediations of reflection transpire formally
but lack any subsistence. They cannot produce things or *res* and hence are
not real. It is ironical that the logic of reflection, which arises from the
axiom of what we may call a thing ontology, leads to the dissolution of
things into a negative process of coming to be and passing away, a process
that can be saved from nihilism only by the logic of process or negative
activity. The determinations of reflection are substrata of the imagination
(*Einbildungskraft*). But ground is real mediation because it is the sublation
of reflection; that is to say, it preserves them as moments in a process of
negative activity. Ground constitutes itself: "it is essence that turns back
into itself through its not-being and posits itself."

I emphasize that the distinction between essence and appearances has
collapsed into contradiction, hence into the identification of essence with
the underlying process of negativity that is subsumed as contradiction. This
process underlies everything; there is from this fundamental standpoint no
separation between essence and appearances. We see here the crucial step

that leads to the subsequent identification of essence as identical with its appearances. Such an identification is no longer external (via reflection) but emerges from the attempt to understand either of its elements independently of the other. In other words, essence is not this or that essence but essentiality. Essentiality is ground or the total process of becoming as the source, structure, and truth of appearances.

Hegel will discuss ground in three stages. The first is absolute ground, in which essence serves as the foundation for the relation of grounding in general; more precisely, it is form and matter arranged as content. The second stage deals with determinate ground, namely, the ground of some determinate content. In the third stage, Hegel treats the *Sache an sich*, "the matter in itself" or the thing that results from the ground through a condition or stipulation (*Bedingung*).[2] Once again,. Hegel's peculiar terminology obscures his point. Stage 3 is the *res* or *pragma* (*Sache*) that results through the modification of ground as such (essence or becoming) by a determination that produces a particular ground out of the universal foundation. Note that *Bedingung* means literally "be-thinging." In order for the ground to serve as the particular ground of some particular thing, it must itself already have manifested itself as other but related things. For example, human beings are born from previously existent human beings, not from the universal ground of essence or becoming. But there is a difference between the general proposition that humans generate humans and the particular generation of G. W. F. Hegel by his parents. Nevertheless, in the concrete instantiation of the relation of ground and consequent, the universal grounding process continues to be visible to the eye of the logician.

In the note appended to the general introduction of chapter 3, Hegel points out that the ground, like all determinations of reflection, is expressed as a law, in this case, the law of sufficient reason: "Everything has its sufficient ground" (65). Hegel interprets this to mean that whatever exists is not immediate but posited, i.e., springs from some antecedent ground (which is in Hegel's account sublated into the product, just as parents are sublated in their children). And this in turn shows that being as immediate is untrue; the truly immediate is the ground. In other words, immediate being is a pure abstraction that cannot account for the coming into existence of a determinate entity. As to Leibniz's teleological interpretation of the law of the ground, we are not yet ready to consider it, since teleology belongs to the concept, which we have not yet reached.

I close this chapter with a general remark. In the subsection on absolute ground, which we will study next, we will be viewing the entire process of self-differentiation or becoming of the spatiotemporal world. In a sense we studied this in our consideration of reflection, which is for all practical purposes Fichte's doctrine of spontaneity, or rather Fichte's revision of the Kantian doctrine of the spontaneity of thinking, now applied to the various positings and self-limitations of the absolute ego through which the subject-object structure of the world of genesis is constituted. Fichte's "activity" of pure thinking was not, however, a genuine process because it was not genuinely dialectical. There was no concept of negative activity; consequently, the various laws of reflection remain independent of one another. The world is produced as a discontinuity, not a continuity; and the absolute ego struggles forever to overcome this discontinuity by ever more complicated reflections. The infinite series of reflections in Fichte is asymptotic; there is no accessible limit.

In Hegel, the ground is the all-encompassing version of Kantian-Fichtean spontaneity. We should therefore not be surprised to learn that certainly in the general case, but also in the particular case as an instance of the general, ground and grounded must be the same. "Same" here is intended not in the static sense of Parmenides or Spinoza but as identity within difference. One could therefore say that in Hegel, spontaneity is absolutized; by this, I mean that the absolute acts spontaneously, and not through the instrumentality of some other, higher ground. What this means is that there is no "reason" for the absolute; to the contrary, the absolute is reason. We cannot therefore ask the famous question, "why is there something and not rather nothing?" because "nothing" is already something. The "why" is furnished by the process of spontaneous world formation, which is its own explanation.

Let me try to make this a bit clearer. How could we go about answering the question just noted? What would count as an answer? A religious person might say that there is a world because there is a God, but he could hardly explain why there is a God. Hegel is not satisfied with leaving the matter at this question-begging level. From his standpoint, all previous philosophies are what Heidegger calls "onto-theo-logies" because they explain the world as the consequence of a God or some other first principle that cannot itself be explained. The result is dualism, the erection of a *Jenseits*, the separation of meaning and value from the world of genesis, and so nihilism. Note that this is exactly the contention of Nietzsche, who repeats in his own way much of Hegel's critical analysis of traditional rationalism but who unfortunately has no solution to the problem.

In his quest for a science of wisdom (as I call his system), Hegel can afford no loose ends, not even the loose end of an unexplained beginning. It is true that we can derive Hegelianism from the fact of thinking, i.e., from the manifest identity within difference of being and thinking. But Hegel does not arbitrarily presuppose that there is something rather than nothing. That is to say, he does not simply rely upon the *fact* of existence, namely, that we are thinking about why there is something rather than nothing. He attempts to explain, not "why" (since there is no higher or deeper level of explanation), but *that* nothing is being. I have already discussed this point. To return now to the question, there *cannot* be nothing rather than something, because nothing is already something. It is an empty abstraction, and as such, a pure concept, the being of which is identical with the pure concept of being. This sounds odd or even question begging, but it is not so. Remember that for Hegel there is nothing outside thinking, not even nothing. Those who believe themselves to be thinking what I will call an ontological nothing (and the expression is already self-contradictory because it attributes being to nothing) are in the first place thinking, and therefore thinking a concept, namely, the concept of nothing, which accordingly cannot be "outside" thinking—for where would that be?

But it is not merely the case that in thinking nothing we incorporate it in thought or conceptualize it. The concept of nothing does not refer to anything outside thinking, any more than does the concept of being. Pure being and nothing are just the pure concept of thinking itself, namely, the concept of the place of anything whatsoever but not of anything in particular. One could perhaps compare it to the *hupodochē* or receptacle of the Platonic *Timaeus*, or to the concept of possibility. Let me restate this crucial point. In ordinary experience we think a tree but would never claim that the tree exists in our thoughts alone. The concept, or more simply, the thought of the tree, somehow connects us to what is outside our mental and physical existence. All this is fine so far as ordinary experience is concerned, but it is philosophically useless. This becomes evident as soon as we attempt to explain how we know external objects. Hegel's reply is much simpler than the ostensibly commonsensical replies of empiricism, pragmatism, hermeneutical perspectivism, and so on. He says rather that common sense is unphilosophical, and that we can think a tree, or know anything at all, because being and thinking are the same, or more fully, an identity within difference. And if we ask what it means to violate common sense and to say that being and thinking are the same, Hegel directs us to his logic rather than giving a short or "clear and distinct" answer.

I have to repeat that in asserting the identity within difference of being and thinking, Hegel does not claim that things are mere thoughts. To infer this from his thesis is to slip from the dialectico-speculative to the traditional mode of rationalism. Hegel does not claim that a tree is a thought;

304 / Chapter Twelve

he claims rather that the being of a tree, and so too the entire categorial structure that articulates the being into a component of *Wirklichkeit*, is the concept that is accessible only to rational thinking. Thinking is the self-consciousness of the concept. A tree is not the concept; it is not even "a" concept, say, the concept of the tree. We are nevertheless dealing with the concept of the tree, not with the tree, when we attempt to understand it, and this attempt leads us by a chain of dialectical analyses to the underlying categorial structure of anything whatsoever, trees included.

The reason why it makes no sense to ask whether trees exist "outside" or "independently of" their concepts is that existence (i.e., being) is a concept. When I decide in the most ordinary ways that a certain object in my experience is not an optical illusion but a tree, I arrive at this decision by thinking; and what I think is the concept, or rather, concepts. Note that those who deny that existence is a real predicate must therefore adopt the Kantian hypothesis of being as position, namely, as positedness within the categorial network that makes up rational experience. But how do we posit something? Or why? Either positing is arbitrary or else it occurs as a result of something outside categorial structure, in particular, via sensation. In either case, it is meaningless to say that something has been sensed to exist but that we cannot say what it is until we apply our scheme of categories to it. In this case, existence or being is not position at all but sensation or arbitrary, i.e., spontaneous creation. It is undifferentiated impressions, and so indistinguishable from fantasies or illusions, exactly as Kant says of Locke. Being is accordingly indistinguishable from not-being. That is, being comes to possess a meaning only through the operation of the categories. But the categories are the conceptual rules for thinking objects. So it turns out that being is a concept after all.

I am not interested here in making a complete analysis of the Kantian doctrine. I wanted to show only that whether or not being is a real predicate, we end up in explaining being by predication, that is, by a doctrine of categories, and so by concepts. There is no explanation of being, or of the existence of things, in classical Greek, i.e., Socratic, philosophy. All explanations are of pure ideas or species forms, and as explanations, they are obviously discursive manipulations of concepts. These discursive manipulations are ostensibly grounded in a nondiscursive, purely noetic apprehension of the idea or form as an eternal entity that subsists outside of thinking, but none of this has any rational content whatsoever from a Hegelian standpoint. Either we can speak of what we see or we cannot. We are ignorant of what we cannot speak; as to that about which we speak, we are able to do so because speaking, i.e., thinking, and being are the same, namely, an identity within difference.

All this being so, as Hegel claims, to ask about nothing is to ask about a peculiar sort of something, namely, the empty something that is pure being. But pure being is an abstraction, that is to say, it is a concept. We cannot explain it by some other word, like "presence" or "being-at-work," since these are themselves instances of being, not something higher than or the ground of being.

In other words, it may be true that being is present, but it is also true that being is absent, as for example in the process of becoming. Presence and absence do not explain being by going deeper, to a more primordial ground; they are in fact more intelligible than being only because they are shallower, closer to ordinary experience. In other words, they are not explanations of the nature of being but exhibitions of some properties that have developed out of being, and hence not exhibitions of pure being at all. Pure being is an empty abstraction; it has no exhibitions as such, although as a category it is certainly present in everything. It would be more accurate to say that pure being is neither present nor absent, if these terms are intended to designate something concrete. But if they are intended as entirely general, namely, as pure presence or pure absence, then again they are not themselves present or absent but are rather concepts of properties of anything whatsoever. If pure presence is itself present, it is in the "concealed" form of this or that, and hence some impure or concrete presence or absence. For reasons like this, when we analyze what Heidegger is saying about Being, I see no difference between the more coherent portions of his doctrine and Hegelianism.

To conclude this remark: the absolute is spontaneous, but not arbitrary or *ex nihilo*. Arbitrariness and negativity are two different things, but both are contained within the absolute; it makes no sense to treat them as the source or the ground for the absolute.

THIRTEEN

Absolute Ground

BOOK 2, SECTION 1, CHAPTER 3, SUBSECTION A, PART A: FORM AND ESSENCE. In this chapter, we will study the first of the three subsections devoted by Hegel to the analysis of the ground; this will give us a general orientation to the structure of ground and grounded. Let me state at the outset the central point of this stage of the argument. The structure of every existing entity consists thus far in the assimilation of identity and difference within contradiction. To be a *res* is to be self-identical, different from everything else, and as both identity and difference in the same respect, self-contradictory. Contradiction as the sublation of identity and difference is the essence of the process of becoming. This process "appears" in the initial sense as a continuum of moments, each of which is grounded by nothing other than the continuum itself. This was basically the situation in book 1, when we arrived at becoming as the identity within difference of being and nothing. At first, there was no content within the continuum of becoming. But now we are going to discover content as prefigured in the dialectic of something and another, and as further developed in the dialectic of essence and appearance, that is, of the collapse of essence and appearance into appearance *as* essence. In other words, "something" and "another" are transformed here into appearances, and hence into forms. We can also say that becoming could not hold itself together without the illicit positing of form, of what shines forth or is identifiable as the content that renders the moments of becoming visible. Now Hegel attacks directly the task of rendering legitimate the earlier illicit introduction of existence or something and another.

The process to which he refers is appearing essence as the ground. Since there is no foundation or principle accessible to us as independent of, and the ground of, what appears, nothing else can serve as the ground of appearances other than the appearances themselves. The ground is thus indistinguishable from the grounded; more fundamentally, essence as ground is appearance in the sense of illusion, inasmuch as what is ungrounded in the traditional sense is inessential appearance.

The dialectical transformation of the determinations of reflection, namely, the laws or principles of traditional rationalist ontology and epistemology, into the negative activity of contradiction has as its result a transition to a new stage of immediacy, in which the process of becoming as a totality shows itself to be essence. There are accordingly no separate, radically detached appearances of which an equally separate essence is the ground. Becoming manifests itself as *Dasein* or determinate being that seems to have spontaneous position rather than to have emerged as a mediation of a previous opposition of determinations. This is because the *Dasein* or moment of existence is the result of a purely negative determination, namely, the sublation of the separate determinations of reflection into the process of negative activity. In simpler language, contradiction as the assimilation of identity and difference is the ontological force that underlies and so grounds every existing thing. In this context, I note that the so-called law of noncontradiction is itself a contradiction. We cannot think the illegality of conjoining p and non-p except by conjoining them and then negating this conjunction. The point is the same as the impossibility of thinking the illegality of thinking the altogether not except by thinking what is forbidden.

At this stage, there is thus no distinction between ground and grounded. These two terms are united by the seemingly spontaneous genesis of *Dasein* (66–67). In more direct language, existence is its own ground. Note that this is quite different from traditional doctrines of creation *ex nihilo*, because for Hegel the *nihil* is part of what it means to exist and not the backdrop against or from which existence emerges as pure positivity. This is what Hegel means when he says that the ground "is essence that is identical with itself in its negativity" (66).

The general theme of this section of the *SL* is to show how the determinations of reflection, namely, identity, difference, contradiction, and groundedness (= "sufficient reason"), or in sum the traditional conceptions of form and intelligibility, are affected by their sublation into the unity of ground and grounded, a sublation that we studied in the previous two chapters. The unity in question is experienced as the spontaneity of existence. Initially, this spontaneity amounts to a shift in perspective by which we conceive of illusion as essence. One could say that most if not all post-Hegelian philosophies of historicity, including the Nietzschean school of hermeneutical doctrines, take their bearings by this experience. The problem with these doctrines is that they assimilate all structural determinations into spontaneous manifestation; such doctrines, as I have pointed out previously, arise from the acceptance of the Kantian thesis of the spontaneity of constructive reason together with the rejection of the transcendental ego. Owing to the lack of a conceptual grasp of negativity, these doctrines are incapable of preserving the stability of formal determinations required to account for the order of experience; spontaneity is thus identical with contingency. But contingency apart from necessity is unintelligible; spontaneity thus dissolves into chaos.

We are therefore not yet free from the sphere of illusion (*Schein*), which does not become transformed into appearance (*Erscheinung*) until the second part of book 2. By "appearance," we recall, is meant "the shining of essence," that is, the appearance of essence as its diverse manifestations. Once again, this should not be taken to refer to individual things like persons, animals, plants, and so on. What is essential in a thing is to possess properties, exactly as in the Aristotelian doctrine of categorial predication. As one could also put this, it is essential that there be contingent or accidental properties; contingency is itself a logical category.

To return to textual analysis, essence is the unity of ground and grounded; as such, its identity is established by the grounded; in other words, the ground "appears" always as some existing thing or another. This is to be expected, since there is no ground apart from the process of grounded elements. The appearing individual is the identifying mark of the ground in each case, but it is not the ground itself, for if it were, the ground would be that particular existent. In simple language: the grounding process is always the same in all groundedness, but the sameness of the process manifests itself as some determinate form or another. The form is the positedness of the ground, but not the ground itself, which is the unity of the various sublated determinations of reflection. As one might put it, the ground is represented by the form of the existing (and so grounded) thing. In this case, however, what is represented has not previously presented itself. We must therefore continue to distinguish between the identity of the ground and the identity of the unification of ground and grounded; this latter identity is the form. But the identity of the ground is negativity, in the sense explicated previously as the assimilation of the determinations of reflection into contradiction. Hegel refers to these two identities as arising from "pure" and "determinate" reflection (67). Their unification is the mediation (*Vermittlung*) of the ground, which, we remember, was first presented as immediate. In other words, the ground, as absolute or total, mediates itself.

This analysis must, however, be refined. Ground and grounded constitute a determination subsequent to essence. Essence is the totality of becoming, and so is exhibited only indirectly by the distinction between ground and grounded, of which it is the unity. I repeat that the ground is essence that is identical with itself in its negativity. The ground is essence at work via negative activity; this work results in the grounded existent. The mark of the accomplished work, the mark by which we identify the product, is form, which can thus be interpreted in an Aristotelian or quasi-Aristotelian sense as *energeia* or "at work-ness." It is only when this process has been accomplished that essence acquires stability (*eine feste Unmittelbarkeit*) as the ground (of some determinate grounded entity) or substratum.

Essence as process is both continuous and differentiated. It is continuous because it is the same process in every case of ground-grounded. But it is differentiated by these very cases and so appears as the heterogeneity of forms. The next point is extremely important, and Hegel does not make it with sufficient explicitness. As continuous, essence is present within every form as the indeterminate underlying ground of all formal determinations (*es liegt ihnen zugrunde*, 68). Hegel is speaking here in the first instance of the determinations of reflection; these are "dissolved" within essence (which is negative activity or contradiction) and are thus the same in all forms (all of which are self-identical, different from each other, and so caught in the contradiction of identity and difference). But the same must hold true of the more concrete formal determinations. In other words, we can see here the paradox of the relation between essence and essential properties. In fact, essence cannot be defined by essential properties for reasons that I have given on several occasions; the same result follows from the continuity or indeterminateness of essence. Strictly speaking, no individual essence can be defined; all we can do is to explicate the categorial structure of anything whatsoever, and so of all individual occurrences of essence as the relation of ground and grounded.

Let me underline this crucial conclusion. Hegel does not actually solve the *aporiai* of traditional rationalism or what I have called Platonic ontology. Instead, he shifts the ground of logical analysis to the formation process. It is not an explanation of the essence of a horse, for example, to explicate the structure of essence. But furthermore, Hegel's explication of the structure of essence gives us no clue as to how a determinate set of properties combine with each other in such a way as to form a determinate essence, a "form" in the Aristotelian sense of the word. I am reminded here of Kant's doctrine of sense perception, which gives us the categorial structure and the role of sensation and imagination within sense perception but does not explain how we can perceive a particular thing as this particular thing of such and such a kind. Hegel's logic is "transcendental" in the sense that it is more like Kant's procedure than Aristotle's. We are told what it is to be an object, but not what it is to be this particular object. Hegel would justify this by reminding us that all explanation, and indeed, language itself, is universal. It is impossible to describe, even to refer with precision by speech alone, to the particular. In sum: we can understand the structure of universal formation process, but not the structure of this or that form. This is Hegel's contention; it remains to be seen whether the contention is reasonable.

The discussion on pages 68–70 repeats in Hegel's technical jargon the situation I have just described. Essence, as continuous or the same in all determinate forms, is identity; but as the different forms, it is obviously difference. The underlying notion is once more of a universal process that manifests itself, or as we might say, "happens," in a particular form, namely, as the moments of the process. For example, becoming "happens" as one moment after another; at no moment do we see becoming as an identity or as that which is the same in all moments. We can arrive at a concept of becoming; but if that concept is accurately formulated, it must bring out the particularity of the process as well as its universality. The accurate concept, in other words, is of a process, hence of an identity within difference, and not of an external combination of static elements. Fichte and Heidegger describe the process as one in which the underlying totality or universality (my terms) is concealed by the particular manifestation. Hegel replaces "is concealed" by "is exhibited."

To summarize the analysis of form and essence, whereas we can explicate the logical movement of identity and difference independently of one another, in each case, this explication turns into its opposite. The result is a work process or self-differentiation of essence into ground and grounded. We can also say that the work process or formation process is identical with itself wherever it exhibits itself, but that it exhibits itself as the heterogeneity of form. The differing forms that the formation process assumes are then precisely how identity shows itself. If we take the "show" in question as merely "differences," the result is *Schein* or illusion. When we come to see that the identity is preserved in and exists as its differences, the show is *Erscheinung* or the appearing, the pointing itself out, of identity; that is to say, it is the appearance of essence as an identity within difference.

Here is another restatement of the analysis of ground to this point. The ground is essence; that is to say, it is essence now understood as the activity of identifying, distinguishing or differentiating, and contradicting. Since essence is becoming as a totality, the ground is a prefiguring of the absolute. Absolute ground is essence as both the origin of genesis and its appearance (as what emerges from the origin). The origin produces appearance spontaneously and is accessible only within or as what it produces. As such, it is pure essence or identity. As produced appearance, it is difference. As both together, it is contradiction or identity within difference. And as identity within difference, it is totality. Note that the term "grounded" refers to appearance in the double sense of illusion and manifestation of essence.

In the discussion of absolute ground, Hegel distinguished between, and therefore joined together, form and essence. "Form" thus corresponds to difference; it is the principle of differentiation and so of intelligibility, since without differences, identity would be everywhere the same and the result would be Eleatic monism. On the other hand, essence is the principle of identity; if it did not inhere in differences, these would dissolve into illusion and so into chaos.

BOOK 2, SECTION 1, CHAPTER 3, SUBSECTION A, PART B: FORM AND MATTER. In the next part ("Form and Matter"), Hegel says that "essence becomes matter" in the sense of formless indeterminateness or pure identity, hence as the substratum of form (70). This reinforces the point that for Hegel, as for the Greeks, form is the principle of intelligibility. But furthermore, essence as pure identity is said to be the substratum of form; Hegel here takes the Aristotelian word *hupokeimenon* (*die eigentliche Grundlage oder Substrat der Form*) to refer to matter. It is not clear whether Hegel is referring here to prime or to noetic matter, that which stands to form as prime matter stands to body. If Hegel is thinking of prime matter, however, the general situation is the same. Matter cannot individuate; this is the task of form.

On page 70 Hegel says that neither form nor matter is *aus sich selbst* or eternal; both emerge from the self-differentiation of essence into ground and grounded. As grounded, essence is matter shaped by form. But the forms do not descend from heaven onto the ground of the earth; matter is a determination of form and vice versa, as was prefigured in the reciprocal determination of identity and difference. Once more, it is important to notice that Hegel does not explain the emergence or genesis of particular forms. The formation process is of no help in our effort to understand how there can be forms of horses, trees, or human beings. But even within the terms of Hegel's own intentions, a serious question arises at this point. How do we account for the emergence of form and matter as such from essence as ground and grounded? Oddly enough, it is easier to answer this question with respect to matter than with respect to form. Matter is not earth, air, fire, and water, and of course not the elements of modern chemistry; it is the sheer identity of the formation process that stands underneath all differences and supports them. Essence as matter prevents the moments of form from simply dissolving. But what produces the moments of form?

It may seem initially as though this is a foolish question. Are not the moments of form the categorial structure of becoming? Did I not myself identify becoming as the formation process? It is true that every form must possess identity and difference, and hence be related to its opposite in contradiction; let us even grant that this contradiction is intelligible as the ground of the abstract structure of form as such. But as the structure that is common to all forms, identity within difference cannot explain the particular look or nature of the heterogeneity of forms. It cannot produce, so to speak, the dog-ness of dogs, the tree-ness of trees, or the personhood of persons. It is at this point that Kantians and their descendants all direct us to take the transcendental turn, or more precisely, to see that philosophers like Kant and Hegel are not concerned with the phenomenal or ontic or contingent world of particulars. But that is not the point. The transcendental or dialectico-speculative exposition of the formation process is designed to explain the conditions for the possibility of a phenomenal world, namely, of the very world that we all occupy, philosophers and nonphilosophers alike. If the dialectical logic of Hegel is no more able to account for particular or concrete forms than is the transcendental ego of Kant to account for particular perceptions of concrete individuals, then the transcendental or dialectical account is defective.

The striking consequence of Kant's doctrine of perception is that the particular sense object must be contingent; and yet it cannot be, since perception is inseparable from cognition, which is in turn grounded in the transcendental constitution of the object. As I have often pointed out, it is also the case that Kant is unable to explain false perceptual judgments, although this is only a corollary of the fundamental problem. It looks very much as if the same problem obtains for Hegel. The heterogeneous forms of objects in the spatiotemporal world cannot be derived from the excitations, dialectical or traditionally logical, of the categories of Hegel's logic. They must therefore be contingent. In a way, this is an advantage of Hegel's doctrine, since it makes his logic to that extent compatible with modern science, as for example with the Darwinian theory of evolution in the case of living forms. But Darwinianism is not an ontological explication of the structure and intelligibility of form; it is a doctrine of the emergence of what the Greeks call the *morphe* or physical appearance of living bodies. Granted that this *morphe* is in the process of evolution from generation to generation, it is nevertheless present, and so visible as a specific kind or look, within each generation and, still more securely, within each living individual representative of a (perhaps contingent) species. How is this possible?

There is no point in turning to science for an answer to this question. Science can provide us with partial explanations of the psychological or neurophysiological processes by which we perceive objects, which are the analogue to Hegel's categories, but entirely apart from the lack of success in explaining such things as the unity of the visual field or the individual object, the question we are interested in is that of the logical or ontological conditions for the appearance (whether as illusion or veridical show) of the perceived looks. Why does the firing of one set of synapses produce the perception of a dog and another the perception of a horse? Are we to believe that the hard-wiring of the brain includes circuits for the production of every possible sense object?

I am very far from claiming that there is an answer to the question of the existence of particular forms or looks. Doctrines like that of the Platonic ideas or Aristotelian forms do not answer the question but turn it into a hypothesis. In other words, Socrates and his students say that particular things participate in, or mirror, the looks of ideas or species forms. But why are there heterogeneous ideas or species forms? Why in particular the look of a horse? It is hardly an answer to the question "why are there horses?" to say "because there is an idea of the horse." And Aristotle explicitly disavows answering such a question; he explicitly begins with the *hoti* or "that," i.e., with what Heidegger calls the "facticity" of existing things of this or that sort. In other words, Aristotle's doctrine of species forms is not an answer to the question why there are horses, but rather an assertion that the existence of horses can be accounted for by the hypothesis of the species form of the horse, together, of course, with the doctrine of matter and the rest of Aristotle's theoretical philosophy.

We should therefore not be surprised to find that the term "form" has suddenly appeared in Hegel's discussion with no genuine preparation. The term "matter" has been prepared by the doctrine of essence as pure negative identity. But "form" is smuggled in by way of its traditional relation of opposition to matter. The closest one could come to giving a Hegelian explanation of particular form is the same as that which is available to modern science. Both Hegelians and scientists would have to contend that the particular sensed form is produced by the interaction of (to put it with maximum simplicity) the motions of matter in the external world and the neurophysiological structure of the human perceptual apparatus. But is there even the possibility of correlating individual motions (in the interaction of world or object and perceiver or subject) with individual perceived looks? And even if such correlations could be established empirically, how would they explain the transformation of motions into horses, trees, and cows? Would this transformation not be contingent in any case, that is, subject to modifications of the interactive motions? What else is being said by those who ask us to imagine methods of sensory perception alternative to those with which we happen to have been furnished by evolution?

On pages 70–72, Hegel presents the following analysis of form and matter. Form presupposes matter or the continuum of identical moments that form differentiates into distinct entities; without identity, there could be no coherent difference, no heterogeneity. On the other hand, matter presupposes form. The reason he gives for this is that matter is not pure negativity, as is essence, but = rather positive or the sublation of this negativity (71). In other words, by reacting to the excitation of its own internal negativity, matter is raised up to the level of form.

Internal negativity refers to the indistinguishability of the items on the continuum apart from form. As Hegel says on page 70, "matter is thus the simple undifferentiated identity that is essence, with the determination of being the other to form." This shows very clearly that form *and* matter have been introduced arbitrarily. Matter is defined as the other to form, but how was form defined? As absolute negativity, as the identity of essence (71), and before this as the determinations of reflection. This comes dangerously close to the definition of form as synonymous with the definitions of matter. It is true that they are coordinate poles of essence. But the question is rather: How are they distinguished? It makes no sense to distinguish them in terms of each other; this says nothing more than that they exist conjointly. We want to know *how* they come into existence. At this point, the evolutionary character of the concept seems to break down.

Hegel would presumably reply that he is referring not to the evolution of everyday experience but to the process by which logical determinations owe their nature to one another. Perhaps Hegel is saying that form is the set of reflective determinations taken in advance of their sublation into the pure negative identity of essence as matter. But as I have already stated, this equates form with the general structure of the logical categories thus far derived. It tells us nothing about form and matter as the two aspects of existing things. Once again: Hegel must provide us with an explanation for the coming into being of the concrete instances of matter as shaped by a particular form. I understand that he is concerned with the structure of a thing as such (his analogue to Aristotle's "being *qua* being"). But a thing as such has particular as well as general formal structure. General formal structure is particularized by heterogeneous looks. There is no logical category corresponding to the heterogeneity of the looks of anything whatsoever. To say this one more time, we cannot explain the general structure of a thing if we have not explained the general property of particularity. So far at least, there is no such explanation in the Hegelian account.

Not only, to continue, do form and matter presuppose one another, but they can also be regarded as indifferent to one another. This means, as usual, that they do not emerge from one another by the dialectical resolution of an initial opposition. For example, since matter is the negative identity arising from the sublation of the determinations of reflection, it is formless, and so cannot be the ground of form (71). Hence form has no ground, or is indifferent to matter. On the other hand, form and matter are related to one another as active and passive or receptive. Hegel's explanation as to why this is so is not very easy to understand, but it has to do with the potential presence of form within matter in the guise of the sublated determinations of reflection. The general point seems to be, however, that form and matter cannot subsist independently of one another, since they are two sides to the same process incorporated within essence as ground and grounded. Their indifference to one another is just an illusion (*Schein*); they are initially united within essence; then they separate out through the ground-grounded distinction, a separation that Hegel calls an externalization. Finally, this externalization is "recollected" (*die Erinnerung ihrer Entäusserung*, 72).

This passage shows us once more that Hegel does not reject reflection, which is a necessary stage in the development of logical structure. Contrary to the situation in Fichte, reflection or externalization is the creation of the world from its spontaneous origin. Before we can see the dialectical relation of contradiction and sublation, we must first see the individual moments or relata. It is reflection that provides us with individual moments like identity and difference. Externalization is thus the necessary preparation for internalization or recollection (*Erinnerung*). In fact, externalization is initially illusion; recollection is the step in which the absolute distinguishes itself from the inside into form and matter.

Hegel then spells out the three major dialectical movements between form and matter. They are initially opposed to one another within the identity of essence. But second, the independence of form is a "self-sublating contradiction," that is, the independence of form is not complete but depends upon the matter that it forms. We may discern here a criticism of the traditional Platonist doctrine of separate forms. As is normally the case, Hegel leans toward Aristotle, whom he interprets from within the perspective of Christian Neoplatonism. In this passage, however, the dependence of form upon matter is finally rooted in essence as negative identity (i.e., in contradiction understood as the ground). It follows that difference (form) is dependent upon identity or in other words that it is matter that unifies the moments of form. Conversely, identity is visible in and through the diversity of form.

Hegel expresses this as follows: "The activity of form, therefore, through which matter is determined, rests in a negative relation of form toward itself. And conversely form relates itself thereby negatively toward matter; only the coming to be determined of matter is just as much the genuine motion of form itself" (73). Form as it were holds itself together by holding itself apart from matter; but conversely, this holding itself together of form is the very activity by which matter takes on the determinateness of form. And this in turn stabilizes form, as just noted: the independence of form "is matter itself, because the first has its essential identity in the second."

In this second stage of the form-matter dialectic, initial independence is overcome from each of the polar standpoints. The working of form thus turns out to be the working of matter; these two work processes are related to one another as the positive to the negative. The terms "positive" and "negative" are preferable to "active" and "passive" because for Hegel, the receptivity of matter to form is itself a kind of activity. "That which appears as *the activity of form* is just as much *the genuine motion of matter* itself. The *ansichseiende* determination or the *Sollen* of matter is its absolute negativity" (73). The absolute negativity of matter is the identity of essence that unifies the moments of form into this or that form of this or that material substrate. At the same time, without the moments of form, matter would work in vain or not at all; it would remain invisible.

As always in Hegel, we cannot understand him by trying to combine from the outside two distinct processes. The two processes are an identity within difference. In order to describe this identity within difference, we have to speak of each element in its turn, and so as apparently separated from the other. In this way the "synthesis" seems to be entirely arbitrary or a mere verbal construction. But the constructive aspect is an illusion of the external discourse of reflection. The actuality is the relation of the two poles, and relations in Hegel are not static syntactical forms but activity, work, excitation, in other words, the process by which the two polar elements emerge from one another, hold themselves apart, and by so holding themselves apart, are each defined by and so transformed into the other.

Let me underline the striking phrase "the *Sollen* of matter." This is a characteristically Hegelian revision of Fichteanized Kantianism. *Sollen* does not simply mean "what ought to be," but it echoes the Fichtean "striving" of the absolute ego to externalize as the world, which in turn is an extension of Kant's moral "ought" to cover all egological activity. The *Sollen* of matter is the striving of essence, or the absolute negativity of interiority to externalize, to come into visibility through the rendering stable of the moments of formation process. This bears upon our previous discussion of why there is anything at all rather than nothing. If there were a *nihil absolutum* (whatever "were" means here), it would succumb to the *Sollen* to exhibit itself in and through being. And this in turn is because nothing, if it were the totality, would be being, which is the same as thinking. One can ask: Why is there thinking rather than no thinking? In other words, why is there a concept of nothing and not merely nothing? Hegel's reply is that nothing achieves its identity by opposition to being; the identity of nothing, to repeat, is "nothing other than" being, or perhaps better stated, nothing, as totality, is "what there is." It is not just a peculiarity of syntax, represented by the copula, that we have to say that nothing "is" or that it "exists." In sum: Parmenides (or Plato) discovered not a destructive contradiction but rather the deepest truth of philosophy when he pointed out the paradox of speaking about nothing or saying that "there is" or "there is not" nothing. We cannot imagine the existence of nothing independent of being; in so imagining, we posit the abstract concept of being.

Now for the third stage in the dialectic of form and matter. First they were separated; next, they turned into one another. What remains is obvious; we must speak of their identity within difference. Hegel calls this a return to original unity, but he does not mean undeveloped unity in which neither is visible. The activity (*Tun*) of form and the excitation (*Bewegung*) of matter are the same, except that the former is position of formal structure and the latter is the negativity of identity (74). The "coming to be determined of matter through form is the mediation of essence as ground with itself in its unity, through itself and through the negation of itself" (74). And the result is the exteriorization or exhibition of interiority; to anticipate, essence is revealed through appearance.

We have now completed our study of the two oppositions of form with essence and matter. There is a third opposition: that between form and content (*Inhalt*). We can see at the outset that essence is becoming or the negative activity of contradiction, that which is always the same in each of its moments and which furnishes identity to individual forms. Essence is both ground and grounded, which correspond to the process of becoming or contradiction on the one hand and the individual moments of that process on the other. Ground and grounded appear as matter and form; we should be careful to notice that it is not form that is the ground but the process of becoming, the prefiguring of the dialectic of form and matter. Form is posited; i.e., it is a positive determination; matter is not posited but is the sublation of the determinations of reflection. It is only through the positing of form that matter comes to be op-posed, and in that sense posited. As to the positing of form, I have already spoken at length about the difficulty this raises for Hegel.

Now what is "content" (*Inhalt*)? Initially, we would tend to think of "content" as neither form nor matter in the general senses of these terms. The content of a box is what lies inside but is not the box itself; the content of a proposition is the thought or truth-value or meaning or something that is not the same as the verbal medium of the proposition itself. What Hegel has in mind here is, I think, the unification of the abstract categories of form and matter into some determinate thing. In the first paragraph of this part (c: Form and Content), Hegel identifies the determinations of form that is opposed to essence as the ground and the grounded; whereas the determinations of reflection are the constituents of form as opposed to matter (75). I note first that these determinations are categorial and so are entirely general; there is no question here of a particular "look" or kind. Second, by attributing the determinations of both ground and grounded to form as opposed to essence, Hegel is saying that essence, understood as absolute negativity and so as identity, has no positive determinations. The ground-grounded distinction is a development of essence that belongs to, and therefore cannot itself produce, form. How then does Hegel explain the emergence of form? There is no real answer to this question in Hegel's logic.

Finally, form stands opposed to content, and in this opposition its determinations are "once more itself and matter." At the end of the preceding part (b: Form and Matter), Hegel said that content arises through the *Aufhebung* of form and matter, that is, through the unification of these two opposing moments within formed matter. Form plays a double role; in general it is the logical structure of difference (to which essence or identity gives stability), but it plays a particular role as the structure of this particular enduring difference. The problem here is that the second role has been left undefined; it cannot be filled by the purely general formal properties that we have studied so far.

BOOK 2, SECTION 1, CHAPTER 3, SUBSECTION A, PART C: FORM AND CONTENT. Hegel analyzes the opposition of form and content from two different angles. In the first analysis, he begins by repeating the point just noted, that "content has initially a form and matter that pertain to it and are essential; content is their unity." This unity is posited; that is, it arises out of the opposition of form to matter, which is in turn distinguished from or opposed to content *as* unity. In simpler terms, the unity is still external; it is as though form and matter were combined by something outside either element to form an artificial unity. Hegel therefore calls it "inessential." In the second analysis, content is the identity of form and matter; in this case the separate moments of form and matter are inessential. Note the shift from unity to identity; the first term is static and the second is for Hegel dialectical.

In the situation described by the first analysis, the content has not yet been shaped into an essential identity as this particular instance of formed matter. The process by which form and matter turned into each other in the previous part has not yet stabilized or been fully integrated. It remains for the unity of form and matter to be itself subjected to a dialectical process like the one that established it. To say that form and matter are indifferent external determinations of content, as Hegel has just done, is to illuminate a more complex version of the "indifference" of identity to difference within the opposition between essence and ground-grounded. In the present context, content is analogous to ground-grounded in the previous dialectic, since it includes both form and matter. Part of the greater complexity is due to the fact that content is here being opposed not to a pure, immediate, and so undifferentiated source like essence, but rather to form, which is (the principle of) difference. In other words, the differentiated identity of content is being opposed to the difference of form.

We can restate the two roles assigned to form as follows. Form is both an essential ingredient in content and also the exemplar or paradigm by which the individual compound is identified. I have insisted that form as defined by Hegel is incapable of identifying any particular individual but can only refer to the general structure of a thing *qua* thing. The paradigmatic role of form is a failure. This to one side, until such time as the unity of form and matter can be both articulated and fused into an identity within difference, the content of anything is unstable and subject to dissolution. It cannot be the case that form is as it were stamped onto matter by some divine artificer, as in the myths of Platonism. In these myths, form is external to its ground. We can go a step farther and say that form is assigned the role of ground, but there is no conception of matter (in Plato) or (as in Aristotle) no conception of matter adequate to stabilize form, to provide it with identity. Hence the content of experience is always collapsing into illusion. So Hegel anticipates the later criticism of two worlds or a Platonic *Jenseits*, but he goes into much greater detail as to why and how this *Jenseits* obtains. It is not simply that in Platonism, form is separate from matter; there is no matter at all, no analysis of essence or becoming as the principle of negative identity, hence no stability to form, which is about to collapse into the sensations or ideas of empiricism.

Now to the second analysis. Content is that which is identical in form and matter. Form and matter, taken as independent of one another, thus become indifferent to that identity. They are significant here only as sublated within content. And this is to say that content now plays the role of ground. In other words, content is the essence of form and matter and provides these "differences" with the stability of identity. In this way, content is indifferent to the identity of form taken apart from it, but it is also the identity of the ground. The entire structure of the determinations of reflection—identity, difference, and contradiction—and so the stabilizing identity of formal difference, in sum, ground and grounded, are all assimilated into the content (76).

As usual, then, we think a pair of opposed terms as both identical and different. At first we view them as distinct. The attempt to see them as distinct unites them. This union is viewed first as external or collapsing and second as sublated into an identity within difference. The collapse of external reflection or traditional rationalism (which, it should never be forgotten, is fulfilled as Fichte's subjective idealism) is necessary in order for us to see how what is a collapse from the traditional standpoint is the formation process or growth of intelligible structure from the dialectical standpoint.

In the last two paragraphs of this part on form and content, Hegel summarizes the analysis of absolute ground. I shall restate his point as follows. Ground is the negative differentiation of genesis or becoming into the substratum that articulates itself via determinations of form; but it is this substratum considered prior to the emergence of these forms into existence. But there is more than one sense of "ground." I believe that we can in fact distinguish three senses:

1. ground as pure immediate essence or source, and so as identity;
2. ground as differentiated identity and so as the potential existing thing;

3. ground as the identity within difference of the grounding-process or work of the absolute, together with the grounded or products of that work.

We should notice two short passages on page 76. Hegel says of formed identity that it becomes *Grundbeziehung*, "ground relation because the determinations of its opposition are also posited as negated in the content." *Grundbeziehung* (like *Grundlage* before it) does not quite mean "ground" in the categorial sense of the term. It refers to the suppression of the separate status of form and matter in content. Finally, Hegel prepares the transition to the next subsection on determinate ground as follows. "On the one hand, content is the essential identity of ground with itself in its positedness." This is the grounding process or work noted in the third sense of "ground" above. "On the other hand, [content] is the posited identity over against the ground relation." This is the product of the work of grounding and the determinate ground of the next subsection. I shall call it a this-such as opposed to a potential anything. A this-such is "form as total relation of ground and grounded" because the work process comes to concrete visibility in the product of its labor. This form "is total positedness that returns back into itself."

The striking, and even surprising, feature of this passage is that, after all talk of form as opposed to essence, matter, and content, and to the apparent triumph of content as the identity within difference of ground and grounded, Hegel reverts back to the traditional language according to which form is the principle of intelligibility. In other words, the formation process acting within the formed entity is itself regarded from the standpoint of the form of the entity. Hegel thus remains, at least in this important sense, within the Aristotelian, and therefore in the Platonic, tradition, as do the Christian Neoplatonists of whom Hegel can be regarded as the last representative—for Heidegger is no Christian but a partisan of Gothic paganism.

I close this chapter with a general remark. Parmenides rejects the *nihil absolutum* as unthinkable and unspeakable; yet he obviously regards the one as both thinkable and speakable, despite the Platonic demonstration that he never succeeded in saying anything about it. Hegel agrees with Parmenides but with an important modification, which we can call his Platonic-Aristotelian (and so perhaps Socratic) heritage. For Hegel it is the activity of thinking and so speaking the one that differentiates it into a many. This differentiation is intended to be the demonstration of the sameness of being and nothing, or the transformation of the *nihil absolutum* into something, namely, not static otherness as Plato thought, but negative activity, "othering" as we might call it. Thinking and speaking could not arise from some source external to the one; there is no such source. For if there were, we would begin with two, not one, in other words, with dualism, and so with incipient nihilism or chaos. Discursive thinking must itself be the differentiating power of the one. In other words, Hegel's "one" is not a unit but an identity, and more precisely, an identity within difference; in the most abstract case, it is the being of the concept of being, which is also the concept of nothing.

The Eleatic one is transformed in Hegel through its identification with the *logos* of the New Testament. The self-differentiation of the one is the self-differentiation of God into his three personae of father, son, and holy ghost. Self-differentiation is also self-manifestation; to manifest oneself to oneself is also to apprehend or grasp, i.e., to conceive oneself. The *logos* is also a concept. We may refer to God, or to the one differentiating itself, or to any of Hegel's central characterizations of *Wirklichkeit*, as the ground, but in no case is the ground "outside" the world. The search for the ground of the world is in fact a search for the world as totality: *das Wahre ist das Ganze*. It is not the one alone, nor is it the many alone. It is the one and the many, and the "and" that joins them is dialectical, not static. What this all means is that the *SL* is not the speech of a finite, temporal, mortal logician named Hegel. It is the conversation of the world with itself, as overheard by Hegel, and we ourselves are eavesdropping on this divine conversation by listening to Hegel's account of it. The situation is thus something like a Platonic myth in which a story about Socrates comes down to us through various intermediaries.

FOURTEEN

Foundationalism and Antifoundationalism

Introductory Remarks

I begin with some general remarks about the ground, which we are now studying. The category of the ground emerges in the middle of the development of logical structure, not at the beginning or the end, where we would expect to find it if Hegel were what is today called a "foundationalist." In fact, he is not; foundationalism is from Hegel's standpoint equivalent to the external reflection by which essence is distinguished in nondialectical logics from its appearances or properties. Since the foundation is introduced arbitrarily, whatever it supports must be arbitrary as well. The deductive structure of such a system is thus separate from the contingency of the system's content. It is a point of view or interpretation, grounded in chaos, exactly as Nietzsche holds is the case with all philosophical doctrines. The problem with the nondialectical substitute for foundationalism is that it simply affirms radical contingency; instead of arriving at nihilism, antifoundationalism begins as its affirmation.

In Hegel, the ground is not the beginning but rather the mediation between two stages. The first stage is the development of the continuum of becoming up to the point at which a world of things is produced. The second stage is the development of those things themselves, that is, of what Hegel calls "content," or a determinate instance of formed matter. In this second stage, the determinate things exhibit not merely their own natures but how they have assimilated the aforementioned development of becoming in the working-out of their individual destinies. The ground is thus not merely "within" the absolute, but the identity within difference of ground and grounded is a stage in the activity of the absolute itself as formation process.

We can therefore say that Hegel rejects the two standard philosophical procedures of attempting to explain the world from the outside, via a transcendent first principle or foundation, and from the inside, as having already been posed from a source that is either inaccessible or to be pursued in an asymptotic process of infinitely more complicated inferences from "the phenomena." This leaves him with a single possibility. He must explain the world from both the inside and the outside, and in such a way as to show that the explanation coincides with the identity within difference of the inside and outside. There must be nothing left over, or not yet explained; the explanation must include not merely the outside and the inside but also their relation. In conventional language, the world must be shown to emerge from principles that themselves emerge from our attempt to explain anything whatsoever.

Let me expand this last assertion. It is one thing for the whole to exhibit an eternal structure, and something else again for a human being to explicate the development of this structure. Our explication proceeds in time, whereas the structure of the whole is eternal. Hegel attempts to reconcile eternity and temporality by showing how the order of exposition of a presuppositionless science corresponds to the eternal process or excitation by which the absolute is exhibited as the world of genesis. The comparison in the introduction (I. 33) between the logic as the system of pure reason and the exhibition of God "as he is *in his eternal essence prior to the creation of nature and a finite spirit*" is of course a metaphor, Hegel's version of a Platonic myth. This is obvious since there cannot be any time "before" creation. Otherwise put, God is not initially a static being who suddenly comes to life and creates the universe. Hegel's God is the absolute, and this means absolute *activity*. But absolute activity is the formation process by which the world is continuously being brought into existence and passing away.

The metaphor must thus be understood to refer to the description of what is in itself a "simultaneous" or eternal process, a description arranged in accord with the human desire to possess a presuppositionless science, that is, a complete systematic account or *logos* of totality. Even if there is a creator-God, then he cannot be thinking the world in some other order that is superior to the one presented by Hegel. It also follows that there can be no creator God and creation *ex nihilo* in the traditional Christian sense; to describe Hegel as an orthodox Christian is nonsense. One could perhaps call him a Christian Neoplatonist, but this is a matter of academic pedanticism. The philosophically relevant question is how Hegel accounts for the creation of the spatiotemporal world, i.e., for the finitude of creation, given the identification of the formation process of the world as the absolute. The customary mantra of "identity within difference" is of no help here, since there is no identity between eternity and temporality other than that of an eternal cycle of creations, more precisely, of coming to be and passing away. In other words, there cannot be any posttemporal "day of judgment" for Hegel. What we have instead is the myth of the eternal return.

This is important, but it is a digression to the main point I wish to make here. And that has to do with the order of exposition of the *SL*. There are no presuppositions in eternity since everything is happening simultaneously. The *SL* is therefore an *analytical* account of the dialectical structure of the eternal process of world formation by which absolute spirit exhibits itself in its work. Despite all the peculiarities of his account, Hegel is giving a *logos* of the divine, but as a human being speaking to other human beings. It is interesting to note that there is a partial similarity between Hegel's account and the biblical (or biblically motivated) story of the creation *ex nihilo*, except that we, as guided by Hegel, replace God. Our task is to create the world out of nothing in the sense that we are to be allowed no presuppositions. In a fundamental sense, Hegel (and we) must begin with *nothing*.

Now we cannot begin with sheer vacuity since we who begin are something rather than nothing. We cannot as it were think away every determination, including the determination of thinking away, i.e., of thinking, and thereby arrive at vacuity. Note that this is a quite different question from that of how we happen to exist at all as thinking creatures. Nor is it the question of why there is something rather than nothing. This last question is answered in a Hegelian manner by seeing that if there is total nothingness, then nothing is, i.e., is the same as being; in other words, being is nothing. That is the first moment of Hegel's exhibition of logic, but it is not fully stated in itself, since as the first moment of logic, it is a *logos*, an instance of discursive thinking. We have to add that we have arrived at the sameness of being and nothing, and so can proceed to the full development of its consequences, by a process of thinking away all possible predicates or formal determinations until we come to the absolute beginning. And "absolute beginning" means here "a beginning of thought that is its own ground and neither can nor must be derived from some antecedent."

In sum: we begin with a concept. Since we shall never be separated from what is after all the substance of the process of giving an account, namely, conceptual thinking, it is clear that the entire logic of Hegel is a concept. We begin with the concept of abstract being, and by "abstract" is meant that there are no determinations whatsoever, other than that of being. As I have previously explained, "being" is for Hegel a logical, not a real predicate. It cannot be derived from anything else or be said to belong to something else; this is another sign of Hegel's Aristotelianism. Whatever is, is; this is a tautology. What is, must *be*. This is not a presupposition; it is the ultimate or absolute tautology. We have no choice but to assert it, and in asserting it, we make no additional assumptions or assertions. This assertion is therefore uniquely fitted to serve as the beginning of a systematic science of totality.

The beginning of science is a concept; in fact, it is *the* concept, but initially in its simplest, purest, or emptiest form, empty in the sense of containing no inner determinations or predicates from which it has been derived or constructed and into which it could be analyzed. It is the concept of being. But is this not a dualism? If we begin with the concept of being, have we not begun with thinking *and* being, and even worse, with the thinking of being rather than with the two as separate? The latter beginning would at least have brought us into direct touch with being, whereas now we seem to have it reflected within thinking or in conceptual form. We have only to ask this question to see that there is no way to begin with being except in thought; to begin with being (or with anything else) is necessarily to begin with the thinking, i.e., the concept of being, as we have just established. This is because "beginning" or for that matter "continuing" is inevitably and intrinsically "beginning to think" or "continuing to think." Thinking is not like a spaceship in which we arrive at being as at a distant planet. We cannot leave the spaceship and walk upon the surface of the planet.

To recapitulate. Someone could suppose that we might not have existed at all, that there might not be any thinking beings whatsoever, and even further, that there might be nothing at all. Let us entertain this hypothesis seriously for a moment. It amounts to the previously noted assertion that nothing is everywhere, i.e., everything, or in other words that nothing is being. But in entertaining the hypothesis seriously, we have been thinking, and so entertaining a concept, namely, the concept, that is, the concept of nothing as totality or being. We cannot entertain the concept of a nothing that is not a concept; this is just impossible. The first step in the operation, entertaining a concept of nothing, cancels out the possibility of the second step, namely, arrival at a nonconceptual nothing.

It is in this sense that Hegel accepts the traditional Parmenidean assertion that being and thinking are the same. What Hegel says explicitly in the exposition of the logic is that being and nothing are the same. But it is understood that this sameness is established by thinking, an understanding to which Hegel occasionally alludes and which is clear from his use of the term "concept."

Hegel is now in a position to explain the world as emerging from exactly the same presuppositionless beginning that is required by the attempt to give a presuppositionless explanation of that emergence. I do not mean by this that totality or the absolute actually begins from the sameness of being and nothing, because the absolute does not "begin." The reference to God prior to creation is a myth. I mean that in order for us to possess systematic or absolute knowledge of the absolute, we must find a beginning that is itself absolute in two senses. It presupposes nothing, and it can be shown to develop, by the very process of thinking or understanding it, into everything, i.e., into the logical structure of totality—not simply of genesis, remember, but of the absolute. The notion of development is crucial here. It is Hegel's surrogate for the deduction of traditional logic. Just as one could say that the derivable consequences of an axiom are implicit in the axiom, so one could say that the totality of logical determinations is implicit in being. But in traditional logic, the logician requires additional technical apparatus, such as a formal language, rules of syntax, or what have you. In Hegel, the claim is made that nothing is required in addition to the natural movement of thought as it entertains the empty concept of being. There is then a creation, not precisely *ex nihilo*, but from the emptiest concept. The empty concept fills itself, whereas the axiom does not produce its own theorems.

To conclude this general remark, the terms "inside" and "outside" require clarification. Hegel is "inside" the absolute, because there is nowhere else to be. But he is "outside" all arbitrary or perspectival interpretations of the world of genesis. And finally, the absolute is "outside" the world of genesis in the precise sense that it is neither this nor that moment of genesis but *the formation process of genesis*. A last observation: the absolute cannot be mere being, i.e., being apart from thinking, because it is self-contradictory in the vicious sense of the expression to attempt to think of being as totally separate from thinking. We arrive at the concept of the absolute as spirit, hence as thinking, and so as alive, from the simple, in a way also presuppositionless fact that we are thinking beings.

Book 2, Section 1, Chapter 3, Subsection B: The determinate ground

Now we come back to the ground. We can consider the structure of the ground from two standpoints: as origin or process and as exhibited within its product. As origin, the ground is very much like the prime and noetic matter of Aristotle. As product, it is form. Form differentiates matter; difference articulates identity. There is, of course, an interaction between matter and form. Each turns into the other through the usual mechanism of reciprocal definition; this "turning into" or "going over" is itself the transformation of reflection into coalescence. Reflection is unstable; the elements that it separates in order to join them are thus separated again, only to dissolve. Rationalism collapses into skepticism and nihilism, and this is once more reconstituted by sublation or negative activity into a higher stage of positive structure, a process that is continuously repeated until there are no more levels of structure and the end point of dialectic rejoins its beginning.

At the end of the discussion of absolute ground, Hegel says: "On the one hand, content is the essential identity of ground with itself in its positedness; on the other hand, it is the posited identity over against the ground relation" (76). So content can be understood both as ground and as grounded, and in the second sense as a particular thing of such and such a kind. Since we identify particular things by their specific forms, which may be said to have the "content" of their defining predicates, form is now identity and content is now difference.

SUBSECTION B, PART A: FORMAL GROUND. The ground has a determinate content that stands as simple immediacy to the mediation of form (76). I have just explained this mediation, but the main point bears repetition: Content is not identity or matter because it has already been shaped in various ways; one might give as examples wood, stone, and marble, all of which are unified into the form of a building. The wood, stone, and marble all have forms of their own when contrasted to prime matter, but as so formed, they serve as properties or differences of a higher, unifying form, such as that of the building of which they are constituents.

Form must therefore be considered as both identity and difference. It differentiates matter, but it unifies content into the identity that it is. But content is itself a mediation of form and matter, as in the case of wood or marble. In my simple metaphor, we have a blueprint for a house, namely, the form of the building we wish to erect, as well as the materials from which we wish to erect it: wood, marble, and so on. When we actually build the house, the wood and the marble will be the matter of the house, but from another standpoint, the form of the house includes the properties of being wooden, marble, and so on.

To begin with, content is immediate with respect to form; it is in this sense the matter out of which forms are constructed. With respect to this functional role only, namely, as the principle of noetic matter (my expression), content is negative identity or the ground. And this in turn constitutes the positive unity of the relation between ground and grounded. In simple English: the content out of which one constructs forms may be viewed in two ways, first as noetic matter (and this is its "negative identity" because it plays the same role in all form, just as did essence in the previous stage of the dialectic); but second, as this particular content, it produces a particular form. So too wood and marble can be regarded as building material or as the particular material for a wooden or a marble house. In the latter role, as contributing to a particular form, content mediates between essence or identity and formal difference. Thus the distinction between the two determinations of ground and grounded disappears in content as the particular stuff of a particular form, as is obvious from the fact that such stuff is both form and matter in its own right. In other words, there are no atoms for building forms that are not themselves already formed and so contain formal elements of their own. But the elements out of which we build forms can be regarded simply as elements, and in that sense as atoms, or they can be regarded as the properties of some definite form (77).

As both noetic matter in general and the formed matter of a particular form, or as one could say, as the essential properties of a given form, content is the negative unity of ground and grounded; it identifies them. One should think here of the essence that is identified by its essential attributes, but an essence that is not something separate from or in addition to, but rather the appearing of, those attributes. Since ground is identified with what it grounds, it has a determinate content (like the appearing essential attribute that is grounded by the essence, namely, by the process through which it appears, and so by its own appearing, i.e., by itself). "Then, however, the negative is the negative relation of form to itself." The negative is content as noetic matter; but noetic matter is precisely what constitutes form; hence it is form. The determinate form thus becomes its ground, whereas the ground becomes the posited determinate form. Hegel calls this process "formal mediation." In it, each aspect of the form is the totality of that form.

This is an extraordinarily obscure passage, even by Hegelian standards. The difficulty arises, in my opinion, because Hegel is trying to account for the coming into being of particular forms by a purely general process of evolving categories, which are themselves too general to do the work assigned to them. Let us grant that the process of ground and grounded is intelligible as an identity within difference of becoming, or the continuum of spatiotemporal points at which anything whatsoever can occur, together with its particular moments. But a particular moment of becoming is not a particular form. Otherwise stated, we can distinguish between form and matter in the following sense only: the categories of logic are like forms and the negative process by which they are transformed into one another is like matter. And the same problem arises when we attempt to understand the distinction between form and content. Content is just the particular mediation of form and matter as a this something. But unfortunately, no such mediation can occur on the basis of the Hegelian distinctions. Each form is structurally the same as every other form. We can say that in general, every instance of formed matter qualifies as content. But from this general standpoint, we cannot tell one content from another.

One way to frame my criticism is to say that there is no such thing as a particular form in general. If we have managed to isolate only the general structure of form, then every form exhibits that structure and none other. But this means that we cannot distinguish one form from another. Suppose one were to offer an analysis of the Platonic doctrine of the pure ideas of phenomenal entities like cows, trees, and human beings by saying that each idea is a harmony or community of one, many, same, other, rest, and motion. We might even be able to describe the process by which these categories combine to form an idea in general, but that would not explain the "formal" differences of one idea from another, e.g., the idea of the horse from that of the dog. Kant in a way attempts to supply this impossible desideratum when he introduces schemata corresponding to perceived objects such as the dog, but this is mere hand waving.[1] He is required to explain to us how there can be schemata corresponding to every conceivable object of perception. What we want is an account of how one schema differs from another; this is not done by telling us that there is a schema for each different object. Kant begs the question.

I must repeat that Hegel does not evade the criticism by saying that he is interested in describing not concrete perceptual forms but only the categorial structure of a particular form. My reply is that the categorial structure of particular form does not describe the particularity of particular form, and this is precisely what we want explained. Hegel can no more explain particularity than Plato can, but because he is wedded to the goal of achieving a complete system of logic, Hegel tries to transform generality itself into particularity. The category of essence, or in other words of negative activity as exemplified in the dynamic interpretation of contradiction as sublation of the determinations of reflection, is pressed into service to furnish us with the distinction between form and matter, and so between form and content. I have already shown that form never genuinely emerges from the inner gyrations of essence, except in the purely general sense that it was already assimilated into those gyrations, namely, as identity, difference, and the ground, alias contradiction. Form stands opposite to matter; content is their unity. But alas, form is introduced here by the magician Hegel who pulls it out of the empty hat of negative activity.

This helps to account for the peculiarly obscure dialectical moves through which Hegel attempts to derive form from content on the one hand and to attribute form to content on the other. But let me now apply my criticism of Hegel to a specific passage in the text. The first paragraph on page 77 begins as follows. "In this content, the determinateness of the ground and the grounded over against one another has at first vanished. But the mediation is further a *negative* unity. The negative element in the above indifferent substrate is the latter's *immediate determinateness* whereby the ground has a determinate content. But then this negative element is the negative relation of the form to itself."

The problem is that none of this is intelligible absent the possibility of particular forms. If we assume their existence, it is then just possible to make sense out of what Hegel is saying here by an analysis of something in particular. I will use the traditional example of the acorn with respect to the passage just translated. The acorn contains both ground or process of growth and grounded or the oak tree. Let us say that the acorn mediates them; we could also ring the other Hegelian changes on this example by noting that the acorn as unity is indifferent to both the process of growth and the tree, whereas from a slightly different viewpoint the process of growth is the mediation of acorn and tree, and so on and so forth. To take a further example, the acorn is a negative mediation of ground and grounded, because it is neither the one nor the other. We could also say that the acorn is being transformed into a tree by the negative activity of growth, and further that this process of growth is visible in and only as the growing acorn. In other words, the ground is visible only in and as the grounded or posited, at first as the acorn and eventually as the oak tree. By the same token, the form "oak tree" is visible not in itself but as the completion of the process of growth, hence as formed matter of this particular kind: this oak tree, which is accordingly content or the unity of form and matter. The form is absent in the growing acorn, but it is negatively present precisely as the growing acorn. Thus the form is negatively related to itself. Let this suffice to show what is possible in making sense out of Hegel, once we have acorns to work with.

Now we shift from the acorn to *das Ganze*, or at least to that stage of totality that we have reached in the chapter on ground. Form is here both implicit or potential within content, which is a content of a certain kind or form, and also distinct from content as one of its two ingredients, the other being matter. So form emerges from content, but content emerges from form. As soon as we strip this circle of all the Hegelian dialectical camouflage, we see that it is vicious. And I have shown that the dialectical camouflage cannot itself furnish us with form in the needed particular sense of that term. In Hegel's account, the absolute has "somehow" (if I may employ Aristotle's favorite technical term) bifurcated into content and form. The form is presupposed within the content to which it is opposed. Now there are no acorns here to help us out, so we cannot say that the acorn is the content and that the form of the oak tree is presupposed by it. Granting the existence of form, it is negative self-reference (to generalize on the example of the acorn}; the form of particularity in general is present as growth into more complex form, but obviously this presence is negative in the sense that the growth has not yet been completed. But what constitutes "more complex form"? The greater complexity that we are developing is that of the general structure of totality, not of the heterogeneity of particulars. But particularity is one stage of the general structure of totality.

To continue with the text on page 77, Hegel holds that ground and grounded are transformed into each other, or stand forth in their difference as identical. This means that it is neither the simpler nor the more complex form (in the illicit example, neither the acorn nor the oak tree) that provides us with the paradigm of intelligibility, but the negative activity of the growth from one to the other, in other words, of the formation process. Hegel intends for this process to pose the moments of becoming, not simply as ontological places or points for something particular to appear, but as *Dasein*, namely, the process as visible in and only as the particular determinate being that "is there" or that occupies a particular point in the spatiotemporal continuum. I will not apply my standard objection to *Dasein* because it is a perfectly general category; something or another exists at each point on the continuum because there is no other way for the continuum to manifest itself.

The identity of ground and grounded, Hegel says, "is the determinate content to which the formal mediation relates itself as to the positive mediator" (77). This means that the determinate content is the unity of the simpler and the more complex form at each stage of development, and so it is not a static form or a finite, independent entity but rather the dialectical process. Hence the expression of form as acting upon content in this process of development is basically form acting upon itself. Growth, development, becoming, negative activity: all these are neither simply form nor simply process or activity, but *form acting upon itself*. Form is as it were the cutting edge of negative activity; if negative activity did not manifest itself as form, it would be sheer identity or the Eleatic one. But the forms so manifested are concretions of absolute activity, by which they are unified in the sense of being kept from disappearing within the excitations of negativity. In earlier terms, matter is *Streben* or *Sollen* whereas form is *Tun* or the fulfillment of the *Sollen*. This is Hegel's spiritualized revision of the *dunamis-energeia* distinction of Aristotle.

I can now be extremely brief with respect to the balance of this part (a: Formal Ground). Since the ground fills its role by sustaining the grounded, it is itself grounded by what it grounds. Ground and grounded are each the other; each has the same content; each is both original and derived. Hence the *sufficiency* of the ground. We do have to look a bit more closely at the final paragraph of part a on page 78. Hegel says here that the identity of ground and grounded means that each is the whole form of the unity. This being so, neither is *real bestimmt*, i.e., neither has independent content or constitutes a *res*. I would take this as an admission that we still lack particular forms. Instead, we have a general structure for the production of particular forms, or as I put it, particularity in general.

In the note that is appended to this part, Hegel emphasizes that the axiomatic deductive method of science should not be applied to philosophy, for the reason I have already given. The ground must be prepared by the self-differentiation of being or the one; it is not immediate or given at the outset.

SUBSECTION B, PART B: REAL GROUND. At the end of the part a, "Formal Ground," Hegel said that ground and grounded are not yet determined in a real manner; they do not have distinct or diverse content. Hence the ground is determined only formally. At the beginning of part b, "Real Ground," Hegel summarizes the previous result as follows. The determinateness of the ground has two different parts; one is the determination of content and the other is the distinctness of content and form. Again we see that form is both contained within and distinct from content. As a result of this distinction between form and content, the relation between ground and grounded "goes astray as a form external to the content" (82). To clarify: the ground-grounded distinction is the general form taken by the process of becoming through which particular existing entities are produced What I call the general form is the negatively activated determinations of reflection, which we may regard as summarized within the sublation of contradiction. This is the basic structure of productive activity differentiating itself into the structure of *res* or things. In this productive activity, we have the form of real structure and the content, namely, some particular thing. But within content, we also have form, since content just is the unity of form and matter.

In order for the form of real structure to play a role in the structure of a particular *res*, it must obviously be particularized. For example, the structure of identity, difference, and contradiction must be, as Kant might put it, "schematized" by the form of, say, a dog. If this does not occur, the general form will be the same in ground and grounded, and there will be no distinction between the two. On the other hand, the general and the particular form cannot be separate from one another but must also undergo an inner or dialectical excitation such that they constitute an identity within difference. I add to this that the absence of such a connection in Kant makes it impossible to understand how perceptual cognition is both transcendental with respect to the general structure of an object and immanent or contingent with respect to the identity of the perceived object. All doctrines that constitute objects out of the cognitive process are faced with this problem. Pre-Kantian or traditional realism does not face the problem since the "object," i.e., the being or *on*, is simply given. But this raises the problem of how to overcome the separation of thing and intellect. Hegel is trying to solve both problems simultaneously.

He therefore says: "In fact, however, both [form and content] are not external to each other, for content is this: the identity of the ground with itself in the grounded and of the grounded in the ground" (82). As we saw at the end of part a, each is the totality (i.e., of process and production). We can now restate Hegel's general point with somewhat greater simplicity. The ground or formation process shows itself initially as what it produces, namely, the grounded. As we begin to grasp the basis for the connection between the two, we come to see that they are united or indistinguishable, since the essence of each thing is just the negative activity by which it is produced. But in seeing this, we run the risk of losing the distinctness of the two sides to the totality. So as usual we have to see them simultaneously as identical and different. Ground and grounded (= process and product) are each the identity of the two taken as a totality, but at the same time each has a distinct content; that is, the nature of the process as such is not the same as the nature of the product as such. On the other hand, if we consider the matter from the standpoint of content, what I have just called "the nature of the process" is like the matter to the form of the nature of the product; the content is the identity of the grounding relation of the one to the other (83).

Since ground and grounded each have a distinct content, their relation is no longer merely formal; i.e., it is no longer a purely abstract structure waiting to be filled with content. "The ground is realized." We make a distinction between process and product without dissolving the inner connection between the two. Hegel then discusses the various dialectical relations that obtain between ground and grounded. We can pass them by, but there is one passage that is of crucial importance for my general criticism of Hegel. In the last paragraph on page 83, Hegel is saying that the grounded contains the ground completely; "their relation is undifferentiated essential purity. What is added to this simple essence in the grounded is therefore an inessential form, external determinations of content, which as such have no ground [*vom Grunde frei . . . sind*] and are an immediate multiplicity."

This passage confirms my distinction between general and particular form, as well as my claim that Hegel cannot explain particular form—the "look" of a perceptually cognized "thing" (or what he will later call a *Sache*). This is for Hegel mere contingency, just as it is for Kant. Strange as it seems, Hegel apparently does not notice that the general form of the ground must then serve as the form of the grounded. He apparently overlooks the inadequacy of this claim because he wants precisely to say that there is an underlying unity to the structure of process and product; but he has forgotten to explain to us how we distinguish the two. Or if he has not forgotten, we are expected to take the presence of the grounded product as explained by the mere fact that the process yields products, i.e., that grounds issue in grounded consequences. But this in turn leaves the inessential, groundless determinations of content, by which the grounded consequences are grasped and understood, entirely outside the structure of logical development. Hegel must sweep all the detritus of particularity into the category of contingency. But this leaves entirely unexplained one of the two fundamental aspects of the whole (*das Ganze*), namely, how the process can concentrate itself into the particularity of its products. Why is not every product, as possessing the same general form with its process, the same, hence indistinguishable? Hegel's doctrine comes down to a revision of Kantian dualism. On the one hand, we have the quasi-transcendental process of the development of the categorial structure of the whole. On the other, we have the particularity of the individual products of the process of categorial development.

In the appended note (84–88), Hegel makes the following point. In the formal ground relation, ground and grounded have the same content. As we can put this, they are only potentially distinct; the grounding process has not yet actually produced its grounded consequence. In the real ground relation, the two have separate content, but for that reason their connection is external. We would have to establish the connection by observation, from outside the process itself. It is thus not clear which of many determinations of content in a concrete thing are essential or grounding (84–85). This is the previously mentioned problem of defining the essential attributes of a spatiotemporal particular, the essence of which we cannot determine simply by observation. Note also the distinction between *Grundlage* or foundation and *Grund* or ground. The former is one of a series of conditions for a concrete thing, for example, weight or gravity in the soil on which a house is built. But this weight is not part of the ground of the house *per se*, whereas it is one of the conditions for many other things or events, such as the falling of a stone. Something further is required for us to consider weight or gravity as the ground of the house. As Hegel says on page 86, "the real ground does not itself indicate which of the manifold determinations ought to be taken as essential."

Hegel gives several other examples, all of them illustrating the point that what counts as the ground of a concrete thing or event depends upon one's viewpoint, that is, upon some third thing external to the ground-grounded relation itself, understood as a real ground in which the content of process and product are distinct. In other words, so long as we regard things in the traditional manner, as external combinations contingent upon our viewpoint of two independent elements, then "the giving of grounds" is an entirely arbitrary process, or what Hegel calls *Räsonnement*, the equivalent to what Socrates and Plato call sophistry (86–87). If we connect this note with my criticism of the Aristotelian doctrine of essences and essential predication, we see that Hegel tries to resolve the problem by setting all categorial distinctions into the reciprocally modifying motion of negative activity. The true is the totality; the truth of each item in the totality is the sum of essential perspectives from which it may be viewed. In sum, the true is the concept, which is alone the "sufficient ground" (87).

SUBSECTION B, PART C: THE COMPLETE GROUND. The formal ground is the identity of form and content; in other words, the distinction between the ground and what it grounds is abstract and so purely general. In the real ground, the distinction is made, but externally; that is, there is no real "grounding" of a variety of possible grounds for any given thing or event. In Hegel's language, we must now find a ground for the real ground that will serve as a unification from within the content that is common to both the process of becoming and its product (87). Note that the two senses of form, general and particular, must both be unified with matter in the particular consequence. In other words, the individual must be both an exhibition of the grounding process and the particular individual that it is.

So long as we have not fixed the specific ground of the item we are considering, the relation between the two is immediate; the two are indifferent to one another or lose the ground-grounded structure, which must now be derived from, i.e., grounded by, some antecedent stage. This is what I meant by the assertion that we have to find a ground for the ground. In other words, without an identification of essence, every specification of essential attributes is contingent. These attributes are the content not only of the essence we are analyzing but also of some antecedent essence that is its hypothetical ground (89).

Nevertheless, attributes, whether essential or contingent, are formally distinct modifications of the content of a particular thing, Note that Hegel explicitly attributes the difference in the content of ground and grounded, and so the transition from formal to real ground, to the form (90). Hegel does not say so explicitly, but this has to be the form of the grounded as a particular that is distinct from the ground, and so from the general structure of the determinations of reflection as sublated into contradiction (= ground). He expresses this point by referring to two distinct "some-things" (*Etwas*), each with a differing modification of the content that is common to both. The *Etwas* that is posited (*gesetzt*) in the other *Etwas* is the grounded particular. The latter is mediated by its ground, the first *Etwas*, in which a connection between A and B is contained *an sich*; this connection is the explicit formulation of the grounding of B and A in the particular product, which is "immediately" only A. In other words, it is not yet the particular that it is until the ground does its work. Conversely, the binding together of A and B in the grounded product serves as the ground of A; A's role as ground is validated by the emergence of the grounded product.

The overall situation is as follows. We start with a formal relation of ground and grounded, in which there is no specification of the particular grounded item; therefore the content of the two poles of the relation is the same, namely, the structure of negative identity or the formation process. Next we identify some ground of a particular *res*, but since many grounds can be given for each item, this relation is external or contingent, i.e., relative to a particular viewpoint. Note that we have shifted from identity to difference. The last step in this stage of the dialectic is to arrive at the identity of identity and difference; this is the complete ground. The latter is thus not some entirely new or distinct stage but rather the sublation of the previous two. Unfortunately, Hegel's explanation of how this takes place is unusually obscure.

Let me first try to illustrate the underlying analysis by means of Hegel's previously introduced example (86) of vengeance and punishment. We may punish in order to extract vengeance; in this case the first serves as the ground of the second. However, we may take vengeance in a variety of ways, such as the imposition of fines, incarceration, or execution. Suppose we happen to execute the prisoner. Since execution is a penalty for other acts in addition to the one we are considering, and because the act under consideration could have been avenged in some other way, the connection between the crime and the punishment is external, contingent, or itself in need of being grounded. Vengeance and punishment are externally related within the *Etwas*, namely, this particular choice of punishment, as two distinct contents of the same thing or event. We need a ground external to the *Etwas* in order to legitimate or make complete the relation of ground to grounded. This role is played by the judge, in contrast to whom execution is not a genuine ground until he has validated it through his persona as the will of society, the agent of the state. The prisoner might have been "executed" by an outraged relative of his victim; in this case the vengeance of society would have been thwarted, not fulfilled.

At this point we can see the distinct character of Hegel's analysis. The judge's decision is the "immediate connection" between the two contents of vengeance and punishment, even though it is formally different from both. As formally distinct, it is not their "absolute relation." What validates the decision of the judge, or "grounds the ground," is the authority invested in him by society or the state. In other words, the judge's intention is the conceptual unification of the state's decision to punish, with the specific determination of the appropriate punishment to be decided by the judge on the basis of the circumstances of the particular case. The judge's decision or intention is the sublation of the formal and the real grounds. It is the complete ground, the synthesis of form and content in the act of execution. This is what Hegel means when he says on page 89 that "the moments of the form reflect themselves into themselves." In other words, they become assimilated into the content; or in slightly different terms, the general form of the ground is assimilated into the particular form of the grounded.

We can schematize the situation as follows, making use of Hegel's abstract expressions on page 90:

A = essential content = vengeance
B = nonessential content = punishment
First *Etwas* = the judge's intention
Second *Etwas* = the act of execution

Note that apart from the intention of the judge, the punishing of individuals is vengeance but it is not rational or fully grounded.

What Hegel refers to as the mediation of completion is thus the reunification of the identity of the formal with the difference of the real ground. In our example, the judge's intention, sanctified by the state, overcomes the externality of the relation between the desire for vengeance and punishment. These two are identified; the difference between vengeance and punishment has been overcome or sublated, i.e., not erased but "reflected" in its difference back into identity. "The ground relation in its totality is therefore essentially presupposing reflection; the formal ground presupposes the immediate determination of content, and this as real ground presupposes the form" (91). In other words, the formal relation of ground and grounded is based upon the conception of the distinction between the two, but the distinction between the two presupposes their formal unity. Ground and grounded must be identical as the expression of a common essence; but they must be different as is essence as activity from essence as the product of that activity.

Book 2, Section 1, Chapter 3, Subsection C: The condition

"The Condition" is the last of the three subsections on the ground, and it will contain a sublation of the absolute and determinate grounds. "The ground is the immediate, and the grounded is the mediated" (91). The ground fulfills its function through the production of what it grounds (e.g., a tree from an acorn), which latter (the tree) is posed by virtue of having been presupposed (in the acorn), albeit only formally, in the initial formal nature of the ground relation. To this Hegel adds in a very confusing passage that the mediation from immediate ground to the grounded is and is not external reflection; that is, it is not simply external reflection but "the genuine deed [*Tun*] of the ground" by which it externalizes the reflexive structure of process and product as both opposed and unified. The immediacy of the ground, the essential presupposition to which the ground refers itself, is called by Hegel the "condition." The determination contained in the ground is "being other than itself" (92).

In straightforward English, the formal structure of ground-grounded is specified or directed toward some particular concrete actualization by a condition. For example, the weight of the earth supports a house, but the earth serves as the ground thanks to the nature of matter, which is a condition for this function but is not itself the ground of the house. More generally, some immediately existing thing (*Dasein*), which is immediate as this independent particular, not with respect to its inner categorial structure, but in the sense that it is not defined as what it is through an opposition to its logical complement, serves as a condition for the existence of something else.

In the example, the existence of the house is conditioned by the nature of matter, but the two are not linked in an identity-difference relation. In its nature as condition, an existing thing is "indifferent" to the existence of that for which it serves as a condition. But it is not simply indifferent to the ground, of which it is the presupposition. Hegel says of this mysteriously: "It is in this determination the form relation of the ground that has returned into identity with itself, and so it is the content of the ground" (92). The nature of matter is certainly the cause of the weight of the earth, and so can be construed as a formal determination of that weight. By functioning as ground through its nature, i.e., through the more general formal structure of matter, the property of weight could be said to return to identity with itself, but it would have been much simpler to say that the nature of matter is the condition for all material grounds. The condition is independent of the particular ground in one sense, but the same as that ground in another. The aforementioned "content" of the ground is thus the formal structure or a three-place relation of the property of some aspect of existence acting upon some other aspect in such a way as to make the latter serve as ground for some third event or thing.

As so distinguished and related, condition and ground have distinct contents that are mediated in the act of grounding (93). The two are both immediate or indifferent and mediated. In the next several pages (93–97), Hegel considers the various ways in which conditions are related to grounds. I call attention to the fact that both are modifications of form (97), which is always for Hegel the dominant principle of intelligibility at each stage of dialectical development. That is, categories and their determinations are all products of the formation process. But this process cannot be "seen" or "grasped" directly. Only forms can be so grasped, and the formation process is the negative activity intrinsic to the visibility, i.e., the being and the intelligibility, of determinate forms. Furthermore, in describing the formation process, we must specify its own "formal" structure. We cannot simply engage in incantations in the manner of the late Heidegger's descriptions of being. This is why the determinations of reflection are absolutely indispensable to the overall dialectic of Hegel's (or anyone else's) logic.

We will examine in detail the last part of the analysis of ground, which is the transition to appearance, that is, the self-presentation of essence within its appearances, not as illusion, but as it truly is. The part is entitled "Emergence of the *Sache* into Existence" (97). The German word *Sache* has a wide range of meanings: thing, affair, matter, concern, the issue under consideration, and so on. It is often used to stand for "things" in general and is, as I noted previously, in this respect like the Greek word *pragma*, from which we derive "praxis." *Sache* is thus more active than *Ding*. If we were to ask in German "How are things going?" we would use *Sachen*, not *Dinge*.

The consequence of the dialectic of condition and ground is that both are fully or essentially present in the existing *Sache*, which was previously called "the grounded" because we were distinguishing it from the formal elements that constitute its production. To go back to a still more general level of analysis, the only way in which to understand the process of becoming is through a grasp of the formal structure of what becomes. There is no "transcendence" in the sense of a being that produces and beings that are produced. But we cannot understand a *Sache* (i.e., what becomes or happens) by reducing it to a *Ding* or inert structure of form and matter. To this I add the following crucial remark. If we start with *Sachen* or *pragmata*, it makes very good sense to hold that they can be understood only as manifestations of an underlying formation process. In this way we could go backward by analysis from the evident looks of things to the underlying structure of the conditions for their appearance, a structure that becomes ever more abstract or general. But this procedure would not explain the evident looks themselves in the sense of reducing them to their inherent processes. When a cognitive scientist says that thinking is electric activity in the brain, this does not mean that the theory of cognition is itself just an electrical field. If that were literally true, then there would be no theories of cognition and no persons who cognize; there would be nothing but electricity.

Hegel's procedure exhibits exactly the same defect that is evinced by contemporary extreme reductivists, although he is moving in the opposite direction. He moves from the presuppositionless or most general to the more concrete, because he wishes to avoid the inductive or empirical and so permanently incomplete nature of modern observational and experimental science. But the starting point is for both Hegel and modern science the same: the given or the looks of things. And this starting point is also the surd or inexplicable point in all analyses, whether reductive or constructive. Hegel is as scornful of the looks of ordinary experience or common sense as the most mathematically oriented philosopher of science is scornful of "the given." The reason for this scorn is extremely simple: The given is a limit to our knowledge and our power. It stands in the path of the human will, not simply to dominate, but also to survive, and to survive well, that is, comfortably and securely. It sets a limit to the satisfaction of our wonder at the nature of things. In our impatience, even our anger, with the given, which is what we set out to explain, we abolish it on the grounds that it does not actually exist, that it is a myth, that it is irrelevant to the grasp of the true nature of things, and so on. All of this is either implicit or explicit in Hegel, who is from this decisive standpoint a modern thinker, like his great predecessors Leibniz and Kant, who also wished to reconcile the ancients and the moderns, a wish that is already the expression of the will to dominate that characterizes modern thought so decisively.

The motto "zu den Sachen selbst" (i.e., away from constructive theory and back to the things themselves) was conceived as a call to return to Kant in a positive or scientifically oriented spirit and so to move away from Hegel, who is ostensibly antiscientific. But this is a misunderstanding. Hegel is not unscientific in any way; on the contrary, he conceives of his system as the incarnation of science. The fact that his definitions of science and so of scientific method differ from those of the conventional rationalists is beside the point; the underlying motivation is exactly the same in both cases. To this I add one further comment. In my opinion the slogan "zu den Sachen selbst" is sound; the error lies in assuming that the way back to the *Sachen* lies in their reduction to something else, or in the equivalent error of thinking that the looks of things can actually be derived from logical rules, categorial tables, or mathematical equations. All this to one side, it is the emergence of the *Sachen* that Hegel must explain if he is to be truly wise. Let us see whether he succeeds in part c.

Part c begins imposingly: "The absolutely unconditioned is the absolute ground that is identical with its condition, [that is,] the immediate *Sache* as the truly essential" (97). Hegel says *die wahrhaft Wesenhafte*; the suffix *-haft* carries with it the note of intimate adhesion, even responsibility. The *Sache* is as it were affixed with and thus responsible for the truth and essential nature of the process we have been studying. All sides of the process adhere to the *Sache*: "This is the totality of the determinations of the *Sache—die Sache selbst.*" I break off the quotation to observe that this strikes my ear as a reference to Kant's *Ding an sich*. The *Sache* of the grounding process is Hegel's replacement for Kant's unknowable thing in itself, which is about, as it were, to emerge into existence, and so to appear. To continue with the quotation: "the *Sache* itself, but as thrown out into the externality of being, into the restored circle of being." The "circle" is the formation process or becoming, not to mention the joining of the future to the past via the gateway of the present.

The condition serves to activate the ground. At this point, Hegel shifts to the plural *Bedingungen,* which are, he says, "thereby the total content of the *Sache,* because they are the unconditioned in the form of the formless being." In other words, the entire process of being is present within each of its manifestations; each *Sache* thus contains all conditions, for otherwise the continuity of the being-process would dissolve. At the same time, the conditions have a different configuration (*Gestalt*) as the determination of the content of the *Sache* from their configuration as "formless" or total being. This distinction corresponds to the one between the general form of anything whatsoever (= the determinations of reflection) and the form of something in particular. It is, however, better justified than the previous distinction, since it makes sense to refer to the totality of conditions as a process and the same totality as concentrated within a product of that process. The so-called "formal" difference is one of *Gestalt* or configuration, that is, of role as universal or particular. But what is still unexplained (and will be from start to finish) is the particular form or look of the *Sache* as this existing or appearing thing.

Understood as formless being, the conditions appear as "an un-unified manifold," where "un-unified" means that they are not brought to a focus by the existence of a particular *Sache.* "As to the absolutely unrestricted *Sache,* the sphere of being itself is the condition." In other words, a *Sache* considered immediately or apart from this or that condition is produced by the entire formation process of being. The form of the *Sache* "sprouts rapidly" as a determination (i.e., as something in particular) of being "and appears thus as a manifold content that is different from and indifferent to the determinations of reflection." Hegel is here describing the crux of the matter, namely, the appearance of the particular form or look as distinguished from the underlying general form of all *Sachen.* But note that he in fact explains nothing; he merely asserts that this particular form appears. On the next page, Hegel makes it explicit that what he previously called "the sphere of being" is becoming (*Werden*), namely, the transition of one determination of being into another (98). The immediacy of the individual existing moments with respect to one another is thus sublated by the inner dynamics of becoming as a process, which Hegel refers to here as "the deed of reflection itself," and which is the underlying structure. Immediacy, or the appearance of the unconditioned nature of existing moments, is only an illusion (*Schein*). In fact, becoming is a process of conditions, and so of grounds being specified to the production of particular grounded *Sachen*.

We can therefore say that the immediacy of existence is in fact posed; everything that shows itself is grounded in the excitation of the total process of becoming. The facticity or apparent immediacy of things—their givenness—is an illusion, beneath which the mediations of condition, ground, and ungrounded disappear or are concealed (99). We see only the flow of becoming, of one *Sache* after another, each of which seems to be immediate and so indifferent to the others. What is for Hegel an illusion is what Sartre described as the discontinuity of each moment of becoming.

"When all conditions of a *Sache* are present, it enters into existence [*Existenz*]. The *Sache* is, before it exists," namely, first as essence or unconditioned, second as *Dasein* or determinate being. This passage implies that *Existenz* is posterior to *Dasein* or corresponds to the appearances of essence as this or that spatiotemporal *Sache*. *Dasein* is then presumably the abstract or general structure that corresponds to existing *Sachen*, just as the structure of the determinations of reflection corresponds to the form of an existing thing. Hegel refers to the presence of the sum of conditions of a *Sache* as an *Erinnerung*, "recollection" in the sense of returning inward of what was dispersed in the immediacy of being. "The *Erinnerung* of conditions is at first the going to ground of the immediate *Dasein* and the coming to be of the ground" (99–100). Immediacy is replaced by the potential ground, which in turn is replaced through its very activity by the reappearance of immediate existence in the circle of being. The cooperation of condition and ground leads to their disappearance before the coming to be of the *Sache* (100). Or as Hegel puts it, "Stepping forth into existence is immediate in this way, that it is mediated only through the disappearance of mediation."

So far as I can see, there is nothing in part c that casts any light whatsoever on the fact of heterogeneity of forms or looks, or why there are any *Sachen* to which we return, or for that matter from which we turn away. The *Sachen* apparently "emerge" by an inexplicable process of contingency upon the backdrop of the general structure of becoming. I can easily understand why Hegel might claim that knowledge of contingent individuals is not a prerequisite for wisdom. But there is something much deeper at stake here. The question is why the formation process manifests itself as the looks of concrete things. Please note that I am not objecting, in the manner of Kierkegaard, that Hegel does not explain the individual as individual. I am asking for his account of the existence of individuality. The Platonic doctrine of ideas is filled with puzzles, but it at least addresses the problem of the specificity of looks, or in other words what it means to say that to be is to be something in particular. Hegel does not assert that axiom, but that is beside the point. He too talks of *Dasein*, existence, and the coming into being of the grounded *Sachen*. It is just these that bring to a focus the underlying universal process of the totality of being as becoming. If Hegel is truly wise, he owes us an explanation of how this happens, and in particular he owes us this explanation because as he tells the tale, these particular forms, although they are clearly ungrounded or contingent as particular, nevertheless emerge as a consequence of the unfolding of the general categorial structure.

FIFTEEN

Appearance

Book 2, Section 2, Chapter 1: Existence

The totality of the categorial determinations of being is essence. To this we may now add that the totality of the determinations of essence is *Existenz*, "emergence from negativity and inwardness." This is what Hegel means by the initial statement of section 2 of book 2, "Appearance": "Essence must appear" (101). The determinations of reflection articulate the fundamental structure of every moment of becoming; these articulations are shown to be dynamic rather than static by the very attempt to think them precisely. Otherwise stated, they are a totality, an identity of identity and difference. The process of coming to be is the rendering visible of dynamic structure, which cannot conceal itself behind its appearances because it is nothing other than the pulse-beat of those appearances. So long as the determinations of reflection are regarded as the static structure of essence, the process of becoming is regarded as an illusion of the externalization of essential inwardness. But the very attempt to separate essence and existence shows that they can neither be nor be thought independently of one another.

I repeat: "Essence must appear." This is already implicit in the inner perturbations of the sameness of being and nothing, or still more radically, in the hypothesis of sheer nothingness, which cannot be the *nihil absolutum* because, as a hypothesis, it is already a concept or manifestation of thinking, and as hypothetical totality, it is being; in other words, the hypothesis amounts to the assertion that being is nothing, or more fully, that the concept of being is the concept of nothing, and so that being and thinking are the same. Hegel claims implicitly that the development of being as essence is the same as the development of subjectivity. We will have to take this up again when we come to book 3 of the *SL*, but there have been numerous indications of this point in the first two books. Hegel's fundamental thesis is that we cannot separate being from thinking. It is obvious that if such a separation is possible, it can be effected only via thinking. But this shows that the separation is impossible.

But what of the time when there were no thinking beings in the physical universe? Hegel's reply should not be formulated as a simple reflection of his ignorance of science because it has nothing to do with cosmology, geology, or biology. The empirical evolution of sentient life from the chemical processes of matter is for Hegel direct evidence of the truth of his thesis that the development of objectivity is also the development of subjectivity. Scientists speak of a chemical transition from lifeless to living matter; Hegel speaks of a "logical" transition or externalization process by which what is implicit in becoming shows itself or appears: "Essence must appear." But note carefully: Hegel does not and cannot claim simply that since sentient beings exist, they must have emerged from the intrinsic or "negative" identity of thought and extension. He goes beyond this in claiming that sentient beings *must* have come into existence. It is not simply that essence must appear but that the absolute "externalizes" in the sense of showing itself to itself, as is represented in the Christian doctrine of the trinity.

In sum: Hegel cannot simply analyze facticity or what Aristotle calls "the that" (*to hoti*). He must explain the necessity of facticity or, in brief, why it is impossible that there might not have been subjectivity. We note here, incidentally, a crucial stage in the prehistory of Heidegger's notorious statement in *Being and Time*: without man, there is no *Being*. But Heidegger was an Aristotelian in *Being and Time*, by which I mean that he begins there with the facticity or "thrownness" of *Dasein*; this in turn is connected to an endorsement of the Aristotelian beginning with *to hoti* as well as to recognition of the centrality of the question "why is there anything at all rather than simply nothing?"

To continue: Stated very generally, existence (not *Dasein*) is "essentiality that has proceeded to immediacy, and [something] existing or [a] thing [*Ding*]" (101). In other words, it is the product of the process of becoming, which process is itself articulated through the dialectical transformation of reflection into essence, and thereby into the conditioned relation of ground to grounded (as is also conveyed by the last sentence on page 100). As such a product, its immediacy is "extinguished" or sublated by the inner structure of reflection. The thing is posed or produced in opposition to this inner structure. As posed, it is not immediate but rather mediated by that to which it is opposed. Existence is the process of essence in the form of a particular, spontaneously present thing.

This is extremely difficult to understand, because the distinction be-

tween existence and appearance is not evident. It seemed that we had overcome the distinction between essence and illusion by showing that all appearances are essential in the precise sense that each exhibits the formation
process of anything whatsoever. But it is now plain that we have not yet
properly unified essence and appearance. Instead, we have arrived at the
existence of essence, that is, the appearance of essence as the existing thing.
The existing thing possesses sufficient stability to convert illusion into appearance (100, bottom). But it is not sufficiently stable to hold together
as a focusing of the underlying process: "Because its ground is essentially
reflection, its immediacy is sublated; it converts itself into something posited" (100–101). That is, it is posited by and thus opposed to its essence
or ground. A possible understanding of Hegel's thought here is as follows:
The appearing existent is still not unified with what produces it; we have
to move from the existence of a thing to the appearance of essence. This
"movement" will take us into actuality (*Wirklichkeit*).

The problem with this explanation is that it leaves obscure the sense
in which existence is no longer illusion. Let us see whether the chapter
entitled "Die Existenz" answers our question. In the opening paragraph,
Hegel associated "the *Satz* of existence" (and *Satz* should be translated
here as "law" or "principle") with the law of the ground. Whatever is is
posed or mediated by its ground. Nothing comes into existence without
a sufficient reason, as Leibniz expresses it. To this Hegel adds that "whatever is exists. The truth of being is not to be an initial immediate [thing]
but rather essence emerging into immediacy" (102). Initial immediacy is
what Hegel called previously *Dasein*; this is the initial sphere of being a
finite something or another as marked by the quality of mere quantitative
extension (102). At this early stage, there is no question of essence and thus
no contrast between essence and its appearances. Existence is a property of
the immediately visible or "appearing" thing as a product of reflection. I
suggest that existence is intermediate between illusion and appearance. It
both is and is not grounded through a condition. That is to say, it arises in
this way, but its immediacy sublates or conceals this groundedness; as Hegel puts it, the emergence into immediacy sublates this emergence itself.

After a short discussion of Kant and the ontological proof for the existence of God, to which I shall refer in a moment, Hegel adds that existence
is not a predicate of essence but "its absolute externalization, beyond which
nothing has remained behind" (104). What is externalized here is the identity of ground and grounded; the result is the existing thing, which in turn
is a product of the grounding process but which, by virtue of its existence,
conceals that process. We can now bring these remarks together as follows.

"Essence must appear," but not immediately as the identity within difference of itself and its appearances. This identity is first accomplished *within* essence; the identity within difference of essence and illusion must then be sublated into the immediacy of externalization (see again the first two paragraphs on page 101). Essence is not itself existence until this externalization occurs. And as a result of this externalization, essence is the immediately existing thing, just as *Dasein* was the immediate moment of being as determined by quality and quantity so as to be something or another.

Accordingly, Hegel both does and does not distinguish between essence and existence. They are distinct logical categories, but the former "goes over" into the latter. Note carefully that existence is not an instance of a concept, as in the dominant modern interpretation from Kant through Frege and into our own time. The "concept," or in Hegel's language the essence, is not separate from but entirely within, and so externalized as, the existing thing, which is not an instance but the existing concept itself.

I want now to make a remark about the discussion of the proof of God's existence. Hegel distinguishes three senses or types of being: the first is the immediate being with which the *SL* begins; the second is existence, or the being that emerges from essence; third is objectivity, which emerges from the concept (102). A proof of God's existence does not furnish a ground for that existence, which is its own ground; instead, it supplies a basis for our knowledge of God (103). It follows that God cannot "exist" in the Kantian sense of being some particular thing that is related to the totality of objects within the phenomenal world, a "determinate *Dasein* . . . in the context of experience as a totality." So the Kantian concept does not exist; it is abstract identity without *Entgegensetzung;* i.e., it is not posited in opposition to something else. But this is precisely what the ontological proof attempts to demonstrate, namely, that abstract or objective being passes over by mediation into existence as *Dasein.* Hegel says that his logic has shown this mediation between the concept and existence; he thereby clearly implies that he has refuted or corrected Kant, as follows in any case from the unity of being and thinking.

Hegel then observes that if the world is contingent or groundless, it cannot be a basis or ground for our knowledge of God's existence (104). At the same time, this apparent cul-de-sac is, when understood dialectically, the basis of the mediation between the identity and difference of God and the world. The ostensibly groundless world slips back into essence, of which it is an illusory appearance, and which is itself thereby reduced to illusion. As we know, but traditional advocates of contingency do not, the dialectic of reflection will propel us from illusion to appearance via existence, and so it will reestablish the exhibition of God in the existing world. This in turn requires us to move beyond the immediacy of existence (in other words to appearance as the exhibition of essence), because immediacy is the domain of faith (*Glauben*), not knowledge (*Wissen*).

The chapter on existence contains three main subsections, all dealing with the (existing) thing. In (A) Hegel discusses the structure of the thing and its properties. The existing thing has the form of negative unity, i.e., a unity of immediacy arising from the negation of the determinate negations that we can call the properties of a thing in contrast to its essence, and this immediacy, we recall, contains within it the mediations of reflection. Therefore, although we can distinguish between existence (as a logical category, and hence as a general process) and the existing thing, this is not an opposition or basis for "going over," that is, for a transition to a higher stage. It is rather an "analysis" of the existing thing into the thing in itself and its external existence (i.e., what Kant calls "phenomenon," 106). Note that Hegel's "thing in itself" is not Kant's. It is both being and *Dasein*, that is, both "nonreflected immediacy" or abstract being and a manifold of determinations that render it other than or external to itself (a product of reflection or positedness). That is, it is "unmoved, indeterminate unity" (as is conveyed by the suffix "in itself"), or what we may call the bare unqualified presence of the thing as a unified something or another, but considered simply with respect to its unity; and it is also the basis for the external reflection of a manifold of existing properties, i.e., properties by which it appears, e.g., to the senses (107). It is not hard to see here the relation of identity and difference in the structure of the thing in itself.

Since existence is external multiplicity only via negative opposition to its unity, and vice versa, Hegel infers as usual the identity of the thing in itself with external existence (108). And things in themselves are related to and distinguished from one another through the medium of external existence, that is to say, through the encounter of individual unities as owners of their properties, an encounter, however, that is carried out at the level of properties (since unities or identities as such cannot be distinguished from one another). Somewhat obscurely, Hegel concludes that there is just one thing in itself "that relates to itself in external reflection" (109); in fact, I have just explained this. As self-identical or negative unity, the thing in itself is a propertyless or unarticulated monad. It is therefore not possible to distinguish one from another.

Are then all existing properties the properties of a single thing? In a sense, the answer is yes, namely, with respect to the underlying unity of the formation process or absolute. But we are still under way toward totality;

at the present stage, we are studying what I called previously the instability of existence. The situation here is reminiscent of the distinction between the totality of essence and its illusory appearances. In other words, the immediate unity of existence, i.e., of the existing thing or thing in itself, must itself be shown to externalize as its properties, and in this way essence will be shown to have overcome illusion entirely within appearance, or more precisely, as actuality.

In the next part, Hegel holds that the thing in itself is visible in its properties and thereby itself (i.e., as unity or identity) externalizes into existence (110). But how are we in a position to identify things in themselves as distinct from one another? Their unity or identity is visible only via their properties. But the properties can be identified as belonging to this or that thing in itself only via the visibility of the respective unities. We seem to be back to the aporia of essences and attributes. Hegel does not explain this at all but simply asserts that "a thing has a property to effect this or that in something else and to externalize itself in its relation [to the other] in a peculiarly characteristic manner," and so on. This is quite striking and is closely connected with the absence of explanation of looks, i.e., of how we perceive looks as distinct, and so as essential unities.

The textual transition to the reciprocal activity of things is interrupted by a note on Kant. The unknowability of the Kantian thing in itself means that all determinations or properties are external to it (111). They occur within the subject, that is, within consciousness. It is therefore I, the subject, that determines the properties of the things of appearance. This characteristic of subjective idealism contradicts the freedom of the subject, which is determined by these object determinations, that is, limited to and by phenomena, and so cannot be free or universal. The problem does not exist in Hegel, since neither the thing in itself nor its properties emerge from consciousness or the I (112). Hegel is referring to the fact that the various categorial codifications of being have been derived entirely from the inner excitation of the sameness of being and becoming. What he forgets to mention is that the excitations are of the *concept* of the sameness of being and nothing; this concept is obviously *my* concept, i.e., it is a modification of the consciousness of the student of Hegel's logic. To be sure, Hegel claims that the excitations are the same from the standpoint of being or thinking. But how does he defend himself from the charge that this standpoint is still within the domain of subjective idealism? Presumably he would do so by referring to the *PS* as the presupposition of the *SL* in which we have been brought to the absolute standpoint. We are then presumably disregarding the content of absolute wisdom, as achieved in the *PS* experientially, and studying only the development of its form. In other words, we are studying the form of the identity within difference of subjective and objective idealism. So this in turn rests upon the thesis that it is impossible to go outside of thinking, i.e., that a nonidealistic objectivism, or what is today called realism, is impossible.

In the final part of subsection A, as just noted, Hegel simply asserts the multiplicity of things, which interact via their properties. Apart from these properties, the thing is mere quantity (113–14). I will not belabor the absence of an explanation of the distinguishability of multiple things, except to note that Hegel unintentionally accentuates this problem when he says that "genuine being in itself is the being in itself in its positedness; this is the property. Thereby thinghood has gone over into the property" (113). Things as opposed to properties are now the inessential (114). They are reduced to the continuum of matter, that is, to an indifferent external form of the property. So properties are themselves freed from the unity of the thing in itself and become independent diverse material for the making of things.

In the next two subsections (B and C), Hegel discusses the constitution of the thing out of differing kinds of matter as an inessential "also." All that we need to say about this is that the instability of the immediacy of existence leads to the dissolution of the thing into its properties, and these in turn are extrinsically or contingently combined types of matter, a mode of analysis that Hegel attributes to chemistry. The thing is both immediate or self-subsisting and also inessential existence. Stated as simply as possible, it is dispersed into appearance (119). One might be inclined to regard this as a deterioration back to the stage of essence as illusion. But we must remember that essence and illusion were shown to be a unity; since essence is defined by illusory appearances, it is itself just illusion as ground and grounded. In other words, essence comes to a focus as the existing thing, which, when it disperses, does not reproduce a distinction between essence and existence but rather transfers essentiality to dispersed appearances. There is so to speak nothing but appearance. "The truth of existence" inheres in its inessentiality or its subsistence in another (appearance), and, indeed, in an absolute other. By this qualification, Hegel means that the "essence" of appearance is *Nichtigkeit*, its nullity when considered from any standpoint other than that it appears (119).

Book 2, Section 2, Chapter 2: Appearance

We can now say that existence is the dialectic of appearance as it works itself out in the immediacy of the thing that is the sublation or preservation at a higher level of the opposition between essence and how it shows itself (a "how" that is initially illusion). If essence is the same as illusion, then what we can call "reality" is nothing other than the immediacy of the appearances of things. These appearances have two aspects, (1) the identity or unity of the thing in itself and (2) the difference of its properties. But the identity of unity is visible only in and as the properties. There is no further illusion of a hidden or inner essence; instead, essence shows itself entirely, and is thereby dispersed, as its appearances. It seems reasonable to anticipate that in the next stage of the logic, Hegel must preserve the dispersion of essence in appearance as an identity within difference. That is, he must return stability or subsistence to things as owners of their properties, even though the owners remain entirely visible in their properties.

In fact, this is impossible. There must remain something contingent about individual subsisting things identified by their looks or particular forms, which we have already discovered to be for Hegel inessential, just as they were for Kant. We can also express this contingency as directly entailed by the nature of the absolute as a formation process. This is why Hegel's honorific term is *Wirklichkeit*, "actuality" in the sense of "working" or "activity" (or a dynamic interpretation of Aristotle's *energeia*), and not *Realität*, the mode of being of *res*. Whereas Hegel does not and would not say that individual things (or more broadly, *Sachen*) are illusions, their independence is contingent relative to the essential character of the formation process. Individual things are not illusory because they are actually how the formation process manifests itself. But the unity of the properties in individual things is certainly contingent in the sense that every attempt to grasp this unity as such (as for example through Platonic ideas or Aristotelian species forms) leads to the dissolution of that unity into a dialectical excitation of identity within difference.

I turn now to the opening statement of chapter 2. "Existence is the immediacy of being, to which essence has once more restored itself. This immediacy is in itself the reflection of essence into itself" (122). In other words, essence is immediate in the form of the existing thing; it emerges "out of its ground," or as we can say, its interiority, and so out of itself as the totality of being. This self-emergence sets up an opposition between essence as ground and essence as grounded, existing thing; Hegel calls this opposition a reflection. Essence emerges "out of" itself because it first turned inward "into itself" by the assimilation of all of its appearances. The emergence is from inner identity or absolute negativity; Hegel calls it "being posed" (*gesetzt*) because it is a difference or attribute, in opposition to identity. It is posed as an appearance, and so as an appearance of essence, namely, as the existence into which essence has been assimilated.

As posed, the appearance is not in and for itself; by this Hegel means that in being assimilated into existence, essence is no longer the stabilizing ground of its appearance, which is merely in itself. We have to reestablish the identity within difference of essence as the process of appearance and the particularity of this or that appearing (= existing) thing. This unity of essence and existence is actuality (156).

The chapter on appearance is concerned with the manifestation of essence as the totality of its existing moments. Essence in this sense is also the ground of those moments. In other words, the structure of the intelligibility of *res* or elements of experience (*Sachen*) is that of the essential existence, the standing out or appearing of things as grounded by the negative activity ingredient in the sublation of identity and difference within contradiction. Hegel has in effect transformed the disintegrating "appearances" (illusions) of the nihilist account of genesis into the categorial structure of the process of world production.

Book 2, Section 2, Chapter 2, Subsection A: The law of appearance

Hegel begins subsection A on the law of appearance by recalling that the existing thing has a determination or property, and so a first negation. But it is also grounded by a conditioned ground, i.e., by some other existing thing; hence its identity lies in that other, or in the negation of the first negation. "Or the existing thing is, as appearing, reflected into another that serves it as ground and that is itself just this, to be reflected in another." The play of appearances makes up the continuum of becoming; one thing grounds another, and all things, as appearances, are posed by the reflection of one within another (124). Hegel calls this aspect of appearance "essential *Schein*," which I would translate here as "show" rather than "illusion," and which is essential because it is total; there is no distinction between essence and appearance because the essence is diffused throughout the flow of appearances. It just is that flow, namely, reciprocal positing, "ein Schein nur in einem Scheine" (a show only within a showing, 125).

There are thus two sides to each appearance: reciprocal positing with another and subsistence through this positing. Each appearance is both positive (as what it is) and negative (as subsisting via reflection in another appearance). But this contradiction of position and negation is sublated in that the passage from one appearance to another is not just the passing away of one but the coming to be of the other (126). This unity of the flow

358 / Chapter Fifteen
of appearances is the law of appearance. It is not a *Jenseits* beyond the appearances, like Platonic ideas but immediately present within them. In a passage reminiscent of the treatment of the inverted world in the *PS*, Hegel says that "the domain of laws is the resting copy of the existing or appearing world. But it is much more the case that both are one totality, and the existing world is itself the domain of laws " (127–28). Hegel develops this pivotal point at some length. The laws of appearance, as for example in modern natural science, are the ground or "essence" of the appearances that *themselves appear*. They are "reflected" within the appearances; or conversely, the appearances copy and so reflect them. The laws are not separate from appearances, because then we would repeat the classical paradox of the separation of essences from their attributes or of paradigms from their instances. But neither are they "merely" apparent; they do not pass away in the passing away of appearances. Rest and motion are thus an identity within difference in the law-abiding flow of appearances (128). The law is the "positive essentiality" of appearances, not their negation or trivialization as merely transient illusions (129).

Book 2, Section 2, Chapter 2, Subsection B: That which appears . . .

In subsection B of chapter 2, Hegel rings the changes on the dialectical relations of a world that both appears and subsists or exists in itself. Appearing things have their grounds and conditions in other appearing things. Not only is each appearing thing other than the others but all are the same because all exhibit the same modifications, which Hegel refers to as their positedness. Hegel plays upon the etymological relation between "posited" (*Gesetzt*) and "law" (*Gesetz*) to make the point that this positedness is just a return by each into itself (i.e., into the sameness of the modifications common to all). "This very reflection of being posited into itself is the law" (130). Hegel thus distinguishes between the existence or immediate being of the world of appearances and its essence as law. This distinction underlies the doctrine of two worlds, one supersensible and the other its sensuous twin. We will see shortly how this separation is transformed into the identity within difference of essence and existence that constitutes *Wirklichkeit*.

Let me interpolate a general remark at this point that is designed to clarify the overall direction of the chapter on appearance. We are studying the dialectic of law and appearance that leads to the split between the sensible and the supersensible worlds. The supersensible world is for Hegel any domain of forms, laws, or principles that are intended both as the essence of appearances and as detached from or beyond those appearances.

Kant's transcendental ego is a *Jenseits* in this sense, as is any conception of scientific laws that has not been integrated into a totality or comprehensive structure of the appearances *as they appear*. In other words, what we call today apriorism is for Hegel a *Jenseits* or detached supersensible world, whereas all nominalist doctrines that reduce laws to points of view or interpretations amount to the dissolution of those laws into the appearances. What is required is the preservation of both aspects of the world within an identity of identity (law) and difference (appearances). Hegel is therefore not saying simply that the supersensible world must be "brought down to earth." It is not enough to posit a totality of appearances if we do not have a comprehensive conceptual grasp of the lawlike structure of that totality. But science can never provide us with such a grasp because it is concerned with the transformations or modifications of appearances as appearances. The laws we seek are of a different order or lie at a different level within the appearances. They are the "laws" of the categorial structure of the intelligibility of totality: the laws of pure logic that underlie the laws of science. But Hegel's is a transcendental logic, not a formal calculus for deriving inferences about the finite manifestations of this or that scientific law or set of laws but the conditions for the possibility of any law whatsoever. And these conditions are "existential" or as we might say "ontological" as well as "essential" or "logical."

I now continue with subsection B of chapter 2. As soon as we shift our attention to the reciprocal positedness of appearances and turn to a consideration of their inner unity, that is, to the domain of law, we find that the same relations of difference and mutual implication or (in Hegel's sense) identity obtain among the laws themselves. "Thus is the identity of law itself posited and real" (131), by which last term Hegel means that laws assume the same kind of determinate structure as things or *res*. More fundamentally, it also means that the domain of laws "appears" as a mirror image of the thinglike heterogeneity of appearances in the sensible or existing aspect of becoming. The domain of laws *duplicates* the domain of existing or immediate appearances; it becomes a duplicate world. But furthermore, that world, having assimilated the motions of appearance into the domain of law, is a world that is detached from the sensible world; essence is once more sundered from existence. "Thus is appearance reflected into itself [i.e., assimilated into the inner identity of law] now a world that gets started *as existing in and for itself beyond the appearing world*" (131).

The domain of laws contains the manifold content of the domain of appearances, but as unchanging. However, it also contains the inessential multiplicity of appearances, i.e., their endless variations, to each of which a scientific law appertains. So it mirrors the properties of the sensible world, or possesses in Hegel's terminology a reflected version of immediacy and existence, albeit an essential existence (in one sense a contradiction in terms, but intended here to bring out the role of the domain of law as the essence of existence, 132).

This world of law is in and for itself, that is, it is the totality of existence but expressed as form. And since form is determination, it is also negation, which means that forms are defined or distinguished by their opposites, and so both are and are not, which is precisely the property of appearances in the world of existence. This is an inner dualism in the domain or world of law. The domain or world of law is both the ground of the world of appearances and itself grounded as the essential existence of that world (133). Or otherwise expressed, it is the totality of the appearances of the sensible world as well as their negative identity or ground. Accordingly, the following inversion has taken place. By both separating itself from existing or immediate appearances and assimilating them as the heterogeneity of law, that is, by becoming a supersensible copy of the sensible world, the supersensible world becomes sensible; i.e., it becomes the sensible world. And the sensible or appearing world, by transferring its essence, form, or as we would say its meaning and value to the supersensible world, has transformed itself into the supersensible world (134). Law, the essence of appearance, is the genuine nature of, and so is itself, appearance. Conversely, appearance is law.

Book 2, Section 2, Chapter 2, Subsection C: Dissolution of appearance

I have discussed the dialectic of the inverted world as it appears in the *PS* in *G. W. F. Hegel. An Introduction to the Science of Wisdom* and will not repeat it here. A few words only about subsection C. Hegel says, quite misleadingly in my opinion, that the inversion of the two worlds means that what is positive in one is negative in the other; e.g., the North Pole in one world is the South Pole in the other, and so on (134). But this surely makes no sense. I take it as a metaphorical expression of the interchange of essentiality and heterogeneity. As Hegel himself says next, "in this opposition of both worlds, their difference disappears; what ought to be the world that is in and for itself is itself the appearing world, and this conversely is the essential world" (134–35). Each is what it is by having come to be the other. Thus each is the totality of existence, but since there are two worlds, the single totality falls apart into two totalities that repel one another (135). The upshot of the dialectic of law in these two worlds is that it serves to relate them to each other in a way that is described in the next chapter.

Book 2, Section 2, Chapter 3: The Essential Relation

Initially law and appearance are sublated into one another, but in such a way that their unity is "broken" (137), by which term Hegel is referring to the continuous transformation of each into the other. "The essential relation is thus not yet the true third to essence and existence, but contains already their determinate unification." We are very close to actuality here, and yet the degree of separation is sufficient to produce the continuous dissolution into the two worlds, each of which claims to be essence through the medium of existence, and existence through the medium of essence, but succeeds in remaining neither the one nor the other. In reading this passage, I am reminded of the contemporary debate in the philosophy of science, in which realists attempt to maintain simultaneously that theory is interpretation but that the entities under interpretation reside in a natural world external to our efforts to cognize them. The similarity is due to the fact that Hegel is implicitly criticizing Kant in this text, who is also the patron saint of twentieth-century philosophy of science in its realist as well as its hermeneutical schools; that is, a Kant as mediated by Wittgenstein.

To come back to the essential relation, it is still appearance; neither side of the relation has genuine existence, but each exists in and through the other. At first the relation is one of whole and parts (subsection A). Each side of the relation is the totality of existence, or essence, but also, as the totality, the diverse appearances or parts. The attempt to think the whole turns into a thinking of the parts; the attempt to think the parts is impossible except by thinking the whole. In an earlier expression, there is no "third" here, namely, the structure of identity and difference that alone constitutes a genuine totality. Such a totality is neither the parts nor the totality or whole, but it is both as exhibited in each. In a sense we have already arrived at this result before, but in a nonessential, unstable manner. We have not yet understood that the apparent flux of the inversion process is itself the stamp of totality rather than the expression of dissolution (138–42).

Hegel expresses this understanding as follows. "The truth of the relation rests therefore in the mediation; its essence is the negative unity in which the reflected as well as the existing immediacy is sublated" (142). This negative unity is not the whole and its parts but the interiority of law that emits appearances. Hegel calls this next stage "force and its externalization" and takes up this new relation in subsection C. The underlying thesis here is that the mutual transformation of the supersensible and sensible worlds is just the process of genesis, the interior unity of which is force externalizing itself as a thing (144–47). I am going to proceed directly to page 150 and subsection C, in which Hegel restates the nature of the first two stages of the relation of the two worlds, i.e., of essence and existence, and their unification at the higher level of actuality.

The relation of whole and parts is immediate; we think of the multiplicity of appearances as constituting a sum. But second, we shift our attention to the inner unity of the parts within the whole, and this is force. The multiplicity of appearances is related now not as the sum of parts to a whole but as the products of a process that is the essence of these products. Third, we come to see that the two sides to this process, the form of reflected immediacy or of the essence (i.e., inner force) and the external manifestations of force taken as the form of being (i.e., of the appearing world), are both one identity. Force is force via exteriorization; external appearances are what they are thanks to the exteriorizing of inner force (151). In the note, Hegel emphasizes that whatever is only inward or immediate and so exists only in its concept has only an immediate or passive *Dasein* (153). Even God is not spirit in his immediate concept. "Spirit is not the immediate opposed to mediation, but rather that which eternally poses its immediacy, and the essence that eternally turns back into itself from out of its immediacy. As immediate, God is only nature. Or nature is only the inner; it is not active as spirit and is therefore not the true God" (154).

And so finally, "What something is is totally in its externalization; its externalization is its totality. It is thus the unity reflected into itself of anything at all" (155). In other words, there is no split between essence and existence; if there were, neither would be what it is but would rather collapse into the show of transient appearances that Hegel calls illusion.

Summary

Let us briefly resume the main stages of the development of the logic to this point. We began with being and nothing, from which becoming emerges as a continuum of moments distinguishable as something or another by a general structure of quality and quantity. The relation of quality and quantity yields measure. That is to say, to be is to be a ratio of quality and quantity. However, these two cannot be preserved in their integrity because there is as yet no essence or ground to the individual being; in fact, quality is initially indistinguishable from quantity. Being thus collapses as the last consequences of its inner categorial development. It cannot preserve the stable existence of any particular thing. But this means that there is no stable distinction between essence and attribute. Accordingly being is equivalent to essence; everything is as it were homogeneous being, but this in turn means that the essence of things is mere show or transient presence. Hegel then demonstrates how the structure of the collapse of essence into illusion is precisely the set of reflective determinations that define the fundamental structure of a being of any sort whatsoever; but these determinations are to be understood as a comprehensive contradiction that is to be viewed in two ways. From the inside, so to speak, the contradiction expresses the aforementioned collapse of being into chaos. But from the outside or above, the contradiction is precisely the expression of the (contradictory) nature of becoming. Differently stated, Hegel shows how we can begin from the chaos of becoming and arrive at the structure of essence, existence, and appearance through the mediation of identity and difference as sublated within contradiction.

Being is transformed into becoming, which collapses into the chaos of "show" or illusion, namely, the production of illusory existing stability by an illusory essence. We escape chaos by the demonstration that the structure of chaos is that of the order of genesis; the key here is to establish that everything is self-contradictory because the formation process of each individual manifestation of totality is itself a contradiction. The Hegelian formula for this contradiction is identity within difference. The pivotal result in this demonstration is that essence and existence are not finally separate from one another; to separate them is to identify them. This identification or more precisely unity of essence and existence is *Wirklichkeit*. If essence is separate from existence, then existence is illusory; but essence, as the essence of illusion, is itself an illusion. This establishes chaos as the essence of things (Nietzsche). But Hegel rescues us from chaos by exhibiting its inner pulse as the same as the determinations of reflection. Chaos, in other words, is the same as world formation.

Since essence and existence cannot be separate without reducing totality to chaos, they must be united. But it is not enough for them to be united, since then they will each turn into the other and thus negate it, thereby reinstituting the process of chaos. They must be united or identical and separated or different, not in such a way as to cancel each other, but so that they are preserved in this reciprocally modifying relation. The study of how this relation is established has taken us through the show of illusion to that of appearance by way of the study of the ground-grounded relation. In the last analysis, we learn that ground-grounded is equivalent to essence and existence, and that both relations are subsumed within the flow of appearances as the exteriorizing or coming into being of moments of interior force, Hegel's way of attempting to express his ontology in the language of contemporary physics. Essence or the interior of appearance is both identical with and different from existence or the immediate exterior of appearance. And this brings us to page 156 and the beginning of the section on actuality.

SIXTEEN

Actuality

Introductory Remarks

"Actuality is the unity of essence and existence. In it the shapeless [*gestalt-lose*] essence and the unsupported [*haltlos*, 'unhalting'] appearance, or subsistence without determination and the unstable multiplicity, have their truth." Essence is "shapeless" because it is the inner unity of genesis; the shapes or forms inhere in the products of genesis, in the grounded *Sache*, not in the ground as the unity of formation process. If this process had a form, it would be static or itself a *Sache*. Let me try to clarify this remark. Although "identity" is a form, it is not visible as something else, just as "being" is a quality or logical predicate that is not analyzable into simpler elements. We "see" identity only as the inner unity of differences. Thus the process of genesis, the formation process, is not visible as some determinate form independent of and opposed to the forms of the moments it generates. What we do instead of analyzing process into static moments is to uncover the general structure of process, a structure made up of moments that are themselves in process, and so that are related, not by some still more comprehensive form but by *nothing* or the work of negative activity, that is to say, by the formation process.

Perhaps the most important consequence of this is that in the last analysis, we cannot distinguish one entity or *Sache* from another as a finite and self-subsisting unity of essential attributes. We can do this at the level of appearance, but not at the level of actuality. This is why Russell's realism ended in Wittgensteinian hermeneutics, to say nothing of what came afterward. Things are *not* intelligible in themselves because we have no knowledge, i.e., no conceptual knowledge, of the inner unity of the essence of anything whatsoever. What we can conceptualize is the general process by which things appear; this general process is total or comprehensive. It is the process of *das Ganze*. "The true is the whole." And by "true," Hegel is referring to the structure of intelligibility. We can say that a thing or entity consists of an essence and a set of attributes, of which some are essential and some not. But all such speeches or definitions are conventional. What is not conventional is the recipe as developed into the general structure of the formation process of the absolute. This is the necessary consequence of the rejection of the Platonic-Aristotelian doctrine of ideas or forms, namely, of the "looks" of particular things as opposed to the general structure of the determinations of reflection, if one does not adopt a dialectico-speculative logic.

For Hegel, the unit of intelligibility is form. But forms are not intelligible simply as units, i.e., in isolation. Particular forms are intelligible only as interrelated, as moments of one and the same form, namely, of the form of the whole. And this form is not really a form, i.e., not the form of a *res*; it is the formation process. When we describe the absolute or formation process as the identity of identity and difference, nothing with a determinate, finite, stable, and independent structure comes before the mind's eye. To state the point in a suitably paradoxical manner, the form of the world has no form. If it did, it would be static, finite, dead or lifeless, not a world, not genesis, not negative activity; there would be no difference, hence no dialectical interplay between its constituent formal elements or atoms, because there would be no thinking. Nothing could be identified in itself as opposed to its logical complement; all distinctions would collapse, and we would return to the Eleatic monad, that is to say, to the unity of being and nothing, but not to their identity within difference.

Hegel's conception of the whole is thus strikingly similar to Aristotle's conception of intellect (*nous*). The intellect, as the place in which forms actualize, has no form of its own but is instead a pure noetic receptivity; this is the so-called passive intellect. The active or poetic intellect that actualizes the forms simply through the process of thinking itself corresponds to the negative activity of the formation process. The passive intellect can be compared to the continuum of becoming within which entities or *Sachen* actualize as existing manifestations of the formation process. Hegel's whole is thus analogous to the Aristotelian "thought thinking itself." Spirit thinks itself *qua* formation process or the absolute and in so doing brings into existence the world of human experience. The net result is a Christianized version of Aristotelian noetics.

To come back to the text, appearances are *haltlos*; they do not cease, nor are they "supported" in the sense that they refer back to a separate or transcendent ground. On the contrary, one appearance is the ground for another; each is grounded by some appearance other than itself. Appearances ground themselves in the double sense that they flow from each other, as just indicated, and also that this flow is the inner unity, the force, the shapeless essence, the negative activity that constitutes the life-pulse of the totality or absolute that Hegel is in the course of developing.

Hegel continues: "Existence is indeed immediacy that has emerged from the ground, but it has not yet posed form in itself. Insofar as it determines and forms itself, it is appearance. And insofar as this subsistence that is determined only as reflection in another builds itself up to reflection in itself, it becomes two worlds, two totalities of content, of which the one is determined in itself and the other is determined as reflected in another" (156). Existence is the immediacy of appearance; it "seems" to be spontaneous, without a ground in relation to which it derives its nature. If the nature or form of the existing thing is itself immediate or spontaneous, i.e., if the existing thing is its own ground, then it is appearance (or what we can paraphrase as inessential essence, existence offered as its own explanation and so not as spontaneous but nevertheless as insubstantial). The subsistence of existence as appearance is insubstantial. It is derived from itself rather than from an independent and nonappearing essence. If reflection in another, i.e., derivation of essence from transition into another appearance, is built up into reflection into itself, i.e., into a return to the inner ground of negative identity that is the nature of essence, then appearance is itself transformed into essence. But conversely, essence is transformed into appearance. This generates the dialectic of the inverted world that we studied previously.

And this in turn leads to the distinction of inner and outer, both of which have one and the same content as foundation. In other words, the inversion process leads to the unification of the two worlds, both of which contain the same flow of appearances (for there can hardly be more than one). "This unity of inner and outer is absolute actuality" (156). Needless to say, as always in Hegel, in arriving at a new category, we have uncovered only the first of three stages of development. The absolute must be articulated by reflection and then united with the results of that articulation.

Book 2, Section 3, Chapter 1: The Absolute

Hegel's use of the term "absolute" in section 3 of book 2 should be distinguished from its occurrence at the end of the *SL* in the expression "the absolute idea." In the present section, the absolute is not the union of subject and object, nor has it achieved the level of the idea. The term refers here to the totality constituted by the identity within difference of essence and attributes, or in other words to the total development of the sphere of essence as the completion of the objective logic. In one more formulation, it is the exhibition of the categorial structure of being as self-manifestation, but not yet as mediated or assimilated by self-consciousness. The absolute is thus here initially the immediate unity of interiority and exteriority. Let us refer to it as the ontological "object" of the external reflection of a thinking that has not yet assimilated its inner excitations as those of reflection, i.e., thinking, itself (156).

Chapter 1 opens as follows: "The simple pure identity of the absolute is indeterminate," that is, as the totality of genesis, the absolute has dissolved the distinctions of the antecedent categories, not by annihilating but by assimilating them to a higher level. Stated as simply as possible, appearance is now preserved from illusion because the relation between essence and appearance has been established as that of the inner unity of genesis or force that externalizes itself in the production of heterogeneous *Sachen*. What is preserved is the independent being and intelligibility not of finite generated things but rather of the process through which appearing things are generated. This process is not visible "in itself," since in itself it is the inner unity of all differences. But we can grasp it in the reciprocal relations of appearances themselves.

The absolute can be viewed from two different standpoints. On the one hand, as the dissolution or sublation of the independence of categorial distinctions, the absolute is without determinations of its own; "it appears only as the negation of all predicates and as the void" (157). On the other hand, the absolute is the "positioning" (i.e., positing) of all predicates. As viewed from external reflection, these two sides of the absolute give rise to a formal or unsystematic dialectic or contradiction that is resolved without a genuine unification. It remains to establish the genuine dialectical identity within difference, or what Hegel calls the "genuine interpretation of the absolute." More precisely, as he makes clear in the next three pages, the genuine interpretation of itself is provided by the absolute rather than being imposed onto it from the outside by external reflection.

To begin with, the absolute unifies being and essence in such a way that each is a part of the totality, while at the same time each is the totality itself. As we try to grasp this part of Hegel's argument, we should be thinking at all times of the play of appearances as a process of externalization through which inner unity is exhibited; this is the totality in which each side or part, process and product, can be distinguished, but only as a presentation of its correlate (158). Next, the unification of being and essence amounts to a canceling of the independence of both these two poles as well as their categorial substructure. This means that the absolute is neither being nor essence, nor any of the other categorial determinations. It is just the absolute; as Hegel puts it, "it subsists at first only in this, to sublate its activity [*Tun*] into the absolute" (159). As Heidegger might say, the absolute absolutizes. Again, the absolute is both all prior determinations and none of these. The prior determinations "appear" as illusorily independent in contrast with the absolute that is their ground. This appearance "shines" or "shows itself" only thanks to the absolute, which, as absolute, is itself shining within them. Hence the absolute as distinct from its determinations is illusory; this interpretation is "a nullity" that is adopted not from within the motion of the absolute but from outside, in the attempt to understand it (160).

The absolute must interpret itself; that is, it must furnish to itself its own structure, via its own inner dialectical motions. Otherwise the absolute will collapse, just as all of Hegel's fundamental structures that consist of complementary categories must collapse so long as their inner relation is viewed from outside by reflection or traditional rationalism, that is, as a combining of elements or a distinguishing of viewpoints into apparent contradictions, viewpoints that are intended to reconcile the contradictory elements or in effect to remove rather than to preserve the contradiction. As the product of an external reflection, the absolute is not yet what Hegel calls the "absolutely absolute," but is only an attribute or determination; it is determined as absolute identity, namely, as that with respect to which the finite is demarcated (see 159).

The absolute as attribute is for Hegel only relatively absolute or a formal determination; it is applied to the negative identity in which all other determinations have "gone to ground" (159, 161). Instead of a relation of opposition between the world in and for itself and the world of appearances, an opposition or totality in which each part is the whole, we have the empty form of the absolute as totality. This point is confusing, because an attribute is a determination that belongs to an essence. One would normally think that the absolute possesses attributes, not that it is itself an attribute. Hegel wishes to say, however, that since the absolute itself lacks attributes or dialectically independent determinations, we can refer to it exclusively as a negative identity, and so as a property of totality. We can say "the totality is absolute," but not "the absolute is so and so."

The last subsection (C) of chapter 1 is entitled "The Mode of the Absolute." The absolute as attribute is negative (indeterminate) identity, but an attribute, even that of negative identity, is a determination; we "determine" or define the whole by calling it "absolute," although the determination that we attribute to it is nothing more than identity (162). But identity is invisible until it exteriorizes or shows itself in a certain manner. Following Spinoza, to whom he is tacitly alluding, Hegel calls this manifestation a mode: "In fact, it is thus first in the mode that the absolute is posed as absolute identity" (162–63). The absolute shows itself or shines forth as its modes. In so shining it is itself present or in other words turns back into itself through the very act of showing itself as this or that mode. Whereas the modes may seem to external reflection to have been discovered outside of or independent of the absolute and then "brought back to" (or attributed to) it (by an act of reflection), it is rather the case that the absolute attribute of negative identity has produced these modes from within itself.

In this rather cumbersome section, Hegel is beginning the process of setting Spinoza's substance into motion. In Spinoza, the modes are mere illusory appearances of substance because not produced by its inner excitation. There is no such inner excitation; hence substance has only one genuine attribute, namely, identity (just as in the case of Parmenides). The modes do not emerge from substance but are found by a process of external reflection and then attributed to substance via the attribute they modify. Differentiation of substance is in Spinoza, as in all forms of Eleaticism, an illusion. Note also that even though the modes are produced by external reflection, Hegel marks as a defect of this version of the absolute that it is "the unmoved, still unreflected absolute" (163). By this he means that the external reflections or attributions of modes have not "gone to ground" or been assimilated into the negative identity of the absolute. When this assimilation occurs, the interiority and exteriority of the absolute unite in absolute self-manifestation or actuality: *Wirklichkeit* (164).

In the note, Hegel confirms that the present discussion is an interpretation of Spinoza. I call attention to page 165. Spinoza, Hegel says, defines attribute as the manner in which understanding (*Verstand*) grasps essence. But the understanding is for Spinoza a mode of an attribute; hence substance is made dependent upon what is external to it.

Book 2, Section 3, Chapter 2: Actuality

Preliminary remarks

"The absolute is the unity of inner and outer as first, *ansichseiende* unity" (169). This is the stage we reached at the end of the previous chapter. In the terminology of Spinoza and Leibniz, the mode is the externalization of the activity of the absolute, and not an external modification of an attribute. The attribute or negative identity of the absolute has been internalized or reflected inward; it is now the inner unity of essence and attribute, here of the absolute understood as substance and attribute. In traditional terminology, it is the ontological subject, not a property predicated of a subject (but not yet "subject" in Hegel's special terminology).

Hegel is about to consider the three modalities of actuality, possibility, and necessity. As a preface to this treatment, I note that as each stage of the dialectic emerges from the previous one, it is initially immediate in the sense that it is the result of the sublation of an antecedent opposition or contradiction but is not yet itself a thesis to an opposing antithesis. Thus actuality is initially the immediate formal unity of the inner and outer dimensions of the process described to this point. As such an immediacy, it must still undergo the developmental excitations of its constitutive categorial moments or produce another opposition from within itself that will be resolved at a yet higher level. At first the constitutive moments are distinguished from the outside, by external reflection. They must then be reflected inward, i.e., rejoin the generative motive power of the interior, and thus be reproduced, literally, regenerated, this time as a consequence of the force or formation process within the unity that we previously overlooked or reduced to a combination of external elements. Hegel distinguishes these two stages as actuality and possibility (170). These are immediate existence and its consequences. "The relation of these two is the third" in which as usual each is, as itself, the other as well. "This third is necessity."

Let us try to formulate this stage as simply as possible. The distinctions between essence and attribute on the one hand and essence and existence on the other are two ways of analyzing the total process of genesis, which consists of a productive force and the things or *Sachen* it produces. Hegel often refers to the two sides of genesis as the inner and the outer. The inner, if taken apart from the outer, is obviously invisible; it shows itself *as* the outer. Conversely, if the outer is taken apart from the inner, it loses its unity, its essence, its ground, its conditions, and it becomes a mere play of appearances that dissolves as it is coming into being. Merely to add them together or combine them in a relation from the outside, or to engage in external reflection, is not enough to achieve a genuine unification of the two dimensions. External reflection is conceptual analysis, but analysis divides and dissolves; it does not unify. At the same time, it is not mere or pure unification that we seek, since this would render the outside as invisible as the inside; it would bring the outside inside, but it would not bring the inside outside. There would be disappearance rather than show,

or rather, there would be an illusory show. So we want a unity that preserves distinctness, or in other words an identity of identity and difference,
or more succinctly, an identity within difference.

The bringing together of essence and existence or inside and outside as
an identity within difference of process and products is itself a process that
has various stages. These stages are in Hegel's terminology the modalities.
Immediate actuality or unity of essence and existence must now produce
from within that unity the existential component; the unification must be
verified as it were by exhibiting itself *as* its products. These products are the
possibilities of actuality, and taken collectively, they constitute the stage of
possibility. They are also the differentiation of inner or negative identity.
As usual in Hegel, we require a third stage, namely, the reunion of identity and difference. This reunion is obviously the identity within difference
of the totality of genesis, the totality that results from the sublation of all
previous stages. As such, it is the formation process as exhibited thus far in
the total articulation of being, or more precisely of the sameness of being
and nothing. But this is the absolute, or the absolutely absolute, or in other
words necessity. There are no possibilities outside or beyond the identity
within difference of actuality and possibility. That which permits nothing
possible beyond itself is the necessary. It cannot be otherwise.

Taking necessity then as the identity within difference of actuality and
possibility, we study the three stages of necessity: formal, real, and the absolute relation of the two (subsections A, B, and C, respectively). It should
come as no surprise that the modalization of actuality must go through
the same three developments that marked the progressive development of
actuality. The formal stage corresponds to the inner unity of identity, the
real stage corresponds to the differentiation by externalization of this inner
unity, and the absolute relation is the two taken together in the usual way
that preserves each as itself and its other. One last word. Actuality is the
unity of essence and existence. But this is not yet the full exhibition of the
domain of genesis as a congeries of appearances of the formation process
working from within the unity of the continuum. Existence is immediate;
it has to develop by the reaction with essence that renders it fully actual.

Book 2, Section 3, Chapter 2, Subsection A:
Contingency: A sketch of the problem

Hegel turns next to the status of contingency, which he locates within formal necessity, or the immediate unification of the actual and the possible.
Whatever is formally actual is possible (171); but it is certainly not for that
reason contingent. At this point, I find Hegel's reasoning unsatisfactory. He

claims that there are two aspects to possibility, of which the first is "actuality reflected into itself." This is the aspect of self-identity or being *an sich*, namely, the immediate existence of the actual considered as a formal structure but not as in dialectical motion. Hegel says that this formal determination or "being in itself" is "determined as sublated or as essentially only in relation to actuality, as the negative of this, posed as negative." What sense can we give to these words? The form is negative because it is mere identity or inner unity and contains no inner determinations that would render it describable in predicative or analytical discourse. "Actuality" thus stands here for the content or differences of actuality, for the heterogeneity of appearances. Corresponding to the positive moment of possibility, then, namely, the possible filling with content of the form of actuality, is a negative moment, namely, the defectiveness of the possible as not yet filled with content, and so as contrasted to actuality as an other, with respect to which it completes itself.

Stated as simply as possible, Hegel seems to say that the formal is not itself actual but possible; that is, it is a formal possibility for actualizing as some concrete thing or event. This is a regular characteristic of modern philosophy, which gives priority to change over rest and to process, temporality, or history over eternity. Hegel sets eternity into motion, thereby synthesizing, or as he would put it, sublating the two component dimensions. Form remains the principle of intelligibility, but it is now understood as a circular or eternal process, namely, the process we are in the course of studying. Remember Heidegger's statement in *Being and Time* that *Möglichkeit* is higher than *Wirklichkeit*.[1] Hegel, of course, is not a Heideggerian. What he says is that actuality is the unity of essence and existence; in other words, when the proper development is understood, actuality is the identity within difference of the inner unity of the formation process as exhibited in the *Sachen* of the products of that process.

As the identity within difference of inner unity and outer diversity, actuality can be described as possessing both form and content. The form is the categorial structure; the content, to repeat, is the product of the activity of that structure. In full actuality, i.e., as both in and for itself, one would expect a unification or identity within difference of the form and the content. But this would render every *Sache* necessary. The identification of the form and the content must be such as to allow for possibility, not merely in the sense that the actual, since it is actual, cannot be impossible, and so is possible, but in the broader sense that the content, which is after all appearance, exhibits contingency. *Die Sachen* could have been otherwise. Note that the same problem exists in Kant, as it must for all transcendental philosophers. How can the structure of the transcendental conditions of existence and intelligibility combine with sensation or the "matter" of experience to produce events that are both necessary and contingent?

We can speak of the "form" of the contingent entity as transcendental or necessary, in distinction to the concrete or material instantiations of those forms, which instantiations are contingent. But this reinstitutes dualism, whether in the classical or in the Kantian sense. The central motive of Hegel's entire teaching is to overcome dualism, that is, to establish "trinitarianism" or the identity within difference of monism and dualism. His problem as we now face it is how to unify monism with dualism in such a way as to avoid chaos without paradoxically reinstituting Eleaticism. That is, how can Hegel preserve the differences of appearance from dissolving into the *différance* of twentieth-century postmodernism without abolishing contingency or relegating it to the domain of illusion? How can he do this without going back to the "two worlds" of classical rationalism?

Hegel takes the following general path to a solution of this problem. The categorial structure of the formation process of actuality is "transcendental" in the sense of eternal and necessary, whereas the individual events or appearances of actuality are contingent. If he stopped here, he would simply accept Kantianism. He therefore goes on to claim that the formation process is fully exhibited in the relative motions of the appearing and disappearing of the spatiotemporal events or content of actuality, and so too in our thinking of these events. In other words, the structure of intelligibility is not separate from (and in that sense "transcendental") but nevertheless imposed onto the motions of sensation, as is the case with Kant. Otherwise put, what Kant calls the phenomenal and the noumenal worlds are for Hegel one and the same world. The two sets of "motions," conceptual and sensuous, are actually one set.

But the problem is still unsolved; in fact, it seems to be worsened by Hegel's procedure, since now the very same motions that are the structure of the absolute are also the structure of the appearances of experience. In fact, these appearances are nothing other than the appearance or manifestation, indeed, the self-exhibition, of the absolute. Hegel responds to the difficulty by making contingency a category of the self-exhibition of the absolute. In principle, this is perfectly intelligible: the absolute exhibits itself, not only as the structure of necessity, but also as contingent instances of that structure. But how precisely does it do this? Remember that for Hegel, it cannot be the case that contingent instances are "images" of the absolute; that is Platonism. Neither can contingent instances be combinations of necessary form and contingent matter; that is the doctrine of the two worlds or two sets of motion. Hegel's solution is to make contingency a modification of the formal property of possibility. Contingency is not separate from yet formed or shaped by formal structure. It is itself a part of the formal process.

As we enter into the details of Hegel's solution, we must remember that we are studying logic, not physics. Contingency could not be anything other than a moment of form in the sense of the categorial structure of intelligibility, because that is what we are studying. We are not studying contingent *Sachen* as such. When I speak of the form and content of actuality, I am therefore referring to what must be called "formal" characteristics of actuality, however confusing the dual use of "form" may be. In other words, the formal structure of actuality consists of the categorial structure of the developing or working formation process, but also of the individual products or manifestations of this process. We are studying what it is to be a manifestation of this process. One aspect of what it is to be such a manifestation is to be contingent.

There is one further difficulty that I want to mention. Suppose that we are able to make sense of Hegel's articulation of the solution just proposed. This still leaves him with the problem of explaining how contingent products of a necessary process can themselves exhibit in the overall configuration of their motions the categorial structure of absolute activity. Granting that each individual thing is contingent in the sense that it could have been otherwise, the overall pattern of genesis, and in particular of human history, is for Hegel itself a direct exhibition of the pattern of development of absolute self-exhibition. World history reflects the transcendental development of the concept. So world history is a necessary development that consists almost entirely of contingencies. I say "almost entirely," because the entrance of God into history in the persona of Jesus cannot be a contingent event, despite Jesus's humanity.

Book 2, Section 3, Chapter 2, Subsection B: Relative necessity

We are in the first stages of our analysis of contingency as a logical category. In the previous section I stated the general problem that Hegel has to solve. How are we to demonstrate that the motion intrinsic to genesis is the same as the dialectical excitations of the formation process or absolute? To say that contingency is a logical category is the same as to say that it is an essential element in the form of actuality. There are no contingent logical categories; contingency itself, namely, as a category, is not itself contingent. Individual *Sachen* or unifications of form and content are contingent in the sense, not that they could have had some other form, but that they could have been some other individual of that form. But this has to be made more precise.

In an earlier chapter I called attention to the distinction between general and particular form and the difficulty that it poses for Hegel. Particular or phenomenal form is contingent or ungrounded and so inessential. Necessary form is general; it is the form of anything whatsoever, and by "anything" I mean any element in actuality. In other words, an individual cow is contingent because it might have been some other cow; the species form "cow" is contingent because the look of cowness is not grounded in the categorial development of becoming. But the cow as actual, and so as woven together by the interrelated dialectical motions of the categorial determinations of becoming, literally exhibits those motions in its existence. These motions are the true essence of any existing thing. And they do not change from thing to thing.

Hegel wishes to account for contingency as what I would call the particular form, and so the content, of the general form exhibited as something or another, i.e., as anything. But since contingency is a logical category, the only thing it can ground is contingent existence, namely, some content or another. Contingency is obviously a property of actuality. Actuality has three modes, absolute, genuine, and their unity. In absolute actuality, we see the unity of inner and outer from the standpoint of the outside, or external reflection. In genuine actuality, this unity is modalized as actuality, possibility, and necessity. This is confusing, because "actuality" as a mode appears as a moment within the more general category of genuine actuality. Note that the particular use of the term is qualified or relativized in subsection A by the adjective "formal," just as in the present subsection (B), it will be relativized by the term "real." Formal actuality pertains to the initial or immediate and unreflected actuality, i.e., to its form as inner unity or negative identity in Hegel's terminology. Genuine actuality pertains to the *res* or diverse exhibitions of negative unity. These will be brought together in subsection C, but that is not yet our concern. Contingency in the first case (formal actuality) is the "actual that is at the same time determined only as possible, whose other or opposite is [i.e., is open for actualization as an existing thing] just as much [as the first formal possibility]" (173). In the second case (real actuality), contingency pertains to content (180). We are dealing here, not with a possible but with an actual existent. But the content of the actual existent could have been otherwise without changing its form.

I repeat: an individual existing thing can be contingent in one of two senses, with respect to either its particular form or its content. A world without cows is as thinkable as a world with cows. So too a brown cow is quite thinkable as a white or black cow. Note that there is no concrete opposite to "cow." For example, "aardvark" is not the opposite of "cow," there are no concrete "non-cows"; that is not the name of an animal. In the case of content, however, there are no existing forms that have no content at all. And content can be specific to individuals of a certain kind; e.g., cows have legs unless they are deformed or maimed, whereas apples do not. Hence there is no possible cow that has no color, but rather cows are possibly white, brown, or some other color. There is no normal cow that has no legs. And no cow has a core like an apple's. So the logical situation is much more complicated with respect to content than it is with respect to particular looks or species forms.

So far so good; now the hard part has to be faced. Nothing as it were emerges from being, difference emerges from identity, and so on. But from what does contingency emerge? This question has two parts. First: from what does the logical category of contingency emerge? Second: whence comes the content of contingent individuals? One could hardly answer the second question, as Hegel in effect does, by saying "from contingency," because contingency is a logical category, not a storehouse of existing contingent forms and properties or content. I don't believe that Hegel has an answer to this second question. This is part of the pervasive difficulty, in fact, aporia, of transcendental philosophy, namely, that it cannot explain empirical or phenomenal form.

Let us therefore concentrate on the first question. And this brings us back to a more detailed consideration of the text. Subsection A is entitled "Contingency or Formal Actuality, Possibility, and Necessity." So contingency is equated with all three of the modes *qua* formal; in other words, it must partake of necessity.

Reconsideration of subsections A and B

Actuality is formal as "first actuality," that is, as immediate and unreflected, but not as totality of form (171). Since "totality" is for Hegel always inwardly articulated, he presumably means here that first actuality is form as "in itself," hence as simply existing or being. And, indeed, he says just that: "It is thus nothing more than a being or an existence in general." However, he qualifies this by saying that immediate actuality is not immediate existence (as it could not be without regressing to that very stage of development). "But as formal unity of being in itself or internality and externality, it contains immediately *being in itself or possibility. What is actual is possible.*" The formal unity of internality and exteriority refers to the form of actuality as not yet *really* externalized. This is an awkward distinction, but I think that it is just possible to see what Hegel is driving at. Form is "of" exteriority, but it is not yet exteriorized or considered as such. Hence it is a formal possibility, a form that can exhibit itself externally as a particular thing. But it could also exteriorize as some other particular thing. That is to say, really *any* two forms are somehow (Hegel never explains how) contained within formal actuality as correlative possibilities.

Possibility, Hegel continues, is actuality reflected into itself as self-identity or being in itself. In other words, the formal dimension of actuality is negative identity; it is not yet articulated, and we do not yet know which particular forms, which appearances, will emerge from it. Nevertheless, form is now totality because all particular forms emerge from negative identity. Differently stated, form is itself posed only in relation to actuality; even as immediate or pure negative identity, form is the form *of* actuality and of nothing else (since there is nothing else of which it could be the form). Form is posed as the negative of actuality; stated simply, it is not the concrete existing things but the inner unity that belongs to each such thing.

Hegel then summarizes the situation. Possibility, as the pure reflected immediacy of actuality, that is, form as identity, is a positive determination. But as opposed to the actual, i.e., the world of existing concrete things, it is something defective in itself. It is , as we might say, "merely possible." And as such, it is negative. With respect to formal identity everything is possible that does not contradict itself; the domain of formal possibility is thus "unbounded multiplicity." As we know, however, Hegel also holds that there is nothing that does not contradict itself. And he says precisely this in the next sentence; every manifold is defined via negation and opposition, which latter is contradiction (171). Hence everything is also contradictory and impossible.

Is this a vicious self-contradiction? No, because the two characterizations refer to two different things. Possibility or nonself-contradiction refers to simple negative identity, A is A, whereas impossibility refers to difference, that is, to the full inner structure of A (172). But this leaves unexplained exactly what Hegel means by saying that the same thing is both possible and impossible, since all actualities are self-contradictory. Every pure form, as an instance of negative identity, is possible in the sense that it might be filled with content. The only impossibility is a nonidentity. But what is that? As pure negative identities, forms do not acquire nonidentity except via difference, and this arises, as Hegel himself points out, only via the development of content. It seems to be impossible to discover a pure form *A* that violates the law of identity but that contains no content. We can think of forms that are logical contradictions, like a round square, but this pseudoconcept consists of two properties or determinations of content. As to empirically impossible things like golden mountains or centaurs, they are patently impossible because of the concatenation of properties attributed to them.

I turn back to the text (paragraph 2 on page 172). The possible, says Hegel, contains more than the mere law of identity. It is "the reflected being-reflected-into-itself or the identical strictly as moment of totality, therefore determined in such a way as not itself to be in itself; it has therefore the second determination to be only possible, and the *Sollen* ['ought' or 'must'] of the totality of form." At first glance, this sentence is completely obscure. It is, however, only Hegel's cumbersome way of redescribing the negative identity of the pure form as possibility, an identity that is a moment of the totality of the fully actualized form. The metaphor of *das Sollen* is a reference to the inner striving of dialectical excitation or the self-exteriorizing nisus of inner unity. "Possibility without this *Sollen* is essentiality as such; but the absolute form contains this [feature], that the essence itself is only a moment, and without being, it does not possess its truth. Possibility is this mere essentiality, so posited that it is only a moment and is not conformable to the absolute form." In other words, pure inner identity is essence, as we learned in a previous section, that is, essence apart from actuality understood as the unity of essence and existence. And this is possibility: the essence has a *Sollen* to actualize, but at this moment it has not yet done so.

Now comes the decisive step; Hegel is about to attribute impossibility to the same complex situation. Possibility "is being in itself that is determined, inasmuch as it is only something posited, as *not to be in itself*. Possibility is therefore in itself also contradiction, or it is impossibility." In other words, possibility is essence or the inner striving to exteriorize or actualize. But as such, it is both being in itself and not being in itself. It is being in itself as the simple determination of reflected inwardness or identity. But it is not being in itself because the full or absolute form, even prior to being actualized via content, has its own inner structure of identity within difference. As merely "in itself," or inner identity, even absolute or not yet dialectically actualized form is not fully itself.

Let us grant for the moment that a pure unactualized form, i.e., one without the content of particularity and contingency that makes it a *Sache* in our everyday experience, contains two moments of identity and difference that correspond to its inner unity or essence on the one hand and its essential attributes on the other. If possibility is equated with the first moment of identity or essence, then I hold that it has no content or conceptual meaning of its own. Since essence is the invisible *Sollen* to exteriorize, it is as such "possible" that anything whatsoever might emerge from it. Hegel says that anything is possible that does not contradict itself. But apart from the fact that everything contradicts itself, we know that something contradicts itself only when it is before our cognitive eye, when it is in other words not sheer possibility, since that is nothing in particular, but it is rather this particular possibility. Could Hegel mean that precisely because from the standpoint of essentiality, identity, or pure inner unity, anything whatsoever is possible, it follows that the impossible is also possible? If essence is then equated with possibility, it still does not follow that what is possible is also impossible, but only that the possible and the impossible are both possible. With respect to essence itself, it must be possible rather than impossible, since it is defined as the inner production of possibility and impossibility.

I suspect that we come closer to Hegel's own thinking if we say that the formal moment of identity is both possible and impossible from the standpoint that it contradicts itself by both being in itself and not being in itself; again, it is itself as the determination of inwardness, but it is not itself because inwardness acquires being through exteriorization. But since contradiction is a fundamental characteristic of every logical category, it is therefore common to the possible and the impossible and cannot be the mark of impossibility. Differently stated, if contradiction is the paradigm, then everything is possible. We still do not know what Hegel means by "impossibility."

This follows from Hegel's next remark as well. He goes on to assert that since it is initially only possible that A is A, it is also possible that not-A is not-A (172). In other words, initially or at the level of essence, both A and not-A are equally possible. But this seems to suggest that the law of non-contradiction is not applicable at the level of possibility. If there is such a thing as impossibility, it seems to be the impossibility of applying contradiction as the criterion of impossibility.

Hegel once more calls the co-possibility of A and not-A a contradiction, but now he says that it sublates itself, i.e., raises itself to a higher level of identity within difference (173). Unfortunately, his explanation of how this occurs is entirely unsatisfactory. He says that the contradiction is itself a self-sublating reflectedness; "it is therefore also the immediate, and thereby it becomes actuality." What is a "self-sublating reflectedness"? It was previously established that reflectedness is turning inward or acquiring the determination of identity. Identity becomes itself by opposition to difference, but this in turn is exteriorization. The contradiction is sublated in the sense that the inner exhibits itself within the immediacy of actuality. This amounts to the actualizing of one particular possibility, e.g., A as opposed to not-A. At this level, there is no contradiction with not-A, but this means that not-A is impossible, given the actuality = possibility of A. So there is really no contradiction at the level of possibility, but rather something is left open or undecided. On the basis of mere identity, either A or not-A might actualize.

This would be a good place for Hegel to introduce contingency (*Zufälligkeit*), namely, as the openness concerning the actualization of A or not-A. Hegel goes on to say that the actuality of the possibility we have just inspected is determined as "only something possible" rather than as possibility. This is because what actualizes is some possible thing, not possibility in general or the negative identity of essence, from which anything might actualize. At this level, according to Hegel, possibility and actuality are formally the same or turn into one another; this is formal actuality or the presence of possibilities for actualization within existence, i.e., within real and absolute actuality. "This unity of possibility and actuality is contingency."

What makes this whole discussion especially difficult to understand, I believe, is the interposition of formal actuality between possibility on the one hand and real or absolute actuality on the other. This difficulty is closely connected to that of the interposition of immediate existence between essence and actualized existence. What we can call "full" or "completed" existence is indistinguishable from actuality. But the existential component of formal actuality seems to have been suspended; it seems to be immediate existence, and yet, since we have passed through the three stages of existence into actuality, it is not clear how we can have reverted to the first of these stages in our new and higher level of development.

If the immediate existence of formal actuality is the same as possibility, it cannot be in the sense of the sheer possibility or undetermined openness of the existence of A or not-A, because this is equivalent not to the existential element in actuality but rather to the essential element. Once A actualizes, it remains true that not-A might have actualized in its place. And in this sense, we can say that the coincidence of possibility and actuality is contingency. It is very important to notice that there is no room for contingency at the antecedent stage of the joint possibility of A and not-A. Where nothing has been decided, nothing is contingent, because "contingent" refers to something in particular, a thing, event, or process.

Unfortunately for the plausibility of this analysis, Hegel goes on to say

that "the contingent is something actual that is at the same time determined only as possible, and whose other or opposite exists [ist] just as
much" (173). I think that this is a slip on Hegel's part. The opposite cannot
exist, as I have just shown. Hegel means that two opposing contingencies
exist at the level of formal actuality, which is, or rather includes, the previous development of essence and existence. But existence is too strong a
term to apply to an open possibility; what exists is an actual possible, i.e., a
contingent actuality that might have been otherwise.

Hegel goes on to generate another dialectical contradiction with respect
to contingency. Insofar as it contains immediate possibility, it is neither
posited nor mediated. This must be because immediate possibility is pure
essence or negative identity, namely, the invisible inner unity from which
possibilities actualize. As such, it is without a ground. But the contingent
is also immediate actuality, and so the latter is also groundless in its role
as possibility, contrary to what we know about actuality (namely, this is
grounded, 174). In other words, the contingent contains both possibility
and actuality. These have opposing or mutually contradictory properties;
hence the contingent is self-contradictory. Hegel concludes that the contingent has no ground because it is contingent, and that it has a ground because it is contingent. This "absolute unrest of becoming" is contingency;
but further, each determination of contingency turns into the other; Hegel
calls their identity "necessity."

Necessity is actual; its possibility has been sublated into actual existence.
To this Hegel rather surprisingly adds that the contingent is also necessary,
a statement he justifies as follows. The contingent is the unity of actuality
and possibility, which is to say that it actually exists. Whereas it might have
been otherwise (and is in this sense contingent), in fact, it is what it is:
"the necessary is, and this existent [Seiende] is itself the necessary" (175).
What Hegel seems to mean here is that since it is the nature of internality
to externalize, all that can be was, is, or will be. Every possibility is actualized. Hence there is nothing that could be otherwise, and so actuality is
necessity. Perhaps one can make this a bit more palatable by adding to Hegel's analysis the observation that the possible is contingent with respect to
what it might have been, namely, some other possibility. But since all possibilities actualize, the possible is necessary with respect to what in fact exists. As Hegel says, the actual is identical with itself through the mediation
of the coming to be of its possibilities; in that sense, it is necessity, because
there is no unrealized part of actuality.

Now we reconsider subsection B, which is concerned with relative necessity, or real actuality, possibility, and necessity. The contrast between for-

mal and real refers throughout the *SL* to the distinction between form as identity and the *res* or formed content, which Hegel here calls the thing of many properties. Bear in mind that form as identity is inner unity and hence has no inner determinations. It is not the species form or look of existing things. Hegel calls it form because it is the formation process, the origination of form. But this form is general or ontologically fundamental; it actualizes or comes to be visible, not as itself (in which guise it is invisible) but as the categorial structure of anything at all. The visible or existing form has as its categorial structure "thing and properties"; but any particular thing possessing properties must already exhibit particularity, and, as I have consistently argued, Hegel cannot explain how things acquire particular form.

Hegel says this, albeit in his peculiar terminology. In the present context, he states that necessity as just attained is formal because its moments are formal, "namely, simple determinations that exist only as immediate unity or as immediate change of one into the other totality and so do not have the *Gestalt* of independence." In other words, the "simple determinations" of formal necessity are constantly losing their "shapes" and exist only as immediate unity, which is itself without inner determinations or shapes; it is negative identity. "In this formal necessity, therefore, the unity is at first simple and indifferent toward its differences." But this means in turn that inner unity depends upon an opposition to difference in order to preserve itself as identity; and therefore, formal necessity is actuality or possesses content, namely, the structure of identity and difference just noted. The argument depends upon Hegel's usual thesis that unity in the sense of simple negative and so undifferentiated identity maintains its nature through an opposition to the very determinations or differences that it negates; in other words, the overall structure is that of a sublation of differences, not their annihilation. So formal necessity turns into real necessity.

More precisely, formal necessity turns initially into real actuality, namely, enformed content or the unity of essence and existence as this determinate thing of multiple properties. And real actuality contains immediately within itself the moment of possibility, as we have already seen in the more general analysis above (176). Formal possibility, we recall, is only abstract identity or noncontradiction. Real possibility is encountered when one considers the properties, circumstances, and conditions of a *Sache* in order to understand its possibility. This treats of particular forms and particular contents, not of simple abstract identity or inner unity. Hegel clarifies: "Real possibility is immediate existence . . . The real possibility of a thing [*Sache*] is thus the existing [*daseiende*] manifold of circumstances that refer to it." This is very similar to Kant's definition of existence as insertion into the web of phenomenal experience. The possibility of some thing y is thus x, which is an actuality in itself (177).

Hegel goes on to say that the real possibility actualizes by contradicting its previous formal self-identity; it becomes another, namely, a real thing with properties. Real possibility is the satisfaction of all conditions for its existence; it becomes the other that, as pure identity, was its formal possibility. It enters into actuality; and as the identity of identity (= inner unity) and difference (its defining properties), it is necessity (178). That is, since all of its conditions have been satisfied, there is nothing lacking in its existence; it is now a necessary element in the totality of actuality. As I understand him, Hegel combines contingency and necessity in possibility, and so possibility and actuality, because for him past and future are modalities of the present moment, which is itself the nexus of the entire categorial structure of the whole. In other words, contingency and necessity stand so to speak back to back in the present moment, but thereby face in opposite directions. The logical structure of the present moment is the nexus of what is a possibility in the past moment but an actuality in the future moment. The same thing is thus contingent in the past and necessary in the future. And past, present, and future are here virtually simultaneous; we are speaking of consecutive moments or instants, not widely separated epochs.

Real possibility is relative to its contingencies; it is therefore not only necessary but contingent (179). As we have just seen, real actuality is the identity within difference of formal actuality and the totality of conditioning circumstances; it is the unity of possibility and actuality. The pole of possibility renders the thing contingent; but the pole of actuality embeds it within necessity. The next step will be for necessity to transform itself into contingency, in order to complement the transformation of contingency into necessity and thereby close this circle of the dialectic. This takes place because necessity, i.e., the actually existing thing of many properties, is dependent upon the satisfaction of the conditions for its existence within the already actual. It is thus contingent upon these conditions (180). This unity of necessity and contingency is absolute actuality.

Book 2, Section 3, Chapter 2, Subsection C: Absolute necessity

The unity of formal and real or determinate necessity contains the moment of contingency in the determinations, which, as we have just seen, are themselves, or are the direct results of, the conditions for the existence of the thing. This is absolute actuality, "which can no longer be otherwise, because its being in itself is not possibility but necessity." In other words, the conditions have been satisfied. Another way to restate Hegel's general point is to say that what has happened cannot be erased; it is in that sense necessary and actual. But that it did happen is due to the satisfaction of certain conditions, which might not have been satisfied. The actual is a result of the possible, and this result is retrospectively contingent but presently necessary. Hegel does not employ the normal strict opposition of necessity and contingency because for him this opposition is static, part of external reflection or traditional, nondialectical rationalism. Since being is actually becoming or process, necessity and contingency are not static but fluid; they are dialectically related or constitute a totality. My previous example of the continuous moments of past, present, and future is a paradigm of what Hegel may be thinking.

Actuality and possibility are sublated within real necessity. Each negates the other in the following sense. Form as self-identical or noncontradictory possibility is realized in or becomes form as actually determinate or possessing real content. Possibility is "actually" an actuality; actuality or the actual thing arises via real possibility, which is some other, previously existing thing or situation that is negated by the coming into existence of its successor. Thus actuality negates a previous actuality and in that way becomes a possibility (181). This reciprocal saturation of possibility and actuality is the flow of becoming, that is, being and its negation. It is the sameness of being and nothing, with which we began, but now as having subsumed all previous determinations (182). This identity of being with itself via its own negation is substance (184). Hegel also calls it the absolute relation of substance to itself; in other words, substance is the whole and thus includes its accidents, with which it is in a dynamical relation of self-manifestation.

Book 2, Section 3, Chapter 3: The Absolute Relation

Chapter 3 on the absolute relation is the last stage in the development of the unity of essence and existence as actuality; with this stage, we conclude book 2 of the *SL*. The absolute relation is absolute actuality. Just as the being of light is not a thing but its very shining, so too is the manifestation of actuality a shining forth as what it is. In other words, we cannot look elsewhere for its essence or nature, which is directly exhibited in the excitation of appearances (185). The shining forth (as I translate *Schein* and *scheinen* in their laudatory senses) of the absolute relation of the whole or totality is thus the show of essence within existence. This show, when fully elaborated, has three aspects. The first is of substance and its accidents, each of which constitutes the whole (i.e., substance is fully exhibited within its accidents). This is the immediate or formal aspect of coming to be and passing away. In its real determination, the absolute relation is one of causality, or the opposition of substance and accident as the structure of the *res*. Finally, the reciprocity of cause and effect or substance and accident is shown to be the concept, and is thus the transition into book 3 of the *SL*.

We begin subsection A with the relation of substantiality (185). This is for Hegel a relatively simple section, and I will be quite brief in my commentary. As we have now arrived at full or absolute actuality, the whole is fully present in its parts, which are obviously fully within the whole. This is the full appearance or shining forth of being as immediate actuality (in other words, as formal process but not yet as articulated into particular things). "The excitation of accidentality [i.e., not of this or that particular accident but of the totality of accidents as a process] exhibits in each of its moments the shining forth in one another of the categories of being and the determinations of reflection belonging to essence" (186). But this is precisely substance or formation process. "This excitation of accidentality is the activity [*Aktuosität*] of substance as *restful emergence of itself*." That is, it is restful because it remains within itself even as changing via its accidents. It is not active with respect to anything but itself. Hegel also refers to the motion of accidents as "the absolute power" (187), by which expression he refers to self-manifestation through the production of accidents, which is at once a destruction of others; "production destroys and destruction produces" (cf. Heidegger's essay *Der Spruch des Anaximanders*).

As I said a moment ago, the self-manifestation of substance in its accidents is the immediate or formal aspect of the absolute relation. We must next articulate this formal process into the relation of causality (subsection B).

Hegel again distinguishes between formal and determinate causality, which two moments he will bring together in the final subsection of the chapter. The first or formal moment is the unity of cause and effect, which is the immediate consequence of the unity of substance and accidents. Each moment implies the whole; each accident exhibits the causality of substance (189–90). The effect contains nothing that is not in the cause, and vice versa, there is nothing in the cause that is not in the effect. Hegel is speaking of the categories or concepts of cause and effect as constituting the causal relation. He does not mean that there is nothing in sunshine, for example, that is not contained in a warm stone. These differences are of contingent content and are not relevant to the present analysis.

Causality as formal, i.e., as just discussed, is universal, or "the endless relation of absolute power, whose content is pure manifestation or necessity. As finite causality, on the other hand," i.e., what Hegel calls the determinate causal relation, "it has a given content and disperses itself as an external difference in this identity that is one and the same substance within its determinations" (192). Note that it is still the case that "the effect is nothing more than the manifestation of the cause" (194). But this generalization has been particularized or instantiated at the present level of analysis. As a consequence of this particularization or manifestation as a particular effect of a particular cause, the effect as external existing thing is separated from its cause or formal reference (as Hegel calls it, 196). Thus both cause and effect are here "positedness," i.e., they are opposed to or separated from one another even as dependent upon each other. The two are united again in the substrate, which, simply stated, is the continuum of causation that underlies each particular instance of cause and effect, and which Hegel calls a "third," not because it is a totally distinct entity but because it is the identity within difference of the cause and effect in question (197). Hegel goes on to discuss the transition of the neutral or passive substratum into cause and effect; the movements are straightforward and do not require special attention.

I turn at last to the final subsection in the chapter, and in book 2 of the *SL*, entitled "Reciprocal Action" (C). In finite causality, i.e., in the analysis of genesis by external reflection, there are multiple finite substances interacting as causal agents but retaining their separation both from one another and from their effects. This is mechanism; the causal relation is external and the effect is transformed into another separate substance (202). Hegel does not explain adequately what he means here. The mechanism is the interconnected activity of separate and internally static substances; the movements are external because they do not evolve from an inner dynamic that is the sign of intelligence or dialectical thinking. We are back in the world of the reflective determinations of essence.

This mechanism is sublated in the reciprocity of substance and accident or cause and effect. Each pole grows out of its opposite; all substances are united by a common form, more precisely by the same formation process that externalizes or exhibits itself in the accidents, just as causes are revealed in their effects and vice versa. Remember the unity or identity within difference of being and thinking; the dialectical excitations of reciprocity between one thought determination and another are activated by the process of thinking the categorial structure of being. It makes no sense to ask whether being exhibits dialectical motion apart from thought, because we are unable to conceive of being as separate from thought. So the excitations of attempting to think being are the consequences of the excitations of being as thinkable. In other words, being and thinking are an identity within difference, and the totality is the common structure of the formation process.

Now Hegel takes a decisive step. The reciprocity of cause and effect is a return to, or arrival at, the absolute concept (203). In the first place, necessity is replaced by freedom. This occurs because the mechanism of rigidly separated and interconnected substances has been transformed into "free actuality" or a creative flux in which causes and effects are no longer separated from one another, hence no longer restrict each other's appearance through the determination of external opposition. One could refer to this as the continuum or seamless web of genesis. I would go a step further and say that Hegel is implicitly thinking here of the shining forth of becoming as a kind of spontaneity, that is, as self-produced, not compelled by anything external to it, and so as free. He goes on to describe the disappearance of the various determinations of this section into one another; his intention is to evoke the sense of a totality that is continuously articulating itself with categorial determinations that, as developed or exhibited, dissolve into the other poles of the structure of the cycle from which they most immediately emerge.

We note the following three characteristics of totality. First: since substance and accident have been reunited, substance does not assert itself as necessity by rejecting its accidents (204). This is universality, or the identification of substance with its posits. Second: substance is universal as opposed to the determinations of accidents, which are posed within substance but as its negation. So substance as universal is also the negation of universality, or the individual. I assume this means that substance is rendered an individual by the determining force of its accidents. In other words, it is this substance, with these accidents, and not just a totality of substance and accidents. Third: substance is both universal and individual; that is, universality or self-identity includes the negativity of the determinations of accidents, which are, to repeat, negative as opposed to substance but included within substance as totality. Hence the negativity of universality is the same as the negativity of individuality (205). So too individuality is a negation in two senses: as an accident it is a determination, and every determination is a negation; but as a determination, it is not the identity of substance, and so it is a negation of the first negation. But accidents are not substance just as substance is not accidents; the "not" is here the *coincidentia oppositorum*. Hegel calls this particularity. The substance, as totality, is universal; as marked by determinations, it is an individual; as both universal and individual, it is a particular, that is, a special individual because one that exhibits universality.

Particularity derives the moment of determinateness from the individual and the moment of reflection into self (as negative identity) from the universal. It contains these two moments in immediate unity. "These three totalities are therefore one and the same reflection, which as negative reference to itself [universality as unity] differentiates itself into those two [namely, individuality and particularity], but as in a completely transparent difference, namely, in the determinate simplicity or in the simple determinateness that is their one and the same identity." But that which is universal and so total, individual and so determinate rather than abstract or merely negative universality, and particular, namely, this individual that exhibits universality through the determinations that it actually possesses, has completed the development of the logical categories of being as sublated into essence and thereby brought into existence, namely, the existence of actuality. There is no room for any other particular whose individuality allows it to express another universality through the determinations that it actually possesses.

In the last sentence of the book, Hegel says, "This is the concept, the realm of subjectivity or freedom." But we are not yet in a position to understand what he means by this prefatory or anticipatory remark. In order to find out, we must study book 3 of the *SL*.

SEVENTEEN

Introduction to Book Three

Transition to the Concept: Foreword to Book 3

At the end of book 2, Hegel asserted that the particular, as the identity of universality and individuality, is the concept, "the domain of subjectivity or of freedom" (205). Let us try to understand exactly what Hegel means by this assertion. To begin with, he does not mean that now, for the first time, at the end of book 2, we arrive at conceptual thinking. In fact, we have been manipulating concepts from the beginning of the logic. A concept is a "grasping" of something in thought. Each of the categorial determinations we have studied thus far in the *SL* is trivially accessible to thought only through thinking. There is no way in which to think something as it is outside or independent of our thinking of it. This is not to say that Hegel regards categorial determinations like being or becoming as "mere" thoughts or *Gedankendingen*. His point is rather that being and thinking are the same from the outset with respect to their form or structure of intelligibility, and he further claims that this is evident from the very fact of ordinary experience. We do in fact think about things that are external to us; these are not phantoms or purely subjective posits as is obvious from their independence and recalcitrance to thought. But this recalcitrance occurs *within* thinking; more precisely, things are recalcitrant as within our thought, not as independent in the sense of inaccessible to it. Recalcitrance is a relation of things to thoughts; independence is in another sense dependence. I can say that a tree is independent of my attempt to alter it by thinking alone, because the tree is present as independent within my thought. This independence is thus not complete but can be overcome by the manipulation of concepts. Even independence is a concept.

What Hegel means by the passage we are studying is rather that we have now arrived at a consideration of the concept *per se*, as distinguished from the concept of this or that categorial determination. Thus far the concepts we have entertained are all categories or determinations of substance. We have been studying the emergence of the distinction between substance and attributes from the self-differentiation of becoming. This distinction is fulfilled in the knowledge that the attributes are not detached from the substance, nor do they constitute illusory appearances of it. The appearances are substance appearing as what it is "essentially." The problem of how to distinguish essential from accidental attributes is thus solved as follows: All attributes are essential or show the essence as it appears, i.e., presents itself. Even accident or contingency is an essential category of substance (although not one that Hegel has successfully defined, as we have already seen). The full presentation of substance thus shows that it externalizes its interiority or possesses no secrets from the logician who thinks it. Hegel holds that substance reveals itself in this way as *subject*. Stated as simply as possible, this means that there is no separation of thought and the content or object of thought. What we can perhaps call the "silent" presence of the subject thus far as that which is thinking the determinations of substance is now revealed as the form of those determinations, understood as content.

Again in a merely preliminary sense, let us ask what it means to say that substance is subject. It does *not* mean that the apparently substantial character of the world is "merely subjective." Hegel entirely repudiates this view, which he associates with subjective idealism, and so with Kant as well as Fichte. That is, the world is not "merely subjective" in the sense that it is a product or posit of the thinking of a transcendental or absolute ego. The world is not a series of self-determinations of an absolute thinker; instead, it is the identity within difference of being and thinking. What we think is indeed as we think it; but we can think it because of an inner connection between being and thinking that externalizes as the relation between the two. We can therefore say that the world, or actuality, is neither subject nor object, that is, neither merely subjective nor objective, but both, and both as identical in their difference. This initially obscure phrase has now been studied by us in extensive detail. It means that subject and object both obey the same rules of dialectical self-excitation, and that this dialectical self-excitation is the negative activity of the absolute.

This, stated as succinctly as possible, is what Hegel means by absolute spirit. No interpretation of Hegel can succeed without acknowledging the fundamental status of this conception of the absolute. One is free to reject Hegel, but in order to do so in a philosophically responsible manner, rather than as an expression of one's own ineptitude, it is necessary to explain the thinkability of things. There are, in other words, three basic philosophical positions, monism, dualism, and trinitarianism. The monist asserts that everything is being, or alternatively that everything is thinking. The first version of monism is refuted by thinking; the second version is refuted by the aforementioned recalcitrance of beings. The dualist says that there is no explanation of the thinkability of things; this leads back to monism, usually to that form of monism according to which everything is thinking, with the added premise that thought is arbitrary or, as we say today, perspectival. In the case of both monism and dualism, the result is the same: the impossibility of philosophy.

It would therefore be quite reasonable to maintain, not only that Hegel is the only philosopher, but that his central thesis is self-evident. It is not philosophy but ideology that denies the difference between being and thinking; as to the assertion of their difference, it is articulated by thinking, which therefore encompasses both in an identity. The task of philosophy is to spell out the structure of this self-evident truth of everyday experience. When therefore Hegel says that substance is subject, he means, despite the cryptic or at least excessively succinct nature of the formulation, to be uttering a truism. The fact that it has not previously been perceived by philosophers is due to the hitherto partial manifestation of substance, and so to the incomplete externalization of interiority. "The true is the whole." There are no truisms until the true has been wholly revealed. Since substance and its attributes are the whole, to think them together is to think everything. But one cannot think everything without thinking; this thinking is the form of the whole. And as the form of the whole, thinking is not detached from it or transcendent of it. It is the form not of some other whole but rather of the one and only whole: Form is the subjective dimension of substantiality.

In my opinion, it is far from easy to refute Hegel's contention that substance is subject, or for that matter what seems to be the still more extreme thesis of the absolute spirit. This doctrine seems preposterous to the post-Hegelian skeptical temperament, but that is a sign of the progressive deterioration of the philosophical impetus, not of the absurdity of Hegel's doctrines. We have today fallen almost entirely into one version or another of subjective idealism; even the so-called realists hold to some version or another of neo-Kantian definitions of reality. But none of these meets the Hegelian challenge, since all of them fail to explain how being is accessible to thought while at the same time retaining its independence or recalcitrance to thinking.

So much for preparation; we are now ready to return to the text. And we begin with the preliminary material, a brief "Foreword" and an extended essay "Of the Concept in General." The foreword is dated 1816, four years after the foreword to the first two books. This temporal disjunction corresponds to a difference in the content. Instead of beginning directly from the conclusion of book 2, and taking up the stages by which the concept unfolds from the moment of its emergence out of the tripartite structure of actuality, Hegel interrupts the flow of categorial development to comment on the difference between objective and subjective logic. Stated with introductory simplicity, this difference corresponds to the traditional difference between ontology and logic. This formulation must be immediately modified with respect to logic, which is not for Hegel "objective" in the sense of constituting a branch of mathematics, or more generally the study of the formal rules of inference. By the same token, Hegelian "ontology" is also not objective in the traditional sense of purporting to state the structure of being as it is in itself, independent of the activity of being thought or grasped within concepts.

In more developed terms, Hegel's "objective" logic traces the development of the concept of pure or abstract being into the categorial structure of actuality. This part of the *SL* is objective in the sense that it concentrates our attention upon the content of actuality or the whole, but not upon the subjective process of apprehending that content. I say "concentrates" but not "restricts entirely" our attention, since Hegel never loses sight of the fact that he is showing us how the very attempt to think pure being, or any undeveloped stage of totality, leads necessarily to the thinking of the subsequent stage, and so in a consecutive order to the formation process by which totality is constituted. One could therefore protest to Hegel that the ostensibly "objective" logic is itself deeply subjective. His reply would be that (in Spinozistic terms) the order of being and the order of thinking are the same. In order to understand anything at all, we must reflect upon the process by which we understand it, that is, we must reflect upon the process of thought that enables us to understand it. This sounds tautologous, and no doubt it is, but the reason is that one cannot think (or understand) that of which one does not think. We should not be misled here by Hegel's criticism of epistemology in the *PS*. Hegel rejects so-called methods of knowledge that are developed independently and in advance of engaging in the activity of knowing. But the activity of knowing is certainly methodical; the method is precisely that of dialectico-speculative logic.

We cannot therefore say merely that the order of being develops together with, in the sense of "at the same time as," the order of thinking. This is already to imply that the two orders are both separate and separately distinguishable, and that we judge them to be the same from a position that is independent of both. We distinguish them as different from the vantage-point of their identity, and *we* are that identity in our persona as locus of the emergence of the idea into its two aspects of subject and object. What the critic of the previous paragraph referred to as the "subjective" nature of the objective logic is precisely this underlying unity of the idea. In the objective logic, we studied the objective side of the idea. In the subjective logic, we are about to study its subjective side. But it is essential to note that our study is *logical* in both parts of the *SL*. We are studying the categorial structure of subjectivity, or in other words the forms by which the subject "grasps" the object. This means that the object reappears in the subjective logic, but now from the standpoint of conceptual knowing. That is why the first two parts of the subjective logic are entitled "Subjectivity" and "Objectivity," respectively.

Let us also note in advance that subjectivity and objectivity are unified (in an identity within difference) in "the idea." Since the objective content of logic has already been sublated into the subjective logic, there is no need for a third stage of logic to unify book 3 with the first two books, "Being" and "Essence," which together constitute the objective logic. As to the idea, it can be characterized for the moment as the logical version of absolute spirit, a term to which no section of the *SL* corresponds. As is obvious from its role in the *PS*, "spirit" conveys the experience of self-consciousness rather than the logical structure of intelligibility.

In the foreword, Hegel speaks of the title "subjective logic" as though it were simply a matter of convenience (*Bequemlichkeit*, 211) for the friends of that science, namely, the science of logic in the usual sense, as distinguished from the logical contents of the first two books, or the Hegelian version of ontology. In a remark that will resonate for the contemporary reader, Hegel says that the "friends" of traditional logic are greater in number than those of what corresponds to the objective logic. There is plenty of material dealing with the logic of the concept, but (in a curiously mixed metaphor) Hegel must restore the heap of its dead bones to fluidity and "kindle once more the living concept in such dead stuff." Two remarks are required here. The first is that Hegel emphasizes the greater difficulty of the objective logic because it had very little in the way of preparation by earlier thinkers. It is not merely that Hegel must introduce fluidity and life into the dead ontology of the past. Clearly he regards the objective logic as different in kind from prior ontologies in a way that the subjective logic is not different in kind from prior logics of the concept. The second remark is that Hegel may be setting the logic of the concept into the motion of life, but he is not inventing the science, as is evident from the mere mention of Kant's *Critique of Pure Reason*.

These two remarks come together when we see that for the German tradition at least from Kant forward, logic is not the study of the deductive connections between propositions; it is the study of the judgment. Whereas a proposition is (ostensibly) detachable in its form from the person who utters it in the guise of a sentence, a judgment is not. To make the judgment so independent would be to convert it into a proposition; but this is not what Kant and his successors had in mind. The logic of the concept is thus the study of the rules by which the ego (transcendental, absolute, or empirical) produces judgments out of concepts. One may therefore apply here Milton's statement in the *Areopagitica* that "reason is but choosing." In the judgment, the judge chooses a better from a worse alternative. The point is not so much that a judgment includes what we call a "value judgment" as that the self-consciousness of the subject is present within the judgment as its motivation or source of validity. In the Kantian ontology, on the other hand, the structure of formal intelligibility is static because, although it is a product of the transcendental ego (to put a complex point in the traditional shorthand), the activity or *energeia* of the production of form is still conceived on the traditional model of pure, eternal, motionless, self-identical, and so abstract entities, like the Platonic ideas or Aristotelian forms and categories.

In other words, Hegel is the first to free the sense of activity in the concept of *energeia* or "being at work" from the static structure of traditional, predialectical ontology. In Hegel, it is not only the projective or constituting activity of thinking that is moving; it is the product of that work or the form itself. Subjective logic thus has its preparation in the logic of judgment of the eighteenth century, and not merely in the doctrine of the syllogism that goes back to Aristotle. It is the interpretation by the German idealists of the doctrine of the syllogism that Hegel has in mind here, since he knows perfectly well that for Aristotle, the syllogism consists of dead or abstract forms. With respect to ontology, however, Hegel is a radical innovator.

The balance of the foreword makes the point that the claim to truth is in Hegel's time characteristic of students of religion, not of professional philosophers and logicians, whom Hegel classifies as disciples of Pontius Pilate (212). He also notes that his own academic duties have prevented him from executing the project of attaining to logical truth with the concentrated exertion that the subject demands. But he makes no apology for the attempt.

Of the Concept in General

However reasonable it may be to infer an underlying unity of being and thinking from the fact of our consciousness of intelligibility, Hegel must still explain how objective logic is transformed into subjective logic, or how, in other words, the Concept emerges from actuality.[1] Is this shift simply one of the attention of the logician? One would almost be ready to answer in the affirmative on the basis of the foreword. To do so, however, would be to admit of the contingency of the division between the two parts of Hegel's logic, and this is entirely contrary to his explicit intentions. In fact, the arrival at the Concept at the end of the previous book was anything but persuasive, and I take it that Hegel is well aware of the difficulty of his presentation of this crucial point. Hence he stops as it were to gird his loins and to interpolate an informal essay that will assist the novice in making this most difficult of transitions. This at least is the symbolic significance of the break between the objective and the subjective logics, which, as we noted above, were published at an interval of four years.

Hegel begins his general essay with an indirect reference to the problem of the emergence of the Concept. On the one hand, the Concept is a "subjective presupposition" and "absolute foundation" (213). In other words, it is present at the outset of the *SL* in the identity of being and thinking; we cannot think abstract being apart from its concept because abstractions are concepts to begin with. Stated colloquially, we cannot leave our thoughts in order to begin with a being that is external to them. Pure abstract being is nothing other, and could not be anything other, than the pure abstract Concept. Each step by which we add content to the former is a step by which we add content to the latter.

On the other hand, the Concept is not a presupposition in some merely given sense, as if it were external to that which it grounds and could not be deduced from the grounded material. It is nothing like logical axioms as applied in geometry to magnitude. One could say that the Concept is immediate in the sense that it grounds logic and so cannot itself be grounded by anything else. But for Hegel, immediacy is always the result of a prior mediation. Again stated colloquially, if the Concept were like a superaxiom that could not be deduced from anything else, it would be entirely arbitrary. We must remember that Hegel always insists upon assimilating intuition into discursive reasoning; he is not content, in other words, to say that the superaxiom is "obvious," that it cannot be refuted, or that it is necessarily presupposed in every attempt to dispense with it. As we saw previously, even the law of noncontradiction is for Hegel a result of dialectical development. At the root of all processes is the fundamental interdependence of identity and difference, neither of which can be asserted except in contrast to the other, and each of which, in Hegel's sense of the term, *is* the other. Identity is identical with itself but different from difference, just as difference is different from identity but identical with itself. This is Hegel's correction of the ontological logic of the Eleatic Stranger in Plato's *Sophist*.

The foundation is immediate, but its immediacy is the result of a process. The process cannot be that of deduction from a still more immediate principle, since this leads to an infinite regression and cancels the claimed immediacy of the ground or principle in question. The only alternative is that the ground must have made itself to be immediate by a sublation from mediateness. In the root example of identity and difference, each is initially mediated by the other. But this does not cancel the two elements; instead, the opposition intrinsic to their reciprocal definition is seen as a productive excitation by which each is exhibited in its self-contradictory nature. The self-contradiction, to repeat, does not cancel either element but implicates it in the conceptual structure of the other. The ground or foundation here is thus neither identity nor difference, but the identity within difference of identity and difference. Otherwise stated, it is the formation process or the pulse-beat of the production of formal elements through negative activity, a negative activity that, viewed from the standpoint of traditional logic, looks like contradiction in the canceling or annihilating sense, and so like nonsense.

When Hegel says that the Concept is the absolute foundation or subjective presupposition, he is not referring to a determinate concept like that of a finite being, or for that matter like that of the intelligible structure of any determinate complexity. The Concept is of totality, but totality is not a finite structure. In colloquial language, the set of all cows is not itself a cow; the set of all sets is not itself a set in the sense that it is a member of itself; the universe is not itself some superelement within the universe, and so on. The Concept is the totality of the logic; it is the structure of thought. This is what Hegel means when he says that it is the foundation and truth of being and essence "as the identity in which they have both gone to ground [*untergegangen . . . sind*] and are contained." Being and essence stand to one another as do identity and difference. The attempt to think either of these in isolation leads directly to the thinking of the other; each is implicated in the intelligible structure of the other, and the truth of this structural implication is the Concept. The Concept emerges as the identity within difference of being and essence. It thus makes its own immediacy through a sublation of mediateness.

As will shortly become apparent, the key to Hegel's understanding of the transformation of substance into subject, and so of the emergence of the Concept, is the infinite self-reflection of what is in and for itself (216, bottom). As Hegel puts this, to be is to be posited. Positing is a result of the inner excitation of logical categories, an excitation in which simpler categories turn into more complex structures that include the simpler elements at a higher level of development. When viewed from the traditional rationalist standpoint, positing is reflection, or the attempt to consider each formal element as an independent determination. But reflection cannot sustain itself; it contradicts itself or sets itself into motion and is sublated into dialectic. I will paraphrase this as follows. Every attempt to assert that a given formal element is static and independent contradicts itself by invoking other formal elements in order to construct the statement of independence. The mutual implication of formal elements might initially be regarded as a property of discursive thinking; in other words, one might wish to claim that in and for themselves, the elements are indeed independent, but we cannot describe their independent natures because description is predicative, and predicative discourse is a weaving together of concepts. Even analysis is synthesis from this fundamental standpoint. To this, Hegel replies that assertions of being as independent of thought are nonsense; to assert is to think, not to cease thinking. When we weave together to describe formal structure, it is the formal structure of our weaving, i.e., of the thought processes, that we are describing, not something else, something external to and independent of these processes.

In other words, identity cannot be thought apart from difference, not because our thinking is defective with respect to the task it is assigned, namely, to capture being in and for itself, but because identity is not, precisely as in and for itself, separate from difference. Hegel claims that thinking is intrinsically adequate to the task it sets itself, provided that it perseveres and actually articulates the formal structure of intelligibility rather than falling back upon common sense. One could therefore cautiously describe Hegel's *SL* as a phenomenological work because it is the precise description of the appearance of intelligibility, where "appearance" refers to the process of self-manifestation, not to a domain of illusion or to a subjective perspective. Whereas finite human existence is undoubtedly perspectival, Hegel's logic is the description of the structure of perspectivism. This is what he means by saying that we must rise to the absolute standpoint.

In Kant and Fichte, but especially in the latter, it is understood that positing is an activity of thinking. What is not understood, however, is the dialectical ground or inner unity of positing and the formal determinations that it produces. One captures the sense of Hegel's criticism of Fichte by saying that Fichte did not fully understand his own doctrine, namely, the doctrine of the positing activity of the absolute ego. Fichte still adhered to the Kantian doctrine of categories and concepts, which is itself still part of traditional rationalism. For Kantians, dialectic exhibits illusion, and contradiction is an unsurpassable boundary or limit. This makes it impossible for logical determinations to be properly or precisely grasped. Kant simply assumed that the contradictions between concepts were a sign of their intrinsic independence as complementary terms. Otherwise stated, he discovered dialectic in the antinomies and paralogisms but took these as a mark of the limitations of human cognition. Kant never noticed that, as posits of thinking, thoughts of form are themselves saturated with the excitation of cognition. He concentrated upon the forms and disregarded the formation process as a process. The excitation of form is more visible in Fichte, who in fact replaces Kant's rigid structure of the phenomenal world with an infinite process of positings or self-limitations of the absolute ego. But there is still a disjunction in Fichte between the excitation of the infinite striving of the human intellect to reduplicate the formation process of the absolute and the static or traditional nature of the forms or posited structures themselves.

Hegel, so to speak, is in the process of bringing together the excitation of Fichtean infinite striving and Kantian dialectic, but in such a way as to transform the pejorative character of the latter while bending infinity into a circle and thereby rendering it accessible to the Concept. As a purely marginal remark, but one that I believe to be intrinsically accurate, Hegel, who knew Greek thought as Kant and Fichte did not, is influenced by the doctrine of the eternal return of the same, which modifies his Christianity. Kant and Fichte, on the other hand, entirely apart from the question of their religious views, were thoroughly saturated with the modern, fundamentally Christian notion of progress, a notion that underlies the modern scientific worldview. Just as Adam and Eve go forth from Eden in Milton's *Paradise Lost* in order to master the world by the sweat of their brows, so Kant and Fichte labor forever to expand our conceptual mastery of creation, an infinite labor that Fichte explicitly identifies as freedom.

We must now return to the Hegelian exposition of the transformation of substance into subject by way of infinite reflection into self. In the objective logic, being and essence unite to produce actuality, or (as we can now call it) the fully articulated structure of the content of the Concept. At this stage, the essence is substance; actuality is the unity of substance and its attributes. This is a radical modification of the situation in Kant. In Kant, the phenomenal world is a product of conceptual thinking and sensation. Kant also starts from the fact of self-consciousness as cognition, or in other words the unity of being and thinking. But this unity is a dualist construction, not an identity within difference. Sensation is itself a production of our cognitive apparatus, which reacts to the noumenal world of being in itself rather than simply receiving or recording it. Nevertheless, it is through sensation that we come into direct contact with what Hegel calls substance, not through conceptual thought. As a result, essence is separated from the constituted being of the phenomenal world (remember that for Kant, to be is to be an object of possible knowledge). Kant never reaches the stage of substance or the unification of being and essence. It is therefore appropriate that Kant refers to predicative knowledge as knowledge of appearances, since from a Hegelian standpoint, this knowledge is of illusion. Substance (the domain of things in themselves) is separated from its attributes (the illusory knowledge of appearances). There is no actuality in the Kantian interpretation of the world.

In Hegel's logic, there is no separation between cognition and sensation, and, indeed, there is no sensation. We are concerned exclusively with conceptual thinking; sensation belongs to the domain of everyday experience that is purified by phenomenological description into the idea of absolute wisdom, which is then articulated into its conceptual structure by the logic. In the *Realphilosophie* we study the externalization of the Concept into nature; sensation reappears, but as thoroughly mediated by conceptual structure. There is no dualism between cognition and sensation; the world is fully accessible, and alienation has been overcome. If this sounds excessively complicated, the difference between Kant and Hegel can be stated quite simply. Kant begins with the dualism of concepts and sensations and is never able to bring them together because he lacks a dialectical logic or understanding of negative activity.

In one more formulation, Kant attempts to ground the modern insight that the world is a project of thought. He succeeds only by alienating the human thinker from the world as it is in and for itself, from which we are separated by the necessary conditions for the production of an intelligible world of experience. Hegel starts from the deceptively simple insight that the world in and for itself is itself a product of thought. The structure of that world is thus conceptual structure. The Concept is the manifestation of what substance is in itself (214). This does not mean that the world, or substance, has suddenly turned into a transcendental or absolute subject. There is no personality or self-consciousness at play here, that is, within the development being studied. And as thinking that development, the student of logic has already risen to the level of the absolute. What is at play, however, is the articulation of the Concept, which has been present from the outset as the concept of abstract being. Our thinking, by which the abstract concept is as it were filled up with content, is now complete. There are no more logical categories to be discovered; what remains is to study the structure of the activity of thinking itself.

The Concept is generated by the dialectical excitation of substance. In his commentary, John Burbidge acknowledges the arbitrary appearance of this shift and explains it by saying that "thought has reached the point where it explicitly thinks itself."[2] I agree with Burbidge's observation, but it unfortunately does not explain why thought should become aware of itself at this stage of the logic. If thought has been present from the outset, why was it not always aware of itself? The explanation I have offered is that once the logical determinations have been fully thought, there is nothing more to think than thinking itself. But this is not what Hegel says. He claims that the Concept is *generated* by the dialectical excitation of substance. In order to preserve my explanation, we must assume that Hegel is referring here to the Concept as a totality, that is, to the "form" of the "content" of the objective logic. "Thus the concept is the truth of substance, and insofar as necessity is the mode of relation of substance, freedom points itself out as the truth of necessity and as the mode of relation of the Concept" (214). The first half of this sentence supports my assumption. The second half expresses Hegel's Spinozism with respect to the identification of freedom as knowledge of necessity. This also supports the assumption, since we cannot be said to be free until we have grasped the truth, and the true is the whole or totality.

Substance develops by positing what it is in and for itself; in other words, the determinations of reflection operate to produce entities or, in Hegel's Spinozistic terminology, attributes and modes. "The Concept now is this absolute unity of being and reflection, that the being in and for itself is first [present] through this, that it is equally reflection or positedness, and that positedness is being in and for itself" (214). Again, "Concept" refers here to the whole Concept, i.e., to the Concept of the whole process of the identity within difference of substance and attributes. As Hegel says next, this process has already been given in the objective logic, and he proceeds to summarize it for the convenience of the reader.

Substance is the absolute, that is, the being in and for itself of actuality. The absoluteness of substance has two different aspects. First, it is in itself as the simple identity of possibility and actuality. In other words, at the level of logical structure, nothing more can transpire. Contingent events will go on unabated, but contingency is itself a logical category. And there are no unactualized essential possibilities. This point is obviously critical for the question of history, which is essentially complete but contingently endless. Second, it is for itself as absolute power or a negativity that refers itself to itself. By this Hegel means that it is not determined or created by something else. This point is crucial for the question of Hegel's religious views. It is impossible to determine these views simply by cataloguing the conventional religious statements scattered through Hegel's works or for that matter by taking literally his metaphorical employment of Christian symbols. Hegel rules out a creation *ex nihilo* by a transcendent God. All "right-wing" interpretations of Hegel as a more or less orthodox Christian, but also the sophisticated Lutheranism of Michael Theunissen, are certainly mistaken.

Hegel proceeds to elaborate on these two aspects with his usual obscurity. The main point here is that in the process of development leading toward substance, all presuppositions concerning a separate creator or an essence detached from its attributes are overcome or sublated within the identity within difference of essence and its appearances (in the veridical or nonpejorative sense of the term). There is a reciprocity of cause and effect: "each becomes the opposite of itself, but in such a way that each remains identical with itself" (216). Otherwise put, the active substance or cause (the God of traditional religion) is revealed within its effects, just as essence is revealed in its appearances and substance in its attributes. *There is no deus absconditus.* The positedness of the world of determinate entities is shown not to be separate from that which posits it. Hegel refers to this as "the revelation of the illusoriness of causality," by which he means that causality is the process of manifestation of posited determinations. In colloquial language, there is nothing behind or above becoming.

"This infinite reflection into itself, that being in and for itself, is [present] first through this, that it is positedness [*Gesetztsein*], is the completion of substance." Again, being shows itself as positedness, as determination or formal structure, but as excited formal structure. In other words, being is the positive self-presentation of the formation process, which is not itself a determinate form but the identity of identity and difference or negative activity, in short, dialectical contradiction. "But this completeness is no longer substance itself, but it is rather something higher, the Concept, the subject." The complete manifestation of absolute substance is the Hegelian equivalent to the completion of the infinite series of positings or self-limitations by which the Fichtean absolute ego produces the world. Whereas Fichte's absolute ego is always hidden, i.e., veiled over by the very limitations or posits that it produces (and so is very much like Heidegger's Being), the absolute is fully visible in Hegel. In the first place, it is fully visible to itself, because it is the actualization or manifestation of all necessary or essential determinations. Second, it is fully visible to us, the logicians who study Hegel's *SL*, because we are able to think through all of the logical determinations that Hegel describes, and thereby not merely to rise to the level of the absolute but to become unified with it, as usual, in an identity within difference.

Substance thus becomes subject because it is the completion of the Concept; nothing can be external to it, including the intellect or subject that thinks the Concept. There is no ontological *Lebensraum* external to substance in which subject may dwell. To repeat, it is not the case that we have at last arrived at the Concept for the first time after a long journey of conceptual determinations; that would be a self-contradiction. We have always been thinking the Concept, but thus far not as itself, because until now it was not complete. It was visible only as its determinations, like the Fichtean absolute ego, and so concealed in its totality, i.e., in its true or essential nature, namely, as the comprehensive structure of becoming. Let me add that it is one thing to say that becoming is the whole and that there is nothing beneath or beyond it; it is something else again to give the structure of the process of becoming, thereby demonstrating its comprehensiveness. It is the latter that Hegel attempts. The paragraph concludes with the previously examined assertion that the transition of substance to subject is via an inner necessity and demonstrates that freedom is the truth of necessity.

Hegel next makes explicit what we have recognized from the outset of the discussion of substance, that he is taking his bearings here by the philosophy of Spinoza. Spinoza's system is not simply false but acquires or exhibits its truth from the place it occupies within the comprehensive system of Hegel (217). Since everything is manifested, and because the manifest is fully captured in Hegel's "phenomenological" description of the complete development of the Concept, this description contains the truth of all previous systems, which, in the case of genuine philosophers, were not false but incomplete. In other words, a genuine philosopher is someone who grasps the totality of logical determinations of the Concept that has appeared in his epoch. Still more fundamentally, the transcendental development and self-manifestation of the absolute are isomorphic to the unfolding of European history from the time that philosophy emerges in its decisive form among the Greeks. Thus Parmenides is the first philosopher because he is the first to grasp the pure abstract Concept of being;

Heraclitus is the second philosopher thanks to his recognition that "being and nothing are the same."[3]

It is not my contention that Hegel carries out this isomorphism with exactness. Nevertheless, the general idea is clear, and is clearly implied by the discussion of Spinoza. Hegel's science is not a new and original philosophical doctrine but the final because comprehensive exposition of what has fully and finally manifested itself: the absolute. And the absolute is accessible because it is the underlying unity of subject and object. The absolute "shows," or as we can also say, "speaks" itself to itself; it is the divine *logos* of Christianity and not the dead or abstract *logos* of Greek rationalism. And the complete speech of the absolute proceeds by repeating the partial speeches of previous philosophers, speeches that correspond to the various stages of the partial manifestation of the absolute. This repetition comes from within each subsequent partial speech and grows into its successor in exactly the manner in which each stage of the development of the concept grows by an inner necessity into its higher and more comprehensive successor. As completely rational, that is, having developed by a necessary process, substance is necessary. As complete, or identical with itself, and so as independent of any further determination or externality, it is free (217–18).

The Concept is the unity of being and essence, or in other words, the complete articulation of substance and attributes as the self-manifestation of the absolute; as complete, necessary, and free, it is the identity of subject and object, or in Hegelian language, substance become subject. As subject, substance explains itself to itself as object. This explanation or *logos* is the sameness of being and thinking; Hegel's Concept is not merely a "grasping" by a finite intellect of an external structure but a self-grasping or externalization of interiority. Otherwise stated, the whole (*das Ganze*) is alive; it is not only absolute but absolute spirit. This is why we are able to think or grasp beings in their intelligibility; there is no separation of being and thinking. Their unification is the Concept, and it is the same Concept in the order of actuality as in our thinking of it.

Hegel then in effect summarizes the content of the general essay to this point in what he calls "the Concept of the Concept" (219). As absolute, it is self-referential determination (i.e., there is nothing outside it to which it could refer as the cause of its determination). Since it is determinate, it is (like all determinations) negation; that is to say, it is individual, or the precise totality that it is. I do not believe that Hegel could explain individuality by holding that totality is this particular totality rather than another, because he has already attributed the identity of possibility and actuality to substance become subject; this is an essential part of what it means to call substantial subject "absolute." There is no room in Hegel for alternative universes or possible worlds in any but a trivial sense of contrary-to-fact conditionals. There could not be in fact some other totality; each thing is essentially what it must be. As to contingency, this is insufficient to define an alternative totality. In sum, the Concept is universal and individual, and each of these is the other; that is, the universal possesses determinateness and so individuality, and each individual determination expresses, i.e.. is, the universal. This is a consequence of the living nature of the Concept; it cannot be analyzed in the literal sense of being dismembered or dissolved into independent formal elements, in the manner of traditional rationalism.

Hegel makes just this point when he says of the Concept as here developed that "insofar as it has achieved such an existence which is itself free, it is nothing other than [the] I or pure self-consciousness. It is true that I have concepts, that is to say, determinate concepts, but [the] I is the pure Concept itself that as Concept has arrived at *Dasein*" ("being there" as some definite moment, 220). The "I" is universal or entirely self-related; but it is so via the negation of all particular determinations, which gives it individuality. In other words, the "I" thinks the whole because, like the Aristotelian *nous*, it is open to the whole and so is not itself limited by any formal determinations. Unlike the Aristotelian *nous*, however, it is self-reflexive, that is, both conscious and self-conscious, and so conscious of itself as personality. It is therefore both universal and individual. All of this follows from the basic insight into the living or spiritual character of totality, that is, via the inference from the thinkableness of being to the identity within difference of subject and object. Hegel is a hyper-Kantian in the following sense. The world is totally constituted by thinking, but this is because there is no separation between being and thinking, no world "in itself" that we apprehend through the filter or screen of our own faculties, faculties that are independent of that world as it is in and for itself. I am the world as it is in and for itself, that is, I as a mode of the attribute of thought am able to think the world, the structure of which is the same as the structure of the activity of my thinking.

Hegel goes on to discuss briefly his relation to Kant's doctrine of the original synthetic unity of apperception, as well as to make a number of other points that I have already covered, such as the irrelevance of sensation and intuition to the logical study of the concept and the pure subject or I (220–24). I cite only the following lines: "The object in intuition or representation [*Vorstellung*] is only external and a stranger" (i.e., to self-consciousness). "The being in and for itself that the object has in intuition and representation is transformed into a positedness through being conceived; the I permeates it by thinking it. As it is in thinking, however, so is it first in and for itself." The objectivity of the object derives entirely from the unity of the I, that is to say, from the "grasping" of the object by the thinking ego (222). This is a Kantian doctrine that Hegel extends to include what is for his predecessor the cognitively inaccessible domain of the thing in itself.

This point is developed by Hegel as a repudiation of the split in Kant between form and content. In addition, Hegel emphasizes that whereas in ordinary life feelings and intuitions precede conceptual thinking, this is of no importance for philosophy, which "is not the recounting of what happens but knowledge of that which is true in" those occurrences (226). One should not make the mistake of regarding Hegel's *PS* as the empirical narrative that precedes the derivation of abstract concepts by the logician. Quite the reverse; the *PS* is already a conceptualized version of experience. The difference between the *PS* and the *SL* lies in the fact that the latter is concerned not with experience but solely with the Concept, or more fully, solely with the elaboration of the Concept from its first appearance as abstract being to its culminating manifestation as the absolute idea.

In sum: Kant was correct to attribute unity to the Concept in the form of the original synthetic unity of apperception, but he was mistaken in distinguishing unity from difference or determination. The Concept differentiates itself in the activity of thinking (227). As to the manifold of intuition and sensation, this is sublated into the concept of the object. "The present standpoint, to which this development has led, is that the form of the absolute, which is higher than being and essence, is the Concept" (229). Through the subjection of being and essence, the Concept has also subjugated the natural starting point in feeling, intuition, and representation and shown itself to be the ground of what are from a prephilosophical standpoint its conditions. Reality has "disappeared" into the Concept; in book 3 of the *SL* Hegel will exhibit the process by which the Concept builds up this reality in and out of itself. It is true that with the Concept we are in possession of abstract truth. But this truth is not to be supplemented by a return to the external or preconceptual stage of experience. On the contrary, reality (the concrete truth of *res*) must emerge from the Concept by its own effort; that is, it must emerge by our thinking of the Concept itself (230).

This does not mean, to be sure, that logic contains the real world of history and the natural sciences. But this higher degree of reality (higher because more concrete) must emerge from the idea, which is the creator of nature. This step takes us beyond the *SL* to the *Realphilosophie*. The idea is the creator of nature; that is, it creates the intelligibility of nature as the identity within difference of its form and content. "Logic is indeed the formal science, but the science of *absolute form*, which is totality in itself and contains *the pure idea of truth* itself" (231). As we can also express this point, the science of logic is not the study of abstract forms of inference that are separate from but applicable to the objects and events of experience. The reason why we can make judgments about things is that the forms of judgment are the forms of the things themselves. Consider Kant's contention that the necessary connection of causality is a rule of thinking that is so to speak built into our cognition of natural events. Hegel extends this point to the rules of syllogistic inference, but with the crucial addition that the forms of logic are themselves dialectical.

It cannot be emphasized too strongly that Hegel's treatment of the concept is not mathematical. He has no interest in what would today be called the "formalization" of syllogistic. Whatever the technical interest of such a formalization, it takes us in the opposite direction from the Hegelian attempt to show the organic development of the concept.

EIGHTEEN

Subjectivity

Introductory Remarks

We are now ready to begin our study of book 3. Book 3 is divided into three sections, subjectivity, objectivity, and the idea. We can express this division in terms of the history of philosophy as follows. The immediate or subjective Concept (i.e., the result of the unification of being and essence) is distinct from external things (Descartes); it moves via its inner determinations (Spinoza) to a sublation of the external, as in Leibniz's monads. But in Hegel's hands, the monad reexternalizes; objectivity emerges from the interior of the monad and becomes the "real Concept that goes over into existence [*Dasein*]" (236). Now, however, as objective or real, it must regain subjectivity, that is, show itself as the identity within difference of internal and external or subject and object. It must show itself as the idea.

The section on subjectivity is divided into three chapters: "The Concept," "The Judgment," and "The Syllogism." Let me repeat and expand on a previous observation. Hegel speaks of "concept" and "judgment" (*Urteil*) where traditional logic speaks of term and proposition. I have already discussed the etymological significance of the word "concept" (*Begriff*); it expresses the grasping of the object by the subject, and so the presence of thinking within being. A "term" or "predicate" is an artifact of the abstractive intelligence that can easily be interpreted as a set of instances that possess a given property. The property is thus separated from its instances but also from the thinking of these instances. Not only is thought rendered external to the being of the things possessing the given predicate, but the predicates are no longer essential elements in the conceptual structure of the entity under analysis. From the standpoint of formal or mathematical logic, one predicate is on the same level as any other, namely, that of an abstract rubric under which to classify instances. Everything is reduced to independent atoms; the difference between essential and accidental attributes is thus abolished.

The same considerations apply to the choice of "judgment" rather than proposition or statement (*Satz*). A proposition is a pure form that is independent of states of affairs; one may or may not apply the proposition to a given state of affairs, but the act of application or thinking is separate from both. From a traditional standpoint, the act of judgment, i.e., the decision that this state of affairs is representable by that proposition, is subjective or a matter of interpretation. The attribution of truth, and judgment of the value of truth, are both separate from and dominate over the purely formal operations of propositional manipulation. This, incidentally, is why theory has gradually been transformed into interpretation in the last two centuries. For Hegel, there is no separation of judgment and proposition; the latter "grows" out of the former. At the same time, the judgment is not "subjective" in the pejorative sense that it replaces an objective theoretical statement with a perspectival interpretation or opinion. This is because the judgment is the constitution of the object, not simply its assessment from outside.

I note parenthetically that this leaves Hegel open to the same difficulty as is faced by Kant: how to distinguish between true and false perceptual judgments. At the level of logic, however, there is no perception but only thinking. By "constitution of the object" is meant the unfolding of the categorial determinations that constitute the ontological structure of anything whatsoever. To judge in this case is to "divide at the origin" in the sense of eliciting the subject and predicate from the very act of conceiving the object; this is what Hegel means when he says later that an *Ur-teil* is an original division of the concept by its own activity (264). At the same time, in thinking an object, we judge it or express its constitution as a product of the activity of our thinking. Thinking is the activity of repositing the objects of the world as *mine*, of re-collecting or repossessing them within the fully developed self-consciousness, so as to overcome the split between subject and object. In this sense, judging is teleological; it aims at a completed return to oneself and so to the overcoming of alienation, to being at home within actuality and "satisfied" to be there, since one now knows that there is nowhere to go outside the whole. In short, to judge is to constitute and to reappropriate.

There is one more objection to Hegel's logic that we have to consider briefly. Hegel, exactly like Kant, assumes that the syllogism is the last and best theory of judging. But even granting that logic is judgment rather than propositional inference, why must we restrict ourselves to the syllogism?

Does not the Fregean functional analysis of the syntax of propositions, as for example with respect to multiple generality or quantification, apply equally well to judgments? The Hegelian response is that dialectical logic applies to all formalizations, whether Aristotelian or Fregean. In other words, not only do formalisms commit the error of transforming the judgment into the proposition, thereby abstracting from philosophical content, but they are themselves conceptual structures that have to be understood, and this means *judged*. One has to reunite the abstract formal analysis with the conceptual content, and this process of reunion is described by Hegel's logic. Let us assume that Frege's logic is superior to the traditional syllogistic with respect to the analysis of nondialectical forms, that is, forms that are conceived on the model of a Platonist ontology of finite, static, self-identical units or atoms. The point is that the paradigm is defective; more precisely, it is philosophically defective, however miraculous its mathematical fruits. To put the point in one last way, Hegel's logic is an analysis of the implications of the Fregean assertion sign.

This points to a still deeper problem that is implied by the aforementioned objection. Hegel, with all of his criticism of commonsense language and the prephilosophical understanding, takes it for granted that the traditional understanding of philosophy as pursuit of the truth about human experience is fundamentally sound. The goal of ontological logic is not to engage in formal analysis of logical categories for its own sake but to make explicit the logical structure of reality in order that human beings may know the truth and be united with the absolute. The goal is science, but science in the sense of cognitive salvation. Salvation is not for Hegel simply the thinking of formal determinations but the satisfaction of desire. Philosophy is therefore rooted in human nature. The deeper objection to the mathematicization of conceptual structure is that it takes us away from the satisfaction of human desire. This is now entirely obvious in the postmodern epoch, which understands itself as a postanthropological, posthumanist epoch, and in which the view that man is a machine is progressing by leaps and bounds. Hegel's full defense of his dialectico-speculative logic must be, not that it is formally adequate to the mathematical analysis of syntax, but that it answers to the inner nature of human existence, that is, to the striving for the satisfaction of desire and. in the highest case, for the satisfaction that comes from understanding. This satisfaction is available only through the understanding of totality, not through mathematics. This does not mean that Hegel would have rejected Fregean logic. It means rather that he would have submitted Frege's conceptual justification for his analysis of the proposition to dialectical excitation. And this brings me to the heart of the problem. It is precisely commonsense or ordinary discourse that is closest to the striving to satisfy desire, because it is only in commonsense or ordinary discourse that the totality of human experience is revealed. The revelation is certainly inadequate and requires all kinds of technical perfecting. But this is where we have to start.

It may seem that Hegel does not start here, or that he begins by an immediate leap to the absolute standpoint. But this is an optical illusion, as is shown by his many prefaces, introductions, notes, and general essays. The only motivation for engaging in the study of Hegel lies in our recognition of the accuracy of the portrait of the human condition contained in Plato's dialogues. Plato may very well require to be completed or perfected by Hegel (and thus by the entire tradition that connects as well as separates them). But it is with Plato that we begin. Otherwise there would be no common denominator of what it is to be a human being. I am not saying that Plato's account in particular is the only legitimate portrait of homo philosophicus. I mean to say that "Platonism" in its deepest and most authentic sense is the thesis that philosophy emerges from everyday life thanks to the nature of the human being as a creature who desires to know the truth about the order of the whole and his place within it.

From this standpoint, the PS is not an adequate introduction or first step in the Hegelian science. We require to be led up to the PS, and I am using the Platonic dialogues as a symbol of the kind of approach that is necessary. In my opinion, something of this sort is evident in the SL itself, not simply in the various interpolations into the main stream of the dialectic but in the nature of Hegel's account of conceptual thinking. The logical categories are not syntactical but ontological. They are designed to explain to us what it is to be a thing, a something or other; and this explanation is predicated upon the availability of ontological structure to discursive thinking. In other words, the whole is accessible at the outset, although we take the conscious step of considering it initially in its most abstract form. But it is also obvious from the beginning that the most abstract form is unsatisfactory. The form has to be developed, that is, not filled in with external content but rendered progressively more determinate. We are moving, however slowly and painfully, back along the road of progressively more concrete conceptual development to the full actuality of human existence: to world history and the Hegelian sage as the human manifestation of the absolute. Our goal is the mastery of ordinary experience, not its elimination. The extraordinary is the complete articulation of the ordinary.[1]

Book 3, Section 1, Chapter 1: The Concept

We will begin with the immediate Concept and proceed to its division into subject and predicate; the dialectical interaction of these two poles produces their unification in the conclusion of the syllogism (238). Hegel employs the Kantian distinction between reason and understanding but gives these terms non-Kantian senses. The understanding is associated with the Concept and reason with judgment and syllogistic inference or the drawing of conclusions. The Concept in turn has three moments: universality, particularity, and individuality. As universal, it is "absolutely infinite, unconditioned, and free" (240). This is the Concept that we met with initially as pure abstract being, which is the same as nothing. It is the pure formal Concept of totality, but considered apart from any determinations whatsoever. The difference between the universal Concept and abstract being is that we have now worked through the determinations of being and essence and risen to a higher level of immediacy, namely, from the Concept considered as being to the Concept considered as thinking. Thanks to the development of essence, we are able to overcome the limitations of appearance taken as illusory or detached from essence, even while reflecting it as hidden. These appearances were determinations and so negations. They are reunified with essence in the Concept, which is the negation of these determinations viewed as finite negations. In other words, the Concept is the universality of totality.

This universality seems to be absolutely simple and incapable of further description. However, as is always the case in Hegel's logic, such simplicity is misleading or only partial. Just as being develops into the structure of becoming and the pure because hidden essence develops through its appearances into the shining (*Schein*) or manifestation of substance as subject, so with the universality of the Concept. "It is the nature of the universal to be that kind of simple which, thanks to absolute negativity, contains the highest difference and determinateness in itself" (240–41). The Concept is the unification of being and essence; it therefore contains the totality of negative determinations that it has negated *qua* universal. There is in other words nowhere else for these determinations to be contained. We can think of being as universality and essence as determinateness; the Concept is both, and so it is both universal and full of logical content.

The universal is thus not compromised by its content, to which it relates as to its other, namely, as that finite content of which it is the universal form, as the content that it itself produces (and indeed that could not be

produced by or emerge from anything else, since again the Concept is totality). Hegel applies various metaphors to the universal; it is "free power . . .
not as exercising force but rather as that which is resting and at home [*bei
sich selbst*] in the other" (242). He also refers to this power as "free love and
boundless blessedness," by which he means that all content flows from the
universal. Thanks to its negative content, with respect to which the universal acquires an identity, it is already particular (capable of differentiating
its universality as determinate content) and individual (identifiable via its
universality and particularity as just this concept, 243–45).

The universal Concept is like the genus of its species; it remains itself
within the exhibition of particularity (245). Hegel repeats this point in a
variety of more or less equivalent formulations for the next several pages.
The universal is the same within each determination; hence its universality
is indeterminateness. From this standpoint, universality stands to particularity as does unity to the manifold it unites. At the same time, universality
appears as this or that particular determination, just as the genus appears
as this or that particular species; to be exhibited as universal is at once to
appear as particular (246). More precisely, the Concept appears in its universality as the series of logical categories or *Gedankenbestimmungen* (determinations of thought) whose development from one another we have
been studying continuously (247). As existing moments of the Concept,
these particular determinations are negations of the universal, with which
they are united by an identity within difference. As to determinate concepts
in the traditional sense, these are abstractions of the understanding, from
which, as we saw previously, they are separate, and so they do not constitute a genuine absolute (248–49). The abstract or finite concept is "empty"
in the sense that it does not contain the totality of the generic Concept.
Stated more simply, just as each logical determination is transformed by
inner dialectical excitation into its successor, and so forms a logical circle
or whole, so no partial concept is intelligible in itself. Hegel is referring
here to the logical structure of totality, not to the intelligibility of this or
that finite entity as an element of experience or object of science. One cannot understand the whole through a part that is not itself grasped in and
through the whole (250).

For reasons of this sort, Hegel modifies the (Kantian) distinction between understanding (*Verstand*) and reason (*Vernunft*). The understanding
provides the Concept with its determinations; the Concept then, thanks to
the universality of reason, "sets fire to itself" or exhibits its dialectical nature (252). He also rejects the thesis that intellectual intuition is superior
to discursive thinking. Intuition, as for example of geometrical figures or

arithmetical symbols, is a sign of the impotence of reason. In other words, formalization is for Hegel silent and requires to be transformed into the explanatory speech of philosophy. This passage (251) casts light on the difference between mathematical science and philosophy. In the former, explanation and understanding are associated with the representation of formal relations in equations. In the latter, we must explain discursively the conceptual significance of the equations.

This point is repeated in the note with respect to the three determinations of universality, particularity, and individuality, which, as we have already seen, are at bottom one, not three. Arithmetic is intrinsically nondialectical; it separates as it counts (253). Hegel associates this with the empirical identification and enumeration of concepts in traditional logic; in other words, just as arithmetically distinguished items do not emerge from and pass into one another, so the traditional logician does not deduce his concepts from an original principle. This objection is often made by the German idealists against Aristotle's rather casual enumeration of the categories, but it is also directed against Kant who, despite the attempt to provide a deduction from the synthetic unity of apperception, actually borrows his categories, as Hegel notes, from traditional logic.

Hegel proceeds to criticize various distinctions employed in traditional logic, of which the first is that between clarity and obscurity. The classification of concepts by clearness is a psychological, not a logical distinction. It leaves unexplained the obscure, since whatever can be explained is presumably clear. He is thinking here of the Cartesian criterion of clarity and distinctness, which is applicable to finite determinations but not to dialectical relations. More generally, however, Hegel's point is that an appeal to clarity leads us to overlook from the outset the deep structure of complex concepts, since we impose onto the material an artificial and external standard of the ease with which we perceive something. The Cartesian wishes to begin with what is indubitable, and so with what is distinct and simple. Not merely does he begin in this way, but he proceeds by the same criterion, as though the formal structure of intelligibility is a smooth deductive chain of simple elements.

From Hegel's standpoint, clarity and obscurity are in the eye of the beholder, not in the structure of the Concept. In other words, we must be free of the subjective desire for immediate clarity in order to do justice to the initially obscure dialectical motions through which, if we exhibit the *Anstrengung des Denkens* (the exertion of thinking), the interior will eventually manifest itself. But manifestation or *Schein* in the sense of shining forth is not clarity in the sense of arithmetical or geometrical representation; it is not a deductive structure of simple atoms but a complex, continuously self-transforming totality of moving rather than static relations (253–56).

Hegel goes on to discuss the difference between his dialectical logic and traditional modes of analyzing concepts. In particular, he explains why a symbolic representation of logical relations is useless; his example is Leonhard Euler, who constructed a calculus of signs for these relations. As Hegel puts it, this is a degradation, not an elevation of the Concept (257). Signs are external to conceptual determinations and furthermore inert; they cannot possibly capture the inner or living dialectical transformations of genuine conceptual determinations. It is essential to bear in mind here that Hegel is not committing the elementary error of failing to distinguish between logic and psychology. On the contrary, he is attributing the creation of logical calculi to the subjective or psychological desire for clarity. At the same time, the distinction between psychology and logic is for Hegel empirical, not philosophical. In a deeper sense, there is no such distinction, because the inner motion of thinking is the same as that of being; if this were not so, we could not think of anything. I note in passing Hegel's criticism of the geometrical thinking that attempts to represent curves by an infinite number of infinitesimal straight lines; he is referring to the calculus as it was prior to Cauchy's use of the limit concept to explain differentiation and integration.

Now we turn to the third of the three united aspects of the Concept: individuality. This characteristic follows directly from particularity. The universal or (in Hegel's example) the genus is revealed as such only with respect to, and so as particularized by, its determinations (or in the example, species). But this identification via particularity, which Hegel calls determinate determinateness, is already the individuality of the Concept (260). Universality and particularity are thus the Concept as a whole; "in individuality, they do not pass over into another." In other words, individuality is not a sublation that moves us beyond the Concept to some more encompassing category. Universality and particularity express within identity what the Concept is in and for itself. Hegel accordingly warns us once more not to pass over to the abstract universal or to attempt to preserve it as separate from and opposed to its content. "Abstraction is incapable of grasping life, spirit, God—and so too the pure Concept, because it removes from its productions singularity, the principle of individuality and personality, and so arrives at nothing but lifeless, spiritless, colorless, and empty generalities" (260–61).

Individuality is "the return of the Concept as negative into itself" (261), that is, it is stamped with an identity by the particular determinations of universality, and determinations are negations in a double sense here, first as delimited from the others and second as a particularizing of universality itself. We can therefore continue to speak of three moments or aspects of the Concept, but the central moment is particularity; it is the ground by which universality is grasped as the individual that it is. Particularity is the totality of the Concept; it therefore corresponds to the middle term in the syllogism (262), which draws together the universal and the individual in the conclusion. But this is by way of anticipation. The next step is to arrive at the judgment through the inner dialectical excitations of the Concept.

This dialectic unfolds from the fact that we are unable to distinguish sharply the three aspects of the Concept from one another. Each dissolves or loses itself in the other two. For example, the Concept passes into actuality via its individuality and thus becomes external to itself. In other words, the various differences each in turn lend a different identity to the Concept as it exhibits itself within human conceptual experience. But this differentiation is a loss of universality. The return of the Concept into itself or the recuperation of universality is conversely a loss of particularity and so of individual identity. Let these examples suffice; the upshot is that "the Concept, as this relation of independent determinations, has lost itself" (264). In other words, by collapsing into one another, they do not subsist in their community as both identical to and different from one another. We get universality, particularity, or individuality, each of which claims to be the whole. The Concept is no longer the posited unity of the individual moments, nor are they the "shining forth" (Miller incorrectly translates *Schein* here as "illusory being") of the Concept.[2] The Concept falls back into its determinations; its totality is its self-division. Hegel says that this is the positing of the judgment (= original division of the Concept).

Book 3, Section 1, Chapter 2: The Judgment

In modern logic, the copula "is" can take one of three different senses: identity, predication, or existence. Of these three senses, predication alone is properly represented by the form "S is p," where S stands for the subject term and p for the predicate. The predicate form is more usually written "$P(x)$" in the functional notation, but the underlying sense is the same, and in the present context the difference between the two analyses is irrelevant. The existential "is" is normally represented today by the existential quantifier and identity by the identity (or equal) sign. Hegel employs the old-fashioned "S is p" form in all three cases. Russell accused him of a failure to distinguish between identity and predication, but, as I have previously noted, this is not correct. Hegel's point is that predication depends upon identity, which is in turn dialectically related to difference. One cannot attribute p to S unless each is identical to itself and so different from the other. Furthermore, to say that p "belongs" to S is itself to say that S is both the same as and other than p. Bear in mind that the standard notation masks the difference between essential and accidental predicates. But whether p is an essential or an accidental property of S, the "belongs to" relation means that p inheres in the identity of S. It is true that p is not coextensive with, and so entirely the same as, S. In that sense, p is different from S. But the difference is not complete. Since no difference is asserted here between essential and accidental properties, to say that p belongs to S necessarily means that it is an element of S and hence a part of its identity; p is part of what it is to be S. Hence p is partially identical with S; it represents the identity of S. To be sure, as was just established, it is partly different from S, but it is also partly identical with S.

Nevertheless, Hegel has made a mistake. The part of S that is identical with p is not the same as the part that is different from p; hence there is no contradiction in the structure of the proposition or for that matter in the judgment. Hegel's error is not due to a failure to distinguish between identity and predication; it is due to an incorrect analysis of their relation. Predication depends upon identity, exactly as indicated above. One could even say that identity depends upon predication since we identify elements by their properties. Thus even in the case of the pure form "$A = A$" one would have to identify the two symbols as "the A on the left of the identity sign" and "the A on the right of the identity sign," or in some analogous manner, in order to ascertain their identity. But predication as such is only partially identical with identity, as I have just shown. As to existence, Hegel understands by it what we call predication; he does not distinguish between existence and predication because he is a Kantian, as I showed previously. That is to say, something "exists" precisely if it has predicates, i.e., if it can be subsumed under a concept that classifies entities of experience, namely, entities that are cognized by sensation and conceptual thinking. For Kant, to exist is to be part of the phenomenal domain and thus a possible object of scientific knowledge. For Hegel, to exist is to be a particular determination of the concept of totality. As we are about to see, the existential judgment has either of two forms: "the individual is universal" or "the universal is individual." This is Hegel's version of the Kantian instantiation of a Concept.

One more reminder. For Hegel the Concept is the cognitive structure of the totality of the identity within difference of being and essence. The universality of the Concept is that of the totality of the essential articulations in being. But the universality as such is other than the determinations, just as for example the abstract concept of pure being is present in every subsequent determination but, *qua* determination, is different from each of these even while remaining the same as itself. The same universality, considered as this or that determination, is then a particular concept. Its form, so to speak, is still universal, i.e., the same as the form of every other determinate concept. And this emerges when we attempt to think the particular concept in itself, an attempt that triggers the inner dialectical excitation by which the particular concept invokes each of the other concepts of logical determinations and thereby the whole or total Concept, i.e., the universal Concept. In short, the universal Concept is multiplied through its determinations into many concepts, but without dissolving the intrinsic universality that is reestablished by the effort to think the many particulars.

Now we return to Hegel's exposition. The judgment is the comprehensive process by which the Concept poses its three moments or aspects of universality, particularity, and individuality (264). Otherwise stated, to judge is to develop the kinds of concepts. These kinds arise from the various relations obtaining between the universal and the individual in the particular concept. These relations in turn are designated by the original division (*Ur-teil*) of the Concept into subject and predicate. In so dividing, the judgment is the "realization" of the Concept to the extent that "reality" refers to entrance into *Dasein* as determinate being (265). In other words, exactly as I stated above, predication and existence are in effect one and the same relation.

The subject stands normally for the immediate existing thing, whereas the predicate expresses the Concept in the sense of the universal or essence (and Hegel is not concerned in the *SL* with contingent predication, which belongs to the domain of intuition, sensation, and perception, 266). From what Hegel calls the subjective standpoint, namely, how things look to us initially, the subject and predicate designate independent entities. The subject stands for an object whose existence would continue even if it did not possess the universal determination named by the predicate, and vice versa (267). This is confusingly stated; what Hegel means, as is shown by the immediate sequel, is that the thinking agent of judgment proceeds as if the predicate names something that lies within his thoughts, and the question is whether it is to be applied to the object that exists outside of those thoughts. This is the standpoint of what is called in 2ook 2 of the *SL* "reflection." From this standpoint, the combination of the predicate with the subject is apparently an act of judgment itself, an operation on two independent entities.

But a sublation occurs when it is realized that the predicate cannot be attached to the subject without belonging to it, that is, without being, as in and for itself, identical with the subject. It is here that Hegel's analysis seems to be erroneous, but we must note that he is explicitly aware of the difference between subject and predicate. This difference is between an individual and a universal, and Hegel never confuses these two relations, however much he insists upon their dialectical relation. He certainly cannot wish to be understood as saying that the universal, through the relation of predication, is identical with the individual to which it is predicated. What he does wish to say, and indeed has already said, is that the individual is identified as this particular thing, thanks to its possession of the universal, and is in that sense itself universal. Conversely, the universal achieves identifiability through its particularization as belonging to this individual, to this thing here (*Dasein*). Accordingly, the universal is individualized through its particularization. The relation between the predicate (= universal) and subject (= individual) is thus dialectical, not logical in the usual sense of the term. Dialectical identity is not the same as logical identity. In my earlier analysis, dialectical identity is partial logical identity. No logical contradiction ensues, whatever Hegel may have thought. But the transformation of universality into individuality does take place through the medium of particularization. In simple language, the genus is universal but becomes individual through the particular identity of this or that species.

Hegel next distinguishes between a proposition and a judgment as follows; in a judgment, the predicate is related to the subject as a relation of conceptual determinations, namely, of a universal to a particular or individual. Hegel's distinction is not quite captured by the distinction between a necessary and a contingent predication. A proposition asserts some singular fact or event, e.g., Aristotle died at the age of seventy-three. A judgment grounds that assertion in a way that renders it universal, as for example by confirming the date of Aristotle's death in the face of doubts as to its accuracy. For all practical purposes, this amounts to the view that judgments exhibit universality, and so necessity, with respect to some property of an individual, whereas propositions assert individual facts about individuals, and so are contingent (268).

Now we come back to the relation between the predicate and the subject in a judgment, which was initially or subjectively viewed as an external connection between two independent entities. The sublation to the objective relation consists in seeing the universal predicate as the expression of the being in itself of the object designated by the subject term (269). The individual subject is raised to universality, whereas the universal predicate descends to individuality. Pages 269–71 serve as a summary of the most important dialectical transition of the first two books of the *SL*. The reciprocal transformation of universal and individual in the judgment is the latest version of a process of "going under" and "going to ground" by which one stage of logical determinations dissolves into a more comprehensive stage but is reconstituted through this assimilation and revealed as an element in that higher stage. In the case of being, "going under" means transition into another stage; in the case of essence, it means "shining" (*Scheinen*) in another. Now the initially separate predicate and subject have "gone over" into one another. The division of the Concept into the "*S-p*" form both specifies the individual and actualizes the universal (i.e., gives it existence as this particular individual that owns it or to which it belongs).

The next stage is to see that the assignment of the universal to the predicate position and the individual to the subject position is arbitrary or only apparent. Each can be the other; the thing without attributes is the universal thing in itself waiting to be rendered determinate by the particularity of the predicate. Hegel says that this capacity to shift roles is already indicated by the form of the judgment, inasmuch as the copula expresses that *the subject is the predicate* (270). In other words, in one sense, the predicate belongs to the subject, but in another, it is the predicate that is the subject. Once more, this makes no sense if we think of the traditional determinations of identity and predication; obviously the *S-p* form does not in the standard interpretation sanction a shift in roles such that the subject is predicated of the predicate. But understood dialectically, the judgment that the subject is the predicate means that the universal is individualized and the individual is universalized. Each term plays both roles; hence the two are both identical and different, and it is in this sense that a contradiction arises. The working out of this contradiction, or the exhibition of the fact that the judgment is the relation of the two terms in the variety of their roles, is also the development of the syllogism (271–72).

So much for Hegel's general treatment of the judgment. In the next chapter, I will turn to his detailed analysis of the four kinds of judgment.

Judgment

Introductory Remarks

Hegel distinguishes four kinds of judgment, those of existence, reflection, necessity, and the concept. He devotes one major subsection, designated by a capital letter, to each of these judgments. Chapter 2 is thus one of only three chapters in the entire *SL* that deviates from the standard "A-B-C" or tripartite structure; the other two exceptions are chapter 2, "The Idea of Knowledge," and chapter 3, "The Absolute Idea," both in the third and final section of the entire work. I am postponing until the conclusion of this study a general consideration of the tripartite structure that normally guides Hegel's exposition in the *SL*. But we have to note here that the chapter on judgment deviates sharply from the norm. Evidently there is no dialectical movement in this chapter from a pair of very general logical complements to a more encompassing stage. The overall movement in chapter 2 is from the simplest element of a syllogism (the concept) to the general form, which is ambiguously represented by the German word *Schluss* ("conclusion" or "syllogism"). As the etymology of the term suggests, the judgment or *Urteil* can be understood as the dialectical bifurcation of the concept into subject and predicate, which are rejoined by the middle term to form the conclusion. In sum, we have three terms, the subject and predicate on the one hand, or the major and minor terms of a syllogism, and the middle term on the other, but four types of judgment. Let us now turn to the details.

I begin by reminding the reader of the central point about contradiction. Hegel does not confuse, or fail to distinguish between, identity and predication in the formalist or nondialectical senses of those terms. When Hegel says that the universal is and is not the individual, or more generally that the subject is and is not the predicate, he means that the same actor can and indeed must play both roles. In other words, the abstract or formal subject term can stand for an individual that is characterized by a universal property as well as for the thing as such or universal owner whose identity is fixed by the individual property named by the predicate. And an analogous duality of roles holds good for the predicate. This may seem initially hard to grasp, but what else does it mean to classify an instance under a general concept? The intended meaning, no doubt, is that the concept is the universal whereas the instance is the individual; e.g., in "the rose is red," "red" is the universal property that particularizes the individual rose. But "rose" can also function as a universal, for example a species of flower, which particularizes the individual property of redness. Stated more fully to bring out the point, the judgment "the rose is red" must then be understood to say "it is the flower called 'rose' that possesses the individual color 'red.'" Note that roses might also be yellow or white. If then the universal can play the role of the individual and vice versa, each is both itself and the other, and in that sense, a contradiction follows. The contradiction is not vicious or annihilating but rather sublates the two terms or raises them to a higher level of determinateness.

This is what Hegel means when he says that "S is p" means that S both is and is not p. As I pointed out previously, even in the case of standard or nondialectical predication, it is correct to say that S is partly identical with p. If this were not so, then p would not belong to S, because "is" means "belongs to" in a structural or ontological, not a purely external, sense. S does not own p in the sense that I own a suitcase. If I own a suitcase, as a matter of fact, then the appropriate judgment is that I am a suitcase owner, and this judgment is true if and only if I do own a suitcase. And in this case, it is part of my identity that I am a suitcase owner. I realize that my example is contingent, but it brings out the point that even in contingent predications, something essential is being asserted about the subject, that is, something that is essential for so long as the predication is true. The fact that my identity as a human being does not depend upon my owning a suitcase is here irrelevant. While I own it, I cannot be correctly described by a judgment that I do not own one. Hegel often speaks as though he takes "S is p" to be a formal contradiction. If this is what he means, then he is only partly right, but not because he failed to distinguish between identity and predication. His error, if it is an error, stems from not having distinguished between formal and dialectical contradiction with sufficient care.

Hegel holds further something like the following. In order to predicate p of S or to say that "S is p," it must be the case that the two terms are different. The intelligibility of "S is p" depends upon the submeaning that S

is not p. (The difference between the capital and the small letters is meant to bring out that we are dealing with items of a different level of generality and so that they cannot be identical—in the standard formal calculus, that is.) One term can be predicated of another if and only if the two terms are distinct in the manner just indicated. So the judgment says both that the terms are different from one another, and that precisely as different, they are the same, that is, not that, e.g., "red" is the same as "rose," but that the predicate role coincides in the relation of predication with the subject role. This coincidence just is the predication relation. This is a separate point from the assertion that what is in one sense a predicate may in another be a subject of predication. I have referred to this coincidence as a partial identity between identity and predication. The element p is part of the identity of S.

Book 3, Section 1, Chapter 2: The Judgment

Book 3, Section 1, Chapter 2, Subsection A: The judgment of existence

Now we can continue with the analysis of the text. As I have already noted, Hegel does not distinguish between predicational and existential judgments, because of his Kantian interpretation of existence by way of predication. We should not be prevented from seeing this by Kant's famous assertion that existence (or being) is not a predicate. It is not a real but a logical predicate, whereas existence requires real predicates. Thus, for example, roses may be said to exist provided that we can establish their color, say, red. This shows that they are part of the phenomenal network that constitutes our experience. Hegel is not a simple or unqualified Kantian, but this doctrine of existence underlies his own doctrine that predication, whether of the individual by the universal or vice versa, taken as immediate or without further development, is an existential judgment (273).

There are three kinds of existential judgments, positive, negative, and infinite. Positive judgments may have the form "the individual is universal" or "the universal is individual," of which the first is for Hegel prior to the second. In his discussion, Hegel makes it clear that he is primarily concerned with the relation of the roles (as I have called them) of the individual and the universal in the dialectical structure of the judgment, and not with the concrete individuals or properties of actual judgments like "the rose is red" (278). He thus warns that it is not a genuine judgment to take both subject and predicate as universal or both as singular, which is possible in the traditional syllogism (276). The kernel of every judgment is the assertion that an individual has a universal determination; in my formulation, it is a something or another of such and such a kind. But the dialectical relation between the two poles of the judgment makes it possible for either to be interpreted as the individual with the other as universal.

The kernel judgment or expression of existence expresses the form of an existential judgment, whereas the converse, "the universal is individual," expresses its content, that is, the predicate of the existing individual. The most important dialectical transformation is as follows. The judgment states immediately that the individual is universal. In fact, however, the individual is not universal, since the predicate is of wider extent than the immediate (i.e., in itself unqualified) individual. Conversely, the universal is not in fact universal but only a single property of those that belong to the subject. Here is a case in which Hegel seems to have confused identity with predication whereas he is actually distinguishing them. The subject "is" the predicate in the sense that it is identified by it; the predicate is an element in the subject's identity. But the subject "is not" the predicate in the sense of being entirely identical with it; the identity of the subject consists of many predicates. We thus have a partial identity of identity and predication. Hegel sees the distinction as one of contradiction or (in the present context) as negation of the two forms of the existential judgment. It would be more accurate, however, to speak of a partial contradiction.

From a Hegelian standpoint, in which the relation between subject and predicate is a judgment that connects individuality and universality, and so expresses something essential about these two aspects of the concept, rather than making a contingent or accidental predication of empirical terms, the sharp distinction between identity and predication cannot be maintained. In the case of an essential relation, predication is a statement of identity. However, it is a statement of partial, not complete, identity. Interestingly enough, this is also necessary for Hegel's dialectical point, since if the universal were entirely the same as the individual, we would have a tautology rather than a judgment, as he himself obviously recognizes. There would be no dialectical transformation of the two roles, because there would be only one role. But if identity and predication were really entirely separate, then all predications would be accidental; and, barring special assumptions, this is the actual consequence of the mathematical approach to logic.

If we then distinguish the properly logical content of a judgment (the relation of individual and universal), and disregard the nonlogical (i.e., the concrete) content, it follows that the existential judgment is not true; its truth is contained in the negative judgment (278). The individual is not universal but is rendered particular by the determination of the predicate.

Hegel's underlying distinction between individual and particular is that the individual is initially immediate or (as we would say) abstract in the sense of being considered apart from any universal properties. It is the substratum for initially independent properties. The donation of a property via predication thus particularizes the individual. But the same is true of the universal. It is not an individual universal but one in particular, namely, the one that allows us to identify, and so to particularize, the individual subject (279). Hegel therefore concludes that "the individual is the particular" is the positive expression of the negative judgment "the individual is not (abstractly) universal." And once more, this in turn means that it is not unqualifiedly true, as the form of an existential judgment asserts, that the individual is the universal. It is true that the individual is identified by the universal, hence that the universal is partly identical with the individual, and that this partial identity is the same relation as predication, not something different or separate. Furthermore, it is true that the subject and the predicate can each play both roles of individuality and universality. Hence each is and is not the other, and in this sense the form of the judgment contradicts or negates itself.

The next point of importance is that in the negative form of the existential judgment, the "not" of the copula is also attached to the predicate, which expresses a not-universal (280). Note once more Hegel's insistence that the logical significance of this operation cannot be derived from consideration of terms designating sensation or intuition (281). Hegel means that the individual, as not-universal, is particular. He wishes to deny the consequence that "not-universal" is indeterminate, e.g., that "not-white" means "either red, or blue, or green . . ." Particularity is a mode of the concept that arises from the positive existential judgment by way of the negation internal to the immediate form of that judgment. Recall also that particularity is a mediation of individuality and universality; Hegel is heading toward the syllogism and, more precisely, the conclusion of the syllogism, in which the particular is the middle term that draws together S and p into a conclusion. In this connection he makes the important distinction between indeterminate nothing, "the thoughtless nothing," and the determinate negativity that is essentially related to a positive. In the present analysis, the "not" that attaches to the universal does not render it indeterminate but gives it a positive identity, namely, that of particularity. It is this particular property, through the possession of which the individual subject itself becomes a particular, rather than an immediate substrate or indeterminate subject.

To continue, the particular is the mediating term between the individual and the universal. It arose from negation; the negative judgment is "the re-flection of the judgment of existence into itself" (283). Reflection is always associated in Hegel with determination; the particular is a determination of individuality and universality. But now things become tricky. We have just established that the individual is the particular. However, it is also *not* the particular, which (exactly like the universal) is of wider extension than it. Previously Hegel equated indeterminateness with universality as opposed to particularity, which latter, in his own example, is expressed by the judgment that the rose is red, as distinct from the indeterminate judgment that, as not-white, it is either red or yellow or something else. Now the fact that the rose is a "particular" color, say, yellow, serves to identify it as an individual, as distinguished from the particularity of being some color or other.

There is clearly some instability here in the account of individuality and particularity. The individual becomes a particular via the universal, but as a particular, e.g., a rose of a certain color, it is an individual, not "a thing of some color or other," which here designates particularity. What Hegel seems to mean is that to be some color or another is to be a particular form of universal, namely, the universal of colored things. However, the individual rose, which is yellow, is not "some color or another" but just precisely yellow. A yellow rose is an individual thing, and so not identical to "a rose of some color or another." It now looks as though a colored rose, namely, one to which we attribute some color or another, but not a specific color, is a particular, whereas a rose with this color here, e.g., yellow, is an individual. In order to bring this passage into conformity with its predecessor, we must take Hegel as follows. Universality is indeterminately some particular universal or predicate or another, of which color is just one. But color is either red or yellow or white, and so on. Hence particularity is also general, albeit not as general as universality.

This is undoubtedly obscure, but it should not surprise us. In Hegel's logic, things are constantly shifting their identity. Particularity is a role that assumes its identity from the context in which it is contrasted with the two extremes of individuality and universality. The roles remain the same, but the players of those roles are constantly shifting, constantly being trans-formed into each other. In Hegel's example, the rose is a determined de-terminate; i.e., it is a rose rather than a nonrose, and it is the color yellow rather than red or white or. . . . There are accordingly two negations built into the assertion "the rose is yellow." To be a rose is already to have un-dergone the first negation of determination. If we say further that the rose is not red, this is equivalent to some positive statement like "the rose is yellow." The denial of redness is thus a second negation, i.e., the application of a determination to the rose or in other words a positive determination. The negation of negation is an affirmation. In Hegel's doctrine, the rose is now certified as an individual because it has been mediated or particularized by negation (284).

We have now traversed the following dialectical trajectory. We began with a simple or immediate existential judgment: The individual is the universal (a subject-substrate possesses a universal predicate). Next we saw that the individual is not the universal but is narrower than it. It was here that the question of the possible confusion of identity and predication arose and was sorted out. Third, we passed from the negative form of the existential judgment to the judgment that the individual is particular, and thence to the assertion that the individual is not particular but individual (since particularity is wider than individuality). Note that this is no longer the mere assertion of a tautology, thanks to the antecedent dialectical development. The individual subject is an individual predicate (the rose is yellow). Fourth and last, Hegel adds that the subject can also be taken as the universal, by which I assume he refers to the immediate substrate of the subject as capable of receiving a multiplicity of predicates. We can then assert that the universal is the universal, if we take the predicate to refer to that multiplicity. I am not entirely sure that this is what Hegel means, but there is no doubt that he wants to arrive at all four possible combinations of the two aspects, individuality and universality (281–84).

There is one more step to be taken here. In the negative judgment, we say that the subject is not a particular universal; alternatively, it does not exhibit a certain particularity. Now we must exhibit the negation of this negative judgment (the positive form of which is "the individual is the universal"). This arises when we deny the predicate as a totality. In other words, the subject is entirely excluded from the range of the predicate and is not rather positively connected with some particular determination of it. This is called "the infinite judgment" (284). Stated with maximum simplicity, an infinite judgment is one in which there is no connection between the subject and predicate other than total exclusion. But this is no longer a judgment, or as Hegel says, it is a nonsensical judgment. Examples are "the rose is not an elephant" and "understanding is not a table." A more sensible example is the committing of a crime; for example, if I steal something from you, not only is it not mine but my act has negated the universal realm of right (285). Since infinite judgments are not genuine judgments, I will pass by their dialectical movements, which are so far-fetched as to be entirely implausible.

Book 3, Section 1, Chapter 2, Subsection B: The judgment of reflection

Also quite obscure, but relevant to the main line of inquiry, is the transition from the judgment of existence to the judgment of reflection. The two poles of the judgment, individuality and universality, have "reflected" themselves into each other; in other words, each moment has taken on its own roles as well as those of its complement. This reached its peak in the infinite judgment, which sunders the subject from the predicate and can thus be understood to say either that the individual is the individual (since it cannot in any sense be the universal or predicate) or that the universal is the universal (since the predicate cannot in any sense be the subject). In either case, the form of the judgment is sublated; we are left with the assertion of the separate identity of each term. At this point, the judgment has disappeared back into the unity of the concept whence it came. It is rather misleading to refer to this collapse as a sublation, which normally implies a rise to a higher and more comprehensive level. In any event, Hegel follows with what must strike the reader as a completely unsupported assertion: "Since this unity is the concept, it is immediately divided again into its extremes, and is [present] as [a] judgment whose determinations, however, are no longer immediate but are reflected into itself. The judgment of existence has passed over into the judgment of reflection" (286).

What Hegel means is that the concept, as we have already studied it, separates itself into the subject and predicate of the existential judgment. When these determinations lose their stability and return to the underlying unity of the concept, the inner motions of the dialectic of the concept once more produce a separation of subject and predicate; but now the determinations of individuality, universality, and particularity have passed through the stages of existential judgment and are no longer present as immediate. Each is determined by the other; this is reflection.

An existential judgment refers to singular existing things that can serve as subjects for predication, e.g., "the rose is red." According to Hegel, judgments of this sort lack genuine content; the predicate is a single property. In the judgment of reflection, the predicate is a combination of various predicates into an essential unity, e.g., "man is mortal," "things are perishable," and so on. Hegel takes predicates like "red" to be less universal than predicates like "mortal" or "perishable." His examples suggest that the difference is one of accidental and essential predication. In language that is closer to Hegel's, the existential predicate expresses just one property of many that belong to the subject (275). It situates the subject within existence. The reflective judgment goes beyond this and characterizes the essential unity of the subject. But, Hegel adds, it is still tied to the immediate subject or *Dasein* as an appearance (*Erscheinung*, 286–87). Judgments of existence are of the inherence of a predicate in an existing individual; judgments of reflection are of the subsumption of an individual entity under a universal predicate. In the first case, the subject is the agent of dialectical transformation; in the second, it is the predicate (287–88).

Hegel distinguishes three kinds of reflective judgments, individual (or better here, singular), particular, and universal. Note that contemporary quantification logic makes no distinction between "one" and "many," whereas Hegel does. We begin again with "the individual is universal," but the universality is now essential. An example is "man is mortal." Hegel says that the general form here is "this is an essential universal." As usual, there is a contradiction between the subject and the predicate. "This" is not universal; the universal "mortal" inheres in the subject term. Hegel's shift to "this" seems to obscure rather than strengthen his point. The subject term "man" can take more than one essential attribution (e.g., rational, political, featherless biped, mimetic being). So man and mortal are not identical. I repeat that they are partially identical, because it is part of man's identity to be mortal. Hegel has not confused identity and predication; he is trying to distinguish them. It is true that man is mortal, and this truth arises from the inherence of mortality in every human being. But man is other things as well; humans have a complex essence. Of course it is true that "mortal" is a predicate of "man," but it is an essential predicate and hence designates a partial identity.

It would probably be better if Hegel were to claim only that the copula is equivocal, rather than to insist upon contradiction between the various senses of "S is p." The dialectically contradictory nature of the judgment comes out much more unambiguously when Hegel speaks of the aspects of individuality and universality. I have called these aspects "roles" in the judgment. Both the subject and the predicate terms can play either of these roles, thanks to their dialectical transformations. One can object that the subject is individual from one standpoint and universal from another, thereby adapting to the context an Aristotelian device for disambiguating complex expressions. To this, Hegel's reply would be that if the same expression is capable of being viewed from two opposing standpoints, then it is intrinsically contradictory. Aristotle focuses on the distinctions, whereas Hegel insists upon the connections.

To come back to the singular judgment, "this is an essential universal" also states that the essential universal is "not a this," i.e., it is the predicate rather than the subject. It is not (in the example) this individual human being *as* an individual but any individual as defined by the essential predicate. Hegel calls this "particularity." One could again object that he has in fact moved from singularity to universality, i.e., to "all men," and in a sense he would agree. But he regards the transition as effected via particularization. His explanation clearly rests upon the unexpressed assumption, not unreasonable in itself, that "some" is conceptually distinct from both "one" or "this" on the one hand, and "all" on the other. Otherwise, he would simply state that in identifying a single person as mortal, we are tacitly referring to the universal class of "all human beings." And this is in fact how he derives universality from particularity. But no plausible reason is given for taking the dialectical negation of "this" in "this is an essential universal" to be "these" or "a particular number of individuals." Since the contradiction turns upon identifying the singular "this" with the universal property, it is hard to see how the contradiction is overcome by shifting to "these individuals."

On balance, I am inclined to take Hegel to be saying that the path from singularity to universality is via particularization of the individual by the particularity of the predicate, which is his standard position. The transformation of a random individual into a determinate particular is for Hegel associated with a multiplicity of individuals of this sort, i.e., individuals that are determined in this manner. It is this intermediate stage that gives rise to universality. As soon as we arrive at "some" or "these" as the negation of "this," it is easy to see that the expression "some men" (not "some *this* man," e.g., "some Gaii") contains an inner allusion to the class of all men (289).

The universal judgment is about the kind (*Gattung*) named by the subject term, and not about the empirical sum of individuals. The kind-subject is no longer subsumed under the universal predicate term. The latter now characterizes the subject term as a particular universal; more generally, each term plays in turn the role of general or universal and particular or a determinate individual. In the example (all men are mortal), "men" is a family or universal, but it is also a particular instance of mortal things (292–93). Since each term plays both roles, the two terms are identical in their roles (and again, this is not the same as to say that "man" is identical with "mortal"). To make a somewhat garrulous story short, we arrive at the necessary judgment via the inference that "what belongs to all individuals of a kind is transmitted to the kind via its nature" (293).

Book 3, Section 1, Chapter 2, Subsection C: The judgment of necessity

Judgments of necessity are of three kinds, categorical, hypothetical, and disjunctive. I can be very brief about the first two. We have just seen that the *Gattung*, normally translated as "kind" or "genus," has the same nature as all of its individuals. *Genos* means literally "family" in the sense of individuals who are related by sexual reproduction. It need not take the sense "genus" as distinguished from "species," and in the previous subsection it was better to translate *Gattung* as kind. But now Hegel shifts to the genus-species terminology. In a categorical judgment, the predicate is the genus under which falls the species named by the subject. But since the genus is not contained entirely within the species, the categorical judgment contains what Hegel calls the necessity of immediate external existence. The subject is a particular with respect to the universality of the predicate. In a hypothetical judgment, "If *A*, then *B*," what counts is the form, not the content. That is, *A* and *B* stand for two immediate existents or external contingencies that do not produce a necessary connection from their inner development.

Hence both categorical and hypothetical judgments are defective with respect to the degree or nature of the necessity they exhibit. In the categorical judgment, species and genus are external to one another since they do not coincide. In the hypothetical judgment, the identity of the two terms is purely formal. We require inner necessity, and this is supplied by the disjunctive judgment (297). The basic point here is that the genus *S* is all of its species, as indicated by the following disjunction: "*S* is either p_1 or p_2 or p_3 or . . . or p_n," where all species are enumerated by p_1 through p_n.

To say that *A* is either *B* or *C* is to express both formal universality and determinate content (assuming that *B* and *C* are exhaustive). It brings out universality (the genus is all of its species) and particularity (the genus is exhibited as either this or that species; i.e., there is no such thing as a single manifestation of the entire genus, 298). By the same token, the judgment is both positive ("the genus *is* . . .") and negative ("it is this but not in this exhibition that species"). To mention just one other characteristic of the disjunctive judgment, the difference of the predicate from the subject is effected by the differences within the subject (i.e., the species are contained within the genus). The copula thus expresses the identity of the subject and predicate, which have returned via their inner development from separation back into each other (299–301). In short, we have returned to the totality of the Concept.

The main purpose of the discussion of the judgment of the Concept is to spell out the conclusion of the previous subsection, that is, to bring out the teleological significance of the disjunctive judgment. The importance of this last consideration is indicated by Hegel's somewhat surprising statement that judgments of existence are trivial and judgments of reflection are more propositions than judgments. The object appears in its objective universality in the judgment of necessity but not yet as coincident with the predicate. In other words, the judgment of the Concept is the first type of judgment that shows its relation to the total concept. As the expression of the total dialectical excitation of the concept, the judgment of the concept is a *Sollen*, an "ought to be" to which empirical reality may or may not conform. In the fully developed concept, however, there is an identity between *Sein* and *Sollen*, that is, between being and thinking. Contrary to what happens in Kant and Fichte, in Hegel there is no *Sollen* that lies beyond the horizon of human conceptual thought. And this in turn means that the whole is good; it has no deficiencies. This refers not to empirical contingencies but to the comprehensive conceptual structure of experience (301–2).

Book 3, Section 1, Chapter 2, Subsection D: The judgment of the concept

The judgment of the concept has three forms: assertoric, problematic, and apodeictic. The main argument of this section can be easily summarized. An assertoric judgment is of the form "*X* is good." It may be true or false depending upon the circumstances; as such, it is subjective in the pejorative or external sense of the term, and so it is problematic. There is no inner connection of subject and predicate (304). Judgments of this sort lose their external subjectivity by becoming a genuine expression of substance as subject. So far as we can tell from Hegel's examples, all these concepts deal with what would today be called "value judgments." The individual subject is what it ought to be; it coincides with its universal (307). In other words, the individual subject remains an individual, but as in accord with its concept, or as entirely intelligible thanks to the dialectical transformations that we have just studied, it is no longer deficient with respect to the universal predicate. Stated colloquially, the fact that there are good things in addition to the house or whatever entity we are evaluating, is overcome in the presence of goodness as the defining predicate of each individual, whether a house or something else, taken as a product of the formation process through which the concept produces its moments. In one more formulation, the house cannot be good as an isolated individual; it is good only as implicated with those who dwell in it, and so with the total environment of human existence. Isolated goodness, to repeat, is subjective or external; it is what contemporary Nietzscheans refer to as "perspectival." Not only is the true the whole, but so too is the good.

The result of this stage of the dialectic is the complete reciprocal mediation of subject and predicate, i.e., of individual and universal, in the particular. This is the middle term of the syllogism, to which we turn next.

Book 3, Section 1, Chapter 3: The Syllogism

General discussion

The German word *Schluss* means both "conclusion" and "syllogism." For Hegel, the two are equivalent in the following sense: The middle term or particularizing element of the judgment unites the subject and predicate as expressed in the conclusion of the syllogism. "*S* is *p*" is fully grounded as an identity within difference. The syllogism as a whole is the complete articulation of the conclusion that we have already reached by studying the judgment. Hegel thus claims that "the syllogism is the completely posited concept; it is thus the rational [*das Vernünftige*]" (308). Hegel does *not* say that the syllogism is equivalent to the logical analysis of argumentation or deduction. He is therefore not at all committed to the thesis that, for the mathematician or logician in the traditional or Fregean sense of the term, the syllogism is superior to, or renders dispensable, such advances in formal logic as the functional analysis of the proposition, multiple general quantification, and so on. What he *is* committed to, however, is the thesis that what is traditionally called "formal" or "mathematical" logic is not in his sense rational. But this means that it is not an articulation of the structure of the concept. We thus come back to what Hegel means by the concept.

To put the point as simply as possible, the concept is the structure of the dialectical relations existing among individuality, particularity, and universality. These in turn are applied to the relations between substance, understood in its complete development as subject, and its attributes. Hegel's logic is thus intimately connected with the traditional analysis of the individual existing entity into subject as owner of properties. This goes back at least to Aristotle's conception of a being (*on*) as a "this thing here of such and such a kind." If one wishes to maintain that Hegel's equation of the syllogism with rationality is challenged by modern or mathematical logic, one must certainly show that the Aristotelian analysis of the fundamental structure of being is erroneous or more precisely that it is surpassed *ontologically* by the Fregean analysis. But this does not square with the facts. Frege never refutes the notion that things are identified by their properties. Take as an example the statement "Socrates is a man." In the Fregean notation, this is written $M(x)$. The predicate is now "(is) a man," and the subject is obviously Socrates. Frege assumes that the concept or, in the older terminology, the predicate is a function that maps objects onto truth or falsehood. He assumes, in other words, that the predicate relation is just that, namely, a relation. Interestingly enough, so does Hegel; we have just finished studying the relations between the predicate and the subject term. But these relations are dialectical, not logical in the traditional or Fregean sense.

The key points here are as follows. First: Frege's reduction of predication to a relation amounts to the abolition of the distinction between essential and accidental predication. Functions are purely arbitrary; they can be invented *ad libitum*. The upshot of Fregean ontology is that the structure of intelligibility is the logic of relations; but this structure has no necessary or essential content. The result is an accidental universe. The situation in Hegel is both different and similar. The major difference is that Hegel retains the substance-attribute ontology that underlies the subject-predicate structure of the judgment. The similarity lies in Hegel's shifting of the relation of essentiality from the properties of individual things to the structure of the whole; in other words, the dialectical structure of individuality is such as to transform it into universality by way of particularity. What is essential in Hegel's world is not an individual essence like that of the Aristotelian *ousia* but the total structure of the concept by means of which we think individual entities. In this light, to be an individual thing is for Hegel a function of the concept of the whole.

In the second place, Frege substitutes propositions for judgments, which is a decisive change because it eliminates the role of the subject in the determination of the function. Frege reinstitutes the separation of being from thinking but thereby leaves it unintelligible how the functions relate to the actual world. Third and in a way first, functions are relations of finite, stable, and independent formal elements that are incapable of expressing the life-pulse of formal production. The ontology underlying this logic remains Platonist-Aristotelian from this standpoint. Very far from being ontologically neutral, as Quine contends, Fregean logic commits us to the traditional ontology of classical rationalism, despite its repudiation of the substance-attribute paradigm. The difference is that substance is dissolved into attributes, which means that all properties are accidental. Since functions are themselves arbitrary, these cannot serve to bind accidental properties into a necessary world order. In the absence of such an order, the world does not constitute a whole; all classical dualisms reappear, and intelligibility dissolves into subjective creation. As to the productions of formalist logical analysis, these are all artifacts of the primitive assumptions intrinsic to the shift from substance to function.

Finally, Hegel tries to explain the syllogism as the unfolding of the concept via the mediation of the judgment. The truth lies not in the immediate concept or the immediate judgment but in the fully developed structure of the possible relations between subject and predicate via the action of the middle term, which is the agent of particularization. There are in Hegel's doctrine no presuppositions, not because there are no starting points, but because these starting points "go to ground" in the course of our effort to think them; they must be reconstituted by their ensuing inner excitations. In a world of irreducibly independent, stable, and finite forms, there cannot be a retroactive validation of first principles or axioms, or whatever one chooses to call the orientating presuppositions, because there is no reciprocal movement from beginning to end and back. The deductive motion is all forward, and there cannot be a deduction of the starting points.

Hegel replaces the role of deduction in his logic by that of development, and most important, by a *circular* development. As Kojève has rightly pointed out, the beginning is validated by the completeness of its conceptual structure, which structure is generated by its own inner movement, a movement, incidentally, that is identical with that of our thinking. This is the Hegelian version of the Spinozist thesis that the order of things is the same as the order of thought. Implicit in everything I have said in the preceding paragraphs is the underlying principle that all "formalizations" of Hegel's logic are intrinsically absurd, as are all attempts to make his views compatible with the ontological consequences of modern logic. It is for Hegel a platitude that mathematics is empty of content; one could say that the content of mathematics is just mathematics, namely, formal relations. But as we have now seen, the formal relations in question are too abstract to answer to the task of thinking the intelligible structure of the whole.

The syllogism is not for Hegel a fortuitous happy technical invention that serves as an external paradigm for the analysis of logical argument. Strictly speaking, Hegel is not considering the syllogism from the standpoint of valid arguments or as a model of deductive inference. Deduction is for him a consequence of the inner structure of the conclusion arrived at by a complete mediation of subject and predicate, or more generally of individuality and universality, through the middle term or particularity. Hegel is concerned to explain how we are in a position to draw valid inferences, that is, what are the underlying ontological, i.e., dialectico-speculative, processes of categorial development that provide us with valid inferences. The syllogism is the set of inner movements contained in the form of the judgment. And the judgment is the articulation of the relations obtaining between substance and attributes, as represented by the subject-predicate structure. As I have emphasized, the syllogism is for Hegel a necessary consequence of the ontology of substance and attributes, provided that both are correctly interpreted in accord with Hegelian dialectic. No formal analysis of the syntax of judgment that discards the ontology of substance and attributes can be conceptually superior to the subject-predicate analysis.

It is therefore quite mistaken to hold, as does John W. Burbidge in his commentary to the *SL*, that Hegel's is a logic of pure thought that has no metaphysical or ontological baggage.[1] It is indeed a logic of pure thought, but pure thinking is thinking of pure being; in other words, the identity within difference of being and thinking requires that the structure of the concept be the same as the structure of being. It is for Hegel, exactly as for Aristotle, fundamental that things both are and are intelligible because they exhibit a structure of owner and properties. There is no way in which to identify something, or to attribute being (or for that matter "existence") to something, unless we can describe the kind of thing we apprehend. And every description of a thing distinguishes between the thing as a unity and as a multiplicity of properties. The crucial problem lies in the attempt to define the relation between the unity and the multiplicity. If the unity is just the set of multiple properties, then how can we explain the necessity of this particular conjunction of properties such that a thing of just this kind is the result? If we cannot explain this necessity, then the thing is a contingent bundle of accidents, so far as our conceptual grasp of it is concerned. On the other hand, if the unity is distinct from the multiplicity of properties, how can we grasp it? What does it mean to speak of a unity, if not to refer to the order of the properties themselves? But in this case, why this particular order?

As we now know, Hegel attempts to solve this problem by shifting our attention from the empirical individual entity to the structure of totality. We cannot, on his analysis, demonstrate that any set of attributes is essential to the nature of a particular individual entity. From this standpoint, Hegel is in agreement with the conclusion of anti-essentialist mathematical logics. What we can do, he claims, is to demonstrate the totality of conditions required in order that any entity whatsoever exhibit itself to our conceptual processes. We can show how substance manifests itself as its attributes, but not how this particular substance or *ousia*, say, of a man or a flower, manifests itself as this thing here of such and such a kind and not as something else. The truth is the whole. All other "truths" are indeed partial or contingent, and so partly untrue, which is to say that they are opinions or historically unfolding occurrences, but not true in the sense of absolutely true. Only the absolute is absolutely true. This is the Hegelian version of Kant's transcendental ego. Rationality pertains to the logical conditions for the possible existence of any empirically accessible individual whatsoever. But these conditions cannot be captured in a formal calculus of abstract symbols and finite or linear deductive principles.

The syllogism, to repeat, grows out of the internal dialectical excitations of the concept, namely, out of our attempt to think substance as subject. This attempt is reflective in the following sense. The concept is not separate from but is the form of substance as subject. We must therefore bend back upon substance in order to see within it the process of thought by which we constituted it. This "bending back" is at first a separating of the moments of the concept from their coordinate moments in the order of being; the section of the subjective logic entitled "Subjectivity" is in this way analogous to the treatment of the determinations of reflection in book 2 on essence. The second section, entitled "Objectivity," is in a similar sense analogous to book 1 on being; in it, the ontological content of the concept is reunited with the form of the concept, a form that culminates in the syllogism.

In the balance of the analysis of chapter 3, I will translate *Schluss* as "syllogism" unless otherwise noted. But it should be borne in mind that for Hegel, a syllogism is primarily a conclusion that grows directly out of the development of the judgment. As he puts it, the syllogism is the "restoration of the concept in the judgment and thus the unity and truth of both" (308). In other words, the concept, as represented by the subject and predicate terms, is now fully unified in the judgment, which is accordingly a conclusion. The syllogism is the complete statement of the inner movement of the conclusion. Hegel then says: "In reason however [as contrasted with understanding, which deals with abstractions], the determinate concepts are posited in their totality and unity. Not only therefore is the conclusion rational [*vernünftig*], but everything rational is a syllogism." We are now in a position to understand what this initially obscure statement means. The rational is the absolutely true, and this in turn is totality or wholeness, namely, the complete development of the concept in the judgment (which judgment is itself of three kinds that we are about to study). Hegel does not mean that partial or contingent truths, or for that matter the abstract truths of the understanding, are all syllogisms.

Hegel goes on to insist that content as well as form must be rational or in other words assimilated into the concept (309). This assimilation is initially immediate and takes the form of syllogisms of existence, in which the two extremes (subject and predicate) are external to one another and united abstractly by the middle term; as we recall, these are syllogisms that amount to predications of qualities (310). This syllogism undergoes dialectical movement that shows us that the extreme terms are in fact not rigidly separate but reflected or transformed into one another, and this result is the syllogism of reflection. When the reflection or mediation of extremes is reflected into itself, the result is the syllogism of necessity. This refers to the recognition that each term is the (dialectical) totality of the syllogism.

One last and crucial remark is in order. The syllogisms that Hegel discusses are diverse, and he provides concrete examples for most of them. What he is fundamentally interested in, however, is the inner unity of all three main types and their subtypes. Different forms of syllogism provide the conceptual structure for thinking different aspects of totality, but in order to think totality, one must think the system of syllogisms as a whole.

Book 3, Section 1, Chapter 3, Subsection A: The syllogism of existence

I will be as brief as possible in my discussion of the particular forms of the syllogism, now that we have clarified the underlying conceptual foundation of the entire chapter. The first figure of the syllogism of existence is I-P-U (abbreviation throughout for "individual-particular-universal"). This is an external or unstable mediation. Hegel's example is the traditional "All men are mortal; Gaius is a man; therefore he is mortal." The I-P-U structure refers to the subsumption of the individual Gaius under the particular "man," which is itself subsumed under the universal "mortal" (314). But "man," the middle term, has many properties, which fact leads to many different conclusions (315). We have seen this same point previously in the analysis of the existential judgment. The judgment is immediate because only one of Gaius's properties is asserted of him; the connection is external because the man and the property are taken as distinct and bound together only in the sense that the subsumption of an instance under a concept is a unification. In other words, there is no dialectical development here. The unification is abstract and a product of the understanding rather than of reason.

In general, the existential syllogism begins from some arbitrary individual, say, Gaius. Accordingly, the middle term is also arbitrarily selected, namely, in order to ground or mediate the particular that one is interested in predicating of the individual Gaius. The middle term is not mediated or grounded in a syllogism of its own, and so it can "wander" through the various positions of the syllogism, subject, middle, and predicate. There is no concrete mediation here; Hegel calls this the "formal" syllogism. It reveals the form of the syllogism but not the inner development that leads to the determination of each term as the totality (311).

Now we come back to the first figure. The general significance of this figure is that it exhibits the emergence of the individual into existence or "being there," i.e., standing forth in the externality of the process of becoming. This emergence is the same as the rendering universal of the individual by its saturation in the particular. In plain English, the individual named Gaius is shown to be mortal through his exemplification of the species "man." This is the basic form that will permute into the other two figures of the three terms I, P, and U.

The following passage provides us with a convenient summary of the main features of the syllogism of existence. "It can be seen as the qualitative syllogism, insofar as the judgment of existence has this same side of qualitative determination . . . The individual is any immediate concrete object; particularity a single one of its determinations, properties, or relations; universality is again a still more abstract, individual determination in the particular," and so on (315). It is entirely arbitrary which of the many properties of the individual subject is selected as the middle term by which it is to be connected with a predicate. And Hegel gives a variety of contingent predications as examples, the point of which is always the same. Whereas it is correct to say that a certain S is p, it could also be false; S might be not-p (316).

Hegel, rather oddly from the contemporary standpoint, associates the syllogism of existence with a bad infinity, on the grounds that one can generate an infinite number of examples. The contemporary logician would distinguish between the form and the content and insist that the form of predication, granting the doctrine of syllogistic in the first place, is perfectly finite. But this is a characteristic example of the difference between traditional and Hegelian logic. There is for Hegel no separation between form and content; the content must be as necessary as the form. Differently stated, the forms are not necessary if they do not yield necessity in the conceptual relations of the content (319–20).

Hegel's discussion of the first figure shifted back and forth between the figure itself and the syllogism of existence as a whole. This is because he sees the first figure as fundamental for the entire species; the contingency of the particular allows it to wander through the three positions of subject, middle, and predicate. We turn next to the second figure, P-I-U (= particular-individual-universal. 320). In the first figure, the connection between subject and predicate was contingent because immediate. In the second figure, one of the two premises, namely, "the individual is a universal," is mediated by the first syllogism, in which it appears as the conclusion. In order to see what this means, we start with Hegel's explanation of "the definite and objective meaning of this syllogism," namely, "that the universal is not a determinate particular in and for itself—for it is rather the totality of its particulars—but is one of its species [Arten] through individuality; the rest of its species are excluded from it by immediate externality" (321).

Figure 2 tells us that a certain species is an individual member of a genus or universal; it makes an advance on the first figure by interpreting the individual as a species or particular, a kind of individual rather than a contingently selected one, as in the first figure. The individual of the first figure has been particularized by its union with the universal in the conclusion; this is what Hegel means when he says that the second premise of figure 2 has been mediated by figure 1. In plain English, the attribution of universal predicates to existing subjects is rendered determinate by the mediation of the particular species through which the individual derives its connection with the universal. Stated with complete generality, in the case of thinking the evolving order of the whole, existent entities are initially picked out by their qualities, but these must be grounded by the dialectical motions through which the two initially abstract or immediately separate terms are bound together by reciprocal transformation. The first stage of this dialectic is the interaction between quality and quantity, which we studied in book 1.

The unification of individual and universal in figure 1 was contingent; hence the mediation it provides for the second premise in figure 2 is also contingent (321–22). For this reason, either term can be the major or minor term, and either premise the major or minor premise. As to the conclusion, it is both positive and negative, as explained above; to repeat, it is positive as stating that the universal is the particular in question, but negative because, taken as that particular, it is excluded from its other instances. This is a characteristically obscure way of restating the contingency of the conclusion. But there is another characteristically Hegelian peripety; as both positive and negative, the conclusion is indifferent to the two types of determinateness, i.e., the subject and predicate terms. And so the conclusion is a universal relation (323).

The main point is as follows. The conclusion of both syllogisms is contingent, but since the conclusion in figure 2 is mediated by figure 1, in the second case the contingency is posited. And this means that the initial immediacy has been sublated or raised to a higher because more complex state. More fully stated, it is individuality that has been sublated along with immediacy, because individuality is the subject term in the first figure that is raised to the status of middle term in figure 2. On the other hand, the individual externalizes or as we can say is marked out as existing through the universal predicate in the first figure. Again in plain English: The individual plays the subject role in figure 1; it is contingently selected and contingently designated as existing via the quality of inhering in a universal. The individual plays the role of middle term in figure 2; it was designated and thus prepared to play that role by the universal predicate. For that reason, the conclusion is universal.

We shift now to figure 3, in which there is no immediate premise; I-U has been mediated by the first figure and U-P by the second figure (324). Figure 3 thus presupposes the first two figures. However, Hegel adds that "in general, each presupposes the other two." Why? Hegel offers no explanation, as though the answer were self-evident. And in a sense it is; we are dealing with the syllogism of existence, which is marked by an intrinsically arbitrary or contingent conjunction of individuals with universals via some particular or another. Hence, as Hegel put it previously, the middle term can wander through the various permutations, each of which presupposes the other two. No one is complete except when taken together with the other two.

The universality of figure 3 is indifferent and external in the sense that the two extremes are not determined within it to play a specific role (owing to the contingency of the predication). This abstract universality provides us with a fourth figure, the mathematical syllogism, so called because it expresses neither subsumption nor inherence, and so no possibility of inner dialectical development, but only formal equality, thereby exhibiting an axiom in mathematics. Its form is U-U-U (326). Hegel calls this relationless because any one of the universal terms can play the role of the middle. It is thus a kind of picture of the "wandering" role of the middle term in the existential syllogism altogether. The sense of this figure is: "if two things are equal to a third, they are equal to one another."

The syllogism of existence has both a negative and a positive result. The negative result is captured in the fourth figure: abstract universality arising from the contingency of the mediation of the two extreme terms. The positive result is that the presupposition of the mediating function of what is a purely formal or abstract conjunction itself serves to mediate the first three figures. By this Hegel seems to mean that we must posit the mediating link or concept of a middle term in order to judge anything whatsoever about existing entities. A judgment is of either subsumption or inherence; a mere statement of mathematical equality is not a genuine judgment; there is no "original division" or separation, no identity within difference, but only identity. The mediation of the abstract structure of the existential syllogism is thus itself based upon the mediation of the presupposition concerning the fundamental role of mediation. We thus arrive at the mediation of reflection, namely, an instance of one determination's defining itself with respect to another. The first three figures each mirror the others (327–28).

Now I want to try to express Hegel's central point about the existential syllogism in more accessible terms. The endless or at least unbounded number of possible predicates contained in the middle term of the first figure leads to a "bad infinity" of possible syllogisms, each expressing some contingent predication of the arbitrarily selected individual. This bad infinity is terminated by the mediations of the second and third figures, of which the practical result is the "distribution" of the role of middle term to all three determinations of individuality, particularity, and universality. The straight line of the bad infinity is thus bent into a circle (327). We end up with reciprocal mediation; but the mediation is purely formal or abstract because it is not grounded in necessary connections that arise out of dialectical transformations of some simple starting point. There is no genuine particularity in the existential syllogism: no inner connection of subject and predicate, understood as individual and universal. The entire family of existential syllogisms belongs to *Verstand*, the faculty of thinking abstract, purely formal, and so external concepts (329).

In the note (328–33), Hegel emphasizes that we must move beyond the standpoint of understanding, which treats the terms of the syllogism as abstract forms or qualities, and regard them as relations. This sounds very Fregean, but Hegel is referring to the dialectical interactions affecting the three roles played by the terms of a syllogism. The figures of the syllogism must be regarded, not as species standing next to one another, but as "necessary alterations" of, i.e., developments from, the first figure (329–30). "The defect of the formal syllogism therefore lies not in *the form of the syllogism*—it is rather the form of rationality [*Vernünftigkeit*]—but in the fact that it is only abstract form, and so lacks conceptuality" (330). This is very important. There is not some way other than that represented by the mediation of subjects and predicates in which to describe the structure of intelligibility. But in order truly to express this mediation, one must make a dialectical interpretation of it.

In this connection it is worth citing Hegel's dismissive remark about Leibniz's idea of a *characteristica universalis* of concepts: "a language of symbols in which each concept would be exhibited as a relation emerging from others or as itself relating to others—as if in the rational connection, which is essentially dialectical, a content retains the very same determinations that it has when it is fixed for itself [i.e., in isolation from the others]" (332).

Book 3, Section 1, Chapter 3, Subsection B: The syllogism of reflection

The main point in the transition to the syllogism of reflection is the same as in all Hegelian transitions from one level to the next. The syllogism of reflection derives its name from the inward turn taken by the totality of existential syllogisms, namely, by what I called the distribution of the role of middle term to all three characteristics of the judgment. But this initial totality is external or contingent. As is usual with Hegel, we begin with an individual form that is shaken apart into its individual determinations. These turn into each other through the activity of negative work; when this process is complete, the result is a totality. But the totality, which has resulted by sublation from the previous level, is initially immediate (although in another sense it contains the dialectical processes as inner mediations). It must therefore rework itself. We first reached the (immediate) totality by thinking through the particulars as individuals, that is, as separate determinations. Next we must consider them as growing together, via the process of reflection, which proceeds from a working out of the individuals as abstractly related, via understanding, to their dialectical relationship. That is, once reflection is overcome by the growing together of the parts, the result must be thought through again, this time from the standpoint of their achieved unification. The separate parts or determinate forms thus have three different "looks": as separate and hence abstractly related; as growing together via reflection; and as grown together or an organic totality.

In the preceding paragraph, I have explained the first type of reflective syllogism, namely, the syllogism of totality. All subjects and predicate are contained externally in the middle term. This externality is manifested, for example, in the fact that the major premise, "all men are mortal," is true, i.e., is a universal truth, if and only if the conclusion ("Gaius is mortal") is true. In Hegel's analysis, the universal is true not through its universality but only through the individuals that are asserted to be subsumed under it (336). In other words, the universal is actually a collection of existing individual truths, so not a genuine universal. And this is to say that the syllogism of reflection is now seen to be a syllogism of induction (337). The middle may here be understood as the family or genus (*Gattung*). Induction works via the assumption that every individual selected for consideration will belong to a given genus; induction therefore assumes its conclusion. As Hegel also puts it, in the reflective and inductive syllogisms, the major premise and the conclusion assume each other. In other words, Hegel asserts that induction is circular or question begging. We say that all men are mortal, but this needs to be confirmed by an inspection of individual human beings. On the other hand, the inspection can never actually be completed, so we assume what we set out to prove. There is a leap or (as Hegel calls it) "a perennial ought-to-be" (338). We simply conclude at a certain point that, since all the human beings we have inspected are mortal, Gaius must be as well, since he is a human being.

The syllogism of induction in effect makes the individual term of its conclusion into its own universality; i.e., we assume that Gaius is mortal or exhibits the universal, not because we have completed the induction, but by analogy between Gaius and other human beings whom we know to be mortal. So the syllogism of induction turns into the syllogism of analogy (339). In this form, the individual, as we have just seen, is assumed to contain, or to function as, its own universal. What counts here is the universal; the individual is sublated within it. More precisely, it is sublated via the dominance of the universal into the particular or middle term. The middle term, we recall, is the genus. If every individual is sublated into the genus via the universal, then we arrive at the syllogism of necessity (343).

Let us see if we can restate the present argument in more accessible English. Hegel's version of what is known today as the problem of induction is at bottom quite simple. There is no such thing as a complete induction with respect to empirical instances. We enter into induction with a presupposition that some universal is going to be confirmed by our inspection of individual cases. But we must inspect the correct cases. Those cases are correct that exhibit the universal that we are trying to confirm. Hence we have a circle: on the one hand, the universal assumption guides us in our choice of cases; on the other, the universal is said to be confirmed by the nature of the cases. Induction is therefore in fact an argument by analogy; we assume that unexamined cases of a certain kind will all turn out like the cases we have already examined. In other words, we assume an analogy between the examined and the unexamined instances. In both induction and analogy, the relation between the individual and the universal is peculiar. The universal is represented by the individual case; that is, it must be reconfirmed in each individual case. Nevertheless, it is the universal that is being represented; so each individual counts as the manifestation of the universal property in play. But this is to say that the individual is stamped by the universal as a particular kind of individual, a species of the genus. The individual is mediated by the universal into a particular.

And this is precisely the goal of logic, namely, to exhibit each individual as a particular kind of individual, namely, the kind that is stamped by universality. In other words, each individual is the whole, or in the usual formula, it is an identity within difference of individuality and universality; this identity within difference is precisely what Hegel means by particularity or, in the case of the syllogism, the middle term. We must show that each individual is the exemplar or representative of universality, and that as such it passes over into particularity. In syllogistic form, this is I-U-P, the syllogism of necessity (343).

Book 3, Section 1, Chapter 3, Subsection C: The syllogism of necessity

There are three kinds of syllogisms of necessity: categorical, hypothetical, and disjunctive. These obviously correspond to the three kinds of necessary judgment. What is going to happen in these three kinds is that the middle term, namely, the universal, will become progressively more concrete. In the categorical syllogism, the individual is bound to the universal by the particular, but only to a part of it, and so as a subgenus. For example, "the rose is a plant." But not all plants are roses. "Plant" is a necessary property of roses but does not exhaust their essence (346). In the hypothetical syllogism, the existence of the individual is not asserted but is conditional; note that Hegel refers to *modus ponens* as a syllogism, in which *A* functions as a middle term: if *A* is, then *B* is; now *A* is; therefore *B* is. This is clearly not a syllogism in the traditional sense of the term, which Hegel has extended to cover all of rationality. The first premise is universal, the second is individual, and the third is particular. But there are no longer three terms.

This "syllogism" exhibits a unity of necessity (the "if . . . then . . ." structure) and external existence (*A* "is" or "exists"), that is, of universality with individuality in the expression of particularity. *A* not only expresses immediacy, however; it is also the middle term. Hegel is referring to the fact that the role played by the assertion of *A* is to mediate between the hypothetical and the conclusion; he is here concentrating on the roles played by the premises. Existence mediates an abstract universal. Hegel claims that either *A* or *B* could play the role of individual; he presumably means that since each refers to the existence of an arbitrary individual, the judgment could also have been written as "if *B*, then *A*" (347). In either case, the ground or cause of the inference is an arbitrary individual, and as such, it expresses negative unity. The individual comes into existence by negating the hypothetical nature of the universal. Since it also represents or exhibits the universal, the premise "*A* is" (or "exists") is both universal and individual. And the same contradiction obtains in the conclusion; "B is" is both immediate (i.e., it expresses the immediate existence of the individual B) and mediated by the premises (348). Furthermore, A and B have the same content. They are both individual existents mediated by a universal; the difference between them is purely arbitrary or contingent, as was just noted. Hegel calls this the mediation of immediate being.

This results in the shift to the disjunctive syllogism. We begin with "A is either B or C or D" and then assert either "A is B" or "A is neither C nor D" and then draw the appropriate conclusion; either "A is B" or "A is neither C nor D" (350). Hegel sees this as the unification of the formal and the concrete. He takes the middle term to be the first premise, namely, the mediation of universality and individuality into particularity. Furthermore, he plainly thinks of this universal as combining both "A is B, C, and D" and the disjunction. In other words, the disjunction already refers to an individual, or rather to a particular case, namely, an existing instance of A taken as genus. A is thus both universal and individual; furthermore, it is the particularity of determinate existence, not of hypothetical or indifferent existence (351). Hegel now summarizes the three functions of the syllogisms of necessity as follows. The categorical syllogism can assert only one necessary property at a time. The hypothetical syllogism asserts all subjects (values of A) and all predicates (values of B), but negatively, formally, or abstractly, in the indifference of "if . . . then." The disjunctive syllogism says everything, both as everything or totality and disjunctively as parts. In so doing, however, it sublates the form of a syllogism.

By this last remark, Hegel means that the distinction between mediated and mediating has disappeared. The concept, as represented by the middle term, was initially abstract or external to the two extremes that it united. But now the concept is totality: A is the genus of all its predicates or species, and it exhibits itself as each of these seriatim. The genus is the individual (and so particularized) species, but it is also not (i.e., not identical with) that species, and so on throughout the list (351). The middle term can then be described as the *Sollen* or ought-to-be of the concept, that is, a striving for totality (understood as identity within difference). We arrive at this totality by moving from singular necessity (the formal syllogism) to external necessity (the syllogism of reflection) and so to the syllogism of necessity. "The concept in general has thereby been realized; stated more generally, it has won a reality that is *objectivity*." And this in turn is a result of the initial inner excitation of the concept, which divided itself into judgments that were then opposed, i.e., distinguished and related, in the various kinds of syllogism.

Hegel thus claims to have presented all forms of organization of judgments into rational patterns of thinking about actuality or substance as subject. "The syllogism is mediation, the complete concept in its positedness" (352). This means that the study of the syllogism shows us that nothing can be thought in isolation of the whole; nothing exists in and for itself; "everything exists only through another." Since we have exhausted in the sense of completing mediation, the result is a sublation of mediateness into immediacy. In other words, the completely articulated concept is the structure of objectivity; there is nothing to think outside of the concept, which therefore cannot be mediated with something else. Stated colloquially, the concept just is fully articulated being or objectivity. At the end of book 2, we arrived at the fullness of being in actuality, and this led us to reflection on the conceptual form of actuality. In other words, at the end of book 2, the concept was completely articulated, not as concept but as being (or more precisely, becoming). Now, in the middle of book 3, the concept has been fully articulated as concept. We must therefore rethink objectivity, that is to say, actuality considered as the content of the concept, and not as the independent development of that content into the concept. In the last part of the subjective logic, we will think the idea, or the identity within difference of subjectivity and objectivity.

One can already discern in the structure of the *SL* the three fundamental circles of organization, represented by the objective logic, the first two sections of the subjective logic, and the last section on the idea. Stated in an oversimplified but thoroughly Hegelian manner, we think being, thinking, and the sameness or identity within difference of being and thinking.

TWENTY

Objectivity

General Remarks

According to Hegel, the transition from subjectivity to objectivity is the same as that which is captured in the ontological proof for the existence of God (353). As is well-known, the proof argues that God's existence or objectivity is contained within, and so guaranteed by, the concept of God. I note, however, the following difference. In the *SL*, we moved from the Concept or subjective side of actuality to the objectivity of actuality, considered, as we are about to see, as the two leading principles of the science of Hegel's day. The subjective and the objective are two sides of the same thing, namely, totality. In the ontological proof, the concept of God is formulated by the human thinker; it is not self-evidently the activity of God thinking himself. If it could be shown directly from the concept that it is God's own conception of himself, then no inference to existence would be necessary. There would be no proof but a kind of intellectual intuition or revelation of the existence of God, simply from thinking his concept.

Otherwise stated, the traditional ontological argument does not assume that man is God, or that human thought is (at least in the argument) the thinking of God. But this is precisely what Hegel assumes about the *SL*. Inside the ontological proof, so to speak, there is a development from the concept of God to his existence. Outside the proof, however, human beings are thinking its structure and content, and there is no identity between the thought of the human being and the content of the proof. One may therefore say that the proof would be shown to be valid if and only if, by thinking it, we ourselves became God. And this is what Hegel is claiming about our thinking of the *SL*. As part of that process, the thinking of God (i.e., the concept) must externalize, as Hegel refers to the process of coming into existence. But it does not externalize as God; God is already present at the outset. What happens is rather that God externalizes as the world. In one last formulation, the ontological argument proves the existence of God as though he were an entity independent of the world. We can therefore say in a Heideggerian spirit that the ontological argument "reifies" God. But this is not true in Hegel; God cannot externalize as distinct from the world because, as so distinct, God is interiority and *does not exist* in the proper sense of the term. God exteriorizes in his divine activity, namely, in the creation of the world, which is not a distinct entity from the equally distinct deity but is rather that divine activity itself.

Hegel says that it might seem that the shift from the concept of God to his existence is not the same as that from the concept into objectivity, but that the logical process is indifferent to the content (354). In this case, every objectification or actualizing within existence of a concept exhibits the same logical development. In the deepest sense, this is exactly what Hegel holds. But I would take issue with Hegel on his own grounds. In order for God to exteriorize as the world, he must already be the world in thought. Since thinking is God's activity, which is eternal, the separation between God and the world that we refer to as creation must be *Schein* in the pejorative sense of the term. In other words, content grows out of the concept. By assimilating it to his logic, Hegel reinterprets the ontological argument, which intends to prove, not the identity within difference of God and creation, but only that God necessarily exists, and that this necessity is intelligible to finite or created beings. The ontological argument does not claim that God grows out of his concept, which is in fact our concept of God's nature. It does not even claim, as does Hegel, that God is known only by his activity.

I leave it to others to decide whether it makes sense to call Hegel a Christian, but it seems evident that he cannot be an orthodox Christian. Let us pass on to the next topic raised by Hegel: the types of immediacy (356). These are the kinds of totality that constitute a transition point in logical development:

1. in the sphere of being: being itself and *Dasein*;
2. in the sphere of essence: *Existenz*, actuality, and substantiality;
3. in the sphere of the concept: objectivity.

Hegel says that these terms are in a way synonyms; notice again that each of these determinations emerged from the necessity of the concept, with which we began and from which we have never departed (nor could we, in the domain of pure thinking).

Let us analyze Hegel's summary in detail. Being is the first immediacy

(357), that of the pure abstract concept which is our presuppositionless beginning, not itself a presupposition but the final and unavoidable residue of the attempt to abstract from all presuppositions. *Dasein*, translated variously as "existence" or "being there," is the first determination of being, i.e., the first articulation of the flow of becoming that stands forth as accessible to conceptual specification as a something or other. *Existenz* is "the absolute externalization of essence" (II. 105); it is *Dasein* understood as a thing with properties in which that process is fully manifested by which the thing has come into appearance; as Hegel says here, it is the thing that has emerged from the ground. Actuality and substantiality are taken together as one stage that emerges from the sublation of the difference between existence and appearance, in other words, from the full working out of the various modalities of appearance. "Objectivity finally is the immediacy to which the concept determines itself through the sublation of its abstraction and mediation." That is: by thinking through thinking, we think *through* it to the object of thought, where "through" means both "by means of" and "passing beyond."

Whereas we cannot derive philosophical language with any exactness from commonsense language, everyone can see that differences are expressed by being, existence, appearance, actuality, and objectivity (357–58). For example, we say that "gold is a metal" but not "gold exists a metal." What Hegel has in mind here is that the "is" in the first assertion serves to define gold by a general concept, whereas "exists" positions it via a predicate (i.e., a name of a quality it possesses) within the structure of experience. To this we can add on his behalf that "gold exists" has a different meaning than "gold appears," as for example in "gold appears to exist." So too appearance and actuality can easily be distinguished; the full sense of appearance is the "shining" of the actual. Fool's gold "shines" but as illusion (*Schein*), whereas "actual" gold shines in two senses; it glitters, but analysis reveals that it is truly an exemplification of the precious metal and not iron pyrites.

Finally, "objectivity" can be distinguished from "subjectivity" but also as that which is "free and beyond all contingency" (358). Thus, even though rational, theoretical, and ethical principles belong to subjectivity or consciousness, what is in and for itself in these principles is objective. Just as for Hegel truth belongs to form, so form is objective. But objectivity is no longer separated from subjectivity. Hegel's doctrine is a revision of the Aristotelian teaching that the species form actualizes within the intellect (and the distinction between divine and human thinking in a way corresponds to Aristotle's distinction between the poetic and the passive intellect). His next step is to rehabilitate the Aristotelian doctrine of the link between the understanding of nature and teleology. Objectivity is the immediate truth of the content of the concept. That content is actuality or the existing world of things; it is substance.

The truth of the world of existing objects is Newtonian mechanics; hence Hegel begins his study of objectivity by identifying the truth of its immediacy with mechanism (359). But even within the science of Hegel's time, there is an "objective" correlate to the dialectical overcoming of the independence of finite bodies: chemical reactions. The immanent law or sublation of the self-subsistence of objects is chemism. Finally, we must take into account the fact that substance is subject, that is to say, that objectivity is the content of the *concept*. The concept is related to the objective content as its end; the third aspect of objectivity is thus called teleology. In the book 3, section 3, the concept overcomes its status as external end (i.e., external to its objective content) and, through its fulfillment within content, achieves the final and comprehensive stage of the idea.

Book 3, Section 2, Chapter 1: Mechanism

Hegel's treatment of mechanism and chemism is very brief, and my analysis will be brief as well. There is no question here, in either Hegel's text or my discussion, of developing a detailed account of Hegel's knowledge of the natural science of his time, or the details of his interpretation of it. That topic belongs to the *Realphilosophie*. The treatment in the *SL* is altogether more general; Hegel is concerned with the concepts of mechanics and chemistry, with a statement of the dialectical significance of the general results of modern science. He lays down the principles for his subsequent interpretation of the details of modern natural science. We should note that even if this detailed interpretation turns out to be forced or erroneous, this will not settle the question of the merits of his general principles. One question that would have to be explored is whether the subsequent discoveries in natural science such as relativity theory and quantum mechanics would require Hegel to jettison his general principles concerning the logical significance of empirical science. This in turn obviously depends upon whether we hold that there is a general concept of empirical science that cannot be essentially altered by any subsequent discoveries, however revolutionary their implications for our understanding of the actual structure of nature. Note that this is not the question whether there exists an objective and already thoroughly understood "scientific method." It is rather the question of whether we know what it is in principle to engage in science, or to acquire empirical knowledge of nature, where "nature" refers to the regular behavior of extension (however we define it, i.e., as matter, force, energy, or something else).

The fundamental character of mechanism is that of a relation that is "a stranger" to the elements it binds together and that does not enter into their nature. This relation is thus a mere combining or heaping up (360). Hegel considers mechanism from three standpoints; the first two are that of the object and the process, and these are followed by what he calls "absolute mechanism." The object of mechanism arises from the completed syllogism, presumably as the initial object of the mathematical and experimental sciences. Just as in the completed syllogism there is no separation of the determinations of reflection (such as thing/properties, whole/parts, substance/accidents, and so on) but rather the totality of the object (as the immediate result of the sublation of all determinations of the concept, judgment, and syllogism), so the object of mechanism has no inner articulation but is indeterminate in the sense that its determinations arise from its relations to objects external to it (361–62). Hegel is clearly referring to the mathematicizing of nature, which is thus conceived as points of force that are defined by their interactions, which interactions, however, are external to these points. They cannot be internal because mathematicized bodies have no inner structure; they are defined by motion that arises from external forces imposed onto inertial movement (which in itself could not cohere in a structured universe or intelligible nature). They are self-subsistent, external, and indifferent to one another, and so identical in their determinateness but also in their indifference. They merely repel one another and so constitute mechanical process (363).

What I have called points of force are lacking in inner structure; hence, they cannot act upon one another but are like Leibnizian monads (364). Attraction, like repulsion, is for Hegel an external relation. Furthermore, the indeterminateness of the objects of mechanism means that any one is indifferently cause or effect; they are thus not substances. There is no grounding of causality within the object. Hegel does not say so here, but it follows that the relation of cause and effect must be purely contingent; despite the so-called laws of motion, the result of mechanism is that we live in an accidental universe. I am suggesting, in other words, that from the Hegelian standpoint there is a disjunction between the human experience of mechanism and its physico-mathematical determinism. Our experience consists of substances and attributes, some essential and some accidental; these substances are engaged in well-defined relations of causality, within which the cause is distinguishable from its effects. In mechanism, objects combine through attraction and repulsion, but these processes are random, not well defined as the consequences of natural kinds, let alone of purposive behavior. Once the objects have been aggregated into externally combined totalities, we can measure their motions. But there are no measurements that define the concatenation of points of force into the objects of human cognitive experience. To give only one example, there is no transcendental ego in mechanism.

This last extended remark is an interpretation of what Hegel says in his opening general comment on the mechanical process (363–65). Hegel describes two kinds of process, universal and particular. The universal process is one in which there is no transition from one nature to another but a communication or penetration by one material force into another; Hegel's examples are motion, heat, magnetism, and electricity. But the mechanistic process can apply to spiritual forces as well, as in the communication of laws, morals, or rational conceptions (365–66). When human beings are saturated by custom, which takes over their spiritual activity without transforming them into better or different personalities, their behavior is as mechanistic as is that of heated material substances.

The second kind of mechanistic process is the aforementioned action and reaction of particular bodies, which demonstrate their self-subsistence (as is not the case in universal communication) even as they take in the universal physical force or transfer it to other objects. In both kinds, the determination of the objects involved is external, and so too is the "rest" (368) that ensues when the object has taken on the transmitted force. In other words, the object of mechanism remains accessible to further external transformations, not by the determination it has assumed but by virtue of its own indeterminate nature. The object is related to the process in such a way as to exhibit both independent individuality and dependent universality. In this context I call your attention to a striking aside by Hegel: "the only consistent defense [literally, 'means'] against reason is to have nothing to do with it" (369). Hegel is comparing the imperviousness of dullards to the influence of noble spirits to the incommunicability of a disproportionately strong force to a weaker one; the example is not precisely his own, but one may think of water not being destroyed by a torpedo that passes through it.

Hegel then takes up resistance, once more illustrating the physical realm with examples from spiritual or human experience. Resistance is the preservation of individuality in the presence of a communicated universal force; it is overcome when the resisting object cannot preserve its singularity and is destroyed by that force instead of becoming the subject to its predicate. When this occurs, power (*Macht*) is transformed into violence (*Gewalt*, 370). Hegel illustrates this result by referring to fate (*Schicksal*). Unlike power, the violence exerted on the object is not addressed to the specific nature of that object; as one could put this, the result is not energy but dissolution. So in life: the fate of the family or genus of living things is achieved through the perishing of the living individual that has no fate but exhibits only contingency. Hegel is not thinking here of human beings, for he adds that only self-consciousness has a fate in the genuine sense of the term, because it is free and hence can oppose itself to its universal destiny.

In sum: the product of formal mechanism is the object as an indifferent totality that possesses a posited determination, i.e., one that has been imposed upon it from outside (371). As lacking inner determination, the objects are united into an empty manifold (i.e., of indistinguishable points of force) that Hegel calls "the center." This negative universality is particularized via obedience to the law (i.e., the laws of motion), which is the truth and foundation of mechanism. This discussion should be compared with the treatment of interiority, force, law, and the inverted world in the "Force and Understanding" section of the *PS*. Let me summarize the main thread of the argument in the present section (371–76).

The mechanist explanation of objects makes the essence external to the object. However, this externality is subject to the following inversion. The explanation in question is by means of equations that necessarily classify objects into types or kinds. These types constitute a genus that is not itself a part of the process of externalization (i.e., the motions or forces to which the physical objects are subjected). The genus (i.e., the forms of the equation) does not move but is at rest; it must therefore lie within the interior (be the actual essence) of the moving bodies. In other words, mechanism reestablishes the world of Platonic forms, or the separation of essence from existence. The interior, separate, and resting genus is the immanent form or order of the external mechanist process. The genus is law. Therefore, the soul of fully developed objective totality is ideal reality (375).

Mathematical physics is thus from a Hegelian standpoint Platonism, just as many of its original practitioners themselves maintained. Each corporeal object, in its obedience to the laws of physics, is obedient to a "center" or soul. The object is the same as or an expression of that soul, but it is also different from it as the exterior differs from the interior. The law can no more explain the external differentiation of individuals than the Platonic ideas can explain the generation of individuals. One may say, on the basis of Hegel's own presentation, that mechanism is closer than Platonism to dialectic to the extent that the bodies are moving; more precisely, there is an inversion process between the exterior multiplicity of random motions and the center of law and unity. As a moving body, the object is an instance or expression of law. But as an expression of law, it is a moving body. In this vein, Hegel interprets the motion of particles toward a midpoint as a striving for their immanent center. This striving is like the *eros* of the Aristotelian beings for the divine *nous*, except that the motion of bodies is in Hegelian language the striving to externalize the interior, i.e., to manifest the law but also to reach it or to return to the center.

The center (= the law) is the "object" of the striving of objects; it is itself objectified. In simpler language, the law cannot be preserved as at rest and separate from motion. The generic determination of the object is now conceived as part of the object *qua* moving, and not as constituting an immanent domain. Hegel calls this "chemism."

Book 3, Section 2, Chapter 2: Chemism

Chapter 2 is an extremely short chapter (376–83). The main point is as follows. In mechanism, individual bodies are rigid, and new objects arise by the concatenation of rigid bodies. The concatenating forces or motions are external to the individual bodies themselves, just as mathematical descriptions of motion are external to motion. As one could put this, mathematics is the outside of the outside, and so it is inside, like Platonism. The chemical object, however, is internally transformed into another object. Hegel compares the chemical process to that of *Erscheinung* or the self-manifestation of the interior of the object. To say this in another way, chemical transformations are obviously for Hegel more like organic transformation than are mechanical processes. As the self-manifestation of the continuum of appearances of the object, the concept *qua* objectivity has freed itself from the external objectivity or necessity of mechanism. Chemism thus serves as a middle term between mechanism and teleology.

Chemism is not the science of chemistry, any more than mechanism should be confused with Newtonian mechanics. Hegel is interpreting the logical or ontological significance of the principles of these sciences. Chemistry illustrates but is not itself identical with the principle of chemism. Chemism is in Hegelian language the "first negation of indifferent objectivity and the externality of determinateness" (382). It represents the totality of the object as expressed in the three syllogisms of existence, reflection, and necessity but has not yet overcome the independence of the individual object. In other words, the object is not yet completely unified with the processes to which it is subjected and that express its inner nature. Complete liberation from externality in the sense of dualism is achieved only through the unification of teleology: the end toward which all objective motions are directed.

Book 3, Section 2, Chapter 3: Teleology

One way in which to characterize the shift from the early nineteenth to the late twentieth century is to say that teleology has deteriorated back into mechanism and chemism. As the first sentence of chapter 3 makes evident, Hegel still shares the Kantian orientation: "Where purposiveness [*Zweckmässigkeit*] is perceived, an intelligence [*Verstand*] is assumed as its author" (383). Hegel goes beyond Kant in shifting purposiveness from a hypothesis of the understanding to "the genuine free existence of the concept." Purposiveness is not assumed by Hegel as a requisite matrix within which we can account for biological processes. It is instead immanent to those processes themselves. Totality is itself purposive. Thus Kant arrived in the vicinity of the correct explanation of the original synthetic unity of apperception in the Third rather than the First Critique. Unfortunately, he did not properly develop his own insight. Schelling introduces and Hegel perfects transcendental history (my expression), namely, the development through which the synthetic unity of apperception itself unifies with teleology in absolute spirit. Kant unites the physical world of intuition with the world of reason (and so purposiveness) in reflective judgment. But this has a regulative, not a constitutive function. It thinks the unity of the physical world and reason as a *Sollen*, a never to be achieved ideal. Hegel makes reflective judgment constitutive; alternatively formulated, he unites reason and the intuited world in determining judgment (387–90).

Discussion of teleology is divided into three parts: the subjective end, the means, and the realized end. "The end is . . . the subjective concept as essential striving and impulse [*Trieb*] to posit itself externally" (391). Hegel distinguishes this impulse from *Übergehen* or transition to another (and higher) stage. In other words, the subjective concept is complete within the dialectic of the syllogism; in its desire to externalize, it strives to achieve objectivity but not to become something other than itself, as for example the effects of a cause or the attributes of a substance. The end is not something external to the subjective concept or some consequence of its striving; it is rather the totality of the concept understood as the impulse of the subject to manifest itself as the object. When this manifestation is fulfilled, the last step will be to grasp the identity within difference of subject and object in the idea.

The end is the manifestation of rationality as concrete existence; in other words, it is the concept as both subjective and objective. As such, it is its own syllogism or includes the various roles of universality, individuality, and particularity (392). Nevertheless, as was noted previously, this totality is still tinged with the externality or separateness of the object as body. In somewhat more accessible language, the end must be realized as activity or the formation process by which the subject objectifies itself as purposive behavior, not just as corporeal objects that are intelligible through purposive activity. The concept of the object must be completely assimilated into intelligent and purposive activity of a living individual.

Hegel expresses this as follows: The end as form (or structure of thinkability) is separate from content, which is equivalent to the external world. But separation from content is also determination of it. In order to be thought, content must be fitted into syllogistic form; universality and individuality are regimented by the needs of conceptual thinking into the particular or middle term, which is the end or target of intelligibility (393). We can thus say that the particular is the end of the striving of the universal to exteriorize itself in the individual. The identity within difference of being and thinking that underlies the intelligibility of anything whatsoever is thus the impetus within the development of subjectivity and objectivity through the determinations of universality and individuality into the particular. Just as the structure of the particular (or in syllogistic terms, of the middle term) is precisely the identity within difference of the individual and universal (that is, of the subject and predicate), so the subjective side of the concept externalizes or fulfills itself in the objective side (395).

Hegel distinguishes between the subjective side of the concept and the objective side as the means to the end (394). Stated as simply as possible, thinking makes use of being in order to manifest itself as absolute spirit. Still more colloquially, God could not be God except as creator of the world. Hegel spells out his distinction between means and end in terms of the syllogism, in a passage that I have just had occasion to analyze (395). Note that the means is the formal middle term of the formal syllogism; in other words, it is the middle or particular as an abstract form of the motion by which objectivity is defined through the predicative determination of the subject (394). In slightly different terms, the middle here expresses an abstract relation of body and corporeal property; this is the object of mechanism. It is only through the completion of the formal syllogism by the internalizing processes of the syllogisms of reflection and necessity that we arrive at the fully determinate means, or in other words at the object that is the totality of the concept and so is identical with the end (396).

The end connects initially with the external object in the form of the second premise of the syllogism, that is, "M is P" (the middle term is the object defined by its universal predicate, 397). But if the activity of the middle term is simply to determine an external object, that object can itself serve as a middle for some other object, and so on forever, as in the unending progress of empirical science. What we are concerned with, however, is not the empirical infinite but the intrinsic dialectical motion of mechanism and chemism, i.e., with the conceptual form of natural science. This (logical) motion is circular, not rectilinear.

I note the following amusing passage in this connection: "That the end relates itself immediately to an object and makes it into a means can be thought of as violence [Gewalt], insofar as the end appears as of a totally different nature from that of the object, and both objects are thus opposed to one another as independent totalities. That the end, however, posits itself as in mediate relation to the object, and inserts another object between this one and itself, can be seen as the cunning of reason" (397–98). In nature, purposes act on bodies through other bodies; in Hegel's metaphor, they duplicitously pretend to be engaged in direct reaction with the particular body but are carrying out their intentions indirectly, with corporeal means. This is either violence or cunning, depending upon one's point of view. In either case, the concept withstands the attrition of bodies. Put somewhat less poetically, the intelligibility of the mechanistic world withstands, because it is the subjective side to, the objective and, as independent, meaningless and destructive processes of physical motion.

This passage is followed by another of perhaps even deeper import. There is a real sense in which the means is more powerful than the end. This is true in the case of finite ends, i.e., those that are directed toward and fulfilled through finite bodies. The paradigm is the worker and his tools, which outlast the immediate fruits of labor, as for example the plow outlasts the consumption of this season's crop. "Man possesses power over external nature in his work tools, even though with respect to his ends he is subordinate to her" (398). In this succinct passage, Hegel indicates why natural science is fated to be mastered by technology. But the logician is concerned with the intelligible structure of the *activity* of science, i.e., with purposive activity, and not with the mastery of finite external objects. The genuine mastery of nature, as one can say on Hegel's behalf, is conceptual, not material or instrumental.

Activity stamps a purpose onto the object or determines it in accord with a purpose; the object is thereby assimilated into purposiveness; the appearance of externality is sublated (399). In other words, the purpose particularizes the individual object by "negating" it in the sense of mediating it with the universality of the concept, purpose, or end. In this way the teleological process translates the concept into objectivity, but also unites objectivity with subjectivity. That is to say, the object has already been presupposed by the subjective side of the concept as its end or objective completion. Externality itself is thus seen to be a moment of the concept; there is no inside without a corresponding outside. Teleological process is thus the coming together of the concept through itself with itself. "One can therefore say of teleological activity that in it, the end is the beginning, the consequence is the ground, the effect is the cause, that it is a coming to be of that which has come to be, that in it, only the already existing enters into existence, and so on. In other words, speaking generally, all determinations of relations that belong to the sphere of reflection or to immediate being have lost their distinctions [*Unterschiede*], and what was expressed as an other, like end, consequence, effect, and so on, no longer has the determination of an other in the relation of end, but is rather posited as identical with the simple concept" (399–400).

This is the heart of the matter; in the remaining three and a half pages, Hegel adds some details that I shall simply summarize.

1. In mechanism and chemism, the middle is unmediated, that is, not presupposed within the concept. Hence the physical relations of objects are not conclusions of conceptualizing spirit but merely external forms (400).

2. If the concept is not prior to the mediation of subject and object (in other words, if there is no sameness or identity within difference of being and thinking), then every connection of subject and object must itself be connected by some other middle term. In sum, the motions of nature are endless and in themselves (apart from the concept) unintelligible (401).

3. Hegel reiterates this point, which is clearly central to his interpretation of natural science; without intelligent purpose, natural processes are an infinite series of means to means to yet other means, and so on forever. Rational purposes, on the other hand, are finite self-determinations of the infinite self-determinability of the concept (402).

4. In sum, the object can be fully understood only as satisfying a human desire or purpose (404–5).

By way of a conclusion to this section of the *SL*, I offer two general remarks. The first has to do with the ostensible incompatibility between Hegel's logic and modern science. I said above that the shift from the nineteenth to the twentieth century is a regress to mechanism and chemism. By this I certainly do not mean to imply that contemporary science is Newtonian mechanism or nineteenth-century chemistry. The terms "mechanism" and "chemism" refer to the fundamental theses of modern natural science, namely, that nature is externality (as Hegel would put it), and so that it cannot be the expression of subjectivity or the concept. The predominant claim in contemporary philosophy of science is surprisingly close to the thesis of Nietzsche that human knowledge is a perspectival interpretation of chaos. Hegel's contention is that this thesis is incompatible with the intelligibility of the natural order. Very far from rejecting science in favor of metaphysics or mysticism, Hegel tries to justify its rationality. But for Hegel, rationality is a property of intelligence; on this point, he is an unreconstructed "ancient" or follower of the Socratic school.

By the same token, Hegel does not "smuggle" spirit into the natural universe or fall victim to a metaphysical ideology rooted in religious dogma. Spirit is for him the necessary prerequisite of intelligibility. For those who speak of "the ghost in the machine," spirit is a ghost precisely because the body, and by extension the world, is a machine. But speech about ghosts in machines cannot be attributed to ghosts; this is a perhaps too succinct way of restating Hegel's point. In more expansive terms, Hegel shows that modern natural science is an intended monism that dissolves into dualism. If the description of the physical universe afforded us by modern science is a merely subjective interpretation, then it is obvious that the subjective interpreter cannot be a part of that interpretation, i.e., subject cannot be "object" in the sense of external, homogeneous, and uniformly moving points of energy, points whose uniform motion is modified only through attraction, repulsion, and chemical interaction. The doctrine of the ghost in the machine, as soon as it becomes self-conscious or reflexive, leads to the doctrine of a ghost outside of, if not above, the machine. That is a good description of what Hegel means by dualism.

This has an important consequence. We tend in our histories of philosophy to distinguish between the ancient and medieval periods on the one hand and the moderns and postmoderns on the other, as though Descartes originated, or is at least paradigmatic of, a radical break with the past. This is not how Hegel sees the history of philosophy. There is no doubt that for him, too, Descartes is the father of modern philosophy and that with Descartes, the voyagers on the ship of philosophy for the first time see land (as he puts it in the *Lectures on the History of Philosophy*). But modernity is the transformation of a continuous growth of the human spirit going back to the Greeks. There is no discontinuity here but rather continuity, as is obvious from the presence of Platonism in modern scientific theories of natural laws or equations.

It will also be helpful to address four possible criticisms of my approach to Hegel's logic and how these may be answered. (1) Objection may be made to the relative paucity of notes and in particular references to contemporary literature, but it should be remembered that my book is an attempt to think along with Hegel, not to provide a catalog or inventory of secondary literature. (2) One reader chastises me for being out of date in my treatment of contemporary logical philosophy. This is a version of the first criticism. More generally, I believe that informed readers will see that considerable attention is paid to what is common to the major schools of philosophical logic. For a Hegelian, all major logical schools may be shown to exemplify the fundamental schools of philosophical logic and not of what is currently fashionable. (3) This is the most interesting objection. I have already shown that the failing or shortcoming of "postmodern" logic is that it cannot be coherently stated by its own premises. To give only one example, in the English literature, I mention that the development, or should one say, the deterioration of analytical or scientific philosophy results in its own incoherence. Hegel himself has suffered the destiny of transformation into the irresistible "eternal recurrence of the same." (4) One or two of my ingenious readers suggest that the being of rationalism is not antinomial and that nihilism can be overcome by other modalities of the human soul. But it is necessary to employ rationalism in order to explain it to them. And so nihilism returns as the freedom of coherent incoherence.

TWENTY-ONE

The Idea

Transitional Summary

As we move into the last section of the *SL*, let us very briefly remind our-selves of the terrain we have covered. We began by articulating the structure of becoming. Hegel then worked out the contradiction between essence and accident, appearance and reality, phenomenon and noumenon, law and instance, or form and content, within the structure of becoming.

The resolution of the contradiction was equivalent to a demonstration that there can be no sharp cleavage between essence and existence; these two are contained or bound together by the concept, as is prefigured in the traditional ontological argument for the existence of God. Furthermore, the concept, namely, the essential, rational, and purposive nature of existence, would not be possible except for the presence of intelligence, which in turn is the activity of absolute spirit.

I called attention to an analogy on this point between Hegel and the Greeks. The intelligibility and order of the cosmos is an argument for its possession of intelligence. The Greeks, however, sundered these two di-mensions by analogy with their conception of the dualism of body and soul in the individual human being. As a corollary, they distinguished not simply or not so much between divine and human intelligence as between divine intelligence and human personality. Hegel unifies these two sun-dered halves, namely, corporeal order and intelligence on the one hand and divine and human personality on the other (and I note in passing that he does so by replacing the Aristotelian *noēsis tēs noēseōs* with the Christian conception of God as spirit).

Hegel thus returns by way of Christianity to the "spirit" if not to the let-ter of the Greek understanding of *to pan* or *to holon* as divine and so as both intelligent and intelligible. In shifting from Zeus to the Christian trinity, Hegel does not say simply that the empirical fact of intelligent life is a basis for inferring the life of the whole. In other words, he says this, but also something much more profound. The central Hegelian contention is that the attempt to separate the empirical fact of human life from the rational reconstitution of nature is impossible. The very analytical procedures we employ in order to separate the two are the medium for their reunification. Dialectico-speculative logic is the *logos* of this reunification. The *logos* begins with the concept of pure, empty, abstract being; and so it begins with the *concept*, not with being as separated from and external to the concept. What Nietzsche calls the interpretation of the world as chaos, and what is for Kant the constitution of the world out of sensation by the transcendental ego, is for Hegel the positing of the concept as the two aspects of subject and object. The process of thinking together the subject and the object is identical with that of thinking through the development of the concept; in understanding the fact that we understand the world, we are directed to the identity within difference of thinking and being, and so set out on the long journey toward absolute spirit. At this juncture, we have reached the idea.

As usual, Hegel begins with a general discussion of the idea. "The idea is the adequate concept, the objectively true or the true as such" (407). In traditional epistemological language, this is the adequacy of the concept to the object. But there is no "correspondence theory of truth" in Hegel because adequacy is for him coherence in the sense of identity. As adequate to the object, the concept is a return to itself via itself, to adapt a previous expression to the present context. To think the truth is for Hegel to be *in* the truth in the Christian sense of that expression. And since the truth is the adequacy of the concept to the object, it is once more seen to be totality, *das Ganze*. The idea is unconditioned because there is nothing outside it to condition it (408). To be in the truth is thus to be identical, via the thinking of the adequate concept, with totality. It hardly needs to be emphasized that "idea" in this Hegelian sense must not be confused with a subjective thought or representation.

The idea is the actualization of reason understood as both subject and object; it is actuality, not a *Jenseits* or ideal *Sollen* that cannot in fact be achieved in human thinking. "That reality which does not correspond to the concept is mere appearance" (409). In other words, the actual is the true, as Hegel says elsewhere. It follows that, instead of measuring the concept by the object, the object is measured by the concept. The concept is thus the soul or life of actuality; its life is to be rational, purposive, spiritual. And the idea is in general terms the unity of concept and reality, whereas in particular it is the unity of the subjective concept with objectivity (410).

In other words, the externalization of the concept in the objective world is precisely the demonstration of the unity of the concept with actuality.

Hegel then derives from these general remarks three more precise definitions of the idea, each of which will correspond to a chapter in this final section of the *SL*. First, the idea is the simple truth, or truth as an immediate universal; this corresponds to life as the universal medium of the idea but not to soul, which is an individual or a subject of the predicate of life. Second, the idea is soul, not in the full or true sense of the term, but as the subject of the true and the good as cognition and volition. This is an initially odd formulation, but its meaning is quite simple. Cognition pursues the truth, and volition pursues the good. These are the two essential attributes or faculties of life. But they are not yet unified; this comes only with the third and last sense of the idea as absolute truth, or spirit's absolute knowledge of itself (412–13).

Book 3, Section 3, Chapter 1: Life

At first it could seem that the topic of life is out of place in a work on logic. We are, however, concerned with absolute truth, and so with knowing (*Erkennen*), which is a function of life. Life is thus the immediate idea or presupposition of the cognitive grasping of the concept (413–14). We see here another sign of the erroneous nature of the view that Hegel's logic has no ontological presuppositions or interests—as though Hegel were a prototypical W. V. Quine. The structure of intelligibility is the same as the structure of intelligence; the *logos* of being is the same as the *logos* of thinking. It is therefore impossible to study the structure of the concept without studying both the subject and the object, which are the two sides of the concept. Let me underline that this is not psychologism; Hegel would agree with Husserl that psychology is an immanent or empirical science that cannot free itself from the natural attitude. The logician is not concerned with natural life and so he cannot be concerned with psychology. Our interest is with the formation process, and it is precisely the living spirit that produces, or even better constitutes, form. To this it must be added that we are also not studying the incorporation of externality into spirit, as in the *PS*. We are not engaging in a phenomenology of the transformation of the natural into the spiritual world of the sage who has overcome the split between subject and object as inner experience. For us, life is a stage of the idea, one that expresses the fact that the concept is thinking as well as being thought (414–16).

Life is for us not exterior but interior; it is the life of the spirit, that stage of the thinking of the idea that corresponds to absolute universality. As such, however, externality is present in life as the *simple determinateness* of its concept. Soul is ubiquitous in this universal life as having spilled out into its multiplicity; in other words, it is everywhere present as the unity within the multiple manifestations of the living being (416). Stated somewhat more concretely, the intelligibility of the external world is due to its having been permeated with the concept through the presence of soul, the representative within the natural domain of genesis of spirit. I would risk the expression that life is the medium or middle term between spirit and nature. But it has to be added at once that for Hegel, life is "absolute universality in and for itself" and not at all a particular so much as the ambient medium through which particular living beings arise in the natural world.

Life is a negative unity because it is everywhere the same, indeterminate and absolutely simple, as opposed to determinate living beings. At the same time it is the negative unity of each individual living being (417). On this score life is like logical unity in all of its manifestations: everywhere the same, yet accessible only through difference as this or that unity (cf. here II. 435). This feature provides us with the structure of our chapter. We must think life first as the living individual and second as the process that sublates its separateness or unity. As this process, life transforms itself into the universal that is the unity of itself and its other. In other words, it is in the third place the genus or kind (*Gattung*) that attempts to preserve itself by individuating itself; the kind manifests itself and persists despite its dispersion in reproduction or the life and death of the individual members of the kind.

The dialectic of life is very similar in structure to that of chemism. We move from the living individual via the process to the genus or family kind. In sum, the individual is taken outside of itself by the processes of life and related to other individuals of its kind. Most dramatically, it is engaged in sexual reproduction, an act that may be said to exhibit in life the unification of the subject and the object. The child is the mediation and sublation of its parents. The individual achieves an immortality in this process of sublation by way of the persisting genus (cf. Plato's *Symposium*). At the same time, since the genus is manifest in each individual, the latter serves as the particular who, in his or her role as parent, mediates the individual child and the universal (417–29).

I call attention to the fact that in subsection B of chapter 1, on the life process, Hegel in effect repeats his analysis of desire and the struggle for recognition that serves in the *PS* to account for the origin of self-consciousness and individual personality. In this strand of the dialectic, the notion of the assimilation of the external object takes the place of sexual reproduction. In the course of this analysis, Hegel notes that the mechanism and chemism of the external world are as it were internalized or rendered rational through the purposiveness of living desire (424–26). Sexual reproduction is the completion of desire in that it takes the individual living thing outside itself and raises it to the level of the activity of the genus. Otherwise stated, the genus is reflected into itself (i.e., via the interaction of two living things, each of which is an instance of the genus) and obtains actuality. The immediacy of life (as undifferentiated unity or what I called ambient medium) is actualized in the particularity of the newborn child (428).

"In the act of procreation, the immediacy of the living individuality perishes; the death of this life is the emergence of spirit. The idea, which is in itself as genus, is now for itself insofar as it has sublated the particularity that constitutes the living species and has thereby given to itself a reality that is itself simple universality" (429). Restated: we acquire self-consciousness in animal desire; but the peak of this desire is the symbolic extinction of our independence in the act of continuing the species (Hegel regularly uses *Gattung*, literally, "genus") by the child who both continues and replaces, or in other words sublates, the parents. The child is thus the universal expression of the idea of life, but it is a universal that has particularized an individual living thing. "Thus it is the idea that relates itself to itself, the universal that has universality as its determination and existence." The child is the existence of the idea of life; it is the universality of life as represented by the fulfillment of the activity of procreation. But this universality is also a particular, which is to say that the particularity of the child contains all of the existential processes we have just studied within its own individuality, as its own determinations. As a result, the child *qua* particular possesses universality as a particular determination.

But Hegel goes one step further: the idea that relates itself to itself is the idea of knowing (or cognition). Hegel's analysis of desire, assimilation, and procreation is, I think, not difficult to understand and in fact constitutes one of the most accessible and initially plausible aspects of his philosophy. Not so easy to see is how the child expresses the shift from life to knowing. Hegel's response seems to be that the child represents the completion of the genus in actual existence as the synthesis of the individual parents. As such a reality (i.e., living being) it has given to itself simple universality; the relation of the idea of life as manifested in the father is related to itself as manifested in the mother through the unity of the child. In straightforward language, the genus comes to life; it is a universal with a determination of universality, namely, the idea of life as itself alive. I take Hegel to mean that the living process is aware of itself as that process through its manifestation as offspring. So *Gattung* is not at all the dead "genus" of traditional logic or ontology; it is a kind of self-conscious *noēsis tēs noēseōs*.

Book 3, Section 3, Chapter 2: The Idea of Knowing

The German word *erkennen* can be translated in various ways, including "to recognize" and "to discern" as well as "to know." In the discussion to this point, the word has certainly been employed in the sense of awareness rather than epistemic knowing. But awareness or discernment develops into the various stages of cognition and eventually into the absolute idea. We are about to follow this development.

In conventional logic, the genus is the essence; for example, in the assertion "man is a rational animal," "man" is the species and "rational animal" is the genus or essence of its species. For Hegel, the essence of man is the soul, of which rationality is a faculty; and by "soul" Hegel means the living spirit, not an abstract concept. One could almost say that there is something of the Heideggerian "bewaying" or sense of *Wēsen* (in Heidegger's antiquarian spelling) as a process in Hegel's logic, which makes no separation between being and thinking, and so between conceptuality and life. In this vein, the soul is the concept or *Begriff* in the sense of *Greifen* or grasping of the identity between being and thinking (and so of their difference). The soul is a modification of the idea. The idea must first be grasped as "grasping" or as the concept that results from this grasping; but the life of the process of grasping is intrinsic to what is grasped. There is no separation of the concept as an abstract form and the conceptual act itself. In understanding this, we are led to the life of the concept, and from there to the soul as the agent of cognition.

When Hegel says that the object (*Gegenstand*) of the concept is the concept itself (429), he is referring to the thinking of the process of life by a living being, but it is the thinking upon which we are to place the emphasis, and not at all upon empirical living or existence. The same is true of Hegel's discussion of procreation, which obviously takes place via living individuals but which is analyzed by Hegel as a symbolic manifestation of the living concept. The concept is concerned with itself, but it itself is the subjective component of an object. There is accordingly a distinction between the subjective concept that is its own reality and the objective concept that is life. Thinking, spirit, and self-consciousness belong to the subjective concept on this point; that is, they are determinations of the idea that have themselves as their object (430).

One may therefore say that Hegel explains empirical existence by way of the concept rather than vice versa. And, indeed, he often complains about those who criticize the concept because empirical reality falls short of it. Traditional metaphysics, on the other hand, as Hegel understands it, begins its study of spirit or soul with the determinations of empirical or subjective consciousness (430). This procedure is entirely inadequate to the richness of spirit, a richness much greater than that of nature. The essence of spirit "consists in the absolute unity of oppositions in the concept, and so it exhibits in its appearance and relation to externality contradiction in its highest determinateness." Hegel illustrates his criticism of traditional metaphysics of the soul by way of Hume and Kant. Hume starts from the empirical representations or appearances of consciousness and is unable to find the continuity of the self in their discontinuity. He has no dialectical logic and so no conception of negative unity. Kant locates this unity in the empty "I think" that accompanies each appearance. He therefore denies, exactly like Hume, that the unity of self-consciousness is accessible within our experience. As the mere form of thinking, self-consciousness has no objectivity (no distinguishing predicates, and so no existence). Hence it is known only via its empirical thoughts that serve as its predicates; not inner predicates, I emphasize, but surrogate predicates of a phantom or unknowable unity. In other words, it is conceived as the subject of judgment, but as one that, even though it both accompanies and synthesizes the object, is itself always beyond the objects and never accessible through the very thoughts that are its predicates (430–35).

To come back now to the main line of the analysis, Hegel has derived the idea of spirit, which in its primary or immediate form is soul, from the idea, but not from the empirical manifestation, of life (435). Experience must conform to the idea, not vice versa. The universal or generic life is the "interior" of the actually existing living being. Truth consists in the exhibition of the identity of individual lives in the genus, and this is spirit. The concrete forms of spirit are studied elsewhere, in particular, in the *PS*. Hegel proceeds to criticize the usual treatment of soul, one of the concrete forms of spirit, in traditional philosophy, where soul appears as a thing (*Ding*) among other things and, as such, subject to spatiotemporal conditions (consider here Descartes's location of the soul in the pineal gland, 436).

We should notice an interesting remark about the science of the phenomenology of spirit. Consciousness is the lowest form assumed by spirit as sunk into matter. Here spirit preserves itself apart from the object but as related to it. The object both shapes or shares in the definition of consciousness and is a negativity for it; i.e., it possesses the appearance of independence from consciousness. This negative aspect of the object precludes any genuine unification with it, and identity with the object remains illusory (*ein Scheinen*, 437). "This stage is the object of the *Phenomenology of Spirit*, a science that stands between the science of the natural spirit and spirit as such." In the *PS*, spirit is studied as appearing in its object; in the *SL*, spirit is studied "as such" or in and for itself; that is, it is studied as emerging from the concept, whereas in the *PS* the concept emerges from consciousness, or more precisely, appears from consciousness, an appearance that is in one sense illusory, since the emergence is empirical or subjective, not logical.

In sum, the concept "for itself" is the idea; "in itself" it is the objective world. These two sides are brought together by *Erkennen*, recognition, awareness, or knowing. Hegel then divides his treatment of *Erkennen* into two parts corresponding to the idea of the true and that of the good. Note that there is no idea of the beautiful, which for Hegel is the appearance or shining of truth (a conception not altogether different from Plato's).

Book 3, Section 3, Chapter 2, Subsection A: The idea of the true

Hegel begins his discussion of the idea of the true by connecting it with *Trieb*, which may be translated as impulse, inclination, but also as germinating root or sprout. This semantic association is interesting, because it suggests the senses of *phusis* as well as *eros*. It is human nature to "germinate" or "sprout" via the impulse toward the object, an impulse that empiricism normally interprets in its primary sense as desire. Despite his oft-noted affiliation with Hobbes, Hegel is here closer to Fichte than to British empiricism, that is, to Fichtean *Streben*, which is not simple corporeal or physiological desire but rather the striving of the ego, the prototype of Hegel's absolute spirit, a striving to externalize itself by a positing of objects through a self-limitation that is also an actualizing of its inner possibilities. This is why Fichte says that freedom is higher than being. Freedom is *Streben* whereas being is merely its residue, and a residue that conceals it.

Impulse, as I shall call it, is the striving to overcome the split between the subject and the object; as such, it is obviously a characteristic of the subjective idea. "Impulse thus has the property [*Bestimmtheit*] of sublating its own subjectivity, to make its at first abstract reality into a concrete reality and to fulfill [or complete] itself with the content of the world that has been presupposed by its subjectivity" (439). In other words, the subject is impelled to realize itself in the object, but in the particular mode of assimilating it into the satisfaction of desire. As manifested in awareness or knowing, this is the impulse to truth. It is interesting to note that whereas Hegel also recognizes objective truth, he holds that "the more determinate sense of truth" refers to the subjective concept. This is because for Hegel, there is no sense of truth as *alētheia* or the openness of the being as *ontōs on*. Being is always conceived, always a function of the concept; hence in the last analysis even objective truth is subjective.

Hegel takes this up obliquely in a discussion of Kantianism, which, in his terms, poses a contradiction between the subject and the thing in itself, and then overcomes it. The thing in itself is the unknowable version of the Greek *ontōs on*, which latter is most fully knowable because most genuine being. Kant is in effect claiming to know, not the most knowable, but the entirely unknowable; this is the contradiction. Nevertheless, by posing the contradiction between the subject and the thing in itself, Kant overcomes it in the sense that the latter is revealed as a *Gedankending*; that is, it is not an *ontōs on* at all, but a product of thought, and, as entirely empty of truth, it is an untruth (441). This same process also shows that truth is not finite in the sense of limited to the phenomena by the unknowability of things in themselves. As we have already seen, the phenomena are the things in themselves, for to be "in itself" in the fullest sense is also to be "for itself," and it is the unity of subject and object that unites being in itself with being for itself. This is what Hegel means when he speaks of the infinity of the idea, "within which the object in itself is sublated and the end is simply to sublate it for itself."

Hegel turns next to the distinction between analytic and synthetic knowing. We normally think of analysis as a cognitive activity in which the subject (to employ Hegel's own terminology) takes apart the object in order to make explicit a hidden inner structure. Hegel's view is more complex. On the one hand the subject or subjective concept is passive toward the object or objective concept and allows it to appear, "not as determined by the subject but as it is in itself" (442). On the other hand this constitutes negative activity, namely, as distancing the object from "a subjective obstacle, an external shell." The active side of analytic thinking is thus for Hegel the analysis of the subject in order to remove it from the object; it is not the analysis of the structure of the object.

Hegel's analysis of analysis can be summarized as follows. Analysis begins from a subjective immediacy of concept and object; that is, it begins with the assumption that what is to be analyzed is already known. We may wish to uncover a deeper structure of the object under inspection, but we cannot proceed in a rational manner if we do not know the object in a preliminary way as being a particular something of such and such a nature, and so to be analyzed in such and such a manner. Analysis begins with entities of everyday experience; this is why contemporary analysts who shun intuition nevertheless regularly begin by giving us an "intuitive" view of the situation to which they are about to apply their analytical tools, and terms like "intuitive" and "counterintuitive" make clear that the most precise analyst is being guided by the givenness of everyday experience.

In short, the assumption of intuitive knowledge is itself never analyzed. To this I would myself add, how could it be, since it orients us as analysts? As soon as we begin to analyze, we have moved beyond the orientating intuition, but on its basis. In Hegel's own terminology, the object is marked initially by "abstract universality" (443) or an immediate identity of its properties. The analyst *qua* analyst does not concern himself with the prior synthesis by which these properties were "mediated" into the object. He isolates them, but thereby simply assumes their initial presence as constituting the object. In fact, however, the properties are not directly given as logical determinations; this givenness follows only from the work of the analyst. Hence the analyst poses the determinations as well as presupposing them. In my own terminology, the analyst begins with an intuition, for which he proceeds to substitute a conceptual artifact. He thus simultaneously invokes the guidance of intuition and replaces it with the artifact.

These determinations (which I have identified as the properties of an artifact) are appearances of a thing in itself, namely, of the given; for example, in ordinary language analysis, they are examples of "how we actually speak," but they are almost immediately repudiated in favor of artificial statements obtained by analysis from everyday discourse. The artificiality can also arise through the procedure of insisting that certain "ordinary" statements are canonical and that others are incorrectly formed. This contention is unintelligible if it is true that "ordinary language is all right." Why should we say that "ordinary language goes on holiday" when certain sentences are uttered that we regard as badly formed but that are immediately intelligible to speakers of ordinary language or even to those who have mastered ordinary language but sometimes communicate with extraordinary utterances? Is not the extraordinary also part of the ordinary? And is it not a reliance upon extraordinary utterances to distinguish between the ordinary and the extraordinary in a systematic manner?

Analysis results in a dualism of the initial abstract identity and a set of (analytically obtained) differences that are opposed to this unity. No account can be given of their unity within the object, because unity is not a product of analysis. Analysis does not proceed syllogistically, via a middle term that unites the two extremes of identity and difference (444). After a remark about Kant, to the effect that he fails to show the development of the I as the unity of self-consciousness into the logical determinations of the categories, Hegel proceeds to take up some examples of analytic thinking from mathematics, one of which, the nature of the so-called infinitesimal, we have already studied (444–50). I note in passing that for Hegel, arithmetic is analytical whereas geometry is synthetic.

Analysis starts with abstract identity; synthesis starts with differences (450). Analysis is the comprehension (*Auffassen*) of what is; synthesis attempts to grasp it via the unification of the manifold of its determinations. But this is also the defect of synthesis, namely, that it constructs the object from the results of analysis, or in other words relates them externally via reflection, rather than deriving the object from a dialectical interpenetration of the separate determinations. This is equivalent to saying that the object of synthesis is still external to the synthesizing subject (451).

Hegel divides synthetic knowing into definition, division, and the theorem. In general, analysis and synthesis are empirical. They begin with appearances, existence, or facticity; hence the definitions to which they attain are equally contingent (452). There are three subcases to be considered here. First are the definitions of self-conscious purposiveness, which simply express subjective intentions (453). Second, geometrical objects are determinations imposed or posited within abstract space, once again by our cognitive intentions; they are thus analogous to artifacts. Hegel means by this not that we literally invent the form of the circle, the triangle, and so on, but that we can inscribe these in abstract space in accord with the problem we are attempting to solve. This way of looking at geometry goes back at least to Descartes, for whom essences can be replaced by geometrical constructions (themselves equivalent to algebraic equations) that are representations of physical ratios; whatever things may be in themselves, the constructed representations allow us to calculate solutions to concrete problems in the world of experience. Think here of the tangent to a circle and the approaching secant, which allows us to calculate instantaneous velocity. The graph of velocity is a human artifact. Its significance is what we intend it to be, or as Hegel puts it, *was sie sein sollen* (453).

Third is the case of the definition of concrete objects of nature and spirit (454). Here the problem is determining which of the many properties of an object belong to its genus and which to the species, as well as which of the latter is the specific difference. Hegel notes that for this, "there is no other criterion as yet at hand than existence [*Dasein*] itself." This statement is very much in the spirit of contemporary analytical philosophy, which cannot, however, move beyond existence except to go in the direction of arbitrary definitions or artifacts. In the remainder of subsection A, Hegel reiterates the point that definitions of concrete existing things or spiritual states are empirical, hence arbitrary; that is, they issue in the construction of arbitrary objects, which might very well have been defined in quite another manner (455–58). Again I call attention to the topicality of this point, except that for Hegel it is a mark of the inadequacy of the methods of analytical and synthetic knowledge as they are practiced by empiricists. As we can put it, the empiricists are correct in their assertion that those who speak of the intuition of essences cannot tell us what they mean; on the other hand, the champions of essence are correct in observing that empiricism leads inevitably to nominalism, subjectivism, perspectivism, and, finally, chaos. This in itself does not prove that Hegelian dialectic is sound, but it provides the motivation for studying that dialectic as a resolution of the fundamental philosophical problem of silence versus infinite chatter.

These criticisms lead into a criticism of division, which we may also understand to apply to Platonic diaeresis. The divisions of diaeresis are defined in advance by the intentions of the interlocutor; each step depends upon antecedent knowledge of the direction in which one wishes to move. In the case of empirical science, this arbitrariness of the beginning point is radicalized by the generation of an infinite regress. The schemata of classification are not only arbitrary but endless (461). Every result of division leads to another configuration of properties. "For the particular that emerges from division, there is present no genuine ground . . . that connects the segments of the disjunction to one another." Division is possible in accord with a variety of principles because "physical nature is arbitrary and offers us from itself such a contingency in the principles of division" (463). Hegel is undoubtedly thinking of the various classifications of natural species in biology at this point. The main point throughout is that "the externality in which the concept is eminently in nature, contains the total indifference of the difference [*die gänzliche Gleichgültigkeit des Unterschiedes*]; a frequent determination for division is taken from number."

Let us summarize Hegel's argument to this point as follows. If nature is defined as extension or externality, as it in fact is by modern rationalism, then there is no possibility of avoiding an endless proliferation of results and viewpoints. We must have recourse to either apriorism or finalism. Apriorism amounts to the arbitrary assertion of a principle or method as the foundation of legitimate scientific inquiry; finalism seeks guidance from some ideal end. But finalism is just another form of apriorism; in other words, either materialism is totally incoherent or it is a rhetorically masked dualism. Contemporary debates in the philosophy of science reflect Hegel's point very well. Empiricist attempts to rescue realism from the today fashionable linguistic or physiological subjectivisms are unsuccessful and have recourse to important elements of the doctrines they are ostensibly rejecting. Or else the realist must give up the attempt to ground scientific inquiry and retreat to common sense and ordinary experience, which is unfortunately not sustained but dissolved by scientific inquiry itself.

In the final subsection of chapter 1, Hegel takes up the scientific theorem (*Lehrsatz*). According to him, the shift from division to the theorem corresponds to that from the particular to the individual (464). Hegel means by this that the definition covers a number of hypothetical or possible instances, whereas the theorem refers to knowledge of the real or existing object. The theorem demonstrates the structure of the individual object before our very eyes, whereas the definition contains the individuals within the particularity of the general concept. There is in fact no sharp distinction between definitions and theorems, according to Hegel, other than that theorems must demonstrate what is asserted with subjective immediacy in the definition (465).

Hegel's main example of theorem reasoning is geometry. This is obviously because in geometric construction, the proof of the theorem also shows the individual object. The triangle is both particular (an object of a certain kind) and individual; it is this triangle in the construction (469). One might, however, say that constructive proofs of geometrical theorems are too perspicuous, too persuasive. It looks as if the process of constructing the proof, thereby laying out as well as showing the unity of the properties of the object, follows automatically from the theorem itself, in accordance with the rules of geometry. Hegel means by this that we forget the working of spirit within the geometrical machinery because we are hypnotized by the power of the formalism, exactly as happens in mathematical logic. For example, we forget the subjective character of the axioms or overlook presuppositions that are discovered by later mathematicians (466). Hegel regards axioms in general, not as "absolute firsts" or tautologies, but as theorems proven by other sciences, and in particular by logic. The ground of logical axioms is then the concept; in other words, a genuine demonstration of geometrical or any other scientific axioms would have to derive them dialectically from the categorial determinations of the concept. Otherwise there would be an illicit circularity in which one science takes in the other's washing, so to speak.

As usual, Hegel objects to the mechanistic character of abstract demonstration, whether it is called analysis or synthesis. Distinctions are arbitrary and external, but so too are proofs of the concatenation of structure, which depend, as we have just seen, upon a variety of presuppositions such as axioms, definitions, rules, and so on, all of which either require demonstration or remain in the last analysis arbitrary starting points that could have been otherwise, depending upon the intention of the investigator. And this is essential for Hegel, as we saw in the chapter on teleology. Science is an activity, not a method; the significance of the activity rests upon human intentions (470–71). More precisely, the analysis and synthesis of the structure of natural objects is grounded not only in human intentions but in the dialectical development of the determinations of the object from its own interior. Objects are not "objective" constructions by a craftsman-nature who labors independently of our attempts to follow his procedures and understand his products. But we must be very clear about the central point: Hegel is objecting not to modern science but to modern philosophy of science. It is not the geometrician who is required to derive his axioms and definitions from the concept of Hegel's logic but the philosopher-logician.

There follows a discussion of the limitations of geometrical science, and more generally of the difference between finite and infinite sciences, in which Hegel repeats themes that we have now studied. Geometry is rooted in the abstract intuition (*Anschauung*) of sensuousness as externalization. But sensuousness is the pure absence of conceptuality: "No science can arise through sensuousness [*das Anschauen*] but only through thinking" (472). Geometry approaches a higher degree of scientificity only through an abstraction from sensuous intuition in the usual sense; at the same time, it is the homogeneous nature of abstract space that permits the geometrician to inscribe his figures into its indeterminateness in such a way that the properties of the figures themselves are free of dialectical motion. In other words, the stability of finite geometrical constructions is due to the artificial abstractness of geometrical space. In this sense, geometry, like all finite sciences, is an artifact of the process of abstraction. It is dialectical logic that is truly concrete, because it studies the conceptual interactions of geometrical determinations as they actually arise from the effort to think, i.e., to understand them, and not simply to construct them.

Thanks to its ungrounded orientation in sensuous intuition, and so with respect to finite determinations, the empirical sciences proceed step by unmediated step into the bad infinity of endless distinctions. Hegel takes up the example of physics, which begins from notions like force that are derived by analysis of everyday experience; these could be justified only as results, i.e., of a science with nonempirical foundations. Instead, they are themselves made the foundation for the subsequent investigation of experience (473). Little wonder, Hegel would no doubt remark if he were alive today, that the definition of matter or extension has changed periodically in the physical sciences; stability seems to arise by a decision based only upon the convenience of the physicist rather than on a clear and stable grasp of the foundations. In sum: there is no unity or wholeness in analytical and synthetic thinking, nor could there be, because the concept is not immanent in its purely external taking apart and putting together of empirical or contingent determinations (476–77).

Book 3, Section 3, Chapter 2, Subsection B: The idea of the good

Hegel's insistence upon the need to ground science in the concept, and so in subjectivity or the idea of spirit, led us previously to intentions or purposiveness; we should therefore not be surprised that the criticism of empirical science as limited by both apriorism and contingency leads him from the idea of the true to the idea of the good. In a striking expression, Hegel concludes the previous subsection as follows: "The idea, now that the concept is *for itself* the determined [concept] *in and for itself*, is the practical idea, activity [*das Handeln*]" (477). We thus see the sense in which Hegel follows Kant and Fichte in subordinating pure theory to practice. It would be going too far to say that practice is higher for Hegel than theory. The correct formulation is that theory is unified with practice in the form of activity. This activity is the production of form or truth in accord with an end, an end that corresponds to the idea of the good.

The subjective concept, as manifested in the individual human being, "is the impulse to realize itself, the intention [literally, 'end'] of giving itself objectivity and to complete itself in the external world through itself." Again, as throughout this subsection, we recognize the anthropology of the *PS*, but here expressed as a development of the concept. Thus far, the activity of the subject provides only a subjective certitude, precisely because the objective world seems to exist only as a project or posit of its own desires (478). Nevertheless, the impulse to enact one's individuality in the external world is called by Hegel the good: "It appears with the dignity [i.e., 'worthiness': *Würde*] of being absolute because it is in itself the totality of the concept and at the same time the objective in the form of free unity and subjectivity" (478). Again it is clear that Hegel is not a Hobbesian but rather that he synthesizes Hobbes and Aristotelian teleology in his anthropology. *Trieb* is not simple and hence intrinsically neutral desire; it is the dignity or worthiness of Platonic *eros* as directed to the end of overcoming the separation of the ideas from the objects of experience (480).

Hegel describes the process of the identification of theory and practice through activity as a syllogism, of which the middle term is the good end, and through which the subject attains (i.e., is mediated with) the external object. At first the end must be actualized in the sphere of external existence, but then it must be internalized or reunited with the idea of totality; finite ends, so long as they remain dispersed in external existence, are contradictory. The idea of the completed good accordingly remains as a *Sollen* or subjective postulate, and the result is a dualism of ideal subjectivity and actual but self-contradictory objectivity (479–80). "This deficiency can also be thought as follows, that the practical idea still lacks the moment of the theoretical." Otherwise stated, there must be an integration of the good and the true, and this takes the form of a syllogism, as noted a moment ago (481).

The first premise expresses the immediate relation of the good end to actuality (i.e., the objective domain in which the end is to be achieved). In the second premise the end is itself externalized through action in the external world. This is a first negation or canceling of the interiority of the concept. The last step or conclusion of the syllogism is the negation of this negation, that is, the reincorporation of the externalized good in its objective form into the subjective concept, which thus becomes absolute (482–83).

Book 3, Section 3, Chapter 3: The Absolute Idea

The absolute idea is the identity within difference of the theoretical and the practical idea, i.e., of truth and goodness. I want to repeat here a point made previously. There is no unity of theory and practice in any simple sense of "unity," nor is there a simple primacy of the practical. Theory is transformed into an activity, which, in order to be fulfilled, must overcome the split between subject and object. In the process of overcoming, one sees the enactment of two central theses of modernity: the mastery of nature and the equation of knowing with making. But these theses are given a peculiarly Hegelian inflection. Nature is mastered through conceptual thinking, and whereas it is true that we know only what we make, making is the formation process that is common to subject and object. Both are made in the same way by the activity of the absolute idea. Furthermore, once the dualism of subject and object has been overcome, dialectic or formation process, and so too any vestige of the primacy of the practical, is sublated into speculation or the pure contemplation that Aristotle calls *noēseōs*. There can be no doubt of the importance of impulse and practical activity for Hegel, but the last and deepest significance of activity is that it is for the sake of contemplation. That is, thanks to our mastery of the Hegelian *logos*, we can think the thoughts of God as he becomes manifest in and as the world.

This last chapter of the *SL* is not divided into subsections because of the aforementioned termination of dialectic. There is no more overcoming or ascent to a higher because more comprehensive level. Our task is now to see the whole. There are nevertheless different aspects to the whole (484). Nature and spirit are different ways (*Weisen*) of presenting its existence (*Dasein*); art and religion are its ways of grasping itself and giving itself an appropriate existence. "Philosophy has the same content and the same end as art and religion, but it is the highest way of grasping the absolute idea because its way is the highest, namely, the concept." Here we see the nonclassical or Christian side of Hegel's grand synthesis. Natural science does not deal with the same content or have the same end as philosophy, because it works with the modern conception of nature as extension or externality, which is separate from and opposed to spirit. In the Greek or at least Socratic philosophical school, which is of paramount importance for Hegel, *phusis* is alive and contains its own goodness or perfection. It is divine. For Hegel, nature is the external dimension of the divine creation; in itself, it lacks all dignity and value. On more than one occasion Hegel says that the humblest thought of the humblest human being contains more worth than all of physical nature. This is because any thought, however humble, is infused with spirit, whereas nature acquires spirit only through being assimilated by the labor of conceptualization.

Whereas logic is in one sense a particular science, in another it is the way of all ways, just as the logical idea is the idea of the whole. "The absolute idea alone is being, perpetual life, *self-knowing truth*, and it is *all truth*." In other words, it is God (it contains *Persönlichkeit*). As such, it contains "every determination" and "its nature is to return into itself." Hegel is not a process theologian. There is no open future with respect to essential truth. This is why the subject finds itself "at home" in thinking the object; there is no alienation or *Jenseits*, no gap between the sage and the impulse to wisdom. Once we see that the world is permeated with spirit, and so that we ourselves, as spirit, permeate or appropriate the world by thinking it, we have thought the whole. What remains to be thought is not content but method, namely, the universality of the form of thinking itself, not a set of epistemological rules (485).

I repeat this crucial point. Method is not epistemological in the Cartesian sense. We do not construct or discover it in advance of thinking and then govern subsequent thoughts by its rules. Method is "the excitation of the concept itself" (486). Since the concept is not empty but contains the object, this excitation is of the object as well. Method is "the highest force, or rather the only and absolute force of reason, and not only this, but also its highest and only impulse to find and to know itself in everything through itself" (486–87).

Hegel turns next to the question of the beginning of the logic. He does so at both the beginning and the end of the SL in order to make explicit that logic is circular and so necessarily complete. The end is transformed into the beginning and so can repeat but not go beyond itself. Logic begins with the immediacy of thinking, which can also be called "a supersensuous inner intuition" (488). In contrast to Kantian intuition of the spatiotemporal continuum, logical intuition is of the continuum of becoming. Accordingly, it makes no difference where or with what concrete determination we begin; the process of stripping the empirical beginning of all presuppositions leads us back in all cases to the same simple universality. In other words, we arrive at a supersensuous intuition of abstract being. In book 1, Hegel tried to show how the logical categories of being and nothing combine to produce becoming, which in turn differentiates itself via these preliminary positive and negative qualitative determinations into something and another; to be is also not to be, and this circular or eternal dialectic of "to be" and "not to be" is the structure of the moments of becoming. In the present chapter, Hegel speaks of the simple universal as containing within itself what is defective, but also as the impulse to carry itself forward, i.e., to develop content (489). The difference between these two formulations arises from the fact that we are now studying the subjective side of the concept, whereas in book 1 we began with the protostructure of objectivity. Deficiency corresponds to nothing; impulse is the inner activity or negative labor of nothing.

In other words, the abstract immediate is already dialectical and so internally complex. "Only in its completeness is it the absolute" (490). It comes as no surprise to us when Hegel goes on to say that "this moment of the judgment, which is as much synthetic as analytic, through which the original universal defines itself from out of itself as the other to itself, is to be named dialectical" (491). Recall here that the German word for "judgment" is *Urteil*, "original division." The absolute is the concept that divides itself into its subjective and objective sides. In the next several pages, Hegel gives us a condensed historical pedigree of dialectic, the logic of becoming that is, or becomes, reason (492ff.). The central point is as follows. In thinking through the dialectic of objects, as in the ontological dialectic of Plato and the Eleatics, we arrive at the discovery that objective determinations are in fact subjective determinations (Kant). But Plato is alienated from the subject and Kant from the object. These two must be reunited in their fully developed articulation.

The movement of dialectic is by way of negations (494ff.). We saw this in the beginning: The universal negates itself or "goes over" into its other, the particular; particulars negate one another through the opposition of their predicates. But these negations are themselves negated or overcome by the negative movement of reciprocal implication or transformation (494). And what is the weightiest aspect of rational knowing is this: "to retain the positive in its negative, in the content of its presupposition, in its result" (495). In other words, it is a mere prejudice to see dialectic as purely negative; quite to the contrary, the negative is in the service of explicating the structure of the positive. To speak of an identity within difference as the fundamental structure of anything whatsoever, and so too of totality, is to place emphasis upon the visible structure or form, not upon absence or annihilation. But one could not call Hegel a representative of the metaphysics of presence, because this fails to do justice to his doctrine of the role played by the negative within presence itself.

Otherwise stated, negativity is "the dialectical soul" (496). Stated with excessive simplicity, what produces continuously cannot itself be a determinate form; even the expression "identity within difference" points us in the direction of a ratio or structure, that is, of the positive aspect of form rather than toward its negative interior. This interior is the conceptual (as opposed to the physical) force that pulls the moments of identity and difference together even as it holds them apart. I believe it remains true that whereas we are subjected to the ceaseless labor of negativity, we cannot see it as such, because whatever we see is already a product, i.e., a positive determination, of negativity. This negative work is what Hegel means when he speaks of negativity as the soul of dialectic. In a deep sense, then, the soul is "invisible" in Hegel, just as it is for traditional rationalism, except (and it is a decisive exception) for the fact that the soul externalizes in the products of its labor. One could therefore say that it is visible as the "mediating" or "middle" term (497), or as I would paraphrase this, as the fact that the object is accessible to the subject, despite the empirical difference and separation of their natures.

Hegel goes on to relate the doctrine of negative spiritual excitation to the form of the syllogism. This excitation occurs within the copula in the judgment that "S is p," which includes the assertion that "S is not p." As a predicate, p is not simply identical with S. But it is partially identical with it because it belongs to or is ingredient within the essential structure of S. So S both is and is not p, exactly as Hegel says, and in conformity with the distinction between identity and predication. The question is whether Hegel is right to call this a contradiction. The simplest way in which to vindicate, or at least to understand, Hegel is as follows. The identity of S depends upon its essential predicates. Hence the difference between identity and predication collapses into an identity. But what is for Hegel the more important point is that the subject is distinguished from its predicate precisely by the statement that connects the two in the relation of owner and owned. And this separation must be overcome dialectically, in order to overcome the dualism between essence and accidents. Man is mortal, but no man is simply the same as mortality. However, in order to understand what man is, we must understand whether or not mortality belongs to his essence. The separation of man and mortality that is intrinsic to predication precisely as distinguished from identity is the opposition or contradiction between subject and predicate that must be overcome in the fully developed concept of man.

Stated schematically, p is other than S and so engages in its own development. But this development turns out to be part of the development of S itself. P is thus reconciled with S, and this reconciliation is a reinstitution of immediacy that can be called a third term. But it could also be called a fourth term. When the split between two terms is overcome, the initial immediacy is restored (the predicate is reunited with the subject). This restoration is the second immediacy, but in the context of the method of dialectic, it is the third term, since the first two terms were the initial immediate and its (contradicting) mediation. Hegel then adds, somewhat confusingly, that since the first negative is already the second term (non-A is second to A), the third term can count as the fourth. Simply stated:

1. the subject is the predicate;
2. the subject is not the predicate;
3. what is not the predicate is not the nonsubject;
4. by substitution, the subject is the subject.

I don't find this of any great interest; and in fact, Hegel's point is only that it makes no difference whether we find three or four elements in each application of dialectic (497–98).

In our consideration of method, to come back to the heart of the matter, we moved from a discussion of immediacy to one of negativity. The dialectico-negative development of immediacy returns us to immediacy, but here to a mediated immediacy; the universal to which we have returned is now particularized as the absolute idea (in the final stage of dialectic). As we have already seen, there is no further sublation or negation because we have now arrived at the totality of truth (498–99), but this truth is not static. Truth is not "a still third, but even as this unity it is an excitation and an activity that mediates itself with itself" (499). In simple terms, the whole contains everything, including all negations. As complete, it negates these negations and is universality or identity. But negations are preserved within positivity; the universal is mediated. And this is to say that it is excited by the very negativities that it has preserved, the negativities that articulate its inner structure as mediated universal. This excitation is the process by which each part is turning into the whole, which in turn is reflected in its parts (something like active Leibnizian monads, except that here we have just one comprehensive monad).

In human terms, if the sage thinks the whole, he must do it one step at a time. But he is able to proceed because each step turns into its opposite, and so by sublation into something higher or more comprehensive, until no more stages are left. But there is no single speech that the sage can deliver that captures the wholeness of the whole. No one can say everything at once. So the last step, although it is a kind of summation or general formula of the whole, does not really express each and all of the determinations that make up the wholeness of the whole. In attempting to understand that last, comprehensive sublating step, the sage finds that he must begin all over again; the only satisfactory explanation of the last speech is the whole series of speeches that led us to the last. Hence dialectic culminates in speculation, but speculation regenerates dialectic. Dialectico-speculative logic is thus circular (500–503).

"By virtue of the exhibited nature of the method, science shows itself as a circle that turns back into itself" (504). And each particular member of this circle is itself a circle, since regardless of where we start, we always return to the beginning. In other words, the structure of anything whatsoever is the same as that of anything else, but beyond this, of the whole. So speculation is the contemplation of the dialectical nature of totality, or the continuous rethinking of what has already been accomplished; and this is "absolute liberation" (505).

Hegel ends the *SL* with a brief indication of the next science, i.e., the science of the emergence of the idea from the subjectivity of the concept. This proves difficult, since there are no more dialectical transitions available to Hegel. He therefore claims that "the idea freely discharges itself in its absolute freedom and tranquility" as external idea. This points us toward the *Realphilosophie*. In other words, we have thought the logical or categorial structure of the world. It now remains for us who are at one with God to create the world.

NOTES

INTRODUCTION

1. Dieter Henrich, *Hegel im Kontext* (Suhrkamp Verlag, Frankfurt am Main: 1967), p. 7.
2. G. W. F. Hegel, *Phänomenologie des Geistes* (Felix Meiner Verlag, Hamburg: 1988), p. 21.
3. See Pascal Engel, *The Norm of Truth* (University of Toronto Press, Toronto: 1991), p. 32, for a brief discussion of Quine-Duhem.
4. It is now fashionable for Hegel scholars to deny that he referred to a divine spirit, and so to maintain that by such terms as the "life" of spirit, Hegel refers to the motion of conceptual thinking, whereas "spirit" refers to intersubjectivity in the sense of the dominant views of a historical period. Perhaps one could call it a form of neo-Kantianism, but it is not Hegel. I will discuss this, together with the question of whether Hegel is a Christian thinker, in the appropriate place. Suffice it to say here that if he is a neo-Kantian, then he falls back into the very dualism that he condemns so rigorously.
5. To avoid misunderstanding, I note that whereas Hegel frequently speaks of the moments of the concept as "categories," he is using the term not in an Aristotelian or Kantian sense as a class of individual entities but rather as a determination of the structure of totality.
6. See Terry Pinkard, *Hegel's Dialectic: The Explanation of Possibility* (Temple University Press, Philadelphia: 1988), p. 4 et passim. Pinkard speaks of Hegel's "explanation of possibility" and I can see why. But it would be better to speak of an exhibition of actuality as the basis for the explanation of possibility.
7. The expression "identity within difference" is a slight abbreviation of one of Hegel's most important technical terms: the identity of identity and nonidentity. This expression is closely related to another Hegelian term, *Aufhebung*, which is translated in a variety of ways. An *Aufhebung* is a lifting up of two contradictory terms to a higher or broader level, at which these terms are preserved or recuperated from their antecedent reciprocal cancellation. "The identity of identity and nonidentity" refers to the inner structure of an *Aufhebung* and, more broadly, to the inner dialectical relation between a term or moment of the concept and its complement. The former expression is thus broader in its reference than *Aufhebung*.

CHAPTER ONE

1. Stanley Rosen, *G. W. F. Hegel: An Introduction to the Science of Wisdom* (Yale University Press, New Haven: 1974).

2. G. W. F. Hegel, *Einleitung in die Geschichte der Philosophie* (Felix Meiner Verlag, Hamburg: 1959), p. 34.

3. For a good study of the connection between the fulfillment of wisdom and the Christian religion, see Peter Cornehl, *Die Zukunft der Versöhnung* (Vandenhoeck & Ruprecht, Göttingen: 1971), e.g., pp. 17–18, 141. In the atheistic version of this interpretation, "salvation" takes the form of satisfaction, which is furnished theoretically by the possession of wisdom and practically by the political (or in the Marxist version, postpolitical) expression of that wisdom. See Alexandre Kojève, *Introduction à la lecture de Hegel* (Gallimard, Paris: 1947), and Reinhart Klemens Maurer, *Hegel und das Ende der Geschichte* (W. Kohlhamer Verlag, Stuttgart: 1965).

4. See Pinkard, *Hegel's Dialectic*, pp. 14, 141–49, and Stephen Bungay, *Beauty and Truth* (Oxford University Press, Oxford: 1987), pp. 27–29.

5. G. W. F. Hegel, *Die Philosophie Platons* (Verlauf Freies Geistesleben, Stuttgart: 1962), p. 18.

6. Immanuel Kant, *Critique of Pure Reason*, trans. Paul Guyer and Allen Wood (Cambridge University Press: 1998). Unless otherwise stated, all quotations of the First Critique are from this edition.

7. Ibid., B455–495.

8. Bertrand Russell, *Our Knowledge of the External World* (Routledge, London: 1993), p. 48, note 1.

9. See G. W. F. Hegel, *Verhältnis des Skepticismus zur Philosophie*, in *Jenaer Kritische Schriften (II)* (Felix Meiner Verlag, Hamburg: 1983), pp. 34–89.

10. For a more detailed treatment of Hegel's development, I recommend Dieter Henrich, *Hegel im Kontext* (Suhrkamp Verlag, Frankfurt am Main: 1967); Manfred Baum, *Die Entstehung der Hegelschen Dialektik* (Bouvier, Bonn: 1986); and a very thorough older Italian study, *Le origini della logica hegeliana* (Feltrinelli, Milan: 1961), by Nicolao Merker, whose Marxism, so far as I can tell, does not interfere with his scholarly merits. Despite its own Stalinist resonances and the extreme nature of its thesis (the young Hegel as an economist), Georg Lukács's *The Young Hegel* (MIT Press, Cambridge: 1966) is unusually interesting. See also Henry Harris's two volumes on Hegel's development: *Toward the Sunlight: 1770–1801* and *Night Thoughts: 1801–1806*, both published by Oxford in 1972 and 1983 respectively. Those who are especially interested in Hegel's early thought should read *Early Theological Writings*, trans. T. M. Knox (University of Pennsylvania Press, Philadelphia: 1948).

11. Walter Jaeschke, *Reason in Religion* (University of California Press, Berkeley: 1990), p. 300.

CHAPTER TWO

1. G. W. F. Hegel, *Phänomenologie des Geistes* (Felix Meiner Verlag, Hamburg: 1988), p. 13.

2. I put "final" in quotation marks to indicate the ambiguous nature of Hegel's expressions concerning the historical future. The end of history seems to be required by the isomorphism of eternity and temporality, or theory and practice. If history is open, then the *SL* cannot contain a complete account of the concept, and Hegel's thought ceases to be a scientific system in his sense of the expression.

3. The page reference is to the 1986 publication of the 1832 revised edition of book 1 of the *SL, Wissenschaft der Logik. Die Lehre vom Sein* (1832), ed. H. Gawoll (Felix Meiner Verlag, Hamburg: 1990).
4. All italics are Hegel's unless otherwise indicated.
5. Fairness requires me to balance the Hegelian criticism of postmodernism in the text with the suggestion that the verbal fecundity of postmodernism, with the accompanying dissolution of analytical philosophy, may well be a sign of a forthcoming return to what Hegel would have regarded as a more serious version of philosophy.
6. G. W. F. Hegel, *Grundlinien der Philosophie des Rechts*, ed. J. Hoffmeister (Felix Meiner Verlag, Hamburg: 1955), pp. 14-15. Nothing is actual but the idea, which is synonymous with the rational.
7. The same point was made with respect to the communist revolution by Georg Lukács, prior to his recantation and submission to vulgar Marxist determinism.
8. All translations are mine unless otherwise indicated.
9. Terry Pinkard is simply mistaken in holding that Hegel can be understood as attributing motion to thinking rather than to the concept: "The movement of concepts on the *Science of Logic* may be taken as a metaphor for their logical relations. What moves in the *Science of Logic* are not the conceptions but thought itself." *Hegel's Dialectic* , p. 14. Pinkard takes this stand because he believes that it makes possible a reading of Hegel that is more congenial to contemporary philosophers. Perhaps so; but the reading is not Hegelian.
10. David Lachterman, "Hegel and the Formalization of Logic," *Graduate Faculty Philosophy Journal* (New School for Social Research) 12, no. 1/2 (1987): 153-236.
11. *Phaedrus* 265d3ff.
12. Thomas Hobbes, *Leviathan* (Clarendon Press, Oxford: 1947), p. 11.
13. F. W. J. Schelling, *Vom Ich als Princip der Philosophie*, in *Ausgewählte Werke: Schriften von 1794-98* (Wissenschaftliche Buchgesellschaft, Darmstadt: 1967), pp. 43-46.
14. See Plato, *Symposium* 187B.

CHAPTER THREE
1. G. W. F. Hegel, *Phänomenologie des Geistes*, ed. J. Hoffmeister (PhB Verlag Felix Meiner, Hamburg: 1948), p. 30.
2. See the excellent study *History and Modernity in the Thought of Thomas Hobbes* by Robert P. Kraynak (Cornell University Press, Ithaca: 1990), p. 101: "The revolutionary aim of enlightenment science . . . is to build a theory of knowledge *without beginning from opinion.*"
3. Compare Socrates's description of dialectic in contrast to mathematics in the *Republic*.
4. *De anima* III. 429a27-29.
5. For further discussion, compare remark 2 to the first chapter on quantity (198) and *Glauben und Wissen*, pp. 31-32.
6. Stanley Rosen, *G. W. F. Hegel: An Introduction to the Science of Wisdom* (Yale University Press. New Haven: 1974), pp. 123-50.
7. H. F. Fulda, *Das Problem einer Einleitung in Hegels Wissenschaft der Logik* (V. Klostermann, Frankfurt-am-Main: 1965), p. 29.
8. Ibid., p. 12; italics mine.
9. Ibid., p. 52.

10. Ibid., pp. 104–5.
11. Ibid., pp. 110ff.

CHAPTER FOUR

1. *Metaphysics Lambda* 1074b29ff.
2. It is characteristic of extreme left Hegelianism to interpret Hegel as a lightly concealed atheist who was accommodating his true views to the doctrines of his largely Lutheran audience. I find no evidence for this reading in the *SL*. But one could certainly call Hegel an unorthodox Christian for whom God is the absolute, and therefore the *Aufhebung* of the separation of God from his creation (and so of God from humankind), as exhibited in Jesus Christ.

CHAPTER FIVE

1. Martin Heidegger, *Gesamtausgabe*, vol. 24: *Die Grundprobleme der Phänomenologie* (Vittorio Klostermann, Frankfurt am Main: 1975), p. 55.
2. Strictly speaking, dialectic does not begin until becoming overcomes, and thus emerges from, the excitation of being and nothing, which do not themselves emerge from anything but are primary and presuppositionless.
3. Immanuel Kant, *Kritik der reinen Vernunft* B626.
4. Ibid., B627.
5. See note 3 above.

CHAPTER SIX

1. Ernst Bloch does a good job in defending Hegel's writing style in his valuable study *Subjekt-Objekt* (Suhrkamp Taschenbuch, Frankfurt am Main: 1962), but I find his comments more successful when directed at the *Phänomenologie* and writings other than the *SL*.
2. Arnold Miller translates: "Determination implies that what something is *in itself* [*an sich*], is also *present in it* [*an ihm*]." *Hegel's Science of Logic* (Humanity Books, Amherst, NY: n.d.), p. 123.
3. Hegel's continuum, the logical presupposition for space-time, is in effect eternal. But the world, in the sense of the content of the continuum, is not necessarily eternal. As I pointed out previously, Hegel's logic analyzes and describes the conditions for the possibility of the world; it does not explain why there is a world. It is difficult to say whether Hegel thinks of the world as eternal. Certainly he never claims that the absolute ceases, or for that matter begins, to function; and this suggests that Hegel accepts the eternity of creation.
4. This is the problematic that Husserl tackles in his *Phenomenology of Inner Time-Consciousness*. See my essay on the lived present in *Metaphysics in Ordinary Language* (Yale University Press, New Haven: 1999).
5. The reference to God's creation seems to be a metaphor for the continuous process of world creation by the absolute.
6. Once again we find in Hegel an anticipation of Heidegger.
7. G. W. F. Hegel, *Vorlesungen über die Philosophie der Religion*, vol. 2, pt. 3 (Philosophische Bibliothek, Felix Meiner Verlag, Hamburg: 1966), p. 124.

CHAPTER SEVEN

1. In *The Question of Being: A Reversal of Heidegger* (St Augustine's Press, South Bend, IN: 1993), I make a similar criticism of Heidegger to the effect that his postontological language is at bottom ontic.
2. Let me repeat that "category" is not used here to designate a member of a list of abstract universal properties of anything whatsoever. The categories are the most general determinations of the concept. As such, they are as it were alive and concrete, and so turn into each other within the structure of intelligibility
3. See again Pinkard, *Hegel's Dialectic* . One must, however, add that the *SL* is intended to actualize, or let us say to exhibit the actualization, of the absolute. Pinkard ignores this aspect of the *SL*, probably because he rejects the attribution of the claim to comprehensive (circular) wisdom.

CHAPTER EIGHT

1. Stanley Rosen, *G. W. F. Hegel. An Introduction to the Science of Wisdom* (Saint Augustine's Press, South Bend, IN: 2000), pp. 92ff.).
2. John Locke, *An Essay concerning Human Understanding*, ed. A. C. Fraser (Dover Publications, New York: 1959). Until otherwise indicated, numbers in parenthesis in the text refer to volume and page of this edition of Locke's *Essay*.
3. For the idealist position, see J. G. Fichte, *Erste und Zweite Einleitung in die Wissenschaftslehre* (Felix Meiner Verlag, Hamburg: 1954), p. 85: *Sein* is a derivative and a negation (because a determination) of *Freiheit*.
4. Leo Strauss, *Natural Right and History* (University of Chicago Press, Chicago: 1953), p. 251.
5. References in parentheses are to the *Wissenschaftslehre* of 1794 are to *Grundlage der gesamten Wissenschaftslehre*, ed. Fritze Medicus (Felix Meiner Verlag, Hamburg: 1961).
6. Fichte, *Erste und Zweite Einleitung*, p. 76; italics mine.

CHAPTER NINE

1. Unless otherwise indicated, numbers refer henceforth to pages in vol. 2 of the PhB edition of the *SL* edited by Georg Lasson (Felix Meiner Verlag, Hamburg: 1934).

CHAPTER TEN

1. Stanley Rosen, *Plato's "Statesman": The Web of Politics* (Yale University Press, New Haven: 19970.
2. I remind the reader that for Hegel, logical motion is within being; the expression is not a metaphor for the motion of thought, as Terry Pinkard takes it.

CHAPTER TWELVE

1. For an extensive discussion of the main technical issues, see my *The Limits of Analysis* (Basic Books, New York: 1980).
2. *Sache* means "things" in a sense that includes objects and events. Cf. the Greek *pragma* or the Latin *res*.

CHAPTER FOURTEEN

1. Kant, *Critique of Pure Reason* B180.

CHAPTER SIXTEEN

1. Martin Heidegger, *Sein und Zeit* (Niemeyer, Tübingen: 1953), p. 38.

CHAPTER SEVENTEEN

1. I employ the capitalized "Concept" from now on because the main sense of the term is now that of the whole, and not a particular modality, as in "the concept of existence." From time to time, Hegel uses the term in this lowercase sense, but it would be too distracting to shift back and forth. I will use the lower case only when the context demands.

2. John Burbidge, *On Hegel's Logic. Fragments of a Commentary* (Humanities Press, Atlantic Highlands, NJ: 1982), p. 111.

3. G. W. F. Hegel, *Vorlesungen über die Geschichte der Philosophie* (Suhrkamp, Frankfurt: 1986), p. 323.

CHAPTER EIGHTEEN

1. From this standpoint, Hegel's intention is not so far removed from the intention attributed to Fichte by A. Philonenko in his heterodox but illuminating book, *La liberté humaine dans la philosophie de Fichte* (Librairie Philosophique J. Vrin, Paris: 1966).

2. *Hegel's Science of Logic*, trans. Miller, p. 64.

CHAPTER NINETEEN

1. Burbidge, *On Hegel's Logic*, pp. 4–5.